Death, Dying, and Bereavement in a Changing World

Alan R. Kemp

Pierce College

Routledge
Taylor & Francis Group

LONDON AND NEW YORK

First published 2014 by Pearson Education, Inc.

Published 2016 by Routledge

2 Park Square, Milton Park, Abingdon, Oxon OX14 4RN

711 Third Avenue, New York, NY 10017, USA

Routledge is an imprint of the Taylor & Francis Group, an informa business

ISBN : 9780205790760 (pbk)

Cover Designer: Salzbach Karen

Library of Congress Cataloging-in-Publication Data
Kemp, Alan R.
  Death, dying, and bereavement in a changing world / Alan R. Kemp, Pierce College.
    pages cm
  Includes bibliographical references and index.
  ISBN-13: 978-0-205-79076-0 (alk. paper)
  ISBN-10: 0-205-79076-3 (alk. paper)
  1. Thanatology. 2. Death. 3. Bereavement. I. Title.
  HQ1073.K46 2014
  306.9—dc23

                                                              2013016789

CONTENTS

PART II   Death   91

PREFACE

Death, dying, and bereavement are different today than in times past. As Dorothy in the *Wizard of Oz* said, "I don't think we're in Kansas anymore, Toto." Before modernization, life was different. Industrialization ushered in a new world of technology. Today, we are arguably on the cusp of yet another change, a postmodern world, in which information technology, globalization, and new ways of relating loom big. The world in which we live has changed. "Back in the day," as they say, someone might reasonably expect to die the "good death," at home, cared for by family and friends. With the arrival of industrialization and advances in medical technology, it has become far more likely to die in a hospital or nursing home, surrounded by the latest medical technology.

Today, we are not always even sure what death is. Do we mean being "clinically dead"—unable to breathe on one's own and have a heart that is still beating? Or do we mean "brain dead," sometimes called being a "heart-beating cadaver"? When I began working on this project I felt there was a need for a book that tried to provide a context for understanding our changing encounters with death, dying, and bereavement.

I also believed there was a need for a book that helps students integrate the various dimensions of experience with death, dying, and bereavement. Indeed, something else I am very concerned about is assisting readers in understanding the topic from a multidimensional perspective. This includes approaching it in an integrated way, looking at the physical, social, psychological, and spiritual dimensions.

Ernest Becker (1973) is credited with coining the term *denial of death* to describe modern-day attitudes toward death. To use the term *denial* also implies that we human beings are somehow at odds with consciousness about the unpleasant reality of death. Although it may be true that human societies engage in all kinds of practices that are designed to protect us from coming too close to this grim eventuality, death's profound presence is never very far away. Regardless of how we choose to relate to it, death is that most universal of all human experiences.

People in all places and at all times have found ways to relate to death and dying. Beliefs, attitudes, and practices about the end-of-life issues are integral to virtually all human cultures. In the modern technological world in which we live here in North America, there exists a highly evolved system of health care that attempts to combat disease of all kinds and ward off death. Our educational system is rooted in a model of "scientific empiricism" that demands that we try to control the variables we study in order to establish cause-and-effect relationships between them. Because of advances in knowledge, technology, and medicine, life expectancy has been increased to a remarkable degree, at least in the technologically advanced parts of the world.

Modern approaches to mental health and self-help promote ways to help people get the most out of life and live it to its fullest. Despite all this, the end of life remains a pervasive part of the human experience. It is not my intent to be morbid in what I have said here. Life is rich, and precious, and wonderful. It is to be appreciated all the more because our days are numbered. The possibilities in life are replete and its dimensions are many. I hope we can find ways to bridge gaps in our understanding and integrate what we know about life and its counterpart, death. To do so, we explore the relationships that exist between the many facets of living and dying. For me, this means delving into beliefs and meaning; aspirations and what people feel drawn to; human experience and emotion; courage, hope, and growth; ritual and spiritual practices; what it means to live in the fellowship of communities; and what it means to exist within the social institutions that are so integral to our society.

WHAT IS IN THIS BOOK?

Death, Dying, and Bereavement in a Changing World has six parts and a total of fifteen chapters. Part I has four chapters that provide an introduction and context. Chapter 1 opens with the topic of "lifting the pall." The pall, a cloth placed over the casket during a funeral, is a metaphor for "denial of death," the title of the Pulitzer Prize–winning book by Ernest Becker. The text introduces thanatology, the study of death, dying, and bereavement; reviews key events in the development of the field; discusses the multidisciplinary nature of the field; introduces the four-facet model (physical, social, psychological, and spiritual dimensions); and explores the present-day conversation between theory, research, and practice. Chapter 2 focuses on our changing experience as shaped by society, science, and technology. Whereas in times past people ideally died at home, surrounded by friends and family, today seven out of ten people die in a hospital or nursing home. Science has increased average life expectancy by 30 years in just a century, and our industrialized and bureaucratized health-care system has changed *how* we die. In Chapter 3, we will look at death and human development, exploring encounters with death across the life span, the nature of children's consciousness about death, and what happens when the life cycle naturally concludes. Chapter 4 focuses on cross-cultural and interfaith dimensions. The title begins with *Coureur de Bois,* a French-Canadian term denoting the idea of travelers sharing stories about all the places they have been and things they have seen. We will look at the relationship between culture, spirit, and death; review theoretical perspectives on the role of spirituality and religion; and survey five key religious perspectives.

The three chapters of Part II examine death itself. Chapter 5 takes a historical and cross-cultural look at the business of undertaking. It begins with a discussion of clinical death and looks at what happens when the heart stops beating, breathing stops, the body cools, rigor mortis sets in, and the body begins to decay. The text reviews burial practices from ancient times to the emergence of the modern "funeral service industry." Chapter 6 begins with a discussion of our contemporary "death system" but also explores criticisms of "McDeath," the corporate commercialization of death. It explores the use and abuse of the Amended Funeral Rule. It also examines alternatives: funeral consumers' societies, home funerals, and green burial. Chapter 7 addresses traumatic death—that is, death that is sudden, violent, and/or inflicted. Within this context, we will explore death from murder, suicide, terrorism, and pandemics, such as AIDS.

Part III is concerned with dying, or the process of getting dead. It has two chapters. Chapter 8 looks at what is involved in facing death and what it means to make the transition from feeling "temporarily immortal" to being "terminal." The chapter discusses Elisabeth Kübler-Ross's classic stages of dying and Dr. William Bartholome's experience with the "Angel of Death," and examines "death trajectories." In Chapter 9 you will learn about "intensive caring," the term I use when discussing modern hospice and palliative care—the "gold standard" when it comes to end-of-life care. We will discuss its evolution and key players. As our discussion draws to a close, we will explore the pitfalls and falling through the cracks.

Part IV, which focuses on bereavement, grief, and mourning, has two chapters. Chapter 10 considers the "normal" bereavement, grief, and mourning. We will look at the classic "grief work" model first articulated by Sigmund Freud and further developed by a whole generation of theorists. Then we will explore the "new science of bereavement research," which may be turning the old ideas on its head. Chapter 11 focuses on complicated grief—what happens when grief is experienced too intensely or for too long. We will investigate the evidence that supports innovative approaches to treatment.

Part V contains two chapters that deal with the legal and ethical borderlands. Chapter 12 explores physician-assisted suicide and euthanasia. You will learn that physician-assisted suicide is now legal in Oregon and Washington state and is tolerated in Montana. Typically, the physician prescribes a drug the patient takes to end his or her life. Some patients, however, such as those suffering from Lou Gehrig's disease, may not be able to act on their own. This is the segue to discussion of the issue of voluntary euthanasia, what happens when someone else takes steps to end the life of a patient who wants to die. Although illegal in all U.S. jurisdictions, it is tolerated in the Netherlands, Belgium, and Luxembourg. Chapter 13 addresses the issues of withdrawing life-support systems and organ transplantation. The text reviews "brain death" and harvesting human organs, and discusses what to do when a person is in a "persistent vegetative state," "coma," or "locked-in syndrome."

Part VI contains two chapters. Chapter 14 addresses a single question, but it is a big one: What happens after we die? According to terror management theory (TMT), discussed in Chapter 1, human beings are different from other animals in that we can conceptualize our own deaths, leading to death anxiety and a host of other problems. Also according to this theory, we have come up with two strategies to deal with it: culture (including the use of religion) and self-efficacy, or the sense of personal empowerment. Most religions tell us that part of us survives death. In this chapter, we will explore in some detail what the various religious traditions say about life after life. We will also contemplate speculations based on the so-called near-death experience. Chapter 15 looks at what is ahead. It reviews the current trends in death, dying, and bereavement and speculates on the future, including the experiences of the "X-ers," "Nexters," and "Texters."

HOLISTIC AND INTEGRATED APPROACH

The field of thanatology is multidimensional and multidisciplinary. It is an enterprise that strives to integrate diverse perspectives and facets of life (Corr, 1992; Canadian Hospice Palliative Care Association, 2004; Ferris et al., 2002; Last Acts, 2003a, 2003b). This makes it unique in academia.

Parker Palmer, an academically trained sociologist, is now more renowned as a social commentator and educational revolutionary. He is among a growing number of educators, spiritual leaders, and researchers advocating for a more integrated, or holistic, approach to education generally (Griffiths & Edwards, 1989; Miller, 2000; Palmer, 1993, 1998). Palmer suggests that in our need to specialize (e.g., psychology, sociology, and thanatology), we have also carved up the pursuit of knowledge, dividing rather than uniting (Palmer, 1993). One of his concerns is that in doing so we have also separated ourselves from each other and become less appreciative of the mysteries of life in general.

Perhaps in an effort to put the whole venture of education into context, Palmer (1993) observes that higher education can trace its origins to the monasteries of medieval Europe, where monks emphasized three key areas of activity: (1) reading scripture, (2) praying and contemplating, and (3) developing spiritual community. He suggests that of these came three key values of academia: (1) respect for the body of scholarly literature, (2) an emphasis on research and analysis, and (3) respect for a collegial community of scholars. Palmer observes that scholars and monks alike had in common a dedication to study, contemplation, and a deep interior life. He laments that when society rejected the excesses of the medieval period and adopted a more scientific approach to knowing, we may have also inadvertently lost something.

With the advent of science, technology, and industrialization came an emphasis on action. Palmer (1993) suggests that in a renewed effort to uncover greater meaning in life, we may want to strike a balance between doing and being. Today, average life expectancy has increased dramatically and infant mortality has declined. However, we may need to ask if how we live and die has really improved.

In pursuit of uncovering new wisdom about life from the study of death, this text intends to both build on contemporary scholarship and endeavor to reclaim our humanity. I like the parallels Palmer makes between academia today and the monastic traditions that gave rise to it. In the following table, I draw some parallels between monastic and academic traditions and extend the model to include several learning tools, or activities, used throughout this text.

This book is committed to the idea that in our quest to uncover wisdom about life through the study of death, we should make it one of both mind and heart. It should, of course, include all the rigors of any other academic pursuit, but also honor our deeply personal quest to understand.

To complement the scholarly literature, I have integrated the concept of *story*, some related to individual experience, others that are more cultural. To balance an

A Comparison of Academic and Monastic Traditions and the Learning "Tools" Integrated into this Text

Monastic Heritage	Academic Tradition	Text Learning "Tool"
Sacred scripture	Body of literature	Story
Prayer and contemplation	Research and analysis	Reflection
Spiritual community	Collegial community of scholars	Sharing that fosters a community of learners

exploration of research and analysis I invite you to *reflect*. I will at times *share* the results of experience and reflections and encourage you to do the same. Although the emphasis in academia today is on the building of a body of knowledge and a collegial community of scholars, I hope we can also cultivate our own community of learners.

A review of the literature can inform us about what others have uncovered; the exploration of story makes us participants. Research and analysis leads to the discovery of new truth; reflection may well lead us to uncover hidden truths about ourselves and events. Interaction within the community of scholars leads to the growth of new knowledge, but sharing experience with each other may contribute to the growth of new understanding.

As we all know, story is one of the most engaging ways to bring ideas to life. It is also among the most ancient and natural ways to learn. To complement the literature, I plan to weave stories generously throughout the text. Some, like the snippets I have already shared, come from my own experience. Some come from the experiences of people I have spoken with or from stories I have heard.

■   ■   ■

Listening to stories and telling them helped our ancestors to live humanly—to be human. But somewhere along the way our ability to tell (and to listen to) stories was lost.

—Ernest Kurtz and Katherine Ketcham
The spirituality of imperfection, 1992

■   ■   ■

Reflection, for the purpose of this text, is the process of exploring one's own experience in conversation with the literature, research, story, and experience of others (for a discussion of theological reflection, see Killen & De Beer, 1999). It should be a give-and-take dialog. Reflection can confirm, challenge, clarify, or expand understanding. It is intended to lead to new truth or meaning. I will share my reflections and at various times invite you to explore your own.

Sharing is central to cultivating the kind of mutual respect and understanding that can lead to building a community of learners. If you do the "object exercise" I suggest in Chapter 1, you will have an experience of the kind of sharing I am talking about here. When people tell about a meaningful object connected with an experience with death, they enhance the understanding of others. I have never ceased to be impressed by the richness of experience that learners bring with them. When sharing occurs, I get the sense that rather than merely hearing about others, we actually have an opportunity to experience a little bit of their lives. What we learn is not usually restricted to a few tidbits of data in a narrow range of "icebreaker" topics. With this, comes respect for, and understanding of, the people with whom we journey.

KEY FEATURES

I hope that *Death, Dying, and Bereavement in a Changing World* will serve as an introductory text to be used by a general population of undergraduate and graduate students, in addition to students of psychology, sociology, human services, social work, medicine, nursing, chaplaincy, and ministry. I believe it provides a venue in which students can do both a personal and academic exploration of the subject. In addition to a "student-friendly," conversational tone, each chapter presents a chapter preview, special feature "boxes" (e.g., with vignettes, stories, or anecdotes), visual data display (tables and charts), photos, chapter summaries, key terms, suggested activities, and suggested reading. Toward this end, the approach I have taken includes:

- *Holistic/integrated approach:* We explore a variety of dimensions, each to be respected for itself, yet treated within a framework that attempts to uncover the relationships that exist between them.
- *Multilevel fabric:* The entire piece of work attempts to delve into the drama from a variety of vantage points. For example, you will find individual experiences of people not unlike yourself, as well as stories about people who seem quite different from your identity; explorations of life and death in distinct communities, subgroups, and special populations; and broader social issues that are played out at the societal level.
- *Story:* It is my contention that stories help bring concepts to life. These chapters weave the accounts of the personal stories of real people into the text.
- *Symbol and myth:* Symbols, myth, and archetypes are interlaced into the text, at appropriate points, in order to arouse the imagination and bring you into contact with a world of enduring themes.
- *Mind-body-spirit:* This book gives respectful coverage of the mind-body-spirit connection, including the influence of such dimensions as hope and faith on health and recovery.
- *Reflections:* The chapters include original research on bereavement and reflections dr.awn from firsthand hospice experience.

STUDENT AND TEACHER RESOURCES

Please visit the companion website at www.routledge.com/9780205790760

GRATITUDES

It was not until I had finished writing this book that I realized just how many people deserved a heartfelt "thank you." First of all, kudos go to my wife, Claudia, and the rest of my family for enduring the 10 years (on and off) it took to complete the writing. I gratefully acknowledge and remember a few loved ones who died during the journey: my mom, Kay Kemp (see Chapter 2); my mentor at St. Stephen's College, Dr. Ric LaPlante; my former Division Chair at Pierce College, Sam Samuelson; and Lisa Gebo, my former publisher at Brooks/Cole, who died far too young from breast cancer.

Thanks go to Karen Hanson, my former publisher at Pearson, and Nancy Roberts, my current publisher there, for believing in this project. In addition, I thank Simone Rico, the former Pearson representative at my school, who thought the project would be a good fit with Pearson's goals. My gratitude also goes to my peers who reviewed the manuscript and offered such thoughtful reflections: Patrick Ashwood, Hawkeye Community College; Gerry Cox, University of Wisconsin–LaCrosse; Lillian Dees, Texas State University; Meredith Martin, University of New Mexico; and Allen Richardson, Cedar Crest College. Their comments and suggestions helped make it a far better book. I am also grateful for the work of my project manager, Mayda Bosco, to Lynda Griffiths, my copy editor, without whose assistance the product would not have been so polished, and to the rest of the world-class team at Pearson.

Special thanks go to my friends Dennis Morton and Pam Slyter, who read and reread the manuscript in its various incarnations. They gave me invaluable feedback and insight, as well as encouragement, support, and the much-needed coaxing to finish. My friend Father Matthew Naumes always gave me great tips and pointed me in the direction of marvelous resources.

I also acknowledge St. Stephen's and St. Andrew's colleges, where an earlier draft of the manuscript served as the project part of my project-dissertation. They provided me with a challenging but supportive and innovative learning environment. Thank you, too, to my colleagues at St. Stephen's for sojourning with me, as well as Clair Woodbury, Cheryl Nekolaichuk, and Daniel Dangaran, who did yeoman's work on my committee, reviewing my work, supporting my efforts, and helping me grow "beyond the boundaries, boldly."

Pierce College, where I teach, also deserves my thanks for its commitment to professional development and for granting me a sabbatical so I could research, reflect, and renew. Several colleagues at Pierce provided feedback on one or more chapters: Jo Davies, Chris Martin, Doug Jenson, Jo Anne Geron, Tom Link, and Marty Lobdell. But I would be remiss if I did not mention the hard work and dedication of Barb Perkins of Pierce College's award-winning library, who went the "extra mile" to track down those hard-to-find resources I needed.

Last but certainly not least, I thank the many people who journeyed with me and shared their experiences: the good people from Compassionate Friends I interviewed for my research on parents who have had a child die; my hospice patients at Good Sam; His Holiness, the Dalai Lama; Hindu holy man Sri Sri Swami Jitatmananda; Islamic religious teacher Abdul Kareem of the Henry Martin Institute; Acharya Francis Mahieu and the monks of Kurisumala Trappist Ashram; pastoral counselor and ethicist Herman H. Van der Kloot Meiburg; theologian Theo A. Boer of the University of Utrecht; Dr. Rob Jonquiere, former Director of the Dutch Voluntary Euthanasia Society; and Nancy Raynolds and all the folks at Good Samaritan Hospice in Puyallup, Washington.

Alan R. Kemp
Pierce College

ABOUT THE AUTHOR

Alan R. Kemp is Professor and Coordinator of the sociology department at Pierce College, Ft. Steilacoom, Washington, where he teaches a course on death, dying, and bereavement. He holds master's degrees in social work and divinity. He earned his doctorate at the then amalgamated colleges of St. Stephen's and St. Andrew's in Edmonton, Alberta, and Saskatoon, Saskatchewan, Canada. Kemp has many years of experience in teaching, ministry, and professional counseling. He is a licensed mental-health professional. He was also among the last American advisors serving on "Swift Boats" (PCFs) in Vietnam. Kemp lives with his wife, Claudia, and a menagerie of "critters" at their cabin in rural western Washington state.

Introduction and Context

ANDREW BURTON/Reuters/Corbis

Part I consists of four chapters that introduce *thanatology*—the study of death, dying, and bereavement—and the social, psychological, and spiritual contexts in which we encounter them.

Chapter 1 is titled "Lifting the Pall: The Quest to Uncover Wisdom about Life Through the Study of Death." The central metaphor of the chapter is the *pall,* a cloth covering placed over the casket during a funeral. To "lift the pall" is to uncover that which is beneath so that we might see it for what it is. The metaphor of the pall is also connected to anthropologist Ernest Becker's thesis, *The Denial of Death* (1973), the title of the Pulitzer Prize–winning book he wrote just one year before his own death. Becker believed that the pervasive denial of death is at the root of many of society's most pressing problems. Chapter 1 introduces thanatology as an emerging academic discipline. We will discuss the multidisciplinary, multidimensional nature of contemporary thanatology. We will also focus on the topic of death education, which can be both a formal and informal area of study, and learn about a few key figures in the death awareness movement. The tensions in the field, particularly between practitioners and academics, will be noted, and we will discuss the "conversation" between practice and research. We will also look at terror management theory, TMT, which evolved from the interest of three graduate students in the ideas of Ernest Becker. To test TMT, this team, whose members became experimental social psychologists, used rigorous experimental method, yielding very strong support for TMT and Becker's pioneering ideas.

Chapter 2, "Death and Dying in a Rapidly Changing World," focuses on how people's changing experience with death has been shaped by society, science, and technology. In the classic deathbed scene, the dying individual has taken to bed and is surrounded by family and loved ones until the last breath. This kind of death may have been common "back in the day," but today most people die in hospitals or nursing homes, often entangled in technology and surrounded by health-care professionals. Although medicine was once more an art than a science, Chapter 2 will note that with modern science the field of medicine has been able to add 30 years to the average life expectancy. On the downside, the industrialization of health care has continued to grow significantly, perhaps further distancing ourselves from the human touch. The chapter observes that today people seem to be experiencing accelerated social change, perhaps moving from the modern to a postmodern era. With it, we are arguably experiencing a new social malaise. Alvin Toffler called it "future shock."

In Chapter 3, "For Everything There is a Season: The Developmental Context," we will look at death and human development. We will begin by taking note of the advances of modern medicine discussed in Chapter 2. As a result, fewer young people and more old people die. We will then survey encounters with death across the life span, first looking at common causes of death in infancy, toddlerhood, and middle childhood. Next, we will examine the nature of children's emerging consciousness about and understanding of death. We will discuss the experience of gravely ill children, taking note that their experiences seem to differ quite markedly from how well children come to think of death. Turning to youth, young adults, adults, and elders, we will review common causes of death and explore the relationship between social development and the experience of death. Finally, we come to the final stage of life. To do so, the chapter will build on a work written by Erik Erikson in collaboration with his wife, Joan, prior to his own death, called *The Life Cycle Completed* (Erikson, 1982; Erikson & Erikson, 1997). For people who live into their eighties and nineties, as he and his wife did, he notes that the very strengths it takes a lifetime to build all too often come undone, potentially sending the elderly person into a state of despair. According to the Eriksons, a lucky few may achieve *gerotrancendence,* a state of equanimity and peace, before death arrives.

"*Coureurs de Bois:* Cross-Cultural and Interfaith Dimension," the title of Chapter 4, uses a French-Canadian expression that connotes the idea of travelers sharing stories about all the places they've been. The chapter focuses on the cross-cultural dimension of death and dying, including spirituality and religion. It introduces some basic conceptual tools for comparing cultural experiences. We will look at the relationship among culture, spirit, and death. We will also review a few theoretical perspectives about spirituality and religion before surveying five key religious perspectives on death: Judaism, Christianity, Islam, Hinduism, and Buddhism. The concept of pilgrimage, using Joseph Campbell's metaphor of the "hero's quest," will be explored. Finally, we endeavor to undertake a "chautauqua," or a sampling of teaching stories about death from diverse cultures. Woven into the discussion are excerpts from interviews with His Holiness the Dalai Lama, Hindu holy man Swami Jittatmananda, Islamic teacher Abdul Kareem, and reflect on the example of Father Francis Mahieu, the late abbot of Kurisumala Trappist Ashram in the South of India.

1

Lifting the Pall

The Quest to Uncover Wisdom about Life Through the Study of Death

- About Self-Care
- Lifting the Pall
- Death Education

- Theory, Research, and Practice
- What about the Denial of Death?

Encounters with death, dying, and bereavement can be the most powerful experiences we have. They can also be the most personal, perhaps even more intimate than sex. Everyone dies. And before then, most will have someone they care about die. When dealing with a topic as sensitive as this one, it may be helpful to get a sense of the depth of one's experience. In the courses I teach, I like to do an activity called "the object exercise." In this activity, my students and I create an "altar in the round"——a table we put in the center of the room with a cloth covering and a lit candle, to symbolize that something important is taking place. Each participant has already been asked to bring an object to the session that symbolizes death, dying, or bereavement. I explain the activity. When they feel ready to do so, each student places his or her object on the table and explains to the rest of the group why that object was chosen. It is a powerful experience that usually creates a bond. By the time every-one has shared, the participants are usually pretty moved by the personal experiences brought to the activity. It is a poignant way to begin. Read more about it in "The Object Exercise" activity shown in Box 1.1.

Objects placed on an impromptu classroom altar concretizes the experiences of class members with death, dying, and bereavement.   *Alan Kemp*

BOX 1.1

The Object Exercise

In order to help build a sense of community and give students an opportunity to express themselves, I've adapted an exercise I learned in my own studies. I ask my students to bring a tangible, physical, object to class that symbolizes for them personally their experience with death and dying. Each student takes turns placing her or his object on a table in front of, or preferably in the center of, the room, explaining the significance of the object as each person does so. It always amazes me how, by making the subject concrete this way, the class is able to partake in the rich experiences of its members. Students have a chance to share in a personal way. I've found that the exercise tends to foster a sense of trust and camaraderie, which deepens the classroom experience.

ABOUT SELF-CARE

Before exploring the field of **thanatology**—the study of death, dying, and bereavement—let's take just a few moments to discuss self-care. Students may decide to take a course on death and dying for a variety of reasons. For some, it may be a way to come to terms with an unresolved loss. For others, the subject is important for a career goal, like becoming a physician, psychologist, counselor, social worker, chaplain, or pastor. And for still others, the course simply fulfills a requirement, one I hope will also enrich. Whatever the reasons, when venturing into territory like this, it is wise to approach the topic respectfully. The topic of death and dying touches poignant human experience, and may have the potential to expose emotionally charged thoughts and feelings that lie just below the surface.

One of the things the object exercise makes abundantly clear is that death is a pervasive human experience. Every reader, and every student, has been and will be touched by it. For some, grief about an important loss lies close to the surface. If this is the case for you, you can expect that delving into the subject will expose your memories, thoughts, and feelings—an experience that can have both positive and negative dimensions. I encourage you to use your own support system of close friends, loved ones, and perhaps even a favorite teacher, counselor, or pastor. Don't let the tender nature of your feelings hold you back.

Just as you may have been touched in some way by death and have had to find ways to handle its impact, people in all places and at all times have found ways to come to terms with death and dying. A friend and colleague, Dale McGinnis, was an anthropologist. I often sat in on his classes. I can recall him saying on several occasions, "Death is something that all cultures have to deal with in one way or another." Referring to funerals, I also remember him saying, "One day we'll all be the star of that show." How prophetic were his words, for Dale, one of the most gifted teachers I've ever known, was battling terminal cancer. He died in less than a year. Fully in character, however, he refused to be the star of "that show" by not showing up. He requested that there be no service.

■   ■   ■

It's not that I am afraid to die. It's just I don't want to be there when it happens.
—WOODY ALLEN

■   ■   ■

LIFTING THE PALL

The key words in the title of this chapter, *lifting the pall,* are pivotal to grasping its central theme: achieving a greater understanding about death occurs when we lift the shroud that covers it.

Military pall bearers lift the pall, in this case an American flag, revealing the casket of a fallen comrade. The flag also evokes feelings of patriotism which may help survivors find meaning in the experience of loss. *David Kay/Shutterstock.com*

A **pall** is a cloth covering placed over the casket during a funeral service. The word is also used to describe a somber mood or tone that pervades a place, as in the expression, "There was a pall covering the whole room." Metaphorically, we can visualize the pall as veiling the casket, symbolically shielding us from the full impact and reality of what lies beneath. Some social scientists believe society in general has a hard time dealing with death and that the difficulties facing up to death may have serious consequences. One of these was Ernest Becker (1973), a cultural anthropologist who coined the term **denial of death** to describe modern death-denying attitudes about death. To Becker's thinking, when people cover up the realities of death, they shield

Interchangeable Parts

During the writing of this text I was granted a sabbatical from the college where I teach. A very competent person was hired to replace me while I was gone. When I was working on the part of the text you are reading now, I thought of Dale McGinnis again. I recall him in his final years speaking to a class about death and the kind of society we live in. Referring to his own potential death he told the class, "If I died today someone would be here the next day teaching in my place."

Dale retired the year previous to his death. The college advertised his position and formed a hiring committee. The following fall, someone new was teaching amidst a classroom cluttered with the artifacts of years of Dale's teaching: handmade Indian masks, glass cases filled with model villages, canoe handles—you name it. Like an archaeological dig, none of the artifacts was situated in a neat, clean, or orderly way. Also like an archaeological site, you could trace Dale's evolution as a teacher through the things he left behind. Someone new was teaching in his place now. Gradually, the fame of this charismatic teacher receded into institutional memory. A scholarship in his name lives on, but those of us who knew him know life at the college was changed—his wit and humor were gone. Yes, the institution could fill the position but it could not replace the person.

themselves from it by using a process of *denial*—an activity that not only shields them from the unpleasant realities of death but also has the effect of eclipsing poignant truths about life. The notion that Western society may be in denial about death implies people are really incapable of dealing with life and perhaps lose out on experiencing important parts of their own humanity.

Although it may be true that people today as inhabitants of the modern (or postmodern) world engage in all kinds of behavior designed to psychologically protect themselves from getting too close to consciousness about death, its presence is never too far away. There is an American adage

There is a spot reserved for each of us.   *Oksana Jancevicl Shutterstock.com*

attributed to Benjamin Franklin that says there are two things in life that are unavoidable: death and taxes. Well, some may be able to find ways to evade taxes—but *nobody* avoids death. As a funeral director once told me, "Really, everyone's a customer."

■   ■   ■

But in this world nothing can be said to be certain except death and taxes.
—BENJAMIN FRANKLIN

■   ■   ■

If we cannot avoid death, perhaps we might try to understand it, which is the purpose of this book. To lift the pall, then, is to take that potentially scary step into the unknown.

Although one may think of the "denial of death" and the notion of confronting fears about death as particularly relevant to life today, it is not exactly new. To make the point, let's recount an ancient story of a young man—a prince, in fact—whose father attempted to shield him from the unpleasant realities of the world. He lived in his father's palace and was showered in luxury. His father's servants were ordered to make sure that the young prince wasn't exposed to any of the unpleasant realities of life. One might envy being in this privileged position, but the young man eventually began to sense that there was more to life than what he understood, and he wanted to learn about it. Ultimately, his father arranged for an excursion, a procession, into a nearby town, but ordered his servants to keep any fearful experiences from his son. Wanting to understand, the young man looked beyond the greetings of the "beautiful people" who were allowed close to the procession. Escaping from his father's servants one day, he encountered a feeble old man. Next, he met a terribly ill and diseased person. Then he came upon a funeral procession and learned that what was under the pall was none other than the body of a dead person. The name of the young man in our story is Guatama Siddartha. Most know him by the name Buddha, or "enlightened one," a name given to him later. Most scholars believe he was born in the year 563 B.C.E. at Kapilavastu, near the India-Nepal border. He is acknowledged as the founder of Buddhism, one of the world's great religions.

What young Siddartha discovered on his trek outside the palace were three basic truths about human life: We age. We experience illness. Eventually we die. In addition, Siddartha chanced on a fourth person, an ascetic, or holy man, who symbolizes a fourth realty—spirituality or the quest to uncover greater wisdom, understanding, and truth.

As we embark on our own journeys, perhaps we might wish to consider that the understanding we seek about death may actually be the quest to uncover higher truth about life and living. Siddartha, having made those initial discoveries, could no longer remain within the guarded confines of the palace. He ventured out. So shall we.

DEATH EDUCATION

Growth of Contemporary Death Studies

The study of death—the field of study we now call thanatology—did not begin to emerge as an academic discipline until the late 1950s and 1960s, when the work of such pioneers as psychologist Herman Fiefel (1959) and psychiatrist Elisabeth Kübler-Ross (1969) first began to appear.

Herman Fiefel was an Army Air Corps psychologist during the World War II when he witnessed the *Enola Gay* take off to unleash a nuclear bomb on the Japanese city of Hiroshima. He later described this and the death of his mother in 1952 as being integral to his interest in the study of death. In 1959, early in his career as a psychologist for the Veterans Administration, he edited his groundbreaking book on the topic, *The Meaning of Death*, which most authorities now believe sparked the present-day scholarly interest in the topic. A significant contribution by Fiefel is the concept of **death anxiety,** or fear of death, which has been the focus of much of the research done in death education ever since.

Ten years later, Elisabeth Kübler-Ross, a Swiss-born psychiatrist who had emi-grated to the United States, was teaching at the University of Chicago's medical school and working with terminally ill patients. As a result of the interest she developed while doing so, she published her own groundbreaking book, *On Death and Dying* (1969). At a time when medical practitioners didn't want to deal with the realities of death, Kübler-Ross taught a seminar intended to help medical students learn how to listen empathi-cally to their patients and thus provide them with better care.

In 1963, sociologist Robert Fulton offered the first modern-day course on death studies at the University of Minnesota (Strack, 1997). In 1969, he founded the Center for Death Education. Upon his retirement, Fulton renamed it the Center for Death Education and Bioethics, moving its operation to the University of Wisconsin–La Crosse, where it continues today as a resource center for academic materials on the subject.

Courses in a variety of disciplines (e.g., psychology, sociology, and educa-tion) became popular at North American colleges and universities. In 1976, a group of educators and mental-health professionals formed the Forum for Death Education and Counseling, which evolved into ADEC, the Association for Death Education and Counseling (2009). This organization continues today as the oldest interdisciplinary association dedicated to the study of death, dying, and bereavement.

Most colleges and universities offer courses on the topic. Today, however, death education is about more than formal coursework. It is about teaching professionals to provide better care. In addition to formal education, it can be an informal activity to help ordinary people face the issues. *Death education* actually refers to a whole range of activities and experiences related to death. It may include helping someone to under-stand their feelings and attitudes about death, coping with the dying process, dealing with death, caring for the dying, or handling bereavement and grief.

The overarching goals of death education include helping people achieve a greater understanding about death, dying, and bereavement as well as promoting the best pos-sible quality of life for all concerned. **Death** is the cessation of life. **Dying,** to paraphrase a now deceased physician, Dr. William Bartholome (2000a), is the process of getting dead. **Bereavement** is what happens as a result of experiencing a loss, usually, but not always from death.

There are two key approaches to death education: the didactic and experiential. In the **didactic** approach, an instructor imparts the knowledge, values, and skills believed to be beneficial to student learning though direct teaching. This might involve the use of lectures, DVDs, audio recordings, and so forth. In the **experiential** approach, the facilita-tor directly engages participants in real-life activities designed to evoke one's feelings and perhaps even change attitudes. Earlier in this chapter, I outlined an experiential activity—the object exercise. If you participated in that exercise, you have already engaged in experiential learning.

Sometimes the most powerful of all educational experiences is the **teachable moment,** or real-life experience related to death, that opens one to learn about death in a personally meaningful way. For example, children often learn about death when a pet or loved one dies. Although neither planned nor desired, such experiences are generally moving and intimate.

A Multidisciplinary, Multidimensional Emphasis in the Field

The pioneers of death education came from a very broad range of professions and academic disciplines—medicine and nursing; psychology and counseling; anthropology, sociology, and social work; theology and chaplaincy; and many others. From its beginnings, the field has always been rather multidisciplinary. It embraces diverse views and experiences. For many, this is part of its appeal.

There is an often-quoted Hindu parable about a group of blind men who are asked to describe an elephant. The first approaches the elephant and grabs its tail. He says the elephant is like a rope. The second puts his arms around a leg and says an elephant is like the trunk of a tree. Then the third man grabs the snout at exactly the same moment the elephant shoots a stream of water, so he says the elephant is like a water hose. The fourth grasps an ear and says an elephant is like a fan that circulates the air. The moral is that each is both correct and incorrect. Correct because the account, as far as it goes, is accurate; incorrect because none was able to understand the totality of the elephant. A solution to the paradox only becomes apparent when one recognizes that the descriptions are really complementary, not contradictory.

The field of thanatology is **multidisciplinary** because people from diverse fields and professions join its ranks. It is **multidimensional** because its practitioners recognize that dealing with death, dying, and bereavement requires them to work with whole persons—body, mind, and spirit—and not only them but also their families, their faith communities, and their networks of friends and colleagues.

Since graduate programs that train thanatologists are a rarity, most people in the field have completed graduate education in other disciplines, each with its own body of literature and preferred research methods: medicine, psychology, sociology, theology, and so forth. This makes a unified, or integrated, approach in thanatology a near impossibility, unless it be one that is very open to diverse ideas, experience, and methods, which I believe to be the case.

Charles Corr (1992), one of the most prolific writers in the field, suggests there are four fundamental dimensions of coping with dying: the physical, psychological, social, and spiritual. Corr uses these within a task-based approach to coping with dying (see Chapter 8). I think we can use the elements more holistically, in a multidimensional approach to the whole field of thanatology—what I like to call the **four-facet model** (see Table 1.1).

The **physical facet** pertains to those aspects of material existence that we experience directly with the senses. It includes the complexities of the human body, survival needs, bodily functions, processes associated with wellness and illness, and how the body adapts to stress and illness. We can include the experience of pain, loss of breath, toileting, and other bodily functions as being part of this facet. We should not think of this, or any facet, however, as being independent of the others, for each one is integral to the whole.

The **social facet** is the dimension of human experience concerned with social relations—family, groups, communities, the culture, social institutions, and the society itself.

TABLE 1.1	Four-Facet Model (Four Key Facets of the Death and Dying Experience)
Physical	The physical dimensions of living: bodily needs and physical distress. Material existence is experienced directly with the senses.
Social	Includes all of one's relationships (i.e., with family, friends, community, culture, and society).
Psychological	The entirety of human subjective experience: thinking, feeling, relating, and human aspiration.
Spiritual	The dimension of life that reflects the need to find meaning or connectedness to a universe greater than oneself, and a sense of transcendence.

The family, perhaps the most basic of social institutions, is where people come together out of mutual care, where children are reared, and where end-of-life issues are played out. More broadly, the social facet includes all the complex social institutions and practices that shape our social interactions (e.g., Macionis, 1999, p. 93; Henslin, 2001, p. 150; Lindsey & Beach, 2002, p. 99). Within the context of death education, the social facet can be thought to include our **death system** (Kastenbaum, 2009)—the ideals, values, and practices that shape how we deal with death; our health-care system, laws, and the funeral service industry.

Culture, which one can think of as everything that is part of the "social environment"—the language, beliefs, values, norms, behaviors, and material objects that are passed on from generation to generation. Another way to think of culture is to think of it as including everything about a collective way of life that is often taken for granted. As anyone who has ever traveled to a foreign country can tell you, we are often unaware of the pervasive influence of culture until we are in a different one. So, we can also think of culture as being like the air we breathe. We don't notice it until it's not there.

The **psychological facet,** the third dimension of coping with dying, includes that most intangible of human phenomena, *human consciousness,* as well as the thoughts, feelings, and behaviors that are integral to human experience. This facet in many ways is more subtle than those discussed so far. The human psyche can inspire the imagination. In many respects, our society is psychologically savvy, deeply interested in all things related to the mind, including the desire to understand end-of-life issues.

Spirituality can be thought of as a sense about that which is beyond the ordinary. It is often linked to thanatology, perhaps because of widespread speculation about what, if anything, happens to us after death. Although **religion**—a set of organized beliefs and practices about the supernatural—embraces the spiritual dimension, not all people who regard themselves as spiritual are necessarily religious in a formal sense. In anthropology and sociology, we use the term *simple supernaturalism* to denote the belief that supernatural forces help shape the course of human events, without making recourse to specific religious beliefs. George Fitchett, a chaplain-educator at Chicago's Rush-Presbyterian–St. Luke's Medical Center, defines *spirituality* as "the dimension of life that reflects the need to find meaning in existence and in which we respond to the sacred" (Fitchett, 1993, p. 16). So then, we can think of the **spiritual facet** of experience as the dimension of human living that is concerned with trying to understand death within the context of intuition about a reality that transcends ordinary experience.

In Chapter 9, we explore **hospice,** a model that is considered the "gold standard" when it comes to providing care to the dying. It reflects the multidisciplinary and multidimensional emphasis in thanatology. It is multidimensional because it attempts to address each of the four facets, as previously discussed. It is multidisciplinary because professionals from diverse fields are brought together with one goal in mind: providing high-quality, compassion-driven, care. These individuals include doctors, nurses, counselors, social workers, chaplains, and even everyday people who want to help.

THEORY, RESEARCH, AND PRACTICE

A detailed discussion of theory, research, and practice is well beyond the scope of an introductory text on thanatology like this. Each element, however, is vital to our knowledge of the field. Indeed, it is impossible to explore it without making recourse to them. So, we only briefly introduce them here.

Academic disciplines (e.g., psychology, sociology, and anthropology) are often defined by the body of theory they have and the research methods they use; *professional disciplines* (e.g., medicine, nursing, and social work) are usually defined by their body of theory, research methods, and practice. It is both a blessing and a challenge for this relatively new field that its practitioners come from such diverse backgrounds—a blessing because its diversity makes it so rich; a challenge because its body of theory seems so diffuse and its research methods are still emerging.

This having been said, I should also point out that research originally done in thanatology has enhanced the knowledge of research more broadly. For example, the pioneering research done by sociologists Strauss and Glaser (1965,1968) on the experience of dying patients in San Francisco led to the development a whole new methodology of qualitative research called *grounded theory* (Glaser & Strauss, 1968).

Carol Wogrin, a former nurse, current practicing psychologist, and well-respected grief educator, observes that even in the field of thanatology there is a divide between its practitioners, researchers, and theoreticians (Wogrin, 2007). Practitioners in the trenches sometimes have a hard time seeing the relevance of the research to their day-to-day work. Researchers complain that the folk wisdom spun off by practitioners seldom contributes much to the scientific understanding of death, dying, and bereavement. So then, let's take a few moments to explore the relationship between theory, research, and practice.

The Theory-Research Cycle

One way to begin this discussion is to introduce the **theory-research cycle.** Think of a **theory** as a tentative explanation for some phenomenon. It is a set of logically interrelated statements that attempts to describe, explain, and predict. Theories make assertions about how things work. For example, Kübler-Ross (1969) theorized that dying people go through predictable stages as they approach death.

A theory may lead to, or guide, **research,** but a theory doesn't in and of itself constitute evidence, or provide proof, of its own claims. This is the job of research, which is a systematic process. In what is sometimes referred to as the *classical research method,* the experiment, researchers test theory to see if it holds up. In contemporary practice, the investigator typically reviews the literature, conducts an experiment, gathers data, and analyzes the data in the search for new knowledge. Without evidence to support it, a theory is just that—a theory.

Theory and research are interdependent. They rely on each other. Although theory often guides research, research is the accepted process for testing current theory, confirming or disconfirming it, which in turn leads to changes in theory or the development of new theory. Walter Wallace (1971) describes the relationship between theory and research as being that of a continuous cycle. For a graphic depiction of the theory-research cycle, see Figure 1.1.

According to the research-theory cycle, the investigator can begin with a theory or observations. If one begins with a theory, the investigator designs research to test it, observes what happens, analyzes it, and then tries to come to some conclusions, or

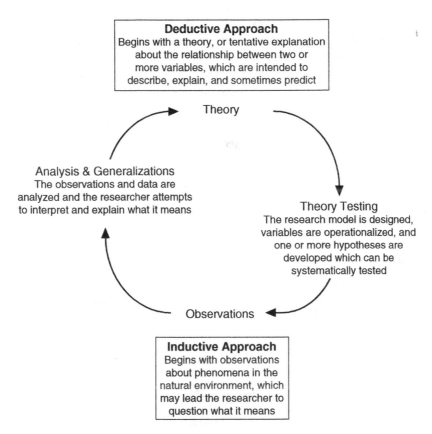

FIGURE 1.1 Theory-Research Cycle   *Source:* Based on Wallace, W. (1971). *The Logic of Science in Sociology.* New York: Aldine de Gruyer. In Kendall, D. (2009). Sociology in our Times, 9th ed. Belmont, CA: Wadsworth/Cengage.

generalizations, about what it means. This is called the **deductive approach**—start with a general idea and try to deduce a conclusion. In the next section, we will look at an impressive body of research done on terror management theory using classical empirical research, an example of the deductive approach.

One can also start on the opposite side of the cycle. Someone makes an observation that gets her or him wondering. The person generalizes what he or she thinks it means, which develops into a theory. This is called the **inductive approach**—beginning with specific observations which then generalize into a theory. For example, Herman Fiefel, the pioneering psychologist who coined the term *death anxiety*, became interested in the topic as a result of his observations of doctors who he thought behaved nervously when dealing with the dying. To him, they seemed *anxious* about dealing with death (Neimeyer & Fortner, 1997).

Diverse Research Methods

In addition to the general deductive or inductive approaches, there are many specific research methods: the experiment, survey, field study, participant-observation, historical analysis, case study, and secondary analysis of existing data. Examples of each are integrated throughout this or any good text on death, dying, and bereavement. Why? It is because the methods of research are important to understand, and researchers from diverse disciplines have used a variety of approaches in this quest. Some methods are better than others depending on what it is we're trying to learn. In the experiment, "classical," or "hard" research, the researcher attempts to establish a cause-and-effect relationship between two variables using the scientific method. This is the benchmark in academia by which all other research methods tend to be judged. For a summary of the key elements of the scientific method, see Table 1.2.

TABLE 1.2 Basic Elements of the Scientific Method	
Description	Information about the phenomena being studied must be both *valid* (accurately related to the focus of inquiry) and *reliable* (repeatable; i.e., consistently yields similar results when following the same procedures).
Prediction	The results of experimentation should be predictable based on the theory used and the hypothesis tested.
Control	The researcher should be able to control at least one variable (the independent variable) in order to test the effect on at least one other variable (the dependent variable). This helps determine if a cause-and-effect relationship exists between the two.
Understanding	Specific criteria must be met before the phenomena under study are said to be understood: **Covariation of events**—The predicted variation of one variable (the dependent variable) in response to the manipulation of the other (the independent variable) must occur as predicted. **Sequence**—The hypothesized cause (the independent variable) must in fact precede in time the observed effect (the dependent variable). **Elimination of alternative explanations**—Steps must be taken to ensure that some other intervening variable did not cause the observed effect.

TABLE 1.3 Comparing Approaches to Research	
Deductive	**Inductive**
begins with theory	begins with observations
forms hypothesis	makes generalizations
makes observations - tests hypothesis	results may help give shape to new theory
generalizes results	
modifies theory	
Quantitative Research	**Qualitative Research**
deductive	inductive
explanatory	exploratory
emphasis on determining cause-and-effect	emphasis on exploration of phenomena
attempts to control variables	naturalistic - no attempt to control variables
natural science world view	anthropological world view
examines behavior of individual variables	holistic
goal: determine cause-and-effect	goal: understand actor's view
focus is on objective reality	focus is on actors' subjective reality
positivistic	phenomenological
outcome oriented	process oriented
reality can be observed and measured	reality is subjective
General Placement of Selected Research Methods	
experiment	field research
survey research	participant observation
secondary analysis of existing data	ethnography
	case studies
	historical analysis

There are also "softer" **qualitative methods** of research, which means nonnumeric approaches in which the researcher tries to get at and describe experiences, perhaps by interviewing people or observing how they behave in real life. **Quantitative methods** emphasize the use of measurement. Generally, qualitative methods are associated with the inductive approach and quantitative methods are associated with the deductive approach. Table 1.3 summarizes distinguishing characteristics of deductive and inductive approaches; quantitative and qualitative research; and the general placement of various research methods on a continuum from deductive, quantitative and explanatory, to inductive, qualitative and exploratory.

WHAT ABOUT THE DENIAL OF DEATH?

Earlier in the chapter, we discussed Ernest Becker's concept, denial of death, and suggested that in "lifting the pall" we take the scary step of gazing into the void. But is it true that denial of death and death anxiety are really that important?

This section will try to answer that question by looking at some interesting theory and research. Beginning in the 1980s, Becker's original work inspired three experimental social psychologists, then graduate students at the University of Kansas, Tom Pyszczynski, Sheldon Solomon, and Jeff Greenberg, to seriously study the denial of death. They took Becker's ideas and tested them in an array of impressive, classical, empirical, research studies (e.g., Greenberg, Pyszczynski, & Sheldon, 1986; Greenberg et al., 1993; Greenberg, Arndt, Simon, Pyszczynski, & Solomon, 2000; Pyszczynski, Greenberg, Solomon, & Hamilton, 1990; Pyszczynski, Greenberg, & Solomon, 1999a; Pyszczynski, Solomon, & Greenberg, 2003; Pyszczynski et al., 2006; Solomon, Greenberg, & Pyszczynski, 1991, 2003; Solomon, Laor, & McFarlane, 1996). As a result, they extended Becker's thinking into a theoretical model that is known today as **terror management theory (TMT).**

In the almost three decades since Pyszczynski, Solomon, and Greenberg began their work, they have developed TMT and amassed an impressive body of research to support the theory. Indeed, they believe the denial of death may be one of the most important psychological principles yet discovered. After the events of 9/11, these researchers published a remarkably jargon-free book, explaining their work, the research, and how it might be useful in explaining events like what happened on 9/11 (Pyszczynski, Solomon, & Greenberg, 2003).

Building on the early work of Becker (1971, 1973, 1975), the trio observed that human beings, like all living beings, share a biological predisposition to self-preservation (Pyszczynski, Solomon, & Greenberg, 2003). This is necessary to promote the survival of the species. We humans are also extremely social and highly intelligent, such that our gregarious nature fosters the ability to cooperate with one another, engage in complex social behavior, and develop the kind of social institutions—political, economic, military, and religious—that make collective survival possible. What makes us different from other animals is our large and very well developed brains, which give us the capacity to do more than just respond reflexively to the environment. We can consider alternatives, reflect, and even imagine desired outcomes.

Not only are we able to imagine but we are also conscious and self-conscious (Pyszczynski, Solomon, & Greenberg, 2003). There are certain cognitive abilities that come with this faculty, such as the ability to reflect on the past and anticipate the future. With this self-awareness comes both awe and dread—awe at the wonders of life and being alive, and dread as a result of the unsettling awareness, to recall the story of Siddhartha, that we will age, experience illness, and one day die. We understand we are corporeal beings—a mixture of flesh and body fluids, which Pyszczynski and colleagues note "makes us vulnerable to potentially overwhelming terror at virtually any given moment" (Pyszczynski, Solomon, & Greenberg, 2003, p. 16).

According to TMT, what saves us from becoming overwhelmed by the awareness of our mortality and corporality are culture and **self-esteem** (Pyszczynski, Solomon, & Greenberg, 2003). In the fields of anthropology and sociology, culture has both material and nonmaterial elements that are passed on from one generation to the next. Material culture includes all the physical artifacts of a people, from the iPods, laptops, and SUVs of today's North American culture to the arrowheads, burial masks, and cooking pots of a bygone era. Nonmaterial culture includes all the nonphysical elements of a people—the customs, beliefs, norms, and values that give them a sense of meaning, identity, and that help them deal with their environment so as to make it possible for them to survive. Self-esteem, according to TMT, involves the ability of individual members of a society to see themselves as valuable and significant players.

At the core of terror management theory is the notion that culture gives people a way of managing the potential terror of death by helping us see ourselves as having enduring significance (Pyszczynski, Solomon, & Greenberg, 2003). Two key implications of this proposition is that we must:

1. Sustain our faith in culturally derived worldviews that give reality a sense of meaning, order, and purpose; and,
2. Maintain a sense of personal worth—the conviction that we really play significant roles in the unfolding drama.

A problem with this twofold strategy for dealing with the fear of death is that we live in a world with diverse cultures, with varying ways of dealing with the problems of living. According to TMT, when differing cultures come in contact with each other, there is the risk they will pose a challenge to each other (Pyszczynski, Solomon, & Greenberg, 2003). If the culturally derived worldviews protect a people from the realities of death, then coming in contact with people with other views can threaten belief in the perceived truth of it. Pyszczynski and colleagues suggest this is why it is so hard to coexist peacefully, and why cultures clash—the strife between American and Arab cultures that erupted in the attacks of 9/11 being one example of how problematic it can be (Pyszczynski, Solomon, & Greenberg, 2003; Yum & Schenck-Hamlin, 2005).

In addition to the challenges posed by culture clash, Pyszczynski and colleagues suggest that since culture is a socially constructed way of coping with the physical problem of death, it is utterly dependent on social consensus. Because social consensus is "socially constructed" and subject to change, it is inherently unstable. As a result, it is never able to completely resolve our fear of death. From the standpoint of TMT, this death anxiety, although it is repressed, is always with us. Pyszczynski, Solomon, and Greenberg (2003) suggest that the challenges to one's own worldview are generally countered by five basic strategies:

1. *Convert:* Change one's worldview when one's existing perspective does not adequately fulfill this need for self-esteem and a sense of meaning.
2. *Derogate:* Belittle or undermine the worth of alternative worldviews.
3. *Get others to assimilate:* Get others to adopt one's own worldview.
4. *Accommodate:* Incorporate appealing aspects of alternative worldviews into one's own perspective while divesting any of the potentially threatening dimensions of it.
5. *Annihilate:* Endeavor to destroy those who persist in keeping their own cultural worldviews.

Empirical Evidence and Key Elements

Now that we have reviewed a few key principles of terror management theory, let's briefly turn to the research that supports it. For over 20 years, Pyszczynski, Greenberg, and Solomon have conducted over 300 peer-reviewed studies supporting the theory using the experimental method (Greenberg, Pyszczynski, & Solomon, 1986; Greenberg et al., 1993, 2000; Pyszczynski et al., 1990, 2006; Pyszczynski, Greenberg, & Solomon, 1999a; Pyszczynski, Solomon, & Greenberg, 2003; Solomon, Greenberg, & Pyszczynski, 1991, 2003; Solomon, Laor, & McFarlane, 1996). Indeed, the very large volume of empirical research they have amassed on the theory is beyond the space available to review here.

Let it suffice to cite a few important studies and key concepts. Pyszczynski, Greenberg, and Solomon (2003) coined the term **mortality salience** to denote the influence of death awareness on human behavior. They use their "classic mortality salience treatment" to accomplish this. This involves asking research participants to describe their feelings when they consider their own death, write down what they think will occur when they themselves go through the dying process, and what they think will happen once dead.

The TMT team describes two general modes of reacting to terror, which they call the **dual-defense model** (Pyszczynski, Solomon, & Greenberg, 1999b, 2003). The two types of reactions are *proximal* and *distal*. **Proximal reactions** are likely to occur right away in response to an explicit threat, such as those that occurred in the wake of 9/11 (Yum & Schenck-Hamlin, 2005). These are conscious and rational, but may have elements of shock and horror. They tend to deny one's vulnerability by indulging in such strategies as distracting oneself or making attempts to understand the situation by relying on logic and evidence. **Distal reactions** are longer term and more likely to emerge

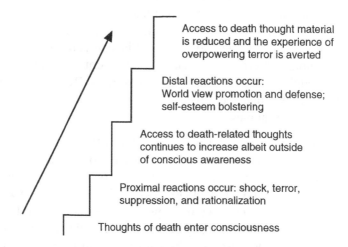

Access to death thought material
is reduced and the experience of
overpowering terror is averted

Distal reactions occur:
World view promotion and defense;
self-esteem bolstering

Access to death-related thoughts
continues to increase albeit outside
of conscious awareness

Proximal reactions occur: shock, terror,
suppression, and rationalization

Thoughts of death enter consciousness

FIGURE 1.2 Steps in the Terror Management Process *Source:* Based on: Pyszczynski T, Solomon S., & Greenberg J., (1999b). A dual-process model of defense against conscious and unconscious death-related thoughts: An extension of terror management theory. *Psychological Review, 106,* 835–845.

over time. Terror management theorists believe these kinds of reactions operate at the unconscious level. It is this type that strives to promote and defend one's cultural world-view and uses self-esteem enhancing strategies. Figure 1.2 is based on TMT theory (Pyszczynski, Solomon, & Greenberg, 1999b). It graphically portrays the steps in the terror management process.

Implications

Concurring with preeminent psychotherapist Irving Yalom (1980), proponents of TMT suggest that the fear of death may be far more important than ever imagined (Pyszczynski, Solomon, & Greenberg, 2003): it is associated with schizophrenia, pho-bias and obsessive-compulsive disorders, neuroticism; depression; and post-traumatic stress disorder. On a practical level, members of the core TMT team suggest three basic strategies that may be useful in helping people (Pyszczynski, Solomon, & Greenberg, 2003), as discussed in Box 1.2.

BOX 1.2

Focus on Practice: Helping People Cope with the Reality of their Finitude

Based on their research on terror management, Pyszczynski, Solomon, and Greenberg (2003) recommended three strategies for helping people with mortality salience in other words, the awareness of mortality. Mortality salience can be expected to increase at times of threat, seri-ous illness, trauma, or loss. Anyone wanting to help others may wish to consider the implica-tions of this research.

1. *Provide social support and caring:* This is something friends and family do naturally; professionals do this from their deep commitment to helping people.
   - Strategies, such as person-centered therapy, or just "thick listening," that focuses on listening intently to the experience of the individual, may be particularly helpful.
2. *Help people achieve a sense of meaning and understanding:* This involves going beyond helping people "connect the dots" to helping them make sense of tragedy and strive to achieve a sense of ultimate purpose.
   - Depending on the person's background, frame of reference, and worldview, anyone wishing to support someone with this may want to consider supporting the religious or spiritual traditions of the individual, perhaps partnering with those who have expertise in this area. Logo therapy and narrative therapy may be well suited to help individuals achieve a greater sense of meaning or purpose.
3. *Provide opportunities for heroism and self-esteem building:* Find ways to help people see themselves and their contributions as valuable to a purpose beyond just themselves.
   - Help engage the person in any practical task or service that assists others or helps resolve a problem—for example, volunteer work, mentoring, or even political action.

Chapter Summary

This chapter began with a few words about the importance of self-care and suggested a classroom exercise that might deepen your understanding through the telling of your own story and listening to the stories of others. I shared a couple short reflections about a friend and colleague—some snippets of insight he related before his own death from cancer—before discussing one of the book's central themes: The idea that learning about death is like "lifting the pall," or the covering that shields us from the full significance of death's reality. I briefly introduced the pioneering work of cultural anthropologist Ernest Becker, who coined the term *denial of death* to describe Western, particularly North American, attitudes about death. The death-denying proclivity is not exactly new or unique to our own culture. To emphasize, I briefly recounted the story of Siddhartha Guatama, who would became known as the Buddha, and how, as a prince living in a palace, his father attempted to shield him from the harsh realities of life. As the story goes, he happened on four people on a journey outside the palace. Three of them represented unpleasant realities of life (i.e., we age, become ill, and ultimately die). The fourth figure, the hermit, represents spirituality or the spiritual path.

We briefly explored the field of thanatology and death education, including an introduction to the work of psychologist Herman Fiefel, psychiatrist Elisabeth Kübler-Ross, and sociologist Robert Fulton. In this context, we explored several concepts important to the field, including death anxiety, didactic and experiential approaches to death education, and the teachable moment. We also explored a four-facet model of death education that organizes the various aspects of death, dying, and bereavement into the physical, social, psychological, and spiritual facets.

The relationship among theory, research, and practice was our next topic, beginning with the introduction of the theory-research cycle. We compared deductive and inductive approaches to research, noting that the deductive, classical, empirical, and scientific methods are the "gold standard" when it comes to academic research. This section made brief mention of various specific research methods.

Finally, following our survey of research, theory, and practice, we looked at terror management theory, or TMT, with an eye to answering the question: Is the denial of death really that significant? We briefly discussed the key tenets of the theory, the research supporting it, and the implications of this work.

Key Terms

multidisciplinary *10*
pall *6*
physical facet *10*
proximal reactions *18*
psychological facet *11*
qualitative *15*
quantitative *15*

religion *11*
research *13*
self-esteem *16*
social facet *10*
spiritual facet *12*
spirituality *11*
teachable moment *9*

terror management theory
  (TMT) *16*
thanatology *5*
theory *12*
theory-research
  cycle *12*

Suggested Activities

1. If you do not already do so, start keeping a daily journal. You might wish to use the journal to process your reactions, insights, and reflections as you move through this text, but start by writing about your own experiences with death or, if you prefer, your inclinations to push such thoughts out of your head.

2. For one week, keep a log of examples of how people you observe respond to topics or experiences related to death.

3. Select an elderly family member or friend and conduct a taped interview (audio or video) with this person about his or her life and whatever reflections the person might wish to share about the future end of his or her life. These kinds of interviews can be powerful bonding experiences. The elderly person has the opportunity to fulfill a mentoring role. Not only will you gain valuable insights but in addition you'll have a permanent audio- or video-recording of the interview with your loved one.

Suggested Reading and Viewing

- Becker, Ernest. (1973). *The denial of death.* New York: Free Press.
  This wonderful, classic book did much to awaken people to the need to pay attention to death. Since the years following its first release it has played an important role in arousing professional awareness.
- Hesse, Herman. (1951). *Siddhartha.* New York: Bantam Books.
  Although this beautifully written novel isn't factually correct about the human being who would be regarded by millions as "Buddha," this book is a wonderful read about the spiritual journey.

- Palmer, Parker J. (1993). *To know as we are known: Education as a spiritual journey.* New York: Harper San Francisco.
  For a compelling book about putting heart back into education, this first-rate book serves as a springboard for much of the direction of this chapter.
- Shen, Patrick (Director). (2005). *Flight from death: The quest for immortality.* Go-Kart Records.
  This insightful documentary is built around the ideas of Ernest Becker, especially the notion that a great deal of human striving and culture revolves around our denial of death and our ambition to make a mark on our world.

Links and Internet Resources

- **The Ernest Becker Foundation**
  www.ernestbecker.org/
  Exclusively devoted to the work of Ernest Becker, this site provides a glimpse into the impact of his work. A description from this website: "To cultivate

and support scholarly work that explores and extends Becker's insights; to disseminate to the public and its institutions the understandings which emerge; to apply these principles to the mitigation of violence and suffering."

- **Association for Death Education and Counseling**
  www.adec.org/
  This website is of the oldest interdisciplinary organization dedicated to the study of death, dying, and bereavement. It includes information of interest to professionals as well as to links to resources.
- **Encyclopedia of Death and Dying**
  www.deathreference.com/
  This extensive, and searchable, online database will take you to a variety of well-written articles on death, dying, and bereavement.

- **Kearl's Guide to Sociological Thanatology**
  www.trinity.edu/~mkearl/death.html
  This website, devoted to the sociology of death and dying, can be both entertaining and illuminating. It contains a student survey as well a large number of links to sources of information on a variety of death-related topics.
- **The Center for Courage and Renewal**
  www.teacherformation.org/html/ctf/index.cfm
  Inspired by the ideas of Parker Palmer, the Center for Courage and Renewal is dedicated to "Help[ing] people reconnect who they are with what they do." It helps foster personal and professional renewal.

Review Guide

1. If your class did the class exercise suggested in the text, describe what you experienced and learned by participating in the exercise.
2. Why should a person taking a course (reading a text) like this take self-care into consideration?
3. Consult the Glossary found at the back of this book, as well as the Key Terms (in **bold**) used in this chapter. Become fully familiar with the definition of each, see if you can find an example for each, and consider how you might apply the concepts to new situations.
4. What is a pall? What is its symbolic significance?
5. What term did sociologist Ernest Becker use to describe how people in our society deal, or don't deal, with death? Discuss why this concept is or isn't important to the study of living and dying.
6. Summarize the main points about the story of Prince Siddhartha. What four figures did he meet on his journey outside the palace? What is the significance of each? Why is Siddhartha remembered today?
7. Who are Herman Fiefel, Elisabeth Kübler-Ross, and Robert Fulton? How have they contributed to the development of death education and thanatology? What is ADEC? In general, what is meant by death? Dying? Bereavement?
8. What is the difference between didactic and experiential approaches to death education? What is a "teachable moment"?
9. Why do we say that thanatology is both multidimensional and multidisciplinary?
10. Summarize the "four-facet model." What kinds of relationships do you see between each of these dimensions? Do some seem more "important" than others? To what degree do your responses to this question correspond with your own biases and lifestyle choices and values?
11. What is hospice? Today, who participates on the hospice team?
12. What is the relationship between theory, research, and practice in thanatology?
13. What is the theory-research cycle?
14. What are the differences between the deductive and inductive approaches to research?
15. What research has been done on Becker's concept, denial of death?
16. What is terror management theory? What two basic ways do we try to manage our own death anxiety? What are the two key implications of this? What are the five basic strategies for countering challenges to our own worldviews?
17. What is mortality salience? What is the "classic mortality salience treatment"?
18. What is the dual-defense model? What are proximal and distal reactions?
19. What are the implications if terror management theory is true?
20. In the quest for a more integrated approach to studying thanatology, what three activities did I suggest might be usefully employed to complement the modern academic ones?

2

Death and Dying in a Rapidly Changing World

- Advances in Medicine
- Western Experience
- Modern Trends

- A Changing World
- Changing Attitudes

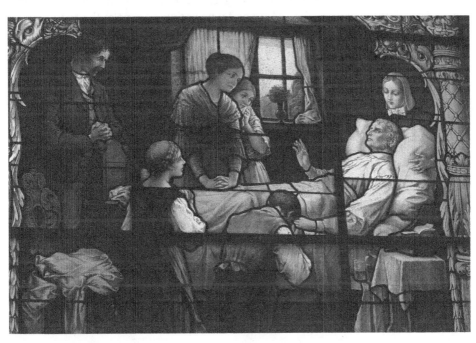

The classic deathbed scene, as shown in this stained glass rendition, is that of the dying person in bed surrounded by concerned loved ones. *jorisvo/Shutterstock.com*

T he classic deathbed vigil looks something like this: The critically ill person has "taken to bed" in her or his own home to await death. It has become increasing obvious that the person is nearing death, so family and friends gather to pay their respects (DeSpelder & Strickland, 2009). It is an intimate experience that gives the dying person and the loved ones one last time to reminisce, perhaps make amends, and say good-bye before the last parting. In an earlier day, most people died at home, often in the company of an extended family that included family members from several generations. Throughout the history of Western civilization, the home was, until recent years, the customary place of passing (Aries, 1974, 1981). This is still the kind of death many of us imagine.

Today, however, it is increasingly common for loved ones to die in a hospital or nursing home. Although it is now more popular to care for a terminally ill loved one at home with hospice services (Sankar, 1993; also see Chapter 9), in reality more than seven out of ten people actually die in an institutional setting—about half in a hospital and another 20 percent or so in a nursing home, cared for by staff paid to look after them (see Figure 2.1).

Perhaps sharing a personal experience may be in order here. The death of my mother is probably the single-most impactful event to happen to me. Her name was Kay. The last time I saw her alive she was in the intensive care unit, ICU, at St. Joseph's Medical Center in Burbank, California. This is in the San Fernando Valley, where I grew up. My sister, Peggy, who had moved to Santa Clara three decades before, drove down. She picked me up at the airport and we went straight to the hospital. I had moved some 20 years before, but came home this time because of a phone call, telling me it was unlikely mom would live much longer. Our brother, Bob, who now lives in northern Idaho, had recently visited Mom and was not able to make the trip again.

Our mom's ICU room was probably like similar ICU rooms across North America. Although "sterile" and tidy, whoever did the decorating seems to have tried to make the room as comfy as an ICU room can be. The appointments—the bedspread, visitors' chairs,

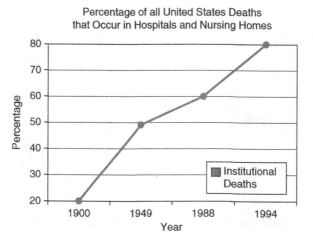

FIGURE 2.1   Percentage of All U.S. Deaths That Occur in Hospitals and Nursing Homes   *Source:* Adapted from Marrone (1997).

and privacy curtains—were done in cheery colors, muted pinks and blues. Mom was fully alert but unable to talk because of the intubation equipment that was helping her breath. An electronic monitor digitally displayed her vital signs—heart rate, respiration, blood pressure, and temperature. She was in exactly the situation she had always said she never wanted to be in—immobile and hooked up to tubes. Her wrists were tied to the bed's railing with "soft ties," put there to stop her from pulling the tubes out. Although she was fully alert and had all her faculties, in many ways our last visit was pretty much a one-sided affair. We could be with her. We could tell her we loved her. We could touch her. Attached to the ventilator, hooked to tubes, and immobilized with the soft ties, all she could do was use facial expressions and touch to respond to our communication. Chatting and sharing—things that make a conversation real and personal—just weren't possible. I knew she was happy to see me by the look on her face when I first walked into her room. Two days later, when I had to leave, she was in tears. Our mom, who was 85 at the time, rallied from that episode but would die in another hospital a few short weeks later.

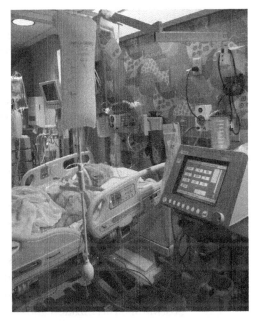

While many people imagine dying at home with loved ones near at hand in reality 7 out of 10 of us will die in an institutional setting, like a hospital or nursing home. *Mediscan/Corbis*

The kind of experience we had with our mom's death is unashamedly anecdotal, but it is also similar to the experiences of many others. Our mom, one of the seven out of ten elderly people who die in an institutional setting, didn't have her family and friends with her when she passed.

Before the beginning of the twentieth century, when our society was more agriculturally based, the **extended family** was common—a family pattern in which grandparents, parents, and children all lived in the same home, or at least in the same community. As we became industrialized, the **nuclear family** emerged—a family pattern in which only parents and their children live together (see, for example, Williams, Sawyer, & Wahlstrom, 2009). In these families, once the children grew up, they generally left home to attend college, take jobs, or start their own families, often far from home. As they became established in their own lives this often meant not being nearby as their parents became elderly. Other social changes contributed to death's move from the home to hospital, including the rise of modern medicine.

ADVANCES IN MEDICINE

Michael Kearl, a sociologist with a keen interest in death (1989, 1996, 2002), comments that until about a century ago, Western medicine was a relatively powerless profession, and physicians often did as much harm as good. Beginning in the latter half of the nineteenth century, with the dawning of industrialization and advances that came with the use of the scientific method, modern medicine began to make significant advances in what became a battle with disease. In 1858, Pasteur had refined his method of sanitizing foods; in 1864, Lister theorized that doctors spread infection by the microorganisms they carried on their hands; and the germs responsible for such diseases as cholera, tuberculosis, and rabies were identified, which would lead to the diseases themselves being subdued (Goldberg, 1998). By 1935, sulfa, the world's first antibiotic drug, came on the market. Within another 10 years, penicillin would follow. An effective treatment for tuberculosis, one of the most lethal diseases of all time, was discovered in the 1950s, a decade that would also usher in the first polio vaccine (Goldberg, 1998).

By the 1930s, the shift in the usual place of death, from home to hospital, would begin. The trend continued, culminating in the 1950s in a pattern that is consistent with what we know today. This shift is also one of the most commonly cited explanations for our changing perspectives about death (see, for example, Aries, 1974, 1981; De Spelder & Strickland, 1999, 2008). At an intuitive level, this makes a great deal of sense, since our entire experience with death has changed. We encounter it less often. When it does occur, it most often happens away from view. We can attribute much of this to the availability of effective treatments and the technological advances that sprang out of an era of booming postwar industrialization and that made heretofore undreamed of inroads possible. Modern science and technology revolutionized the treatment of disease and increased life expectancy, and as a hallmark of our culture they also helped bring about substantial changes in the way we think, how our families are organized, and how we relate to each other socially.

As you can see from a quick perusal of Figure 2.2, life expectancy in the United States rose dramatically from 1900 to the year 2000. The average person born in 1900 could expect to live about 47 years, whereas those born in the year 2000 can expect to live to about 77 years, depending on race and gender. Not only has life expectancy increased, but advances in medicine have influenced the kind of death we encounter. Whereas in previous eras child deaths were quite common, this is much less the case today in developed parts of the world because of the availability of drugs for treating infectious disease that are highly effective and because sophisticated technology is

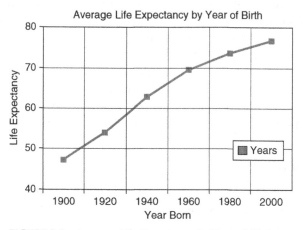

FIGURE 2.2 Average Life Expectancy by Year of Birth.

increasingly effective in fending off premature death. As a consequence, the most usual category of persons to die in North America today is the elderly. And, as we previously discussed, because technology is so integral to the way we treat the seriously ill as well as the seriousness of their disabilities by the time of death, they usually die in an institutional setting. The less common deaths that occur among the nonelderly happen in a variety of settings and by a number of causes, including accidental injury. In North America, death due to natural catastrophe, war, and violence are much less common and public—the events at the World Trade Center Twin Towers, the Pentagon, and in a field of Pennsylvania on September 11, 2001, notwithstanding.

WESTERN EXPERIENCE

With the shift in how we experience death has come a shift in our perspectives about it. Phillipe Aries (1974, 1981), a French historian who was among the first to conduct historical analysis on Western attitudes about death, comments that although attitudes have always undergone change, it has invariably been gradual—that is until now.

■   ■   ■

In our day, in approximately a third of a century, we have witnessed a brutal revolution in traditional ideas and feelings...an absolutely unheard of phenomenon....Death, so omnipresent in the past that it was familiar, would be effaced, would disappear. It would become shameful and forbidden.

—PHILLIPE ARIES
*Western Attitudes toward Death: From
the Middle Ages to the Present*, 1974, p. 85

■   ■   ■

Although a thorough discussion of Aries' work is beyond the scope of the present discussion, his work does offer a glimpse into perceptions about death that were once experienced as culturally "real" in western Europe. I hope this recognition also reminds us that our own beliefs and perceptions are conditioned by culture and experience. The five historical perspectives, as outlined by Aries are the tame death, the death of self, the remote and imminent death, the death of other, and invisible death.

The time of the **tame death**, according to Aries, may be the most benign of all with respect to the beliefs and attitudes people had about death. Taking place during the early Middle Ages, this was time when death was experienced as a community event. When someone died, everyone was somehow involved. The dying invariably accomplished the person's final act at home, surrounded by family, friends, and neighbors. The religious vision underlying the tame death reflected the theology expressed in the Revelation of John, where death was seen as a time of sleep before Christ's second coming. In Aries' description, this was also a fairly benign occasion with respect to expectations of what would happen in an afterlife. Aries tells us that people during this era believed salvation came not so much as a result of their deeds, but by virtue of their baptism and membership in the church.

During the late Middle Ages, the time of **death of self**, Aries (1974, 1981) tells us of a highly individualistic age in which people paid a great deal of attention to how they lived their lives. Saint Benedict, considered by many as the father of Western monasticism, suggests, "Keep death daily before you" (Delatte, 1950, pp. 72–74). His message seemed to be that life is all the more precious because the number of days of one's life are numbered. It was a time of personal responsibility. Western society was still very much intertwined with the ethos of the Christian religion, but in contrast to the era of the tame death, the vision of this next era was more reflective of the kind of *eschatological* (last things) thinking expressed in the Gospel of Matthew, with its imagery of Christ on his judgment seat. It was during this era that Dante Alighieri (1265–1321) wrote *The Divine Comedy* (Alighieri, 1982), with its allegorical vision of the afterlife, which some believe was both the culmination and a reflection of the medieval worldview. Influenced by the theological currents of the time, people in Europe during this era were quite concerned about whether they would spend eternity in heaven or hell.

In Aries' (1974, 1981) scheme, the **remote and imminent death** is characteristic of the period of time from roughly the beginning of the Renaissance period through the seventeenth century or a little beyond. During this era, Aries tells us, people paradoxically attempted to push death out of consciousness yet were also strangely fascinated by it. The attitudes during this time, he suggests, were similar to those of the present era.

Aries (1974, 1981) describes the **death of other** as an eighteenth- and nineteenth-century attitude toward death that was highly sentimental. It focused not so much on the dead as on the survivors, emphasizing the emotional experience of bereavement.

The type of attitudes toward death we are now encountering in the developed West, Aries (1974, 1981) calls the **invisible death** or **death denied**. Possibly compounded by the youth-oriented nature of society, it is an attitude toward death that sees it as being ignominious and taboo. Aries contrasts it with the perspectives of earlier eras, which he tells us experienced death as a more common, accepted, visible, and visceral part of everyday life.

Table 2.1 visually summarizes key elements in each of the five Western historical perspectives on death, as outlined by Aries (1974, 1981).

Whereas the rate at which perspectives about death have changed in modern times may be an unheard of phenomenon, as Aries puts it, it does parallel the rise of industrialization in the West.

⸙ ⸙ ⸙

But our machines have now been running seventy or eighty years, and we must expect that, worn as they are, here a pivot, there a wheel, now a pinion, next a spring, will be giving way; and however we may tinker them up for a while, all will at length surcease motion.

—Letter of Thomas Jefferson (age 71) to
John Adams (age 78), July 5, 1814
Sherwin B. Nuland, *The Way We Die*, 2000, p. 44

⸙ ⸙ ⸙

TABLE 2.1	Five Historical Perspectives on Death In Western Society	
Perception	**Historical Period**	**Theme, Emphasis & Theology**
Tame death	Early middle ages	• Death is an unavoidable 6th–11th centuries and normal part of life • Death is a community event • Members of the church go to heaven • Gospel of Matthew—we sleep until the second coming
Death of self	Late middle ages 12th century to Renaissance	• Personal accountability and responsibility for one's life are crucial • Individuals attempt to master their own deaths through the practice of *ars moriendi,* the art of dying • Apocalypse of John-judgment day; heaven or hell
Remote & imminent death	Renaissance (14th–17th c)	• Death is paradoxical-both near and distant; both enticing and to be feared • God is imminent and transcendent
Death of the other	Enlightenment period on 18th–19th centuries	• A romantic period in which the focus is on the one loved and lost • Death of the other is experienced emotionally and sentimentally • Death is a family affair • Evil exists, but outside self
The invisible death	20th century on	• Medicine successfully battles disease • Death itself becomes invisible in day-to-day life • Human beings perceive selves as masters of their own fate

This table is based on Aries, Phillipe. (1981). *The hour of our death.* New York: Alfred A. Knopf.

MODERN TRENDS

We often regard Thomas Jefferson, the author of the earlier quote and a founding father of the United States, as a visionary figure. Although the technological age did not fully kick into to gear, so to speak, until about the mid-nineteenth century, the words Jefferson put to paper in 1814, with their mechanistic metaphor, have a prophetic ring, presaging the dawning of an industrial age—a hallmark of life in the modern era.

In the United States, widespread adoption of modern science and research in medicine was facilitated by the publication of the **Flexner Report** in 1910 (Kendall, 1980, 2009). Its author, Abraham Flexner, met with a group of faculty from Johns Hopkins School of Medicine to develop a model for medical education. This established the principle that a medical school should be a full-time, research-oriented, laboratory facility. The report served as a guide for evaluating all 155 medical schools then conducting medical education. Previously, medicine was as much an art as a science. With the wide-scale adoption of the Flexner Report, medical education became transformed. As mentioned earlier, one measure of a nation's health is average life expectancy. Since the publication of the Flexner Report, the average life expectancy in the United States has climbed and infant mortality has declined sharply. We can probably credit the widespread adoption of scientific medicine as being largely responsible.

Jean Quint Benoliel, a long-time nursing educator at the University of Washington, and Lesley Degner, a researcher at St. Boniface General Hospital in Winnipeg, Manitoba, are part of a growing band of investigators who are also concerned about the adverse consequences of rapidly changing cultural values, uncritical acceptance of technology, and the dispassionate way we care for the sick and dying (e.g., Callahan, 2000; Cassell, 1993; Kastenbaum, 1993; Kearl, 1996). Benoliel and Dregner (1995) observe, "People's attitudes and behavior in relation to death and dying have been affected by the secularization of society, the dominance of science over medical practice, and the pressure of an expanding population" (p. 118). They applaud the many advances brought about by science and technology that none of us would want to give up, but they lament the emergence of troubling social consequences: "The creation of an assembly line model of work production that operationalizes the historical values of hard work, pragmatism, control over nature, and action…encourages a depersonalization of work through fragmentation of the tasks to be done, leading to monotony in many people's lives" (Benoliel & Dregner, 1995, p. 119). This sounds a lot like the observations made by sociologist Emile Durkheim, who made note of the rising sense of alienation and anomie that came into being with industrialization (Durkheim, 1893/1964; 1897/1951).

Benoliel and Dregner express concerns about the general dehumanizing side-effects of industrialization, but they are particularly troubled by its impact on the way we provide health care and tend to the dying. A large part of this concern revolves around how the principles of scientific empiricism have come to dominate the healing arts through the **biomedical model**, a scientifically based approach to health care that is now the accepted paradigm in Western medicine. The researchers comment, "Applying the reductionistic principles of the physical sciences to the study of disease has led to an objectification of the doctor-patient relationship and a disregard for the social and behavioral factors that affect illness" (Benoliel & Dregner, 1995, p. 120). In short, they express concern that the human element is being lost to a process they call the "industrialization of disease management."

One of my favorite stories is about a person whose given name was Israel ben Eliezer. He lived from 1700 to 1760, and was more commonly known by the title Baal Shem Tov, which means "master of the holy name." The Baal Shem Tov is the acknowledged founder of the Jewish Chasidic movement. The story is called "The Baal Shem Tov and the Doctor" and appears in Box 2.1. I think it helps bring the scientific and spiritual world views into relief, and speaks to a certain tension between scientific and person-centered orientations—between the ostensibly objective and the admittedly subjective.

BOX 2.1

The Baal Shem Tov and the Doctor

The highly respected doctor of a certain town had met a patient of his on the street—a man whom he had diagnosed just days before with a broken leg. Seeing that the man was walking about without his crutches, which he had been told not to do, the doctor chewed him out. The man explained that the holy Baal Shem Tov had healed his leg so the crutches were now unnecessary. The doctor was outraged that the Baal Shem Tov was misleading people and giving medical advice without a license, so he went directly to his home to confront him. "Israel ben Eliezer, I want to talk to you," the doctor shouted through the door. The Baal Shem Tov opened the door. After hearing why the doctor had come, the Baal Shem Tov suggested a contest. Whoever could correctly diagnose what was wrong with the other would prevail in the dispute. The doctor performed a series of tests but could find nothing wrong with the Baal Shem Tov. "You are incorrect. There is something terribly amiss with me," said the holy man, who then looked deeply into the doctor's eyes. "I am separated from God and I ache every day of my life because of it. What is wrong with you is that you have even forgotten that you ache." At this moment the doctor was reminded of something deep and primal in his soul and he began to weep at the realization of what he'd lost.

Source: Adapted from a version told by Doug Lipman; retold with permission. See http://hasidicstories.com.

■   ■   ■

Death was not considered the enemy of ancient medicine. It could not be helped.
Only with the modern era, and the writings of Francis Bacon and René Descartes
in the 16th and 17th centuries, did the medical struggle against death emerge.
—Daniel Callahan
The New England Journal of Medicine, March 2, 2000

■   ■   ■

There are those who are deeply concerned about what we may have lost as a consequence of the uncritical acceptance of scientific empiricism and the abuses of the biomedical model. At the heart of these concerns is something one might call an "institutionalized attitude" that became pervasive in our culture (Engel, 1977), especially so in modern medicine. It is a perspective that seemed to define health almost purely in physical terms, often as an absence of disease (Benoliel, 1997; Benoliel & Dregner, 1995; Dossey, 1982; Hewa, 1994; Johnson, 1995; Nuland, 1994); that looked on the human body as a machine to be repaired (Benoliel, 1997; Benoliel & Dregner, 1995; Hewa, 1994); that sought to combat and control disease and death as if they were some sort of enemy to be conquered (Callahan, 2000;

Hewa, 1994; Nuland, 1994); and that was biased in its priorities by dependence on the requirements of its funding sources (now largely controlled by a system of managed care), the financial concerns of pharmaceutical companies, and the allocation of governmental research dollars (Ebert, 1986). Nevertheless, the biomedical model continues to guide the health-care industry as well as its professionals and technicians (Cassell, 1993).

In the Preface, I briefly review some of Parker Palmer's work. Palmer has been concerned about the adverse effects of our modern educational system as detached and focused on the external. Palmer (1993) believes that the capacity for compassion and empathy is not addressed with students, and that inner subjective experience is devalued. He also states that today's educational system promotes the separation and compartmentalization of disciplines and encourages people to become manipulators of the environment instead of its stewards.

Sherwin B. Nuland is a physician who wrote a best-selling book on dying, titled *How We Die* (1994). In this book, Dr. Nuland talks about his own frustrations, for instance, at having to go along with a system that insists that each person who dies must have a specific medical "cause"—an imperative of empiricism and the biomedical system, which likes to establish clear-cut, cause-and-effect relationships. Bridling at the requirement, Nuland comments that although "old age" sounds too imprecise, the reality is that as we age, our bodies wear out, and if we don't die from one thing it'll be another. He says, "Whatever scientific diagnoses I have been scribbling on my states' death certificates to satisfy the Bureau of Vital Statistics, I know better" (pp. 43–44).

The modern, mechanistic, empirical, model that has exerted such a strong influence on science, the social sciences, our biomedical health-care system, and indeed our culture. It is now being challenged, however, by new questions and paradigms that are exposing problems on the edges of modernity and calling into question some of the old assumptions. The sense of certitude that came from the use of science and the scientific method may be taking on a new cast in the light of new discoveries from quantum physics about the remarkable complexity, potentiality, and unpredictability of life. Today, we may be awakening to new realities, in which we have come to recognize that we live with a high degree of uncertainty amidst of a maelstrom of change.

A CHANGING WORLD

To help provide a "frame" for these rapidly changing social realities, sociologists sometimes think of societies in relation to one of the most revolutionary events in human history: industrialization. It is the process by which a society uses science and technology to extract raw materials and convert them into finished products. With industrialization, jobs move from the farm to the city and people move with jobs, giving rise to urbanization, or city living. Today, many believe we are experiencing yet another change, a postindustrial era of rapid change, digital technology,

TABLE 2.2 Summary of Distinctive Characteristics of Premodern, Modern, and Postmodern Societies

	Economic focus	Characteristics
Premodern	Hunting & gathering Horticulture Pastoring Agriculture	Nonscientific world view. Religion is central to way of life. Simpler division labor. Individual members essential to the survival of the group. Relationships often stable & emotionally close. Roles stable. Environment is insurmountable. Strong sense of identity and purpose but social mobility is more difficult.
Modern	Use of advanced technology & manufacturing Urbanization	Acceptance of (Newtonian) science and the scientific method. Individual less crucial to group survival. Industrialization. Complicated division of labor. *Anomie and alienation*. Rise of capitalism. Overt manipulation of the environment. Mix of formal and informal relationships.
Postmodern	Information, communication, & service	Quantum science. World experienced as more ambiguous, with fewer certainties. Communication and information more important. Rapid rise in new knowledge. Increase in consumerism. Recognition of global interconnections." Future shock." Recognition of human impact on the environment. Relationships often diverse, but also more fluid and less clear.

and globalization (Best & Kellner, 1991, 1997, 2001; Kellner, 1990; Ritzer, 1997; Seidman, 1994). These shifts not only influence the way we live but they also change the way we die. Since industrialism is also referred to as modernism, we might wish to refer to these eras as *premodern, modern,* and *postmodern.*

An emerging postmodern perspective in many fields now uses industrialization and modernity as a point of reference. The postmodern perspective questions the assertions of modernity, suggesting they are really just social constructs that may need to be reconsidered. Table 2.2 attempts to highlight some distinguishing characteristics.

Industrial Revolution and Modernity

We can think of modernity as the era spanning the period between the dawning of the industrial revolution in the mid-eighteen century until a little after the middle of the twentieth century. One can argue that the modern social sciences (e.g., anthropology, psychology, and sociology) emerged during this time as the result of the desire to understand human behavior at a time of rapid social change (Kendall, 2010). Émile Durkheim, an early sociologist (1858–1917), thought that the rapid social changes that were taking place caused a sense of confusion, or "normlessness," which he called **anomie** (Durkheim, 1893/1964, 1897/1951; see also Ritzer, 2000, p. 82). Closely akin

We live in a rapidly changing world that can lead people to feel anxious and uncertain about what comes next. *iStock © DRAWbyDAR*

to the concept of anomie is the notion of **alienation**, a term Durkheim used to denote the sense of estrangement that results from industrialization.

Peter Berger (1977) suggests that because of modernization, four major social changes have occurred: (1) the decline of small, traditional communities; (2) an expansion of personal choice; (3) increasing social diversity; and (4) a "future orientation," with a growing awareness of time.

The shift from premodern to modern was made possible by the acceptance of Newton's physics, a cornerstone of modern science. With it came the conviction that we could uncover the secrets of the universe and unleash new power. This made the industrial age possible. Ultimately, it would lead to the development of modern medicine, and with it the ability to fight disease effectively and to prolong life.

Quantum Change

Arguably, we are on the cusp of yet another time of change. It may be more accurate to say we are now living in a postmodern world, not a modern one, which is marked by the emergence of quantum science, an emphasis on information, the growth of digital technology, increasing reliance on computers and communication, globalization, the rise of consumerism, and a preoccupation with personal choice (Best & Kellner, 1991, 1997, 2001; Kellner, 1990; Ritzer, 1997; Seidman, 1994).

So, what do these changes mean? The terms *postmodernity* and *modernity*, in contrast to their counterpart *postmodernism* and **modernism**, refer to eras, or periods of time, and not to the worldviews that characterize them (Best & Kellner, 1991, 1997, 2001; Kellner, 1990). **Postmodernity**, as implied by the term itself, is understood as the epoch following **modernity**—that period in history when modern empiricism as a philosophical paradigm reigned in the West (see Grassie, 1997; Wilson, 1997). It can be counted as a span of about 200 years between 1789 and 1989. It is sometimes thought to have had its inception in the same Zeitgeist that inspired the American and French revolutions. **Modern*ism*** is a perspective, or worldview, that is associated with the scientific model and the Enlightenment era emphasis in Europe on reason. Modernism, which originated in the West, is a systematic way of thinking that was itself a reaction to the excesses of an earlier paradigm, or model, referred to as medieval Christianity. Some suggest that modernity culminated in the collapse of the Berlin Wall—an event some say marked the end of the Cold War and the start of a new era (Fields, 1995; Oden, 1992).

■   ■   ■

Postmodernism looked at the culmination of modernity in the 20th century—the results of forces such as nationalism, totalitarianism, technocracy, consumerism, and modern warfare—and said, we can see the efficiency and the improvements, but we can also see the dehumanizing, mechanizing effects in our lives.
—Brent G. Wilson
in Dills and Romiszowski (Eds.),
Instructional Development Paradigms, 1997, p. 299

■   ■   ■

Stepping out of the vortex and into this age of the postmodern can give rise to a sense of **future shock**, to use a term first coined by futurist Alvin Toffler (1970). It refers to the natural human reactions to the kind of breakneck change characteristic of life after the mid-twentieth century. To use a metaphor from the motion picture, *The Wizard of Oz*, we may well resonate with the words of Dennis Okholm (1999), professor of theology at Wheaton College, when he says about the postmodern, "I don't think we're in Kansas anymore, Toto!"

The advances made in science, technology, and marketing may have outpaced our ability to comprehend and deal with the unanticipated consequences. You may recall the personal tragedy and public turmoil that ensued when the husband of Terri Schiavo, a woman diagnosed as being in a "persistent vegetative state," asked that her feeding tubes be removed (Weijer, 2005). The strife between family members became fare for the nightly news and a battle on the floor of Congress. The competing social values played out in the media and in the respective positions of her various family members. Terri's birth family decried the proposed action as murder by starvation while her husband defended his decision as an act of love that honored her previously stated wishes.

What to do, or not do, with technology when one is critically ill is one kind of issue. What to do after death is another. There is an inherent conflict of interests between funeral homes, which must face the realities of surviving in the modern business world, and the loved ones of the deceased. The funeral homes must recoup their overhead expenses and make a profit to stay "alive." The consumer—often dollar-strapped and grief-stricken survivors—may face a different reality: profound feelings of loss, grief, and sometimes even guilt, at a time when funeral directors are offering a range of expensive goods and services.

Modernity made advances in medicine and technology possible. With modernity also came a rise of capitalism with the demand for profit, a pharmaceutical industry to meet growing needs, and in the United States, the debate over the most appropriate way to fund health care. These and related issues in the health-care and funeral service industries have helped create a climate of change.

Today, when someone is diagnosed with a life-threatening illness, the individual can locate a range of information online—some excellent, some not so good—bout diagnosis, prognosis, course of treatment, innovations, debates, and even links to support groups. Physicians, treatment centers, hospice programs, and other resources frequently have websites. To counter the rise of a corporate funeral service industry, loved ones of the newly dead can now get abundant information online or over the phone: price surveys of burial and cremation information in the local area, discounted caskets, and local regulations.

Concepts such as premodern, modern, and postmodern simply give us a way to talk about the so-called big-picture view of change. It is at the level of individual attitudes and experience, however, where "the rubber meets the road." In the final section, we explore changing attitudes of key professionals who are regularly called on to encounter death.

CHANGING ATTITUDES

Human beings may be vulnerable to anomie, alienation, and future shock, But we are also quite capable of embracing those changes that enhance our lives and adjusting to those that don't. Examples of innovations that have emerged in response to change include the hospice movement, which emphasizes quality of life and comfort care as one approaches the end of life; increasing recognition by health-care providers about the importance of the patient's right make his or her own decisions about care; and consumer protections against funeral industry abuses.

Professional Attitudes

Health-care providers, therapists, and chaplains are practicing their professions during this time of rapid change and uncertainty. When you think about it, it's something like playing a high-stakes card game when the rules are changing in the midst of play.

Here, we explore the professional attitudes of those who care for the dying and their loved ones—people such as physicians, nurses, social workers, and chaplains. As I began the research on this topic, I expected professional attitudes to more or less reflect the roles of the players (for example, the doctor), the expectations we have of them, and the situations they're faced with; however, I learned that trying to get a clear sense of professional attitudes about death and dying from the literature wasn't nearly as easy as I had hoped.

LITERATURE ON PROFESSIONAL ATTITUDES In psychology, an *attitude* is considered to be a combination of thinking and feeling that influences behavior (see Kalat, 2002). Understanding the attitudes of professionals is important because we will be in a better position to understand why they practice as they do.

When I went looking in the literature for insight about professional attitudes, what I did not find was a body literature on the global attitudes of health-care providers about their work, or their general attitudes on death and dying. What I did find was a range of material on attitudes relating to very specific, narrowly circumscribed, topics. For example, I found articles on medical students' attitudes about end-of-life decision making (Hayes, Stoudemire, Kinlaw, Dell, & Loomis, 1999), medical staff's attitudes toward the distress of cancer patients (DeWalden-Galuszko, Majkowicz, Trzebiatowska, & Kapala, 1998), medical students' attitudes toward the autopsy (Conrad, Nowacek, Adams, & Smith, 1996), and the personal fear of death among physicians (Hamama-Raz, Solomon, & Ohry, 2000)—a favorite topic of psychologist Herman Feifel, who is often considered a founder of the modern-day field of *thanatology* (see Neimeyer & Fortner, 1997, p. 18).

In the early 1950s, Herman Feifel (see Chapter 1) became interested in the attitudes of physicians because of his experience with them when he wanted to talk with patients about thoughts and feelings about death. Neimeyer and Fortner (1997) commented, "Feifel experienced repeated rebuffs by powerful physicians who blocked his access to patients." They suggested that as a result, Feifel became interested in studying the attitudes of the very people who were making his research efforts so difficult.

Despite the patients being eager to talk about end-of-life issues, these physicians restricted Feifel's access to patients on the grounds they (the physicians) were looking after their patients' best interests. Neimeyer and Fortner (1997) said that as a result of this experience, and some pilot research that provided tentative support for the idea, Feifel developed a hypothesis that physicians were motivated by their own heightened fears of death—a view consistent with Becker's (1973) thesis, now supported by the research done by proponents of *terror management theory* (Pyszczynski, Greenberg, & Solomon, 1999a; also see Chapter 1). Not a few thanatologists suspect that at least part of the medical profession's frenetic efforts to conquer disease is related to death anxiety. To paraphrase medical ethicist Daniel Callahan (2000), it sometimes seems as if the field of medicine is attempting to eliminate death one disease at a time.

Fiefel's explorations into the suspected death anxiety of health-care providers marked the beginnings of modern-day research into professional attitudes about death. From the time of Fiefel's early investigations, the lion's share of research has been done on the suspected *death anxiety* of physicians and other health-care providers. Now, an interesting twist is that this research, which began as an open-ended search to understand the blocking behavior of physicians, became a weighty body of work focused on the suspected culprit—death anxiety—a hypothesis that despite having had a fairly long period of time to hatch has gotten only equivocal support from the evidence (for a review, see Neimeyer & Fortner, 1997). Although I know it's easy to look at how all this unfolded with the 20-20 vision of hindsight, it seems a loss that so little research attention has been given to other approaches to understanding professional attitudes about death and dying.

Although Feifel was interested in psychological explanations for the attitudes and behavior of health-care professionals, particularly their suspected fear of death (conscious or unconscious), this topic, like so many others, seems broader and more complex. Attempting to look at it with "fresh eyes," we can also look see the health-care industry, with its many providers and technicians, as not only playing a critical role in safeguarding the public health but also as being integral to our "death system" (Kastenbaum, 2010) and the very fabric of modern-day societal life. Perhaps because of its important function, and the success with which it's able to prevent premature death and extend life, the health-care industry enjoys considerable social influence and a high degree of prestige.

We can look at the resistance Feifel experienced in response to his pioneering research on physician attitudes about death and dying as being fairly consistent with what generally happens in large organizations when they feel challenged in some way. By doing direct research with the dying, Feifel was cutting across the grain at a time when death was being pushed out of view. Since part of the medical mystique is that modern medicine prevents, or at least forestalls, death, putting the spotlight on it exposes the blemishes of the mystique that lie in its shadows. From this perspective, the dream slips away—into a reality, warts and all, that conflicts with the promises of the medical miracle.

Professional Socialization

Social institutions, like the health-care system, are complex, abstract, and very real parts of our social life. But they can't continue to exist without the human beings who play important parts in making them work. To bring all this down to the level of the individual physician, nurse, psychologist, social worker, and chaplain who work in the system, we might say that each enters her or his chosen field for a variety of reasons. Some are personal—for example, there are individuals who are motivated by their own experiences with severe medical challenges who might either want to give back or fight back. Many choose a career field simply because they want to help. Others are attracted by the prospects of achieving high status or secure incomes. Some very bright and honest people are simply interested in taking advantage of their natural curiosity and interest in solving problems. Whatever the motivation—personal, social, or even spiritual—each individual will need to prepare for her or his career and will need to learn to play his or her role within the larger professional culture of their chosen fields.

Health-care providers, human service professionals, and pastoral care givers are socialized into the beliefs, norms of behavior, values, knowledge bases, and attitudes that are integral parts of their respective professions. And this plays no small role in the attitudes these recruits develop and how they play out their roles when they become full-fledged professionals. In North America, the socialization begins with undergraduate education and, depending on the profession, generally culminates in graduate or professional school.

Physicians, nurses, and human service professionals, in particular, are steeped in scientific method, since medicine, the allied health professions, and the social sciences rest solidly on a foundation of scientific empiricism, as we discussed earlier in the chapter. Pastoral care providers are probably somewhat less influenced by the empirical model since theology has traditionally had closer links to the broader discipline of philosophy, which is more deeply rooted in the humanities. Even this is changing, however, since programs that train chaplains to work in hospitals are usually hosted at major medical centers, and because the programs themselves often borrow counseling theory and methods that come out of the social sciences.

■   ■   ■

The medical profession embraces—indeed endorses—technology with little critical examination. It rewards overtesting and overtreating. And worst of all, it has trained an entire generation of doctors—mine—in certain attitudes and thought patterns that are often detrimental to patient care.

—DAVID HELLERSTEIN, M.D.
Technology Review, Alumni Association of the Massachusetts
Institute of Technology, August/September, 1983

■   ■   ■

Technology Dependence

Earlier we discussed how professionals have been socialized to play their respective roles in our health-care and death systems. In this section, we shift gears a bit, turning our attention to the topic of technology and technology dependence. The previous quote from Dr. Hellerstein's article speaks to a troubling paradox. On one hand, we are enchanted with modern technology, a child of science. On the other, many of us have a gnawing sense of frustration and concern about the potential consequences of our dependence on this irksome creation of ours.

■   ■   ■

Like the broom in "The Sorcerer's Apprentice," technologies come to have a life of their own.... Technologies come into being to serve the purposes of their users, but ultimately their users redefine their own goals in terms of the technology.

—ERIC J. CASSELL
Professor of Public Health Cornell University Medical College
Hastings Center Report, November–December, 1993

■   ■   ■

No matter how we may feel about technology—excited, concerned, or both—one thing seems certain. It has changed the way we provide health care and can be expected to continue to do so for the foreseeable future. Eric Cassell (1993), who is quoted above, comments that technology is "one thing that can be singled out as the engine of the medical economic inflation now occurring everywhere." It has also changed the attitudes and behavior of the physicians and other health-care professionals who provide care. The extensive use of technology is now considered essential to the state of the art when it comes to the standards of medical practice. Conforming to the prevailing standards of practice is not only consistent with medical ethics but it is also vital to clinicians who want to avoid malpractice suits.

The Research Imperative

Medical ethicist Daniel Callahan (2000), who is quoted elsewhere in this chapter, comments, "For several years, there has been an awareness of the often harmful power of the 'technological imperative' in the care of dying patients.... There is another imperative that now deserves more attention...the research imperative. It stems from the view that medicine has a sacred duty to combat all known causes of death." Callahan suggests there is a natural tension between this research imperative and what he calls the clinical imperative, which ultimately sees death as a natural part of the life cycle. The research imperative, however, seems to go much further than just this. It is at the core of the natural and social sciences, and as a consequence the way helping professionals understand human nature.

Research produces the knowledge on which most of the helping professions are based. Chapter 1 briefly introduced the topic of research in thanatology, including the topic of research in thanatology includes quantitative (explanatory) and quantitative (exploratory) approaches. Although there may be a renewed interest in qualitative research methods, at least in certain quarters, the quantitative approach to research and the scientific method are still the "cat's meow" in the sciences—and for good reason. There is no better research model that we know of for determining specific cause-and-effect relationships between variables. There is no doubt whatsoever that the knowledge that has come from this model has made possible the phenomenal advances that have taken place in medicine in the last hundred or so years.

The scientific model is parsimonious—simple, effective, and "elegant." When done well, research using this model leads to results that are highly relevant (valid) to understanding our experiences, as well as being reliable in establishing isolated cause-and-effect relationships between variables. But that word, *isolated,* is also a clue to something else. The model assumes the need to artificially take whatever phenomenon we want to study out of its natural environment in order to examine it in a controlled atmosphere, often dissecting it in order to do so. If we're not careful we are likely to end up learning about abstractions in a lab instead of truths about real life.

We tend to train future researchers, clinicians, and helping professionals that in order to find scientific truth, they need to isolate complex phenomena, remove them from their natural surroundings, and study them in aseptic environments. Indeed, every person who earns an academic degree from a North American college or university will have been indoctrinated, to at least some degree, into its tenets by virtue of graduation requirements in the natural and social sciences. This approach to truth-finding, while admittedly leading to remarkable advancements, may in some ways be at odds with the more holistic and humane approach to end-of-life care now gaining acceptance.

The Human Imperative: Competence in End-of-Life Care

There seems to be an increasing recognition that in its almost single-minded effort to eradicate disease and stave off death, our health-care system may have lost touch with the importance of considering the human dimensions of death and dying.

As discussed briefly in Chapter 1, Elisabeth Kübler-Ross (1969), herself a physician and psychiatrist, was a pioneering figure who has been a powerful voice in the cause of understanding and humanizing the experience of death and dying. She deserves much of the credit for ushering in a more integrated approach to dealing with end-of-life issues. She asked us to put a personal face on the experience, astutely subtitling her ground-breaking book (1969), *What the Dying Have to Teach Doctors, Nurses, Clergy and Their Own Families.*

■ ■ ■

If we could combine the teaching of the scientific and technical achieve-
ments with equal emphasis on interpersonal human relationships we would
indeed make progress.
—ELISABETH KÜBLER-ROSS, M.D.
On Death and Dying: What the Dying Have to Teach Doctors,
Nurses, Clergy and Their Own Families, 1969, pp. 11–12

■ ■ ■

Out of the ground-breaking efforts of pioneers such as Elisabeth Kübler-Ross, Herman Fiefel, and Ernest Becker (see Chapter 1), there are some hopeful signs of change in the attitudes of health-care professionals. The EPEC Project (1999 and 2003), an acronym for Educate Physicians on End-of-Life Care, is one such sign. Spearheaded by the American Medical Association with the support of the Robert Wood Johnson Foundation, it attempts to provide high-quality training to physicians on caring for those who are at the end of their lives.

Recognizing the omissions of the past, the EPEC Project acknowledges "until recently, formal education in end-of-life care has been absent from medical school and residency training.... most physicians feel ill equipped, if not fearful, to care for the dying" (p. P1-7). This project seems to have evolved out of a maturing awareness within the medical community itself about disturbing gaps in the ability of physicians to competently and sensitively care for people at the end of their lives. As outlined in the *EPEC Participant Handbook*, the EPEC Project's primary goals are aimed at enhancing physician competence in end-of-life care, strengthening relationships with patients and their families, and enhancing the physicians' own sense of satisfaction in their work with the dying.

An important part of the EPEC ethos has to do with rediscovering and reclaiming certain core values of medicine that are concerned with care and healing, as well as fostering a collaborative approach to providing treatment, in partnership with nurses, social workers, chaplains, and child life specialists. The kind of collaborative ethos expressed in the EPEC Project and the curriculum developed at Stanford University (Stanford Faculty Development Center, 2003) probably reflects the values embodied in the holistic, organic, and ecological principles at the heart of an arguably more enlightened approach to working with death, dying, and bereavement that is emerging in the field today.

Chapter Summary

We began this chapter by recalling the "classic" deathbed scene, in which the dying person takes to his or her bed, and is surrounded by loved ones until the last breath. I recounted our family's very different experience, where the last time I saw our mother was in the intensive care unit, ventilator dependent, and restrained with "soft ties" to prevent her from removing the tubes she was connected to. She was one of the seven out of ten people who die each year in a hospital or nursing home. We briefly explored the changing nature of the family, from the extended family with several generations living together, to the modern nuclear family.

Advances in medicine have extended average life expectancy from about 47 years a hundred years ago to about 78 today. These include adoption of the scientific method and resulting in improvements in food sanitation, infection control, medications to treat acute illnesses, and vaccination against disease. We noted that with the ability to manage disease, we moved the location of treatment, and ultimately death, from the home to the institution.

Next, we explored Western attitudes about death, profiling the historical analysis of Phillipe Aries, who described five eras, each of which can be understood within the context of distinct attitudes about death, from the relatively benign tame death to today's invisible or denied death.

Then, we explored developments that occurred during industrialization, noting the impact of rapidly changing cultural values, technology, and social organization on the way we care for the sick and dying. We noted here the evolution of an almost assembly-line model of work through the fragmentation of tasks coupled with a strong work ethic, pragmatism, and a desire to control nature. With this came increasing use of the biomedical model, a scientific approach to health care that became the accepted paradigm in Western medicine.

We also explored the experience of death within the context of a rapidly changing world. With broad strokes, we looked at how the experience with death has changed. With the shift from industrial to postindustrial living, we explored Alvin Toffler's concept of future shock, which attempts to describe twentieth-century reactions to the quantum changes that seem to characterize life in a postmodern world.

In the concluding section, we looked at the changing attitudes of practitioners, since they both reflect the social milieu and also help shape it. We learned about a previous generation's denial of death, professional socialization, technology dependence, the research imperative, and finally the human imperative—a movement that puts the human person at the center and that strives for competence in end-of-life care giving.

Key Terms

alienation *34*
anomie *33*
biomedical
   model *30*
death denied *28*
death of other *28*

death of self *28*
extended family *25*
Flexner Report *29*
future shock *35*
invisible death *28*
modernism *34*

modernity *34*
nuclear family *25*
postmodernity *34*
remote and imminent
   death *28*
tame death *27*

Suggested Activities

1. Try to imagine how you would prefer to die, if you had a choice in the matter. What kind of death would it be? Where would it take place? Who would be there? How would the experience unfold? Engage your imagination as much as you can. To the degree you feel comfortable with this, you may wish to use whatever experiences you already have with death. For instance, you might wish to reflect on your experience with the death of a relative or friend. Again, depending on the level of trust that's been established in your class, it might be meaningful to share this exercise in a small group or within the context of a class activity.

2. Put aside about 20 minutes and find a quiet, private, place where you can spend some time recollecting any religious or spiritual, thoughts, feelings, or experiences that have helped form your own attitudes about death and dying. Perhaps you'll just want to brainstorm the topic and write down as many thoughts as you can. Reflect on them. Write about them in your death and dying journal.

3. Take five minutes and write a paragraph about your personal views of death. What is death? What does it mean to you? You might wish to consult the guidelines found in Neimeyer, Fontana, and Gold (1984).

Suggested Reading

- Aries, Phillipe. (1982). *The hour of our death.* New York: Vintage Books.
  Now considered a classic that should be read by serious students of thanatology, this book traces the changes in Western attitudes toward death and dying from the earliest Christian times to the present day. Taking two decades to complete, it explores everything from religious rituals to grave robbing.
- Nuland, Sherwin B. (1994). *How we die.* New York: Vintage.
  This now classic book was the winner of the National Bookseller's Association award for best nonfiction in 1994. Nuland draws from his own vast experience as a physician, bringing to life what it means to be doctors, nurses, the patient, and the family.
- Strack, S. (Ed.). (1997). *Death and the Quest for Meaning.* Northvale, NJ: Jason Aronson.
  This anthology of readings is dedicated to furthering the clarion efforts of Herman Fiefelk. It is a collection of veritable gems written by of a panel of thoughtful contributors. The five-section compendium contains diverse essays on historical and religious perspectives, caregivers, children and adolescents, grief and bereavement, and current issues.

- Toffler, Alvin. (1984). *Future shock.* New York: Bantam. Published 30 years ago, fans believe Toffler's predictions have largely come true. Toffler marshals a virtual mountain of argument to make his point that a rising flood of technological, social, and economic change is influencing virtually every facet of our lives.
- Best, Steven, & Kellner, Douglas. (2001). *The postmodern adventure: Science, technology, and cultural studies at the third millennium.* New York: Guilford.
  The authors analyze a broad array of literary, cultural, and political phenomena—from fiction, film, science, and the Internet, to globalization and the rise of a transnational culture. According to these writers, the postmodern, dramatic developments in computerization and biotechnology herald the transformation from the so-called modern era into a postmodern age, replete with nuclear weapons, genetic engineering; and even cloning.
- Capra, Fritjof. (1982). *The turning point: Science, society, and the rising culture.* New York/Toronto: Bantam Books.
  For those of you who are interested in learning more about the new discoveries in science that are literally causing waves, this is a good place to start.

Links and Internet Resources

- **The Death Clock**
  www.deathclock.com/
  Here you will find the Internet's friendly reminder that life is slipping away. At this site, enter your birthday, body mass index, and whether or not you smoke, and the website will calculate a future death date.

- **Hasidic Stories Homepage**
  http://hasidicstories.com
  This is a first-rate website devoted to the telling of Chasidic stories. In addition the story, "The Baal Shem Tov and the Doctor," which is featured in this chapter, there are numerous others stories in the Chasidic tradition at this site, in addition to other resources.

- **The Fritjof Capra Home Page**
  www.fritjofcapra.net/
  Fritjof Capra is the author of several international bestsellers, including *The Tao of Physics*, *The Turning Point*, and *The Web of Life*.

- **The EPEC Project: Education in Palliative on the End-of-Life Care**
  www.epec.net/
  This remarkable website is devoted to educating physicians on how to provide high-quality end-of-life care. An inspiring effort, it was supported by a grant from the Robert Wood Johnson Foundation. There are any number of really fine resources available at, or linked to, this site, but one of the most precious gems to be found here is a complete "Participants' Handbook," which can be downloaded as a series of PDF files.

- **Growth House**
  www.growthhouse.org/
  This site contains an array of online resources, including a "Handbook for Mortals" and a link through which you can access the complete end-of-life curriculum developed by Stanford University School of Medicine (Stanford Faculty Development Center, 2003).

Review Guide

1. Consult the Glossary found at the back of this book, as well as the Key Terms used in this chapter. Become fully familiar with the definition of each term, determine an example for each, and consider how you might apply the terms to new situations.

2. How and where does death usually occur today? What social and historical forces have contributed to this?

3. How does family structure influenced our experience with death, dying, and bereavement?

4. How have advances in medicine influenced how we experience death, dying, and bereavement?

5. Phillipe Aries conducted some ground-breaking historical analysis on death in Europe from the Middle Ages to modern times. Briefly summarize the key eras, their themes, and how people during the various eras understood death. How does this compare with Becker's "denial of death," as discussed in Chapter 1?

6. What modern trends occurred in medicine influencing life expectancy? What impacts did these developments have on how we see illness and provide care? What is the biomedical model? What are its advantages and disadvantages?

7. Briefly describe Herman Fiefel's contributions to our understanding of "death anxiety."

8. Summarize the characteristics of premodern, modern, and postmodern eras. How do these influence our experience of death? According to sociologists such as Emile Durkheim and Ferdinand Tonnies, what happened as a result of industrialization? What are anomie and alienation?

9. What is "future shock" and how does this concept compare with Durkheim's notions of anomie and alienation?

10. Who is Ferdinand Tonnies? What does he say about rural versus urban living? How do his ideas differ from those of Durkheim?

11. What are modernity and postmodernity? How might we use these concepts in our quest to understand death, dying, and bereavement?

12. Be able to discuss changing attitudes of health-care providers toward death, dying, and bereavement.

3

For Everything There Is a Season
The Developmental Context

- Children's Deaths
- Learning about Death
- A World of Seriously Ill Children
- Helping Children Cope

- Death among Youth
- Death in Adulthood
- Social Development
- Life's Final Stage

■ ■ ■

For everything there is a season, and a time for every matter under heaven…a time to mourn.
—ECCLESIASTES 3:1, 4

■ ■ ■

Ecclesiastes, that often quoted and poetic book of the Hebrew scriptures, which is cited above, tells us, "For everything there is a season, and a time for every matter under heaven." It suggests that certain events in human living are part of the natural course of events, including death, grief, and mourning. When an elderly person dies, it may seem fitting because we expect life to come to an end with old age. The very concept of the death of a child, in contrast, by its very nature suggests a death that is unnatural, simply because it is so out of season.

In Chapter 2, we discussed advances in modern medicine that have been so effective in treating infectious diseases, reducing infant mortality, and increasing average life expectancy. As a result, we no longer anticipate that a child will precede his or her parents in death (Sanders, 1989, quoted in Oliver, 1999). Today, of the slightly more than 2.4 million Americans who will die in one year, relatively few will be young people. The vast majority—about 1.8 million people—will be people age 65 and older (National Center for Health Statistics, 2011).

In this chapter, we will provide a developmental context for understanding experiences with death, dying, and bereavement. We will explore the likely types of death when children do die, and they are different in infancy, toddlerhood, and childhood. There will also be a brief look at how healthy children acquire their conception of death. Also, the emotionally moving topic of gravely ill children will be explored. Then, we will discuss another particularly poignant topic: the experience of parents who have had a child die.

Death among older teens and young adults is qualitatively different than it is for children. We will look at the common causes of death in these age groups before exploring the nature of our social development. To do this, we will use Erik Erikson's eight-stage model. In addition, we will survey the common causes of death among adults and older adults before attempting to move beyond Erikson's original model of social development, to explore a proposed ninth stage, which he and his widow, Joan, suggest is life's "final stage." According to the Eriksons, in this final stage, people in their eighties and nineties, which is far more common now, have to face the challenge of coming to terms with the disintegration of the very strengths it took them a lifetime to develop. If they are lucky, the Eriksons suggest, a fortunate few will find a way to rise above this humiliating state of affairs to achieve equanimity before dying.

▪ ▪ ▪

A riddle of ancient times: What moves on four legs at dawn, two at midday, and three at sunset?
Answer: A human being. At the dawn of life, we crawl; as we mature we learn to stand upright; at the end of life we must use a cane.

▪ ▪ ▪

CHILDREN'S DEATHS

In 1994, physician Sherwin B. Nuland wrote a best-selling book on the topic of *how* we die. In this remarkably readable book, he explains what actually happens as people die from

In the first year of life infants are actually quite vulnerable.   *Randy Faris/Corbis*

various causes. In this section, we briefly explore *what* we encounter at various ages.

In an earlier day, it was quite common for many children to die young from infectious diseases. With the advances that came with modern medicine, this is far less so now (see Chapter 2). Today, slightly fewer than 2½ million people die in the United States each year (Xu, Kochanek, Murphy, & Tajada-Vera, 2010; also see Table 3.1). The vast majority are older. Table 3.1 provides a breakdown of the number of deaths in 1980 and 2007. As you can see, although death is far more likely to occur in old age, it actually strikes at every age. Table 3.2

TABLE 3.1 Number of Deaths in the United States, 1980 and 2007	
1980	
Under 1 year	45,526
1–4 years	8,187
5–14 years	10,689
15–24 years	49,027
25–44 years	108,658
45–64 years	425,338
65 years and over	1,341,848
TOTAL	1,989,273
2007	
Under 1 year	29,138
1–4 years	4,703
5–14 years	6,147
15–24 years	33,982
25–44 years	122,178
45–64 years	471,796
65 years and over	1,755,567
TOTAL	2,423,511

Sources: Centers for Disease Control/National Center for Health Statistics (1985); Xu, Kochanek, Murphy, & Tajada-Vera (2010). Available from www.cdc.gov/nchs/data/nvsr/nvsr58/nvsr58_19.pdf

provides a summary of the three leading causes of death in each of the age groups used by the National Center for Health Statistics (2011).

Newborns

In the first year of life, infants are actually quite vulnerable. In the United States, infant mortality rates have been dropping. Nevertheless, more than 29,000 newborns die each year.

The leading cause of death for children under 1 year of age are **congenital malformations**, or birth defects. Congenital malformations are characterized by structural deformities in the developing fetus. They may have various causes, including harmful genetic variations; certain conditions in the womb, such as poor nutrition in the mother or the presence of drugs or alcohol; problems during development; and infection.

TABLE 3.2	Leading Causes of Death by Age Group		
	First	**Second**	**Third**
Under 1 year	Congenital malformations	Sudden infant death syndrome	Respiratory distress syndrome
1–4 years	Unintentional injuries	Congenital malformations	Homicide
5–14 years	Unintentional injuries	Malignant neoplasms	Congenital malformations
15–24 years	Unintentional injuries	Homicide	Suicide
25–44 years	Unintentional injuries	Malignant neoplasms	Heart disease
45–64 years	Malignant neoplasms	Heart disease	Cerebrovascular disease
65 & over	Heart disease	Malignant neoplasms	Cerebrovascular disease

Source: Xu, Kochnek, Murphy, & Tajada-Vera (2010). Available from www.cdc.gov/nchs/data/nvsr/nvsr58/nvsr58_19.pdf

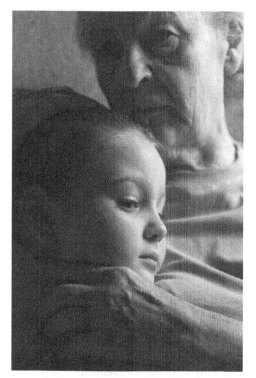

Although we usually expect death to occur among the elderly it can, and does, happen to people of all ages. *Vladimir Godnik/moodboard/Corbis*

The second leading cause of death in infants is **sudden infant death syndrome (SIDS)**, sometimes called *crib death.* It is an umbrella label used to describe the sudden death of an infant that is not expected based on medical history and that often remains uncertain, even after a thorough postmortem examination. Much remains to be learned about SIDS, but generally experts now believe it is the result of the interaction of an unstable developmental period, environmental stressors, and preexisting pathology (Krous, 2010).

The third leading cause of death among newborns is **infant respiratory distress syndrome**. This syndrome begins to unfold shortly after birth and is characterized by irregular breathing and heartbeat. Experts think it is a complication of premature birth and the inability of the lungs to develop properly (Rodriguez, Martin, & Fanaroff, 2002). The chest wall recedes and there is difficulty in breathing. It results in prolonged periods in which the baby cannot breathe and there is an increase of carbon dioxide concentrations in the blood.

Toddlers

Somewhat fewer than 5,000 children aged 1 to 4 die each year. In this age group, the leading cause of death is unintentional injuries, more than half of which can be attributed to automobile accidents (Xu, Kochanek, Murphy, & Tajada-Vera, 2010). The second leading cause of death in

---

The Death of Eli Creekmore

Approximately 1,000 children die each year from abuse or neglect, few get the kind of attention as the case of little 3-year-old Eli Creekmore, which became the focus of a documentary film, *The Unquiet Death of Eli Creekmore.* Eli took one beating after another from his father Darren, an ex-con with many other problems. There were repeated complaints to the authorities by people who knew what was happening—Eli's grandmother, emergency room doctors, and even a waitress who watched Eli bleeding from his mouth as he tried to eat ice cream. Children's Protective Services (CPS), who had removed Eli three times and put him in temporary foster care, had returned him to his parents once again. On September 26, 1986, Darren, angry that Eli was crying, kicked him in the stomach, beat him with a belt, and left him in the bathroom on the toilet. His mother, who heard Eli gasp when kicked, finally took him to the emergency room at the local hospital. Just days before, Eli had been seen in the emergency room with two black eyes, which the doctor suspected was caused by a fracture to the base of the skull. This time it was too late. He died in the ER. Darren was later convicted of second-degree murder and sentenced to 60 years in prison. Eli's mother, Mary, who said she was too afraid to help, would get 10 months.

Source: Kemp, A. *Abuse in the family: An introduction.* (1998). Florence, KY: Brooks/Cole (Cengage Learning, Inc.).

---

this age group is congenital malformations. The third leading cause of death for preschoolers is homicide. Indeed, more than 1,000 children die each year from physical abuse or neglect (see Kemp, 1998). Of those who die from direct physical abuse, over half are children under age 2. One particularly heart-wrenching story is that of the death of Eli Creekmore, a 3-year-old little boy kicked so violently by his father that his intestines ruptured, leading to his death a few hours later (see vignette).

Close on the heels of homicide are **malignant neoplasms** as the fourth leading cause of death for preschool-aged children (Xu et al., 2010). Malignant neoplasms, more commonly called *cancer,* is a class of diseases in which cells experience uncontrolled growth, destroying adjacent tissues, and sometimes spreading, or *metastasizing,* to other locations through lymph fluid or blood.

Middle Childhood

Over 6,000 children aged 5 to 14 die. Unintentional injuries are the leading cause of death for this age group (Xu et al., 2010). Again, injuries from automobile accidents are the most common. Cancer, or malignant neoplasms, moves into second place. The effects of congenital malformations is the third leading cause of death for this cohort.

LEARNING ABOUT DEATH

Elsewhere in this text, I asked you to imagine your own death. When I did so, I clearly made some assumptions about where you might be in terms of your cognitive maturity, or thinking. Because the text is written for an adult audience about a mature subject, I assumed you could participate in such an exercise at an abstract level. To borrow a concept from developmental psychology, I assumed you were able to use a thinking process called "formal operations," which we discuss later. This section explores how perspectives about death and dying change over time depending on maturity. To frame the discussion, we begin with the topic of human development, which we can also think of as the study of growth and living. For the purpose of trying to understand how children learn about death, we begin with process called **cognitive development.**

Cognitive Development

Cognitive development is a term used to refer to the process by which one's thinking matures. For example, a toddler has a different way of conceptualizing than does a child in middle school. Adolescents think differently than older people. It is a rich field of study. We barely scratch the surface here, merely as a way to begin the conversation about how we learn to understand death.

Jean Piaget, who died in 1980, was a Swiss developmental psychologist and philosopher who believed that cognitive development is at the very center of the human experience. He became interested in the development of children's thinking early in his career, partly because of informal observations of his own daughter. Later, he conducted systematic observations of her and other children at various ages, which developed into the stage-based theory of cognitive development that remains a bedrock in the field to this day (Piaget, 1937/1954). See the top portion of Table 3.3 for a linear display of Piaget's four key stages.

TABLE 3.3	Visual Summary of Developmental Schemes Articulated by Piaget, Nagy, and Tamm & Granqvist			
Piaget	birth–1.5 years	1.5–7 years	7–11 years	11 years up
	Sensorimotor	Preoperational	Concrete oper.	Formal oper.
	Simple motor responses to environment	No understanding of transformation of objects	Object permanence Beginnings of abstract thinking	Able to think abstractly
Nagy	Under 5 years No concept of permanent death	5–9 years Death is tentative & personified	9 years up Death is an event governed by natural laws	
Tamm & Granqvist	9-year-olds Death is a concrete, biological, event	12-year-olds Death is also a psychological & emotional experience	15-year-olds Death can be understood abstractly & metaphysically	18-year-olds

In Piaget's model, human thinking unfolds in a series of stages, as a result of the child's interaction with the environment, each of the later stages being dependent on the development of earlier ones. There are four basic stages in this model (see the upper portion of Table 3.3) (also see Piaget, 1937/1954; Craig & Baucom, 2002; Kalat, 2002; Santrock, 2002). The first stage, the **sensorimotor**, begins at birth and continues roughly to about age 18 months. Next is the **preoperational** stage, which unfolds in toddlerhood. It lasts from about age 18 months to around age seven years. In the school years, the model suggests, the **concrete operations** stage appears. Piaget thought it was dominant from approximately age 7 to 11 years old. According to Piaget, the emergence of the **formal operations** stage does not begin until about age 11 years and continues to be a critical part of thinking for the rest of one's life.

You might think of the sensorimotor period as an early time characterized by simple motor responses (Piaget, 1937/1954). During this period, the child is not yet able to truly understand existence outside of his or her own experience. In the preoperational stage, children begin to form stable mental concepts and begin to reason. It is also a time of "magical thinking." With respect to their understanding of death, sometimes preoperational children who have become angry with someone who later dies might think they were to blame because of a secret wish to cause harm. In the concrete operations stage, children are able to understand that people and things exist apart from the self, and that people and things change yet continue to retain their basic nature. They begin to think logically, and perhaps appreciate the significance of loss. One would not necessarily expect very young children to understand death as a permanent event until concrete operations is achieved.

It is not until about age 11 that an individual begins to form the ability to think abstractly, as adults do, that he or she reaches the formal operations stage (Piaget, 1937/1954). It is here when the person learns to integrate information, draw conclusions, and apply one's understanding to hypothetical situations. It is also when a person begins to understand such experiences as love and character, tolerate ambiguity, and imagine future possibilities. We would probably not expect a young person to fully understand the implications of death until he or she reached this stage.

Children's Understanding of Death

Piaget's theory of cognitive development provides a general framework for talking about children's thinking. Maria Nagy, a Hungarian psychologist, was among the first to explicitly attempt to "connect the dots" between age and the comprehension of death. In research done before the onset of the Second World War, she used the medium of drawing with younger children and written descriptions with older children to explore their understanding of death.

Nagy (1948/1959) identified three stages in a child's understanding of death and dying (refer to the middle portion of Table 3.3). In the first stage—generally seen in children under 5 years of age—the child doesn't really have an appreciation of death as a regular and final process. Death is experienced as a separation, or the individual is thought of as being asleep. In the second stage—generally, children ages 5 to 9—the dead are truly dead, but death itself is personified, perhaps thought of as a person, like the "grim reaper," that one might or might not be able to keep at bay. In the third stage—found in children after about age 9—the children are able to recognize dying as a normal and natural part of what it means to be human and mortal.

Three important concepts emerged from Maria Nagy's original research: the irreversibility, universality, and inevitability of death, although not exactly expressed in these terms (Speece & Brent, 1984, 1992, 1996; Candy-Gibbs, Sharp, & Petrun, 1985). **Irreversibility** refers to the notion that death is permanent; **universality** refers to the fact that death happens to everyone; and **inevitability** refers to death being a natural result of the breakdown of the body. We can think of these concepts as being the basic elements of a mature understanding of death.

In addition to these basic elements, other concepts associated with an awareness of death have since attracted the attention of investigators (e.g., nonfunctionality, causality, personal mortality, and noncorporeal continuity (Speece & Brent, 1984, 1992, 1996). The term **nonfunctionality** refers to the understanding that with death comes the utter cessation of all body functions. The concept of **causality** refers to the conceptualization of what causes death. **Personal mortality** refers to the deeper understanding that not only do all living things eventually die, but that all of us, *personally*, will die. **Noncorporeal continuity** is a more abstract concept that connotes belief that some form of personal existence—a self, soul, or psyche—will continue to exist after the demise of the body.

Based on concepts and methods originally developed by Maria Nagy (1948/1959), two Swedish researchers, Tamm and Granqvist (1995), asked a large sample of Swedish children in four age groups (ages, 9, 12, 15, and 18) to draw their impressions of the word *death* and provide a verbal commentary. Three major categories of perceptions about death, and ten subordinate categories, emerged from this research. Generally, most children in the 9-year-old group tended to see death as a biological event (exemplified by ideas of violent death, the moment of death, or the state of death). This was somewhat true for the 12-year-old group, too, although these children also described death in more psychological terms (emotional reactions, mental imagery, and a sense of emptiness). The 15-year-olds were more abstract and metaphysical in their descriptions (concept of the tunnel phenomenon, the mystery of death, notions of heaven or hell)—a pattern that was even more pronounced among the 18-year-olds. The lower portion of Table 3.3 is relevant to this discussion. Table 3.3 arrays key elements of each of the three models reviewed here.

Piaget explored the broad subject of cognitive development, which opens the conversation about how children think. Nagy (1948/1959) specifically looks at the acquisition of children's mature conception of death—irreversible, universal, and inevitable—which she suggests forms at about age 9. Tamm and Granqvist (1995) looked at four age groups, starting with a 9-year-old cohort, suggesting further development from about age 9. The 9-year-olds saw death as a concrete, biological, event, as discussed by Nagy; the 12-year-olds saw it more as a psychological and emotional experience; and the children age 15 and older saw death more abstractly and metaphysically.

A WORLD OF SERIOUSLY ILL CHILDREN

The discussion about children's conceptions of death so far has been based on the reports of healthy children. For the most part, it is consistent with our generally accepted under-standing of how children conceive of death, which is called the **standard developmental account** (Matthews, 1989). The actual experience of seriously ill children, however, does not seem to follow the standard account (Bartholome, 1995; Spinetta & Maloney, 1975; Stevens, Rytmeister, Proctor, & Bolster, 2010).

It is now well documented that gravely ill children as young as age 4 are aware they are dying despite the efforts of their caregivers and families to keep it from them (Stevens et al., 2010; Waechter, 1971, 1984, 1987; Bluebond-Langner, 1978, 1989). The early research done by Waechter (1971) was definitive. She studied 64 children, ages 6 through 10, in four equally sized groups: (1) those with a fatal disorder, (2) those with a chronic nonfatal disor-der, (3) those with a brief illness, and (4) a group of well elementary-aged children who were not hospitalized. Pictures of hospitalized children, their families, and caregivers were shown to each child. Stories were elicited from the participants to get at fantasy material relating to any concerns they might have. Only 2 of the 16 gravely ill children knew of the likely out-come of their illnesses. The generalized anxiety of all of them were more than twice as high as the other two groups of hospitalized children and three times that of the well children. A very high proportion of their stories included explicit references to death.

Parents and caregivers were working overtime to keep the bad news secret. Gravely ill children pretended not to know, keeping their fears, struggles, and loneliness to them-selves. It turns out that "children as young as four were able to piece together informa-tion from treatments they were undergoing, from their observations and conversations with other children, from overheard conversations between adults, and from their par-ents' nonverbal behavior" (Bartholome, 1995, p. 139). The multidisciplinary oncology team at the Children's Hospital in Westmead, Sydney, Australia, reported that although these children do not very often share this knowledge with their parents or caregivers, most, if not all, are well aware of it (Stevens, Rytmeister, Proctor, & Bolster, 2010). To drive this point home, the team recounted several moving stories of such children.

As a result of this emerging awareness that even very young children with poor prognoses know they are going to die, there appears to be more emphasis on taking steps to tell them about the seriousness of their illness, improve communications, involve them in making decisions about their treatment, gain their assent, and even help them take charge of their own dying, to the extent they are able to do so in a meaningful way (Bartholome, 1995). Although children often dislike formal psychotherapy, especially as understood by adults (see Sourkes, 1995), there are creative approaches to doing this work that promote self-expression. See Box 3.1 on the use of creative therapies.

HELPING CHILDREN COPE

Death is tough for adults to cope with. Imagine how it is for a child, especially if the adults around the child have a difficult time accepting and coping with the loss. To add to the difficulty, adults sometimes try to exclude children from conversations and

BOX 3.1

Focus on Practice: Using Creative Therapies

Many therapists have come to recognize that the kind of talk therapy that has been useful in work with adults may not be as effective with children (Axline, 1947; Kalff, 1980; Oaklander, 1988; Sourkes, 1995; Weinrib, 2004). Indeed, some of these same authorities find that the creative therapies—drawing, sculpting, storytelling, dramatization, and playing with figures in the sand—provides a way into deeper levels of consciousness even for adults (Kalff, 1980; Oaklander, 1988; Weinrib, 2004).

Often, children hate therapy, the way adults think of it. They do like to be listened to, though. Even better, they like to play, and are only too open in expressing what is really going on when given an opportunity to do so. Creative therapies, in which the child is given the opportunity to do art, engage in music, or even play in the sand gives them a place to do precisely this.

One particularly well-developed approach, called Sandplay, was developed by lay Jungian analyst, Dora Kalff (1980). In this approach, it is the job of the therapist to say as little as possible, but to create a safe and protected space, while the person selects miniatures from shelves and then creates a world, a story in the sand. It was Kalff's belief that the unconscious helps the individual express what is going on deep in his or her psyche, thereby fostering the natural process of healing.

Creative approaches to psychotherapy, like this Sandplay, are often easier for children to engage with than traditional talk therapies. This tray was done by Isabel, a nine year-old girl. iStock © Blair_witch

experiences because they want to protect them (Moore & Moore, 2010). They may try to shield the child from places they think will be scary for the child, such as hospitals or funeral homes. And they may even become uncomfortable around the child for fear they may say or do something "wrong."

Many bereavement professionals now seem to agree that there are no "cookie-cutter" formulas for how to help bereaved children. Each child is different, just like each adult and each relationship is different. How a child experiences loss depends on a great many things, including the child's developmental level, the nature of the relationship the child had with the deceased, the circumstances of the death, and the other experiences the child has had with death, dying, and bereavement. As suggested earlier, younger children experience loss differently than do older ones. Some children have experienced death primarily through the death of a pet or grandparents, but for others, it's a far more poignant affair, perhaps involving a parent or sibling. As is also true for adults, it may be more difficult if the death was traumatic (Kastenbaum, 2009; also see Chapters 7 and 11).

According to William Worden's handbook on grief counseling (1991, 2002, 2008) three common questions for bereaved children are: Did I cause it? (perhaps because I got angry with the person and willed it), Will it happen to me? and Who's going to take care of me? To help bereaved children, Kastenbaum (2009) suggests that responsible adults try to build an open communication pattern with these children; give them the opportunity to decide about attending the funeral; check out what the child is thinking and feeling; encourage them to express their feelings; reassure them that someone will be there to love and care for them; consider professional counseling if there are special risks; use age-appropriate books about children's experience with death and loss (for a few examples, see "Suggested Reading" at the end of this chapter).

Jane and Clint Moore (2010) suggest four general strategies when trying to talk with children about death-related issues: Be real, use appropriate and simple language, have an open agenda, and listen and observe. To "be real" means being who you are, including being a person with your own life experiences, feelings, and thoughts about what happened. This having been said, one should also be sensitive to what the child is thinking and feeling. In our efforts to explain what has happened, Moore and Moore remind us how important it is not only to include children in our conversations about death and loss but also to make sure we use language the child can understand. Having an "open agenda" means not imposing our own ideas about how the grieving process ought to unfold for the child. Don't assume just because you're an adult that you know what's best for grieving children. Follow their lead and explore their experience in a nonintrusive way. Let them express themselves in their own way, and then be sure to listen carefully and observe. Children are quite likely to communicate what's going on with them, but they're likely to do it in their own way and in their own time. Too much pushing or prying can actually get in the way of understanding what they're going through.

In Chapter 10, we discuss bereavement, grief, and mourning, including what the "new science of bereavement research" has to say about it. Most bereavement experts now seem to agree that with the help of family and friends, most bereaved people cope fairly well after a significant loss (see, e.g., Bonanno et al., 2002; Bonanno, 2004; Jordan

& Neimeyer, 2003; Bonanno, Wortman, & Nesse, 2004; Wortman & Boerner, 2007; Stroebe, Abakoumkin, & Stroebe, 2010). Unfortunately, the time-honored "grief work" model we've come to accept emphasizes "moving on" with life as quickly as possible. Katrina Koehler is the Executive Director at Gerard's House in Santa Fe, New Mexico, which is dedicated to supporting children and teens who have experienced the death of someone significant. She observes, "The very thing we have been pushing away—the natural grief process—is the very thing that can restore us after loss" (Koehler, 2010, p. 314). She believes that the natural grief process is a built-in phenomenon. Unfortunately, it doesn't feel good (see Chapter 10). What we as adults need to do is honor it.

DEATH AMONG YOUTH

Information from the *National Vital Statistics Reports* lumps high school youth and young adults into an age cohort of 15- to 24-year-olds (Xu et al., 2010). Approximately 34,000 young people in this age grouping die each year (National Center for Health Statistics, 2011). Of those, unintentional injuries are the most common cause of death. Motor vehicle injuries are implicated in most, males being twice as likely as females to die from traffic accidents.

The Shot Went Straight to the Heart

Joan, a white woman in her early forties, lives with her husband, their small child, and exchange students from Japan, in a suburban community. She is a woman who pulls no punches. When I contacted her by phone about an interview, I told her that I was doing research on the experience of parents who had "lost" a child. She agreed to the interview but wasted no time in telling me that she certainly hadn't lost her son. "It's not like he went the wrong way in the grocery store one day and I lost him," she told me. "That's not what happened. He died."

Joan's son, Zach, was apparently a lot like many other teenagers in North America. He was age 18 the year he died. It was April. He had just gotten his first real job—the kind you get without the help of your parents—busing tables at the Olive Garden, a nice Italian restaurant that sits next to the freeway in a busy part of town. He was starting to be grown up, his mother said. He had the use of a car and his mom and stepfather pretty much let him come and go as he pleased. It was a little after ten at night. He and a friend drove over to a restaurant that stayed open late. It was the time of night when the management was kicking under-aged kids out of the restaurant. Zach and his friend brushed up against two other kids, a 14- and 15-year-old on their way in. There was a minor altercation.

Later that night when Zach and his friend were driving to the friend's apartment they saw the two other boys. They pulled over, locked the car, went over to where the kids were standing and the altercation continued. One of the younger boys pulled out a gun, aimed it at Zach, and said, "Don't you think I'll shoot you?" Apparently, Zach tried to brush the gun away. As he did so, the angry youth pulled the trigger. The shot went straight to the heart. With the help of search dogs, the boys and the gun were found that same night. At 6:30 in the morning a sheriff's officer was at Joan's door. "I have a death notice to deliver," he said. Joan looked out the window. Zach's car wasn't there.

Death by homicide moves into second place for this age group. In the previous vignette is the story of one mother whose son died from homicide. The homicide rate for males is six times higher than that for females, and is significantly higher for African American and Hispanic males than for whites.

Although the suicide rate for persons aged 15 to 24 has declined slightly between 1997 and 2007, it is the third leading cause of death for those in this age group. As is true for suicide more generally, males are far more likely victims than females. Indeed, in this cohort males are five times more likely to commit suicide than females (Berman et al., 2006; Miller & Eckert, 2009; Xu et al., 2010). In Chapter 7, we explore suicide in more detail. At this point, it may be enough to say that suicidal behavior is complex (Berman et al., 2006). Many experts, however, suggest that the root of the problem can be attributed to psychological pain (Miller & Eckert, 2009).

DEATH IN ADULTHOOD

Approximately 122,000 adults, ages 25 to 44 die each year. Unintentional injuries remain the leading cause of death for this age group (Xu et al., 2010). Over 40 percent of these are related to unintentional poisoning (possibly including accidental overdoses of prescription and nonprescription medications). Cancer is the second leading cause of death for this cohort. For men, the chief culprits are lung, brain, and colon cancers. For women, it is breast, lung, and cervical cancers. The third leading cause of death for this age group is heart disease.

In the older age groups, the number of people who die rises dramatically. Nearly half a million adults ages 45 to 64 die each year (Xu et al., 2010). Cancer moves into first place as the leading cause of death among those in this age group (33 percent), followed by heart disease (22 percent), and finally by unintentional injuries (7 percent).

Understandably, the single largest number of people who die each year are those age 65 and older. Each year, more than 1.8 million people in this age group die (Xu et al., 2010). Heart disease moves into first place as the leading cause of death in this age group (23 percent), with cancer coming in at a close second (22 percent), followed by stroke (7 percent), a distant third.

SOCIAL DEVELOPMENT

This section explores the kinds of goals, struggles, and strengths that seem to emerge at different junctures in people's lives as we relate to death and dying. The focus is on the experiences and perceptions formed beginning in adolescence and continuing through late adulthood.

Erik Erikson, a luminary in the field of social development, pioneered a well-known model that attempts to explain development as a social process, involving passage through a series of eight developmental crises and eight stages of social development, from infancy through old age. In this model, each stage comes with its own life tasks, which Erikson refers to as **syntonic**, and their related struggles, which he calls **dystonic** (Erikson, 1963, 1982; Erikson & Erikson, 1997). The syntonic tasks exist in dynamic tension with the opposing, dystonic, challenges as the person moves through successive developmental stages. In addition, each stage has an existential question, such as, "Is the world a safe place?" "Who am I?" "Has my life had meaning?"

In his last major work, Erikson suggested that as people successfully navigate through each stage, there is the potential to achieve a new strength. As a result of successfully getting through infancy's struggle—one that centers on the question of whether or not the world is a safe place—the new strength that emerges is a sense of hope. Similarly, for the toddler what emerges is will; in the preschool years, it is purpose; in middle childhood, competence; in adolescence, fidelity; in young adulthood, love; in middle age, care; and finally, in old age, wisdom. In Erikson's scheme, people carry the strengths they acquire for the remainder of their lives, using them as needed to overcome life's many challenges.

For the sake of providing a touchstone, I've summarized Erikson's model of social development in Table 3.4. If you are not already familiar with the model, you may wish to take a few moments to acquaint yourself with it. If you are already familiar with it, this will be a review. Erikson proposes a model on how social development unfolds from childhood, young adulthood, middle age, and elderhood.

We previously discussed childhood experiences. In this section we pick up the discussion with adolescence, giving only brief mention of childhood social development. Adolescence, in Erikson's view, is a time of striving to find a sense of personal identity, but it is also a time of struggle with the countervailing dynamic of role confusion (Erikson, 1963, 1982; Erikson & Erikson, 1997). As we commonly understand it, adolescence is also an occasion of transition between childhood and adulthood, and is associated with a heightened sense of turmoil and uncertainty. The existential issue, in Erikson's view, has to do with the question, Who am I? In relation to death, this period is a time when death often feels remote and not personally meaningful (Santrock, 2002).

■ ■ ■

Adolescents...show a sense of invincibility, believing that they themselves will never suffer the terrible experiences (such as deadly car wrecks) that can happen to other people. This sense of invincibility likely is involved in the reckless behavior of some adolescents, such as drag racing, drug use, suicide, and having sexual intercourse without using contraceptives.

—JOHN W. SANTROCK
Life-Span Development, 2002, p. 331

■ ■ ■

The term **adolescent egocentrism** is a term that is sometimes used to explain the sense of invulnerability that seems so characteristic of adolescence and adolescents.

TABLE 3.4	An Overview of Erikson's Developmental Model		
	Life Task (syntonic)	**Struggle (dystonic)**	**Existential Questions/Emergent Strengths**
Infancy	Basic trust	Mistrust	Is my world the kind of place that is predictable and safe? Emergent Strength: Hope
Toddlerhood	Autonomy	Shame & doubt	Can I function independently or must I always rely on others? Emergent Strength: Will
Preschool Years	Initiative	Guilt	Am I good or bad? Emergent Strength: Purpose
Middle Childhood	Industry	Inferiority	Do I have value and worth? Emergent Strength: Competence
Adolescence	Identity	Role confusion	Who am I? Emergent Strength: Fidelity
Young Adulthood	Intimacy	Isolation	Will I find depth in a committed relationship or live life in isolation? Emergent Strength: Love
Middle Age	Generativity	Stagnation	Will I pass along something of worth or just take up space? Emergent Strength: Care
Old Age	Integrity	Despair	Has my life had meaning or has it been all for naught? Emergent Strength: Wisdom

Sources: Erikson (1963, 1982); Erikson & Erikson (1967).

John Santrock (2002), one writer on human development, comments that adolescents all too often seem preoccupied with themselves and in "their belief that they are invincible and unique" (p. 609). "I know everybody has to die, but what does that have to do with me," Santrock quips in parody of the kind of comment an adolescent might make. Adolescent egocentrism is a heightened sense of self-consciousness experienced by adolescents, he suggests. Elkind and Bowen (1979) break adolescent egocentrism down into two types: imaginary audience and personal fable. In **imaginary audience**, adolescents imagine that others are as preoccupied with themselves as they are, always thinking about them. We can think of **personal fable** as the adolescent's sense of uniqueness and invincibility.

The sense of invincibility may be understandable, especially if one considers the actual lack of experience most adolescents have with death, the invisibility of death today, and the death-denying proclivity of the culture. Depending on circumstances, young people are not usually at very serious risk of experiencing death personally (although some adolescents are all too familiar with it). This is a far different reality from what existed a mere hundred years ago (and by young people who live in other parts of the world today), when a youthful death from a variety of infectious diseases was much more common. As discussed earlier in the chapter, statistics suggest that of the approximately 2.4 million deaths we expect will take place in the United States each year, about 34,000 will involve persons ages 15 to 24 (Xu et al., 2010).

As you can see from a review of Table 3.2, among chief causes of death among young people in the United States are accidents, homicide, and suicide, depending on age bracket and social circumstances (e.g., cancer, or malignant neoplasms, is the second leading cause of death for youth ages 5 to 14). Although there is a dearth of literature on the subject, when adolescents do encounter death, they can be profoundly impacted. Such an observation has tremendous contemporary implications. When a young person dies for any reason, its impact can reverberate throughout his or her school. When we consider the phenomenon of school shootings, we are reminded of the far-ranging impacts of youth violence and death (see links given at the end of this chapter).

If we can describe adolescence as a time of personal fable, we might depict young adulthood as the era of Romeo and Juliet. Although we can readily sense the implications of death at this age (e.g., it is the time when the young go to war; also when they are infected with HIV/AIDS), there is a paucity of research about young adult perspectives on death (Santrock, 2002). In Erikson's model (1963, 1982), this is the stage of social development in our society in which the search for intimacy is the prime imperative—love, the strength that emerges when intimacy prevails over isolation. The death of one's beloved is a particularly poignant and heart-wrenching experience. The now classic 1970 movie, *Love Story,* starring Ali MacGraw and Ryan O'Neal, is an especially touching work on this theme. Perhaps the acclaim the film received reflects our natural sensitivity to this kind of tragedy. Although admittedly anecdotal, I recall a young man who worked for my brother and who died in a tragic bicycle riding accident. He left a young, beautiful, and pregnant widow behind. It was only recently that I learned that devastated by the death of her husband, she raised their only child alone. She never remarried. Tragic accidents continue to be the leading cause of death among young adults, but as you can see from glancing at Table 3.2, both homicide and suicide drop away as the leading causes of death in adulthood, to be replaced by cancer (malignant neoplasms), the cause of the heroine's death in *Love Story*, and heart disease (cardiovascular disease) (Xu et al., 2010).

In Erikson's model, midlife is the season of life when one becomes concerned with generativity, or passing something along for posterity (Erikson, 1963, 1982; Erikson & Erikson, 1997). It is also a time in life when one has lived long enough to have lost friends and acquaintances, not to mention the quite common experience of losing one's parents. This can bring home in a real way the message that life as we knew it comes to an end.

During middle adulthood, or middle age, cancer becomes the leading cause of death, followed by heart disease (Xu et al., 2010). Cerebrovascular disease appears in third place. A whole generation of baby boomers is now in midlife. Perhaps the experience of seeing one's friends and parents die is contributing to a process of self-examination and reevaluation among this group—the flower child generation—which came of age in the 1960s.

Some suggest that with midlife comes a rise in consciousness about death and dying that springs from an increasing awareness about one's aging (Santrock, 2002). Old age is described by Erikson as the era when people strive to find integrity (meaning and purpose in their life) (Erikson, 1963, 1982; Erikson & Erikson, 1997), but perhaps we can say midlife is the starting point for this process. In fact, several excellent books describe midlife as a time of reawakening and new development—a time for a personal quest or spiritual journey (see Brehony, 1996; Moody, 1997; Rupp, 1996).

My mid-life journey has taken me deeper than I ever dreamed I would go. It has not always been a journey that I have chosen. I have felt, at times, that I was being pushed and shoved forward on the road that would set me free. At other times, I relentlessly pursued the path that led down to the darkness where wisdom waited to greet me.

– JOYCE RUPP
Dear Heart, Come Home: The Path of Mid-Life Spirituality, 1996, p. 10

The end-stage of life has been dubbed by Erikson as a season of integrity or despair (Erikson, 1963, 1982; Erikson & Erikson, 1997). Often we think of people who are coming to the end of their lives as needing to reflect on their lives, their triumphs, and their disappointments. Santrock (2002) suggests that as a result of engaging in the process of reflection, one's death can take on a dignity that it may have lacked in earlier years. How one dies, according to this view, can in some ways be as important as how one lived.

The term **life review** is sometimes used in the field of thanatology to describe the process of reflecting on one's life at the end of it (Butler, 1968, 1980–81), as cited in Craig & Baucom, 2002). It is often felt that this process can result in new "grace." From this perspective, old age need not be a stagnant time of waiting for an inevitable, dreadful end. Indeed, it can be seen as a time when a person finds a fresh resolve to move toward self-awareness, leading to new growth, resolving "unfinished business," finding a renewed sense of meaning in life, and making fresh discoveries about the self.

The standard version of *The Life Cycle Completed* was Erik Erikson's last major work on human social development (Erikson, 1982). Although he did not substantially alter his original model, he did revisit it, this time starting from the standpoint of old age. Eighty years old when he wrote this, Erikson says, "I...begin my account of the stages with the last one, *old age*, to see how much sense a re-view of the *completed* life cycle can make of its whole course" (p. 12).

The struggle that characterizes old age in Erikson's model is that of *integrity* versus *despair* (1963, 1982; Erikson & Erikson, 1997). Given the nature of old age as a time when a person experiences losses in body, mind, and relationships, Erikson suggests that the dystonic element—*despair*—can sometimes be more pronounced

(Erikson, 1982; Erikson & Erikson, 1997). Rather than gaining *wisdom*, it is all too easy for elderly people to find its opposite, *disdain*. He attributes this to the many negative experiences associated with old age: declining body functioning, receding mental acuity, or even the experience of utter helplessness. The despair people confront in old age, according to Erikson (1982; Erikson & Erikson, 1997), is inversely related to hope, a strength that comes into being as a natural outcrop of achieving basic trust. Hope, when experienced in its mature form at the end of life, Erikson tells us, can also contribute to a sense of coherence and wholeness that are hallmarks of integrity.

Even the best cared for bodies begin to weaken and do not function as they once did. In spite of every effort to maintain strength and control, the body continues to lose its autonomy. Despair, which haunts the eighth stage, is a close companion in the ninth because it is almost impossible to know what emergencies and losses of physical ability are imminent. As independence and control are challenged, self-esteem and confidence weaken.

—JOAN M. ERIKSON
The Life Cycle Completed, 1997, pp. 105–106

LIFE'S FINAL STAGE

We'll now look at a proposed ninth stage in Erikson's model of social development, but you might also think of it as life's final stage, in the sense of a drama that plays out in life.

Based on years of personal discussions, Erik Erikson's wife and long-time collaborator, Joan Erikson, expanded *The Life Cycle Completed* and proposed a ninth stage of development, which she suggests completes the model her husband had worked on all of his life (Erikson & Erikson, 1997). Both she and Erik Erikson lived into their nineties. She suggests old age in one's eighties and nineties, an experience that is becoming far more common, brings with it difficulties she believes can only be adequately addressed by a new ninth stage of development.

Based on a careful review of the notes Erik scribbled in the margins of his own copy of the original edition of *The Lifecycle Completed*, as well as her own understanding of her husband's thinking, Joan Erikson describes this ninth stage, focusing on coming to terms with the disintegration of the very strengths that had developed over the course of an entire lifetime (Erikson & Erikson, 1997).

In the ninth stage of development, Joan Erikson writes that hope often gives way to despair as the elderly person experiences chronic and sudden indignities. Shame and doubt return, she writes, when elders can no longer trust in the functioning of their bodies or the soundness of their choices. Guilt often reemerges, she suggests, when elderly people become too focused on topics that amuse themselves, forgetting they are engaged in a dialog involving others. She continues, the elderly are vulnerable to a feeling of inferiority, which results when the nagging inadequacies of old age reveal themselves. Identity confusion, a problem originally associated with adolescence, reappears in old age, she writes, when the social status and roles the elderly once held are lost. *Isolation* versus *intimacy*, a focal point for young adults, again becomes an issue for elders who have lost their life partners, therefore barring them from expressing themselves within the context of an intimate relationship. In addition, many live in isolation, left home alone or forgotten in long-term care facilities. *Generativity,* the process of making contributions to society, is no longer expected when one is 80 or 90 years old. It can also leave a person feeling useless and unimportant.

The litany of challenges is daunting. Joan Erikson, however, suggests that if a person can somehow come to terms with all the troubling issues of his or her eighties or nineties, the individual could be on the path to **gerotranscendence**, a state that only a minority of elderly people are able to achieve. She suggests, one can think of it as a state of equanimity—a strength that is unique to the ninth stage. Based on the work of Tornstam and colleagues, Joan Erikson says *gerotranscendence* has five key characteristics (Tornstam, 1993):

1. There is a feeling of cosmic communion with the spirit of the universe.
2. Time is experienced in the present.
3. The experience of space begins to coincide with one's physical abilities.
4. Impending death is understood as a natural event.
5. One's sense of self expands to include a wider range of interrelationships.

Here, it may be appropriate to share a story about the last days of Ernest Becker's life (Craig & Baucum, 2002). Becker, who, you may recall from Chapter 1, was the thanatology pioneer who introduced the term *denial of death.* When the story unfolded, Becker was hospitalized, in the final stages of dying of cancer. Surviving a series of end-of-life crises, he is said to have finally achieved a state of transcendence—a heightened sense of awareness and peace, in which he told an interviewer that he was able to find meaning in his death only through faith in life, which understands that "the creative energies of the cosmos" is using each of us for a purpose we may not fully comprehend (pp. 634–635).

Chapter Summary

The chapter began by surveying encounters with death at different times of life, according to age group. We then explored our cognitive understanding of death and dying across the life span, beginning with an application of Piaget's model of cognitive development. We reviewed Maria Nagy's model on the acquisition of the conceptual understanding of death. This was followed by a brief review of some work by Swedish researchers who extended Nagy's model. All of this work was done with a focus on well children. Then we turned our attention to research done with critically ill children, noting that some of the assumptions of cognitive theory appeared not to hold.

Finally, the discussion moved to social development, the part of the field of human development that examines how human beings interact with each other and develop socially. Beginning with adolescence, the period when people are first able to use abstract thinking, this section reviewed some of Erik Erikson's seminal ideas and we attempted to apply Erikson's model of social development to issues of death and dying across the life span. Erikson's model proposes that people confront a sequence of unique crises at each stage of life. The chapter explored the nature of the life tasks, the struggles confronted, the existential questions posed, as well as the strengths that develop at the various stages of development. While Erikson developed his model when he himself was in midlife, he revisited it when he and his wife, Joan, were quite elderly. We also looked at the work of Joan Erikson, who attempted to complete her husband's work after he died by writing about a ninth, and final, stage of development.

Key Terms

adolescent egocentrism *58*
causality *52*
cognitive
    development *50*
concrete operations *51*
congenital malformation *47*
dystonic *58*
formal operations *51*
gerotranscendence *63*
imaginary audience *59*

inevitability *52*
infant respiratory distress
    syndrome *48*
irreversibility *52*
life review *61*
malignant neoplasms *49*
noncorporeal
    continuity *52*
nonfunctionality *52*
personal fable *59*

personal mortality *52*
preoperational *51*
sensorimotor *51*
standard developmental
    account *53*
sudden infant death syndrome
    (SIDS) *48*
syntonic *58*
universality *52*

Suggested Activities

1. Draw a time line of your life. On a piece of paper draw a line that represents birth to the present. Indicate years along the line and include significant events. Consider "where" you were "at" in terms of your development, awareness, and state of mind. What sorts of things were influencing you? What kind of impact were you having on others?

2. Make a list of people you have personally known who have died. Consider their age and the kind of death they experienced. What happened? Who was around? Did they become ill or did they die suddenly and unexpectedly? Did the manner of death make a difference to them and those around them?

3. Reflect on your relationship with a dying person, or a person you know who has died. Did you and the person who eventually died know she or he was dying? As a result, what did you experience? How has this person's death impacted your own life? Did you learn anything from the experience?

Suggested Reading

- Boritzer, E. (2000). *What is death?* Santa Monica, CA: Veronica Lane Books.

  A children's book that tries to explain the concept of death with examples from diverse cultures and religions. This book tries to encourage children to see the positive in life while also learning about its realities.

- Jukes, M. (1985). *Blackberries in the dark.* New York: Dell Yearling.

  This is a small little book about Austin, a young boy who had spent many summers with his grandparents, picking blackberries among other things. But Grandma is now alone on the farm and everything is different. Grandma and Austin have to learn to create some new traditions in order to keep Grandpa's memory alive.

- Zotovich, K. D. (2000). *Good grief for kids.* Los Osos, CA: Journal Keepers.

  This focus of this book is to guide children through grief associated with various losses through a process of journaling. It is designed to help children create their own books in which to express and work through their grief.

- Fry, V. L. (2005). *Part of me died too: Stories of creative survival among bereaved children and teenagers.* Montpelier, VT: Phoenix Rising Press.

  Eleven true stories about children and teens who experienced the death of family members or friends may be found in this book. Through the use of writing, drawing, games, projects, and rituals, these stories tell of the loss of pets and grandparents, as well as more troubling and complex experiences, such as losses that result from accidents, HIV/AIDS, suicide, and abusive parents.

- Sourkes, B. M. (1995). *Armfuls of time.* Pittsburgh: University of Pittsburgh Press.

  This enormously moving book takes us into the psychological world of children who are facing life-threatening illnesses. It artfully reveals the things these children do to learn how to live with their illnesses.

- Brehony, K. A. (1996). *Awakening at mid-life: A guide to reviving your spirit, recreating your life, and returning to your true self.* New York: Riverhead Books.

  Written by a Jungian psychologist, this highly readable and enjoyable book attempts to combine Jungian archetypal concepts about life's journey with practical steps that can further a person's development during midlife, including the spiritual and physical aspects of aging.

- Erikson, E. H., & Erikson, J. M. (1997). *The life-cycle completed: Extended version with new chapters on the ninth stage of development.* New York: Norton.

  This book, coauthored by the husband-wife team of Erik and Joan Erikson, reviews Erikson's theories of human development and discusses a proposed ninth stage of human development.

Links and Internet Resources

- **The Dougy Center**
  www.dougy.org/
  This site provides resources for families dealing with the loss of a loved one. There's advice for parents on how to talk with children about death and dying, and a special section just for kids.

- **Gerard's House**
  gerardshouse.org/
  Gerard's House is a center in Santa Fe, New Mexico, that supports children and teenagers who have experienced the death of someone significant in their lives through free weekly peer support groups. Youth ages 3 through 20 are together with other young people while their parents or caregivers conduct their own group experience at the same time.

- **Starbright World**
  www.starbright.org/projects/sbworld/
  Starbright World (SBW) is a website that tries to create a safe and secure online community for kids and teens living with serious illnesses. Kids on SBW can chat, read, and post to bulletin boards, e-mail, search for friends with similar illnesses, participate in fun events and contests, surf prescreened websites and play games.

- **Children's Hospice International**
  www.chionline.org/
  This is the website for Children's Hospice International (CHI), a nonprofit organization that was founded in 1983 to promote hospice, encourage the integration of children in hospice programs, and include the hospice perspectives in all areas of pediatric care.

- **Sandplay Therapists of America**
  www.sandplay.org/
  This site is dedicated to promoting Sandplay therapy and the legacy of Dora Kalff. The site contains a number of resources, including a directory of STA practitioners across the United States.

Review Guide

1. Be familiar with the definitions of each of the concepts that were printed in **bold** in the chapter.
2. Be familiar with the basic demographic information about death at various ages. What are the leading causes of death in each age range?
3. Be familiar with the key stages in Piaget's model of cognitive development. What role does cognitive development play in the perceptions of children about death and dying?
4. Be familiar with children's conceptions of death and dying. What are the key differences, depending on age and stage of development?
5. What is the scientific evidence for how children acquire a concept about death? Briefly summarize Piaget's system. Why is the concept of formal operations significant?
6. What do you know about the experience of children with a terminal illnesses?
7. What are the most common causes of death for youth and young adults? How do these differ from those of children? What are the qualitative differences between youth/young adults and children in terms of what they experience?
8. Briefly discuss Erik Erikson's stages. What are the differences between cognitive and social development?

According to this model what happens at each stage? What are the goals? Struggles? Existential questions? What does it mean to say that these crises involve *dystonic* and *syntonic* features? What strength is learned as a result of passing through each stage? What are the challenges associated with the eighth stage of development? What is a "life review"?

9. What is the ninth stage of development? What is gerotranscendence, and under what conditions does it emerge?
10. What do the official data say about causes of death for each major age group discussed by Erikson? Discuss any developmental issues raised in the chapter that you felt were significant.
11. Do you think Erikson's model adequately explains what actually happens as people progress through our lives? Explain.
12. Be familiar with the mortality statistics included in the chapter. What do researchers know about the age at which people die? What does it mean in terms of the types of death most commonly experienced by people in North America today? How has this changed from previous eras?

4

Coureurs de Bois

Cross-Cultural and Interfaith Dimensions

- **Conceptual Tools**
- **Culture, Spirit, & Death**
- **Key Religious Perspectives**

- **The Hero's Quest**
- **Chautauqua**

The term *coureurs de bois* is a French-Canadian expression that literally translates as "runners in the woods." It has a rich meaning in Canadian history, harkening back to the early days of colonization, when the fur traders who ventured throughout the back woods came together each year, sat in a circle, and shared stories about all the places they had been and the things they had seen during the previous year. I would like to recapture something of that pioneer spirit, making this chapter a sort of worldwide *coureurs de bois,* with the chance to hear the stories of other sojourners, people from other parts of the world, on their experiences with death and dying.

■   ■   ■

I know death hath ten thousand several doors for men to take their exits.
—JOHN WEBSTER (1580–1625)

■   ■   ■

In previous chapters, we've discussed "lifting the pall" (i.e., the "denial of death" and reality of death); explored our changing experience of death, from premodern times to the present; and looked at the experience of death across the human life span. In this chapter, we explore the cultural and religious dimensions. To better accomplish this, we will review a few conceptual

Although experiences with death, dying, and bereavement can be among the most powerful and intimate experiences we one can have, in cultures like ours we often try to distance ourselves from the realities of death. *JORGE SILVA/Reuters/Corbis*

tools I think may help you understand your worldview and the perspectives of others. The overriding question is, How does one's worldview affect the understanding of death? This part of the journey begins with an exploration of insights coming from the fields of anthropology and sociology on the role of religious belief and spirituality in relation to experience with death. In this regard, the chapter briefly reviews a few key religious perspectives. Then it explores a possible role for myth and the "hero's quest."

The chapter concludes with a collection of cross-cultural stories and teachings about death—what I'm calling a *chautauqua*. By stepping into diverse cultural and spiritual perspectives, the aim is to come to a better understanding of others and ourselves. In addition to situating North American society in a cross-cultural and interfaith context, in this chapter you will have the opportunity to sample a few different ways of relating to death. We will review a literary vision of death, "the call of the owl," inspired by Native American tradition. There are also short excerpts included from interviews I conducted with a number of spiritual leaders on the Indian subcontinent, most notably with Tenzin Gyatso, who is better known as His Holiness the Dalai Lama of Tibet. In conclusion, the chapter explores the traditions of Oaxaca, Mexico, during *dias de los muertos*—"the days of the dead."

CONCEPTUAL TOOLS

Let's begin with a discussion of a few basic concepts—conceptual tools—from the social sciences that I think might help you better understand the cultures we will explore. I am introducing these now so they are available when we move into the discussion of various cultural and religious views. But, before we begin, I'd like to ask you to participate in a short exercise from Box 4.1. The exercise is designed to provide a simple experience that might move you to become a bit more aware of the role of worldviews—in German, this is called *weltanschauung*. I think this kind of activity works because it makes its point with a minimum of jargon and explanation.

Each of us has a worldview that is shaped by individual experiences, what we are taught by our parents and learn in our culture. *Culture* is an all-encompassing concept that relates to a total way of experiencing life. It includes everything within the "social environment"—language, beliefs, values, norms, customs, as well as the material objects that are passed on from one generation to the next, becoming integral to heritage. You can think of it as being like the air around us—something that you might not even pay much attention to it unless it's not there. It pervades everything. It provides a framework for understanding the entirety of experience. It gives meaning.

Although personal experience, family upbringing, and culture inform the interpretation of experience, there is a down side. They can also limit the ability to appreciate perspectives

BOX 4.1

From Your Place in the Circle

Take a piece of paper and fold it in half, then in half again so that you've created four quadrangles. In the corner of the fold, tear out about a one-inch piece. Unfold the paper, revealing a small empty patch, where the corner had been. Everyone get in a big circle. Now, hold the paper a few inches away from your face. Carefully observe what is framed by the hole in the paper. Take note of what you see. Try to take in as much of what is exposed in the small window, ignoring the paper itself and anything else. Take in only one piece of the picture. Focus on one area. Do not rotate your field of vision. Now, take about 10 or 15 minutes and write a paragraph about what you saw.

Break into small groups and read your paragraphs to one another (or if you have a small class, you may want to do this with the entire group). Did everyone "see" the same thing? Did everyone share the same perceptions? Did everyone accomplish this task in the same way? If you took this exercise seriously, I suspect that each of you wrote about something quite different. Not only am I fairly certain each of you had a slightly dissimilar field of vision, each of you interpreted what you saw individually, and each of you wrote about it in your own way. To use a Native American way of expressing it, we see a different aspect of "reality" depending on what part of the circle we happen to be sitting in.

that are different from our own. At an individual level, when one meets someone who is very dogmatic or self-centered in her or his views, you might describe that person as egocentric. This is the kind of person who always insists on being "right," and who can't seem to listen to or respect the views of others. Anthropologists use the word **ethnocentrism** to describe group attitudes when a people in one culture become so caught up in their own invisible biases that they fail to appreciate the contributions or worth of people from a different culture. This is also where our exercise ties in. Unless one spends time in other cultures and takes steps to learn about them, there is the danger that one will fall victim to *ethnocentrism*—using the beliefs, norms, and values of one's own culture to judge another.

People in a society organize themselves in order to deal with their life circumstances—coping with outside dangers, procuring the necessities of life, and forming mutually beneficial relationships with others. *How* they accomplish basic life tasks—what tools they use and what attitudes, values, norms, and behaviors they adopt—constitutes the essence of the culture. In the social sciences, culture is commonly thought to be of two basic types: *material* and *nonmaterial*. When an archaeologist, a specialist within anthropology concerned with the study of the physical remains of human settlements, digs up a grave site (**material culture**)—head dress, weapons, and other valuable items—from an ancient site, he or she will use what is unearthed, the technology, so to speak, of the culture, to learn something about the people who were a part of that culture, including how they memorialize their dead. When we explore the behavior, beliefs, values, or norms, of a people in relation to death and dying, we are delving into the **nonmaterial culture**—the aspects of death and dying for that group of people, including their beliefs about the afterlife.

This brings us to another pair of conceptual tools. These are called the *etic* and *emic* approaches to documenting living cultures. In the **etic** approach, the social scientist uses the concepts and categories of one's own culture to describe that of another. It is a type of analysis done from the theoretical frame reference of the social scientist. In the **emic** approach, the emphasis is on attempting to uncover explanations that come from the perspective of the culture one is studying. Rather than trying to impose an outside perspective, in the *emic* approach we attempt to understand why people do what they do from their frame of reference. Max Weber, a pioneering sociologist, used the term *verstehen*, the German word for "understanding," to describe insight about social experience (Henslin, 2005). By adopting the emic approach, it is easier to plumb the depths of subjective experience.

When exploring culture, it is often important to understand the differences between the ideal and the real aspects of culture. As implied by the name, **ideal culture** represents the values, beliefs, and behavior the culture aspires to. No culture is able to actually perform to the full extent of its ideals, however. **Real culture** reflects the beliefs, norms, and values that are actually played out. For example, in North America we might like to think we are very open and accepting of differences. In reality, there is still a great deal of prejudice and discrimination, even if less open and overt than in times past. Virtually every society has both ideal and real aspects of its culture.

The last pair of conceptual tools are those of *culture contact* and *cultural diffusion*. **Culture contact** refers to what occurs when the people from one culture come in contact with those from another. For example, culture contact between Europeans and the aboriginal peoples of North America occurred in 1492, when Columbus set foot on Hispanola. **Cultural diffusion** occurs when the exchange of cultural elements between cultures takes place. These could be material objects—muskets or steel knives, for instance—or nonmaterial things such as concepts, values, or even a religious creed. When culture contact occurs, both societies are likely to be changed in some way. Most social scientists believe it's unlikely for culture contact to occur without at least some cultural change, even if minimal. Sociologist George Ritzer (1998) coined the term *McDonaldization*. The term serves as a symbol of contemporary cultural diffusion, referring to the diffusion of one piece of popular North American culture through the international marketing of such fast-food products as the "Big Mac" hamburger, which, of course, is also part of the modern *material culture*. Although this diffusion is sometimes indigenized (e.g., mutton may be substituted for beef in Delhi, or the *ham*burger may be called a *beef*burger in parts of the Arab world), it is a feature of what many now call **globalization**. Verstehen? In Chapter 6, we discuss "McDeath," or the corporate commercialization of death, which began in the United States and which appears to be spreading.

CULTURE, SPIRIT, AND DEATH

Culture and Spirit

The nonmaterial dimension of culture embodies all the common beliefs, values, and norms of a people that are passed on from one generation to the next. Religion may be what social scientists refer to as a **cultural universal**—one of those few elements that exists in virtually every society (Murdock, 1945). Indeed, every known society has had an explicitly religious or spiritual dimension (Faiver, Ingersoll, O'Brien, & McNally, 2001; Parsons, 1952). It is integral to the *nonmaterial culture*, providing a way to understand an otherwise incomprehensible world. Religion functions to guide human behavior, endows a sense of meaning, and unifies a people into a community of believers (Durkheim, 1912/1995). The culture itself gives a people a sense of common identity. It distinguishes them from others and it serves as a source of dignity and self-respect.

■   ■   ■

Given the biological and social nature of man on this planet, some kind of religious system is a cultural universal; no human society can get along without a religion any more than it can survive without an economic system.
—WILLIAM A. LESSA AND EVON Z. VOGT
Reader in comparative religion: An anthropological approach, 1979, p. 36

■   ■   ■

One early approach to understanding the role of religion in relation to death came out of an exploration of belief in the existence of a soul. Edward Tyler (1873) thought that this belief sprang out of the need for people to explain such events as death, sleep, dreams, hallucinations, and so forth (Lessa & Vogt, 1979). From his perspective, the belief in a soul evolved into the worship of ancestors, spirits, deities, and finally a monotheistic creator God. Other early theorists (e.g., Frazer, 1909, 1911–1915) took a different tack, looking to the awareness of death, fear of death, and fear of *the* dead to explain why people come to believe in the existence of a soul.

As you recall from Chapter 1, *terror management theory* suggests that at the core, cultural worldviews help shield human beings from the awareness of their own vulnerability to death (Pyszczynski, Greenberg, Solomon, & Hamilton, 1990; Pyszczynski, Greenberg, & Solomon, 1999a; Pyszczynski, Solomon, & Greenberg, 2003; Solomon, Greenberg, & Pyszczynski, 1991, 2003). Based on field research done in the Trobriand Islands, early social anthropologist Bronislaw Malinowski similarly suggested that human beings use religious beliefs and practices in an attempt to bridge the gap between what they can control and the enormity of their actual finitude (Malinowski, 1931). He concluded that a people will turn to magic (the attempt to use supernatural powers) as a way to forestall anxiety and regain a sense of control when confronted with forces they cannot otherwise manage. Figure 4.1 lists the four elements of Durkheim's definition of religion.

Early social scientists, such as Tyler (1873) and Frazer (1909, 1911–1915), were concerned with such questions as the how and why of religious belief. Later social thinkers (e.g., Durkheim, 1912/1995; Malinowski, 1931; Parsons, 1952, 1963), who are often called *functionalists,* were more interested in the social functions of religion. **Functionalism** is less concerned with explaining the *why* of religion and more interested with the role it plays in society. Max Weber (1905/1976, 1922/1991, 1947), who was not a functionalist, per se, was among the very first to systematically explore the role played by religion in our modern capitalist society. He concluded that religious

- Has a system of beliefs
- Includes religious practices or rituals
- Has a sacred or supernatural focus
- Brings a people together and is expressed within a community or social base

FIGURE 4.1   The Four Elements of Durkheim's Definition of Religion.   *Source:* This table is based on Durkheim, Emile. *The elementary forms of religious life,* K. E. Fields (trans.). New York: The Free Press, 1995. (Work originally published in 1912.)

belief satisfies a need to achieve a sense of meaning. From his perspective, religion helps people interpret, or make sense of, their experiences (also see Parsons, 1952, 1963). By emphasizing meaning, Weber diverged from the emphasis on objective, or *etic*, criteria and toward greater stress on the subjective, or *emic*. For this reason, we may wish to think of Weber's work as a bridge. Table 4.1 shows a quick summary of anthropological-sociological perspectives on religion and spirituality.

The growth of the emic orientation among new generations of social scientists has contributed to a shift toward interpreting religious experience from the frame of reference of the people themselves. Instead of trying to unearth some religious missing

TABLE 4.1	Quick Summary of Anthropololgical-Sociological Perspectives on Religion and Spirituality	
School	**Key theorist(s)**	**Message about religion (or the spiritual)**
Early Social Anthropology	Tyler (1873) Frazer (1909; 1911–15)	Religious systems have their roots in the experience of people in societies. They change and evolve with time.
Early Sociology & Functionalism	Durkheim (1915) Weber (1922, 1947) Malinowski (1931) Radcliffe-Brown (1939) Parsons (1952, 1963)	Religious systems play one or more important roles within a society. They provide a sense of meaning, guide human behavior, and foster a sense ofcommunity.
Symbolic Interaction	Mead (1934) Goffman (1959) Geertz (1973)	To understand the power of religious systems it is vital to understand the meaning of religious symbols to the people who use them.
Conflict Theory	Marx (1867)	Religion is used by those in power to stay in power. It is the "opiate of the masses." It supports the established order and stands in the way of change.
Postmodern Theory	Foucault (1980) Baudrillard (1983) Lyotard (1984)	Each religious tradition is potentially helpful to the believer. "Grand narratives" that claim an exclusive claim on the truth are problematic. Diversity and mutual understanding should hold sway in religious matters.

link, or decipher the functions religion plays in some grand but invisible social system, there was a shift in social science thinking. This more recent trend finds expression in the **symbolic interaction** perspective of sociology (Blumer, 1969; Goffman, 1959; Mead, 1934/1962; Ritzer, 2000). It strives to understand religious symbols and practice.

The functionalist is interested in *what* a religious system does; the interactionist is interested in discerning the depths of its meaning, coming full circle to the *why* of it. On the journey toward greater understanding about the spiritual or religious dimensions of death, we can conceptualize religions as complex symbolic systems, with material and nonmaterial elements that include sacred objects, artifacts, scriptures, concepts, beliefs, creeds, codes, and anything else that is imbued with religious or spiritual meaning. We can also say religious systems are culturally rooted social institutions that try to articulate a plausible **cosmology**–theory about the nature of the cosmos, or the universe. Religious systems assert a vision of reality that reaches beyond the physical, however.

A third way of understanding the role of religion comes from the **conflict theory**. Derived from, and drawing on, the work of social critic Karl Marx (1818–1883), the *conflict perspective* is far less positive in its outlook on religion. Indeed, it contends that rather than playing a critical role in society, religious ideologies are used to justify the status quo and impede social change (Kendall, 2005). It suggests that those in power use religion, including fear about what happens after we die, to control and manipulate the people. In Marx's view, religion is also like a drug that dulls the consciousness of people. He referred to it as the opiate of the masses (Marx, 1843/1970).

In contrast to Marx (1843/1970), the conflict perspective, and science, all of which tend to rule out religious ideologies as valid ways to explain phenomena, a **postmodern theory** is inclined to see diverse religious and spiritual ideologies as potentially valid (also see Chapter 2). Although the perspective eschews any ideology, religious or otherwise, as a "grand narrative" best avoided (Lyotard, 1984), the postmodern perspective accepts all religious traditions as potentially helpful to the believer—to a point. It draws a line, however, when it comes to intolerance, which it rejects as antithetical. Advocating a "cafeteria-style" approach, in which the religious consumer is encouraged to pick and choose, it fosters an ecumenical and interspiritual attitude. The perspective strives to promote mutual understanding and respect. Many of the new religious currents of the postmodern era reflect the desire to promote an appreciation for the commonalities of the world's religious traditions, deemphasizing the differences (Beversluis, 1995; Gyatso, 1999; Teasdale, 1999).

The fact of human mortality (death) and the belief in immortality (life after death) have served as the nucleus of an elaborate system of beliefs, customs, laws, and social practices that constitute social life in Western societies.
—Robert Fulton in Strack (Ed.),
Death and the quest for meaning, 1997, p. 331

Spirit and Death

Robert Fulton, is renown in the field of modern thanatology as the first educator to have offered a course on death at an American university (Strack, 1997). The year was 1963. The preceding quote is significant. It bears witness to the considerable influence of the Judeo-Christian ethic on contemporary Western culture.

Fulton alerted the reader to an important feature in the dynamic tension between religious and secular influences on the understanding of death and dying. Fulton looked to the work of sociologists Robert Blauner (1966), Talcott Parsons (1963), and Peter Berger (1970) to help bring these dynamics into relief. Blauner's observations seem quite consistent with themes already highlighted in this text. The increases in life expectancy, rise of medical bureaucracy, isolation of the dying from the rest of us, and the use of euphemisms by the funeral industry (see Chapters 5 and 6) has worked to dull the experience of death and grief. Parsons deals more directly with the tension between scientific and religious worldviews. He suggests that with the increasing faith in science and diminishing belief in the soul and immortality, a blunting in the personal awareness of death has occurred. Commenting that although there may be a rise in participation in organized religion and a more prominent role for organized religion in politics, Berger suggests it is often less relevant in the day-to-day lives of its practitioners because it is arguably experienced with less depth and intensity. Despite playing a more limited role in secular affairs, Fulton (1997) suggests that religious paradigms, which have been such significant influences on our North American culture, exercise a much more profound influence on our understanding of death than we may have come to appreciate until now.

It is commonly thought that human beings are the only known creatures with the ability to reflect on the eventuality of their own death. Indeed, coming to terms with this awareness seems part of the human condition. With this comes an unsettling thought: the very possibility of nonexistence or chaos. Arguably, it then becomes the job of religion to cast out the demon of chaos and transform the cosmos into a universe endowed with order and purpose.

In contrast to an earlier period, when people presumably relied on religious tradition, the spiritual and religious impulse seem overtly less central to everyday life. In modern cosmology, science has largely taken the place of religion, by making the mysteries of the universe more intelligible. Many people, however, continue to experience the world as a tenuous place. Philosopher George Allan (1994) uses the word *whirl* to describe the experience, suggesting it is the role of tradition, religion included, to provide a place of safe harbor.

KEY RELIGIOUS PERSPECTIVES

Each of the world's major religions traditions recognizes human existence on at least two levels: the physical and spiritual. A key point when considering religious perspectives about death relates to belief about what happens after physical death to the **soul** (Abrahamic tradition), **atman** (Hindusim), or **continuity** (Buddhism). In Judaism,

Christianity, and Islam (Abrahamic tradition), the soul is thought to reside in another realm. Their religious books speak of such places "the kingdom of God," "heaven," "paradise," and "hell," which believers regard as a reward or punishment for the way people lived their lives.

Abrahamic Tradition

The **Abrahamic** family of religions—**Judaism**, **Christianity**, and **Islam**—have come to believe in a soul that continues to exist spiritually after the body dies (Toynbee, 1968). **Judaism** integrated belief in a soul and an afterlife late in it development. There now is good reason to believe the very concept of a soul did not enter Jewish religious consciousness until the Greek occupation by Alexander and his successors (Bowker, 1993). Judaism places an emphasis on community life in the here and now, but belief in an afterlife, and even belief in a resurrection of the body, became accepted tenets of rabbinic Judaism, which had inherited it from its predecessors the Pharisees, after the destruction of the temple in Jerusalem in 70 C.E. (Gillman, 2000; Toynbee, 1968).

Although Judaism emphasizes life in the here and now, it began to integrate beliefs about a transcendent place into its theology some 200 years before the current era (Bowker, 1997; McDannell & Lang, 2001; Toynbee, 1968). In addition, although not very well known, there are also certain mystical expressions of Judaism, including some Chasidic and Renewal sects, that teach a doctrine of reincarnation (see Cooper, 1997).

As a sect of Judaism, **Christianity**, initially inherited Jewish beliefs about an afterlife, which became further elaborated on in New Testament scriptures. The general belief in resurrection, and the resurrection of Jesus in particular, is a defining characteristic of Christianity. As you may recall from Chapter 2, Phillipe Aries (1974, 1981) suggests that in the late medieval period in Europe there was an emphasis on the Christian vision of death described in the Gospel according to Matthew, with its depiction of the second coming of Christ (Matthew 23: 39–24, 31) (see Chapter 2). The period between death and the second coming was seen as a period of rest and waiting (Aries, 1974, 1981). In Roman Catholic tradition, this life has sometimes been thought of as a "valley of tears," as is expressed in the "Hail Holy Queen," a revered Catholic prayer (usually the concluding prayer of the traditional rosary).

> Hail, Holy Queen, mother of mercy, our life, our sweetness, and our hope. To you we cry, poor banished children of Eve; to you we send up our sighs, mourning and weeping in this valley of tears. Turn then, O most gracious advocate, your eyes of mercy toward us, and after this, our exile, show us the blessed fruit of thy womb, Jesus. O clement, O loving, O sweet Virgin Mary.

The Prophet Mohammed, before founding the religion of **Islam** had explored and rejected both Judaism and Christianity. Islam professes belief in a soul even more explicitly than is expressed in Judaism and Christianity, as is articulated in its holy book, the *Qur'an*. There is the belief in a soul that is thought to wait in the grave from the time of death until a day of judgment, at which time it is believed it will go directly to heaven or to hell until it can be purified (Bowker, 1997; Murata & Chittick, 1994; also see Chapter 14).

Hinduism and Buddhism

India is the acknowledged birthplace of two of the world's great religions: Hinduism and Buddhism. **Hinduism**, arguably the most ancient of the world's major religions, acknowledges the *atman*, a term that can be roughly translated as the "soul" (Bowker, 1993, 1997). Hindus believe the atman survives the cycles of death and rebirth. In Hindu tradition, a chief goal of religious devotion is to realize one's true nature, which is thought to be identical with the divine, which is immortal. What we experience in daily life in the physical world, according to Hindu tradition, is really just a very persistent illusion, called *maya*.

Growing out of Hinduism some 2,500 years ago, **Buddhism** has no belief in an immortal *atman* or soul. Instead, it has the notion of an **anatman**, the "not self"or "not soul." As with Hinduism, Buddhism includes teachings of reincarnation, but it suggests that the "self" we subjectively experience is in reality a mere transient state of consciousness, or subtle mind (Bowker, 1993, 1997). Whatever part of the self that persists from one lifetime to another is abstractly referred to as a mere *continuity* (Bowker, 1993; Gyatso, 2001).

In Hinduism, the afterlife is thought to be **samsara**—the cycles of birth, death, and rebirth—that revolve until the soul is able to realize its basic unity with the divine and find release, or **moska**, from reincarnation. Similarly, in Buddhist belief, reincarnation continues until consciousness achieves **nirvana**, the merging with the cosmos that can take place only when one's (selfish) desires completely dissolve (Bowker, 1997). Rather than seeing death as a sorrowful event, Buddhist teachings suggest that when death results in the complete cessation of a separate existence, it is also released from the cycle of rebirth. To use a Buddhist and Hindu term, it is the **liberation** from suffering (Bowker, 1997).

THE HERO'S QUEST

One can think of the trek through life as a quest, pilgrimage, or sojourn, with a beginning, middle, and an ultimate end. Indeed, the idea of *pilgrimage* is a feature of Christian "folk religion," which, although it is a very real part of the faith tradition, is not explicitly spelled out in scripture nor is it well articulated in formal theology (Naumes, 2002). In the Christian tradition, which is said to have originated with the mother of Emperor Constantine, Empress Helena, who made an extensive pilgrimage to the holy sites in Jerusalem after Constantine adopted Christianity as the state religion of the Roman empire (Jarrett, 1999). At least from the time of her pilgrimage in the fourth century, C.E., the idea of going on a pilgrimage has been an important part of Christian tradition, particularly a pilgrimage to Jerusalem, which for Christians also symbolizes an earthly counterpart to "New Jerusalem," the Kingdom of God, the sought-after spiritual destination (Naumes, 2002).

A pilgrimage seems to be very much a part of the Western tradition, the inspiration to go on a pilgrimage may be a universal spiritual impulse (see Jarrett, 1999), arising spontaneously in the heart and found in all religious traditions. It is often associated with particular shrines, oracles, or places in the religious history of diverse faith traditions. Those hoping for a miracle flock to Lourdes; Christians of all denominations journey to the holy land; Jews to the wailing wall; Buddhists to Bodh Gaya (the site at which tradition says the Buddha delivered his first sermon); Hindus to the seven sacred cities that dot the river Ganga; and Muslims to Mecca for the Haj, a pilgrimage that each of the faithful is expected to make at least once during their lifetime. While we may think of pilgrimages as being linked to particular places, one can also envision it more broadly as a movement from the ordinary to extraordinary–to a state of wholeness, holiness, or healing (Bowker, 1997).

In his classic book, *The Hero with a Thousand Faces,* Joseph Campbell (1949), considered by many to be the preeminent twentieth-century scholar of myth, suggests that pilgrimage—the story of the hero and the quest of life—really belongs to each of us, for it is the great *monomyth*, to use a term coined by James Joyce in his classic novel, *Finnegan's Wake* (Joyce, 1939). Famed psychoanalyst Carl Jung pictures it as an *archetype* of the journey to the true self (Jung & Reed, 1981), a successful journey representing the triumph of consciousness over the dark forces of the unconscious. Joseph Campbell (1988) comments that it appears in the mythology of virtually every culture of the world.

In the story of the hero's quest, the protagonist ventures forth from the everyday world, is initiated in a world of supernatural wonder, and ultimately returns to bestow the boons of the experience on his fellow human beings (Campbell, 1949). In the first stage, the stage in which our hero embarks on the journey, there is a calling, often an initial refusal to heed the call, the appearance of unexpected aid from supernatural forces, crossing a threshold of no return, and a passage into darkness. In the next stage, a period of initiation, the hero encounters various dangers, gets a taste of bliss, experiences temptation, finds reconciliation or atonement, achieves **apotheosis** or the experience of a divine state, and ultimately finds the great boon. In the final stage of the adventure, the hero returns, but not to life as it was, for our protagonist has become transformed in the process and has returned with a message, gift, or blessing. In the end, the sojourn benefits the world from which the hero has come and to which he or she will return.

Although the hero of legend typically features a bigger-than-life figure, it can be about regular people, like you and me, who live ordinary lives, but who embark on a quest or are thrust into one through extraordinary circumstances. One way of looking at the journey is to see it as one in which the hero's main challenge is to overcome some peril—like a great dragon or perhaps the incarnation of evil itself, which looms in the shadows. Along the way, our hero (each of us) encounters unavoidable dangers and obstacles, yet if we are open, we also find allies who help us on our path, and perhaps even some supernatural tool—for instance, special wisdom, a magic ring, or some elixir—with which we can prevail over forces we had previously experienced as insurmountable.

For ourselves, we can think of the journey to find meaning and purpose in this life as a pilgrimage; our eventual journey through the experience of death as either the conclusion of the quest here on earth or a pilgrimage in its own right. If you believe "you"—your soul, spirit, or continuity—existed before this lifetime, then you may see death as a necessary step before experiencing a "return." If you have no such belief, you might envision death as the conclusion of your journey in this world, or the beginning of a new life that will take place in the next world.

CHAUTAUQUA

This section explores a sampling of stories, teachings, and reflections on life and death from around the world. I'm using the term **Chautauqua** for the meanderings here. *Chautauqua* is a lot of things: a place, a philosophy about lifelong learning, and a state of mind (Maxwell, 2002). Located in the westernmost part of the state of New York, Chautauqua County was probably named after the lake that rests placidly within its environs. It seems that the word itself has Native American origins, meaning something like "a bag tied in the middle," describing the shape of the lake.

In the years to come, a rich philosophy of education and lifelong learning took root there. It came to embody the highest ideals of adult learning, and took in a diverse range of subjects: art, education, literature, music, religion, patriotism, science, and anything else that might inspire people through a world of culture, ideas, and values. Epitomizing the best in adult education, *Chautauqua* has become a watchword for quality learning in the United States and Canada. Since its inception, the idea has grown in all kinds of ways: through various regional institutes that sprang up via traveling chautauquas that brought enrichment to outlying areas, in the theatrical portrayal of historic and cultural figures, into cyberspace through an Internet-based forum for teachers hosted by the National Science Foundation, and even into the annals of modern literature. It became an integral theme of Robert Persig's 1974 classic book on pilgrimage, *Zen and the Art of Motorcycle Maintenance*—the story of a person's quest for truth and an inquiry into values. I aspire to draw inspiration from the ideal of *chautauqua* as we embark on our own pilgrimage into the cultural stories and teachings that follow.

The Call of the Owl

European explorers first came in contact with the Kwakwaka'wakw, a confederation of tribes that share a language and culture, in the late eighteenth century. There are Kwakwaka'wakw villages in northernmost Washington state in the present-day United States, but most are found on Vancouver island, the Queen Charlottes, and other rural parts of coastal British Columbia. In the late nineteenth century, a number of anthropologists, including Franz Boas, often considered to be the father of American anthropology, began to write about these people, who we now know as the Kwakiutl. The tribe, whose name is spelled in a variety of ways, is but one of many tribes that comprise the Kwakwaka'wakw nation.

Oral tradition has it that there was once an anthropologist, who, deeply challenged by the difficulty of pronouncing Kwakwaka words, called them the "Quackadoodles." The story of the Kwakwaka'wakw people has found its way into the consciousness of nonaboriginal people through a book by Margaret Craven (1973), titled *I Heard the Owl Call My Name*. It also seems appropriate to mention that not just a few aboriginal artists of note have sprung from the ancestral roots of this people.

Craven spent several months among the Kwakwaka'wakw at the village of Kingcome, where she did the research for her book. The story begins in the white man's world. Mark Brian, a young Anglican priest, unbeknownst to himself, has been diagnosed with a terminal illness. His bishop, who once served as the pastor of the parish at Kingcome, assigns the young priest to be the new vicar, hoping his young charge will learn enough about living to be ready to die.

By embarking on his journey to the village, the protagonist begins another kind of pilgrimage through the experience of living and dying. As he makes the transition from the white man's world into the world of the Kwakwaka'wakw, his own ethnocentrism, his preconceived ideas about the aboriginal people, begin to change and he himself starts to undergo a transformation. From his first day at the village, he learns that death is a very real part of life for the Kwakwaka'wakw people. The salmon, called "swimmer" by the Kwakwaka'wakw, are born, meet their destiny by venturing out into the ocean, and return again to Kingcome inlet, where they fight their way upstream, spawn, and then die. In the story, Mark seems to sense that he too is a swimmer, one of the salmon people, as indeed he is. The title of the book refers to Kwakwaka'wakw tradition, which suggests that when the time of death draws near, we hear the owl call our name. By the time Mark hears the owl call his name, he finds that he is home, perhaps for the first time, with his true self, in a community with people who love him. He finds peace in the realization that with his passing he will live on in the hearts of the people of the village.

Considering the realities of life and death is a regular part of the religious practices of Tibetan Buddhist monks, like His Holiness, the Dalai Lama, pictured here. He is the spiritual leader of the world's estimated 20 million Tibetan Buddhists. *Hanan Isachar/AGE Fotostock*

The Dalai Lama Speaks about Life and Death

India is the birthplace of two of the world's great religions, and the country has major centers of other religions as well. In the quest to learn more about different views on death and dying, I spent time visiting with several Indian religious leaders, including His Holiness the Dalai Lama (Gyatso, 2001). His Holiness went into exile in 1959, nine years after the Chinese occupied his native land. The Chinese occupation has been particularly harsh, the culture and people of Tibet nearly decimated, but His Holiness has persisted in nonviolent struggle. Awarded the Nobel Peace Prize in 1989, he now lives in Dharamsala, a small town in the North of India, which also serves as the capital of the free Tibetan government-in-exile. The following is a short excerpt from my interview with His Holiness.

AUTHOR: On a televised broadcast, I've heard Your Holiness say you meditate about death. From the perspective of a Tibetan Buddhist, why do you think it is important?

DALAI LAMA: To remember...death is useful....Things are always changing... that's a reality. In order to know that reality, that aspect of reality, look first to the end of life....Without...changing there is no death. If something exists without changing then there is no course. If there is no course...there is no reason....So, I think it is simply the realization of this reality.

Then second...to reduce too much attachment...to this life. For society...in one city we visited...there was a fortress for a king....There are so many [such] castles on this planet. The Great Wall. The Taj Majal. I think the rajas, the kings, or emperors, when they were constructing them...they didn't care about the hardship of the people. But, in those days there was much emphasis on these...because they felt their own kingdom or their own life [was more important]....They never thought anything about life. So, because of that attitude...Hitler, Stalin, and Honeker of East Germany...tried to save their systems...thought they would last a hundred years or a thousand years *(laughter from His Holiness)*. So, those beliefs created a lot of problems. For...practitioners, in order to practice contentment, self-discipline, it is important and useful to know about the end of life. Death. Yes, I think these are the main reasons. Buddhists, of course, accept life after life.

AUTHOR: Reincarnation?

DALAI LAMA: Rebirth. So, the future life means endless. This life is a maximum of one hundred years. So, anyway, in this life difficulties or problems [exist] so we can learn from these experiences. But the future life is more serious. Therefore, think about a long future....

AUTHOR: If I could ask a more personal follow- up, what sort of experience has Your Holiness had as a result of your practice of meditation on death?...

DALAI LAMA: Certainly, meditation on death has an impact. But some other factors, the practice of altruism...practice on the suffering nature, of this very life, this very existence is [also] important.

AUTHOR: Has Your Holiness thought about your own...eventual death?

DALAI LAMA: Of course, daily...in meditation....There is actually a visualization of the process of death....The different stages of death. So that...in my daily prayer...eight times *(laughter from His Holiness)*....Out of eight I may do one or two. *(laughter from His Holiness)*....So, that is supposed to be the preparation for my actual death. If death comes tonight...I don't know if I'm fully prepared or not. *(laughter from His Holiness)*....These practices...remain at the intellectual level. Not actual...experience.

AUTHOR: Your Holiness, I know you have traveled very extensively to many different parts of the world since you've gone into exile from Tibet, and I know you must have come in contact with many practitioners of Western medicine, psychology, and religion. What do you think of the attitudes about death of these Western practitioners?

DALAI LAMA: Serious discussions about death, so far, no. But, serious discussions about the practice of love...on several occasions....One time...I met one Catholic monk who lived at Montserrat. That monk, I was told, had remained for five years in that mountain....He came to see me. So I asked, "I heard you've remained in the mountain for five years as a hermit...what do you do?" He told me he meditated on love. He had a different robe...a different concept, but the same practice.

AUTHOR: Compassion, love?

DALAI LAMA: Yes, compassion, love.

Los Dias de Muertos

Los dias de muertos, or the "days of the dead," is a Mexican folk tradition honoring the dead. It is celebrated with special gusto in Oaxaca, the second most southern state of Mexico (Andrade, 1996; Greenleigh & Beimler, 1998; Mendoza, 2001). I made the trek to Oaxaca during the days of the dead to experience the celebrations for myself. A blend of pre-Columbian and Spanish Catholic traditions, the fiesta begins each year, late on October 31st, when the *angelitos* (spirits of the dead children) arrive. Local tradition holds that the spirits of adults arrive the day after the angelitos come (Mendoza, 2001). The days of the dead extend through the first and second of November—in the Catholic liturgical calendar, on the feasts of All Saints and All Souls days. During the days of the dead, the people welcome their dead relatives home for a fiesta celebrated in their honor. Although the festive nature of the memorial might seem odd to their neighbors to the North, the celebrations do have a parallel in Halloween, but with a difference. Visitors are often struck by the mingling of heartfelt reverence for the dead and fiesta celebration.

During the week prior to the fiesta, the stalls of the open-air market in the city of Oaxaca are filled with food of all kinds, bright arrays of flowers, masks, skulls made from sugar, and little skeletons depicting all kinds of human activities. For example, you can find the scene of a skeletal couple getting married; a mariachi band, made up entirely of the dead, playing in concert; or a long dead priest presiding at a funeral. In this tradition, the dead don't stop doing what they did in life just because they've moved on.

Shops display **calacas**, or skeletons. For the local shopper, it is the time to get ready for the annual arrival of some very special visitors—departed friends and loved ones. Various living members of the family construct special altars, called *ofrendas* (literally "offerings"); prepare special dishes, including rich *molé*, a sauce made with chocolate; and create special paths bounded by the bright orange *cempasuchitl*, a local wild flower, and marigolds that lead to the family homes and *ofrendas*. According to tradition, the dead use the bright orange flowers as something like runway markers to guide them to the correct house on their return flight home. In addition to incense, water, and a special bread for the dead, there are candles and candy skulls, often with the names of the dead written on top with icing, that are placed on the *ofrendas*. For the spirits of the returning dead, these things apparently mark the way for their arrival and affirm that they've come home to the right landing pad.

The paradox of solemn remembrance and fiesta celebration seem to have their roots in the pre-Columbian civilizations of the Zapoteca and Mixtec and two mesoamerican gods, Quetzalcoatl and Mictlantlecuihtl (see Andrade, 1996; Greenleigh & Beimler, 1998). Quetzalcoatl was the ancient god of life, who governed earth and sky. Mictlantlecuihtl was god of the underworld and keeper of the dead. Each of these gods, despite ostensibly having disparate functions, were often thought to be mutually dependent on the other—and, in the stone reliefs, they were always carved in profile, joined together at the spine (Mendoza, 2001).

In pre-Columbian tradition, life is considered an illusion on the path toward death (Greenleigh & Beimler, 1998). The illusion could be harsh, and death was sometimes viewed as a release. Reflecting on the custom of awaiting the return of the dead, it is said that in ancient times, family members would squat reverently as they waited for the dead on the appointed days, eyes cast down, lest those returning sense any sign of disrespect.

Today, the relations between the living and dead are more festive, although families still gather solemnly in the graveyards at night awaiting the arrival of their loved ones during the days of the dead. Whole families spend the night at meticulously cleaned and festively decorated graves to celebrate a family reunion with their departed kin. The traditional belief is that the dead stay with the living until November 2nd, when they leave—but only after having had a good meal and spending some quality time with their kin, of course. As the festivities draw to a close, the memories of the celebrations fade. Life begins to return to normal—until next year. Sweets purchased for the fiesta are consumed, but not the offerings that were placed on the *ofrendas*. "What would be the point," I was told by a local, "all the taste has already been consumed by the dead." *Ofrendas* are taken down. The lacy *papel picados*—intricately cut decorative tissue paper used as trim—eventually falls apart. They were never intended to remain forever.

▪ ▪ ▪

She couldn't stop complaining about "clinging."

▪ ▪ ▪

Mejo Ma and the Dilemma of Maya

The word *asramas*, in Hindu tradition, refers to the four stages of the spiritual life cycle. The term literally means a "residence" or "house" in which spiritual goals are pursued. These stages are **brahmacarya**, **grhasta**, **vanaprastha**, and **samnyasa**. They are integral to the Vedic social system. The idea is that human life should extend 100 years, 25 years in each stage. For the sake of visual clarity, the four are summarized in Table 4.2.

▦ ▦ ▦

As a child living in northern California, I had observed a grandmother and great-grandmother, each widowed and living alone in a big, separate house. The older adults, like my parents and adults in general, struck me as very independent beings whose dwindling relations with others left them too isolated for their own or anyone else's comfort.

Soon after I settled as an anthropologist in the village of Mangaldihi in West Bengal, however, I met an aged, white-clothed widow called Mejo Ma ("Middle Mother") sitting beside the dusty lane in front of her home. She could not stop complaining about clinging. *Her connections to her family, to things, to good food, and to her own body were so tight, she said, that she was afraid of lingering for years in a decrepit state, unable to die. She feared that after her body died, her soul (atma) would not ascend but would remain emotionally shackled nearby as a ghost* (bhut).

—Sara Lamb
"The making and unmaking of persons," 1997, p. 279

▦ ▦ ▦

Anthropologist Sara Lamb (1997) suggests Mejo Ma is in the last phase of life *(samnyasa)*. She has shaved her head and wears the white garb thought appropriate in her culture. While Mejo Ma is a *samnyasa*, she is also part of a *jal*, an intricately

TABLE 4.2	Hindu Vedic Divisions of the Human Life-cycle
Stage of life	**Description**
Brahmacarya	Student. Period of celibacy and religious study under the tutelage of a guru. Generally, study takes place at the residence of the guru, often called a *guru-kula*. First 25 years of life.
Grhasta	Householder. Adult married life. Second 25 years of life.
Vanaprastha	Recluse or retirement. May be compared to midlife in the West. Generally conceived of as a time of retreat to the forest. Takes place after the children are grown, and is considered the beginning phase of disentanglement from this world. Third period of 25 years of life.
Samnyasa	Ascetic. Traditionally, considered a time of complete renunciation of family life and material obligations. Final 25 years of life.

It is customary in Hindu tradition for the loved ones of the deceased to carry the body to the 'burning ghats' where it will be cremated on the banks of a sacred river. *Anders Ryman/Corbis*

connected network of relationships with people, places, and things. Lamb writes, "By sharing and exchanging bodily and other substances through acts such a sex, touching, living together, sharing food, owning things, and eating the fruits of village soil, people saw themselves as forming substantial-emotional bonds." To them these relationships are *maya,* which, as already discussed, is considered nothing short of illusion in Hindu tradition. And for Mejo Ma and people in her West Bengali village, these bonds, which become stronger over time, not weaker, pose an additional challenge during the final phase of life, when such bonds are supposed to be dissolved.

Near the Burning Ghat

The city of Varanasi, mistakenly called *Benares* in the West, is one of the seven sacred cities of Hinduism. Often called Khasi, the holy city of light, Hindu tradition says that a person can find *moska,* (eternal liberation), if death should occur here. *Manikarnika Ghat*, the main **burning ghat**, is the place on the banks of the sacred river Ganga where most cremations take place. Within walking distance is the Ramakrishna Mission, a Hindu monastery, or *mat,* which has a hospital, and several social service programs. Because of a curious series of events, I met up with His Holiness Sri Sri Swami Jitatmananda, a Hindu monk, scientist, and teacher, who spent much of his morning sharing a few thoughts with me on death and dying. Here, I include a short excerpt from the transcript of that discussion.

SWAMI: The inevitability of death. This thing has been dear to all religions in this way or that way. The Hindu say, "Don't fear death." Conquer death before death comes. How? Hindu spirit has a route to conquer death before the death comes.

AUTHOR: What would be the elements of that?

SWAMI: Very simple. If you become one with the whole universe...if you feel your oneness with the whole universe. If you feel yourself one with...the world population...there is no death for you....

That is what the Upanishads...the Indian Upanishads say. Realizing yourself in all the other living beings...or nonliving beings in this universe. The moment you realize it you touch immortality. Death has lost its power. Its fear. Because you are not dying. You are going to be one with the whole universe....It is life.

What happened to Buddha when he was dying? He was not dying. He was dissolving himself in the whole universe....

God realization...self-realization...means this, feeling one's presence in the whole universe....

It is a holistic universe. It is one single universe. Modern physics have shown it....This whole universe is inextricably interconnected. Not just spiritually but physically. And the connection...the only connecting link is not the speed of light but consciousness. They've found superluminal connections...more than speed of light connections. How is it possible? In the physical world, according to Einstein...more than the speed of light is not possible. Then what connects two particles...?

AUTHOR: It would have to be consciousness.

SWAMI: Consciousness. They have to come to consciousness. There is one single consciousness in the whole universe. I'm a wave...on that infinite ocean of consciousness. You are a wave on the infinite wave of consciousness. Christ is a bigger wave. Buddha is a bigger wave. We are all waves...one single consciousness.

Reunion with Allah

Every evening at mosques around the world you can hear the call to prayer. Now thought to be the second largest religion on earth, Islam is an impressive religious force in the world today. In history, Islamic moguls and emperors have reigned from Morocco to the Indian subcontinent. Hyderabad, in the South of India, famous for its impressive tombs, buildings, mosques, and diamond markets, was founded in 1589 by the fifth Sultan of Golconda (Bradnock & Bradnock, 2000). It continues to thrive as a major center of Islamic culture in India. I was there during the holy season of **Ramadan**. I met Abdul Kareem, a teacher of Arabic and Islam at the Henry Martin Institute, an organization that is dedicated to Christian-Muslim dialog. We spent several hours discussing Islamic views on death and dying. I include a short except from the transcript of these discussions here (Kareem, 2001).

AUTHOR: All people everywhere. And, people in different places approach the subject of death and their practices related to death in different ways...I'm interested...trying to learn...as much as I can...about Islamic perspectives about death...

ABDUL: Dying or death is the fact of the world. Whoever is born dies....In Islam, the death is...you want to listen to very simple or pure words...just separating the soul from the body. That is...death. This body is not ourselves....Actually, my self is that soul, which works in combination with this body. In this world.

AUTHOR: ...In Islam, you would say that the body is not regarded as who the person is, and you very much have the idea of a soul, which exists as a distinct something within the body.

ABDUL: Yes. God mixes...both things, the soul and body, together and He will send the person to this world.

AUTHOR: So, you would say the person's soul exists with God before the person is even born?

ABDUL: Yes.... And this period in which the soul will live in this world with a body...we will stay here as a human being...this is a life...and when God wants to separate them again...because in the first the soul and body was not together...when they separate...we will say the person died. That is just the transferring of soul from this body to another place....

AUTHOR: ...I...understand that the word *Islam* itself means to submit. So, what God wants us to do is to submit to His will for us?

ABDUL: Because we are the creations. We must submit....

AUTHOR: That is the proper relationship between the creator and the creation?

ABDUL: Yes...

AUTHOR: What sorts of...insights do you think the Islamic mystics have about death? The experience of death?

ABDUL: The person who is Sufi or mystic...he...will be pleased...or happy...if his life is ending. Death is coming. Because he knows because of his experience...trying...to understand God, to understand himself, to understand this life. "This life is given to me. What do I have to do with this life? Which kind of works should I do? What should I think?"...How do God's guidelines bring him towards God?...Death is actually leaving this earth. Leaving this life—which is kind of having a distance from God...or God's wishes....The Sufi feels that when he is in this world, he is in a period of test. But, God is with him, and he is trying to experience Him....Sometimes, some mystics will wait [for death]...because they know that after this period of testing...there will be just a loving period. A period of being close to Him....

Chapter Summary

The chapter began with a reference to *coureurs de bois*, a French-Canadian expression. It gets at the idea of a gathering of travelers who share stories of the things they've seen and heard from far-away travels. In preparation for our own journey into the hinterlands of a multicultural and interfaith exploration of death and dying, I asked you to participate in an informal exercise. Then, I shared a few anthropological conceptual tools I thought might be helpful on the trek.

To explore the relationship between culture, spirit, and death, the chapter reviewed the development of key social science views about the relationship between culture, religion, and spirituality. It explored the work of early anthropologists and briefly reviewed insights offered by four key theoretical perspectives:

functionalism, symbolic interactionism, conflict theory, and *postmodern theory*.

Recognizing that it may be dangerous to try to synthesize key religious perspectives, I nevertheless tried to condense a few concepts from Christianity, Hinduism, Islam, and Judaism. We surveyed Joseph Campbell's work on the "hero's quest" and the work of psychoanalyst Carl Jung, who used the metaphor of the hero's quest, spoken of in the myths of virtually every culture on earth, to symbolize the individual's own pilgrimage through life to death.

In the last part of the chapter, the section titled "Chautauqua," I shared a few words from three religious leaders: the Dalai Lama of Tibet, a prominent Hindu swami, and an Islamic teacher. I asked you to explore a story inspired by a Native

American experience. Also, I shared something of the experience of the "days of the dead." You heard from Sara Lamb, an anthropologist who describes the plight of Mejo Ma, a Hindu woman who is struggling to let go of the worldly attachments she believes are binding her.

It was my hope that in this literary *coureurs de bois* that you might have the opportunity to look on the North American experience of death with greater awareness that ours is but one of many ways of addressing this most human of experiences—death.

Key Terms

Abrahamic *75*

anatman *76*

apotheosis *77*

atman *74*

brahmacarya *83*

Buddhism *76*

burning ghat *84*

calacas *82*

Chautauqua *78*

Christianity *75*

conflict theory *73*

continuity *74*

cosmology *73*

cultural diffusion *70*

cultural universal *70*

culture contact *70*

emic *70*

ethnocentrism *69*

etic *70*

functionalism *71*

globalization *70*

grhasta *83*

Hinduism *76*

ideal culture *70*

Islam *75*

Judaism *75*

liberation *76*

material culture *69*

moska *76*

nirvana *76*

nonmaterial culture *69*

postmodern theory *73*

Ramadan *85*

real culture *70*

samnyasa *83*

samsara *76*

soul *74*

symbolic interaction *73*

vanaprastha *83*

Suggested Activities

1. Go to the phone book under the headings of churches, synagogues, mosques, and religious organizations. Select a religious community that is different from your own faith tradition, yet one that you are interested in or curious about. Contact the faith community and make arrangements to attend one of their services. After you've attended the service, reflect on your experience and write in your journal about your experience in relation to the material covered in this chapter.

2. The following is appropriate for a class activity, perhaps an end-of-term project. Break up into small groups, according to interest in one or more religious or cultural traditions. Some may be interested in various Caribbean traditions; others might find African or Asian or North American or other traditions interesting. Each group should extensively research the beliefs, philosophies, and practices related to death and dying. This should not be restricted to a review of the literature alone, but it should also include as many firsthand accounts from people of the culture or tradition being explored. Audiotaped, or even better, videotaped interviews would be one way to record the story as a living record. Each group should create a poster that summarizes what the group has learned. Sufficient class time should be set aside for poster presentations and perhaps short clips from tapes.

3. Write in your journal about any reflections, thoughts, or feelings you may have experienced as a result of your study during this part of the course. You may wish to reflect on your own learning. In what ways, if any, does the material you were exposed to in this chapter compare to your own life experiences? Were there any parts that triggered uncomfortable feelings? If so, what was that about? Were you able to catch bits and pieces of your own ethnocentrism? In what ways, if any, has the material enriched your understanding of your own attitudes and beliefs about death and dying?

Suggested Reading

- Bowker, J. (1993). *The meanings of death.* Cambridge: Cambridge University Press.

  In this important book, John Bowker challenges certain revered intuitions that came out of early anthropology about the meaning of death. Based on a comparative study of the world's great religions, he suggests that rather than being created to deal with our fears about death, religion emerged into human consciousness as a way to help human beings with day-to-day issues of living.

- Craven, M. (1973). *I heard the owl call my name.* New York: Laurel, a division of Doubleday.

  A now classic novel, this book is about a terminally ill Anglican priest who is assigned to Kingcome village, a remote aboriginal settlement in British Columbia. The young vicar reexamines his own beliefs, values, and behavior in the light of what he learns at Kingcome. Ultimately, he finds out how to live and die well.

- Moody, H. R. (1997). *The five stages of the soul: Charting the spiritual passages that shape our lives.* New York: Anchor Books.

  An exploration of spiritual passages, this book describes the spiritual quest as a normal part of human development. Based on several years of research, Moody attempts to chart the search for meaning and self-discovery. Rich in stories about the experiences of real people, it unveils both the challenges and opportunities.

- Sogyal, R. (1992). *The Tibetan book of living and dying.* New York: HarperCollins.

  This beautifully written book, rich in Tibetan wisdom, is about learning how to come to terms with death. From the Tibetan Buddhist perspective, learning how to die well also means learning how to face death as expected with learning about day-to-day life.

- Gyatso, T., 14th Dalai Lama. (1996). *The good heart: A Buddhist perspective on the teachings of Jesus.* Boston: Wisdom Publications.

  Invited by Dom Laurence Freeman, a Benedictine monk, His Holiness the Dalai Lama went to England in 1994 and participated in a seminar dedicated to Christian meditation. His Holiness was asked to comment on eight specific passages of the Gospels. This book lays open the reflections of His Holiness about the message of these Christian teachings.

Links and Internet Resources

- **Government of Tibet in Exile**
  www.tibet.com/
  This is the official website of the Government of Tibet in exile. In addition to news releases, the political status of Tibet, and the government in exile, this site can serve as a starting point in the quest for understanding about Tibetan culture and religion.

- **Day of the Dead Index**
  www.mexconnect.com/tags/day-of-the-dead
  This site is an excellent entré for information about Mexico's days of the dead. It includes first-rate articles, beautiful reproductions of days of the dead art, and a range of information about days of the dead activities such as making a personal altar, or *ofrenda*.

- **Death on the Ganges**
  www.time.com/time/magazine/article/0,9171,5010206 17260751,00.html
  This is a short but nicely written article about funeral practices at the burning ghat in Varanasi. It provides the reader with an overview of Hindu philosophy and practices relative to death and dying.

Review Guide

1. Be prepared to discuss why it is important to be sensitive to the issue of ethnocentrism when exploring other cultures and belief systems.
2. Describe what is meant by the term *weltanschauung*, and discuss how this concept can be used to understand human experience.
3. Be able to define, explain, and employ the following terms: *material* and *nonmaterial culture; etic* and *emic perspectives; verstehen; ideal* and *real* aspects of culture; *culture contact* and *cultural diffusion.*
4. Offer an informed opinion about why it may be helpful to consider the role of religion and spirituality in human societies.
5. Be able to retrace the evolution of social science perspectives about the role of religion and spirituality in human society. Who are the key theorists? What did they

say? What pitfalls did some of them fall in? What did
Durkheim have to say about what constitutes religion?
Compare the functionalists and those who more closely
resemble the symbolic interactionists. What insights are
offered by conflict theory and postmodernism? Where
do they agree, and on what points do they differ?

6. Be able to summarize the key religious perspectives
discussed in this chapter and discuss how differences
in religious perspective might impact one's cultural
experience with death.

7. Briefly describe what is meant by the "hero's quest,"
and discuss how this metaphor might or might not
be helpful in understanding our experience of living.
What is meant by the great monomyth? How does this
relate to Carl Jung's archetypes?

8. What happened when you tried to do the visualization
at the beginning of the chapter on your own death?
Were you able to visualize your own death? If so, what
did it look like?

9. What is meant by chautauqua? Briefly summarize the
contents of the interview excerpts, the story, and cross-
cultural material presented in this chapter. In what
ways do these relate or not relate to the key religious
perspectives surveyed earlier in the chapter? Can you
identify any patterns? Do they relate to the great monomyth of the "hero's quest?"

10. Please discuss the concept of immortality. Explain
why you think human beings have beliefs in immortality despite a lack of clear scientific evidence of its
existence. Do you think scientific method can explain
belief in immortality? Be sure to support your position.

11. Briefly outline the major tenets of the major religious
traditions discussed in the chapter. Compare and
contrast.

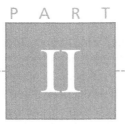

II

Death

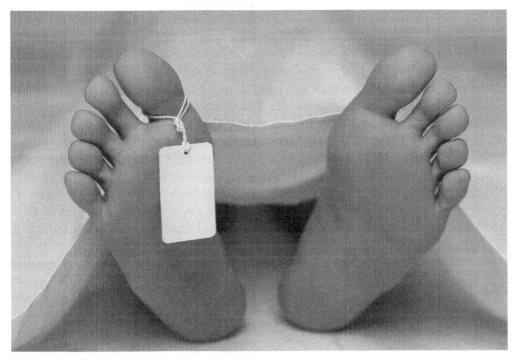

jedi-master/Fotolia

Part II contains three chapters, each focusing on death itself. Chapter 5, titled "The Grim Reaper through Time: Historical and Cross-Cultural Look at Undertaking," begins with the definition of death we now call *clinical death,* the cessation of heart beat and respiration, cooling of the body, rigor mortis, and decay, the reason why it is so necessary to dispose of human remains. We will review burial practices from Neanderthal times, ancient Egypt, and the American Civil War. During the Civil War, the bodies of battlefield dead were embalmed to preserve them long enough to be transported back to their families. The practice spread to the civilian community. From this emerged the profession of funeral director. The chapter will conclude with a look at its legacy: today's funeral service industry.

In Chapter 6, titled "The Grim Reaper Today: Death on the Cusp of a Changing World," we discuss death in twenty-first century America, beginning with a look at our contemporary "death system": the people, places, things, and so on that are integral to how we manage death. We will take a peek at the HBO TV series, *Six Feet Under*, which has become part of thanatology's pop culture underworld. We will review the work of Jessica Mitford, a critic of the funeral industry, with attention to "McDeath," the corporate commercialization of death. In this context, we look at the FCC's Amended Funeral Rule as an effort to protect first the consumer, but ultimately the funeral industry as well. Also, we will vvisit a cultural icon—the traditional Amish way. The chapter concludes with a discussion of today's "alternative death movement": funeral consumers' societies, home funerals, and green burial.

Chapter 7 examines the topic of traumatic death–death that is sudden, violent, inflicted, and/or intentional, or encountered as shocking. The chapter, suitably titled "Traumatic Death," surveys several specific examples of traumatic death: terrorism, suicide, murder, and AIDS. We apply terror management theory (TMT) to the topic of terrorism and explore what at least one national security expert has to say about religious terrorism, both domestic and international. We will also learn about the collective trauma caused by large-scale trauma. The chapter looks at suicide with both psychologically and sociologically oriented theory: Freud's anger-turned-inward hypothesis; Beck's identification of hopelessness; suicide as an intrapsychic drama played out on an interpersonal stage; and Emile Durkheim's model for understanding the influence of social integration and regulation. We will also discuss "anger turned outwards" (i.e., murder and the impact on those left behind). Finally, we will address the topic of HIV infection and AIDS. Although it may now take longer to see the impact of HIV and AIDS, we note that the spread of the HIV virus and death from AIDS continues to create a pall in the lives of sexually active young people.

5

The Grim Reaper through Time

A Historical and Cross-Cultural Look at Undertaking

- ■ **Historical Undertaking**
- ■ **Modern Embalming**

- ■ **Trends in Burial and Cremation**
- ■ **Commemorative Customs**

■ ■ ■

Any day above ground is a good one.
—NATIONAL MUSEUM OF FUNERAL HISTORY

■ ■ ■

With the exception of portrayals in the media and infrequent encounters, death has been largely removed from day-to-day life—a far cry from the way it used to be. In a previous time, people encountered death almost as a matter of course. It was familiar. Today, we even have different names for two distinct categories: clinical death and brain death. In Chapter 10, we discuss the significance more fully. For now, it will be sufficient to discuss **clinical death**—the only kind people of a bygone era knew anything about. The person stops breathing and the heart stops beating. As a result, the body begins to cool, the blood settles, the tissues begin to decompose, and foul-smelling gasses build up. It becomes important to dispose of the body.

We begin with a historical look at undertaking–the business of dealing with the bodies of dead people. Then we will explore what today's undertakers, people we now call **funeral directors**, actually do. This will be followed by an exploration of contemporary trends in burial and cremation. Next we'll briefly look at the "best practices" of the funeral service industry through a short profile of Lynch and Sons, family undertakers. Finally, we will survey how selected religious traditions deal with the disposal of the body and remember the lives of the deceased.

HISTORICAL UNDERTAKING

Evidence from a prehistoric past suggests that ritualized burial has been practiced since the time of the **Neanderthal**, a distinct species of people, *Homo sapiens neanderthalensis,* who appeared in Europe as early as 250,000 years ago (Solecki, 1975). The Neanderthals died out after the last great ice age, some 27,000 years ago, arguably because of interbreeding and rivalry with our own ancestors, *Homo sapiens.* Although it is still debated in the field of archaeology, it appears they may have cared for one another, going to the trouble of burying their dead with ceremony, constructing grave sites adorned with flowers and prized belongings (Solecki, 1975; Sommer, 1999). Whereas the meaning of the Paleolithic evidence continues to be hotly debated, ritualistic burial, which seems to have been practiced by the Neanderthal, may also be suggestive of a link between burial customs and belief in an afterlife (Bowker, 1994, 1995; Trinkaus & Shipman, 1993).

Taking care of the remains of the dead is a practical and essential feature of any death system. How human beings accomplish this is far more varied than it might at first appear. Many people living in North America may think of burial and cremation as natural, but there are actually many diverse ways of dispatching the departed.

Aboriginal groups in the frozen North have encased the dead in special igloos. Some North American plains Indians exposed the remains of their dead in trees or else on biers elevated above the ground on poles. Vikings of old put the remains of respected leaders in burning ships. The Tibetan people, and others, have long employed "sky burial"—a practice that involves chopping up the bodies of the dead and feeding them to waiting vultures. In our own time, Hall of Fame slugger Ted Williams willed that his head be surgically removed from his body after death, and that both be frozen and stored in liquid nitrogen—a process called *cryonic suspension*, in the hope that he might someday be "reanimated," when technology has advanced (Associated Press, 2002). Although belief in eventual reanimation, espoused by the so-called

While the Neanderthals may have been a less intellectually or technologically advanced species than *Homo sapiens*, our species, there is evidence to suggest that they may have grieved the deaths of their loved ones, perhaps even burying their bodies with valued things. *Bastos/Fotolia*

transhumanists (see Chapter 13), might seem a little "out there," in reality, it may not be much different from other beliefs and practices, such as those of the ancient Egyptians.

Ancient Egyptian Funerary Customs

Some 5,000 years ago, in a time known as the predynastic period, a civilization began to develop in Egypt that put extraordinary emphasis on preparing the human body for burial. Society believed that the fate of the soul in the next world depended on the state of the body in this one. The Egyptians believed that the body, soul, and spirit were mystically interconnected. The spirit of the person, they thought, could return to animate the mummy, causing it to come back to life and that life in the nether world was dependent on the continued existence of the body in this one (see Chapter 14).

Burial practices and customs in Egypt evolved over time, so there is no single set of beliefs and practices that applied in all periods (Mackenzie, 1907; Schumann-Antelme & Rossini, 1998). Embalming ultimately became general practice throughout Egypt. The embalmers who were entrusted with the care of the body were apparently well trained and credentialed to practice their craft. In a now classic work, Mackenzie (1907) described the embalming process they used. The embalmers removed the brain through the nostrils with a hooked tool after being treated with a special preparation. They then used a stone knife to make an incision on the left side of the body. This gave them access to the liver, heart, lungs, and intestines, which they removed. After cleaning, the organs were steeped in palm wine and perfumed before being covered with nitre, a semitransparent salt that they left to cure for 70 days. While the internal organs were curing, the rest of the body was prepared and dried. When the organs were ready, they were put in four canoptic jars, which were placed in a special chest. The body was wrapped with bandages that were treated with a strong gum.

Civil War Roots of Modern Undertaking

Prior to the American War Between the States (1861–1865), disposing of the remains of the dead was a home-spun affair. People usually took care of their own dead. If an undertaker was called in, this individual would have most likely been someone at the local general store, a carpenter, or a cabinetmaker who provided a coffin for burial. Most often, burial would have taken place soon after death, so preserving the body was rarely a major concern. If there was a delay, the body was exposed to the elements during the winter, or packed with ice at other times to retard the process of decomposition.

During the American Civil War, large-scale death was occurring far from home. As a consequence, preserving the bodies of the dead so they could be returned to the families became a matter of concern. Dr. Thomas Holmes, considered the father of American embalming, was employed by the Union Army to set up battlefield embalming stations (Konefes & McGee, 1996). Dr. Holmes was a well-educated physician who had been a coroner in New York City before the war. Indeed, this may have contributed to his interest in **embalming**. He became well-known for having developed a nonpoisonous embalming fluid that was widely sold.

As a result of massive death occurring on the battle field during the American Civil War, the bodies of the dead were embalmed at make-shift field embalming stations, like this, so they would be preserved long enough for the bodies to make the long journey home for burial. *CORBIS*

Had it not been for a chance event, we might never have known of Dr. Holmes. On the morning of May 24, 1861, Colonel Elmer Ellsworth, a former clerk in Abraham Lincoln's Springfield law office, was killed by an innkeeper with southern sympathies (Lee, Nelson, Tilden, Ganzini, Schmidt, & Tolle, 1996). The distraught president authorized a White House funeral. Through the offices of the Secretary of State, Holmes got permission to do the embalming. Distinguished guests paid their respects. When Mrs. Lincoln viewed the body, she is said to have commented on how natural it appeared, as if he was merely asleep. The Washington press corps reported on the Ellsworth funeral, giving it and Dr. Holmes glowing reviews (Lee et al., 1996).

Dr. Holmes's services were in demand. It is reported that by the end of the war he had embalmed as many as 4,000 bodies. In addition, Holmes helped to train many other battlefield physicians. During the Civil War era, only physicians were believed to be qualified enough to do embalming. The process involved making a small incision near the collar bone, opening the carotid artery, pumping embalming fluid into the artery, and draining the blood from the veins. It was not long, however, before anyone willing to buy a patented embalming fluid could get free training in its use and a certificate from the seller to establish one's qualifications. Thus began the profession of **funeral director**. On January 14, 1880, a group of 26 undertakers held the first meeting of what would just two years later become the National Funeral Directors Association (2006a), or the NFDA.

Many embalming fluids contained arsenic, a deadly poison, but in 1868, a German chemist, August Wilhelm von Hofmann, discovered a new preservative called *formaldehyde*. After 1910, commercial chemical companies increasingly turned to a mixture of formaldehyde, methanol, formic acid, and other chemicals (Museum of Funeral Customs, 2006). By 1906, the recently established National Funeral Directors Association had published several formulas for embalming fluid, as shown in Table 5.1.

MODERN EMBALMING

Although embalming is rarely done in most other parts of the world today, it continues to be routine in North America and Australia, and now seems to be catching on in England, where despite the high cremation rate, it is now more common.

In essence, the process of embalming involves draining the body's natural fluids and replacing them with chemical preservatives. Its purpose is to retard the process of decomposition, reduce the presence of bacterial microorganisms, make the transportation of bodies easier, and preserve the physical appearance for the sake of mourners

TABLE 5.1	National Funeral Director's Association Embalming Fluid—Formula #3 (1906)	
Ingredient	**Quantity**	**Percentage**
Formaldehyde	11 pounds	14%
Glycerin	4 pounds	5%
Sodium borate	2.5 pounds	3%
Boric acid	1 pound	1%
Sodium nitrate	2.5 pounds	3%
Eosin, 1% solution	1 fluid oz.	
Water	10 gallons	

Source: Museum of Funeral Customs. (2006). Formaldehyde: Its development and history since 1906. [Online]. Available: http://www.greatriverroad.com/quincy/kibbemuseum.htm

who may wish to view the body before burial (Iserson, 2001). The funeral industry suggests that even healthy people play host to a wide variety of potentially infectious organisms, especially so for the dying. The industry has apparently been quite concerned about the spread of the disease organisms, especially the HIV and Hepatitis B viruses. Critics argue, however, that while the public health advantages of embalming bodies is questionable, funeral industry profits from the practice appear all too real (Carlson, 1998; Iserson, 2001; Mitford, 1998). There may be a public perception that embalming is required by law, but few states and provinces actually demand it under most circumstances. Indeed, some religions—including Orthodox Judaism, Islam, and Baha'i—forbid the practice of embalming except in special situations.

When embalming is done, the body is usually "laid out" at the funeral home on a stainless steel or porcelain embalming table (Iserson, 2001). The funeral home personnel may then remove and inventory the clothing and other personal effects. The body is often sprayed with a disinfectant solution and sponged down. Any fluids, called **purge**, that may be seeping from the lungs, stomach, or intestines are suctioned or wiped away. This prevents further purge from seeping out the mouth or nose. To relieve the **rigor mortis**—the stiffening of the muscles that occurs after death—the mortician may flex and massage the limbs to keep them pliable so they can be worked with easily.

In a common method of embalming, the mortician uses a pump to inject several quarts of chemicals (often a solution of formaldehyde or methyl alcohol) into the large arteries, such as the carotid (neck), femoral (groin), or axillary arteries (upper arm) (Carlson, 1998; Iserson, 2001). They will simultaneously drain as much blood as possible

A new class of professionals called funeral directors have emerged to take care of our dead for us.   *Lisa F. Young/Fotolia*

TABLE 5.2 Estimated Cemetery Costs		
Item	**Casket Burial**	**Urn Burial**
Lot	$1,000–$3,000	$850–$2,550
Endowment Care	10% of lot price	10% of niche price
Administrative Fee	$95	$95
Grave Liner	$595	Not applicable
Vault (instead of liner)	Not needed if vault used	$300
Opening & Closing	$850	$150–$300
Flat Marker	$150 or more	$150 or more
Monument/Headstone	$4,000 or more	Not commonly used
Engraving	Variable	Variable
Placement of Marker/Headstone	$195	$195
TOTAL Cemetery Cost	At least $3,000	At least $1825

Source: People's Memorial Society. (2004). Sample cemetery cost calculation. [Online].
Available: http://www.peoples-memorial.org/cemetery.html

through the major veins. Often a **trocar**, a pointed hollow surgical instrument approximately two feet long and three quarters of an inch in diameter, is used to pierce and then suction any gas or fluids from the body's organs to further slow the process of decay.

When the embalming fluids begin to infiltrate into the body tissue, the muscles begin to firm up or "set" (Iserson, 2001). Morticians use plastic or rubber eye caps and mouth formers to position the eye lids and lips in place. Sometimes they are sewn shut or glued with modern quick-setting products. The body is cleaned, dressed, made up, and put into the casket—referred to as **casketing**—for viewing or the funeral.

TRENDS IN BURIAL AND CREMATION

In North America, commemorative services often precede the disposition of the body. This section discusses contemporary burial and cremation practices.

More than 70 percent of human remains in the United States are buried; in Canada, over half of human remains are buried. The North American way of death, which commonly includes burial, generally necessitates the services of a funeral director. Unless the funeral is held within 24 to 48 hours, either embalming or refrigeration will usually be required. With the price tag of the average funeral being now well over $5,000, cost has become a huge issue. In addition to the funeral director's fees and embalming costs, the casket (or coffin) and burial plot are among the most costly expenses to be incurred (see Figure 5.1).

The pricing of even inexpensive caskets (often made deliberately unattractive to discourage people from buying them) begin at a few hundred dollars. Top-of-the line models, such bronze caskets with sealed gaskets, can cost upwards of $25,000. The high profit margins on caskets (a tenfold markup are not unheard of) make them

The goods and services shown below are those provided to customers. Customers may choose only the items they desire. However, any funeral arrangements selected will include a charge for basic services and overhead. If legal or other requirements mean you must buy any items you did not specifically ask for, funeral home will explain the reason in writing on the statement we provide describing the funeral goods and services selected.

Basic Services Fee... $1,213.00

Services include: conducting the arrangements conference; planning the funeral; consulting with family and clergy; shelter of remains; preparing and filing of necessary notices; obtaining necessary authorizations and permits; coordinating with the cemetery, crematory, or other third parties. In addition, this fee includes a proportionate share of funeral home's basic overhead costs.

This fee for basic services and overhead is added to the total cost of the funeral arrangements selected. (This fee is already included in the charges for direct cremations, immediate burials, and forwarding or receiving remains.)

Embalming.. $420.00

Except in certain special cases, embalming is not required by law. Embalming may be necessary, however, if certain funeral arrangements selected, such as a funeral with viewing. If embalming not desired, customer usually has the right to choose an arrangement that does not require a fee, such as direct cremation or immediate burial.

Other Preparation of the Body $150.00

Transfer of Remains to the Funeral Home.......................$154.00

Use of Facilities and Staff For Visitation/Viewing.........$275.00

Use of Facilities and Staff for Funeral Ceremony at the Funeral
Home $350.00

Hearse (local)...$185.00

Service car/van..$85.00

Acknowledgment cards...$18.00

Casket...$2,800.00
[A separate casket price list is required to be provided at the funeral home]

Total average cost $5,650.00
[Does not include cremation or burial costs]

FIGURE 5.1 Sample General Price List Based on U.S. National Averages   *Source:* Federal Trade Commission. (2004). *Sample price lists.* Available at www.ftc.gov/bcp/conline/pubs/buspubs/funeral. htm#samples. Prices based on National Funeral Directors Association. (2001). *General price list survey.* Complete GPL Report may be purchased from NFDA, InfoCentral: http://www.nfda.org.

lucrative commodities for those in the funeral industry. In the United States, the federal **Funeral Rule** requires funeral directors to fully disclose their basic fees, casket prices, and quote prices over the phone. The rule came about because of disclosures of widespread abuse within the industry. The rule also requires funeral homes to use caskets purchased elsewhere without charging additional handling fees. Recent conflicting

Simple and Cheap

Josephine Black Pesaresi, the daughter of former U.S. Supreme Court Justice Hugo L. Black, wrote a story about the time she needed to shop for her father's casket. Her father, the second longest sitting justice in the history of the Court, died in 1971 at the ripe old age of 85. He left three instructions on the funeral arrangements: simple, cheap, and no open casket. Evidently, Justice Black had been appalled over the years by the high cost of funerals. He opined that funeral homes were often guilty of taking advantage of bereaved people when they were most vulnerable. An unassuming person, he was apparently not impressed by so many people who seemed puffed up by their own sense of importance. He wanted none of it.

As Josephine Black Pesaresi writes, she went to Gawler's Funeral Home in Washington, DC—a mortuary often used by high government officials. She was accompanied by members of her family and two sitting Justices of the U.S. Supreme Court, Byron White and William Brennan. The casket room was elegant, with piped-in music, wood-paneled walls, and thick carpeting. On entering, one's eye was immediately drawn to a superbly crafted dark wood casket framed in white light. In contrast, the first casket in the room was a tasteless, frilly thing, covered with pink organza, satin bows, and ruffled skirting.

When Justice Black's funeral delegation finally learned the price of the room's center-piece, they recalled the justice's instructions: simple, cheap, and no open casket. It was clear that the magnificent casket in the center of the room was out of the question, and so were the other polished wood beauties. It would be a cloth covered casket. When they learned there was a basic pine box concealed beneath the fabric of each, they decided on the cheapest in the room—the pink monstrosity—but they wanted to see beneath the cloth. Someone pulled at the pink fabric, exposing a small patch of wood. Off came the pink bow. Off came the skirting. Before long, a perfectly fine, plain, pine box stood before them. It was in this coffin that Justice Black would rest, unadorned even by a flag, at the National Cathedral in Washington, DC, where over 1,000 people—family, friends, the President, Supreme Court Justices, and members of Congress—all gathered to say good-bye. For the Black family, the price tag of the coffin did not express the depth of their love, nor did it reflect the stature of the man.

Source: Adapted from Funeral Consumer's Alliance of Connecticut (FCA-CT). (2004). *Simple and cheap my father said.* Available on www.funerals.org/faq/judge.htm. Adapted by permission.

federal court decisions on the legality of Oklahoma and Tennessee laws, which require consumers to buy caskets from state licensed funeral directors, make these protections less secure. Many people are still unsure of where to start looking for a casket, although high-quality and low-cost caskets are available from a variety of sources (including through the Internet). For a few suggestions, refer to the links at the end of this chapter. Figure 5.2 shows a sample price list form for a casket.

Today, low-cost caskets suitable for a funeral are often made of fabric-covered pressed board. Even less expensive **alternative containers** made of cardboard are available to use when the body will be cremated or the loved-ones aren't concerned with the appearance. More costly caskets are usually made of hard woods or steel, and are generally lined, often with adjustable mattresses, although it is still possible to find simple, unlined, pine caskets. As discussed later, in Judaism it is customary to bury the dead in a simple unlined

Alternative Containers:

1. Fiberboard Box.. $_____

2. Plywood Box.. $_____

3. Unfinished Pine Box... $_____

Caskets:

1. Cloth-covered softwood...................................... $_____

2. Oak stained softwood... $_____

3. Mahogany finished softwood............................... $_____

4. Solid White Pine.. $_____

5. Hardwood casket... $_____

6. 18 gauge steel (available in a variety of interiors)......... $_____

7. 20 gauge steel (available in a variety of interiors)......... $_____

8. Solid Bronze (16 gauge) with brushed finish (available in a variety
   of interiors)...................................... $_____

9. Solid Copper (32 oz.) with Sealer (Oval Glass)............... $_____

FIGURE 5.2 Sample Casket Price List Form   *Source:* FTC (Federal Trade Commission). (2004). Sample Price Lists. [Online]. Available: http://www.ftc.gov/bcp/conline/pubs/buspubs/funeral.htm#samples

wood coffin. In Islam and Hinduism, a shroud is all that is required. Contemporary metal caskets are made in varying gauges, or thicknesses (with a corresponding difference in the price tag). The more expensive ones are often gasketed to make them air tight (to prevent moisture from getting in—but in actuality, they are likely to contain the seeping purge, effectively speeding rather than slowing the process of decomposition).

Grave plots are sometimes located in public cemeteries, although it is far more common these days to purchase a plot at a private cemetery. It can be a significant expense. In the United States, eligible veterans may be buried on a first-come first-served basis without charge at one of many national cemeteries located throughout the country. (Please refer to links at the end of chapter.) Although many of the older cemeteries have a variety of above-ground monuments, or markers, newer memorial parks, such as southern California's Forrest Lawn, strive for a pastoral appearance, and require that plots have simple flush-mounted plaques that do not extend above the surface.

Today, in addition to the basic plot, cemeteries may require the use of a **grave liner** or **burial vault**—usually concrete liners that enclose the body in the grave completely or on three sides. These prevent the earth above from sinking *when (not if)* the casket and body decompose, thereby preserving the desirable smooth, rolling, appearance the modern memorial park is striving to create. For an estimate of potential costs, see Figure 5.2.

In addition, casketed bodies are sometimes placed in special above-ground buildings called **mausoleums**. The fronts of these crypts are often faced with marble. Internment in buildings like this tend to be far more costly than traditional below-ground plots.

Cremation

Cremation can be an alternative to the high cost of burial, and indeed, it can be far less costly. With the increasing number of people who choose cremation, the funeral industry has been quick to find other ways to increase its market share—often by promoting a full range of services that are packaged with the cremation itself. Although there are freestanding **crematoria**, many funeral homes, especially those affiliated with the large funeral chains, have their own facilities. A high-end cremation arranged through a traditional funeral home can cost well over $1,000—a figure that does not include other funeral home fees. **Direct cremation**—the practice of cremating the body after death without benefit of traditional mortuary services (embalming the body; viewing or visitation; conducting a funeral prior to cremation)—is an alternative. When the cremation is done by a discounter or is arranged through one of the nonprofit consumer funeral societies that exist throughout the country (please see Chapter 6), the fee for direct cremation in the United States can be as little as $250, but more typically it costs $500 or more.

Before cremation can take place, a permit is usually required, since it is impossible to determine the cause of death after cremation. There is often a 48-hour waiting period before a permit is issued. In many parts of North America, the law requires that a **medical examiner** or the **coroner** determines the cause of death before remains can be released, especially if the deceased was not receiving medical care at the time of death.

Cremation is now used about 99 percent of the time in Japan, 70 percent in the United Kingdom, 43 percent in Canada, and 29 percent in the United States (Cremation Association of North America, 2004b, 2004c). When cremation is to occur, special medical devices (e.g., heart pacemakers, which can explode during cremation), and any other noncombustibles (e.g., metal casket handles or jewelry) are removed. The casket or other container is placed in the cremation chamber, called a **retort**, where gas or electric burners raise the temperature to a range of 1,400 to 1,800 degrees Fahrenheit (Cremation Association of North America, 2004, 2004a). With some advance notice, the staff of the crematory can generally accommodate loved ones who wish to witness the cremation.

The body and container rapidly catch fire. The skin and hair scorch, char, and burn. The muscles slowly contract, and occasionally there will be abdominal swelling, due to the formation of steam and expansion of gasses in the belly (Evans, 1963, cited in Iserson, 2001). The destruction of the soft tissue gradually reveals the skeleton, which falls apart when the tendons connecting the bones are consumed. The tissue of the stomach, lungs, and brain (encased as it is in the cranium), evaporate as the process continues. The cremation, which usually takes between 1½ to 3 hours, consumes everything except bone fragments, dental gold, and any other noncombustibles that were not removed before cremation (Cremation Association of North America, 2004). The metal objects are removed by hand or with a magnet. Large bone fragments are pulverized and mixed with the other body residue (the wood casket or cremation container will be completely consumed). Depending on the size, age, gender, and bone structure of the individual, the cremated remains, called **cremains**—a white-, yellow-, or gray-colored mixture with a texture ranging from that of sand to powder—will weigh between 4 and 8 pounds.

What happens to the cremains? Many people are under the impression that cremains must legally be handled in a specialized manner, but cremains can be and are disposed of in a variety of ways. In 1997, the Cremation Association of North America conducted a study looking at the kind of container used for cremation and what was done with the cremains afterward.

In 1996, about 41 percent of cremains are delivered to cemeteries, 36 percent are taken home by the family, and about 18 percent are scattered directly by the crematory staff. Of the cremains delivered to a cemetery, approximately 57 percent were buried, 26 percent were placed in a **columbarium** (a special building at a cemetery or church with niches for cremains), 15 percent were scattered on dedicated property, and 2 percent were buried in a common grave.

State of the Art

There have been concerns about funeral industry practices that have led to adoption of federal regulation. However, many funeral directors are sensitive and concerned people, who recognize the profound power of death to impact lives of the living. They do yeoman's work in assisting them during their time of sorrow.

Thomas Lynch is a poet, author, and a funeral director. He and his family run Lynch and Sons, headquartered in the community of Milford, Michigan. They are perhaps the largest remaining family-owned funeral home company in the United States. They are probably also the best of the best in the industry. Thomas Lynch writes eloquently about serving the needs of his neighbors, and the experiences of those who grieve. In 2007, his work was featured in a PBS documentary on the funeral business as well as in other educational offerings, such as the Bill Moyers series on death and dying, *On Our Own Terms*. Lynch is frequently invited to speak at national gatherings, and has published many of his poems in collected works (see links at the end of this chapter). Box 5.1 discusses the physical, social, psychological, and spiritual aspects of dealing with death.

BOX 5.1

Focus on Practice: Dealing with Death

When death occurs, its realities quickly become manifest. The survivors will need to care for the body; interface with the society's "death system" and work out relationships; cope with loss; and negotiate how to handle the spiritual dimensions.

Physical

Body decomposition. The human body begins the process of breaking down as soon as death occurs. Loved ones of the deceased will have to decide how to deal with this. Some religious traditions (e.g., Jewish and Islamic) require quick disposal of the body without attempts to preserve it in any way.

If there is a need to preserve the body, there are two basic methods: refrigeration and embalming. Some legal jurisdictions require this be done soon after death. When preservation

(Continued)

is not a consideration, "direct cremation" may be an option. In this event, the body is taken directly to the crematorium.

All of these matters should be addressed directly with the survivors. If the deceased has specified preferences, these may make decisions easier.

Social

Relationships. Relationships in families are often complicated and sometimes conflicted. If there is conflict in a family, it is likely to get played out when a loved one dies, sometimes in the context of trying to make a variety of decisions.

Anyone working with families following a death would be prudent to consider the nature of the family relationships. Close family ties may foster continued bonding. Conflicted ones present both challenges as well as opportunities for healing, depending on the inclination of the parties, the nature of whatever issues surface, and astuteness of the intervener.

Psychological

Grief. Following a loss, grief is a normal human response yet the strong emotions associated with it can nevertheless be distressing.

If the family has very strong cultural or religious traditions, how the mourning process is to unfold will be clearer to the parties. It may quite well provide a structure that will direct and contain the grief. However, clearly defined mourning rituals are less common today. Providing for emotional support and taking practical steps to help might, nevertheless, soften the trauma.

Mental illness and complicated grief. The death of a loved one is arguably one of the most stressful experiences a person can have. If the individual is already mentally or emotionally compromised, it may be experienced more profoundly. About 20 percent of bereaved people experience complicated grief (Jacobs, 1993; Middleton, Burnett, Raphael, & Martinek, 1996; Shear, Frank, Houck, & Reynolds, 2005). Intense yearning, anger, strong emotions, and preoccupation are characteristics. The risk is increased when the bereaved person was highly dependent on the deceased, intense caregiving stress existed before death, and the nature of the death was traumatic (Bonanno et al., 2002; Bonanno, Wortman, & Nesse, 2004).

Spiritual

Spirituality and religion are important elements of culture that provide considerable support to bereaved persons. In addition, many now feel that "meaning making," an important feature of religious and spiritual systems, makes significant contributions to the process of recovering from loss (Neimeyer, 2001).

When there are different religion opinions in the family, the meaning making contribution can get complicated or confused. Finding commonalities and congruencies can sometimes, but not always, help with this.

COMMEMORATIVE CUSTOMS

The primary reason for embalming and cosmetic restoration is to prepare the body for viewing and the commemorative service. Today, there are three common types services held to honor the dead: **funeral**, **memorial**, and **committal** services (Searl, 2000). A key difference between a funeral and a memorial service is that at a funeral, the body is physically present; at a memorial service, the body is not present. In our society, having a funeral, especially an open-casket service, generally requires the body to be embalmed or refrigerated to retard decomposition. After a funeral, a committal service may held at the cemetery. Unless the funeral is held on the grounds of a cemetery, the family and friends usually follow the hearse carrying the body to the cemetery in a motorcade. When there are no other services, the type of service usually held at the cemetery is often called a **graveside service**. When direct cremation occurs, a funeral with the body present is not possible. Under these circumstances, a memorial service may be held without the body or the services may be held with the cremated remains present.

Typically there is a period between death and disposition. In the Western tradition (and many parts of the world for that matter), friends and family gather in the presence of the body prior to burial to hold a **wake**—a term that hearkens back to days before medicine was a scientific undertaking. It was customary to accompany the body. In the Christian tradition, the wake, especially in Ireland and Scotland, was a vigil held before the funeral, usually in the home of the deceased person (Cross & Livingstone, 1997). The idea was that mourners would watch and wait in the presence of the body, perhaps to ensure the person was really dead, but mostly just to gather, share stories about the deceased, and provide each other with emotional support. There are many reports suggesting that wakes sometimes became uproarious parties—the departed being celebrated as guest of honor.

There is considerable variation in Catholic tradition, but the vigil for the dead remains the principal rite celebrated after death and before the final rites (International Commission on English in the Liturgy, 1990). In addition, it is also common for the faithful to gather to pray the rosary. At the conclusion of the rosary there is a very beautiful traditional prayer, called the Hail Holy Queen, which refers to this life as a valley of tears.

With the displacement of the home by the funeral home as the place where the body lies until the funeral, the wake seems to be on the decline, replaced by the practice of a **viewing**, where family and friends come to see the body at the funeral home—a chief reason to embalm and prepare the body. In the Tibetan Buddhist tradition, it is thought that the 49-day period after death is crucial to the transition of the person from this life to the next one. The rituals used during this time—a period called the **bardo**—are intended to help the departed journey safely through the experience, a passage that includes potentially frightening encounters (Gyatso, 2002; Goss & Klass, 1997; Sogyal, 1992; Thrangu, 1999).

In North America, it is still traditional to hold funeral services at a place of worship, yet it has become increasingly common to hold services at funeral home chapels—a practice encouraged by the industry. In addition, it is not altogether uncommon for services to be held at rented halls, club houses, fraternal lodges, or even private residences. When the funeral is held somewhere other than the funeral home, the body will need to be transported there by hearse. Depending on the religious affiliation of the deceased and individual choice, the casket may be greeted at the door by the officiant, who escorts the casket and close family to a place in front of the congregation.

Although religious traditions are intertwined with funerary customs, North American culture has become increasingly secular—less explicitly religious in its orientation—and as a result there are many families without any affiliations to traditional religious institutions. Survivors in these circumstances are sometimes faced with the task of arranging an appropriate commemorative service. Lacking other clear options, they may opt for a traditional service, perhaps by seeking a sympathetic clergy member or using a referral provided by the funeral director. It is the baby boom generation—the generation that launched the practice of writing their own wedding vows—that is increasingly in need of last rites. For them, the solution may lie in an alternative service, which may focus more on consoling the bereaved and less on the departed.

Nontraditional commemorative services often include a simple entrance, perhaps with the officiant escorting the immediate family and casket, followed by a few words of welcome and thanks for the people present. Photographs of the deceased may be displayed, photo albums put out, or photo collages posted on the walls for the guests to look at as they mingle. There might be times of informal remembrances, prayers, or meditation; readings of various kinds; and music to help give voice to the feelings of the day. There may or may not be a traditional sermon or homily, but one or more individuals who knew the deceased well might deliver a **eulogy**, which is a talk about the person. The service might end by sharing a few final words and thanking those who came.

Included next is a short discussion of how a few major religions handle the traditions of the disposal of the body and commemorate the life of the deceased. We will begin with the three religions of the Abrahamic tradition: Judaism, Christianity, and Islam. It is called *Abrahamic* because each accepts Abraham as a spiritual ancestor and patriarch. We will then turn to a brief discussion of Hindu and Buddhist beliefs and practices.

Jewish Custom

In Jewish tradition, it is customary for someone to be with the **mit**, or body, of the individual constantly. This is usually done by members of the **chevra kadisha**, or burial society (Getzel, 1995; Goodman, 2003; Ponn, 1998). Members of this society will not only stand vigil but will also wash and dress the mit for burial, men caring for the bodies of men and women for those of women. The mit is put on a plank and washed from head to foot while prayers for the dead are recited. Then, the mit is dressed in special burial clothing—a simple white shroud of cotton or linen—which is identical for members of all social classes. The person's prayer shawl, or **tallit**, is wrapped around the shoulders. Any fringe on the tallit is clipped. Embalming and any type of cosmetic preparation of the mit is prohibited. Once the mit has been prepared for burial, it is sealed within a simple, unlined, wooden casket. The casket is made without metal nails, screws, or handles, so that it and the mit can return to the earth. If soil from the holy land is available, a small bag of it is placed at the foot of the mit, inside the casket.

Last rites in the Jewish tradition are generally divided into two parts (Ponn, 1998). The first is the funeral service itself, which is usually held at the synagogue or mortuary. Typically, it includes a composite of psalms and prayers; a eulogy; and the *el malei rachamim*, beseeching the Almighty to accept and protect the soul of the dead (Getzel, 1995; Ponn, 1998). The next part of the last rites is the committal service, held at the graveside, which concludes with each mourner shoveling a small amount of soil into the grave, thereby returning the mit to the earth (Ponn, 1998). At the conclusion, a special prayer, the **kaddish**, is recited in a dialect of Aramaic. This is a special prayer—an affirmation of God that does not specifically mention the dead. The next of kin return home where they receive well-wishers and share a meal. For a week after burial, the bereft will sit **shiva**, a strict period of mourning, when the mourners refrain from work, staying at home to receive the condolences of visitors. When shiva comes to an end, there is an additional 30-day period, **sheloshim**, when the restrictions on activities are relaxed and the bereaved may begin to resume their usual activities. For a year after shiva, it is traditional for the principal mourners to continue to mourn, reciting the Kaddish regularly. At the end of the year, the formal period of mourning concludes.

Christian Tradition

ROMAN CATHOLIC   In the Catholic tradition, the celebrant, usually a priest, will greet the casket and family at the door of the church. If there is a viewing before the service, the attendants will close the casket before putting a cloth pall over it. A priest will sprinkle it with holy water, which is a symbol of baptism. A processional cross will precede the casket into the church, followed by the Paschal (Easter) candle, book of Gospels, and other sacred items, some of which may be carried by members of the family. The casket will be put at the front of the church near the altar. The Paschal candle, a symbol of resurrection, will be placed near the head of the casket and lit.

In the Catholic tradition, a full **funeral mass** is preferred since the eucharistic celebration is at the heart of Catholic worship, although a more simple funeral, memorial, or committal service may be celebrated instead (International Commission on English in the Liturgy, 1990). In addition to the entrance and preparatory rites, the service typically includes offering prayers for the soul of the dead and consolation of the bereaved; readings from scripture; hymns; a homily (a short sermon); one or more eulogies (although many celebrants like to limit this); communion; and a final blessing or benediction. The theme is one of resurrection, for the Catholic faith holds that human beings are baptized in both the death and resurrection of Christ. Since the Second Vatican Council, which concluded in 1965, cremation has been permitted so long as it is not intended to deny the credal belief in the resurrection of the body. When burial is to occur, a brief committal service may be held at the cemetery.

PROTESTANT SERVICES   Protestant services may be similar to Catholic practice, especially for Lutherans, but Protestant worship, with its deemphasis on ritual, tends to be simpler (Anderson, 1995; Olbricht, 1998). It generally puts more emphasis on scripture and the sermon, which is usually longer than a homily. Communion is not as likely to be a feature of Protestant commemorative services. Some churches insist on a closed casket; in others, there is often greater emphasis on confronting the realities of death, to include stressing Christian conversion in the service, and the presence of an open casket. The African American funeral is likely to put more emphasis on the idea of "coming home to God," encourage more open expressions of feeling, and make greater use of music than services held in most white Protestant churches (Bolling, 1995; Sullivan, 1995).

Islamic Tradition

In Islam, as in Judaism, burial is to take place soon after death, on the same day if possible (Sakr, 1995; Smith, 1998). Tradition requires that men wash the bodies of men; women wash the bodies of women, except a husband may wash the body of his wife, and vice versa. According to tradition, the body is washed three times, followed by an anointing with nonalcoholic perfumes. The body is then wrapped—for men, three pieces of cloth are used; for women, five pieces of cloth are used. When five cloths are used, they include a full-body sheet, head wrap, chest wrap, body wrap, and **kafan** (shroud). Four cloth ties, seven feet in length, are used to tie the shroud bundle. No part of the body is left exposed. Special prayers, **salatul janazah**, are said without bowing or prostration, but with special supplications called **du'a**. Often, there is a funeral at the mosque and a brief service at the cemetery. Traditionally, the body is carried in procession to the cemetery (cremation is forbidden) by rotating teams of pall bearers. No music or singing is permitted. After a brief eulogy, the body is placed in the grave, and put on its right side, with the head facing Mecca. Each mourner puts three handfuls of soil into the grave while special verses from the Qur'an are read. When the body is covered, the Imam, or religious leader, recites special prayers, reminding the deceased of the creed and about the two angels, Munkar and Nakir, whose task it is to question the deceased in their graves, examining the sanctity of their faith and the nature of the lives they lived.

Hindu Tradition

In contrast to Islam and Judaism, which forbid cremation, in the Hindu tradition, cremation, **antyesti**, is the usual way of disposing of human remains and is considered the sixteenth sacrament of Hinduism (Bowker, 1997). Hinduism is both a complex and paradoxical religion with both a pantheon of divinities and belief in the one Brahman; a fusion of sacred scriptures (Vedic, Grhya, Puranic); and a diversity of devotions that have evolved over the course of 3,500 years (Pearson, 1998; Sanskrit Religions Institute, 2003).

Hindu culture is complex. It includes belief in reincarnation, the idea that each of us has a spiritual path, called **dharma**, based on certain obligations and one's position in the society. A caste system that demarks four social strata (Brahmin: the priestly caste; Kshaatriyas: the ruling or military caste; Vaishayas: the merchant caste; Shudras: the labor caste; in addition to a category of persons regarded as being outside the caste system, outcasts, or "untouchables") and generally recognizes four divisions in the life cycle. These are brahmacarya (student), grhasta (householder), vanaprastha (recluse or retirement), and samnyasa (ascetic). (For more information, see Table 4.2.) Depending on one's status (or caste), the life cycle is being divided into four parts. During the first part, one is a student. Then, one becomes a householder with adult responsibilities. Next, one enters midlife, a time of reflection. And finally, as one prepares for death, it is a time to withdraw from the concerns of this life. This emphasis on life as lived in a cycle acknowledges that carnal life is transitory. It also provides structure and guidance on what sorts of things people should concern themselves with at various times in the life cycle.

Similar to Judaic and Islamic practice, Hindu tradition requires that the last rites be done quickly, within 12 hours of death, if possible. When a person is believed to be dying, he or she is laid out with the feet facing South, the direction of death. Those present read sacred verses so the person will hear the name of God when he or she dies. A lamp is lit near the dying person, indicating to the atman, or soul, that it should go straight up (Pearson, 1998). When it is clear the person is dead, the individual's domestic fire is put out. The chief mourner, usually the eldest son, bathes the body in water, clips the hair and nails, and puts a few drops of water from the holy river Ganga and perhaps a few basil leaves in the mouth of the corpse. Small bits of gold and other precious stones, representing the five elements, are put on the body. Sandalwood paste may be applied. Perhaps some kusa grass is placed in the hands. Sesame seeds, grains of barley, and some clay from the holy river Ganga may be used to help protect the remains from evil spirits. The mourners then wrap the body of a man in an unbleached white cloth; a woman is wrapped in an orange, red, or gold cloth). They put the corpse on a simple bamboo bier, which is covered with flowers and marigold garlands.

The bier is carried on bare feet by male relatives, headed by the chief mourner, who leads the way with a torch lit from the domestic fire (Pearson, 1998). As the procession weaves its way through town, the name of God is chanted. The procession traditionally stops six times, and special **shraddh** rituals are performed. In India, it is desirable for the cremation to occur at one of the burning ghats, cremation grounds near a river. The bier is put on a pyre of wood, preferably sandalwood, as mourners chant verses from the sacred **Vedas**. The pyre is sprinkled with ghee and water before the principal mourner ignites the pyre with the torch from the deceased person's domestic fire or one lit from an eternal flame, such as that kept perpetually burning at Shiva's shrine near the burning ghats in Varanasi (Benares). When the cremation rites have concluded, the chief mourner ritualistically bathes while facing South.

Death and contact with the corpse creates ritual defilement of the family, which may last up to 10 days (Pearson, 1998). During this time mourners are considered to be in a liminal zone, when they may not visit temples, the homes of friends, or take part in social functions; forego normal comforts; and restrict their diets. In the complex Hindu religious system, it is thought that when death occurs, the atman of the deceased goes through a stage called **ativahika**, when the deceased has a vaguely formed subtle body (Sanskrit Religions Institute, 2003). A function of the rites performed during this period is to feed the subtle body until it can sever the last remaining ties to this world and cross over to the world of the **pitr**, or ancestors. On the eleventh day, a feast is prepared, the mourners put on fresh clothes, and a new domestic fire is ignited. The atman of the deceased is thought to be free to abide now in the world of the ancestors where it may rest until it is reincarnated.

Buddhist Customs

Buddhists, like Hindus, believe in reincarnation, holding that the consciousness of the individual continues to be reborn until the person achieves liberation from suffering. They differ from Hindus in that they do not believe in an atma, or soul. For them, the consciousness dissolves with death and is reformed in new life. Although Buddhism has several key precepts that most Buddhists agree on (e.g., the Four Noble Truths and the Eightfold Path), there is also great diversity in emphasis and practice (Society for the Promotion of Buddhism, 1966). There are two major branches (Theravada and Mahayana) and numerous sects. The Theravada branch—"teachings of the elders"—is rooted in the most ancient of scriptures written in the Pali language. It is widespread in Thailand, Cambodia, Sri Lanka, and several other parts of Southeast Asia. Mahayana Buddhism, which is sometimes called that of the "greater vehicle," spread to Tibet, China, Mongolia, Korea, and Japan, adapting to the local cultures as it dispersed. The Mahayana sutras, or texts, were first written in the more recent Sanskrit language, and have been widely translated. The Vajrayana branch—the leading tradition in Tibet, Nepal, Bhutan, Sikkim, parts of Mongolia, and some other areas of the world—grew out of Mahayana Buddhism. As discussed in Chapter 4, I had the opportunity to interview with His Holiness the Dalai Lama, about his views on death. Shortly after I returned from India, His Holiness published a book on dying and living (Gyatso, 2002), which is reviewed more fully in Chapter 14.

Buddhist burial customs vary depending on the customs of the country and the form of Buddhism practiced. In Tibetan Buddhism, for example, the 49-day period of time after death is considered crucial. The present Dalai Lama and other authorities suggest that during this time, consciousness dissolves step by step and the deceased emerges in the intermediate state (Gyatso, 2002). In all forms of Buddhism the funeral rituals are intended to help the deceased make the passage from this incarnation to the next. In the Tibetan tradition, a monk or another adept may read passages from the *Bardo Thodol Chenmo (Tibetan Book of the Dead)*, to remind the deceased of what to expect so as to make the transition more safely and achieve a good reincarnation. In the Theravada tradition, the Bhiksus, or monks, chant a formula of faith with the people, recite the Five Precepts, and deliver a sermon on the nature of death and impermanence (Bowker, 1997; Kariyawasam, 1995). One part of the Theravada ritual includes a water ceremony in which the merit earned from their ritual efforts are transferred to the departed person. The person is buried or cremated, depending on the individual's status and local custom. Because tradition has it that Guatama Buddha was cremated, it is customary for monks to be cremated as well.

Chapter Summary

We began the chapter with the definition of clinical death–when the person's heart stops and the person stops breathing–and a discussion about why all societies need to deal with the disposal of the body. We noted evidence to suggest that as early as the time of Neanderthals, people have buried their dead with ceremony.

We next summarized one of the most sophisticated death systems that have ever existed—that of the ancient Egyptians. A review of their practices provides one with the sense of the relationship between their religious beliefs and burial customs. Their embalming practices were actually quite sophisticated, and not that much different from practices that evolved in our own society.

The origins of modern embalming trace practices that began during the American Civil War. Until that time most deceased persons were cared for by their own families at home, but with death occurring at far off places during the war it became important to preserve the body so the families could see their deceased relative one last time and bury them at home. In this regard, we noted the contributions of Dr. Thomas Holmes, Colonel Elmer Ellsworth, and President Abraham Lincoln. German chemist August Wilhelm von Hofmann discovered formaldehyde, a relatively nontoxic substance that made the practice of embalming safe enough to be practical.

We also reviewed the practice of embalming, burial, and cremation in society today. We discussed in some detail what actually happens when a funeral director prepares the body of a deceased person for viewing and disposition. Taking brief note of abuses that led to the adoption of federal regulations, we also paused to reflect on the many funeral directors who regard what they do as a compassionate service to neighbors. Briefly, we profiled Thomas Lynch, a poet, author, and funeral director.

Next, the chapter turned to the practical and financial aspects burial and cremation, exploring the cost of caskets, funeral directors' fees, burial plot, and cremation. Various tables and figures were included, listing common burial items and their cost. You read about how U.S. Supreme Court Justice Hugo L. Black asked that he be remembered in a service that was both "simple and cheap." The chapter looked at a few options and compared costs, for example, between burial and cremation, immediate cremation or burial, and burial in a public or private cemetery.

We then turned to trends in burial and cremation. We looked into burial commemorative customs, including a brief survey of the beliefs and practices of the religions of the Abrahamic tradition: Judaism, Christianity, and Islam. We also briefly examined Hindu and Buddhist customs.

Key Terms

alternative container *100*
antyesti *108*
ativahika *109*
bardo *105*
burial vault *101*
casketing *98*
chevra kadisha *106*
clinical death *93*
columbarium *103*
committal *104*
coroner *102*
cremains *102*
crematoria *102*
dharma *108*
direct cremation *102*

du'a *108*
embalming *95*
eulogy *106*
funeral *104*
funeral director *96*
funeral mass *107*
Funeral Rule *99*
grave liner *101*
graveside
  service *105*
kaddish *107*
kafan *108*
mausoleum *101*
medical examiner *102*
memorial *104*

mit *106*
Neanderthal *94*
pitr *109*
purge *97*
retort *102*
rigor mortis *97*
salatul janazah *108*
sheloshim *107*
shiva *107*
shraddh *109*
tallit *106*
trocar *98*
Vedas *109*
viewing *105*
wake *105*

Suggested Activities

1. Using the blank form provided in Figure 5.2, go to the Internet or call funeral homes in your area and get prices on the various types of alternative containers and caskets.

You may also wish to inquire about simple cardboard burial containers (which wholesale for about $35). In a short reflection paper or journal, discuss what you learned.

2. Conduct a search on the Internet or at your library on the topic of the eulogy. See if you can track down a range of eulogies online. You may wish to collect several of these, perhaps of the famous. What can we learn about the dead from these eulogies? What do they say about the living?

3. Using examples from the paper or a book, write your own eulogy.

4. Find your local funeral consumers' alliance chapter on the Internet. Each conducts a local survey of prices in the local area. You may also wish to call several local funeral homes. Compare prices for funeral services. If there are significant differences, what explains them?

5. Your class may wish to arrange a visit to the office of the local medical examiner or coroner. You might be surprised to learn about both the human and scientific aspects of this kind of work.

Suggested Reading

- Iserson, K. (2001). *Death to dust: What happens to dead bodies* (2nd ed.). Tucson, AZ: Galen Press.
  This tome, with a whopping 821 pages, contains more information on what happens to dead bodies than any normal person should ever want to know. Written by a physician, it includes detailed, but easily understood, information on virtually every facet of what can happen to the human body after death.

- Laderman, G. (2003). *Rest in peace: A cultural history of death and the funeral home in twentieth-century America.* New York: Oxford University Press.
  This book traces the origins of U.S. funeral practices and the U.S. funeral industry from the time of the American Civil War to the dawning of the twenty-first century. It includes a discussion of the impact Jessica Mitford's book, *American Way of Death*, has had on the funeral industry. Indeed, Laderman's book paints a far more complimentary picture of the funeral director's role in society than do others.

- Lynch, T. (1997). *The undertaking: Life studies from the dismal trade.* New York: Norton.
  This American Book Award winner was authored by Thomas Lynch, a second-generation undertaker and first-rate writer. In this collection of essays, Lynch chronicles the life of the community he serves and the story of the couple hundred people he buries each year.

- Matson, T. (2000). *Round-trip to deadsville: A year in the funeral underground.* White River Junction, VT: Chesea Green.
  Tim Matson, a pond designer and author of six books, spends a year exploring the funeral underground as a way of confronting his own angst about death. He visits and interviews a variety of individuals, each of whom he assigns a descriptive pseudonym, such as "Coffin Maker," "Graveyard Guide," "Crusader," and "Cremator." In his journalistic account, he attempts to take the reader into the ordinary lives of human beings who inhabit this extraordinary world.

- Searl, E. (2000). *In memoriam: A guide to modern funeral and memorial services* (2nd ed.). Boston: Skinner House Books.
  Edward Searl, a Unitarian minister with many years' experience, offers some practical tips on organizing a funeral or memorial service.

Links and Internet Resources

- **National Funeral Directors Association**
  www.nfda.org/
  The National Funeral Directors Association (NFDA) describes itself as the largest association of funeral directors in the world. Although large portions of this site are open only to members, the site hosts a number of links and pages that may be of interest to the student of thanatology. Although difficult to find on the site itself (I found it through a search engine), it contains guidelines on how to comply with the amended FTC Funeral Rule.

- **Cremation Association of North America**
  www.cremationassociation.org
  This is an international organization of over 1,200 members, composed of cemeterians, cremationists, funeral directors, industry suppliers, and consultants who are committed to the idea that cremation can be preparation for memorializing the deceased. The site contains some excellent reference materials, particularly about trends in the use of cremation, which are downloadable as PDF files.

- **Thomas Lynch**
  www.thomaslynch.com
  This is the website of Thomas Lynch—poet, author, and funeral director. Included at the site are excerpts and reviews of his work.

- **The Undertaking**
  www.pbs.org/wgbh/pages/frontline/undertaking/
  This is the site of the PBS documentary, *The Undertaking*, which profiles the work of Thomas Lynch and Sons, funeral directors. Lynch is both an undertaker and poet who speaks eloquently about his work in caring for the dead, but most of all, caring for the living. The full program is available for viewing online at this site.

- **The Dash**
  www.lindaslyrics.com/
  This is the website of Linda Ellis, author of a remarkable poem about life. As the author explains in the poem, the dash represents the life lived between the dates of birth and death. Included at the site is a full text version of the 36-line poem, slide show of the same, and the author's blog.

- **Federal Trade Commission, Funerals: A consumer's guide**
  www.ftc.gov/bcp/conline/pubs/services/funeral.htm
  This online guide provides basic information about funerals. It includes a summary of the federal Funeral Rule, which spells out the consumer's right to a written price list, the right to use a casket purchased elsewhere, and the right that alternate containers may be used when the body is to be cremated.

- **Trappist Caskets**
  www.trappistcaskets.com
  The Trappists of New Melleray Abbey produce beautiful, simple, and reasonably priced caskets (coffins) that can usually be shipped anywhere in North America within 48 to 72 hours. A simple pine one costs less than $700. Proceeds help support the ministries of the abbey.

- **B'nai Shalom Memorial Chapels**
  www.jewishfuneralsforless.com
  This site provides information and caskets for traditional Jewish burials. The caskets conform to Jewish religious traditions. A simple unlined pine casket is available for about $400 and can be shipped immediately.

- **ClevelandCasket.com**
  www.clevelandcasket.com
  This is a supplier of caskets and other funeral goods through the Internet. Specialty caskets include steel caskets with various painted scenes, including "The Race Is Over," "The Last Supper," "Going Home," and "Firefighter." Pricey, but if you're interested in something a little different this site might be for you.

Review Guide

1. Review the material on early examples of ritualized burial. Do such burials prove a relationship between burial practices and belief in an afterlife? Explain.

2. After considering ancient Egyptian burial practices, what would you say we can learn about them? What might they teach us about Egyptian spiritual and religious beliefs? To what degree are their customs similar to and different from modern-day funerary customs?

3. Modern embalming may be used somewhat differently than such practices were by the Egyptians. Although some claim that embalming protects the public health, there is good reason to believe modern embalming practices merely strive to preserve the body just long enough for viewing. Review the material on embalming. Do you agree or disagree? Why? How did the material on embalming "fit" with your prior understanding of what this process entails?

4. Compare the diverse ways of commemorating deceased people. In what ways are these practices different from and similar to each other? What can we learn from an understanding of them? Based on what you now know, have you given serious thought to your own funeral? Do you think the funeral is important? Why or why not?

5. Be sure to review the material on North American burial customs. Consider the kinds of products and services available to the public. You may wish to compare prices and then reflect on the purpose of funerals, burial, and memorialization of the dead. To what degree do modern practices meet these needs?

6

The Grim Reaper Today

Emerging Trends in Contemporary "Deathcare"

- **Our Changing Death System**
- **Commercialization of Death**

- **Flashback**
- **Alternative Death Movement**

This chapter explores the experience of death in the twenty-first century, with special attention to the North American death system—that largely invisible but ever-present social reality that mediates our experience of death and dying. We will begin with a review of an avant-garde example of how the media treats the topic of death via a brief review of the HBO series *Six Feet Under*. Next, we will discuss how life imitates art with a brief look at mortuary services and the "commercialization of death." By way of contrast, this chapter will also look at the way the Amish, a traditional people, have dealt with death, and the ways in which this is changing because of contact with contemporary society. We will also explore some present-day alternatives to the "North American way of death" (i.e., using low-cost memorial societies, the do-it-yourself home funeral, and "green burial").

OUR CHANGING DEATH SYSTEM

Although it is not immediately apparent to the casual observer, we have an entire system in our society devoted to dealing with death. This should come as no surprise, since for many reasons all human societies must find ways to deal with the realities of death. This is precisely because death is such a ubiquitous part of life. Many details must be tended to when death visits—for instance, for sanitary and aesthetic concerns, the remains of the dead have to be disposed of; survivors need to grieve; and whatever wealth the person may have accumulated before death must be redistributed to the living.

How society handles death says something about its character and nature. As briefly mentioned in Chapter 1, Robert Kastenbaum, a pioneer of contemporary thanatology, coined the term *death system* to denote the complex system society uses to deal with death (1998, 2001). He suggests that many aspects of dealing with death, such as medical care for people with terminal illness, doing business with a funeral home, or recovering from a loss, do not exist as isolated, separate, realities but as a network of connections that more or less function as an integrated death system (Kastenbaum, 1998, 2001). In an essay written for a collection of readings, Kastenbaum (1995) offers the following pithy definition of a death system: "Society's multifaceted, multilevel attempt to mediate our relationship with mortality" (p. 9). Kastenbaum (1995, 1998, 2001) sees the death system as intertwined networks, but he outlines several identifiable components and functions. See Table 6.1 for a summary.

The HBO television series, *Six Feet Under,* is a show that ran for five seasons, until 2005. Now available on DVD, it continues to enjoy a "cult" following. The series depicts the life and times of the Fishers, an all-American family who, like many others, is described as "dysfunctional." What's different is the nature of the family business and where they live. For those of you who aren't familiar with the series, the Fishers ran a funeral home, a veritable symbol of our modern death system. Much of the action took place upstairs, "above the shop." In the premier episode, the family patriarch dies in a quirky automobile accident. In the ensuing episodes the story unfolds as the patriarch's widow, two adult sons, and one teen-aged daughter are left to deal with the "ordinary" and not-so-ordinary aspects of life in the "deathcare" business. What emerges is an eccentric, sometimes disturbing, but often touching story of a resilient American family. (Home Box Office, 2003).

I wouldn't claim the show is an accurate or "real" portrayal of life at a funeral home, but I think I can say that through this show, death became a "prime time" part of our culture. Whether out of curiosity or a genuine openness to the subject of death or dying, there's no denying the critical acclaim and popular appeal of the show. In 2001, when the series opened, the show won a Golden Globe award for best television series (Home Box Office, 2003). In the following year, it earned six Emmy awards.

In contrast to an earlier period, when observers such as Ernest Becker (1973) suggested we were an overtly death-denying society, the success of *Six Feet Under* seems to suggest that times and tastes may have changed. From the safety of our living rooms we can peer into the fictional lives of the Fishers. Either we are a less death-denying society today, or we're actually titillated by flirting with the hidden and forbidden.

Pictured here is the set of the HBO TV series, *Six Feet Under*, that attempts to portray death, dying, and bereavement issues played out in the lives of members of a 'dysfunctional' funeral home family.   *CORBIS*

TABLE 6.1	Components and Functions of a Death System

Components of a death system	Examples
• People	Medical examiners, funeral directors, life insurance agents, attorneys, clergy members, florists
• Places	Hospitals, nursing homes, funeral homes, cemeteries, roadside shrines, memorials
• Times	Anniversaries, memorial holidays, certain religious commemorations (e.g., "All Souls Day")
• Objects	Body bags, caskets, hearses, death certificates, tombstones
• Symbols	Religious anointing of the sick, wearing black clothing (Western culture) or white clothing in certain other cultures, black arm bands

Functions of a death system	Description
• Warn and predict	Publicize risk of death in order to encourage people to change behavior (e.g., cigarette and poison warnings)
• Prevent death	The techniques or strategies used by a people to prevent death (e.g., a health-care system designed to fight contagious diseases)
• Provide care for the dying	Provide care for the dying consistent with the values of a given society (e.g., hospice care)
• Dispose of the dead	The system or process in which the remains of the dead are disposed of, and the deceased is memorialized
• Social consolidation	The process or system used to help a people cope and regroup after having experienced a loss
• Make sense out of death	The process of attempting to reconcile perceptions of what is good in terms of life with the realities of death
• Killing	The process, methods, or systems by which a society deliberately takes the lives of human beings (e.g., through war or the execution of certain law violators)

Source: Based on Kastenbaum (1972, 1998, 2001).

As discussed in Chapter 2, one of the characteristics of life today—perhaps a transitional period between modern and so-called postmodern times—is that the boundaries between reality and make-believe are blurred. What we vicariously experience through the media is also part of our collective consciousness, saying something about the society in which we live. Jean Baudrillard (1983), regarded as a prominent postmodern theorist, claims that technology and modernity have brought us into an age in which the simulated realities we experience have actually become more real than what we experience in our daily lives. If we extend this principle to our death system, the simulated realities we get through the media have in large part replaced firsthand experience with death.

In contrast to a time before the baby boom generation, when there was an almost unfettered belief in science, progress, and reason, the world, including the world of death and dying, doesn't seem so certain, positive, or clear any more. The media, information, and communication seem to have transformed the present one. Smart phones, i-Pods, laptop computers, and 24-hour programming piped in through our TVs have changed the way we talk to each other, manipulate information, and conceptualize the world. We can speculate that since we rarely experience death firsthand, information technology gives us our experience of death, thereby transforming the way think about it. We need not look any further than *Six Feet Under* for an example–its avant-garde tone, humorous and dramatic brushes with death, and playful explorations into the dark side of life.

COMMERCIALIZATION OF DEATH

As discussed in Chapter 5, prior to the American Civil War, disposing of the remains of the dead was a homespun affair and most families took care of their own dead. Since those early days of the funeral business, the family-run funeral home became part of almost every North American community. In certain respects, many were much like to the one run by the Fisher family, as depicted in *Six Feet Under*.

Death, Incorporated

I was told that the dramatized image of the funeral business depicted in *Six Feet Under* wasn't popular with members of the funeral trade. When I inquired why, I was told, "It's a soap opera that happens to take place in a funeral home…but it doesn't deal at any depth with the real issues in the business."

Fictionalized it is. But, from an academic perspective, the fact that the show had popular appeal does raise questions about the nature of our culture. Is curiosity about death and the public fascination with such media representations as presented in *Six Feet Under* really new? Why do people in our society want death-oriented entertainment? What's the role of this kind of entertainment? The age-old horror stories and the ghoulish B-movies of an earlier generation serve as reminders to realize there is enduring interest in the topic.

Journalistic interest in the funeral industry began in the early 1960s. The early writings of authors such as Harmer (1963) and Mitford (1963) contributed to an increased public awareness of the industry as well as new concerns about some exploitative practices perpetrated by funeral directors. Jessica Mitford, a renowned writer even before she began digging into the burial business, took on the task of investigating and reporting on the practices of the funeral industry with great aplomb and biting humor. In 1963, she authored *The American Way of Death,* a book that has become a classic exposé. Climbing to number one on the *New York Times* bestseller list, it would send the mortuary world reeling.

Mitford (1963) took the public into a world few people really knew—a world in which funeral directors carefully choreographed each part of their encounters with the bereaved with an eye to profits. She examined a range of practices that may seem a bit bizarre to the average person—the walk through the display room to select a **casket** (not a coffin); the use of **wound filler** to hide injury and to promote restorative services

Jessica Mitford, shown here, was among the first journalists to expose abuses in the funeral home industry. In her final exposé on the topic she expressed concern about the corporate takeover of the industry. *Hulton-Deutsch Collection/CORBIS*

to make the body fit for viewing; the display of bodies in rooms with names like the **slumber room**; the use of special shoes and **hostess gowns** for the departed; the use of euphemisms like **floral tributes** instead of flowers; insistence on the use of concrete or fiberglass grave burial vaults, grave liners, and **lawn crypts** (pre-dug multiple units) to prevent the earth from sagging after the casket and body disintegrate; as well as the use of earth dispensers to insulate the bereaved or officiating clergy from dirt when committing the body to the earth.

In 1975, after much fanfare, the Federal Trade Commission (FTC) proposed regulations to deal with the most serious concerns. In 1984, the regulations, which are called the **Funeral Rule**, were finally implemented. As a consequence of later dialogs between the FTC and National Funeral Directors Association (NFDA), a softened and **Amended Funeral Rule** went into force on July 19, 1994 (Federal Trade Commission, 2003; National Funeral Directors Association, 2003) and is still in effect today. See Table 6.2.

The Funeral Rule addressed the most serious concerns raised by the industry's critics. Chief among the concerns was that the loved ones were being manipulated when

TABLE 6.2 Disclosures Required Under the Amended Funeral Rule

Item	Disclosure
• General Price List (GPL)	• Must be provided to all consumers • Must also be provided to people who call on the telephone • Stipulates the right to select only goods and services needed (with certain limitations) • Notification about alternative containers for direct cremation • Price range of caskets • Price range of outer burial containers • Special price lists for government and certain groups
• Embalming	• Prohibits mandatory embalming or telling consumers embalming is legally required unless it really is
• Alternative containers	• Consumers must be told they may use alternative containers for direct cremations
• Basic services fees	• Non-declinable fee added to the total cost of the funeral arrangements to cover expenses and overhead
• Casket price list	• Consumers must be told that a casket price list is available
• Outer burial container price list	• This applies when the cemetery requires a vault or similar case to prevent the earth from sagging in when the casket and body deteriorate.

Source: Based on Federal Trade Commission. (2003). Complying with the Funeral Rule. Available: http://www.ftc.gov/bcp/conline/pubs/buspubs/funeral.htm

they were most vulnerable. Among other things, the rule required funeral directors to give customers a general price list, provide it over the phone if asked, inform consumers they had the right to choose only the goods and services they actually needed, inform them about less-expensive containers to use for cremation, and provide them with various price lists. Although the funeral home industry acceded to the requirements of the funeral rule, they lobbied for the right to charge a "nondeclinable" **basic services fee**. This gave the industry the right to pass on the cost of doing business, assuring them a profit.

The Funeral Rule may have been a step in the right direction, but industry critics have raised new concerns. They argue that undertaking has gone "corporate" (Harmer, 1963; Mitford, 1963, 1998). In the early episodes of *Six Feet Under* we have art imitating life. The Fishers fend off the encroachments of a large funeral home chain bent on expanding its corporate empire (Home Box Office, 2003). In this case, art highlights a tension that exists between the old and new—between the "mom and pop" funeral home of days gone by and the modern, efficient, systematized, corporate model, in which high-quality, but impersonal and expensive, goods and services are packaged and marketed to consumers. Critics, such as the late Jessica Mitford, argue that the mortuary industry continues to evolve, finding new ways to maximize profits.

Writing years later, and shortly before her own death, Mitford would recall the initial reasons for her first foray into the world of the North American undertaking business:

> *To trace the origins of the book: my husband, Bob Treuhaft, got fired up on the subject of the funeral industry in the mid-to-late 1950s. A labor lawyer...he began to notice that when the breadwinner of a union family died, the hard-fought-for death benefit...would end up in the pocket of the undertaker.* (Mitford, 1998, p. xiii)

In the sequel to her best-selling exposé, Mitford (1998) laments that while some changes had taken place since the early revelations about the industry—notably the involvement of the Federal Trade Commission in providing oversight—the overall situation had actually worsened rather than improved. In explaining her reasons for writing an updated version of *The American Way of Death,* Mitford (1998) says,

> *More recent changes on the funeral front should go far to dispel any feeling of complacency on the part of consumers.... Cremation, once the best hope for a low-cost, simple getaway, has become increasingly expensive.... The Federal Trade Commission's much heralded trade rule has huge loopholes. Most sinister of all is the emergence over the last fifteen years of monopoly ownership of hitherto independent mortuaries and cemeteries.* (p. xix)

Just as chains such as McDonald's have gobbled-up a huge bite of the world's fast-food market, we could say McDeath is engaged in much the same undertaking. While acknowledging that the vast majority of funeral homes are still small operations, Mitford's last and latest book on the topic (1998) heralds the appearance of corporate death tapping at the door.

Indeed, there are now at least three large publicly traded mortuary service corporations operating in North America: Service Corporation International (SCI), the Alderwoods Group (formerly the Loewen Group), and Stewart Enterprises. In addition, there is the NorthStar Memorial Group, a large privately held company. Service Corporation International, a Texas-based concern, is the largest of the big publicly traded mortuary service corporations, boasting of over $2.2 billion in income from over 3,000 "affiliate" funeral homes (only a few of these are not fully owned by SCI), crematoria, and cemeteries in North America, the United Kingdom, France, and South America (Service Corporation International, 2003). The Alderwoods Group, a reorganized company that was coping with financial problems related to numerous lawsuits and being overextended, has its executive offices and operations center in Canada. It counts about 950 funeral homes and another 200 or so cemeteries among its assets in the United States, Canada, and the United Kingdom (Alderwoods Group, 2003). Stewart Enterprises, the smallest of the industry conglomerates, is a Louisiana-based company that boasts a solid financial footing and about 450 funeral homes and cemeteries in the United States (Stewart Enterprises, 2003). If you are interested in finding out if there's an affiliated branch funeral home or cemetery in your community, you may wish to use a favorite search engine to search the Web for the sites of the funeral industry big three—SCI, Alderwoods, and the Stewart Group. From these pages, a branch office in your neighborhood could be just a "click" away.

You probably would not be able to find a branch office of any of the big three in your local phone book. As Mitford observes, when the industry giants buy out one of the small, privately owned funeral homes, they invariably continue to use its old name. From a business point of view, there is a very important reason for this. The conglomerates naturally want to take advantage of whatever goodwill may have been established by the previous ownership. In addition, they may also wish to foster the public perception that the funeral home is a small concern that exists to provide a service in time of need—not a big business that exists to generate profits for the parent corporation and its investors.

Mitford (1998) suggests that conglomerates often use two linked strategies in their business practices. She refers to these as *clustering* and *anonymity*. By **clustering**, she is refers to the practice of buying up several funeral homes within the same area and then centralizing its key services—such as cremation, embalming, and restoration—at a single location. By controlling several funeral homes in an area, competition is minimized, as is the need to have specialized mortuary services at each location, thereby reducing the overhead. **Anonymity**, as Mitford explains, is the practice whereby the company continues to use the old name of the funeral home, not publicizing the new affiliation of the funeral home to the parent corporation, or its connection with other funeral homes in the area.

Service Corporation International has taken the additional step of "branding" their service model. They use the registered trademark *Dignity Memorial* for the services it provides and as a way to identify members of its network of fully owned and affiliate funeral homes. Were you to visit an SCI funeral home near you, the staff might very well give you promotional materials with the Dignity Memorial brand name on it, but in keeping with the principal of anonymity, the funeral home probably wouldn't provide you with any literature that might alert you that the home is actually part of the SCI conglomerate.

The amended Funeral Rule does not address the issues that have surfaced as a result of practices engaged in by large funeral corporations (i.e., clustering, which effectively creates monopolies in certain communities, and anonymity. However, there have been numerous lawsuits filed against large funeral corporations, as well as legal actions initiated by various state and federal agencies in the United States.

Cemeteries and Crematories Loopholes

Although funeral homes have been subject to the FTC Funeral Rule since 1984, the same rules do not apply to cemeteries. Numerous reports from consumers state that cemeteries have been engaging in some of the same predatory practices that the Funeral Rule was intended to alleviate in the funeral home industry. In response to these consumers' complaints, the Funeral Consumers Alliance has been expressing its concerns to regulators (Funeral Consumers Alliance, 2009, 2010). Illinois Congressman Bobby Rush has introduced legislation that directs the FTC to expand the Funeral Rule to cover cemeteries, crematories, and merchandise retailers (Funeral Consumers Alliance, 2009, 2010).

Industry Perspective

From the perspective of the funeral home industry, they have worked hard to reform their image and in fact are responsible members of the professional community. The National Funeral Directors Association, which boasts of being the oldest and largest funeral directors association, describes its mission as being devoted to providing advocacy, education, programs, and services to help members enhance the quality of service to families (National Funeral Directors Association, 2006a).

The National Funeral Directors Association supplies information to consumers; furnishes publications, meetings, research projects, and continuing education opportunities for members; as well as provides services of the Funeral Service Foundation, which supports grants and gifts to help grieving children. The organization has developed a code of professional conduct, and in 2004, mandated a conduct enforcement procedure. The code of conduct emphasizes the industry's responsibility to families, the decedents, the public, governmental regulatory bodies, and the profession itself (National Funeral Directors Association, 2006b). The code articulates the need for transparency, candor, and honesty in all matters. It specifically prohibits deceit and fraud of all kinds, including misleading advertising. The organization's enforcement procedure provides a way to file a complaint, investigate, mediate, and ensure the discipline of its members (National Funeral Directors Association, 2006c).

FLASHBACK

Window into the Past

The current situation—that is, our distant relationship with the experience of death, the commercialization of funeral services, and the limited governmental protections available to us—can leave one feeling a bit morose and discouraged. When faced with such a disturbing present, we can sometimes find solace by turning to a safer, gentler, past. In this section, we briefly explore the experience of life and death among the Amish, a traditional people, who until recently have been successful in maintaining a way of life and death that has been largely unchanged for about 400 years.

Although we can glimpse into the past, or even go in search of a nostalgic sense of what life and death may have been like in earlier times—perhaps through old movies, books, or memorabilia—we don't often have the chance to look into the realities of a previous era in "real time." Through the efforts of Kathleen Bryer (1979) we may have one such opportunity. Bryer, a psychologist practicing in Lancaster, Pennsylvania, conducted an interesting study. Immersing herself in the nearby Amish community, she interviewed two dozen Amish families on five areas of Amish life: the family structure, group structure, funeral customs and mourning rituals, personal experiences with death, and personal feelings about death.

Commenting on the contrast between the modern whir and the Amish way of life, Bryer (1979) suggests, "Science and technology seem to have replaced belief and ritual . . . and the high rate of mobility of the nuclear family lessens the opportunities for experiencing life and death within an extended-network support system" (Bryer, 1979, p. 255).

Descendants of Swiss Anabaptists, the Amish fled from religious persecution in Europe, settling in Pennsylvania as early as 1727 (Bryer, 1979). They've dressed traditionally, in a manner most of us probably associate with a bygone era. They continued driving horse-drawn buggies well after the likes of Henry Ford gave us the assembly line and mass-produced automobiles. The Amish eschewed modern conveniences and appliances in favor of their traditional ways. So unchanged was their lifestyle that the term *time warp* formed in my mind when I first began to think about the contrast between the Amish way of life and our modern experience.

As described by Bryer (1979), the Amish traditionally form family-oriented, agrarian, communities that emphasize traditional religious values, respect for authority, separation from "the world," and assistance to others in the community at times of need. Time seems to be experienced differently. To use an example from one source, you would normally find a digital clock in a modern automobile but you'd likely find a calendar tacked to the dash of a traditional Amish buggy. As introduced in Chapter 4, Ferdinand Tonnies, a pioneering sociologist, uses the term *gemeinschaft* to describe the close relationships fostered in such communities—characterized by a sense of kinship and a shared tradition (Tonnies, 1887/1963). He contrasts this to *gesellschaft* relationships, which are characterized as being generally weak and remote—the kind we often think of in connection with complex, urban, societies like our own.

The traditional Amish way of death seems to reflect the closeness and intimacy so characteristic of their way of life. According to Bryer (1979), friends and neighbors take charge of notifying other members of the community about a death. Two or three families will take responsibility for making the funeral arrangements and making up a list of families to be invited to the funeral. The community takes care of all aspects of the funeral, except embalming, the coffin, and the horse-drawn wagon. These goods and services are apparently provided by Amish-friendly funeral directors in the area. The embalmed body is returned quickly to the community, where members prepare and dress it in accordance with tradition.

In contrast to the modern North American way of death, a traditional part of Amish culture is the practice of lifelong preparation for death and life after death (Bryer, 1979). To illustrate this point, it is customary for an Amish woman to be buried in a special white dress she has put away for the occasion of her own death. The apron and the cape worn on top would be the same ones she would have worn at her baptism and marriage. In a similar way, men are dressed in white trousers, shirt, and vest when they die. Man or woman, it is traditional for members of the family to make burial clothes for their loved ones. After the body has been dressed, it is put in a simple wooden coffin, which is then placed in a room without furniture, where friends and family can view the body and say their good-byes. The funeral service itself, Bryer tells us, has traditionally been held in the barn, when weather permits; otherwise, the service is held in the house. Traveling in horse and buggy, the guests follow the bier (a horse-drawn wagon carrying the coffin) in single file to the cemetery.

The old mode of transportation, manner of dress, and form of religion vary considerably from what most of us are accustomed to in our day-to-day lives, yet in many respects what Bryer (1979) describes is really very similar to the modern North American experience of death we spoke of earlier—particularly the practice of embalming and the use of professional funeral directors. When she mentions the use of commercial funeral directors and embalming, Bryer also reveals a crack in our fantasy about the undisturbed nature of the Amish way of life. As you might recall, embalming was not a practice that was generally used in North America until the American Civil War—something that did not take place until about 150 years after the Amish settled in Pennsylvania.

What distinguishes the Amish way of life is their acceptance of death as a normal part of the life cycle and the intimate *gemeinschaft* relationships experienced by members of the community (Bryer, 1979). And it is this kind of experience that many of us nostalgically long for—the very thing that may in fact spell death for the Amish way of life— something that many of us so admire. In 1997, for example, 4.5 million tourists visited Lancaster County to observe the Amish way of life (Eitzen, 1998). Anthropologists use the term *culture contact* to describe what happens when distinct cultures encounter each other (see Chapter 4). The anthropologists suggest that culture contact will inevitably change the various cultures.

Unfortunately, this seems true for the Amish as well. Although the dollars tourists spend on various Amish-made products is sometimes described as a boon to Amish families, who can no longer make a living on farming alone, it has disrupted the traditional patterns of life (Eitzen, 1998). The escalating price of land and the slow but steady encroachment of the suburbs on Amish territory make it increasingly difficult for new generations of Amish to continue in the old ways. In response, the Amish, like so many other groups, have divided into factions—the traditionalists, who are trying to hold out against the onslaught, and those who feel the need to accommodate the changing social realities.

ALTERNATIVE DEATH MOVEMENT

Whereas traditional patterns of life and death seem under siege, the yearning for greater emotional warmth and intimacy in relation to death has not waned. In this section, we take a look at three present-day movements happening in North America that attempt to reclaim a more personal way of dealing with death: funeral consumers' advocacy, home burial, and green burial.

As we discussed in Chapter 5, the large-scale commercialization of death is a relatively recent phenomenon that can be traced to the American Civil War—a time when a great many soldiers on both sides died far from home. Embalming, the practice of draining the blood from the body and replacing it with embalming fluid, came into common use. It preserved the body for transit and minimized the normal smells that result from decay. Since then, the practice of embalming bodies and preparing them for public viewing has become a feature of the North American death system—a practice not commonly employed in other parts of the world.

Although embalming has the advantage of preserving the body for transit and viewing, it is also a costly process that requires the use of special equipment. It is not something that can be easily done at home. With the widespread use of embalming, the task of preparing the body and burying the dead became the province of this new breed of professionals. No longer wanting to be called "undertakers," these new professionals—now referred to as "funeral directors"—have become an increasingly important part of our present-day death system. Working hand in hand with them are the florists, casket makers, and those who manage cemeteries and crematoria.

Funeral Consumers' Advocacy

The expensive services of the funeral directors and embalmers, the use of high-end caskets, and high-priced cemetery real estate have all combined to drive up the price of the North American burial. Starting in the late 1930s, a number of people began to explore alternatives. One expression of this is the evolution of a grassroots *funeral consumer's rights movement.*

The People's Memorial Society (PMS) of Seattle is the oldest local funeral society in the United States. Dedicated to providing low-cost alternatives to high-priced funerals, it was formed on January 12, 1939, originally for the purpose of making relatively low-cost direct cremation available to its members (cremation following death, done without embalming or a formal viewing). Since then, People's Memorial, like other memorial societies, has expanded its services, contracting with local funeral homes to make a full range of low-cost funerals and inexpensive burials available to its members (Hayek, 2003). In Seattle, a member can arrange for direct cremation (there is a one-time $25 membership fee) for about $650, and a full burial with funeral and basic casket for about $1,500. This compares to the national average of approximately $7,400 (People's Memorial Society, 2011). In an article titled, "How to Plan an $800 Funeral," published by MSN-CNBC (Solomon, 2003), the author includes joining a memorial society among his tips.

Although nonprofit funeral societies are still not well known, they do exist as a viable alternative. People's, for example, has enrolled more than 178,000 members since it began. There are similar organizations serving nearly every state and over 125 U.S. cities. The Funeral Consumers Alliance (FCA) (formerly the Funeral and Mortuary Societies of America) is a loose-knit federation of these groups (Funeral Consumers Alliance, 2011). It serves as a national clearinghouse, dedicated to protecting the consumers' right to a meaningful, dignified, and affordable funeral. It monitors the funeral industry, testifies before Congress and other regulatory bodies, provides information to the public, and serves as a point of contact for some 150 affiliated local groups.

If you are interested in finding one in your area, check the organization's website (at the end of the chapter). Regardless of whether or not you choose to join a memorial society, most groups do regular comparison price surveys that compare the prices charged by various mortuaries in the local area. This information is available to the public, often published online.

Home Funerals

Another development in the twenty-first century experience of death isn't really new at all. It is that of the do-it-yourself burial, or **home funerals**. Funny as the concept may sound to twenty-first century North Americans, Lisa Carlson (1987), the survivor of her husband's suicide, wrote a how-to book titled *Caring for Your Own Dead.*

Based on Carlson's experience with making the final arrangements for her husband, John, without the benefit of a funeral director (she didn't have the money), she not only reviews how we as a society got to where we are but she also outlines what we can do to manage death on a practical level—getting the death certificate, handling and moving the body, reporting fetal deaths, and arranging for cremation or burial. Carlson has now partnered with the Funeral Consumers Alliance to publish a successor book (Slocum & Carlson, 2011). It describes how to preserve the body until disposition; the use of public, religious, and family cemeteries; body and organ donation; necessary information related to managing death; home funerals; green burial; as well as a state-by-state summary of laws relating to burial in the United States. Although there is now some "push back" by the funeral industry, the book points out that burying your own dead is perfectly legal in 45 of the 50 U.S. states (with some qualifications).

> ## We Wanted to Keep Him with Us...
>
> Bill was a health-conscious, middle-aged vegetarian who was an avid outdoors man and athlete. A human service professional for most of his adult life, he had made a career of working with domestic violence abusers to overcome their insecurities and violent behavior. One day Bill, a nonsmoker, developed a cough that wouldn't go away. This would eventually be diagnosed as mesothelioma, a rare and especially virulent form of lung cancer, which is usually associated with asbestos exposure. Within nine months of diagnosis it would take his life.
>
> Bill and his wife, Circe, were active practitioners of a nature-based religion. Circe refers to their spiritual tradition as Pagan or neo-Pagan, but others sometimes refer to it as "Wiccan" (Santaniello, 2003). The day Bill died, after a long and uncomfortable illness, he was surrounded by Circe, his friends, and his loved ones who were with him, chanting at the moment he drew his last breath. Although not using the expression employed in this text, Bill's family and friends would care for and bury their own dead.
>
> Pagan spiritual traditions hold that the spirit of the deceased remains close to the body for three days (Starhawk, 1997). When Circe told me her story, she explained that she and the rest of Bill's loved ones wanted to keep him with them the whole time (between the time he died and was cremated), despite laws that required embalming or refrigeration within 24 hours. They washed each part of the body, once symbolically, while one of those caring for Bill read blessings from a blessing poem she had written. After washing the body, they used a variety of oils on his skin. These included the natural essential oils of frankincense, myrrh, lavender, and white sage. In addition, they had prepared natural vegetable juices to help color his skin, but did not actually use them because Bill's body retained its natural color after he died. Folks from all over brought boughs made from various plants—rosemary, thyme, and other natural herbs—that were growing in their gardens. They wrapped Bill's body in sheets made from soft Egyptian cotton. It was November and cold, and they left the windows to the bedroom open, to slow the process of decay. He lay swaddled on his bed in front of their personal altars for two nights and three days, as a steady stream of well-wishers came to pay their last respects, pray, or just be with Bill and Circe. Everyone who entered Bill's bedroom commented on how they experienced it as a sacred place, Circe told me.
>
> Bill had become a member of the local funeral society when they learned about the prognosis. When it came time to transport Bill's body for direct cremation, Circe and the rest of his loved ones accompanied it to the funeral home, where they chanted in a sacred rhythm, as Circe pushed his body into the cremation chamber to finish the journey.

Green Burial

Also called *natural burial,* **green burial** is an attempt to dispose of human bodies without harming the environment. "What's become known as 'green burial' is what people throughout history have called, simply, burial... but the full-service formaldehyde funeral has been the new 'normal'...so getting people to think outside the box isn't easy" (Slocum & Carlson, 2011, p. 139).

So far, we've discussed concerns about the funeral service industry in relation to consumer protection, but one may also ask, What does it do to the environment when we put nonbiodegradable caskets and embalmed bodies into the earth? For now, we don't know for sure what the potential impacts of modern burial and cremation practices on the environment are.

What we do know is that there are over 20,000 cemeteries in the United States that bury over 30 million board feet of hard woods, 100,000 tons of steel, 2,700 tons of copper and bronze, 1.6 million tons of reinforced concrete, and over 800,000 gallons of embalming fluid, most of which contains formaldehyde. Although formaldehyde is a known carcinogen, and a danger to those who do embalming, we don't know its impact on the environment. Similarly, cremation releases about 350 pounds of carbon dioxide per cremation, in addition to soot particles, sulfur dioxide, and trace metals, including mercury from dental fillings (Tweit, 2010).

In response to these concerns, there are now some organizations devoted to promoting a return to green burial practices. One of these, the Green Burial Council, has established standards for "green" cemeteries. A concern, however, is that in their efforts to win over the

Green burial is becoming more popular with families concerned about the effects of modern burial practices on the environment. Depicted here is a pastoral setting with a more natural grave marker. *michaklootwijk/Fotolia*

funeral industry, they have not set the standards very high. Another concern is that cemeteries and funeral homes can use the "green" label as a way to market their products and services to environmentally sensitive consumers without making real changes to how they do business, sometimes referred to as **greenwashing** (Slocum & Carlson, 2011).

The desire for a healthier and more wholesome approach to death seems real, however. Billy Campbell, a small-town doctor, and his wife, Kimberly, have established a preserve called Ramsey Creek, in Westminster, South Carolina. Begun in 1996, it has been hailed as the first intentionally "green cemetery" in the United States. The couple embraces what they describe as a philosophy of high "conservation ethics." Their organization aspires to protect, restore, and permanently endow a million acres of wilderness. Here is a summary of the basic guidelines for burial at the Ramsey Creek preserve (Memorial Ecosystems, 2011):

- No embalmed bodies are permitted. This is primarily out of concern that embalming fluid, containing formaldehyde, may seep into the ground water and contaminate it. They note that with dry ice or a cooler, to body can be sufficiently preserved for up to three or four days prior to burial.
- Caskets are not required. Using a shroud, or even a favorite blanket, to wrap the body is encouraged. Families wanting to use a casket or alternative burial container must ensure they are made from biodegradable materials, such as untreated wood or cardboard, with no glue, lacquer, or metal.
- Burial vaults are not permitted. Bodies go directly into the ground to decompose naturally.
- Graves are hand dug, with some exceptions. This minimizes the impact on surrounding land and protects native plants.
- Grave markers are made from native stones, which can be engraved, but which lie flat, consistent with the geology of the site. Putting in other plants requires permission.
- Burial is combined with ecological restoration. It is hoped that the site can be used by people for a variety of social activities, and with links to area sacred spaces and the community. Indeed, the Campbells have restored an old schoolhouse for use as a chapel, which is situated on the premises.

Chapter Summary

In this chapter, we endeavored to explore the experience of death in the twenty-first century in North America. We began with a discussion of the U.S. death system, a largely invisible but pervasive social reality that mediates our experience with death and dying. We began with a look at the award-winning HBO series, *Six Feet Under*, which became a segue into discussion of the U.S. way of death. While clearly fictional, we noted how we can think of the show as a pop culture example of twenty-first–century art speaking to a postmodern world.

Next, we reviewed the work of Jessica Mitford and others who described the commercialization of death, particularly in North America. In this connection, we briefly looked at modern North American funerary practices,

abuses identified by critics, as well as steps taken by the Federal Trade Commission to address these concerns. This included the adoption of the Funeral Rule, establishing minimal consumer protections, and an Amended Funeral Rule that guarantees funeral homes a basic services fee.

For contrast, we briefly looked at death among the traditional Amish people, but noted that even the Amish culture has been affected by tourism and the high cost of land. Indeed, the Amish now feel the need to use the services of funeral directors instead of caring for their own dead at home. After exploring the traditional Amish way of death, we surveyed an emerging alternative death movement, including the use of nonprofit funeral consumers' alliances, burying your own dead, and green burial.

Key Terms

Amended Funeral
  Rule *118*
anonymity *120*
basic services fee *119*
casket *117*

clustering *120*
floral tribute *118*
Funeral Rule *118*
green burial *126*
greenwashing *127*

home funeral *125*
hostess gown *118*
lawn crypt *118*
slumber room *118*
wound filler *117*

Suggested Activities

1. Review the components and functions of our death system, as outlined in Table 6.1. Identify as many of these in your local community as you can.
2. Make a deliberate search for television shows and/or movies that deal with the topics of death and dying. What do you think how they deal with death tells us about the way our culture understands death and dying?
3. Contact one or more local funeral homes and request a copy of their price lists. You may also wish to know if any or all of those you call are affiliated with a national chain such as Service Corporation International, Alderwoods, Stewart Enterprises, or NorthStar Group.
4. Go on the Internet and look up "Amended Funeral Rule." If you can find a full-text version, review it. Ask yourself about the ways in which it protects the funeral consumer, as well as the ways in which it doesn't.
5. Conduct your own explorations to see if you can find groups or communities that handle death and dying in a more traditional way than we do today.
6. Using the links cited at the end of this chapter, visit the website of the Funeral Consumers Alliance. Using links found at this site, see if you can find a funeral society in your community. If you like, contact it and inquire as to how the alliance attempts to help consumers. Is it able to provide you with a set of prices for various funeral homes in your community?
7. Using the Internet, see if you can find someone who does workshops on how to care for your own dead. What are the workshops like? Would you or anyone you know want to care for your own dead? What are the rules for doing so in your state, province, or territory? How can you learn about these rules?

Suggested Reading and Viewing

- Mitford, J. (1998). *The American way of death—Revisited.* New York: Vantage Books.
  This is an updated version of Mitford's classic 1963 exposé of the undertaking business, *The American Way of Death.* Written just before her own death in 1996, Mitford reviews developments during the intervening years from 1963 to 1996. Included is an exploration of the rise of large international funeral service conglomerates, and the involvement of the Federal Trade Commission in consumer protection.
- Slochum, J., & Carlson, L. (2011). *Final rights.* Hinesburg, VT: Upper Access.
  A successor to Lisa Carlson's two previous books on funeral rights for consumers, this book is an updated reference. It provides a thoughtful and provocative discussion of funeral practices. In addition, it covers the alternative home funeral and green burial movements. Included is a compendium of up-to-date information on the laws of each of the 50 states.
- Westrate, E. (Producer & Director) (2003). *A family undertaking.* [Film]. (Available from Fanlight Productions, P.O. Box 1084, Harriman, NY 10926)
  This gripping and touching film takes the viewer into the world of home funerals. Through a blend of home video clips and film shot by Emmy Award–winning cinematographer, Scott Sinker, the film chronicles the truly touching experiences of several families who chose to care for their own dead.

- Mark Harris. (2008). *Grave matters: A journey through the modern funeral industry to a natural way of burial.* New York: Scribner.
  Written by a former journalist, this slim but insightful book gives an up-close look at current practices and an insiders' exploration of the stories of 12 families who have opted for this more natural approach.

Links and Internet Resources

- **HBO Six Feet Under**
  www.hbo.com/sixfeetunder/
  This is the official website of the acclaimed HBO television series, *Six Feet Under.* On this site, you will find links to information about the show, an episode guide, information on the cast and crew, as well as links titled "The Wake," "Obituary," and "Postmortem."

- **Funeral Consumers Alliance**
  www.funerals.org/
  Formerly known as the Funeral and Memorial Societies of America, this is a federation of nonprofit funeral consumer societies. Often staffed by part-time employees and volunteers, local funeral societies endeavor to help consumers arrange for low-cost mortuary and funeral services. You can find a nonprofit funeral society in your community through this website.

- **Service Corporation International (SCI)**
  www.sci-corp.com/
  As described on this website, "Service Corporation International is the largest provider of funeral, cremation, and cemetery services in North America. Generating more thant 2.2 billion dollars of revenue annually, SCI boasts of a network of over 3,000 'affiliate' funeral homes, crematoria, and cemeteries in North America, and around the world."

- **Dignity Memorial**
  www.dignitymemorial.com/
  This is a network of over 1,800 SCI "affiliate" (subsidiary) funeral homes, crematoria, and cemeteries operating in North America. Through this website you will be able to locate the SCI-affiliate funeral homes doing business in your community.

- **Discount Caskets and Containers**
  www.funerals.org/caskets.htm
  Although there is often a 300 to 700 percent profit margin on caskets purchased from funeral homes, it is perfectly legal in most states to purchase a lower-priced casket elsewhere, which can be shipped in time for the funeral. Check out this page, located on the website of the Funeral Consumers Alliance, which contains listings for a large number of low-cost options: do-it-yourself coffin kits; cardboard caskets; local casket and urn artisans; and discount retailers.

- **Paper Coffins and Body Bags**
  www.browncaskets.com/
  Brown Caskets is a provider of paper coffins and polyethylene body bags. They advertise their paper coffins as an alternative to the high cost of wooden caskets—they are cost efficient, strong, easy to assemble, and environmentally sound (100 percent recyclable material and 100 percent safe for the environment).

- **Natural Burial Company**
  funerals.naturalburialcompany.com/
  This is the largest collection of biodegradable caskets, urns, and shrouds available. Sells to funeral homes and the public.

- **Green Burial Products**
  www.kinkaraco.com/
  This San Francisco company makes natural body shrouds, herbal body wash, and natural herbs used in burial.

- **Crossings: Caring for Our Own at Death**
  www.crossings.net/
  Beth Knox and the people at Crossings, a nonprofit corporation, headquartered in Silver Spring, MD, provide workshops and resources for people interested in caring for their own at the time of death.

- **Final Passages**
  www.finalpassages.org/
  Final Passages is a grassroots organization, funded largely from donations, educational materials, and workshop fees. Founded and directed by Jerri Lyons, it promotes the use of dignified and loving home funerals.

- **Green Burial Council**
  www.greenburialcouncil.org/
  This website provides established green burial certification standards, information to the public, and resources to funeral directors who wish to accommodate the wishes of their clients for sustainable death care.

- **Centre for Natural Burial**
  http://naturalburial.coop/
  This organization is dedicated to providing resources and information for those interested in natural burial.

Review Guide

1. Be sure to review Table 6.1. It contains brief descriptions of both the components and functions of Kastenbaum's death system.
2. Reflect on the way death and dying are depicted in the media. How does this "fit" with the real experience of people today with death and dying?
3. Be familiar with criticisms of the North American funeral industry, brought to bear by Jessica Mitford and others. What does "the commercialization of death" mean? What is McDeath? Who are the key funeral service corporations in North America? What is meant by the terms *clustering* and *anonymity?* What is the Amended Funeral Rule and why was it enacted? What is the nondeclinable *basic services fee*? What disclosures are mandated under the Amended Funeral Rule?
4. Who are the Amish? What can their way of handling death teach the rest of us? What has happened to the Amish way of life as a consequence of their contact with the broader North American culture?
5. What are the two primary alternatives to the "American Way of Death," as described by Jessica Mitford and briefly reviewed in this chapter? What is direct cremation? What are the legalities about caring for your own dead?

7

Traumatic Death

- ■ **Trauma & Traumatic Death**
- ■ **Terrorism**
- ■ **Suicide**
- ■ **Homicide**
- ■ **HIV/AIDS Pandemic**

Today, in this time of digital technology, 24-7 cable news, and round-the-clock access to websites across the world, we are exposed to tragedy and death on an unprecedented scale–popular uprisings in the Middle East and deadly suppression by the powers that be, wars, suicide bombings, hurricanes, like Katrina; the Japanese earthquakes, tsunamis, and near-meltdown at the Fukushima nuclear plant. Indeed, if we attempt to take in the full impact of the tragedy with empathy and feeling, the enormity is too much to bear. We end up asking ourselves what we can do, which usually is not much. Often we pitch in with a contribution, then follow the story, hoping the situation normalizes and everyone is able to get back to life as usual. These tragedies invariably involve death, loss, and heartbreak, and often enough we have stories of hope, too.

This chapter explores a few selected encounters with traumatic death: terrorism, suicide, homicide, and death from AIDS. Each speaks of flesh-and-blood experience with traumatic death in this 24-7 digital world of ours. Terrorism has a long history, yet today its impact on us and the world looms large in our consciousness, perhaps because of the destruction of the Twin Towers in New York, the damage to the Pentagon, and the plane crash on a field of Pennsylvania on September 11, 2001, and the killing of Osama bin Laden, its mastermind. The problem of suicide began to take on new dimensions as society has become infused with global consumerism, information, communication, and computers, which are more central than ever before (see Chapter 2). For example, witness the death of the young man who committed suicide because his roommate planted a camera in their room and posted a video on the Internet of him having sex with another man. Homicide, although small in terms of actual numbers, is huge in terms of its impact on others and what it says about who we are. The pandemic of HIV infection and death from AIDS is a relatively recent global phenomenon. In the West, it was only in the mid-90s that we became somewhat successful in managing it. In Africa, its spread is wide and its impact remains huge. Massive numbers of children are living as orphans. Older children are caring for the little ones, and grandparents step in to take care of their grandchildren because their own adult children have died.

TRAUMA AND TRAUMATIC DEATH

The term **trauma** connotes the idea of shocking injury (Leppaniemi, 2004). It is the exposure of an individual to an event outside the ordinary, which is experienced as traumatic (Meagher, 2007). "Packed" in the term is the idea that it is devastating, is acutely suffered, and involves intense emotions and strong reactions. The Association for Death Education and Counseling (ADEC) describes **traumatic death** as a major topic in the field's collective body of knowledge (Balk, Wogrin, Thornton, & Meagher, 2007). The ADEC defines *traumatic death* as death that is sudden, violent, inflicted, and/or intentional, and encounters that are shocking. Sometimes it involves widespread devastation, such as what happens as the result of a natural disaster. The 2011 Japanese earthquake and the tsunami that crashed in on coastal communities, for example, is estimated to have killed over 20,000 people (*USA Today*, 2011). At other times, it is an isolated event experienced intensely by individuals, or small groups.

In recent years, we have become far more sensitive to the impacts of traumatic events, such as natural disasters, war, and terrorism (Pfefferbaum et al., 2001; Bonanno & Kaltman, 1999; Green et al., 2001; Neria & Litz 2004). As a result, a whole new field of traumatic response intervention (Gray, Prigerson, & Litz, 2004; Boelen & Prigerson, 2007) and psychological first aid has come into being (Brymer et al., 2006). In Chapter 11, we discuss the assessment and treatment of complicated grief, which is a risk of traumatic death. In the major sections that follow, we discuss several types of encounters likely to cause traumatic death and traumatic reactions.

TERRORISM

Terrorism: Foreign and Domestic

Terrorism is an excellent example of a present-day experience that is changing the way people understand death in the twenty-first century. What happened on September 11, 2001, provides compelling testimony of this. Not only was it an act of suicide on the part of the Islamic fundamentalists who carried it out but it was also an act of terrorism, intended to evoke fear and tilt the balance of power. Indeed, for many of us, the world was turned upside down

Traumatic death often involves widespread devastation, such as what happens as the result of a natural disaster, like the Tsunami that destroyed the coastal Japanese city of Fukushima on March 11, 2011. *Christophe Fouquin/Fotolia*

on that day when Mohammed Atta and the other 21 Islamic fundamentalists hijacked four commercial jets and then aimed them at targets in New York and Washington, DC.

The world as we knew it changed. In addition to such things as changes in airport security, what emerged from the aftermath was a new awareness that those of us living comfortably in North America are not immune from the kind of danger that has been part of life in other parts of the world. On that one horrific day, 2,829 people died at the World Trade Center Twin Towers in New York, 189 others died at the Pentagon, and another 44 died on a field in Pennsylvania, when passengers attempted to retake control of the plane from the hijackers (Fingerhut, Hoyert, & Pickett, 2003). Since then, the events of 9/11 seem to have crystalized into a new recognition of our vulnerability. A chief goal of terrorism, of course, is to arouse fear and to intimidate.

This most dramatic of terrorist events, however, is perhaps just the most recent, devastating, and dramatic of attacks on America, although certainly other terrorist acts have followed. There have been many in the nation's history. In the modern era, however, 1979 seems to have been a pivotal year. It was then that the United States, one of the last remaining superpowers, came face-to-face with its own powerlessness to control terror. In that year, 52 U.S. citizens were taken hostage by militant students at the American embassy in Tehran, Iran (Public Broadcasting System, 2001). Since then, there have been several other terrorist attacks, including bombings at the U.S. embassies at Beirut and Kuwait (1983); the hijacking of TWA flight 847 in 1985; the bombing of Pan Am Flight 103 at Lockerbie in 1988; and in 1995, the destruction of the Alfred P. Murrah Federal Building in Oklahoma City, which was leveled by an explosive-laden van put there for that purpose by two native-born White extremists, Timothy McVeigh and Terry Lynn Nichols (Federal Bureau of Investigation, 2000). More recently in the United States, two brothers, Tamerlan and Dzhokhar Tsarnaev, natives of Russia but long-time residents of the United States, set off two explosives near the Boston Marathon finish line, killing 3 and wounding 260 others (CBS News, 2013).

Although of terrorism will surely vary, perhaps it will be useful to take a look at how it is defined in the United States *Code of Federal Regulations* (Federal Bureau of Investigation, 2000). This definition contains the following basic three elements:

- Terrorism is the unlawful use of force or violence against persons or property;
- to intimidate a government or the civilian population, or any segment thereof;
- in furtherance of political or social objectives.

The attacks on the Twin Towers and Pentagon and other recent attacks were acts at least partially motivated by Islamic religious fundamentalism, but terrorism can and has been inspired by religious extremism of all types. In addition, it can be politically or economically inspired, and can be of either the domestic or international variety (Federal Bureau of Investigation, 2000).

Chapter 1 introduced *terror management theory* and the work of Tom Pyszczynski, Sheldon Solomon, and Jeff Greenberg (2003). As you may recall, they suggest the events of 9/11 can be largely explained as a clash of cultures. Jessica Stern (2003), a former National Security Council staffer and Harvard lecturer, did something others had not. She spent four years interviewing Islamic, Christian, and Jewish religious terrorists in such places as the Palestinian refugee camps, religious schools in Pakistan, and prisons around the world. Interviewing these terrorists, both foreign and domestic, she wanted to find out what inspired them to do what they did.

■ ■ ■

Religious terrorism arises from pain and loss and from impatience with a God who is slow to respond to our plight, who doesn't answer. Its converts often long for a simpler time, when right and wrong were clear, when there were heroes and martyrs, when the story was simple, when the neighborhood was small, when we knew one another.

—JESSICA STERN
Terror in the Name of God: Why Religious Militants Kill, 2003

■ ■ ■

What Stern learned is that religious terrorists often experience grievances that give rise to deeply felt feelings of **alienation** and **humiliation**, which Stern (2003) suggests festers until it results in terrorism. *Alienation* refers to the experience of being cut off from the mainstream of society, perhaps because of unconventional religious convictions or social or racial attitudes. In her view, alienation is more likely to be a factor in home-grown brands of terrorism, such as that which was perpetrated by Timothy McVeigh in Oklahoma City. Humiliation, in Stern's view, relates to the perceived degradation experienced by an entire group, such as what might be felt by members of such groups as Palestinian refugees or Iraqi Baathists as a consequence of what they understand to be the occupation of their homeland.

According to Stern (2003), charismatic leaders, such as Osama bin Laden, then exploit such feelings to further their cause. She believes that grasping these dynamics can help us understand why people are willing to become "holy warriors." Shifting population patterns, a highly selective reading of history, and territorial disputes are then used, Stern tells us, to justify the so-called "holy wars," which when repeated by both sides have the effect of perpetuating a cycle of violence.

Examples of persons who start off their terrorist careers as a result of alienation might include such home-grown extremists as Timothy McVeigh and Ted Kaczynski. Kaczynski, also known as "the Unabomber," may have been mentally ill, but he was clearly an alienated individual who was obsessed with an antagonism to technology. McVeigh was executed for bombing the federal office building in Oklahoma City. He was a fan of William Pierce's novel, *The Turner Diaries,* a racially charged, anti-semitic work that articulates a vision about an armed underground resistance to the government. The book seems to have become a "cult classic" among members of certain right-wing, extremist, religious groups. McVeigh and Pierce apparently believed they were living in the end times and that it was the duty of "called" Christians, such as themselves, to fight an armed war of resistance against what Pierce refers to in *The Turner Diaries* as the "Zionist Occupied Government," or ZOG (Stern, 2003, p. 11). Examples of terrorism that result from perceived humiliation include many of the various international attacks by Islamic extremists, including the attacks of September 11, 2001.

Understanding the Events of September 11, 2001

Hans-Jurgen Wirth (2003), a German psychoanalyst, suggests that we might best understand 9/11 as involving both a **syndrome of fanaticism** and **collective trauma**.

In the syndrome of fanaticism, we encounter individuals who have a firm belief in absolute truth, great zeal, utter faith in their view of good and evil, a standardized way of thinking, an aversion to anything contrary to their vision of truth, and such a complete commitment to an ideology that they are willing to end their own lives and partake in acts they might otherwise regard as criminal. Wirth (2003) suggests that these fanatics cut off normal human feelings of affection for most other people and reserve their positive sentiments for members of the group whose ideology seems good and reasonable to them. He suggests that the ideology and the group become an ideal, or idol, for which the fanatic is willing to utterly submit. Full-fledged fanatics lack the capacity to feel for any but their own, Wirth says. They come to cherish ideas over people. For the fanatic, normal human feelings—such as those of love, fear, shame, and guilt—are experienced as dangerous weaknesses when they pose the slightest challenge to the guiding ideology.

To provide some insight into the mind of the fanatic, Wirth briefly explores the psyche of Mohammed Atta, who left his last will behind. This, Wirth (2003) tells us, reveals something of Atta's inner world. In it, Atta, who did have a girlfriend, expressed concern about Western influences, egalitarian attitudes, and the potential contamination of his memory by the presence of women at his funeral or their mourning of his death.

The psychology of the 9/11 terrorists, as delineated by Wirth (2003), can provide us with fascinating glimpse into the inner world of the fanatics, but it tells us only about half the story. The other half comes with reflection on the impact of the events on the consciousness of the society that was the intended victim. Wirth uses the term *collective trauma* in his description of the impact.

■   ■   ■

A trauma is an experience of such intensity as to overwhelm the mind's capability for dealing with it. The trauma is accompanied by feelings of extreme fear, frequently, the fear of death, terror, powerlessness, and total hopelessness. This leads to a collapse of central functions of the self, and a fundamental shock to the entire personality. If this happens to a large group simultaneously, it is called "collective trauma."... The destruction of the World Trade Center in New York and the partial destruction of the Pentagon represent a collective traumatization of the American nation.

—Hans-Jurgen Wirth
"9/11 as Collective Trauma," 2003, p. 377

■   ■   ■

Wirth (2003) continues, "In terrorism and its opposition, the…delusions of…the powerless, and the smug…self-image of the powerful act in disastrous collusion" (p. 386). The result of the attack, Wirth suggests, was that the United States came face to face with its own vulnerability, the finality of death, and its own powerlessness in the face of evil. The key to recovery, he tells us, is in how one deals with the trauma. He cautions that there is a great danger in constantly ruminating on the trauma, becoming fixated on it, and violently acting out against others in retaliation. To recover, he advises, Americans should be prepared to come to terms with what happened, endeavor to understand it, be prepared to undergo a long grieving process, and be willing to undertake positive, thoughtful, steps in an effort to come to terms with the reality of the experience.

Unresolved Questions Arising from the Boston Marathon Bombings

The Boston Marathon bombing raises perplexing questions. The Tsarnaev brothers were long-time residents of the United States although they had their roots in largely Islamic portions of southern Russian. Although the older brother, Tamarlan, had apparently become quite religiously Islamic, both brothers seemed socially well integrated into American culture. Tamerlan had been active in Golden Gloves boxing and was married to an American woman. Dzhokar was still enrolled at the University of Massachusetts and was observed at parties near campus even after the bombing. It seems that the motivation behind the attack may have been something of a hybrid of international and domestic terrorism. Religious fundamentalism may have been partly responsible but one cannot ignore possible resentment from Tamarlan having been denied the opportunity to compete for a spot in the U.S. Olympic boxing team because he was not a U.S. citizen (Hummell, 2013).

SUICIDE

Today, the estimate is that one person takes his or her own life every 13.7 minutes in the United States (American Association of Suicidology, 2013). Information from the Centers for Disease Control and Prevention suggests that about 30,000 of the 2.4 million Americans who die each year intentionally take their own lives (Crosby, Ortega, & Stevens, 2011; Hoyert, Arias, Smith, Murphy, & Kochanek, 2001; Minino & Smith, 2001). It has been the eleventh leading cause of death for some time now.

Information published by the American Association of Suicidology (AAS), indicates that for each completed suicide, there are approximately 25 attempts (American Association of Suicidology, 2013). Women attempt suicide two to three times more often than men, but men complete suicide almost four times more often than women (American Association of Suicidology, 2013), possibly owing to the method chosen (Crosby et al., 2011; Hoyert et al., 2001; McIntosh, 2002; Minino & Smith, 2001). Guns are the most common method used by men (nearly 56 percent) whereas poisoning is the most common method used by women (over 40 percent) (Centers for Disease Control, 2010). Overall, guns are the most common method of committing suicide, followed by hanging, then poisoning (National Institute of Mental Health, 2010).

Impact of Suicide

Although the number of suicides that occur in a given year might be few when compared to the total number of deaths, the count of people who have died from suicide in recent years is dismaying. The AAS estimates that there were over 738,000 completed suicides between 1976 and 2000 (McIntosh, 2002). The AAS reckons that for each completed suicide, at least six people are profoundly affected (McIntosh, 2002). Each is poignant. Each tells a story.

As you can tell from Sophie's story, the impact on the lives of the survivors is profound. The American Association for Suicidology estimates that over 4.4 million people have been so affected (McIntosh, 2002).

Over the years, it has been commonly understood that the loved ones of persons who die of suicide almost always have an extremely difficult time dealing with the experience. The classic work on the subject is consistent with the general understanding (e.g., Cain, 1972; Lindemann & Greer, 1972; Wallace, 1973). More recently, Barrett and Scott (1990), suggest that while many aspects of grief may be similar to what occurs after other kinds of losses, survivors of suicide seem to face a greater number of issues. These include (1) issues related to the death of a person with whom one has been close, (2) issues that arise from the unnatural nature of the death, (3) issues related to the experience of sudden loss, and (4) issues associated with the uniquely suicidal character of the death—that is, the rejection of life itself and the abandonment of those left behind.

Tomorrow Never Came

Georgina is a retired professional woman. During her life she had four children—three daughters and a son. All of them grew up to become adults. Three of them survived. One of her daughters, Sophie, became terribly depressed after the birth of her own daughter. Diagnosed with postpartum depression, Sophie struggled with her psychic pain for about two years before her death. As Georgina tells the story, Sophie went to visit her sister in a nearby city for a few days prior to leaving on trip to Los Angeles for a visit with her uncle. When she returned, Sophie called her sister to say she'd gotten back okay. She put a message on her father's answering machine, just saying she'd called. In addition, she called her other sister, who, apparently beleaguered by her sister's long depression, suggested they speak about it "tomorrow." Georgina had seen Sophie the day before she died, just like she did almost every Thursday, when Georgina babysat Sophie's little girl, Perpetua, while mommy went to see her psychiatrist. As Georgina put it, "Tomorrow never came." During the night Sophie's husband, George, awoke to find that his wife was dead. With her bags packed for Los Angeles, Sophie wrote a note and then ended her life using the many pills that were prescribed to control her various psychiatric symptoms. Georgina got a call from her son-in-law saying, "Sophie died…she ended her own life." "I can still hear a tape of that call in my head," Georgina said, even though several years have now passed.

Although we certainly want to avoid stereotyping survivors, one often hears reports that suggest survivors are left feeling numb and bewildered, perhaps struggling with such questions as "Why didn't I do more?" and "How could this have happened?" According to one study, the survivors often have an intense need to fathom why the suicide had occurred, what it means for themselves and their families, and what it portends for the future (Dunn & Morrish-Vidners, 1988; Silverman, Range, & Overholser, 1994; Van Dongen, 1990, 1991, 1993). Feelings of rejection, guilt, and the need to blame are commonly reported by survivors. Those left behind may also feel ashamed and judged by friends and family (Dunne, McIntosh, & Dunne-Maxim, 1987), especially if they had relationship problems with the deceased or were one of the parents (Reynolds & Cimbolic, 1988–1989).

Completed suicides can be devastating in terms of their impact, but the survivors of attempted suicides—an event that took place more than 700,000 times in the year 2000 (McIntosh, 2002)–are also impacted, although perhaps differently. The loved ones of attempters, especially chronic attempters, often live on an emotional roller coaster, never knowing when the bearer of bad tidings will show up at the door or call on the phone. Even for mental health professionals, suicidal verbalizations and attempts by clients are among the most stressful experiences they face in practice.

Explanations of Suicide

Suicide is a topic of interest to clinicians, research psychologists, and sociologists. There is no consensus about its causes. The contributions of thinkers from diverse fields, however, have added to a rich body of literature on the subject.

PSYCHOLOGICALLY ORIENTED THEORIES   Among the first psychologically oriented theories about suicide comes from the work of Sigmund Freud (1917/1959a). Freudian theory on human motivation, proposes the twin drives *eros* and *thanatos,* which he believed could explain why people behaved as they did. **Eros**, a word that derives from the Greek for sexual energy, represents the life instinct. **Thanatos**, the Greek word for death, signifies the death instinct. These twin drives are in dynamic opposition, in Freud's model, and a constant force in our lives. Thanatos, representing as it does, aggressive and destructive impulses, are generally directed outwardly in order to tackle the problems of day-to-day life. Eros is the drive at the center of the search for pleasure. Freud believed human beings naturally experience anger as a consequence of the loss of a desired person or object, with one big difference: The anger is generally turned inward, manifesting itself as depression.

Although there is only limited support for Freud's **anger turned inward** hypothesis, it has nevertheless found a home in pop psychology, often cited as the very definition of depression. Regardless of its source, there is little doubt that depression, including postpartum depression (as in our story of Sophie), is implicated in suicide. It is commonly understood in clinical circles that a very high proportion of depressed people also experience suicidal thoughts. Clearly then, it is a risk factor for suicide (American Psychiatric Association, 2000; Kaplan, Sadock, & Grebb, 1994).

Perhaps related to depression is the concept of hopelessness. Aaron Beck, an acknowledged pioneer in research on suicide and depression, led a 10-year longitudinal study of over 200 depressed and suicidal patients (Beck, Steer, Kovacs, & Garrison, 1985). In this study, an alarming 90 percent of the patients he studied who had high levels of hopelessness eventually killed themselves. Only one who didn't similarly have a high score for hopelessness eventually committed suicide. Beck's results, which have been confirmed by other studies, clearly seem to implicate a sense of hopelessness as a predictor of eventual suicide (Beck & Weishaar, 1989). In addition, others who are at an especially high risk for suicide include individuals who have previously attempted to commit suicide, those who have a family history of completed suicides, who have psychotic features, and those who have ongoing substance abuse problems (American Psychiatric Association, 2000).

Although depression, and especially a sense of hopelessness, are risk factors for suicide, we should also acknowledge that suicide is a complex phenomenon with many facets. Whereas suicidal people invariably experience unbearable pain, it isn't always depression or hopelessness. It can also be experienced as outward hostility or rage, anxiety, despair, shame, or guilt. Antoon Leenaars (1995), a psychologist who has done extensive work on the subject, suggests that suicide is an intrapsychic drama that is played out on an interpersonal stage. (See Table 7.1.)

In reviewing each element of the intrapsychic drama and the stage on which it is played out, what seems to emerge from Leenaars's model is one in which, because of a combination of personal frailty and life's blows, the person comes to see suicide as the only option available to him or her in order to find relief from unbearable psychic pain.

SOCIOLOGICALLY ORIENTED THEORY   Chapter 2 briefly discussed the work of the pioneering sociologist, Émile Durkheim. As you may recall, Durkheim coined the term *anomie* to describe the sense of alienation—a feeling of rootlessness, normlessness, lack of intimacy, or belongingness—that all too often seems to be a feature of modern living (Durkheim, 1893/1964; 1897/1951; see Ritzer, 2000, p. 82). He suggests that there's a profound relationship between the kind of society we live in and the incidence of suicide. Next, we will review Durkheim's sociological theory—a model that is still influential today. It constitutes one way of thinking about suicide. There are other approaches, most notably theories that tackle the problem from clinical and psychological points of view. Following an exploration of Durkheim's sociological ideas, we will turn to these other approaches.

There are two key concepts that are important in understanding Durkheim's explanations of suicide: *social integration* and *social regulation* (Durkheim, 1897/1951). **Social integration** is a term that refers to the degree to which individuals are included, or integrated, into the fabric of the society of which they are a part. When there is a

TABLE 7.1	Suicide as Intrapsychic Drama Played Out on an Interpersonal Stage

The Intrapsychic Drama

1. Unbearable psychological pain	According to Leenaars, unbearable psychological pain is the common stimulus in suicide. The person feels boxed in, hopeless, and helpless.
2. Cognitive constriction	In cognitive constriction, the person experiences his or her situation as one in which fewer and fewer choices are open to them *except* suicide. The person has tunnel vision, a narrowing focus, and inflexibility in his or her thinking.
3. Indirect expression	Plagued by ambivalent, contradictory feelings, the person expresses the turmoil without clarity and focus, perhaps because much of what is going on is unconscious.
4. Inability to adjust	Leenaars suggests that suicidal people themselves acknowledge their inability to adjust to their circumstances. Feeling too weak to overcome their severe difficulties, they come to reject everything but the inevitability of death.
5. Ego deficits	"Ego strength," the ability to react and adjust to reality, is impaired in suicidal people. With an ego weakened by the traumas of life, the suicidal person becomes unable to cope.

The Stage on Which the Drama Is Played Out

1. Weak/troubled relationships	The social situation in which the suicidal person lives may be one in which there is unbearable pain or conflict. Perhaps because of difficulties in forming or maintaining strong personal relationships, the person may become suicidal because of thwarted or unfulfilled human needs.
2. Rejection-aggression	Rejection by another may be experienced as utter abandonment, an unbearable narcissistic injury. Suicide then, may also be an attempt to retaliate, or reject, the very person who has rejected her or him—to use Freud's phase "murder in the 180th degree."
3. Identification-egression	Identification-egress ion is a complex expression. It refers to Freud's idea that because of a painfully experienced loss to a person or object with which the person strongly identifies, the suicidal person wishes to leave, egress, or in other words be elsewhere. To use Leenaars' own words, "Suicide becomes the only egress ion or solution, and the person plunges into the abyss" (p. 361).

Source: This table is based on Leenaars, A. A. (1995). Suicide. In H. Wass & R. A. Neimeyer (Eds.), *Dying: Facing the facts, 3rd ed.* Washington, DC: Taylor & Francis.

high degree of integration, closeness, or connection, we also say that there is high degree of social solidarity or cohesiveness. The lack of cohesiveness can be experienced as isolation or loneliness. **Social regulation** refers to the process by which a society is able to manage, or regulate, the behavior of its members and their relationships with each other. When it is too tight, life within the society can be experienced as rigid and oppressive. When it breaks down, one may experience life as an uncertain endeavor in a chaotic world.

Using the concepts of social integration and regulation, Durkheim postulates four different kinds of suicide. To streamline our discussion, these four types are presented in Table 7.2.

Referring to Table 7.2, **anomic suicide** relates to motivation to commit suicide as a reaction to a sense of normlessness that is experienced in a world in which the traditional social structures, roles, or rules have broken down. Using Durkheim's theory, this kind of suicide might occur at times of great social stress or upheaval. Social regulation has broken down. Perhaps experiencing life as chaotic, an individual under these conditions might commit anomic suicide as a response to a void—perhaps owing to such circumstances as the collapse of one's government, or the loss of one's faith, job, or marriage.

Although mentioned only in passing, Durkheim (1897/1951) describes **fatalistic suicide** as being at the opposite end of the spectrum. In this form of suicide, the person is not so much reacting to a breakdown of society, but the reverse. Social regulation is excessive, not absent or chaotic. A person faced with excessive social control, in Durkheim's view, might choose to commit fatalistic suicide in an effort to escape. Conditions that might foster this kind of response could include such experiences as life in the Nazi death camps, the Soviet Gulag, or the Cambodian killing fields. Survivors of the holocaust, in fact, report that one of the easiest ways to end one's misery was to grab the barbed wire on the forbidden perimeter of the compound so as to be shot or electrocuted (Frankl, 1984).

Turning from social regulation to social integration as an influence on suicide, **egoistic suicide** is the type that might occur as a consequence of a lack of close ties with others. In Durkheim's theory, the kind of person likely to commit this kind of suicide would be a socially isolated individual with little feeling of connectedness with the society. The sense of community that comes with purposeful involvement with others

TABLE 7.2	Suicide Matrix Based on the Work of Emile Durkheim	
	Social Regulation	**Social Integration**
Low	Anomic Suicide	Egoistic Suicide
	Society unable to help individuals regulate their desires	Society fails to assist the individual in finding his or her place in the world
	Individuals experience a sense of "normlessness" in a chaotic world	Isolated individuals experience a lack of closeness and connectedness.
High	Fatalistic Suicide	Altruistic Suicide
	The society is excessive or oppressive in the regulation of its members	The society or group has high ideals that contributes to suicide under certain conditions.
	The individual, feeling oppressed, commits suicide as an escape	Individuals feel honor bound to commit suicide for various ideological reasons.

Source: This table is based on Durkheim, E. (1897/1951). *Suicide.* New York: The Free Press.

is diminished in such persons. Cut off from close social ties, the person experiences a sense of distance from the care and social influence of others, which may contribute to an excessive individualism and obsession with the self.

Whereas egoistic suicide may arise from weak ties to the group, the final category in Durkheim's model, **altruistic suicide,** can be thought of as coming out of an excessive, perhaps idealistic, sense of social responsibility. The most commonly cited examples of altruistic suicide include the practices of **seppuku,** or hari-kiri, and **sati,** or sutee (Corr, Nabe, & Corr, 2003; DeSpelder & Strickland, 1999, 2004, 2008; Kastenbaum, 1998, 2001, 2003, 2006, 2008, 2009). In feudal Japan, seppuku, or hari-kiri, was a form of suicide most often used by the ruling warrior caste, or Samurai, who would commit ritual suicide as an act of honor in certain circumstances. Likewise, in pre-colonial India, widows, especially the widows of prominent figures, were expected to throw themselves on the funeral pyres of their departed husbands as an act of devotion (sometimes with a little help from others).

Some cultural examples that might fall into Dukheim's category of altruistic, or idealistic, suicide include:

- *People's Temple.* On November 18, 1978, 914 people, 276 of them children, were found dead at a place called Jonestown in Guyana. The dead were members of the People's Temple, a group led by their charismatic leader, the Reverend Jim Jones. Members drank a soft drink laced with cyanide and sedatives. A taped message from Jones claimed the suicide was an act of political protest. It followed in the wake of the killings of five people, including Congressman Leo Ryan, by members of the group at a nearby airstrip. Ryan was there to investigate human rights abuses by Jones and his group (British Broadcasting Corporation, 2003).
- *Heaven's Gate.* Marshall Applewhite and the 39 other members of the Heaven's Gate cult committed mass suicide on March 26, 1997, near San Diego, California. A videotape from Applewhite, and messages posted on the Internet, said they hoped to find redemption through the intervention of a flying saucer they believed was awaiting them behind the Hale-Bopp comet (Robinson, 1997).
- *9/11.* On September 11, 2001, Mohammed Atta and 21 other Islamic fundamentalists hijacked four commercial jets and diverted them to targets in New York and Washington, DC (September11News.com, 2003). At 8:46 a.m., American Airlines Flight 11 crashed into the North Tower of the World Trade Center in New York. Seventeen minutes later, all doubt about the cause of the crash disappeared. United Airlines Flight 175 crashed into the South Tower. At 9:45 a.m., American Airlines Flight 77 slams into the East wall of the Pentagon. Some 20 minutes later, the South Tower of the WTC collapses. At 10:10 a.m., United Airlines Flight 93 dives into a wooded area in Pennsylvania. The cockpit recorder and cell-phone messages from passengers of Flight 93 indicate that a number of passengers stormed the cockpit in an effort to retake the plane.

All the hijackers, passengers, and crews of the four planes perished in the suicide attacks, together with nearly 3,000 victims at the Twin Towers (Fingerhut, Hoyert, & Pickett, 2003).

Suicide Awareness

When mental-health professionals assess the mental status of new or continuing patients, they routinely look for mood disorders, such as depression, feelings of hopelessness, and psychic pain (Kaplan et al., 1994). The average "person on the street" might be surprised to learn this, but suicidal people will often tell professionals about their suicidal thoughts and plans, if asked. Although not everyone who commits suicide is crazy, people with a variety of psychological disorders—especially mood disorders and psychotic conditions—are at especially increased risk. This is consistent with observations made by Leenaars (1995)—that is, unbearable psychological pain can drive a person to suicide. Mental-health professionals are only too familiar with how much pain such people have.

The kinds of contextual things we want to be watchful for when considering suicidal risk include specific precipitating events, such as job loss, relationship problems, divorce, or even the suicide of another person; feelings of hopelessness; depression; the presence of advanced age, the disabilities, and serious illness; and family background (including a family history of suicide) (American Psychiatric Association, 2000; Kaplan et al., 1994; Leenaars, 1995).

The individual factors we should consider include prior attempts; verbal threats or even expressing thoughts about not wanting to be alive (*contrary* to the myth that suggests people who talk about it don't do it); cognitive constriction, or the belief that there are few options left in life; emotional turmoil, especially hopelessness, depression, anxiety, rage, shame, or guilt; sudden changes in behavior (including sleep, appetite, and activity level); and engaging in high-risk activities (American Psychiatric Association, 2000; Kaplan et al., 1994; Leenaars, 1995).

Preventing Suicide

Whereas about 20 percent of people who attempt or commit suicide show no advance warning signs, the other 80 percent do (Fisher, 2006). Despite the old myth that people who talk about suicide don't do it, verbalizing suicidal thoughts or feelings is actually an important early warning sign. As previously discussed, many people who commit suicide feel as if they've run out of options (Leenaars, 1995). By telling others about their suicidal thoughts and feelings, the part of the individual that wants to live may actually be reaching out. Other early warning signs include having trouble eating or sleeping; drastic behavior changes; withdrawing from friends and family; giving away prized possessions; being preoccupied with death and dying; losing interest in things that used to be pleasurable; and letting personal hygiene decline.

Being aware of the risks gives potential helpers the "heads up" they need so they can try to help the suicidal person before he or she acts. One of the most important things others can do is to care and be willing to listen. This does not mean doing therapy. It does mean giving a person the chance to share so that the individual doesn't feel he or she has to bear the burden alone. Hearing a person talk about such things can make one uncomfortable. However, once one knows what's going on, it will be easier to find other sources of support. For anyone who knows a suicidal person, acknowledging the pain and finding competent assistance is often critical in getting that person the help he or she needs.

Although the community mental system is far from perfect, the resources they provide often include suicide hotlines, support groups, and crisis screening for at-risk people. In most jurisdictions, designated mental-health professionals can help those who are at immanent risk of hurting themselves, even if they are not willing to accept the help voluntarily. Even if intervention is required, family, friends, and peers may hold the keys to supporting suicidal persons until the crisis passes and the person is able to resume normal activities.

Survivors of Suicide

One suicide survivor told me that the experience is more sudden, traumatic, and stigmatized than other losses. A handbook published by the AAS concurs and suggests that suicide bereavement is like no other (Jackson, 2003). The reason for this is fairly simple. The victim of suicide has chosen to die. Those left behind are called survivors because they are left to deal with the aftermath. Many survivors become angry at their loved one for what he or she is putting them through. Many also report that they feel stigmatized, perhaps because of the misconceptions that still exist in the general population or because they fear others might have lingering questions about the role they may have played in the life of the deceased before the person died. Survivors often feel disconnected because the hurtful way their loved one died is so painful they psychologically distance themselves from the person and what happened. As a result, some survivors end up feeling separated or "divorced." Unlike other bereaved people, every time survivors think of their deceased loved one, they also have to think about *how* that loved one died.

Edwin S. Shneidman is considered by many as the father of modern suicidology (Leenaars, 2010). Indeed, he was the founder of the American Association of Suicidology. Shneidman (1975) coined the term **postvention** to distinguish what we do to help after suicide, and what we attempt before suicide (prevention and intervention). His suggestions for how to respond include the following: Begin as soon as possible; explore the negative emotions the survivor has; be a voice of reason; monitor the survivors' physical health and overall mental well-being; and be prepared to be patient with a grieving process that is likely to take some time.

Today, most people in the know believe that suicide survivors never really get *over* it. The good news is that they do get *through* it (Jackson, 2003). Although Shneidman thought that psychotherapy was the best way to accomplish this, we now know that survivors do "their work" in a variety of ways. Survivors are individuals and they are often both resilient and creative. Some deal with it in their own way (perhaps by using friends and family for a support); some seek out information, including from books or the Internet; some get help from their pastor or a pastoral counselor; some engage in counseling with a mental health professional or use a support group made up of others who have gone through the same kind of experience; and some never deal with it at all.

The suicide survivor is likely to face a range of difficult emotions and experiences. As with other types of bereavement (see Chapters 10 and 11), the road to "recovery" is not likely to be a straight path with predictable stages. It is more like riding a roller coaster, with many emotional ups and downs (Jackson, 2003). Any number of reminders—running across some belonging of the deceased, a birthday or anniversary, a song, a photograph, or a favorite place—can trigger memories and sad feelings. Friends and relatives may or may not "be there" to provide the support the survivor needs. People who don't know, or who don't understand, might make insensitive or "stupid" remarks. And survivors sometimes report that they go through life having to contend with the perceptions or misperceptions of others, making it hard to relate to them.

In addition, some survivors might be unable to "move on" emotionally until they grapple with the question, "Why?" *Good* answers are hard to come by. Instead, many survivors have to settle for *good enough* explanations, or else learn to live with the ambiguity of having no clear answer at all—at their own pace and in their own way. When the dawn begins to break, so to speak, and recovery is on the horizon, survivors may also have to grapple with their internal judgments about whether or not they are truly worthy of the benefits they have fought so hard to achieve (Jackson, 2003).

What others can do to help is "be there" and be willing to just listen and be supportive. As Shneidman (1975) suggests, these "helpers" might also try to be the voice of reason that listens (sometimes to far-fetched concerns of the fearful sojourner) but also asks the practical questions that helps ground the grieving person and bring her or him back down "to earth." If the survivor has her or his own fleeting, or not so fleeting, thoughts of suicide or other serious problems, formal therapy and a professionally trained counselor might prove to be that much needed safety net.

HOMICIDE

Over 18,000 homicides occur each year in the United States. Each homicide is violent, leaving in its wake countless others to live with the memory of how their loved one died. *dmitrimaruta/Fotolia*

If suicide is anger-turned-inward, to use Freud's term, murder is anger-turned-outward. Although homicide rates have been going down slightly in recent years, more than 18,000 Americans are murdered each year (Logan, Smith, & Stevens, 2011). For persons ages 1 to 40, it has been among the fourth leading cause of death for a decade, or so.

When looking at homicide rates by age group, we see relatively high rates of homicide among children, ages 0 to 4; low rates for children ages 5 to 14; then a rise, peaking among those 20 to 24 years old (Logan et al., 2011). As already discussed in Chapter 3, over a thousand toddlers in the United States are murdered each year from child abuse, most of them under age 2. Homicide is the third leading

Smoke Him

Tariq Khamisa grew up in Seattle, but he moved to San Diego after high school to attend San Diego State University, near his father's home. "TK," as his friends called him, joined the Delta Upsilon fraternity and became active at the Jamat Khana Center, a worship center for local followers of the Ismaili Muslim sect (Dibsie, 1995). During his first year at San Diego State, TK met Jennifer Patchen. They fell in love and told their families they planned to wed. While his father, Azim, had encouraged TK to pursue a business major, he ended up dropping his business classes to follow his passion for art, a love both he and Jennifer shared. He moved out of the dorm. They rented their own apartment and formed a pact. They would take turns being the breadwinner while the other attended school. Initially, she worked at a photo shop while he took art and photo classes (Dibsie, 1995). Then, they swapped roles. He took a job at DiMille's Italian Restaurant delivering pizzas, so she could attend classes.

On January 21, 1995, three 14-year-old boys and Antoine Pittman, their 18-year-old leader, had been "partying." They were members of a little known street gang called the Black Mob. They decided they wanted pizza. Antoine decided it was time for his "little homies" to carry out a mission (Hasemyer & Cantlupe, 1995). They asked a girl to call in an order for two extra-large pizzas and have them delivered to a bogus address. "It was supposed to be a hit and run—get the pizzas and run," the mother of one of the 14-year-olds later told the police.

Tony Hicks, one of the 14-year-olds, was carrying a 9mm handgun. When Hicks demanded the pizzas, TK uttered an expletive, threw the pizzas on the backseat of his tan VW Hatchback, and started to leave. Pittman issued a kill order, "Smoke him." Hicks fired a shot through the driver's side window. The boys took off. A Catholic priest, who happened to be in the area, heard the shot. When he got to TK, the priest realized the shot was fatal. He said a final prayer for TK and blessed him.

Antoine Pittman was convicted for his role in ordering TK's murder, as well as for the murder of a homeless man Pittman had shot weeks before the pizza escapade. Tony Hicks, the boy who actually pulled the trigger, became the first youth under age 16 to be tried as an adult in San Diego under a new California law. Eventually, he pled guilty and was sentenced to prison for 25 years to life. The two other 14-year-olds previously confessed to their parts in the crime and were sentenced in juvenile court.

TK's father, Azim, decided to do something positive. He founded the Tariq Khamisa Foundation and befriended Hicks's grandfather, Ples Felix, who had been trying to provide a structured home for his grandson. The two of them began visiting schools, telling their story, and preaching a message of forgiveness and healing. The foundation continues its work (see "Links" at the end of the chapter), and Mr. Khamisa has now written three books (see "Suggested Reading" at the end of the chapter). Jennifer continued to work at her art, but it took on a disturbing edge. She drifted, became increasingly troubled, and eventually moved to be with her family. In late 2001, in a small apartment in Lakewood, Washington, she put a gun to her own head and ended her life.

cause of death in toddlers. Approximately the same number of women are killed each year by their intimate partners, a much lower number of men meeting the same fate (Kemp, 1998). Homicide is the second leading cause of death among youth, aged 15 to 14, especially so among ethnic minorities (Xu, Kochanek, Murphy, & Tajada-Vera, 2010).

Many of the homicides among the 15- to 24-year-old age group is from youth violence. Violent crime rates in the United States are generally at all-time lows, but homicide rates in dense urban areas are high, much of it related to gang activity (Kingsbury, 2010). While extreme violence may be a taboo in the society generally, violence itself is often glorified, as reflected in the popular media. What we call "gangs" make the use of extreme violence a virtue, such that it brings status within the group to the perpetrator, and in intergang violence, honor to the victim as well. The memory of deceased gang members live on in the consciousness of members who remain. Leak & Sons Funeral Home, on Cottage Grove Avenue, on the South side of Chicago, is doing a booming business these days, largely because of youth violence (Burden, 2009). On any given day, they might host funerals honoring the memories of victims of rival gangs, each beautifully casketed and adorned with the symbols of their gang affiliation.

Gang violence is often played out between rival groups, but sometimes "civilians" also suffer. The following vignette tells the story of one such civilian, Tariq Khamisa, or TK, an unfortunate 20-year-old college student who had the bad luck of crossing paths with a nest of gang members when trying to deliver pizza.

Regardless of whether your child is an innocent victim, as was TK's father and Jennifer's mother, or simply got caught up in a neighborhood spiral of violence, the impact is devastating (also see Chapter 3). We do not know how many other lives are affected by homicide: the parents, siblings, peers, and countless, nameless, faceless others who we never hear about but whose lives are touched by the victims and perpetrators of these crimes. The loved ones of the perpetrators are often hurt as much as loved ones of the victims. However, their grief is less likely to be met with the same degree of support. They have what has been termed **disenfranchised grief**—grief that is socially disallowed, hidden, and unaffirmed (Doka, 1989, 2002).

One of the ways those who experienced a loss from the AIDS pandemic addressed their grief was to create the AIDS quilt, -a patch work of cloth sections, each of which was crafted by those who were bereft because of AIDS. It was their way to memorialize their loved one and make the public more aware of the magnitude of the problem   *Mark D. Phillips/Photo Researchers, Inc.*

HIV/AIDS PANDEMIC

Just as people no longer accept the death of children as normal, they don't generally countenance the premature illness and death of young adults. In recent times the emergence of the AIDS epidemic–often called the **AIDS pandemic**–has changed that.

In the early days of the pandemic, to get an AIDS diagnosis was a death sentence. Today, AIDS is no longer an automatic death sentence, but the pandemic prevalence, lethality, and widespread fear of HIV infection and AIDS continue to make it traumatic, particularly among populations most at risk. According to information gathered from the CDC, or the Centers for Disease Control (2011a), each year over 34,000 persons are infected with HIV, the virus that causes AIDS (the Acquired Immune Deficiency Syndrome). Even though treatment for AIDS is much better than ever, about 18,000 persons still die each year from it. There are approximately 1.1 million Americans currently living with HIV infection (Hall, Hughes, Dean, Mermin, & Fenton, 2011). About 350,000 of them have full-blown AIDS.

Early Days of the AIDS Pandemic

Beginning in 1981, physicians in Los Angeles began to notice deadly episodes in which a small number of young gay men were infected with two unusual diseases: **pneumocystic carinni pneumonia,** or **PCP**, and **Kaposi's Sarcoma** (Centers for Disease Control, 1981a, 1981b, 1981c). PCP, an unusual form of pneumonia, is caused by a protozoan parasite. Kaposi's Sarcoma was thought to be a relatively rare cancer, which until then had been associated with elderly Jewish men living near the shores of the Mediterranean. Both are now counted among the 21 **opportunistic infections** that characterize AIDS (Castro et al., 1993). They erupt when a person's natural immune system is compromised. At around the same time these then atypical infections were detected in Los Angeles, similar outbreaks were popping up among gay men in other cities, particularly in the San Francisco Bay area and New York (Centers for Disease Control, 1981b, 1981c).

As a result of the puzzling infections that seemed to afflict a disproportionately high number of these young men, research efforts were launched in several parts of the world to find its cause. In late 1983, scientists came to the conclusion that the devastation exacted on the immune systems of these otherwise healthy young men was caused by a parasitic retrovirus. By 1986, the virus was discovered was given the name that is still in use today: Human Immunodeficiency Virus, or HIV (O'Donnel, 1996). As mentioned earlier, the life-threatening illness caused by HIV is called AIDS, or Acquired Immune Deficiency Syndrome.

The Progression of HIV/AIDS

A person can get AIDS from anyone infected with HIV, even if the infected person doesn't currently show signs or symptoms of the disease. Not only this, but the person may not even test "positive" for the virus. HIV is transmitted via the blood, semen, vaginal secretions, or the breast milk of an infected person, often through sex, sharing intravenous needles, living in the womb of an infected mother, breast feeding, or, until tougher screening standards were imposed on the medical blood supply, through contaminated blood used in transfusions (AIDS Treatment News, 2003a).

After HIV enters a new host, it replicates itself very rapidly. During the first 2 to 4 weeks, the concentration of the virus in the bloodstream will be very high, and the person may experience flu-like symptoms. Whatever symptoms become present will subside as the body fights off this first onslaught. The microbes of the virus, however, hide in the CD4 helper cells (also called *t-cells*), lymph nodes, bone marrow, central nervous system, and spleen. The CD4 helper cells are essential to the body's immune system. By the time HIV has invaded the CD4 helper cells, the body is producing HIV-antibodies in an effort to try to fight it. The HIV screening procedures that have been developed to test for HIV key in on these antibodies. At this stage, the tests would likely detect the antibodies. A person whose screening comes up positive for the antibodies is classified as being **HIV-positive**.

The microbes of the HIV can lay dormant like this for 3 to 10 or more years. The HIV hides quietly, but it is nevertheless attacking the CD4 helper cells, doing substantial damage to the immune system (Nuland, 1994; summarized in Dean, 1995). In addition, remember that an infected person can pass on the virus at any stage of the infection, even before the body develops antibodies against the infection—in other words, before the person shows up as HIV-positive. The mere absence of HIV antibodies, which do not develop until after the initial onslaught of the infection, is no guarantee the person is not infected.

When the immune system becomes sufficiently compromised, blood tests may reveal that the count of CD4 helper cells has dropped from a normal count of 800 to 1,200 per millimeter of blood to 400 or less (Nuland, 1994; summarized in Dean, 1995). When the count drops below 200, or the person gets a specific opportunistic infections identified by the Centers for Disease Control, the person can be said to have full-blown AIDS (Castro et al., 1993; Hall et al., 2011).

AIDS Lethality

Since the onset of the AIDS pandemic, more than a million cases of AIDS have been reported in the United States since the beginning of the pandemic (Centers for Disease Control, Divisions of HIV/AIDS Prevention, 2003a; Centers for Disease Control, 2011b); 55,000 cases have been reported in Canada (UNAIDS/WHO, 2003). In the early years, people diagnosed with AIDS generally died within six months to a year (O'Donnel, 1996). Nearly a half-million AIDS victims in the United States have in fact died from the disease since the beginning of the pandemic (Centers for Disease Control, Divisions of HIV/AIDS Prevention, 2003a).

Worldwide, the picture is even more troubling, especially since the funding to pay for the newer sophisticated anti-HIV drugs now on the market is far more difficult. Estimates from the chief international authority—the Joint United Nations Program on HIV/AIDS and the World Health Organization (UNAIDS/WHO)—suggest that over 36 million people across the globe have contracted AIDS since the onset of the pandemic. Of these, nearly 22 million have died from it (UNAIDS/WHO, 2003).

It seems that Brother Dale from the vignette was quite right. The most recent data from the Centers for Disease Control (2003b) shows that in 1994, about 48,500 people died from AIDS. The next year, deaths peaked with slightly more than 49,500 deaths from AIDS. In 1997, the year Brother Dale closed St. Christopher's, AIDS deaths dropped to less than half that amount, or about 21,500. Data from UNAIDS/WHO estimate that in 2002 there were approximately 15,000 people who died from AIDS in the United States (UNAIDS/WHO, 2003). The number of people staying alive has shot up. The CDC estimates that today there are well over 350,000 people who are living with AIDS in the United States (Centers for Disease Control, 2003c). This is a figure that

St. Christopher's House

St. Christopher's House, a six-bed hospice for AIDS victims, was established in a large, private residence by Brother Dale, a professional nurse by training, and his domestic partner, David. They wanted to make a difference, he said, and do something for the community. Brother Dale was then a member of an ecumenical, or interdenominational, Christian religious order—the Ecumenical Order of Charity. When they opened St. Christopher's House in 1993, it was at a time before the really effective treatments for AIDS were on the market. "People were still dying fairly regularly from AIDS," he said.

There were only limited resources for people dying from AIDS. St. Christopher's House took as it its spiritual mission, or apostolate, the job of taking in AIDS victims who had nowhere else to go. The residents of St. Christopher's House were in the end-stages of the disease, afflicted with some very serious impairments, including dementia, severe discomfort, nausea, diarrhea, and wasting. The aim of St. Christopher's House was to minimize the suffering and provide a first-class place for them to live until they died. "Everybody who sent us patients loved us," Brother Dale told me. "We had a wonderful place," he said, "decorated with some very nice Queen Ann furniture, crystal chandeliers, and we provided excellent care...people couldn't believe it was a hospice," he quipped.

Although Brother Dale and David had a policy of never asking the residents how they got AIDS, those whom they cared for in the early years seemed to be mostly gay men, he said, including some very well-known people in the local gay community. In later years, the face of the residents began to change and included more straight men and women, even including one woman who contracted the disease from a man who had deliberately gone around trying to infect others.

When St. Christopher's House closed in 1997, more effective drugs and combinations of drugs, called "cocktails," had been developed to treat AIDS. AIDS victims got healthier, stopped dying in such great numbers, and started living longer. Many small AIDS hospices like St. Christopher's began to close. "They simply didn't need all these hospices anymore," Brother Dale explained, "They needed more community-based programs and supported living situations."

does not include the 1.1 million people who are infected with HIV but who haven't yet developed full-blown AIDS, not to mention the many who are infected but haven't yet tested positive for the AIDS antibodies (Centers for Disease Control, 2011a, 2011b).

The Anti-HIV Drugs

The development of more effective drugs has had quite an impact on the lives of people infected with HIV/AIDS. Although there is no known cure for AIDS, quite a diverse array of anti-HIV drugs have appeared on the market that work well at containing the infection and prolonging life (AIDS Treatment News, 2003b). The numerous drugs on the market fall into three major categories of anti-HIV drugs. In addition, there are several categories of new pharmaceuticals in the clinical trial phase of their development.

The three major categories of drugs currently in use are: "nukes" (nucleoside and nucleotide analog reverse transcriptase inhibitors), "non-nukes" (non-nucleoside reverse transcriptase inhibitors), and protease inhibitors (AIDS Treatment News, 2003b). "Nukes" were the first class of anti-HIV drugs to be developed. Among them is a well-known anti-HIV drug called AZT, or zidovudine, which first appeared in 1987. Nukes provide "decoy" DNA building blocks, which confuses the virus as it tries to replicate itself. The non-nukes began to appear in about 1996. They also interrupt replication, but do so by attaching themselves to a viral enzyme, thereby restricting its activity. Protease inhibitors first appeared in about 1995. They block the action of protease, an enzyme that cuts the DNA strings of the HIV into specific proteins. Blocking the action of protease also prevents the virus from replicating itself.

Complacency Creates New Dangers

The successes in treating AIDS eventually lapsed into complacency. Parts of the gay community, a community that responded well to the call to engage in safer sexual practices, again began to flirt with unsafe practices—sex without condoms. Beginning in 2003, reports started to surface in New York, sounding alarm bells that it was becoming popular in some quarters of the gay community—especially the "club scene"—to combine the use of methamphetamine with recreational sex (Gorman, Nelson, & Applegate, 2003; New York Voice, 2004; Quittner, 2004). "Meth" a powerful stimulant, kept these men awake and in a state of heightened sexual arousal, leading to sex binges that sometimes lasted for days. The friction between the male organ and soft tissue during these sprees caused minor tears and abrasions to the tissue, providing an opening for the virus and thus increasing the risk of infection. The drug, sometimes called "club meth," confers a false sense of invulnerability, reducing inhibitions and thereby increasing the risk the men will want to "bareback" (i.e., have sex without condoms, further raising the risk of infection). Coinciding with the spread of "club meth" is a potentially more serious development—the appearance of new strains of HIV. One found in New York rapidly progresses into full-blown AIDS and is highly resistant to the drugs that were previously effective against HIV (Agence, 2005; Chua, 2004/2005; Ludden, 2005).

Chapter Summary

In this chapter we endeavored to explore encounters with death in the twenty-first century North America, beginning with the experience of parents who have had a child die. Although the death of a child may have been common in earlier times and is not uncommon in faraway places, the experience is particularly tragic today because it seems so premature and out of season. In this regard, we looked at the experience of parents who have had a child die with due concern for its poignancy.

We began the chapter with a discussion of a phenomenon that has begun to loom in the public consciousness because of the events on 9/11: death and terrorism. We briefly defined terrorism as the use of violence to intimidate in furtherance of political or social objectives. While the events of September 11, 2001, may have been a twenty-first century turning point, we briefly discussed terrorism as an age-old phenomenon. After surveying a few recent episodes of death and terrorism, we turned to the inner world of the terrorist, pondering why terrorists do what they do. We briefly reviewed the work of former National Security Council staffer, Jessica Stern, who has identified two basic types of religious terrorism—international and domestic—and two basic reasons for perpetrating it—alienation and humiliation. Venturing deeper into the mind of the terrorist, we also surveyed the work of German analyst Hans-Jurgen Wirth, who suggests that terrorism involves both a syndrome of fanaticism and the reactions of the people at whom it is directed. When, as in the case of 9/11, it involves a nation, or large group of people, he refers to the reaction as collective trauma. Finally, we noted that recovery from events, such as those of 9/11, may need to involve coming to terms with the events and finding constructive ways of healing.

First identified as a modern malaise by sociologist Émile Durkheim, we next turned our attention to the problem of suicide. At a personal level we explored the impact of suicide on its survivors. Turning to Durkheim's work, we reviewed four types of socially mediated suicides, as suggested by Durkheim. The text then discussed a few psychologically oriented ways of tackling the problem. We began with Freud's ideas about depression as "anger turned inward." Next, we looked at the role of the experience of hopelessness. Finally, we reviewed some of the ideas of Antoon Leenars, an eminent psychologist who has worked extensively on this issue. He has identified unbearable psychological pain and cognitive constriction—the sense that there

are few ways out—as key factors bearing on the actual completion of suicide.

We then turned to the topic of homicide, which we might call anger-turned-outward, to contrast it with suicide, which Freud called anger-turned-inward. We note that this form of traumatic death is increasingly familiar to some populations of young people. In this context, it is called youth violence. Some of this violence is related to gangs. We looked at the murder of Tariq Khamisa, a 20-year-old college student who had the misfortune to be called on to deliver two large pizzas to youthful gang members who had no intent to pay for them.

Finally, we tackled death and HIV/AIDS. Death from infectious disease may have been quite common at one time, but the lethality and resilience of the Human Immune Virus has had its effect on twenty-first century death and dying. Beginning in the early 1980s, when it was first identified, AIDS has killed nearly a half million people. Many of its early victims were gay men, intravenous drug users, and blood transfusion patients, but it is becoming more and more common among heterosexual young people. Although there is still no cure for HIV infection, fewer people are dying in North America, in large part due to the effectiveness of new drugs and new drug "cocktails" that have become available. People are staying alive longer, and today there are more than 350,000 people living with AIDS.

Key Terms

Suggested Activities

1. Check your phone book or the Internet to see if you can find a local chapter of Compassionate Friends. If so, you may wish to contact someone from the organization to find out more about the experience of parents who have had a child die.
2. In your community, inquire into the services and programs that are available to help people living with AIDS. In what ways are persons living with AIDS supported? What challenges remain? What do they have to do in order to survive?
3. Inquire into suicide prevention programs in your area. What do they suggest in terms of identifying and working with persons at risk for suicide? How is involuntary commitment of persons at risk managed? Are there cases of suicide you are familiar with in your community? If so, what can we understand as a result of these suicides?
4. Make yourself familiar with the popular literature dealing with terrorism. Pay attention to newspapers, magazines, and television reports on the subject. Perhaps you might even wish to start a "media file" of what you find. What do these reports say about the causes of terrorism? What strategies, if any, might help us manage the problem and reduce the risks?

Suggested Reading

- Stern, J. (2003). *Terror in the Name of God: Why Religious Militants Kill.* New York: HarperCollins.
  This is an artfully written book about religiously inspired terrorism by someone who not only has professional expertise but is the only writer I know of who has taken to the streets of the world to interview the terrorists. A thoughtful book that explores the grievances that give rise to religious terrorism as well as the organizations dedicated to "holy war."
- Saul, D. (2008). *Did You Know I Would Miss You: A Healing Journey.* West Vancouver, BC: DSaul Journey Publishing.
  Donaleen Saul, the brother of a person who took his own life, wrote this combination memoir and self-help journal as a way both to tell the story and heal from the grief through the question, "Did you know I would miss you?"
- Jamison, K. R. (2000). *Night Falls Fast: Understanding Suicide.* New York: Vintage.
  Suicide is a particularly awful way to die. "There is no morphine equivalent to ease the acute pain, and death not uncommonly is violent and grisly." Jamison has studied manic-depressive illness and suicide both professionally and personally, having attempted suicide at age 17.
- Khamisa, A. (1998). *Azim's Bardo.* San Diego: Tariq Khamisa Foundation.
  A compelling story of a father's journey from the initial shock of the loss of his son to forgiving the murderer, teaming up with his grandfather to teach young people about the real impact of youth violence.
- O'Donnel, M. (1996). *HIV/AIDS: Loss, Grief, Challenge, and Hope.* Washington, DC: Taylor & Francis.
  An extremely informative and practical book on HIV/AIDS. Although the book is getting a bit dated, this is one of the few good general resources on the market. The reader should be aware that there is more recent information about pharmacological therapy available, yet should not be reluctant to make use of the other information, suggestions, and resources outlined in the book.

Links and Internet Resources

- **September 11 Digital Archives**
  http://911digitalarchive.org/
  In partnership with the Library of Congress, the September 11 Digital Archive has preserved a moving collection of stories, e-mails, photographic images, video clips, audio bites, documents, and information about the 9/11 terrorist tragedy. The September 11 Digital Archive is funded by a major grant from the Alfred P. Sloan Foundation and organized by the American Social History Project/Center for Media and Learning at the City University of New York Graduate Center and the Center for History and New Media at George Mason University.

- **American Association of Suicidology**
  www.suicidology.org/
  The American Association of Suicidology (AAS) is dedicated to fostering understanding about and preventing suicide. It promotes research, public awareness programs, public education, and training for professionals and volunteers. A handbook for survivors, discussed in the chapter, is available as a free download at this site. The site also has extensive links, including resources for survivors.

- **American Foundation for Suicide Prevention**
  www.afsp.org/
  This organization, with chapters around the country, is dedicated to the prevention of suicide and helping friends and family of suicide victims get the help they need. The site has extensive links, including resources for survivors.

- **MurderVictims.com**
  www.murdervictims.com/
  This site is dedicated to preserve the memories of innocent victims of violent crime, to serve as a resource to help murder victim survivors, and to provide information to interested persons on murder statistics, news items, and an opportunity for discussion.

- **Tariq Khamisa Foundation**
  http://tkf.org/
  The Tariq Khamisa Foundation (TKF), begun by Tariq's dad, is dedicated to transforming violence-prone, at-risk youth into nonviolent, achieving individuals and to create safe and productive schools.

- **AIDS.org**
  www.aids.org/
  Here is an online journal of the nonprofit organization, aids.org, which is a leader in providing online AIDS education and prevention programs, and essential HIV resources. It describes itself as always looking for ways to help people to communicate with each other, and to share HIV and AIDS in the battle against AIDS.

Review Guide

1. Be fully familiar with all the terms and concepts in this chapter set in **bold**. See "Key Terms" at the end of the chapter and the Glossary at the back of the text.

2. Be able to explain what trauma and traumatic death are. How is traumatic death diagnosed and assessed? What is PTSD? What are the elements of PTSD? Complicated grief? Complicated grief syndrome? What are dissociative symptoms? Dissociative disorders? Dissociative identity disorder? What general strategies can we employ to help traumatized people? What is the complicated grief treatment protocol?

3. What is terrorism? Domestic terrorism? International terrorism? What are the basic elements of the definition offered in this chapter? According to Jessica Stern, what are the grievances that can give rise to terrorism? What are alienation and humiliation? What roles do they play, respectively, in domestic and international terrorism? What is the syndrome of fanaticism? Collective trauma? What does Wirth suggest in terms of the collective recovery of Americans from the 9/11 terrorist attack?

4. What is the personal and social impact of suicide? How many people are affected? What additional challenges are posed from death from suicide in contrast to other forms of death? What do social explanations for suicide have to say about why it occurs? What is social integration? Social regulation? What are the four types of suicide suggested by Durkheim?
   What do the psychologically oriented theories have to say about the causes of suicide? What are eros and thanatos? What is anger-turned-inward? Review Table 7.1. Be able to briefly describe the elements of the intrapsychic drama and stage on which the drama is played out. What steps can we take to prevent suicide? What can we do to help survivors after suicide occurs?

5. What age groups seem most affected by homicide? Who are the victims? The perpetrators? As discussed in the text, what does this suggest in terms of what's happening in our society? Also, consider the experience of the loved ones of perpetrators and disenfranchised grief.

6. What is HIV? AIDS? What is PCP? Kaposi's sarcoma? How did the appearance of PCP and Kaposi's sarcoma lead to the discovery of HIV/AIDS? What are opportunistic infections? What can happen to the immune system of a person infected with HIV? What does it mean to be HIV-positive? In recent years, what has happened to the death rate from AIDS? How do the various anti-HIV drugs work?

Dying

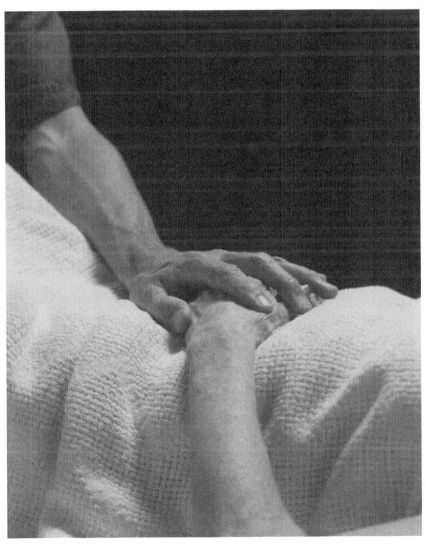

tomas del amo/Fotolia

Part III of this text has two chapters. They address dying, or what Dr. William Bartholome (1999) calls *the process of getting dead.*

Chapter 8 explores what is involved in facing death—walking through the "Valley of the Shadow" of death, so to speak. We will look at what happens when one makes the transition from feeling "temporarily immortal" to becoming aware that one is approaching death's door. We discuss Dr. Elizabeth Kübler-Ross's stages of dealing with death; learn about life from the "Angel of Death"; examine the most common "death trajectories," or paths to death; and look at a little of what is involved in attempting to fight a life-threatening illness. Also we briefly review some of the practical matters that have to be attended to, as well as delve into both two special topics "spiritual pain" and "hope." And finally, we learn from someone who has been there what it is like to live in the light of death.

In contrast to intensive care, which has become almost an icon of the battle to fight off death, Chapter 9 deals with intensive caring. Specifically, we learn about hospice and palliative care—an approach that has been described as the "gold standard" in end-of-life care. We contrast it to what is practiced in the so-called biomedical model (see Chapter 2) and contrast it with the wellness paradigm that is so characteristic of hospice and palliative care, intended to help achieve a "good death." We introduce the chief players in this drama, what they do, what actually happens as we approach death, and finally some of the pitfalls and gaps in today's end-of-life care system.

8

In the Valley of the Shadow
Facing Death

- Walking in the Shadow
- The Course of Dying
- Kübler-Ross' Stages
- Task-Based Approach

- Spiritual Pain
- Hope
- Living in the Light
- Wills, Trusts, and Life Insurance

Most of us don't give much thought to dying—it doesn't seem real. So, in this sense, we are temporarily immortal. Dr. William Batholome was a pioneering pediatric medical ethicist at a time when we didn't pay much attention to the experience of dying children. After he was himself diagnosed with terminal cancer, he came to realize that the difference between being "terminal" and being "temporarily immortal" was really just a matter of how much time you have left and whether or not you realize you are dying (Bartholome, 2000a, 2000b). In this chapter, we explore what it means to be terminal—in other words, to live in the valley of the shadow. We look at what we know about how human beings conceptualize their dying, comparing this with actual "death trajectories."

We also review Dr. Elisabeth Kübler-Ross's stage-based model about dealing with dying, as well as a more recent task-based approach to coping that takes in the physical, social, psychological, and spiritual dimensions. Metaphorically, we walk with critically ill people "in the valley of the shadow." In the process, we explore the role of hope. We conclude with a review of reflections about learning lessons of living directly from the "angel of death."

WALKING IN THE SHADOW

■ ■ ■

Why did I feel like such an outcast, such an "Other"?...It's hard to start new friend-
ships. It's hard to get people willing to invest in a relationship with you when they
know your limited future.... I began to resent that and to wonder about the relationship
between being terminal and being mortal.... Yet I, the terminal one...was living in a
society of people who considered themselves to be temporarily immortal.... "You're
mortal" to my "terminal,"...It's not all that much different.

—WILLIAM G. BARTHOLOME
"Lessons from the Angel of Death," *Bioethics Forum*, 2000, p. 35

■ ■ ■

The preceding quote was written by Dr. Bartholome before he died on August 2,
1999. The point he makes so well is that life itself is "terminal." No one gets out
alive. Unlike the rest of us, people living with a terminal diagnosis know they are
dying.

Everyone dies. Based on recent data, we can project that death will visit about 2.4
million people in the United States this year (Xu, Kochanek, Murphy, & Tajada-Vera,
2010; Minino & Smith, 2001). While each experience of dying and death is unique
and personal, we can make two generalizations (see Chapter 3). First, it is clear that
infancy seems particularly precarious. If a child survives the first year of life, however,
the outlook for those next years of childhood are fairly secure—deaths are few during
this period. Second, although death occurs among people in every age range, it becomes
significantly more frequent as people age.

Death is relatively rare among the young and much more common among the old.
This is actually something of a recent phenomenon in the West. Since so few young
people die, people today live longer and become older. This state of affairs has resulted
from innovations in public health and medicine that unfolded in the second half of the
twentieth century—better sanitation, improved nutrition, the discovery of antibiotics,
the widespread immunization of children, and other advances in science and medicine
(see Chapter 2; Goldberg, 1998; Wilkinson & Lynn, 2001). The life expectancy of a
person born in the United States at the beginning of the twentieth century was 47 years;
for persons born at the dawn of the twenty-first century, it is about 77 years, depending
on race and gender.

When life expectancy increases, we can say that the **mortality** rate decreases.
With a decreasing mortality rate there is also an increase in the age at which people die.
So far, so good. But with aging comes greater **morbidity**—the occurrence of chronic
illness and disability—which significantly impacts the *quality* of life (see Callahan,
1990; Sankar, 1993; Verbrugge, 1984; Wilkinson & Lynn, 2001). This is one of the
ways in which dying at the beginning of the twenty-first century is different from what
it was at the beginning of the twentieth. With some exceptions, instead of dying in

one's prime from an acute infection or injury, people in North America are now far more likely to die at an older age. When they finally do succumb, they tend to be sicker than ever before. With this change in who dies (the old) also comes a change in *how* we die.

In Chapter 3, we discussed the leading causes of death in the United States by age group. To summarize here, infants are most likely to die from the complications of birth defects, SIDS, and respiratory distress syndrome, a complication of premature birth. For toddlers, causes of death are likely to be accidents, cancer, and homicide (from child abuse). For children ages 5 to 14, it is accidents (often auto accidents) and cancer. For those aged 15 to 24, causes are likely to be accidents, homicide, and suicide (also see Chapter 7). For adults in the 25- to 44-year age range, it is accidents, cancer, and heart disease. Among middle-aged people, ages 45 to 64, it is cancer, heart disease, and stroke. Finally, for those over age 65, causes of death are likely to be heart disease, cancer, and stroke. To generalize from these rankings, we can say a smaller number of young people die from cancer, accidents, and violence. A much larger number of older people die from the effects of a debilitating illness, such as cancer, heart disease, and stroke (Eberhardt, Ingram, & Makuc, 2001).

The Messengers of Death

Once upon a time, Death confronted a giant while trekking through a mountain pass. Rather than succumbing to Death, the giant wrestled with Death, ultimately overcoming him. Death was left lying near a rock by the side of the trail, exhausted, thirsty, and so weak he was unable to rise. It was at this moment when Death wondered what would happen to the world if he was unable to do his job. Soon, he thought, there will be so many people they would be unable to stand next to each other. Just then, along came a healthy, young man. Taking pity, the young man comforted Death and gave him food and water.

Soon, Death recovered and was grateful. He said to the young man, "Do you know who I am?" The young man said he didn't. "Well, I'm Death," he said. "I can't spare anyone, not even you. However, to show that I'm grateful, before your time comes, I will send messengers to warn you so that you will not be taken by surprise." The years passed and the young man aged and became ill, but recovered. Then, Death appeared, tapping him on the shoulder. "But you said you'd send your messengers to warn me before it was my time," the man said. "I did," chimed Death. "I sent Sickness and Infirmity, not to mention my brother, Sleep, to remind you nightly of my coming." To this the man could say nothing, so he went away with Death and gave up his life.

Source: Adapted from *Grimm's Fairy Tales.*

THE COURSE OF DYING

Ann Wilkinson and Joanne Lynn (2001) comment that various writers have applied a range of terms to patterns of dying. For instance, Elisabeth Kübler-Ross (1969) coined the term *stages of dying*. Pattison (1977, 1978) uses the phrase *phases of dying*. Schneidman (1977) refers to what people experience at the end of life as *responses to challenges*. Glaser and Strauss (1965, 1968), followed by Benoliel (1987–1988), who worked with them, use the term *dying trajectory*.

Dying Trajectories

Sociologists Anselm Strauss and Barney Glaser were among the first modern thanatologists to systematically study the experience of people facing death (Glaser & Strauss, 1965, 1968). As part of their research at several San Francisco Bay area hospitals, they coined the term, **dying trajectory.** Many years later, Strauss explained that what they wanted to convey was the concept of the course of illness, without resorting to any kind of medical thinking or clinical terminology (Strauss, 1985).

There are two dimensions involved in their concept of death trajectory: *certainty of death* and *timing*. Four basic trajectories, or courses, can be discerned as a result of the interaction:

1. Uncertain death at an unknown time
2. Certain death at an unknown time
3. Uncertain death with a reasonable estimate of when the outcome would be known
4. Certain death within a generally known time frame

I've attempted to outline a rough approximation of the four basic trajectories in visual form (see Figure 8.1).

Glaser and Strauss were interested in learning how the awareness of death influenced the interaction between dying people and those around them. They identified four patterns: closed awareness, suspected awareness, mutual pretense, and open awareness. In the closed awareness pattern, the dying person does not know she or he is dying. In the suspected awareness pattern, the dying person suspects what is happening but this is not confirmed by those who know. In the mutual pretense pattern, everyone knows about the likely outcome but no one is talking about it openly. One could say this pattern leads to an indirect, or even devious, way of relating. Finally, in the open awareness pattern, death is acknowledged and discussed. It makes sharing, and even enhanced intimacy, possible for all concerned.

One of the problems with any model that attempts to simplify complex experiences like dying is that they tend to generalize. Death is messy. It rarely seems willing to fit easily into existing paradigms. Each death, like each life, is in important ways individual and unique. We tend to idealize one kind of death—the kind in which a person dies a natural, and predictable, death at the end of a disease process. As you can see in Figure 8.1, however, only one of the four basic trajectories lends itself easily to this ideal—that is, an illness with a *certain prognosis* of death, usually cancer, that can be expected to unfold in a *predictable time* frame.

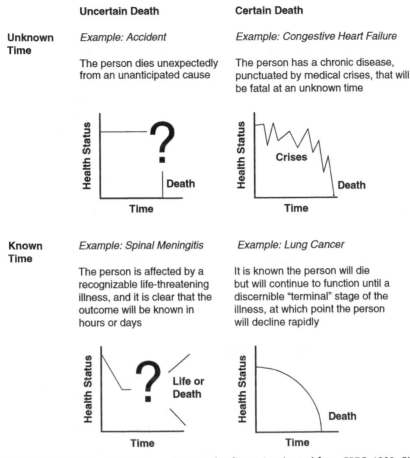

FIGURE 8.1 Dying Trajectories   *Source:* This figure is adapted from EPEC, 1999; Glaser, B. G., & Strauss, A. L.,1968. *Time for dying.* Chicago: Aldine.

There is probably no life-threatening illness as predictable as **amyotrophic lateral sclerosis,** or **ALS,** more commonly known as Lou Gehrig's disease. It is a disease of the nerve cells in the brain and spinal cord that control voluntary muscle movement (PubMed Health, 2011). In ALS, the nerve cells waste away, losing their ability to send messages to muscles. This leads to the inability to move arms, legs, and hands, and eventually to paralysis. The symptoms usually do not develop until after age 50. Death usually occurs within three to five years, although about 25 percent of ALS patients live longer than five years after diagnosis.

Lou Gehrig's disease and the topic of facing death took on a courageous face in the story of Morrie Schwartz, a retired sociology professor from Brandeis University who wrote several articles for a local newspaper. As a result, Ted Koppel, then of *ABC's Nightline*, got interested in his story. They aired an interview with Morrie, which was seen by a former student of Morrie, Mitch Albom, a sports writer who later went on to write a best-selling book about the time he spent with Morrie before he died (Albom, 1991). Not to be outdone, Morrie wrote the story in his own words (Schwartz, 1996).

> ## Morrie Schwartz
>
> Morrie Schwartz (1916–1995) was a much beloved professor of sociology at Brandeis University before he retired. He contracted ALS (amyotrophic lateral sclerosis), or Lou Gehrig's disease, soon after. ALS is a progressively degenerative and fatal disease of the central nervous system that causes the person to increasingly lose control of his or her muscles. Morrie appeared on an episode of *ABC's Nightline* and was interviewed by its then-host, Ted Koppel. One of Morrie's former students, Mitch Albom, who was then a successful journalist and broadcaster, saw his old professor on TV. Albom then recalled that 16 years earlier, the day he graduated, Morrie asked, "You'll stay in touch?"
>
> He hadn't. As a result of the *Nightline* appearance, Mitch did get in touch with Morrie and the two of them began to spend Tuesdays talking about old times and the meaning of life. Their experience evolved into a collaboration on a best-selling book, *Tuesdays with Morrie*, that would then become a movie. Morrie wrote his own book, *Letting Go: Morrie's Reflections on Living While Dying* (1996). He died on November 4, 1995. In 1999, his publisher reissued the book under a new title, *Morrie: In His Own Words*.
>
> Since publishing *Tuesdays with Morrie*, Albom has written three books, including, *The Five People You Meet in Heaven* (2003) and *Have a Little Faith* (2009).

Dealing with Life-Threatening Illness

Although stories like Morrie's are gripping dramas, the most common type of life-threatening illness is cancer. Indeed, cancer remains the most common diagnosis for persons referred to hospice (National Hospice & Palliative Care Organization, 2010; also see Chapter 9). The National Cancer Institute (NCI) estimates there were over 1.5 million new cases of cancer diagnosed and a half million deaths from it in 2010 (Edwards et al., 2010). The good news is that it is no longer the automatic death sentence it once was. When there appears to be a reasonable chance of survival, patients and their health-care providers will usually opt to pursue treatment intended to cure the illness.

While there are many different cancers, the most common cancer treatments are *surgery, cryosurgery, chemotherapy,* and *radiation therapy* (National Cancer Institute, 2011). Surgery can be effective in the treatment of cancers that have not spread, but it is usually used in conjunction with other therapies. **Cryosurgery** is often less invasive than traditional surgery. It is the use of extreme cold produced by liquid nitrogen or argon gas to kill abnormal tissue.

Chemotherapy is a type of treatment that uses drugs to destroy cancer cells. It works by stopping or slowing the growth of the cancer cells (National Cancer Institute, 2011). Because chemotherapy is designed to kill fast-growing cells, like cancer, it also affects other fast-growing cells in the body, like bone marrow; the cells that grow hair; and those that line the mouth and the intestines. This helps explain some of the common side-effects of "chemo," including fatigue, nausea, hair loss, reduced blood cell counts, and sores.

About half of cancer patients receive some type of **radiation therapy** at some point during treatment (National Cancer Institute, 2011). Radiation therapy involves the use high-energy radiation to shrink tumors and kill cancerous cells. The types of radiation delivered include x-rays, gamma rays, and charged particles. Sometimes, radioactive substances, like radioactive iodine, are introduced into the bloodstream to kill the cancer cells. Depending on the patient's condition, radiation can be curative (be used to help cure the illness) or palliative (intended to alleviate unpleasant symptoms), or both. Fatigue and nausea, depending on the site of the radiation, are among the most common side-effects. In addition, radiation therapy can damage healthy tissue, which can lead to a variety of other possible complications.

In addition to the conventional cancer therapies described here, many people also choose to explore complementary and alternative medicine. According to the National Cancer Institute (2011), this is a group of medical and health-care systems, practices, and products that are not presently considered to be part of conventional medicine. Conventional medicine is medicine that is practiced by physicians and by health-care professionals who work with them, including physical therapists, psychologists, and registered nurses.

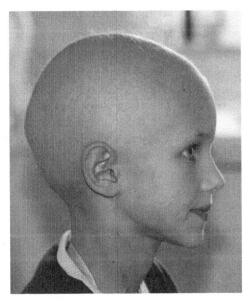

A young person undergoing chemotherapy, which attacks fast growing cancer cells. Unfortunately, it also affects other fast growing cells, such as hair. *Frantab/Fotolia*

Prognosis

Reflecting on the available literature as well as their own work, Wilkinson and Lynn (2001) note that there seems to be a clear "terminal" phase in only about 23 percent of deaths. In 58 percent of cases, death occurs suddenly within the context of a serious chronic illness, such as chronic heart disease or dementia. In 17 percent of cases, death strikes with no apparent warning. Wilkinson and Lynn comment, "Only a few patients will have a short, well defined period that justifies special services or special attention.... Most people with chronic illnesses never have a defined time in which to 'wrap up' their lives, plan for death, or consider hospice care" (p. 447).

The term **prognosis** is a commonly understood medical term that denotes an estimate about the likely outcome of a patient's case. Although most of us have a sense that prognoses are only estimates, we still seem to want to rely on these physician estimates. Indeed, Medicare uses estimates about projected longevity in determining funding eligibility for hospice programs. As we discuss more fully in the next chapter, Medicare will provide hospice funding for persons who have a prognosis of six months to live or less. In the mid-90s, an investigation called the Study to Understand Prognoses and Preferences for Outcomes and Risks of Treatment (SUPPORT) was undertaken in an effort to better understand problems in providing end-of-life care (Connors et al., 1995). We will discuss the SUPPORT study in more detail in the next chapter, but what I'd like to say here is that Joanne Lynn, one of SUPPORT's principal investigators, did some additional analysis using data from the study, partly in an effort to get a better handle on the efficacy of prognosis (Lynn et al., 1996, 1997).

Using both the prognostic methodology of the SUPPORT study itself as well as the estimates from physicians, Lynn and her colleagues (Lynn et al., 1996; Lynn, Harrell, Cohn, Wagner, & Connors, 1997; Wilkinson & Lynn, 2001) came to the startling conclusion that most seriously ill patients die sooner than predicted; and, that physicians and patients alike tended to avoid describing what was happening as "dying" until this outcome was unambiguously clear. Using SUPPORT criteria, Lynn and her colleagues were able to determine that 17 percent of those who actually died within one day were estimated to have had two months left. Using the same SUPPORT methods, they found that of those who actually died within a week, 51 percent were thought to have had two months to live. Median physician estimates were comparable. In 10 percent of cases, physicians wrongly prognosticated that those who actually died within a day would live for two more months. They similarly estimated that 30 percent of those who died within a week would live for two months.

KÜBLER-ROSS'S STAGES

There is undoubtedly no more famous model for understanding the experience of terminally ill patients than Elisabeth Kübler-Ross's stage-based model of dealing with the awareness of dying. A psychiatrist who had recently begun working at the University of Chicago Hospital, Kübler-Ross was approached by four students from the Chicago Theological Seminary who were interested in undertaking some research on dying. As she recounts in her classic book, *On Death and Dying* (1969), she spoke with a colleague, Dr. Sydney Margolin, about the request. As a result, they decided to approach the task by directly interviewing terminally ill patients in the presence of the students.

No one in recent times has probably done more to make us aware of the kind of experiences people have when nearing death than psychiatrist, Dr. Elizabeth Kübler-Ross, who is pictured here in an early photo. *Jack Moebes/Corbis*

When Kübler-Ross began to approach attending physicians about speaking with their patients, she ran into unexpected problems, much as Herman Feifel had a decade earlier (see Chapter 2; Neimeyer & Fortner, 1997). Recalling the reactions of her medical colleagues, Kübler-Ross stated, "I did not get one single chance to get near such a patient. Some doctors 'protected' their patients by saying that they were too sick, too tired or weak, or not the talking kind; others bluntly refused to take part in such a project" (Kübler-Ross, 1969, p. 23). Undaunted, Kübler-Ross continued on and would eventually get access to terminally ill patients. As time went on, their simple idea would evolve into what has come to be called the "Chicago Seminar," a fully sanctioned class, in which

TABLE 8.1	Summary of Elisabeth Kübler-Ross's Stage-Based Model on Dealing with Dying
Stage	
Denial and Isolation	After the initial shock, this is the first response. As a way of protecting the self from the devastating news, the patient denies the reality of the situation. According to Kübler-Ross, the reaction of the patient is, "No, not me. It cannot be true!"
Anger	When denial can no longer be maintained, and the reality sets in, it is replaced by feelings of anger, rage, envy, and resentment. No longer able to deny the reality of the situation, the question for the patient becomes, "Why me?"
Bargaining	According to Kübler-Ross, the next stage of adaptation is one that involves trying to bargain, perhaps with health-care personnel or with God, to postpone the inevitable. Kübler-Ross suggests that when anger fails, it may be an attempt to ask more nicely.
Depression	Feelings of hopelessness and depression are natural responses that ensue when the effect of other emotions has worn off, and the patient comes face-to-face with the reality of his or her situation. In addition to the future prospect of dying and the present loss of functioning, the depression is a response to such things as the lengthy treatment, hospitalization, and financial burdens. Kübler-Ross describes two types of depression: reactive and preparatory. In the reactive type, the patient responds to losses already experienced. In the preparatory type, the patient responds in the present to losses that are anticipated to occur in the future.
Acceptance	In some respects, depression prepares the way for acceptance, the final stage in Kübler-Ross's model. In this stage, the patient, having worked through feelings of anger and depression, is able to come to terms with fate. During this stage, Kübler-Ross observes, the person may be in and out of sleep. Acceptance is not a necessarily a happy state of affairs, merely one of recognition and resignation.

Source: This table is adapted from Kübler-Ross, E., (1969). *On death and dying: What the dying have to teach doctors, nurses, clergy and their own families.* New York: Collier Books.

students would observe as Kübler-Ross thoughtfully interviewed dying patients. The idea caught on, and before long not only did she have students attending her seminar but physicians and staff began showing up, too, now eager to listen to these fascinating exchanges.

By the time *On Death and Dying* (1969) was published, Kübler-Ross had interviewed over 200 patients about their experience. As a consequence, she would develop the stage-based model for which she has become so well known (see Table 8.1). Because of the popularity of this model, many people are familiar with the five stages of dealing with death she proposed: denial and isolation, anger, bargaining, depression, and acceptance. In describing the work of dying, she suggests that the process of moving through these stages begins when the patient learns of the fatal prognosis.

In thinking about Kübler-Ross's work, one of the things we might keep in mind is that she was deeply interested in learning from and affirming the experience of the terminally ill people with whom she worked (1969). During a period when it was all too common for professionals to "pathologize" patients, she expressed a great deal of concern about the importance of understanding the experience of the dying in a way that respected what it was like for them. According to Kübler-Ross, moving through the stages is a normal process—one that forces the patient to respond to the prospect of death as well as the realities of his or her current circumstances. Herself a practicing psychiatrist with a deep interest in the human psyche, Kübler-Ross was a leader in interpreting what dying patients experience as a normal part of a dreadful process. Commenting about denial, she stated that it is "a healthy way of dealing with the uncomfortable and painful situation with which some of these patients have to live for a long time" (p. 39).

Critiques of the Model

Over three decades after it was introduced, Kübler-Ross's work has continued to have an undisputed appeal to the imaginations of sincere people who wish to understand the plight of the dying. According to one text on the subject, "It has directed caregivers and lay people alike to thoughtful consideration of issues related to dying patients, as well as to the universal human confrontation with death." (Despelder & Strickland, 1999, p. 157). I think we could take this a step further to say that Kübler-Ross's stages have become part of our culture that is commonly understood, or misunderstood. While she had argued for fluidity, give and take, the possibility of experiencing more than one response at a time, and the feasibility of going back and forth between stages, many professionals have expressed considerable concern about the model and how it has at times been inappropriately, indiscriminately, and thoughtlessly used (Corr, 1993; Corr, Nabe, & Corr, 2003; Kastenbaum, 2001). For a summary of key criticisms identified by Robert Kastenbaum (2001), a thanatology pioneer and important author in the field, see Figure 8.2.

---

1. The existence of discrete stages has not been clearly shown.
2. No evidence has been offered to show that people actually move from stage to stage in the dying process.
3. The limitations of the model have not been acknowledged.
4. There is insufficient distinction between description and prescription.
5. The totality of the persons life is neglected in favor of supposed stages of dying.
6. Other influences, such as resources, pressures, and characteristics of the immediate environment can also have a considerable impact on a person's responses to dying.

FIGURE 8.2 Kastenbaum's Criticisms of Elisabeth Kübler-Ross's Stage-Based Model *Source:* Adapted from Kastenbaum, R. (1998, 2001). *Death, society, and human experience, 6th & 7th eds.* Boston: Allyn & Bacon.

Kastenbaum (2001) points out that although dying people sometimes use denial, become angry, try to bargain with fate, or fall into depression, these are experiences that are not unique to dying people, nor do they constitute the full range of experiences they undergo. He also points out that in addition to interviews with dying patients, there are other sources of information that might help us test the model and better understand the experience of the dying.

Kastenbaum (2001) and Corr (1993, 2003) suggest one of the greatest misuses of Kübler-Ross's model has been to imply that the dying process, as outlined in the model, is **normative** or **prescriptive**—in other words, it has been used as the standard for how the process *should* unfold. As a result, well-meaning but misinformed helpers have abused it. The behaviors dying people use to cope have been, and continue to be, at risk of being misunderstood or adjudged as being "dysfunctional" when they don't conform to Kübler-Ross's stages. Kastenbaum (2001) also cautions that by putting so much emphasis on what happens in the supposed stages of dying, the person is treated primarily as a *dying* person, with the emphasis on dying, and *not* as a complete human being. Dying people are more than their diagnosis, Kastenbaum points out. Finally, he tells us, there are other circumstances that can exert a tremendous influence on how the dying process unfolds. It isn't just about internal processes. We ought to pay attention to these factors as well, he insists.

In an essay written about a decade ago, Charles Corr, the chief author of another text on death and dying (Corr et al., 2003) suggests we consider that there are both things that we should and should not learn from Kübler-Ross's work (Corr, 1993). See Table 8.2.

Rather than thinking of the dying process as something that happens in stages, Corr suggests we might be better off if we framed the whole experience as a special category of coping. He generally agrees with Kastenbaum's list of concerns. Indeed, he says, "As we develop our alternative model, we might turn Kastenbaum's (1998, 2001) criticisms into positive guidelines for our work" (Corr, 1993, p. 80). Using Kastenbaum's criticisms of Kübler-Ross's framework, Corr (1993) suggests that we may wish to make use

TABLE 8.2 A Summary of Corr's Suggestions about Lessons We Should and Should Not Learn from Elisabeth Kübler-Ross's Work	
Lessons We Should Not Learn	**Lessons We Should Learn**
1. There is no reason to believe there are only five way of coping with dying	1. Those who are dying are still alive and often have unfinished needs they want to address
2. There is no reason to think that those five stages are interrelated as stages in some more encompassing dying process	2. We cannot become effective helpers unless we listen actively to those who are dying
3. There is no reason to think that the stages Kübler-Ross proposed ought to be normative or "prescriptive"	3. We need to learn from the dying in order to know ourselves better

Source: Adapted from Corr, C. (1993). Coping with dying: Lessons that we should and should not learn from the work of Elisabeth Kübler-Ross. *Death Studies, 17*, 69–83.

of the following principles as we attempt to develop a new model to help guide us in working with the dying:

1. Set aside stages.
2. Refrain from thinking about dying as a linear process.
3. Try to be clear about methods.
4. Emphasize describing what happens and forbear from prescribing what *ought* to happen.
5. Consider the totality of the dying person's life.
6. Attend to the influences that emanate from the dying person's immediate environment.

In concluding our review of Kübler-Ross's stage-based model, we may wish to put it in a broader context. Corr (1993), I think, astutely observes that we should consider the person of Kübler-Ross when we consider the model she has made famous. A psychiatrist, she developed professionally in her native Europe, where psychoanalytic theory has played a dominant role. Corr (1993) notes that Kübler-Ross's model is based on the patient's use of **defense mechanisms**, including denial, as a way of dealing with threats to the psyche that result from impending death. I agree with Corr when he suggests that it is well to consider the potential biases of theorists when weighing the implications of applying their work. He comments that "a careful examination of *On Death and Dying* reveals that its emphasis, not surprisingly, is on defense mechanisms" (Corr, 1993, p. 72). Remarking on Kübler-Ross's use of psychotherapeutic language when she suggests it is important for dying patients to work through their issues, Corr observes, "Dying is not a psychiatric illness" (Corr, 1993, p. 72).

Task-Based Approach

Based on an address he made to the Annual Conference of the Association for Death Education in 1991, Charles Corr wrote a rather compelling paper calling for a newer and better model to replace Kübler-Ross's decades-old stage-based model (Corr, 1992). A key element of his proposal was the assertion that we needed a model that accurately describes coping with dying. He suggests it is a process that goes beyond being a reaction to the threat of death or a defense against psychic trauma. Coping with dying is an active process, he suggests. It involves awareness of, and efforts to contend with, the many events and challenges that confront a person who is dying. The differences between the two models pivot on the premise that reacting is a negative, passive, process; coping is an active one that involves taking steps to manage what happens.

Corr (1992) suggests that any adequate model about coping with dying ought to do four basic things:

1. Provide a basis for understanding all dimensions, and all the individuals involved.
2. Foster empowerment by emphasizing the options available to the dying person.
3. Emphasize participation—the shared aspects of coping with dying—those aspects in which people come together to help each other.
4. Provide guidance for care providers and helpers.

TABLE 8.3	Dimensions of Coping in Corr's Task-Based Model of Coping with Dying			
	Physical	**Psychological**	**Social**	**Spiritual**
Types of Tasks	Nutrition Hydration Elimination Pain control Nausea	Security Autonomy Richness of living	Relationships Significant others Social networks	Sense of integrity Acceptance Reconciliation Self-worth Life-review Hope

Source: This table is adapted from Corr, C. (1992). A task-based approach to coping with dying. *Omega, 24* (2), 81–94.

Corr (1992) endeavors to accomplish these four things through what he calls a task-based approach. The way he portrays this model, tasks represent work that may, or may not, be undertaken by those who are coping with dying. In Corr's view, they aren't prescriptive—in other words, the tasks are not things that must be done, or ought to be done, by the dying person. Rather, they are things that may be helpful or desirable. Corr says, "I prefer to describe them as discretionary, although I realize that some may be more or less necessary and others recommend themselves more insistently" (p. 83).

Describing the genesis of his task-based model, Corr (1992) notes that the hospice and death awareness movements sprang forth from the realization that dying people are still living, breathing human beings. He describes his own model as being rooted in the same understanding. He comments that although it may seem obvious that the dying are still people, this is all too often lost within the complexities of the modern health-care milieu. Consistent with the holistic philosophy introduced in Chapter 1, Corr suggests that we look to the needs of dying patients in four basic areas, which he refers to as dimensions of coping with dying. They are:

1. Physical
2. Psychological
3. Social
4. Spiritual

Table 8.3 is a visual representation of the four dimensions, together with examples of tasks Corr associated with each.

This four-pronged approach is both simple and compelling. The physical dimension certainly includes such tasks **hydration** (providing fluids), elimination, and the management of pain. These are discussed in more detail in the next chapter. For now, it may be enough to note that because pain hasn't always been properly attended to, many concerned health-care providers are advocating that it be monitored as a **fifth vital sign** (the other four being temperature, heart rate, blood pressure, and respiration). Corr (1992) suggests that such issues as that of autonomy, security, and the richness of life (also known as quality of life) falls within the psychological sphere. Relationships are a feature of the social dimension. Corr identifies two key types: (1) those with close, significant, people and (2) those with other people that take place in one's broader social network (e.g., people in the neighborhood, congregation, or community). Corr does not attempt to define the spiritual dimension, although he does note it's a broader concept than religion. He points to such deeds as attempting to find a sense of meaning as the kind of thing that falls within the spiritual domain.

SPIRITUAL PAIN

Richard Groves is a former Roman Catholic priest and long-time hospice professional whose wife was facing a life-threatening illness. He believes that the spiritual dimension includes several discrete types of pain that can motivate us to find practical ways to end suffering (Groves & Klauser, 2005). He suggests that these aspects of spiritual pain cause an individual to live out his or her days in a state between extreme anxiety and utter peacefulness. They are:

1. *Meaning pain:* Encounters with truth such that the person experiences life on a continuum from meaninglessness to a state of being filled with a sense of meaning and purpose.
2. *Forgiveness pain:* Arising from the estrangement from self and others in which the person experiences varying degrees of unforgiveness or reconciliation.
3. *Relatedness pain:* Stems from taking leave from others and things that are important. It is experienced on a continuum from alienation or relatedness.
4. *Hopelessness pain:* The sense of trust or despair in relation to the goodness of the ultimate outcome.

Groves suggests that each of these elements of spiritual pain can be put on a Likert scale, similar to other pain scales (Groves & Klauser, 2005). When addressed with a dying person, these aspects can serve as a starting point for a discussion about each of the four parts of one's spiritual pain, perhaps providing the impetus to work toward resolution, heal rifts, and achieve a greater sense of peace before one's death.

HOPE

In the social sciences, **hope** has sometimes been thought of as an elusive, mysterious, or "soft" concept (Farran, Herth, & Popovich, 1995). Used as a verb, a noun, and an adjective, Ronna Jevne and Cheryl Nekolaichuk (2003) comment, "Its descriptions have spanned *soul* and *goal*, *being* and *doing*, *process* and *outcome*, and *state* and *trait*" (pp. 189–190). According to Farran, Herth, and Popovich (1995): "Hope constitutes an essential experience of the human condition.... A way of thinking, a way of behaving, and a way of relating to oneself and one's world...has the ability to be fluid in its expectations, and in the event that the desired object or outcome does not occur can still be present" (p. 6). Farran and colleagues suggest that hope is a process with at least four clear attributes: experiential, rational, relational, and spiritual (transcendental).

TABLE 8.4	Four Attributes of the Process of Hope	
Experiential	The *pain* of hope	Grounded in an inescapable trial
Rational	The *mind* of hope	Rooted in subjectively desirable and objectively possible goals
Relational	The *heart* of hope	Influenced by a sense of caring or love
Spiritual (transcendental)	The *soul* of hope	Sense of certainty about the uncertain

Source: This table is adapted from Farran, C. J., Herth, K. A., & Popovich, J. M. (1995). *Hope and hopelessness: Critical clinical constructs.* Thousand Oaks, CA: Sage.

As you can see from Table 8.4, the attributes of hope in this model are somewhat similar to the dimensions of coping seen elsewhere—with a twist (Farran et al., 1995). Jevne and Nekolaichuk (2003) suggest, "Hoping and coping are intricately intertwined" (p. 11). Note that the *experiential, rational, relational,* and *spiritual* (*transcendental*) attributes of hope in Table 8.4 are beautifully and poetically expressed in this model as being the *pain, mind, heart,* and *soul* of hope. In a paradoxical way, hope comes into existence only as a result of coming face-to-face with some undesirable and unavoidable trial or threat. The individual subjectively desires a positive outcome that may not always be likely but is nevertheless objectively possible. Other people can foster the hope by their own love and caring, as expressed by projecting a positive attitude and confidence, or simply being truly present for the person. Farran and colleagues describe the spiritual or transcendent aspects of hope as being related to faith about oneself, a higher power, or a sense of confidence in a positive outcome that has not yet become an eventuality.

Ronna Jevne, the former director of the Hope Foundation in Edmonton, Alberta, suggests that whatever else hope is, it is capable of changing lives and enabling affected individuals to "envision a future in which they are willing to participate" (Jevne & Nekolaichuk, 2003, p. 190). In relation to the experience of cancer, it seems that not only is hope important because of the now well-documented relationship between hope and one or more positive health outcomes but also because of its intrinsic value (Farran et al., 1995; Jevne & Nekolaichuk, 2003). Hope can be directed at a *particular* outcome, such as cure, remission, or freedom from pain, or it can be experienced as the desire for some *generalized*, albeit unspecified, future good (Dufault & Martocchio, 1985). Because of hope, life is enriched and made more bearable.

LIVING IN THE LIGHT

We now turn from the experience of living in the shadow of death to living in the light of death (Bartholome, 2000b). You may recall that we began the opening section of this chapter with a quote from Dr. William Batholome. Early in his career, Dr. Bartholome was thrust into the arena of pediatric bioethics, when, as a pediatrics resident at the Johns Hopkins Hospital, he was involved in the landmark 1970 Baby Doe Hopkins case, which involved a child born with multiple birth defects that was allowed to die. In the ensuing years, he would to devote much of his career to helping dying children, medical bioethics, and teaching—until, that is, he himself succumbed to metastatic adenocarcinoma of the esophagus, an especially lethal form of cancer.

People with the type and severity of cancer experienced by Dr. Bartholome usually die relatively quickly. He would live on for five more years—a span he would refer to as a gift beyond his wildest imaginings. By his own account, he would be transformed during this time. In a meditation he wrote several months after "getting the bad news," he used the expression, "living in the light of death" to describe his metamorphosis. It has also become the inspiration for this, the concluding section of the chapter. It is about hope and transformation as much as it is about dying.

Lessons from the Angel of Death

In the case of Dr. William Bartholome, the particular hope for a cure from his cancer would not have been a very reasonable one. With the cancer having spread to several lymph nodes and his liver, his doctors were very clear that it wasn't a matter of *if* his cancer would end his life, as his doctors expressed it, rather, it was a matter of *when*. He underwent "radical palliative surgery" with the hope that it might buy him some time. The surgery and other "intangibles" gave him a little over five more years of living. Without hesitation, Dr. Bartholome attributed this lengthy respite to his experience of getting married again. Between the time of his surgery and his death he would celebrate five "last" Christmases with his new wife, Pam, his children, and many friends. By his own account, this was a remarkable gift of time. During the interval, he lived his life—enjoying time with family and friends, worked as long as he could, and became a teacher to us, leaving several reflections and an essay titled, "Lessons from the Angel of Death" (Bartholome, 2000a).

As Dr. Batholome recounts, his life began to change from the moment he realized what he was up against. As you might imagine, his life was turned upside

While the idea of the 'Angel of Death' may conjure up a sense of foreboding, Dr. William Batholome believed he learned important lessons from the 'Angel of Death' that made his final days profoundly more meaningful. *umbertoleporini/ Fotolia*

down. To use his words, it was "a world unraveling" (Bartholome, 2000c). Almost from the outset of learning of his diagnosis, however, Dr. Bartholome looked beyond the specter of death, which as he described it, was sitting on his shoulder, to how he might live until he died. From the unraveling strands of his old life, he would weave a new one. "I have no desire to go back to the frantic life I was living before—a life dominated by things-to-do lists and organizers and calendars; a life in which I did little more than juggle an almost overwhelming burden of things that needed to get done" (Bartholome, 2000d, p. 19). Four years later, he wrote, "I don't want...to go back to living the life I was before...now every aspect of my life is miraculous. I want to live each day...as if it will be the last time I am 'above ground'" (Bartholome, 2000e, p. 25).

■   ■   ■

*In June of 1994, my life was visited by a teacher, the likes of which I had never previ-
ously encountered. From this teacher I have been taught lessons in a way that I had
never learned before....*

   *I have learned about what illness means in a way that I couldn't possibly
learn from textbooks or professional journals or even by carefully listening to
patients and families describe their illness experiences.*

—WILLIAM G. BARTHOLOME
"Lessons from the Angel of Death," *Bioethics Forum,* 2000, p. 29

■   ■   ■

Dr. Bartholome articulated seven lessons he learned from the angel of death.
Although you miss out on the joys of reading these lessons directly, and in the prose
style of its author, I nevertheless include a brief summary in Figure 8.3.

The metaphors of living in the shadow and living in the light of death provide a distinct contrast and way of looking at the complexity of the experiences of dying. There is no
single such experience, but rather a variety of them, each being individually and uniquely
different. Only a small proportion of people are lucky enough to know in advance that
they will die soon, yet the "deathbed scene"—the veritable model for terminal illness—
has become the social norm. Those who have an illness with a clear "terminal stage,"
have, if they are told, the opportunity for consciousness about their impending death, and
a period of time to suffer, to hope, to plan, and to live until they die. Such was the stuff of
Dr. Bartholome's dying. As odd as it may sound, death was like "sugar" to him (2000e).
Although perhaps bittersweet, he wrote that the awareness of dying nevertheless enriched
his life. With little future to consider, there was only the present. He used it as an opportunity to learn a new way of living. With no clear-cut terminal stage—the experience of
most people—dying is often a less certain and more lingering affair.

LIFE INSURANCE, WILLS, AND TRUSTS

Included in Lesson 1 that William Bartholome learned as he was drying was how
important it is to get your affairs in order for the sake of those left behind. This
means making your wishes known and providing for your loved ones. A **will** is a
legal document in which you declare what will happen with your assets and who
will manage your estate after you die (American Association of Retired Persons,
2011). The person you appoint to manage your affairs after you are gone is called
the *executor* because he or she executes what you have already decided. The will
generally specifies who inherits large assets—such as homes, retirements funds, and
bank accounts—but it can also specify who you want to get such personal things as
particular photographs, mementos, and automobiles. It addition, it can specify who
you want to become the guardian of any minor children who might still be at home.
Although laws vary from jurisdiction to jurisdiction, people with simple estates can

Lesson 1	*The value of dying.* Knowing that one is dying can be valuable information. "Living in the light of death" may actually be the best ways to live because we can then learn to become more focused on the only thing we truly have—the present. In addition, it provides time for taking care of all the necessary details so that arrangements can be made and loved ones are provided for after one's death.
Lesson 2	*No space in our lives for the dead.* We have failed to make the dead part of our ongoing lives. This lesson came to Dr. Bartholome when a friend died during his illness and he "discovered" the value of keeping the dead, or the memory of the dead, with us.
Lesson 3	*Limitations of the hospice solution.* For a long time hospice has set the standard when it comes to end-of-life care. As someone who had cared for dying children, Dr. Bartholome came to believe that he would be able to avail himself of hospice, a movement that was spearheaded by volunteers. With Medicare funding for hospice, a movement predicated on voluntary caring has become a major industry. Two major problems became apparent to him: (1) The program requires that physicians certify that patients have less than six months to live—some physicians refuse to acknowledge the existence of such patients; (2) Hospice serves only a small fraction of people who die. For him, this raised the question about unequal care. Some people get "Cadillac" end-of-life care; some get very little.
Lesson 4	*Physician duties owed to the dying.* Based on what he learned in Lesson 3, Dr. Bartholome came to believe that physicians needed to take more seriously their responsibility to tell patients when they have a life-threatening condition and make sure all patients have adequate end-of-life supports to help them through the dying process.
Lesson 5	*America's need for "rituals of withdrawal."* As an alternative to assisted suicide, Dr. Bartholome came to believe that we needed to support dying people when it came time for them to withdraw from their social responsibilities, and eventually from food and fluids. Instead of imposing life-sustaining activities when the person has already begun the process of dying, he proposed that we start learning how to help the dying by letting them withdraw from life-support measures when they are ready to die.
Lesson 6	*Existential questioning.* The only difference between being "terminal" and being "mortal" is the span of time until death and the awareness of its impending approach. In order to live more fully, we need to cultivate a relationship with the skeleton (death) we are becoming and to acknowledge and value that skeleton in others.
Lesson 7	*Spiritual hounding.* Allowing the specter of death to haunt one's life can also open a person to the presence of the spiritual side of life. As a result, life can be experienced as richer, deeper, and fuller than ever before.

FIGURE 8.3 Summary of Dr. William Bartholome's Seven Lessons from the Angel of Death
Source: This figure is adapted from Bartholome, W. (2000a). Lessons from the Angel of death. *Bioethics Forum, 16* (1), 29–36.

usually make use of online resources or do-it-yourself will kits, which are widely available. For those with more extensive estates, the services of an experienced attorney are often a good investment.

A revocable **living trust** is a written document that designates a person to manage your property (American Association of Retired Persons, 2011), including yourself. You create a trust while you are living. So long as you are legally competent, a person can change or dissolve it at any time for any reason. Once you die, it cannot be changed. While still living, people generally appoint themselves and their spouses as the trustees, or persons designated to manage your affairs. Both wills and trusts establish who gets what, when, and how. The advantages of a trust are that they are private while you are still alive and they provide a way to avoid probate court after you die. Living trusts can be more complicated than wills and may require the services of an attorney. However, just as with wills, there are a wide ranges of online resources that can help most people put one together.

Life insurance is something of a misnomer. It is really a contract between a policy holder and the insurance company, in which the insurance company agrees to pay a designated beneficiary a sum of money upon the death of the insured person. Insurance of various kinds are frequently offered to eligible employees as a benefit, so you should check with the human resources department of any present or future employer to determine the benefits and eligibility requirements.

Life insurance is a complicated topic, and you are cautioned to explore the options carefully before purchasing any form of life insurance. However, we can generally say there are two basic types of life insurance: *term insurance* and *whole life* coverage. **Term insurance** provides life insurance coverage for a specified period of time in exchange for the payment of a regular premium (Insurance Information Institute, 2011). The policy cannot be cashed in; it buys protection in the event of death and nothing else. With **whole life** coverage, there is a fixed annual premium, guaranteed death benefits, and guaranteed cash values, depending on when the policy is cashed out. In addition, there are relatively low-cost accidental death policies that pay off only in the event of accidental death. Most policies assess the risk of death and base insurability and the cost of premiums on the likelihood of death. Many policies have exclusionary clauses. For example, they commonly will not pay out in the event of suicide.

BOX 8.1

Focus on Practice: Dealing with the Dimensions of Dying

In 1969, Dr. Elizabeth Kübler-Ross ignited the social consciousness about end-of-life issues. Based on her work with dying patients, she suggested there are five stages in coming to terms with dying. Charles Corr (1992) observed Kübler-Ross's model had been often misused. He suggested a task-based model as an alternative that includes attention to the physical, social,

(Continued)

psychological, and spiritual dimensions. Richard Groves and his colleagues advise attending to three aspects of the spiritual experience (Groves & Klauser, 2005).

1. *Coming to terms with dying:* Kübler-Ross's work should inform us that those facing death wish to come to terms with and share their struggle.

   We can help by being present, listening, and allowing the dying person the opportunity to share her or his experiences and struggles. Without imposing any expectations, you may wish to consider the degree to which the person is accepting of her or his situation. Resolve to support the person as the person contends with whatever end-of-life issues he or she may struggle with.

2. *Tasks of dying:* Corr (1992) helps bring focus to the many issues faced at the end of life: physical, social, psychological, and spiritual.

   As you journey with the dying person, make sure you attend to such physical issues as pain and shortness of breath. A simple pain scale, rating it from 1 to 5, can be used to monitor physical pain. Consider the social dimensions, such as family issues and funding realities. Pay attention to emotions, thoughts, and behavior. How might these things inform ways to help?

3. *Spiritual pain:* Groves and Klauser (2005) suggest there are at least four dimensions of spiritual pain. These relate to issues of finding meaning, forgiveness, relationships, and hope about the future.

   Use the poles on the end of each spectrum as a way to dialog about the person's experience. You may be surprised at what you learn.

Chapter Summary

This chapter began with a brief quote from Dr. William Batholome in which he writes about what it's like to have a terminal diagnosis in a world full of people oblivious to the prospect of death. We then focused on causes of death in the twenty-first century at various ages, noting that our present-day experiences are quite different from those in earlier times. Today, it is common for old people to die, but death is rare for the young. It was not always so. With this change came a change in *how* we die—now more commonly with chronic disease. We looked at a model of dying trajectories, first developed by Glaser and Strauss (1968). Using a matrix, we differentiated these dying trajectories and noted that while we generally imagine the deathbed scene and think of the kind of death as being

associated with a terminal stage as the norm, most people actually die at an unpredictable time from chronic illness.

We looked anew at Elisabeth Kübler-Ross's famous (1969) model about stages of dying, which she developed after interviewing over 200 dying patients. We also explored criticisms of the Kübler-Ross model and then reviewed an alternative, task-based, model, articulated by Charles Corr (1992). We noted that this new model is in important ways more holistic and inclusive, encompassing the physical, emotional, social, and spiritual dimensions of dying, much like the four-facet model offered in Chapter 1.

We shifted our attention from living in the shadow to living in the light of death. We briefly explored some recent work on the role of hope, noting that even in the case of terminal illness there is room to hope for some general, albeit unspecified, future good. In this light, we heard the story of Dr. William Bartholome, who left us an account of his own experiences as a dying person—a legacy of lessons he learned from the angel of death. And finally, we discussed some of the practical realities for anyone facing death (all of us): life insurance, wills, and trusts.

Key Terms

amyotrophic lateral sclerosis (ALS) *163*

chemotherapy *164*

cryosurgery *164*

defense mechanisms *170*

dying trajectory *162*

fifth vital sign *171*

hope *172*

hydration *171*

life insurance *177*

living trust *177*

morbidity *160*

mortality *160*

normative *169*

prescriptive *169*

prognosis *165*

radiation therapy *164*

term insurance *177*

whole life *177*

will *175*

Suggested Activities

1. Draw a time line of your life. On a piece of paper draw a horizontal line, representing birth to the present. Indicate years along the line and include significant events. Consider "where" you were in terms of your development, awareness, and state of mind. What sorts of things were influencing you? What kind of impact were you having on others?

2. Make a list of people you have personally known who have died. Consider their age and the kind of death they experienced. What happened? Who was around? Did they become ill or did they die suddenly and unexpectedly? Did the manner of death make a difference to them and those around them?

3. Reflect on your relationship with a dying person, or a person you know who has died. Did you and the person who eventually died know they were dying? As a result, what did you experience? How has this person's death impacted your own life? Did you learn anything from the experience?

Suggested Reading and Viewing

- *Albom, M. (1997). Tuesdays with Morrie.* New York and Toronto: Doubleday.
  This deeply moving book recounts the lessons taught by Morrie Schwartz to the author during the last days of Schwartz's life. Mitch Albom, a student, begins to meet with Morrie after seeing him appear with Ted Koppel on an episode of *ABC's Nightline*.
- Schwartz, M. (1996). *Morrie: In his own words.* New York: Delta Trade Paperbacks.
  Morrie Schwartz, the subject of the book, *Tuesdays with Morrie*, endeavors to teach us lessons of living while he is dying. With warmth, wisdom, and humor, Morrie shares his thoughts on such things as what it means to live with physical limitations, handle frustration, grieve losses, maintain one's involvement with life, and consider death at the end of life.
- Moyers, B. (2000). *On our own terms: Moyers on dying.* [Video series]. (Available: Public Affairs Television, Inc., www.films.com)
  This is a series of four videos, first aired on PBS in 2000. Bill Moyers takes us into the world of the dying and those who care for them. Program 1 focuses on

living with dying; Program 2 deals with a different kind of care; Program 3 focuses on a death of one's own; and Program 4 deals with a time to change.

- Bosanquet, S. (Producer), & Nichols, M. (Director). (2010). *Wit.* [Motion picture]. United States: Home Box Office, Inc.

  This is an intense and moving portrayal of a university literature professor diagnosed with life-threatening ovarian cancer. The protagonist discovers a fine line between life and death that can only be walked with wit.

- Rosenberg, L. (2000). *Living in the light of death.* Boston: Shambhala.

  Noting that getting older, becoming ill, and dying are difficult subjects in today's Western world, Larry

Rosenberg, a Buddhist practitioner, teaches us about an ancient Buddhist path to liberation—death awareness. He suggests that becoming intimate with aging and mortality, we can uncover greater understanding of ourselves, relationships, and all things, thereby achieving a measure of freedom from suffering.

- Sourkes, B. M. (1982). *The deepening shade.* Pittsburgh: University of Pittsburgh Press.

  This book deals with the medley of issues that confront patients, families, and caregivers when they face a life-threatening illnesses. Written as a resource for psychiatrists, psychologists, social workers, and other professionals who encounter patients like these in their practices, it helps professionals put a human face on this troubling experience.

Links and Internet Resources

- **Center for Practical Bioethics**
  www.practicalbioethics.org/
  This freestanding practical bioethics center is dedicated to raising and responding to ethical issues in health and health care. It serves as a resource center dedicated to educating and empowering health-care professionals and their institutions, advocating for patients' rights, training ethics committees, and supporting change though ethics education and leadership. Resources on aging and end-of-life care are available. See "online store" in the "resources" tab for video and print materials, including some featuring Dr. William Bartholome.

- **On Our Own Terms: Moyers on Dying**
  www.pbs.org/wnet/onourownterms/
  This PBS-sponsored site is the online home for the pioneering four-part, six-hour, series *On Our Own Terms: Moyers on Dying.* The website contains a vast array of articles (many written by professionals featured on the series) and other resources of interest to any student of death and dying.

- **Sacred Art of Living**
  www.sacredartofliving.org/
  Founded by Richard and Mary Groves, the Sacred Art of Living Center was begun as a one-of-a-kind school for spiritual formation. They offer a range of programs and

services, including an acclaimed workshop on the Sacred Art of Living and Dying, America's first comprehensive training program on spirituality in end-of-life care.

- **Hope Foundation of Alberta**
  www.ualberta.ca/HOPE/
  Affiliated with the University of Alberta, the Hope Foundation of Alberta is dedicated to understanding and enhancing hope in individuals, families, and institutions. It offers opportunities for research, specialized counseling, speakers, workshops, and hands-on experience.

- **Nolo Press**
  www.nolo.com/
  Nolo Press was born out of the frustration of two legal aid lawyers in California out of concern for people who didn't qualify for free legal aid but couldn't afford lawyers. They offer do-it-yourself books, PC software (but not for the Mac OS X), and online legal forms to help people get quality legal information.

- **American Association of Retired Persons–Estate Planning**
  www.aarp.org/money/estate-planning/
  AARP, the largest organization in the United States representing elderly people, offers a variety of free resources on its estate planning pages. Included are articles on insurance, wills, and trusts.

Review Guide

1. Be familiar with the definitions of each of the concepts that were printed in **bold.**
2. What are the four basic dying trajectories in the dying trajectories matrix, drawn from the work of Glaser and Strauss (1968)? About what percentage of people die with an illness in which there is a clear terminal stage? What proportion of people die as a result of complications during the course of a chronic illness?
3. What is prognosis? How accurate is prognosis? To what degree can we rely on them?
4. Be familiar with each of Kübler-Ross's five stages in the process of dealing with impending death. In what ways was or is this model helpful to people? What are the key criticisms of this model?
5. What are the four key elements of Charles Corr's task-based model? What kinds of things are subsumed in each? How does this model differ from the stage-based model? What does it say about what a model ought to do? Does the model accomplish these? In what ways is this model more holistic?
6. What is the spiritual dimension? How is spirituality defined?
7. What is hope? How can it be defined? What are the faces of hope? What is the difference between *particular* and *generalized* hope? Why is it important to understand the distinction?
8. What are the lessons we can learn from the experience of people like Dr. William Bartholome? To what degree is their experience like and unlike what is outlined in the models of dying we discussed in this chapter? What lessons did Bartholome say he learned from the angel of death?

9

Intensive Caring

Hospice and Palliative Care

- **Changing Philosophies**
- **The Hospice Story**
- **Spread of Programs**
- **The Hospice Team**

- **Providing End-of-Life Care**
- **World with Good Death?**
- **Falling through the Cracks**
- **On the Horizon**

In this chapter, we turn our attention to the topic of *intensive caring*, an expression that denotes high-quality, compassion-driven care for people with life-threatening illness (Bartholome, 1999). The term stands in contrast to *intensive care*, which is associated with the biomedical model, high-tech life-support and heroic efforts to preserve life at all costs (see Chapter 2). Intensive caring expresses a philosophy about enhancing the "quality of life" for as long as the person is alive. Today, we do this through hospice and palliative care.

In the United States, **hospice** usually refers to end-of-life care for people who are not expected to live longer than six months. Hospice patients have to abandon further efforts to cure their illness. **Palliative care**, on the other hand, is intended to relieve suffering, but it does not require patients to forego curative therapy. In Canada, the expression **hospice palliative care** is used to denote all care provided to alleviate the suffering of those afflicted with life-threatening conditions. It has no expectations about abandoning curative therapy, nor does it embrace any specific requirement about how much time the patient is expected to live.

CHANGING PHILOSOPHIES

According to David Barnard, the former chair of the Department of Humanities at Pennsylvania State University College of Medicine, we are the cusp of the change from the unconditional acceptance of the biomedical model (see Chapter 2) to insistence on a more person-centered approach to care that has come about in response to three conditions (Barnard, 1998):

1. The effects of medical technology that has blurred the line between life and death, making the end-of-life an expensive time that is often lived out in pain, with intrusive medical procedures, and an increasing sense of helplessness
2. The devaluation of symptom control in medicine in favor of treatments intended to cure disease and prolong life
3. The loneliness of dying arising out of the awkward, distant, and evasive relationships between dying people and their loved ones with their care givers

One way to conceptualize this shift is to contrast the modern biomedical model with the newer wellness philosophy, which reflects the *dying-well ethos* that has been emerging within the past couple decades (see Table 9.1).

Hospice is a person-centered, compassion-driven model of care for people nearing the end of their lives, which also tries to support families during a difficult time. The National Hospice and Palliative Care Organization (NHPCO) (2004b) describes it as an approach that focuses on caring, not curing, and constitutes a "gold standard" for

TABLE 9.1 Contrasting Old "Biomedical Model" and the "Wellness Paradigm"	
Old Biomedical Model	**Wellness Paradigm**
A–Attitude about disease and death: Disease and death are regarded as enemies that should be attacked and defeated	**A–Attitude about disease and death:** Disease and death are accepted as a normal part of life
B–Belief about health: Health is thought of as a physical state, characterized by the absence of disease	**B–Belief about health:** Health is thought of holistically, as a state of total well-being, including the physical, social, psychological, and spiritual facets
C–Care: Care is aimed at curing disease and prolonging life as long as possible	**C–Care:** Care attempts to promote total well-being–body, mind, and spirit–balancing efforts to prolong life with activities intended to foster quality of life
D–Dealing with death and disease: Treat chronic disease processes and episodes of acute illness	**D–Dealing with death and disease:** Attend to the physical, social, psychological and spiritual needs of the person, including the individual's acute and chronic illnesses
E–Efforts aimed at: Defeating death one disease at a time	**E–Efforts aimed at:** Caring for the whole person; promoting health; preventing illness; relieving suffering; and comforting those who can't be cured

treating people with life-threatening conditions. It is a multidisciplinary and team-oriented approach to alleviating **suffering**, broadly defined, including the physical, social, psychological, and spiritual dimensions.

As you can see from Table 9.1, the biomedical model and so-called wellness paradigm reflect different assumptions, ideals, attitudes about death and health, goals of treatment, emphasis, and values. In an article on aging and dying, Marshall and Levy (1990) suggest that all societies have idealized concepts about proper and improper ways to die—the preferred manner of death being called the **good death**. Today in North America, a new approach to the good death is in some ways a return to the old—that is, being at home, surrounded by friends and family; a minimum of technological intrusion; good pain management; achieving "closure" with respect to unresolved personal affairs; and experiencing some level of dignity in the dying process (Erikson & Erikson, 1997; Levy & Gordon, 1987; Lofland, 1978, cited in Marshall & Levy, 1990).

Although more people are now dying at home, the reality is that about two-thirds of us still die in the hospital or a nursing home (National Center for Health Statistics, 2011). As a result of the awareness that there continues to be a "disconnect" between the ideal of the good death and what really happens probably helps account for the surge of interest in the "dying well" movement.

With increased life expectancy and overall better health, many of us have come to see nearly all technological progress and scientific innovation as good. With respect to end-of-life issues, however, it has contributed to the expectation that we can and should preserve life itself at all costs. The newer paradigm defines a good death, as previously described, as the ideal. Although it recognizes that advances in medicine have improved our lives, it also acknowledges that the end of life is normal and should be allowed to unfold naturally. It paradigm asserts, however, that when death does come, the process should be as meaningful and as pain-free as possible.

THE HOSPICE STORY

Hospice Heritage

The terms *hospice, hospital, hostel,* and *hotel* all have their roots in the Latin word *hospitium,* which conveys the idea of providing hospitality (Phipps, 1988; Saunders, 1998; Sloan, 1992). Bill Phipps (1988) observes that although many people often use the term *hospice* for innovative approaches to patient care, most people have probably forgotten its roots in early Christianity.

In the year 335 C.E., Constantine, the Emperor of the Roman Empire, decriminalized Christianity. Indeed, he would later make it the official religion of the empire. In contrast to Roman society, which paid little or no attention to the plight of the underdog, adherents of this new religion were known for caring for the poor and the sick. Consistent with this tradition, Constantine ordered the construction of infirmaries in all Roman cities throughout the empire. In Greek-speaking parts of the empire, Bishop Basil of Caesarea in Cappadocia founded a place of healing. Ephraim, of Syria, did the same in Edessa. And Fabiola, a wealthy Roman widow, brought the idea of hospice back to her native Italy after visiting St. Jerome in Bethlehem (Phipps, 1988; Sloan, 1992). In medieval Europe, it became a fundamental part of the monastic tradition, which even today provides hospitality to pilgrims of all kinds (Phipps, 1988; Saunders, 1998).

Modern Hospice

Today's hospice movement has led the way to the new dying well paradigm, discussed in the previous section. The term *hospice* now embodies the very idea of specialized and compassionate care for the dying. Dame Cicely Saunders founded St. Christopher's Hospice, now considered the first in a long line of modern hospices. Describing the beginnings of St. Christopher's, Saunders (1977) states,

> St. Christopher's Hospice was originally founded in 1948 with a legacy of 500 Pounds given by a man who, having escaped from the Warsaw Ghetto, died of cancer in a busy surgical ward in London at the age of 40.... He died in peace, leaving a heritage that went far beyond his 500 Pounds—a vision of what could be done to help people like himself to die in peace and dignity. (p. 160)

Saunders started her career as a nurse before becoming a qualified social worker. In 1948, she fell in love with a patient, David Tasma, a Polish-Jewish survivor of the Warsaw ghetto, who was then dying of cancer (Barker, 2005; British Broadcasting Corporation News, 2005; Richmond, 2005). When Tasma died, he left her the 500 British Pounds, a considerable sum in those days, and asked that it be "a window in your home" (Saunders, 1977). It was not until 1967, however, that St. Christopher's would finally open its doors. In the intervening years, Saunders gained additional experience caring for dying patients, earned a medical degree, and ultimately organized the committee that would establish St. Christopher's (Saunders, 1977).

Unlike the hospices in the United States today, which generally provide care in the homes of patients, Dame Cicely's hospice was a specially designed facility with 54 beds. Later, St. Christopher's developed an outpatient service (Ingles, 1980; Phipps, 1988; Saunders, 1977). Although Dame Cicely did not invent the term *hospice*; she renewed and renovated it at a time when providing intensive caring was a lost art. Indeed, St. Christopher's became an icon for intensive caring (Phipps, 1988; Saunders, 1977, 1998; Sloan, 1992). Today, a simple glass window remains at St. Christopher's to honor David Tasma's memory. Dame Cicely died there in 2005.

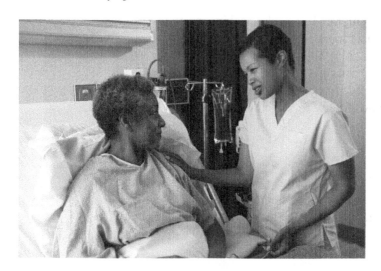

Hospice has become the 'gold standard' of the contemporary 'dying well' movement. In the United States, a team of hospice providers -nurse, social worker, volunteer, and chaplain -usually come into the person's own home to give physical, psychological, social, and spiritual care. iStock © monkeybusinessimages

Hospice in North America

Dame Cicely Saunders's work prepared the way for the rise of the modern hospice movement. The diffusion of hospice, like other social movements, is a phenomenon that spread in a series of stages (Sloan, 1992). In 1963, Dame Cicely Saunders, Elisabeth Kübler-Ross, and Colin Murray Parkes met at a workshop on death and dying being held at Yale University. Florence Wald, the Dean of the School of Nursing at Yale, had also attended. Impressed by her vision, Wald brought Dame Cicely back to Yale to deliver a series of lectures on hospice (National Hospice and Palliative Care Organization, 2004a). In 1968, Wald visited St. Christopher's just a year after it opened. The next year, Elisabeth Kübler-Ross's book on death and dying hit the shelves, and was greeted with an enthusiastic response. Dame Cicely credits this book and its popular appeal with the surge of interest in death and dying that made North America ripe for the hospice movement (Saunders, 1998; Sloan, 1992).

The ethos of the death awareness and dying well movements, which was embodied in Kübler-Ross's book, mirrored other societal changes that were unfolding in North America at the time—for example, concern for individual rights as well as consumer protection, and an eagerness to challenge the status quo. Sloan comments, "The larger sociological trends of the 1960s were beneficial in persuading adopters…to embrace the hospice concept" (1992, p. 26). Dame Cicely, indeed, became a catalyst for change. When Wald returned from her visit to St. Christopher's, she formed a committee that started the first hospice in the United States: The Connecticut Hospice. Staffed by volunteers with medical support, it began providing in-home care in 1974 (Saunders, 1998).

Across the border to the North, Dr. Balfour Mount, who had also visited St. Christopher's, brought its philosophy back to Canada. In 1975, he started Canada's first hospice service at the Royal Victoria Hospital in Montreal, Quebec (Mount, 1976; Saunders, 1998). Unlike the Connecticut Hospice, which provided in-home care, or St. Christopher's, which gave care in its own freestanding facility, the program at the "Royal Victoria" operated in a special ward of the hospital. Dr. Mount coined the term *palliative care* to describe what they did. He preferred *palliative care* to *hospice,* since for hundreds of years the latter had been used in French-speaking parts of the world to denote a place of last resort for the poor and derelict (von Gunten, Ferris, Portenoy, & Glajchen, 2001). The term *palliative care* seemed to him a good alternative, since it was acceptable to both the English and French-speaking communities.

Palliative Care

The term *palliative care* also has Latin roots, denoting that it is aimed at alleviating suffering (Doyle, Hanks, & Macdonald, 1998b). In the United States today, how the term is used makes some subtle distinctions between it and hospice. According to the National Hospice and Palliative Care Organization, palliative care extends the principles of hospice to people much earlier in the disease process. In the United States, providing hospice is begun only after efforts to cure have ended. As discussed next, the rules of the American Medicare program, which funds most hospice care in the United States today, actually requires that all attempts to cure have stopped.

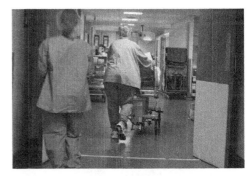

Hospital based palliative care teams work in dedicated palliative care wards or in specialized consultation services that provide expertise to the patient's primary care provider. *Shuva Rahim/Fotolia*

In contrast, palliative care programs typically permit continued efforts at curing while still providing comfort care. The World Health Organization (WHO) defines palliative care as having two features: (1) it strives to improve the quality of life for patients and families facing a life-threatening illness and (2) it endeavors to relieve suffering of all kinds (World Health Organization, 1990, 2004). A set of attributes of palliative care are articulated by the World Health Organization and are summarized in Figure 9.1.

- Provides relief from pain and other distressing symptoms
- Affirms life and regards dying as a normal process
- Attempts to neither hasten nor postpone death
- Integrates the psychological and spiritual aspects of patient care
- Offers a support system to help the family cope in time of both illness and bereavement
- Uses a team approach to address the needs of the patient and the family
- Will enhance the quality of life, and may sometimes treat in ways that will positively influence the course of the illness
- May be applied during the early course of illness, used in conjunction with therapies intended to prolong life, and includes doing investigations that are needed to better understand and manage distressing complications

FIGURE 9.1 Summary of World Health Organization Attributes of Palliative Care. *Source:* This figure is based on: WHO, World Health Organization. (2004). WHO definition of palliative care. [On-line]. Available at: *http://www.who.int/cancer/palliative/definition/en/*

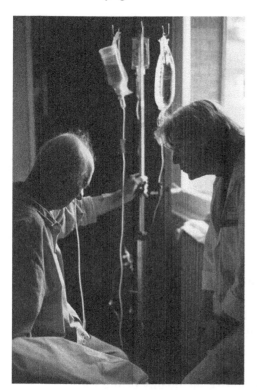

Today, palliative care physicians are attempting to do a much better job partnering with dying patients and their families to enhance their experiences while the gravely ill person is still alive   *BSIP SA/Alamy*

Palliative Medicine

Palliative medicine is an emerging specialty of medicine devoted to alleviating suffering, which grew out of the hospice and palliative care movements. A closer examination of Figure 9.1 will reveal that palliative treatments can sometimes go further than mere symptom management used to "positively influence the course of the illness."

SPREAD OF PROGRAMS

From the mid-1970s to today, the number of programs offering end-of-life care have grown tremendously. Hospices, palliative care programs, and physicians qualified in palliative medicine have proliferated. Information on the growth of programs is briefly summarized here. Keep in mind, however, that while there is growth in all facets of palliative care, recent studies affirm there are still large numbers of dying patients who don't get adequate relief for their symptoms (Field & Cassel, 1997; Singer & Bowman, 2002; Teno, Clarridge, Casey, & Welch, 2004).

In 2009, based on figures published by the NHPCO, there were more than 3,200 hospices in the United States that provided care to over a 1.5 million people (National Hospice and Palliative Care Organization, 2004c, 2010). In 2009, hospice programs cared for over 40 percent of all persons who died in the United States. Over 80 percent of people receiving hospice care are age 65 and older. Also, over 40 percent of everyone receiving hospice care in the United States were living in their own homes when they died; fewer than 20 percent were in nursing homes; and fewer than 9 percent were in residential facilities (National Hospice and Palliative Care Organization, 2010). In contrast, official government data indicate that in the general population about 35 percent of Americans over 65 years of age die in a hospital; 28 percent die in nursing homes; and 24 percent die at home (National Center for Health Statistics, 2011). Figure 9.2 graphically compares the place of death for hospice patients with those in the general population who died in 2002.

Today, we refer to hospital-based comfort care programs as **hospital-based palliative care programs**, or **HBPCP**. Most often, they take the form of inpatient units or specialized consultation services made available to the patient's primary health-care providers. Sometimes palliative care is provided on specialized units. When it is, the service may or may not be called an inpatient hospice. At other times, palliative care patients are mixed-in among the general hospital population. In this situation, they are cared for by palliative care teams that rotate in to look after them, or by their regular providers who

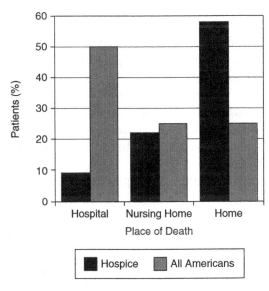

FIGURE 9.2 Comparison of Place of Death Hospice Patients and All Americans   *Source:* Based on NHPCO. (2004c). *HHPCO facts and figures*. Alexandria, VA: National Hospice and Palliative Care Organization.

make use of a palliative care consultation service. Sometimes terminally ill patients, especially those suffering from cancer, are served in hospitals by pain-management services, although it is well understood that pain is just one of many distressing symptoms associated with life-threatening illness.

Hospital-based programs are becoming more widespread (Billings & Pantilat, 2001; Center for the Advancement of Palliative Care, 2003; Center for Health Workforce Studies, 2002; Pan et al., 2001). Some estimates suggests there are between 350 to 800 programs operating in the United States (Pan et al., 2001; Center for the Advancement of Palliative Care, 2003). Most of these are hospital-based consultation services. A particularly exemplary program exists at Mt. Sinai Medical Center in New York. A self-report done by the American Hospital Association suggests that up to 20 percent of American hospitals now offer a palliative care service of some kind. A slightly larger proportion of teaching hospitals, 30 to 35 percent, have such programs (Billings & Pantilat, 2001).

In 2006 and after a long battle, the American Board of Medical Specialties (ABMS), the group charged with certifying medical specialties and subspecialties in the United States, finally granted recognition to the subspecialty of hospice and palliative medicine (American Academy of Hospice and Palliative Medicine, 2011). Opponents to recognition had contended that all physicians should be better trained in providing this kind of care. They suggested that palliative care should be the province of all medical doctors, as it once was, and not the domain of a select group of specialists (Center for Health Workforce Studies, 2002).

Convergence

With all the discussions of hospice, palliative care, and palliative medicine, some of the perceptions about the distinctions may be evaporating. The Canadian Hospice Palliative Care Association (CHPCA) suggests there may be a convergence when it comes to the meaning of the terms *hospice* and *palliative care.* Indeed, CHPCA had adopted the term *hospice palliative care* to describe the many facets of high-quality end-of-life care. "The term 'hospice palliative care' was coined to recognize the convergence of hospice and palliative care into one movement that has the same principles and norms of practice" (Ferris et al., 2002, p. v).

You might think of the unifying principles and norms of hospice palliative care as an expression of the paradigm shift that has been the topic of this section. *The Last Acts State of the Nation Report* contrasts key features of the old biomedical model and the holistic principles that are thought to underlie the wellness ideal—an ideal that seems so important to the hospice palliative care movement (Metzger & Kaplan, 2001). Please consult Table 9.1. I am suggesting that this ideal as well as the cultural norm of the good death are at the very heart of the present-day paradigm shift.

Figure 9.3 graphically portrays the evolution of the hospice palliative care movement in North America. I use *hospice palliative care,* the term minted by the

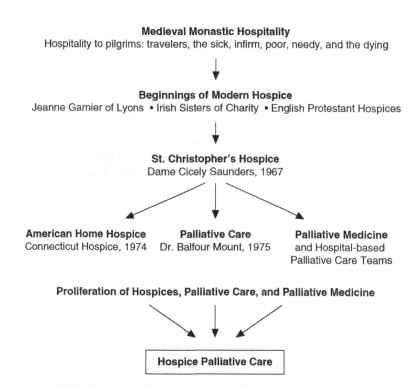

Medieval Monastic Hospitality
Hospitality to pilgrims: travelers, the sick, infirm, poor, needy, and the dying

Beginnings of Modern Hospice
Jeanne Garnier of Lyons • Irish Sisters of Charity • English Protestant Hospices

St. Christopher's Hospice
Dame Cicely Saunders, 1967

American Home Hospice
Connecticut Hospice, 1974

Palliative Care
Dr. Balfour Mount, 1975

Palliative Medicine
and Hospital-based
Palliative Care Teams

Proliferation of Hospices, Palliative Care, and Palliative Medicine

Hospice Palliative Care

FIGURE 9.3   Evolution of Hospice Palliative Care in North America

CHPCA, as the end-point of the diagram. I do so because the unifying concept embraces both the holistic philosophy and integrated approach that seems so characteristic of the movement today. It concludes our discussion of changing philosophies in end-of-life care.

The Hospice Team

In order to ensure the kind of coordinated care previously discussed, there is a general consensus in the field that good palliative care requires a team approach. A hallmark of hospice, the team concept has been adopted by each of the key professional associations (e.g., Canadian Hospice Palliative Care Association, 2004; International Association for Hospice and Palliative Care, 2004; National Hospice and Palliative Care Organization, 2004b) and is also required under Medicare and Medicaid rules (Moon & Boccuti, 2002; Tilly & Wiener, 2001). The team, whose members may visit on different days and times, typically includes such key professionals as physicians; nurses; social workers; counselors or chaplains; personal care aides; various other kinds of special providers (e.g., physical therapist, occupational therapist, speech therapist, or dietitian); and volunteers, who are counted as full-fledged members of the team (Beresford, 1993; Cummings, 1998; Sheehan & Forman, 1996).

The physician, who usually serves as the medical director, has an obviously important role in supervising the treatment of pain and other symptoms (Beresford, 1993; Cummings, 1998; Sheehan & Forman, 1996). Palliative treatment frequently involves the use of pain medication, but it can include a wide range of other methods including surgery, radiation, or even chemotherapy.

The nurse, often the lynchpin of the entire team, frequently functions as treatment team leader or coordinator. Nurses are also the team members most likely to have regular contact with patients and families, monitor symptoms, administer medications, and report changes in the patient's condition.

The social worker is often the person who helps the patient and family deal with the personal and social aspects of the advancing illness and impending death. The social worker routinely helps support the patient and family, coordinates with funding sources, locates community resources and makes referrals, and often provides personal and family counseling.

The chaplain or counselor typically supports the patient and family personally and spiritually by listening nonjudgmentally. Often, they are called on to help resolve old emotional injuries and feelings of guilt. They often assist patients in talking about their lives and helping them achieve a sense of meaning and purpose. Volunteers, some of whom were themselves helped by hospice, are there to support the patient and family in practical ways, such as relieving the primary caretaker so he or she can run errands or simply take a break. Sometimes the volunteers are there just "present" for the dying person and the family as they go through the experience.

PROVIDING END-OF-LIFE CARE

What Hospice and Palliative Care Actually Do

Simply put, end-of-life care is an approach to treating patients with far-advanced disease and a short life expectancy for whom the focus of care should be on relieving suffering and enhancing the quality of life. There are four key tasks involved in accomplishing this (International Association for Hospice and Palliative Care, 2004):

- Relieve pain and other physical symptoms.
- Maximize the quality of life while neither hastening nor postponing death.
- Provide for the patient's psychosocial and spiritual care.
- Support the family during the patient's illness and the bereavement process.

Most professionals now think of high-quality care as an approach where there is good communication between health-care providers and patients; the best possible medical, nursing, and allied care is available; a comprehensive plan is in place and a multidisciplinary team addresses all aspects of the patient's suffering; consistency and continuity of care exist across treatment settings (home, nursing home, or hospital); steps are taken to anticipate crisis situations and prevent them; caregivers are supported (especially by making respite, or breaks, available); and there is ongoing assessment of the challenges that face the patients and their families (International Association for Hospice and Palliative Care, 2004).

The Experience of Pain

Pain can be defined as the unpleasant sensory and emotional experiences associated with tissue damage (International Association for Hospice and Palliaive Care, 2004). It is always subjectively experienced, but there are a variety of ways to classify it. Differentiating various types of pain and understanding their causes sometimes helps guide what to do about it. One way to think about pain is to break it down into four broad categories: acute pain, chronic pain, incident pain, and breakthrough pain (International Association for Hospice and Palliative Care, 2004).

Acute pain is usually due to a clearly identifiable injury or illness, with a definite onset and predictable duration. It is accompanied by easily recognizable distress and clear signs of heightened sympathetic nervous system activity. **Chronic pain**, in contrast, is caused by the effects of a long-term illness process. It generally has a gradual or poorly identified onset, continues without relief, and may become progressively more severe with time. **Incident pain** occurs only under certain circumstances, such as when some body part is in a particular position. It is often best managed by such simple techniques as repositioning the person or body part to minimize the effects. **Breakthrough pain** is very common. It only occasionally erupts, or "breaks through," the otherwise effective treatment of chronic pain. It requires temporary additional measures to control it.

Untreated pain can be a threat to the well-being of terminally ill people. It hastens dying by wearing the person out, impacting appetite, and interfering with sleep (Bailey, 2000). Patients and family members are justifiably concerned about unbearable pain. It is always appropriate to be vigilant, although they should be reassured to know that severe pain can be treated effectively.

In 1986, the World Health Organization developed a three-step model to help guide the management of cancer pain (1990, 1996). Today, there is widespread acceptance of this simple model (EPEC Project, 1999 and 2003), shown in Figure 9.4.

Most professionals now understand that pain is always experienced subjectively and can never be measured objectively by outside observers. Because of the impact on the quality of life, a key goal of care is learning how to assess it. As briefly mentioned in Chapter 8, there is an emphasis on considering pain to be a fifth vital sign (Lynch,

STEP 3 - Severe Pain
Morphine
Hydromorphone
Methadone
Leorphanol
Fentanyl
Oxycodone
(*with or without "nonopioid analgesics"*)
(*with or without "adjuvants"*)

STEP 2 - Moderate Pain
Aspirin or Acetaminophen
Codeine
Hydrocodone
Oxycodone
Dihydrocodeine
Tramadol
(*with or without "adjuvants"*)

STEP 1 - Mild Pain
Aspirin
Acetaminophen
Nonsteroidal anti-inflammatory drugs (NSAIDs)
(*with or without "adjuvants"*)

FIGURE 9.4 The WHO 3-Step Ladder: A Guide to Using Medications to Control Cancer Pain

2001a, 2001b; Lanser & Gessell, 2001; Torma, 1999). Health-care professionals should routinely check on pain in addition to the other four vital signs: pulse, blood pressure, temperature, and respiration (National Pharmaceutical Council & Joint Commission on the Accreditation of Healthcare Organizations, 2001). It can be monitored by simply asking patients to rate their pain on a scale from 0 to 10 (International Association for Hospice and Palliative Care, 2004).

Concerns about Addiction

Patients and families are sometimes very concerned about using strong pain medications out of fear of addiction. Rarely is this concern necessary. While physical dependence on opioids is a normal physiological response to chronic use of opioids (International Association for Hospice and Palliative Care, 2004), the withdrawal is easily done in stages. Also, patients and families might be reassured to know that addiction requires more than physical dependence. It also involves a pathological pleasure-seeking pattern. Patients with severe pain who are treated with opioids for a life-threatening illness need not be concerned about this occurring.

Other Physical Symptoms and Their Treatment

In addition to pain, there are a number of other distressing symptoms associated with the last stages of illness. These fall into four general types (International Association for Hospice and Palliative Care, 2004):

- Breathing difficulties
- Gastrointestinal problems
- Weight loss and weakness
- Reduced consciousness and restlessness

Among the breathing problems associated with the dying process are dyspnoea, cough, and terminal respiratory congestion (International Association for Hospice and Palliative Care, 2004). **Dyspnoea** is experienced as severe shortness of breath (Ahmedzai, 1998). As anyone who has ever experienced difficult breathing can attest, anxiety quickly erupts. It is sometimes caused by an obstruction to the trachea or bronchia; the reduction in the ability of the lung tissue to process air and distribute oxygen to the body; circulatory problems (including heart); the loss of red blood cells; and anxiety.

Once the cause of the breathlessness is understood, the therapy is aimed at the source of the problem, whenever possible. Reassuring the patient as well as repositioning the person can also help, but there are a number of other techniques that can be used to improve the condition. These include administering oxygen, using opioids (sometimes infused into inhalers), as well as giving medications that dilate the bronchia, relax the patient, or reduce secretions.

Terminal respiratory congestion, often called the "death rattle," is the noisy, gurgling, respiration heard in some people when they are dying. It is caused by the accumulation of fluids on the trachea in patients who are unconscious or semiconscious, or who are too weak to spit (Ahmedzai, 1998; International Association for Hospice and Palliative Care, 2004). Placing the individual on her or his side, suctioning, and using medications to reduce secretions can help, although these measures are used more to comfort loved ones than the dying person.

Gastrointestinal symptoms associated with the end-stage of life include nausea, vomiting, bowel obstruction, and constipation (International Association for Hospice and Palliative Care, 2004). Nausea and vomiting can have many causes, including cancer and the side-effects of radiation or chemotherapy, as well as the use of certain pain medications (Mannix, 1999). Nausea and vomiting can be treated with diet, reducing unpleasant smells, using relaxation techniques, and administering an anti-vomiting medication. Bowel obstructions can be effectively treated with a variety of medical interventions (see Reinhold, 1993), surgery, and various medications.

Constipation can have many causes, including inactivity, diet, metabolic changes, obstructions, and various medications, particularly using opioids to control pain. In contrast, there is diarrhea. It is not as common as constipation in most types of cancer but it can occur among persons infected by HIV (Sykes, 1998). Often caused by infection, it can be either short lived or chronic and persistent. The recommended treatment varies depending on the cause but can include using agents that absorb intestinal fluids, or opioids. Weight loss and weakness among terminally ill people can result from diarrhea. It requires medical intervention.

Weight loss and weakness can have other causes as well. These include anorexia and cachexia (Bruera & Fainsinger, 1998; International Association for Hospice and Palliative Care, 2004). **Anorexia** is the reduced desire to eat. It often contributes to the problem. When this is the case, such simple remedies as providing dietary advice, preparing visually appealing meals, and including favorite foods in the diet can help. When weight loss and weakness among cancer patients doesn't get better with improved diet, it may signal the existence of a more troublesome condition called cancer **cachexia**—a kind of wasting associated with the cancer itself. It is characterized by abnormally low weight, weakness, and a general bodily decline that interferes with the quality of life (Bruera, 2001; Bruera & Fainsinger, 1998; Kotler, 2000; Martignoni, Kunze, & Friess, 2003; Tisdale, 2001). Medical experts don't understand the condition very well but believe it may be due to tumor metabolism and the person's body spending large amounts of energy trying to fight off infection and fever (International Association for Hospice and Palliative Care, 2004; Martignoni et al., 2003). It remains very hard to treat. Even feeding the person artificially doesn't generally help.

Impaired consciousness, delirium, and restlessness sometimes occur among terminally ill people (International Association for Hospice and Palliative Care, 2004). Delirium is a condition in which there is a global change in thinking and consciousness that is characterized by disorientation, fluctuating levels of consciousness, and impaired thinking (EPEC Project, 1999 and 2003). It can come on quite rapidly.

Depending on its origins (it can have multiple causes), it can sometimes be reversed (International Association for Hospice and Palliative Care, 2004). When the origins of the delirium are determined, the benefits and risks of trying to reverse it should be explored (EPEC Project, 1999 and 2003). When delirious dying persons are agitated, restless, moaning, and groaning, it's very likely they have **terminal delirium**, which is not reversible (EPEC Project, 1999 and 2003). In these cases, providers and caregivers may wish simply to make the dying person as comfortable as possible, continue speaking to him or her (many believe hearing is the last sense to go), reassure the person as much as possible, and perhaps reduce disquieting stimulation until death occurs.

Providing Psychological, Social, and Spiritual Care

Not all suffering is physical. Dame Cicely Saunders is credited with first using the term **total pain** in her effort to encourage physicians think about suffering as involving much more than just physical pain (Clark, 1999). To her, it includes the physical, yes, but it also embodies the psychological, social, and spiritual aspects of experience.

Because of the multidimensional nature of the dying experience, the team approach is integral to hospice palliative care. Treating pain and other symptoms certainly helps reduce suffering, but fear, anxiety, and depression in relation to loss—of control, dignity, independence, and the ability to direct the course of one's life—also affect the dying person psychologically. The level of psychological well-being (or distress) is interwoven with the ability to cope. This coping depends on a number of factors, including how well the person has learned to deal with other illnesses and stresses; experiences with the illnesses of others; losses; family stress; personality development; psychiatric and substance abuse; social supports; economic status; culture; and spirituality (International Association for Hospice and Palliative Care, 2004).

Many terminally ill patients suffer from depression, a bona fide psychiatric malady characterized by pervasive feelings of sadness; lack of energy; changes in appetite; the loss of interest in pleasure; feelings of helplessness, hopelessness, and worthlessness; and often a diminished sense of self-esteem (American Psychiatric Association, 2000). In contrast to popular belief, intense depression is not "normal" for anyone, even people with a terminal illness. It is a source of psychic pain and suffering that if left untreated can deprive the person of the energy needed to fight his or her illness. Personal psychotherapy, social support, as well as the use of medications, can often help.

As discussed in the introductory chapter, spirituality is an aspect of life that has to do with meaning and transcendence (Fitchett, 1993). It can be experienced as a connectedness to God, the infinite, one's fellow human beings, or one's true inner-self (Ley & Corless, 1988). Whereas most chaplains have their own religious affiliations and "spiritual paths," they are trained to be "present" for the patients' experiences, to support them in finding meaning in their experience and nurture their relationship with what the patient experiences as sacred. Peter Speck (1998) suggests there is good evidence to believe that the subjective experience of well-being is enhanced by the ability to engage in activities that give one's life a sense of meaning (Reed, 1986, 1987), and that a deeply personal experience of spirituality may enhance this (Watson, Morris, & Hood, 1988). The spiritual issues a person deals with when preparing to die are sometimes grouped into three types (International Association for Hospice and Palliative Care, 2004; Speck, 1998)—those connected with past, present and future experience.

Those linked to the past include dealing with feelings of guilt and shame; understanding one's relationships; reevaluating achievements; and coming to terms with past failures and unfulfilled aspirations. Concerns associated with the present include dealing with changes in one's health; reconciling oneself to current suffering; and learning how to accept rising dependency. Some future-oriented issues include struggling with a sense of hopelessness; anticipating the loss of loved ones; thinking about the dying process; and contemplating an afterlife or nonexistence (International Association for Hospice and Palliative Care, 2004; Speck, 1998).

WORLD WITH GOOD DEATH?

There are many groups today that are devoted to promoting excellence in palliative care. They envision a time when everyone who comes to the end of their life can expect to experience the kind of good death discussed so far in this chapter (e.g., American Geriatrics Society, 2002; Ferris et al., 2002; Connors et al., 1995; Field & Cassel, 1997; Jennings, Ryndes, D'Onofrio, & Bailey, 2003; Last Acts, 1997, 2003a, 2003b; Metzger & Kaplan, 2001). *Last Acts*, a national coalition of over 50 such groups, developed a set of principles it hopes will lead to high-end end-of-life care. It integrates these principles into five *Precepts of Palliative Care* (Last Acts, 2003a, 2003b).

In addition, there are several other groups committed to similar aims. Among them are the Milbank Memorial Fund (Cassel & Foley, 1999) and CHPCA (Ferris et al., 2002).

Advance Directives, Living Wills, Medical Powers of Attorney, and Do Not Resuscitate Orders

The sophisticated technology we have today has created choices we never had before. Medical personnel can resuscitate a person whose heart has stopped beating, keep the person breathing with a machine, and give him or her the needed nutrition with a feeding tube, even if the individual lacks consciousness or brain functioning. The person can physically survive this way. The question becomes, Would the person want to? In Chapter 13, we will discuss various forms of "brain death," human consciousness, and providing or not providing life support. If you end up in such a state, how could you communicate your wishes? An **advance directive** is a general term for two kids of legal documents: the *living will* and *medical power of attorney* (National Hospice and Palliative Care Organization, 2011).

A **living will** is a document in which the individual provides specific information about the course of treatment to be followed by health-care providers if he or she is at the end of life or is unable to communicate. It is the oldest form of advanced directive used in North America, first proposed by Illinois attorney Luis Kutner (1969). It is called a living will because it is created by the individual while he or she is still alive. It can be called various things, depending on the legal jurisdiction in which the person lives, including "advance directive," "health-care declaration," and "medical directive" (National Hospice and Palliative Care Organization, 2011).

There is a specialized living will called **Five Wishes**, valid in all but eight U.S. states. It addresses an individual's personal, emotional, and spiritual needs as well as her or his medical wishes. The five wishes specify: (1) who will be empowered to make medical decisions when the person can't, (2) what medical treatment the person wants and doesn't want, (3) how comfortable the person wants to be, (4) how the person wants to be treated, and (5) what the person wants their loved ones to know (Aging with Dignity, 2011).

A **medical power of attorney**, sometimes called health-care power of attorney, health-care proxy, or durable power of attorney for health care, is a document that allows you to appoint someone to make health-care decisions for you, should you be unable to do so for yourself (National Hospice and Palliative Care Organization, 2011). The reason it is sometimes called *durable power of attorney for health care* is because general powers of attorney generally cease to be legally binding when the person is no longer competent to make decisions for herself or himself. Language can be added to make a document "durable" (or effective) even when a person becomes incompetent. There is a link for a free PDF version of an advance directive and durable power of attorney for health care in the "Links" section at the end of this chapter.

A **do not resuscitate order**, or **DNR**, is a written document directing health-care providers not to attempt cardiopulmonary resuscitation (CPR) if a patient stops breathing or if her or his heart stops beating (National Hospice and Palliative Care Organization, 2011). Although the document is written at the request of the patient or the family, the order must generally be signed by a physician in order for it to become valid. These orders may be written for both a person in a health-care facility or at home, such as someone who is in home hospice care. A DNR allows a person to make her or his wishes about end-of-life care known ahead of time in case the person is unable to participate in making these decisions at a future time.

Some Present-Day Realities

As discussed elsewhere in this text, about two-thirds of all Americans die in a hospital or nursing home (National Center for Health Statistics, 2011). As you may have discerned from the previous discussion, a small proportion of those who die in health-care facilities receive specialized end-of-life care, as are provided by hospital-based palliative care programs. While we may hope these patters will change, it is still the exception for hospital and nursing home patients to receive specialized end-of-life care (Billings & Pantilat, 2001; Center for Health Workforce Studies, 2002; National Hospice and Palliative Care Organization, 2004c; Pan et al., 2001).

One of the implications is that only a few patients who die do so with the kind of palliative care that meets their physical, social, psychological, and spiritual needs. Often patients who die in hospitals or nursing homes don't get the kind of help and support they need. This came to light with the publication of the highly respected SUPPORT study, the earliest modern study to explore the experience of the dying in North America (Connors et al., 1995). The records of over 4,300 patients with life-threatening illnesses were reviewed in this study. In addition, both patients and loved ones were interviewed. The results showed that communication between providers and patients (and their loved ones) was generally rated as being poor; aggressive treatment was routine; providers weren't aware of the resuscitation preferences of patients in nearly half the cases; over one-third of patients who died spent at least 10 days in an intensive care unit; and, among patients who were conscious when they died, over half experienced moderate to severe pain.

A more recent study suggests that the problems with hospital-based care continue (Teno, Clarridge, Casey, & Welch, 2004). Fewer than half of the families whose loved ones spent their last days in health-care facilities were satisfied with the care the patient received. In contrast, about 75 percent of family members whose loved ones received hospice care reported that their loved ones got "excellent" care. The chief complaints included inadequate symptom relief, limited or poor communication with their physicians about medical decision making, too little emotional support, and they were not treated with the dignity warranted by the seriousness of their situations.

In addition to the location of death, the kind of care a dying person gets also depends on the nature of the person's illness and the prognosis, or anticipated outcome. Heart disease, cancer, and stroke continue to be the three leading causes of death in the United States (Arias, Anderson, Hsiang-Ching, Murphy, & Kochanek, 2003). In Canada, they are cancer, heart disease, and stroke (Statistics Canada, 2002).

As discussed in the previous chapter, estimating prognosis is an uncertain business at best. Whereas it is easier to estimate the prognosis in cancer cases, with congestive heart failure, the precise course of the illness is notoriously hard to predict. Heart failure is the leading cause of death in the United States, and a significant cause of death in Canada, but a far lower percentage of heart patients die with hospice or palliative care than those with cancer. Over half of the hospice patients who died in the United States were cancer patients; about 11 percent were suffering from heart disease (National Hospice and Palliative Care Organization, 2004c). Owing to the nature of the malady, relatively few stroke victims received hospice.

Eligibility, Access, and Referral

Getting into hospice, like access to all health care, depends on meeting eligibility requirements and having funding. The United States has no universal health-care coverage and no universal coverage for end-of-life care apart from the Medicare and

Medicaid programs. **Medicare** is a federally funded program that covers people over age 65 and those with disabilities (Moon & Boccuti, 2002). Hospice became a Medicare benefit in 1982, in large part as a result of advocacy efforts and strong public support for better end-of-life care for the elderly. Estimates are that over 70 percent of hospice funding in the United States is now provided by Medicare (National Association for Home Care and Hospice, 2002).

Medicaid, which is a joint federal–state program, covers low-income people who have few assets (Tilly & Wiener, 2001). For people with assets and good incomes to qualify, they must first "spend down," or use up, their own resources to pay for care before becoming eligible. The Medicaid program is administered by the states, which use federal guidelines to determine eligibility.

Both Medicare and Medicaid require that persons be diagnosed as having six months to live or less and be willing to forego all medical care aimed at curing their illness (Moon & Boccuti, 2002; Tilly & Wiener, 2001). In addition to Medicare and Medicaid, most private insurance programs cover hospice. For a visual representation of hospice funding sources in the United States, see Figure 9.5.

In Canada, hospice palliative care is a benefit provided in a variety of settings: hospital-based palliative care units, stand-alone facilities, acute care facilities, continuing care beds, and at home. Services are sometimes coordinated by regional teams who attempt to find a fit between patient need and available resources (e.g., Edmonton Regional Palliative Care Program). Canada has universal health coverage for its citizens, but waiting lists are sometimes a problem and hospice palliative care isn't always available. As in the United States, Canada is struggling with how to make access to hospice palliative care more available (Canadian Hospice Palliative Care Association, 2004). In 2002, the Kirby Report, an official government review of the Canadian health-care system, lamented that "palliative care services in Canada are often fragmented and frequently nonexistent" (Senate of Canada, Standing Committee on Social Affairs, Science & Technology, 2002, *6*, 9.l).

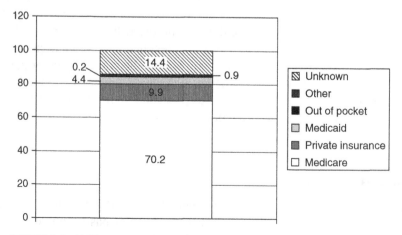

FIGURE 9.5 U.S. Hospice Funding Sources.

FALLING THROUGH THE CRACKS

Because of the humanitarian philosophy, patient and family focus, team approach, and insistence on providing comprehensive care, hospice palliative care has been called the "gold standard" when it comes to end-of-life care. There are gaps, however, in both the American and Canadian systems. Many people fall through these cracks. In this section we briefly explore some of those fissures. We begin with a story about John and Sarah.

Although the biomedical model can do a lot in terms of preventing an untimely death, the reality remains that we human beings are mortal. The best efforts of the system cannot overcome this truth. The complexity of the system and division of labor created a condition where the key actors weren't properly communicating with one another. No one told John and Sarah that he was not expected to live more than six months. They were victims of a compartmentalized and impersonal system.

In some ways, however, John and Sarah were among the "lucky" ones. They were referred to hospice. He died at home with the benefit of good symptom management. Most of his medical expenses were covered by insurance—a benefit of his job. Others aren't so lucky. Please see the vignette below, titled I didn't Even Know What Hospice Was.

Medicare

As you may recall, Medicare is the largest funder of hospice care in the United States. Hospice became a Medicare benefit in 1983 (Moon & Boccuti, 2002). Under this benefit, persons diagnosed as having six or fewer months to live can elect to

---

I Didn't Even Know What Hospice Was

John was a 45-year-old man when he began to notice blood in his stool. Eventually diagnosed with colon cancer, John underwent extensive radiation treatment and chemotherapy. In and out of the emergency room for various complications, John was eventually given a referral to hospice. "I didn't even know what hospice was," Sarah, John's wife, said, "until the day the hospice intake worker came out to explain the program." It was not until the worker explained that hospice was for people with six or fewer months to live that she found out John was "terminal."

By the time John and Sarah were referred to hospice, he had undergone long bouts of illness caused by his cancer as well as the side-effects of chemotherapy and radiation. In an effort to eradicate the cancer, his intestines were inadvertently burned by the radiation. After several medical emergencies and many visits to the emergency room, he would eventually die at home with support from a local hospice program. John's infected bowels, which would no longer function properly, began forming abnormal little tunnels, called fistula—his body's attempt to provide for drainage. One of these fistula eventually found its way from John's intestines to his kidney. When it did, his kidney could no longer function and he died. Heavily sedated for pain, John spent the last days of his life at home, in and out of consciousness.

receive hospice under Medicare Part A (the part that covers hospitalization) if they agree to give up on efforts to cure their illness. In 1995, Pam Miller and Paula Mike, of the School of Social Work at Portland State University, did a 10-year follow-up on the program (Miller & Mike, 1995). They identified four problem areas with Medicare:

1. *Home care requirement:* Medicare hospice benefit requires that almost all care be provided at home. A large number of elderly people don't have a person who can be with them 24 hours a day, and 18 percent of men and 41 percent of women live alone. The cost of long-term care in a skilled nursing facility or around-the-clock care at home aren't covered by Medicare.
2. *Resources of small communities:* Medicare rules require programs to use a professional team. It is hard for small, rural, communities to afford this.
3. *Estimating prognosis:* Medicare rules require the patient to be certified to have six or fewer months to live. Estimating how much time a terminally ill person has left is difficult, with the possible exception of patients with certain forms of cancer. As a result, most people who get hospice will be suffering from terminal cases of cancer; others will be left out.
4. *Funding is capitated:* This means that programs get a daily fixed rate (see Table 9.2). That doesn't offer much incentive to take on the tough cases, provide higher levels of care, or use helpful but expensive palliative procedures (Miller & Mike, 1995; Moon & Boccuti, 2002).

Medicaid

Medicaid uses Medicare's hospice requirements, but unlike Medicare, which covers all people *over* 65 years of age, Medicaid covers people of *any age* who have low incomes and few assets, including those who have become impoverished by the high cost of health care. Also unlike Medicare, Medicaid does pay for long-term nursing home stays and in-home services for those still able to live at home. Although expanded eligibility and nursing home coverage are boons to people who need them, there are other concerns about the end-of-life benefits available through Medicaid. In order to expand the limited research available on end-of-life care for

TABLE 9.2   Capitated Medicare Hospice Reimbursement by Level of Care

Level of Care	Comments	Daily Rate
Routine home care	Provided by the hospice team at home	$110
Continuous home care	Round-the-clock care provided at home	$644
Inpatient respite care	Maximum of five days of care at this level	$114
General inpatient care	Limited to 20% of time in hospice program	$491

Source: This table is based on Miller & Mike, 1995; Moon, M. & Boccuti, C., 2002.

Medicaid beneficiaries, Tilly and Wiener (2001) of the nonpartisan Urban Institute, interviewed 23 national experts in a qualitative study of Medicaid. Their findings suggest four problem areas with Medicaid:

1. *Estimating prognosis:* The requirement that beneficiaries must have a prognosis of six or fewer months to live creates the same kind of barriers as are created by Medicare rules.
2. *Pressure to get pain relief:* Like Medicare patients, Medicaid patients must agree to forego efforts to cure their illness in order to qualify for hospice. Nursing home patients often have had difficulty getting adequate pain relief. Some will choose hospice, even if they might otherwise want to continue efforts at a cure.
3. *Conflicting standards of care:* The rules governing nursing home care, where many Medicaid patients live, and those controlling hospice care aren't consistent. Nursing homes that might otherwise want to use hospice to help care for their terminally ill patients may be reluctant to do so out of fear of going out of compliance with these regulations.
4. *Reduced payment:* When nursing home residents get hospice, the Medicaid payment is switched from going directly to the nursing home to going to the hospice. The hospice receives only 95 percent of the nursing home rate, and must then pay the nursing home directly. The hospice must offer the nursing home the reduced rate, which few are willing to accept.

The eligibility realities of Medicare and Medicaid are such that people under age 65 aren't eligible for Medicare and those with income or assets but without insurance, are required to "spend down" their assets before they can qualify. They must, in effect, become medically indigent. Because of the high cost of care, the *spend-down* process typically unfolds rapidly. Since both marital partners hold their assets in common— savings, securities, house, and vehicles—and since these assets must be liquidated to pay for care, when death comes, the surviving spouse is often left with large burial expenses but few means with which to pay them.

ON THE HORIZON

The dream of hospice is that everyone will be able to have a good death and do so without bankrupting their heirs. In Chapter 2, we discussed the efforts of a growing band of people who have become concerned about the excessive use of technology, medicalization, and depersonalization in the way we care for dying people (Benoliel & Degner, 1995; Callahan, 2000; Cassell, 1993; Kastenbaum, 1993; Kearl, 1996). It is this concern, together with the efforts of a corps of pioneers and present-day leaders, that are responsible for the more holistic treatment climate that exists today. Although problems persist, we now have the resources, know-how, and technology to resolve them—if, that is, we also have the will.

Chapter Summary

This chapter began by recalling lessons learned by William Bartholome, a physician who wrote about his own experience as a terminally ill person. He used the term *intensive caring* to contrast the kind of high-quality care he thought was desirable at the end of life with *intensive care*, a term from modern medicine that conjures up images of intensive care units and the sort of high-tech approach that strives to prolong life at all costs.

Discussion then turned to changing philosophies of care—a movement of consciousness away from putting one's total faith in the biologically based biomedical model toward accepting a wellness paradigm. The chapter traced the evolution of this caring ideal—now embodied in the hospice concept—from its ancient religious roots, through medieval monastic expressions, to Dame Cicely Saunders and the founding of St. Christopher's Hospice, which most sources agree marks the beginning of the present-day dying-well movement, which proliferated in home-based hospice programs, hospital-based palliative care units, and the new specialty of palliative medicine.

We also discussed some of the present-day realities in end-of-life care. People still fall through the gaps, sometimes because of problems in communicating, sometimes because of barriers in the system itself. Among the barriers to accessing U.S. programs, we observed a lack of universal health insurance and eligibility restrictions in accessing public health insurance.

Finally, we looked to a horizon where everyone can have a *good death* without bankrupting those left behind. Reflecting on the existing problems surveyed in Chapter 2, we might take solace in knowing that there is a band of concerned people out there who want to humanize our system. The concerns of those early hospice pioneers gave rise to the dying-well movement we have today. What remains to be done is nothing short of fulfilling the promise.

Key Terms

acute pain *192*
advance directive *197*
anorexia *195*
breakthrough pain *192*
cachexia *195*
chronic pain *192*
do not resuscitate order
   (DNR) *198*
dyspnoea *194*

Five Wishes *198*
good death *184*
hospital-based palliative care
   program (HBPCP) *188*
hospice palliative care *182*
hospice *182*
incident pain *192*
living will *198*
Medicaid *200*

medical power of attorney *198*
Medicare *200*
palliative care *182*
palliative medicine *188*
suffering *184*
terminal delirium *196*
terminal respiratory
   congestion *194*
total pain *196*

Suggested Activities

1. Write about whatever experiences you may have had with a dying person. As you reflect, consider the things that made the experience of dying difficult or that made a difference to the dying person. What lessons can you find in your experience?

2. Consider the ways in which religion, science, and medicine have influenced your life. What tensions between these two systems do you experience because of their differing ways of understanding the world, if any?

3. Reflect on whatever changes in thinking you've experienced as you've gone through life. Why did your thinking change? How was life different? What do you think of paradigm shifts?

4. Browse the Internet. Using your favorite search engine, type in such terms as *hospice, palliative care,* and *palliative medicine.* Explore the websites you find. Then explore links you find at those sites to other sites. What do you suppose the existence of all these resources say about our society's interest in end-of-life care?

5. Write a one-page essay about some experience you had with pain. How did it change life for you? How did you cope? Also consider other physical discomforts you've experienced. How have they affected you at various times?

6. Reflect on your experiences with bureaucracies—for example, schools, government, hospitals, the military, and so forth. What kinds of experience did you have? How would you describe these systems? What are the advantages and disadvantages of having them?

7. Interview a person with a serious illness or who is elderly. Spend an hour or so listening to the person tell her or his story without offering your own opinions, reflections, or conclusions. Just listen. You may want to tape record it, particularly if this is a person you care about. Wait a day. Listen to the tape if you recorded your interview. Then write a short summary of what you learned about the person.

8. Chart a "life line." Make a list of all the significant events in your life. On a piece of paper draw a horizontal line. On the line plot these events from beginning to present. You may also want to anticipate the end of your life. What would you like to accomplish between now and then?

9. Make a collage. Using copies of old photos or pictures from magazines, piece together a collage that portrays the important experiences of your life. What was it like as you arranged the pictures in a collage?

10. Put together a family genogram. Chart whatever you know of your family. Use squares to depict males and circles to depict females. Draw lines to show connections such as marriages and children. To indicate death, use an X. Breaks in lines can show breaks in relationships. Strong connections can be depicted with bold, or double, lines; weak ones can be represented with dotted lines. Reflecting on the genogram, what does it say to you about your past, present, or future?

Suggested Reading

- Byock, I. (1997). *Dying well: Peace and possibilities at the end of life.* New York: Riverhead Books.
  In this touching book, Dr. Ira Byock shares the experiences that led him to become one of today's leading palliative care practitioners. He infuses the book (which is really about learning to live while dying) with the wisdom that can come from only a caring practice. Included in this edited volume are chapters written by Byock as well as people with special sensitivities to such topics as finding dignity in disease, accepting the gift of dependence, and letting go and growing on.

- Lynn, J., & Harrold, J. (1999). *Handbook for mortals: Guidance for people facing serious illness.* New York & Toronto: Oxford University Press.
  This thoughtful book was written by doctors Joanne Lynn, Director of the Center to Improve Care of the Dying, and Joan Harrold, the Medical Director of the Hospice of Lancaster County, PA. As the *Journal of the American Medical Association* puts it, the book warmly addresses all who want to approach their final years with more awareness and make the end of life a time of growth, comfort, and reflection.

- Lynn, J., Schuster, J. L., & Kabcenell, A. (2000). *Improving care for the end of life: A source book for health care managers and clinicians.* New York & Toronto: Oxford University Press.
  This practical book will help professionals improve the quality of life for the dying. It includes text on improving care and care-systems, promoting reform, and managing specific diseases. It also summarizes key instruments for assessing quality standards, pain, spirituality, and grief. In addition, the book contains important resources, such as *Five Wishes, Elements of Care Checklist, Precepts of Palliative Care,* and *Interdisciplinary Care Competencies.*

Links and Internet Resources

- **Palliative Care Service–Mt. Sinai Medical Center**
  *www.mountsinai.org/patient-care/service-areas/
  palliative-care*
  Doctors, nurses, social workers, and massage therapists help patients with advanced illnesses and their
  families make informed decisions about their health
  care when curative measures are no longer effective.
  The goals are to relieve suffering and attain optimum
  quality of life. The service works with the primary
  doctor, providing in-depth consultation with patients;
  pain management; 24-hour coverage; visiting doctor;
  social services; and social, spiritual, and bereavement
  support.

- **American Academy of Hospice and Palliative
  Medicine**
  www.aahpm.org
  The AAHPM is the only organization of physicians and
  other medical professionals in the United States that is
  dedicated to excellence in palliative medicine. It is committed to the proposition that the proper role of the physician is to help the sick, even when cure is not possible,
  and it recognizes that death is a natural and inevitable
  part of life. The organization strives to provide physicians with educational opportunities, peer support and
  exchanges, support for research; promote careers in palliative medicine; develop standards of practice, accredit
  trainings, and publish a journal.

- **Americans for Better Care of the Dying—ABCD**
  www.abcd-caring.org/
  The stated goals of Americans for Better Care of the
  Dying (ABCD) is to improve end-of-life care. The site
  includes links to a variety end-of-life care topics. It also
  contains a "reading room," which includes an online
  version of *Handbook for Mortals: Guidance for People
  Facing Serious Illness.*

- **The Center to Advance Palliative Care (CAPC)**
  www.capc.org/
  This organization is dedicated to increasing the availability of quality palliative care services in hospitals
  and other health-care settings for people with life-
  threatening illnesses, their families, and their caregivers. It is a national initiative supported by the Robert
  Wood Johnson Foundation, with direction and technical assistance provided by the Mount Sinai School of
  Medicine.

- **DyingWell.org**
  www.dyingwell.org/
  This is a highly valuable site with first-rate resources
  for people facing life-limiting illness, their families,
  and their professional caregivers. This site is sponsored
  by author Dr. Ira Byock, a preeminent palliative care
  physician and advocate for improved end-of-life care.

- **Growth House**
  www.growthhouse.org/
  This serves as your international gateway to resources
  on life-threatening illness and end-of-life care. The primary mission of Growth House is to improve the quality
  of compassionate care for people who are dying through
  public education and global professional collaboration.

- **Last Acts**
  www.rwjf.org/pr/product.jsp?id=20938
  This original site closed in 2005, but a number of
  resources developed by the project on end-of-life care,
  pain management, and making life better for individuals facing death and their families are maintained on a
  "mirror site."

- **National Hospice and Palliative Care Organization**
  www.nhpco.org
  This website serves as a clearinghouse for general
  information on hospice and palliative care, particularly
  in the United States. The site contains a number of links
  and resources, including questions and answers, guidelines on selecting a provider, as well as an overview of
  the Medicare hospice benefit.

- **Canadian Hospice Palliative Care Association**
  www.chpca.net/
  The Canadian Hospice Palliative Care Association
  (CHPCA) is a national association providing leadership in hospice palliative care in Canada. Materials
  are provided in English and French. A copy of the
  Model to Guide Hospice Palliative Care is available as a free download from the resource section of
  the site.

- **Free Living Wills**
  www.doyourownwill.com/living-will/states.html
  This website provides a listing of state-specific *living
  will* forms in Word (.doc) for mat. Once opened, you can
  then save and edit on your computer. Once saved, you
  may edit and fill in the forms with your word-processing
  software.

- **Aging with Dignity**
  www.agingwithdignity.org/five-wishes.php
  The Aging with Dignity organization provides a way to purchase the Five Wishes document online for a fee of $5. It has also created an online version that allows those interested in using *Five Wishes* to complete the form online and then print it out.
- **Free Advance Directive & Durable Power of Attorney for Health Care**
  www.practicalbioethics.org/FileUploads/ DPOA.121406.pdf
  The Center for Practical Bioethics provides free *advance directives* and *durable power of attorney for*

health care forms in PDF format (valid in most jurisdictions) on their website. Simply print the form, fill it in, sign it in front of witnesses or a notary public, and keep it in a handy place. *Note:* There are many other so-called free forms available that a person can fill out online and then print. However, some of them require credit card information and a "free trial membership" in their service, which is renewed automatically unless you take the trouble to cancel before the end of the trial period.

Review Guide

1. Discuss the significance of the paradigm shift between the modern, scientifically based biomedical model of care and the wellness paradigm.
2. Explain the tensions that seem to exist between the cultural concept of the *good death* and the way a terminally ill person dies when aggressively treated with the best of modern technology and sophisticated medications.
3. Identify three reasons for the shift from the biomedical model to a wellness paradigm.
4. Outline the key people, events, places, and ideologies in the history of the modern hospice movement, discussing the role of each.
5. Analyze how the hospice ideal found different expressions in Canada, England, and the United States (i.e., as free-standing facilities, home-care programs, and hospital-based services).
6. Compare and contrast the concepts *hospice* and *palliative care*.
7. Identify the key components of contemporary hospice and explain the basic principles that guide this model of care.
8. Describe the proliferation of end-of-life programs, taking note of whatever holes still exist in the availability of services.
9. Discuss the convergence of hospice and palliative care conceptions into hospice palliative care.
10. Summarize the precepts of palliative care and discuss how these might, or might not, work in concert to improve the quality of end-of-life care.
11. Identify the most common places for death to occur. Discuss how location can influence the experience of dying.
12. Know the eligibility requirements, access points, and referral process for getting into end-of-life care. Be able to map out the process.
13. Identify four key tasks involved in providing high-quality end-of-life care.
14. Identify the various hospice team members, discussing the role of each.
15. Define pain.
16. Identify and differentiate the four broad categories of pain.
17. Identify and describe three types of pain that can be distinguished on the basis of their neurological causes.
18. Summarize how different types of pain can be managed.
19. Discuss pain as a fifth vital sign.
20. Reproduce the WHO three-step model guiding the medicinal management of pain.
21. Explain why it is unlikely for pain patients to become addicted, even when given large doses of opioid medications.
22. Identify each of the four major categories of physical symptoms associated with dying, besides pain. List the particular maladies within each category. Discuss how they are treated.
23. Summarize ways in which the psychological, social, and spiritual needs of the dying are addressed by the hospice palliative care approach.
24. Identify the various gaps in coverage for terminally ill persons.

Bereavement, Grief, and Mourning

Petair/Fotolia

Part IV has two chapters that take on the issue of what happens to those who are left behind when someone they love dies. Chapter 10 explores "normal" bereavement, grief, and mourning. In it, we will look at the "grief work" model first developed by Sigmund Freud, Elizabeth Kübler-Ross's famous stage-based model, Bowlby's attachment theory, and some pioneering work by Colin Murray Parkes, who was the first contemporary bereavement expert to distinguish between ordinary and "complicated" forms of grief. After reviewing the established grief-work models, we will look into the "new science of bereavement research" that challenges the old assumptions. We will also examine new research about what happens when we experience loss. For example, we will find out that most people get through this painful experience quite well. Then we explore some cross-cultural examples, and what it means to enter into the story of the person who has died.

In Chapter 11, we will look at what happens when grief goes awry—the topic of complicated grief in its various forms. We will also review what we know about grief that can erupt in response to traumatic death. Two types of mental conditions associated with this: postraumatic stress disorder and dissociative disorders. In this context, we also look at evidence supporting specific approaches to their treatment. In addition we will learn about a new diagnosis being proposed for a forthcoming edition of the American Psychiatric Association's *Diagnostic and Statistical Manual*, tentatively called "bereavement-related disorder."

10

Life after Loss
Bereavement, Grief, and Mourning

- ■ **Core Concepts**
- ■ **Grief Work**
- ■ **Having One's Child Die**
- ■ **Shifting Paradigms**

- ■ **New Knowledge**
- ■ **Mourning**
- ■ **Telling the Tale**

When a loved one dies, those left behind may experience a roller-coaster of sometimes confusing, often powerful, twisting, turning thoughts and feelings: shock, feelings of being ripped apart, profound sadness, confusion, guilt, loneliness, and sometimes even relief and hope. These, of course, are all just words. The experiences that go with the words, however, are profoundly personal. They vary from person to person and from situation to situation. What they have in common is that they are all linked to encounters with loss.

In this chapter, we will endeavor to make sense out of the often powerful, usually inimitable, experiences of the people left behind. The text begins with a discussion of three essential concepts: bereavement, grief, and mourning. We will then review several key classical theories that have been used to explain grief, including the concept of "grief work." We will also look at some problems associated with the classical models. Also we will explore revelations from "the new science of bereavement" and briefly look at mourning from a cross-cultural perspective. Finally, we will discuss "telling the tale"—what people seem to do naturally to keep the memories of their loved ones alive.

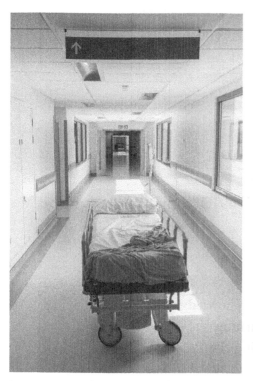

Bereavement is the experience of a severe loss, usually from death. *spotmatikphoto/Fotolia*

CORE CONCEPTS

Although the terms *bereavement, grief,* and *mourning* are sometimes used almost interchangeably, the terms actually signify quite different things. The word **bereavement** has old English roots connoting the idea of being despoiled or left destitute (Onions, Friedrichsen, & Burchfield, 1966). Today, the term is used to indicate the objective fact, or reality, of a loss sufficiently severe to cause significant disruption in the lives of the bereaved, usually involving the death of a family member or a close personal friend. Corr, Nabe, and Corr (2003) suggest that for bereavement to occur, three elements must be present:

1. A relationship with a valued person or thing
2. The loss of that relationship
3. A survivor who is now bereft of it

Bereavement is not only a personal experience but it is also a social one. Kastenbaum (2001), author and noted thanatologist, reminds us that depending on the nature of the relationship, the social status of the bereaved also changes, since the survivor is left as an orphan, widow, or widower.

In the field of death studies, it's commonly understood that **grief** is the reaction to bereavement (Corr, Nabe, & Corr, 2008; DeSpelder & Strickland, 2008; Kastenbaum, 2008). Although there are many variations, and no one has exactly the same experience, grief is often associated with physical sensations, strong emotions, changes in thinking, behavioral reactions, altered social relations, and spiritual or existential struggles. For a brief overview of adverse consequences, see Figure 10.1.

Grief is also commonly associated with a cluster of distressing reactions that often occur in waves (Lindemann, 1944; Lindemann & Greer, 1972). Some of these unpleasant reactions mirror the signs and symptoms of clinical depression (American Psychiatric Association, 2000), but even acute, or intense, grief is not usually seen as pathological but rather as a normal reaction to a very troubling experience. Complicated grief—the form of grief that lasts longer than normal or that is more destructive—is usually regarded as unhealthy and worthy of professional intervention (see Chapter 11; Ginzburg, Geron, & Solomon, 2002; Parkes, 1998a).

Although the terms *mourning* and *grief* are often used in similar ways, **mourning** doesn't so much refer to the reactions or experiences that come as a result of loss; rather, it refers to a *process* that survivors go though as they attempt to cope with loss (Corr, Nabe, & Corr, 2003; DeSpelder & Strickland, 2005). This, however, doesn't tell the whole story. As with grief, mourning has an important social dimension, with

Physical	Loss of energy, muscle weakness, loss of coordination, shortness of breath, tightness in the chest, lump in the throat
Behavioral	Crying, disturbance in sleep, appetite, loss of interest in usually pleasant activities, avoiding reminders of the deceased, excessively returning to places of shared memories, clinging to objects that remind of the deceased person, dreams
Social	Social isolation or withdrawal, irritability, difficulty performing usual social roles
Emotional	Shock, sadness, anger, relief, guilt, anxiety, numbness
Cognitive/Thinking	Confusion, disbelief, difficulties concentrating, disorganization, preoccupation, paranormal or "hallucinatory" experiences of the deceased
Existential/Spiritual	Anger toward God, need to find meaning in the experience of grief, new questioning of one's values, views, and priorities

FIGURE 10.1 Manifestations of Grief   *Source:* This figure is based on Robinson & Fleming, 1989, 1992; Worden, 2002.

religious, spiritual, cultural, and practical implications. So, you may also want to think of mourning as the culturally patterned process through which bereaved people deal with their grief (Kastenbaum, 2001). How people mourn in Papua, New Guinea (Brison, 1995) is different from how it's done among the Hmong of Indochina (Adler, 1995), or in Japan (Yamamoto, Okonogi, Iwasaki, & Yoshimura, 1969).

GRIEF WORK

If you are like many people living in North America today, when you consider coping with a significant loss you might very well think in terms "working through" your grief. As a creature of your culture this is quite understandable. If observers and critics of modernism can claim we live in a medicalized society (see Chapter 2), they might just as well say we live in a highly "psychologized" one. There is probably no one who can claim more credit for our psychological mindset than Sigmund Freud. The very concept of **grief work**, which has been at the heart of how we approach the mental-health care of grief-stricken people, traces its origins to Freudian ideas and the psychoanalytic model (Freud, 1917/1959a).

Grief is the emotional reaction we have when we experience a severe loss. *iStock © Deborah Cheramie*

Freudian Perspective

In classical Freudian psychoanalysis the patient must learn to uncover, confront, and work through emotionally threatening material from the unconscious (Freud, 1917/1959b). This is especially so in Freud's view of successful grief work. At its core, this involves learning to confront and deal with one's losses. In his classic paper on the subject, Freud suggests that there are actually six interlocking principles involved in this process (Freud, 1917/1959b). For a summary, refer to Figure 10.2.

According to Freud, grief *work*, emphasis on work, involves getting past one's own resistance, facing the realities of loss through a series of confrontations, ultimately freeing oneself from the strong emotional ties to the lost person, and opening oneself to new life and new experiences (Freud, 1917/1959b).

Stages of Grief

In Chapter 8, we briefly looked at Elisabeth Kübler-Ross's stages (Kübler-Ross, 1969). There is good reason why it was addressed there. While Kübler-Ross later *applied* her stage-based model to *grief*, it was not initially intended as a way of understanding grief. Rather, it was developed as a way to understand the reactions of people who had been informed by their physicians that they were going to die. According to her stage-based model, people respond to the bad news in a sequence of stages. As discussed in Chapter 8, the process as described by Kübler-Ross begins with denial and isolation, followed by the experiences of anger, bargaining, depression, and finally acceptance.

Broken Bonds

Freud and Kübler-Ross focused on the internal struggle. In contrast, John Bowlby, a British psychiatrist, put more emphasis on the *inter*personal dimension of grief, what some refer to as the **broken bonds** theory (Bowlby, 1969, 1973, 1980). While he was quite willing to use and build on Freud's theoretical foundations, he was also a creative thinker interested in real-life experience (Ainsworth, 1992), including grief. He

1. The experience of grief is adaptive. It is more than the expression of feeling; it is an experience one must work through.
2. Grief work takes time and is arduous. Neither the individual nor the society should expect the bereaved person to be fully functioning after only a short time.
3. The purpose of grief work is to confront the realities of death and free oneself from the strong emotional ties that binds himself or herself to the lost object (person).
4. Grief work unfolds through a series of confrontations with the reality of loss.
5. The process also involves getting past one's own resistance, which involves the natural struggle to hang on to the attachment with the lost object (person).
6. Failing to complete grief work is likely to result in continued suffering and dysfunction.

FIGURE 10.2   Freud's Principles of Grief Work   *Source:* Adapted from Freud, S. (1917/1959b).

believed, with some justification, that human beings naturally seek to form bonds with others, and likened the experience of grief in adults to what children experience when they are separated from their parents. Bowlby's key concept was **attachment**. According to Bowlby, *attachment*—the natural capacity and inclination to form emotional *bonds* with others—is essential to social relationships and human survival. Indeed, his work on attachment has become a pillar in recent moves to understand troubled children who—because of early separation, abuse, or neglect—have difficulty in forming meaningful relationships with other people (Kobak, 2002; Page, 1999; Steele, 2002).

According to Bowlby, the reason grief work is so painful for the bereaved is because the very purpose of attachment is to provide for the emotional security that is uniquely found in the bonds of a significant interpersonal relationship (Bowlby, 1980). He believes that strong emotion, such as that which occurs upon the death of someone close, reflects the importance of the emotional attachment. Like the child who acts out when she or he feels abandoned, the bereaved person may turn to whatever primal behavior he or she knows—crying, begging, clinging, and even threats—in a futile effort to restore the lost relationship. According to Bowlby's attachment theory, the pressure to withdraw one's psychological investment of **libido**, or emotional energy, from the lost relationship comes into dynamic conflict with the human need for the social bond. As the conflict persists, and as the bereft person does his or her grief work, the previous emotional investment is eventually detached from the loved one, freeing the person to invest in a new relationship.

The Work of Colin Murray Parkes

Colin Murry Parkes is another one of those iconic figures in the history of thanatology. He is British psychiatrist who, at this writing, is quite elderly but still living. He drew extensively from Bowlby yet worked quite apart from him. He was an early convert to the hospice movement of Dame Cicely Saunders. Indeed, Parkes worked with her at St. Christopher's Hospice until her death, and is still affiliated with the organization as a consultant (Parkes, 1998a, 2001). Like Freud, Kübler-Ross, and Bowlby, Parkes maintains that dealing with grief is a process. He is best known for three major contributions to the study of bereavement, grief, and mourning: (1) a rich description of the grieving process, (2) the recognition that grief affects both one's mental and physical health, and (3), the distinction between normal and complicated grief.

PHASES OF GRIEF   Parkes tells us there are three elements of grief present from the outset, but that they ebb and flow as the process unfolds. He asserts that each is more or less prominent at different times after loss (Parkes, 1998a). Like Freud, Kübler-Ross, and Bowlby, Parkes believes the process of grief unfolds in a sequence of phases, but describes them differently (e.g., Bowlby, 1980; Parkes, 1998a, 2001). See Table 10.1

The *numbness and blunting phase* is a response to the initial shock after the loss, especially if death occurred suddenly and unexpectedly. It is an immediate reaction characterized by feelings of unreality, which unfold in the hours and days after the loss

TABLE 10.1 Elements and Phases of Grief	
Elements of Grief	**Phases of Grief**
The urge to cry and search for the lost person	Numbness and blunting
The urge to avoid and repress the urge to cry and search	Pining and yearning (pangs of grief) Disorganization and despair
The urge to review and revise internal conceptualizations	Reorganization and recovery

Source: This table is based on Parkes, 1998b.

(Parkes, 1998a, 2001). The *pining and yearning phase* emerges as the reality sets in. The loss is felt. This period is one in which there is a fluctuation between intense pining interspersed with periods of relative quiet, a time when emotional turmoil, anger, self-reproach, and bewilderment dominate the emotional landscape.

Physical signs and symptoms may be present to such an extent that the bereaved and others may have doubts about their psychological health—concerns that could themselves contribute to anxiety at such a level that it may lead to panic attacks. As the "pangs of grief" diminish, the *disorganization and despair phase* may arrive. During this phase, there are longer periods of apathy and despair. The bereaved may exist from day to day, remain disengaged, feel physically depleted, and lose interest in food. During the *reorganization and recovery phase,* the appetite returns, lost weight is gained back, and life returns, more or less, to normal. According to Parkes, it is a time when a new internal model of the world is built alongside the old.

COMPLICATED GRIEF   Parkes (1998b) identifies two possible outcomes of the process: normal grief and complicated grief. Reflecting on his experience with bereaved people, he observes that sometimes they aren't able to negotiate what he calls the **psychosocial transition**. He describes the normal psychosocial transition as being similar to the kind of relearning that must take place when someone becomes disabled or loses a body part (Parkes, 1998b).

Although Parkes is aware that the relationship between risk factors and the outcome is complex (Parkes, 1998a), he is, nevertheless, also convinced there are factors that predispose some individuals to have **complicated grief** following loss. He suggests that complicated grief, sometimes called *pathological grief,* poses a threat to both the physical and emotional health of the individual. In addition to the psychological or emotional impacts, Parkes suggests that bereavement can cause temporary impairment of the immune system, endocrine changes, and increases in the production of human growth hormone, all of which, he suggests, contribute to depression and feelings of distress (Parkes, 1998b).

Parkes suggests that if professionals know more about the risks and risk factors, they may be able to predict, intervene, and prevent the adverse effects of complicated grief. He identifies three key risk factors: the existence of traumatic circumstances, personal vulnerability, and the nature of the relationship with the deceased. He ties these risk factors to three types of complicated grief:

1. Traumatic
2. Conflicted
3. Chronic

Traumatic grief is a type of complicated grief characterized by the way the death occurred; it involves trauma of some kind, perhaps due to sudden occurrence, its unexpected nature, mutilation of the body, or some other such circumstance (Parkes, 1998a). Parkes suggests that as a result, the immediate reaction may be numbness and blunting, which may persist for a long period of time, perhaps leading to social withdrawal and interfering with the completion of grief work.

Conflicted grief, another type of delayed grief, refers to the conflict-ridden nature of the relationship that interferes with accomplishing the grief work. According to Parkes, the conflicted or ambivalent nature of the attachment can result in an immediate sense of relief that often gives way to "unfinished business," haunting memories, anger, and guilt.

Parkes suggests there is a danger of **chronic grief** when a very dependent, or mutually dependent, relationship existed between the deceased and the bereaved. According to Parkes, this type of grief can be prolonged and unhappy, but sometimes there is also a manipulative dynamic, as when comforting gestures of others become reinforcing to a very dependent, or needy, bereaved person. Figure 10.3 presents an overview of risk

Traumatic circumstances	Personal vulnerabilities
Death of spouse or child	Low self-esteem
Death of a parent (especially if in childhood or adolescence)	Low trust in others
Sudden, unexpected, untimely death (especially if associated with horrific circumstances)	Previous psychiatric disorders
Multiple deaths	Absent or unhelpful family
Death by suicide	
Death by murder or manslaughter	
Relationship issues	
Ambivalent attachment Dependent or interdependent attachment Insecure attachment to parents in childhood (particularly learned fear or learned helplessness)	

FIGURE 10.3 Factors Identified by Parkes as Increasing the Risk of Complicated Grief after Bereavement *Source:* This figure is based on Parkes, 1998b.

factors Parkes (1998b) suggests are associated with the three forms of complicated grief in his model.

A Task-Based Approach

William Worden suggests an alternative to stages and phases, which he calls a task-based approach (Worden, 1991, 2002, 2008). He frames the process as one that involves tasks that can be accomplished, which puts responsibility on mourners to take a more active role doing the grief work. He also suggests this can provide the mourner with a sense of empowerment or reassurance to know there are things she or he can actually accomplish. Worden also suggests that identifying specific tasks can provide professional helpers more clarity on how they can help.

In Worden's task-based approach, there are four basic **tasks of mourning** and seven factors he calls **mediators of mourning**. The tasks are more or less universal, things that most everyone should accomplish. The mediators are variables that help explain individual differences and needs. Refer to Figure 10.4 for a quick overview of tasks and mediators. As you can see from even a casual perusal of this figure, Worden has developed a rather comprehensive model that is intuitive, easy to follow, and comprehensive in scope.

HAVING ONE'S CHILD DIE

According to Therese Rando (1986), a pioneering investigator on the topic, "Parental loss of a child is unlike any other loss. The grief of parents is particularly severe, complicated, and long lasting" (p. xi). Not only is this loss difficult for the parents to cope with, but it seems as though the kind of society in which we live has its own peculiar difficulties, which exacerbate the challenges faced by the parents. As a reflection of this, Rando suggests that even the kind of language we use may tell us something about the difficulty with which society has in dealing with the death of a child. She points out that although we have a word to denote the status of a child who loses a parent, *orphan*, a spouse who loses their partner, *widow* or *widower*, we have no word for a parent who experiences the death of a child.

Cultural attitudes toward death are extremely important (Aries, 1974, 1981; Becker, 1973; also see Chapter 4). In a previous time, before the technological advances of the modern world, death may have been more a part of day-to-day life (see Chapters 2 and 5). As we've already discussed, when someone died in an earlier time, it was often at home, and it became the task of the family to deal with its aftermath, including the process of preparing the body for burial and actually disposing of it. This experience was not limited to the deaths of adults. Perhaps because of more primitive conditions, and the general hardships of life, the death of one or more children was a more common experience. Frank McCourt's (1996) book, *Angela's Ashes*, is about growing up poor, Irish, and Catholic. In it, McCourt writes about his childhood in Ireland during hard times, and about the deaths of a sister and two brothers. Indeed, the untimely deaths of many children continue to be an experience of poor families and those who live in the developing world.

Tasks of mourning

I. Accept the reality of loss

II. Work through the pain and grief

III. Adjust to an environment in which the deceased is missing

IV. Emotionally relocate the deceased and move on with life

Mediators of Mourning

1. Who the person was	• Strength of attachment
	• Security of attachment
	• Ambivalence in the relationship
	• Conflicts with the deceased
	• Dependent relationships
2. Nature of the attachment	• Kinship (nature of relationship)
3. Mode of death	• Natural
	• Accidental
	• Suicidal
	• Homicidal
	–Proximity–location of death
	–Suddenness/unexpectedness
	–Violent/traumatic
	–Multiple losses
	–Preventable deaths
	–Ambiguous deaths
	–Stigmatized deaths
4. Historical antecedents	• Previous losses (and how grieved)
	• Prior mental health history
	• Unresolved loss and grief
5. Personality variables	–Age and gender
	–Coping style
	–Attachment style
	–Cognitive style
	–Ego strength: self-esteem; self-efficacy
	–Assumptive world (beliefs & values)
6. Social variables	• Support availability
	• Support satisfaction
	• Social role involvement
	• Religious resources
	• ethnic expectations
7. Concurrent stresses	Concurrent changes and crises that follow in the wake of the death (those with the greatest number of changes have the most difficulty with adjustment

FIGURE 10.4 Worden's "Tasks" and "Mediators" of Mourning   *Source:* This figure is based on Worden, 2002.

Cowboy in the Sky

Michelle is the director of a social service agency in a large metropolitan community. When I interviewed her, she told me she sought out a career in the helping fields because of her own experience with the death of her little boy, Justin. "I wanted to help other people who are going through the same thing I went through to get through the system," she said.

When Michelle was just 28 years old and living in San Diego, she went to Justin's preschool to pick him up and was confronted by one of the teachers. It was the afternoon of New Year's Eve; 1993 was just around the corner. The very young preschool teacher commented on the lump Justin had on his head. Reflecting on it in my office several years later, Michelle said she felt accused of child abuse. Driving Justin home, she wondered if her boyfriend's teenaged son might have "dumped" Justin when he took him to preschool. They got home and Michelle went to the boy and asked him. "He swore up and down he hadn't," Michelle said.

On New Year's Day, Michelle took Justin to the emergency room. Over the previous few months Justin had been a little crabby at times. Michelle had thought he'd had ear infections, and the pediatrician had prescribed antibiotics on and off by phone. At the emergency room that New Year's Day they thought Justin might have had a cold or flu, and indicated that he probably had a salivary gland infection. On the tenth day, when the infection didn't resolve itself, Michelle took Justin to the pediatrician. The doctor looked at him and said, "Oh no, this isn't an ear infection." She looked alarmed. "This was a little bit scary for me," Michelle explained, "You don't anticipate a doctor being alarmed."

The situation became even more grave when the ear, eye, and nose specialist, who their pediatrician referred them to, found significant hearing loss in one ear and the presence of a tumor showed up on the ultrasound. He gave Michelle a phone number and advised her to make an appointment within 10 days. "They answered the phone 'UCSD Cancer Center,'" Michelle related. Michelle said that although all kinds of things had run through her mind about the possibilities, "I had no idea this is where I was calling. I was shocked. I hadn't been warned." The situation intensified. She had been told that getting Justin in for a CT scan and biopsy was urgent, but there was a mix-up at the hospital that led to a confrontation with the medical team, which resulted in the intervention of the hospital's president. When the CT scan was done, the medical team reassured Michelle that she was being a good mom by kicking up a fuss. She got the news the next day. Justin had a soft tissue cancer called embryonal rhabdnomyosarcoma.

The system that Michelle had run up against would become the world she and Justin would live in until a few short months later. After aggressive attempts at treatment with chemotherapy and radiation, Justin, a little boy who above all things wanted to be a cowboy, died as the result of a 28-day medically induced coma. As Michelle put it, he had lived "three years, nine months, twenty-eight days, eight hours, and fifteen minutes" when he passed away.

In our society today, the parents of critically ill children, and the children them-selves, have contact with legions of professionals (doctors, nurses, and therapists) who perform various specialized tasks associated with the attempt to treat the child. The fol-lowing vignette tells one such story.

Simply explaining to readers that the "parental loss of a child is unlike any other loss" cannot begin to touch the actual impact of having one's child die. Michelle, whose little cowboy, Justin, died, would eventually join an organization called the **Compassionate Friends**, in order to begin healing from her agony. This is a self-help group of parents who have had a child die. As Michelle and several other members told me when I was conducting a piece of qualitative research on their experiences (Kemp, 2001), "It's a club no one wants to join."

Although categorizing is always tricky, the kind of loss that Michelle describes in the vignette is one of two types of loss commonly experienced by parents whose child has died—that of an **expected loss**. It is the kind of loss usually experienced after a lengthy illness. Parents who have a **sudden loss** generally experience it in a different way. (For an in-depth exploration of the distinctive experiences of parents who have suffered both types, refer to Bolton, 1986; Kupst, 1986; Nichols, 1986; Sanders, 1986; and Schmidt, 1986). It is the experience of loss that is common to both groups.

With loss comes the necessity to somehow deal with the stark reality of death. Parents who have had a child die commonly report a sense of shock—the sense of living in a dream world (*unreal* and *surreal* were words that were used), and having difficulty accepting and integrating the experience (Kemp, 2001). Dennis Klass (1997), a well-known figure in the field who has extensive experience working with Compassionate Friends, uses the concept of **disequilibrium** to describe the kind of disruption that takes place in the lives of bereaved parents. As the parents told me, "Your whole life changes forever."

Grief is the process of mourning the loss, which is required in order to find a new equilibrium. Once the reality of the loss sets in, shock turns to grief (see DeSpelder & Strickland, 1999, 2004, 2005; Corr, Nabe, & Corr, 2003; Kastenbaum, 1998, 2001; Sormanti & August, 1997). For parents who experience loss after a child's lengthy ill-ness, some of this grieving—aptly enough called **anticipatory grief**—may actually start before the child's death.

The reality of the lives of those parents whose child has died suddenly and unex-pectedly changes radically from one moment to the next (Kemp, 2001). Parents whose loss occurs from illness have a much longer period of time to contemplate the ultimate possibility of death. They commonly face other challenges, however, such as living a roller-coaster existence in which they are constantly subjected to the shifting tides of their child's illness. As some parents told me, life is experienced from one crisis to the next. At one moment there is a time of great peril and crisis, sometimes followed by a rally, and even long periods of remission, when there seems to be a realistic hope that the illness might recede into a more or less permanent remission if not an actual cure.

As suggested earlier, the experience of grief, what parents have to go through after the death of a child, is commonly suffered at a profound level. It also seems to be unbelievably complex, since parents deal with loss in so many ways (see Bolton, 1986;

Dyregrov & Dyregrov, 1999; Klass, 1997; Kupst, 1986; Milo, 1997; Nichols, 1986; Oliver, 1999; Sanders, 1986; Schmidt, 1986; Schwab, 1996; Van Dongen-Melman, Van Zuuren, & Verhulst, 1998; Van Setten, 1999). Survivors commonly feel shock, isolation, anger, distrust, and an inability to communicate, and sometimes resort to the use of alcohol or drugs and "unhealthy" behaviors like workaholism, and you name it.

In contrast to such so-called stage theories, like the classic model developed by Kubler-Ross (1969) (also see Chapter 8), in which the person is believed to psychologically work through the dying process one stage at a time, one of the little things I learned from talking with parents who have had a child die is that the grief recovery process never really ends. Although originally developed to understand the process of coming to terms with dying, Kubler-Ross's model has often been applied, erroneously I think, to the experience of grief. Certainly the experience of parents who have had a child die is varied, but one thing seems fairly clear: It is so profound there is rarely a complete resolution of the grief, even years later (Arbuckle & de Vries, 1995; Dyregrov & Dyregrov, 1999; Farrugia, 1996; Gillis et al., 1997).

Dennis Klass (1997) suggests, however, that a transformation does eventually take place in the lives of parents who has had a child die—from having a concrete, physical, relationship with the child, which is truly ended forever, to a symbolic one, in which the child assumes a new place in the parents' lives.

At the risk of stepping on the sensibilities of parents who are newly bereaved, the veteran survivors I spoke with also told me that although they never would have wished for the experience, it has left them changed in profound ways (Kemp, 2001). For the first time, some said, they felt as if they truly understood the stark reality of death. Several indicated having an enhanced appreciation of how temporary life really is, and how critical it is to use every minute well. There was general agreement among them about an enhanced capacity to feel empathy and compassion. Their lives were different, they told me—more people oriented. One parent, who described himself as being basically modest, shy, and retiring, told me he had discovered a boldness in sharing his vision of what's really important in life.

SHIFTING PARADIGMS

Our discussion so far may seem very intuitive and familiar. This is precisely because the stages, phases, and tasks of grief have become so integral to our cultural world view. But now, I need to shake you up a bit. Thomas Kuhn, in his ground-breaking book, *The Structure of Scientific Revolutions,* argues that science doesn't evolve in a gradual, predictable, path toward truth, but instead develops as a result of alternating periods of relative peace and intellectual revolution (Kuhn, 1962; Walker & Pomeroy, 1996; Wikipedia, 2004). Kuhn (1962), who is credited with coining the term *paradigm shift,* suggests that when scientific revolutions occur, one conceptual worldview is often effectively replaced by another.

One such shift may involve rethinking the classic grief-work paradigm, inaugurated by Freud and further developed by succeeding generations of theorists—Kübler-Ross, Bowlby, Parkes, Worden, and others—who took his basic ideas and refined them into new theories about attachment, and the stages, phases, and tasks of grief work. One review comments, "Over the years, the stage theory of grief resolution...described for dying patients...and for adjustment to bereavement....has had enormous appeal among bereavement experts and lay persons" (Zhang, El-Jawahri, & Prigerson, 2006, p. 1189).

Problems with the Grief-Work Paradigm

Torill Christine Lindstrom, a psychologist at the University of Bergen in Norway, suggests that the traditional theories about grief and bereavement have by now been so thoroughly challenged by new research that we need to reevaluate them (Lindstrom, 2002).

The opening volley of this revolution was fired when three teams of investigators revisited the familiar models we just discussed, conducted independent research, and began looking at the familiar grief-work paradigm with new eyes (Bonanno & Kaltman, 1999, 2001; Stroebe & Stroebe, 1987; Wortman & Silver, 1987, 1989).

Margaret and Wolfgang Stroebe (1987) were among the first to suggest that despite a considerable body of literature and public acceptance, the actual benefits of grief work aren't scientifically well established (Lindstrom, 2002; Stroebe, 1992–1993; Walker & Pomeroy, 1996). Wortman and Silver (1989) challenged key notions of the grief-work paradigm—that depression is inevitable following loss, that distress is necessary, that the failure to experience them is indicative of pathology, that it is essential to work through personal loss, and that the bereaved should expect to achieve resolution following a severe loss. Bonanno and Kaltman (1999) supported Wortman and Silver's findings, but went a step further, suggesting that doing grief work can sometimes even *interfere* with making a healthy adjustment.

Broken Bonds or Broken Hearts?

Margaret Stroebe and her colleagues (Stroebe, Gergen, Gergen, & Stroebe, 1992) describe traditional grief-work theorists as creatures of their own culture and era. They contrast the zeitgeist of modern society with that of the previous age, the so-called *romanticist* era (Stroebe et al., 1992). As you may recall from Chapter 2, according to historian Aries, the *romanticist* era is the time that roughly spanned the end of the eighteenth century to the beginning of the twentieth century, and which Aries calls the era of *death of the other* (Aries, 1981). It was a sentimental time, when there was a great deal of emphasis on the emotional aspects of grief. To grieve intensely, from this perspective, was thought to be an expression of great respect for the deceased and a reflection of the depth of that relationship. In contrast, the modern perspective may be thought to have medicalized, psychologized, and pathologized it (Stroebe et al., 1992).

Stroebe and colleagues (1992) use the metaphors *broken bonds* and *broken hearts*, respectively, to describe the modern and romantic views of grief. From the romanticist perspective, the human spirit is at the center of love, creativity, and the human imagination. Marriage, in this view, is a communion of souls. Because love is seen as being a human experience of profound depth, having a broken heart upon the death of one's beloved is an understandable, poignant, and human, response—not grist for the therapist's couch. Grief isn't an illness, they suggest, and breaking a love-bond is not a task to be accomplished, but an unpleasant fact of life to be endured.

Challenging Prevailing Theory and Clinical Lore

Camille Wortman and Roxane Silver observe that professionals and laypeople alike make assumptions about how people ought to cope based on the tenets of prevailing theory and clinical "lore" (Wortman & Silver, 1987, 1989). For this reason, they felt it was important to revisit five basic assumptions prevalent in both the professional literature and the culture:

1. Grief, which involves significant emotional distress, necessarily follows in the wake of loss.
2. Not having such a grief experience is indicative of either a weak relationship with the deceased or psychological pathology.
3. Grief routinely involves the unavoidable experience of psychic pain, often accompanied by physical distress.
4. In order to get through grief successfully, one must engage in grief work, fully exploring one's feelings and expressing them, with the goal of releasing the attachment to the deceased.
5. Avoiding doing the grief work merely delays the inevitable and could contribute to more serious problems (i.e., complicated grief).

Wortman and Silver did a careful review of all the available empirical research in a quest to determine how valid these assumptions really were (Wortman & Silver, 1987, 1989). Although the research on major loss showed there are often feelings of sadness or what appeared to be a depressed mood following loss, there was no universal experience of significant distress. Indeed, only a minority of participants were distraught enough to warrant professional attention. For the majority that did not experience significant impairment, there was little support for the notion that those who don't become distraught, sometimes called *absent grief*, either develop problems later on or else had a weak relationship to begin with. Likewise, they found very little evidence that trying to "work through" one's grief was actually beneficial. Finally, the convergence of literature was fairly clear. Contrary to clinical lore and popular belief, people never seem to achieve a satisfactory "resolution" of their grief over a significant loss, even many years later.

Quest for an Integrated Framework

George Bonanno and Stacey Kaltman, like Wortman and Silver, challenged the claims of classical bereavement theory, which asserts that recovery from loss requires accomplishing grief work, which itself is aimed at the ultimate goal of severing one's emotional attachment to a deceased loved one (Bonanno & Kaltman, 1999). Like the other two teams, they point to the surprising absence of empirical evidence to support this

Context of the Loss	**Sudden or unexpected; timely or untimely**
Meaning	The subjective significance of the death to those left behind
Representation of the Lost Relationship	Whether or not the bereft maintains a relationship with their lost loved one, and the nature of that relationship over time, e.g., guide, role model, supporter from the other side, and so forth.
Coping or Emotion Regulation	Managing the strong up and down waves of emotion that follow in the wake of the loss

FIGURE 10.5   Integrated Components of the Grieving Process   *Source:* This figure is based on Bonanno & Kaltman, 1999, 2001.

view and explore several alternative perspectives. They sought to develop a conceptually sound and empirically testable framework in which to explore the many individual differences in the grieving process. They identified four integrated components of the grieving process: context, meaning, representations of the lost relationship over time, and coping or emotion regulation. See Figure 10.5 for a brief description of each.

What We've Learned

Now, after more than twenty years have passed since the first volleys in this paradigm war were fired, we have amassed a large body of impressive empirical research on the experiences of people who suffer loss (see, for example, Bonanno, Wortman, & Nesse, 2004; Stroebe, Abakoumkin, & Stroebe, 2010; Wortman & Boerner, 2007). As a result, the smoke is clearing and a consensus seems to be forming among today's generation of bereavement experts. From the remains of the old stages, phases, and tasks, something new seems to be emerging.

Consensus in Bereavement Research

Most bereavement researchers now seem agree that with the help of family and friends, most bereaved people actually do pretty well after a significant loss (Jordan & Neimeyer, 2003; Wortman & Boerner, 2007). Bonanno and colleagues call this ability to bounce back **resilience** (Bonanno, 2004; Bonanno et al., 2002). Certainly there are many emotional ups and downs during the grieving process, but it seems that bereft people often have positive feelings and experience humor, which actually seems to help them get through it. Not everyone needs to do "grief work"—that is, actively confront their difficult feelings. Indeed, two independent reviews of the research now suggest that grief counseling, the way it has been done, tends to be ineffective (Kato & Mann, 1999; Neimeyer, 2000). Indeed, one study suggests that up to 38 percent of bereaved people who had this type of treatment would have been better off without it (Neimeyer, 2000). This new grief research also suggests that it is not only normal but also healthy to keep a deceased loved one alive in memory (i.e., attempt to maintain a bond, a relationship with them, after they have passed).

Although bereft people do very well, on whole, it also seems true that people who have significant losses never completely get over it. In one national prospective study of over 1,500 couples—the Changing Lives of Older Couples study—we learn that it is quite common for bereft spouses to maintain memories and thoughts, and even to have complete conversations with their deceased mate, which has left them with poignantly sad feelings (Carnelley, Wortman, Bolger, & Burke, 2006, cited in Wortman & Boerner, 2007).

Perhaps most important of all, this new generation of bereavement researchers now suspect, in contrast to popular thinking, that the experience of loss may in some ways be a good thing. For instance, it may very well help bring about "enduring positive changes, such as increased self-confidence and independence, altered life priorities, and enhanced compassion for others suffering from similar losses" (Wortman & Boerner, 2007, p. 312).

Significance for Helpers

Researchers are concerned about whether or not the accumulated wisdom from over 20 years of research has actually filtered down to therapists, counselors, and other helpers—the "boots on the ground" who actually work with bereaved people (Wortman & Boerner, 2007). Although clinicians are well-meaning and the research seems clear, studies suggest that as many as 65 percent of those who practice grief therapy continue to subscribe to the old assumptions of the grief-work paradigm (e.g., Middleton, Moylan, Raphael, Burnett, & Martinek, 1993).

With inaccurate assumptions being rampant about how people ought to grieve, one can only imagine the potential impact of the expectations of physicians, nurses, therapists, and even family, friends, and clergy. The problem seems to be a one-size-fits-all mentality (Bonanno, 2004; Wortman & Boerner, 2007). We previously came to believe that if therapy is good, we ought to offer it to everyone. As alluded to in this chapter, what we now know that this is not true for everyone. Resilient grievers do very well with just the support of friends and family. For them, formal grief therapy is generally ineffective and can be even harmful. Grief treatment for traumatized or chronically grief-stricken people, on the other hand, may be highly appropriate. However, we are coming to the position that their needs probably demand that treatment methods be precise and targeted. Those who have been traumatized may need intervention akin to that used for post-traumatic syndrome disorder, whereas those with chronic grief may need help with finding meaning in their loss (Neimeyer, 2000, 2001).

NEW KNOWLEDGE

The Work of George Bonanno

George Bonanno began his career in bereavement research right out of graduate school in response to a job offer. He describes himself as a relative outsider who never intended to make grief a career. Now a professor of psychology at Teacher's College, Columbia

University, he has been at the forefront of grief research and practice. His research publication record is impressive, but what may be even more impressive is that he has been able to take some fairly complex theoretical material and make it understandable to everyday people. In 2009, he published *The Other Side of Sadness*, an immensely popular book in which he shares the stories of bereft people and what the new science of bereavement can tell us about life after loss (Bonanno, 2009).

One of the problems is that concepts have gotten confused. Bonanno points out that grief, depression, and post-traumatic stress are three different things (Bonanno et al., 2007), and depression and sadness are different things (Bonanno, 2009). *Depression* is a clinical syndrome of related signs and symptoms, which is described in the *Diagnostic and Statistical Manual* of the American Psychiatric Association (American Psychiatric Association, 2000). "The emotion of sadness occurs when we know we've lost someone or something important and there is nothing we can do about it" (Bonanno, 2009, p. 31). About the only thing that sadness has to do with depression is the experience of feeling "blue." Other basic emotions that might be encountered during grief are anger, fear, or even relief, depending on the person and the circumstances.

A function of sadness is to turn our attention inward so we can take stock, reflect, and adjust to our changing circumstances (Bonanno, 2009). After a loss, sadness helps us accept what has happened and accommodate to it. In addition, it tends to evoke a supportive response from others. A person who is sad needs support and time to herself or himself so she or he can sort things out. A person who is depressed, on the other hand, may need clinical intervention, usually some combination of medication and supportive psychotherapy.

Another problem relates to confusion between different patterns of grief reactions (Boerner, Wortman, & Bonanno, 2005; Bonanno et al., 2002, 2004). Bonanno's basic premise is that grief, even though the experience itself is common, is experienced differently by each of us. No two people go through it exactly the same way. Nor does a single individual go through each experience of loss the same way. This having been said, there do seem to be some common patterns. In a prospective study of 276 persons who had a spouse die, Bonanno and colleagues looked at depressive symptoms three years prior to the loss, then at six and eighteen months afterward. The results reveal five distinct **grief trajectories** (Bonanno et al., 2002). Figure 10.6 visually summarizes them.

Resilient (46%)	While individuals who fall into this pattern probably have emotional ups and downs, they tend to function fairly well, with support from friends and family
Chronic grief (16%)	Grief that does not get better with time
Common grief (11%)	The type of grief discussed in the prevailing model, in which an individual has significant problems adjusting to loss, followed by recovery and an eventual return to normal functioning
Depressed-Improved (10%)	Depression, which improves after the loss
Chronic depression (8%)	Depression, which is present both before and after the loss

FIGURE 10.6 Grief Trajectories   *Source:* This figure is based on Bonanno, et al., 2002.

As discussed earlier, the *resilient grief* pattern is actually the most common, with nearly half of all bereaved people falling into this category. The *common grief* pattern—the type of grief described in the classical grief literature—as it turns out, is really not so common, with only about 16 percent of bereaved people following that pattern. It can be described as the kind of grief where the surviving spouse has time-limited impairment in functioning–elevated depression, disorganization, and health problems (Bonanno & Kaltman, 2001). The *chronic grief* pattern is said to exist when symptoms persist for an extended period. In addition to these three categories of grief, Bonanno and colleagues take note of the existence of two distinct categories of depression. In the *chronic depressed* category (8 percent), the spouse has symptoms of clinical depression both before and after the death of their partner. In the *depressed-improved* category (10 percent), the spouse has significant depression before the spouse's death coupled with marked improvement afterward. Why?

In a follow-up study, Bonanno and colleagues concluded that those in the resilient group tended to have long, satisfying, marriages (Bonanno, Wortman, & Nesse, 2004). They also tended to cherish the memories of their spouses. Even though they experienced grief-related symptoms—yearning, emotional pangs, and distressing thoughts and emotions related to their spouses—they were able to bounce back. They needed the continued love and support of their friends and family—not therapy. Those in the *chronic grief* group did seem to need professional help. Those in the *chronic depressed* group were depressed before and after the death of their spouses. They got worse when their spouses died and then returned to their previous level of depression. Their underlying depression was a separate matter. Those in the *depressed-improved* group were relatively unhappy in their marriages and were often long-term caregivers. The death of the seriously ill spouses came as a relief. Months afterward, they looked a lot like the resilient group, needing little or no outside intervention.

Dual-Process Model

Many people have observed that the strong feelings associated with grief after a major loss often come in waves. A Dutch team of bereavement researchers—Stroebe, Schut, and Stroebe—developed what is now called the **dual-process model (DPM)** of coping, which is quite consistent with these informal observations (Stroebe & Schut, 1999; Stroebe, Schut, & Strobe, 2005). The model proposes that following the death of a loved one, bereaved people alternate between two different kinds of coping: loss-oriented and restoration-oriented coping. *Loss-oriented coping* relates to such things as the loss of the person, yearning and rumination, and trying to find a new place in their consciousness for the deceased loved one. *Restoration-oriented coping* relates to factors that are secondary to the loss of the person, including such things as adjusting to one's new role as "widow" or "widower"; mastering the skills that used to be provided by the other person, such as cooking, taking care of the finances, and so forth; and restoring one's worldview.

An interesting feature of DPM is the concept of **oscillation**, the idea that bereft people go back and forth between processing emotionally painful aspects of loss and distancing themselves from those feelings of loss, which is referred to as *confrontation* and *avoidance* (Stroebe, Schut, & Stroebe, 2005). In the researchers' view, it is "a matter of slowly and painfully exploring what has been lost and what remains; what must be avoided or relinquished versus what can be retained, created, and built on" (p. 52). A group of clinicians helping survivors of sexual abuse to cope began from the premise that post-traumatic "symptoms" are actually necessary attempts to deal with traumatic experience (Patten, Gatz, Jones, & Thomas, 1989). They found it helpful to encourage their clients to balance between "processing" emotionally charged material with needed recuperative rest periods called *respite.*

While not calling them stages, phases, or tasks, Stroebe and colleagues seem to envision oscillation as being part of a process that has both short-term, moment-to-moment alternations and a longer-term shift, from the early period after the death, when there is an emphasis on loss to a later time period when it seems more important to deal with the stuff of everyday life (Stroebe, Schut, & Stroebe, 2005).

MOURNING

The shifting paradigms in the West about the experience of grief can be seen as a change between a worldview based on Freudian psychoanalytic theory to a newer, but still emerging one, based on the use of science and new theory. You might want to remember, however, that the debate has occurred, and continues to occur, within the Western cultural worldview. As we make a shift between our discussion of grief to an exploration of mourning, you should consider that mourning, by definition, occurs within a cultural context.

Although death seems difficult for people in virtually all cultures—as expressed in tears, anger, confusion, depression, or difficulty functioning—there is ample evidence to show there is a great deal of diversity in terms of how human beings grieve across time, place, and the society. Paul Rosenblatt comments that whatever anyone writes about bereavement, it is in essence a culture-bound viewpoint (Rosenblatt, 2001). As we discussed earlier, mourning is both a *process* people go though as they attempt to cope with loss and a culturally patterned way of dealing with it.

A feature of culture in North America today is that we put a premium on diversity and multiculturalism. Diversity is a thing to behold, but embracing it also means rejecting universals, including universals about how we deal with death. In our own circle of friends and family, my wife and I have been dealing with a lot of life-threatening illness and death lately. One of our friends made the comment, "Where are all the rituals that

While bereavement is the experience of loss and grief is what we experience because of that loss, mourning is the culturally pattered way in which we go about doing this. *ckellyphoto/Fotolia*

tell you what to do when the people you know get sick and die?" Indeed, many of us are uncertain about this.

Dennis Klass began his career in 1968 as one of the four chaplaincy students recruited by the late Dr. Elisabeth Kübler-Ross to help interview dying patients for her project on death and dying. In addition to his impressive work with parents who have had a child die (see earlier text), he has also gone on to do some interesting work in the study of cross-cultural bereavement (Goss & Klass, 1997; Klass, 1996; Klass & Goss, 2000a, 2000b).

In 1996, he wrote an article that explored ancestor worship in Japan, *sosen suhai*— a tradition he says that could help explain the role played by the dead in Eastern cultures (Klass, 1996). Klass notes that the veneration of ancestors in Japan is an important feature of its culture, which at its core is an expression of a shared sense of community that is not broken with death. He suggests that there is no autonomous, independent, *self* in the Japanese tradition, as there is in the West. In Japan, one's identity, one's self is understood primarily as a function of membership within a family, which itself is deeply rooted in an ancestral system. This system is intertwined with Japanese religion—a blend of indigenous traditions and Buddhist religion, a religion that came to Japan through China. In Japanese Buddhism, the individual is not regarded as having a soul, or *atman*, as in Hinduism, but rather is understood as a paradoxical *anatman*, or identity, that comes into being as a result of the interaction between physical form, feelings, perceptions, and complexes (response patterns) and that takes place in the context of higher consciousness.

When people die in Japan, they are thought to become a part of the spirit world unless they achieve Buddhahood, or enlightenment, in the present lifetime (Klass, 1996). The spirits of the dead progress through the spirit world, starting out as *shirei*, or newly dead sprits, and ultimately achieving the status of *kami*, or deity. The spirits of the dead are thought to be available to the living, who may converse with and venerate them as members of the family ancestral system. Indeed, they are at its core, giving the family its very identity. Figure 10.7 gives a brief description of the spirit categories in this system.

In this system, the *shirei* are considered closest to the living (Klass, 1996). Indeed, of all the spirits they are thought to be closest, and remain available to the living for 35 to 50 years, effectively for the remainder of the lives of those who knew them. These

Shirei	Spirits of the newly dead
Ni-hotoke	New Buddhas
Hotoke	Buddhas
Senzo	Ancestors
Kami	Gods

FIGURE 10.7   The Names for the Spirits of Japanese Deceased   *Source:* This figure is based on Smith, 1974, cited in Klass, 1996.

shirei will eventually become *ni-hotoke*, new Buddhas, as they become more a part of the spirit world, then Buddhas, *hotoke*, and finally deities, or *kami*.

It is not until the annual *O Bon* festival, celebrated each summer, however, that *shirei* will loosen, but never completely sever, their bonds with the living (Klass, 1996). The *O Bon* seems to have much in common with how *Los Dias de Muertos*, the days of the dead, which as we discussed in Chapter 4, is celebrated in Oaxaca and other parts of Mexico. *O Bon* is rooted in indigenous tradition and Buddhist religion, much as *Los Dias de Muertos* is rooted in a mix of indigenous traditions and Catholic faith. Also similar to what occurs during *Los Dias de Muertos,* at *O Bon,* members of Japanese communities prepare for the return of their ancestral spirits by gathering wild flowers; clearing the paths to the graves; washing and decorating them; and lighting lanterns, fire, and incense to guide the spirits home. Like what occurs at the days of the dead, Japanese families prepare favorite foods and beverages for the spirits, offering them to the spirits on specially erected shrines or the family *Budsudan*, the Buddha shrine traditionally found in Japanese homes. Whereas in Mexico the name differs (the altars for the dead are called *ofrendas*)—the practice is familiar. As the *O Bon* celebration draws to a close, the *shirei* loosen their attachments to the physical world and the bereaved loosen their ties to the dead, but keep their spirits firmly rooted in their memories as revered beings in the ancestral system, where they will forevermore occupy a place of honor.

The Western Penan people are a small band of hunter-gatherers, living in remote parts of Borneo (Brosius, 1995). They have a complex system of using death-names— names that denote the status of the dead person and others. Using death-names instead of usual names is their way to protect the feelings of the bereft (using the name of the dead might arouse sad feelings). It is also their way to keep the spirit of the dead person at a distance. In their worldview, the dead are as sad as the living about their demise. The Western Penan believe that using the name of the deceased can only disturb them further, perhaps inciting them to return and make trouble for the living.

In contrast are the practices of the Yoruba people, who live in southwestern Nigeria (Adamolekum, 1999). They believe in explicitly showing their support to the bereft by special greetings they extend to mourners—greetings that acknowledge the grief, *ikedun*, that ask blessings, *iwure*, and that make analogies to other similar or worse experiences a person might have, *iferowero*.

In some traditional Gaelic traditions, death was regarded as a natural extension of life, albeit an existence that would continue in the spirit world (Donnelly, 1999). The community showed its support to the bereft by active involvement in the wake (included sharing stories), walking in the procession to the cemetery, and keening (wailing), and through their music.

Raymond Lee, a social theorist at the University of Malaya, suggests there are important distinctions in how premodern peoples—for example, the Western Penan, Yoruba, and Celtic peoples of old—and modern people approach mourning (Lee, 2002). He suggests there are several key distinctions, including how the self is conceptualized, the disenchantment of death, and the significance of mourning.

The premodern self can be understood as a being that is subject to the changing tides of nature and demands of an all-encompassing community, in which the survival of the group depends on each of its members doing his or her part. In contrast, the modern self can be conceived as a highly autonomous and individualized entity endowed with inherent rights and privileges—the kind of self that can take charge and play an active role in writing his or her own biography or even changing the course of history. It is also this kind of self that finds it extremely difficult to face the reality of its final destination.

One of the features of life today is that we have stripped death of its spiritual and religious significance. In premodern culture, death is seen as the culmination of a journey—perhaps involving the release of the soul from the body or reunion with the divine. In our modern worldview, Lee (2002) suggests, metaphysical meaning dissolves and death becomes instead an obstacle that gets in the way of what we want to accomplish. Lee (2002) also believes that how a people mourn says a great deal about their society. For premodern people, the purpose of mourning—the rituals and practices concerned with death—are deeply imbued with spiritual meaning and sacred significance. For them, ritual helps reaffirm their relationship with the universe, provides a sense of community, and helps maintain their relationship with the dead. In the modern context, our rituals are much abbreviated. The few that remain have often become secularized, their cosmological significance now reduced to providing for the psychological and emotional well-being of the living.

The late Greg Palmer, formerly a journalist and PBS personality, produced a TV mini-series and wrote a book titled *Death: The Trip of a Lifetime* (G. Palmer, 1993). In the process of working on the show he made an interesting observation. He said our death rituals and practices help us accomplish three things: get rid of the body, work out our feelings, and tell the tale about the life of the person who died. In Chapters 5 and 6, we already discussed getting rid of the body. In this chapter so far, we have discussed how we work out our feelings. In the final section of the chapter, we conclude with a few words about telling the tale.

TELLING THE TALE

Tony Walter is a thanatologist currently teaching at the University of Bath in the United Kingdom. In a 1996 article for the journal, *Mortality*, he movingly addressed the importance of "telling the tale" by sharing two stories of his own grief experience (Walter, 1996). At his father's funeral, Kingston, a long-time black Zimbabwean friend of the family, had been asked to give the memorial address. Kingston was from the Shona tradition, a very different cultural heritage than that of the rest of the mourners. What he did was read a passage from Henry Scott Holland's poem, "What Is Death?" The chosen passage invites mourners to keep the name of the deceased alive in their hearts. As Walter describes it, what Kingston did was give permission to the rest of the mourners to do what they wanted to do naturally—remember. He recounts that it changed the entire tone of the ceremony from a stiff, formal event to be endured to one in which everyone had the opportunity to reminisce and share their own stories of the deceased.

In a second "case study," Walter (1996) tells of an experience he had after the death of his best friend, Corina, who had once been his lover. After her tragic death, it fell to him to contact her many friends and coordinate the arrangements. Actually, a great deal more unfolded. Using her address book, he contacted each person by phone. He noticed that after he gave them the bad news, they would often begin to spontaneously share their stories and experiences of Corina. When they came together for the funeral, he noticed that they filled in the holes of her story for each other, providing rich new detail and in a sense rewrote her biography.

Walter's comments that the two "experiences," so briefly sketched, are quite natural examples of the healing that can take place when people gather after the death of a loved one (Walter, 1996). He laments, however, that in today's modern, individualistic society, it is often hard to find others with whom to share stories like these. He identifies five factors that interfere with this (Walter, 1996):

1. Since in the West most individuals die in hospitals or nursing homes, those most capable of telling how the person died—the health-care providers—are not personally connected with the family, and may be too busy caring for others to converse with them about what happened.
2. There are no common denominators in grieving. Members of the same family may grieve in different ways, or different times, making it difficult to engage in a *recreative* process together.
3. The religious and cultural ambiguity of our times creates uncertainty about how to behave. Whereas in the past people may have shared a common religious tradition and cultural heritage, in our more pluralistic society it is more uncertain as to how to behave.
4. The compartmentalization of home and work life often means that the various people involved in a person's life are less likely to know each other, making communication on a personal level difficult.
5. Social mobility and increased life expectancy means that people live longer and move. The bereaved are therefore often separated geographically and emotionally from each other.

BOX 10.1

An Important Person Who Has Died

Consider the contrast between the *broken bonds* and *broken hearts* perspectives. Now, I would like to ask you to participate in an activity. It is a similar activity to one that was done with a large group of students as part of research on withdrawing ties to the dead (Marwit & Klass, 1995, cited in Klass & Walter, 2001; Walter, 1996). Take out pen and paper and write about an important person in your life who has died. Consider the role, if any, this person plays in your life today. After finishing, review what you wrote. How does your paper square with what you might have expected based on the "broken bonds" model? Perhaps you will want to share and compare your response with others.

Walter (1996) speculates about whether or not professional counseling and the proliferation of self-help groups is not somehow a natural consequence of not having other opportunities in which to tell the tale.

In the classes I teach on death and dying, I sometimes like to have students do a short "seat writing" assignment that I refer to as "An Important Person Who Has Died." It provides students with an opportunity to share a story. If you are reading this text in connection with a course, perhaps your instructor will include it as a class activity.

When Marwit and Klass (1995) asked students to participate in a similar activity, they were initially uncertain about whether or not their students might see the request as odd, and perhaps even have difficulty with it. As it turned out, no one had any trouble writing about a deceased loved one. Many, in fact, wrote extensively. Marwit and Klass (1995) identified four possible roles played by the deceased in the lives of the living:

1. *Role model:* Defined as a global identification with the deceased
2. *Situation-specific guidance:* Defined as the living calling on the deceased for guidance in specific situations
3. *Values clarification:* Defined as adopting a moral position identified with the deceased
4. *Part of survivor's biography:* In this continuing role, the deceased becomes an important part of the survivor's own story

I would like to conclude by sharing a story from my own experience. During the writing of this text, Ric LaPlant, a valued mentor, advisor, and the chair of my doctoral program, died suddenly of a stroke. As sometimes occurs when someone you love dies, I've periodically found myself reflecting on my memories of Ric. When I do, I can hear his words reverberate in my mind—"Trust the process"—or I just reminisce about his manner and tone. While working on this chapter, I've sometimes found myself thinking about Ric, wondering what he might think or how he would suggest handling a particular topic or issue.

Chapter Summary

We began this chapter by outlining a few basic definitions of bereavement, grief, and mourning before embarking on a review of traditional ways of approaching the subject: the Freudian perspective, Bowlby's contributions on attachment, the elaborations done by pioneer Colin Murray Parkes, as well as a model developed by William Worden. With this exploration came a lot of exposure to theories about the impact of bereavement. We briefly looked at one particularly difficult form of bereavement—the kind parents experience when a child dies. Then we discussed criticisms of classical theory and revelations from new theory, including the work of George Bonanno. In the context of discussing mourning, we looked at the work of Dennis Klass on ancestor worship in Japan as contrasted to the Western worldview on mourning. We also briefly sampled the practices of three other peoples from around the world: the Western Penan of Borneo, the Yoruba of southern Nigeria, and the traditional Gaelic people from Ireland and parts of Scotland. This also provided context for a discussion of the work of sociologist Raymond Lee of the University of Malaya, who helps contrast premodern and modern mourning. Finally, we turned to the topic of telling the tale, with some speculation about what people today can learn from those of yesteryear. For this, we briefly explored what British sociologist, Tony Walter, has to say about the value of story.

Key Terms

anticipatory grief *221*
attachment *215*
bereavement *212*
broken bonds *214*
chronic grief *217*
Compassionate Friends *221*
complicated grief *216*
conflicted grief *217*

disequilibrium *221*
dual-process model
  (DPM) *228*
expected loss *221*
grief *212*
grief trajectories *227*
grief work *213*
libido *215*

mediators of mourning *218*
mourning *212*
oscillation *229*
psychosocial transition *216*
resilience *225*
sudden loss *221*
tasks of mourning *218*
traumatic grief *217*

Suggested Activities

1. Using pictures from old magazines, put together a "grief collage." Cut out whatever pictures seem to represent aspects of any bereavement experiences you may have had. Paste these images onto a large piece of colored construction paper. This is an activity you can do by yourself or with others.
2. Think of a loved one of yours who has died. Reflect on the time you had together and write a biography about this person's life, or about the time you shared with this other individual.
3. If you become aware of things you'd like to say to someone you care about who has died, consider writing a letter to that person. You may either save the letter or destroy it, depending on what seems most appropriate for you.
4. Journal about any losses you may have experienced. In what ways is your own experience similar or different

from what is proposed in the various models? What approach to healing from the loss seems best suited to your needs?
5. Using the Internet or your library, search out poetry or stories with bereavement themes. What do you notice about what the poets try to communicate about their experience? Are you able to relate to their experiences?
6. Draw a time line of the life of a person whose death you are grieving. Include the significant events in that person's life. Draw a parallel line with world events during the same time frame.
7. Write a story, fairy tale, fable, song, or poem about a deceased loved one.
8. Write a story from the point of view of a deceased person you know who has died.

Suggested Reading

- Bonanno, G. A. (2009). *The other side of sadness*. New York: Basic Books.
  This moving and insightful book written for the popular market reveals new scientifically based discoveries about the human grieving process. Bonanno points out that most people travel the road of normal grief pretty well. The book includes lots of case examples, humor, and anecdotes.

- Rando, T. A. (1986). *Parental loss of a child.* Champaign, IL: Research Press.

  This is a very informative, albeit scholarly, piece of work devoted to the experience of parents who have had a child die. There are a variety of essays written by eminent people in the field. It is a worthwhile read for anyone interested in understanding more about this issue.

- Klass, D., Silverman, P. R., & Nickman, S. L. (1996). *Continuing bonds.* Oxford and New York: Taylor and Francis.

  This volume gives voice to some fine work by respected grief scholars who challenge the old grief-work model and show how the healthy resolution of grief can also empower the bereaved to maintain continuing emotional bonds with the deceased. Included is the essay by Dennis Klass on ancestor worship in Japan that was highlighted in this chapter.

- Lewis, C. S. (1961). *A grief observed.* New York & Toronto: Bantam Books.

  In this autobiographical account, C. S. Lewis, author and essayist of unusual distinction, tells the story of his own grief experience. A confirmed bachelor, Lewis married Joy Davidman, an American poet, in April 1956. After four intensely happy years, Lewis found himself alone again when Joy died painfully from cancer. To help combat encroaching doubts about his own religious faith, he wrote this book.

- Remen, R. N. (2000). *My grandfather's blessings.* New York: Riverhead Books.

  This is an extraordinarily moving book of "stories of strength, refuge, and belonging." Drawing on her relationship with her grandfather, an Orthodox Rabbi with a mystic's sense, Rachel Naomi Remen, herself a cancer physician, uses story and her deep appreciation of the sacred to remind us of our many blessings and how we can draw on them as we endeavor to contend with life's diverse challenges.

- Worden, J. W. (2002). *Grief counseling and grief therapy: A handbook for the mental health practitioner* (4th ed.). New York: Springer. Considered a "Bible" of bereavement work, this concise, practical volume serves as a guide for counselors.

- Walter, T. (Ed.). (1999). *Mourning for Diana.* Oxford and New York: Berg.

  Considered a "Bible" of bereavement work, this concise, practical volume serves as a guide for counselors. The shocking death of Princess Diana on August 31, 1997, led to an especially poignant time of mourning. Sociologist Tony Walter and the other contributors to this book explore what happened in those days. The book is filled with rich detail and thought-provoking analysis.

Links and Internet Resources

- **GriefNet.org**
  http://rivendell.org/
  This site, designed to serve as a venue for an Internet community of persons dealing with grief, death, and major loss, contains 47 e-mail support groups. It boasts of an integrated approach to on-line grief support that provides help to people working through loss and grief issues of many kinds. Its companion site, KIDSAID, is intended to provide a safe place for kids and parents to get information and ask questions.

- **Cruse Bereavement Care**
  www.crusebereavementcare.org.uk
  Cruse is the largest bereavement charity in the United Kingdom. It provides direct care as well as information, support, and training through a network of volunteers. Its website has extensive resources for young people.

- **Medline Plus–Bereavement Page**
  www.nlm.nih.gov/medlineplus/bereavement.html
  This webpage is hosted by the National Library of Medicine and the National Institute of Health. It contains a wide range of resources on bereavement topics, links to organizations, and resources.

- **WidowNet**
  www.fortnet.org/WidowNet/
  WidowNet provides information and self-help resources for, and by, widows and widowers. The topics covered include grief, bereavement, recovery, and other information helpful to people of all ages, religious backgrounds, and sexual orientations who have suffered the death of a spouse or life partner.

Review Guide

1. Distinguish between and compare the concepts of bereavement, grief, and mourning.
2. Discuss the concept of complicated grief.
3. Describe what is meant by the term *grief work*. What role does this concept play in the traditional approaches to understanding the experience of bereavement and grief?
4. What are the basic propositions of Freud's model of mourning and melancholia?
5. Put into your own words Bowlby's basic proposition on the role of *attachment*. If he is correct, what are the implications in terms of how one should handle bereavement, grief, and mourning?
6. Briefly summarize the model of grief developed by Colin Murray Parkes. How does he build on the work of Bowlby? What do you think of his concept of psychological transition? What three types of grief does he propose exist? How would you go about dealing with each type? Why?
7. Summarize William Worden's model. How does it differ from other traditional models? What do you think of his concept of tasks? To what degree do you think the concept of task is tied to the dominant culture in North America?
8. What have we learned as a result of working with parents who have had a child die? In particular, what conclusions did Dennis Klass come to?
9. What are some of the key criticisms of traditional approaches to understanding bereavement, grief, and mourning? How would you evaluate them in light of recent scholarship?
10. In what ways can cross-cultural comparisons and contrasting different eras in time help us locate our own culture's approach to bereavement, grief, and mourning?
11. What does current research have to say about the effects of bereavement on the lives of mourners? Which of these seem most relevant to understanding your own experiences? How helpful is the current research to your own understanding? Why?
12. What do you think the new research on coping and adaptation tells us about the human capacity to learn and grow?
13. Briefly summarize the integrated family model proposed by Nancy Moos. What gaps do you think this emerging model fills? What limitations do you think it has, if any?
14. What are the criticisms of the traditional grief-work models? What is the support for this position? What do the so-called thanatology revolutionaries propose as an alternative?
15. According to critics of the traditional models, what continuing roles can the dead play in the lives of the living?
16. According to Tony Walter (1996), what can Westerners learn from people from other cultures about how to mourn? What five factors does he suggest get in the way of this occurring in Western society? What do you think might be done to overcome these obstacles? What are second best alternatives to being able to share intimate stories of the deceased with others who knew the person?
17. What role might postmodern counseling approaches play in helping people more productively grieve their deceased loved ones? Why might these approaches be particularly well-suited for individuals who are grieving a significant loss?

11

When Grief Goes Awry
Complicated Grief

- **Nature of the Beast**
- **Traumatic Loss**
- **Prolonged Grief**
- **Risks and Risk Factors**

- **Disenfranchised Grief**
- **Coping**
- **Emerging Models**

All of us have or will experience significant loss. Profound grief is a normal reaction. As discussed in Chapter 10, it is physically, emotionally, and psychologically challenging, but most of us get through it. The focus of this chapter is on what happens when grief goes awry—that is, when people for whatever reason can't bounce back from their losses.

As you may recall from Chapter 10, Collin Murray Parkes, one of the true pioneers in the field, coined the term *complicated grief* to describe reactions to loss that are experienced more severely or for a longer period of time than normal (Parkes, 1998a, 1998b). He has suggested that experiencing a traumatic death, having had a conflicted relationship with the deceased, or having been overly dependent on the deceased puts bereaved people at higher risk for three forms of complicated grief he referred to as *traumatic*, *conflicted*, and *chronic*. Based largely on firsthand clinical experience, Parkes was the first modern grief expert to raise concerns about the possible health consequences of complicated grief, including early death, immune system impairment, post-traumatic distress, and feelings of profound depression.

In Chapter 10 we also discussed the new body of bereavement research, which has largely challenged the old grief-work model—the stages, phases, and tasks of grief work—that has until recently been so influential in our thinking about the experience of normal grief (see Stroebe & Stroebe, 1987; Wortman & Silver, 1987, 1989; Bonanno & Kaltman, 1999, 2001). What does this emerging body of research have to say about complicated grief?

NATURE OF THE BEAST

It seems quite clear that there is indeed a form of grief that is more troublesome than normal grief. Although most bereaved people get through the roller coaster of emotions associated with acute, or normal grief, bereavement experts now believe that about 10 to 15 percent of bereaved people experience complicated grief—grief so severe that it may require professional attention (Bonanno et al., 2002; Bonanno, Wortman, & Nesse, 2004; Ginzburg, Geron, &

As discussed in Chapter 7, we think that experiencing traumatic death, such as what happens as a result massive devastation, puts us at greater risk for experiencing the traumatic form of complicated grief. *iStock © Vadim Svirin*

Solomon, 2002; Mancini, Prati, & Bonanno, 2011). The term *complicated grief* usually refers to reactions to loss that are debilitating or that last for a significant time.

Generally, persons with complicated grief seem to experience a persistent and disturbing disbelief about the loss and are resistant to accepting its painful realities (Byrne & Raphael, 1994; Middleton, Burnett, Raphael, & Martinek, 1996; American Psychiatric Association, 2011; Prigerson & Jacobs, 2001; Prigerson et al., 2009). The intense yearning and longing for the deceased often involves frequent waves of powerful, painful emotions, including anger and bitterness. The bereft tend to be preoccupied with thoughts of the deceased loved one, which are distressing and intrusive. As a result, people with complicated grief tend to avoid a range of situations and activities that remind them of their painful loss. As a result, their interest in, and engagement with, the usual activities of daily life are often limited or absent, making it hard for them to function in their usual roles. The reality of the death is not well integrated, and the powerful feelings people experience with normal grief is intensified and prolonged (Shear & Shair, 2005).

The definitions and terminology associated with complicated grief are still in flux (Prigerson & Maciejewski, 2006; Neimeyer, 2006; Walter, 2006). The terms *pathological, abnormal, morbid, neurotic, chronic, complicated, traumatic, prolonged,* and several others have all been used to refer to approximately the same phenomenon. As a result of over a decade of focused research on complicated grief, there is now good evidence to support the existence of a bereavement-related grief disorder distinct from major depression and posttraumatic stress (Bonanno et al., 2007; Prigerson et al., 2009).

Research on complicated grief has focused on testing the proposition that it is a bona fide mental-health disorder that can be distinguished from other pathological reactions to loss—for example, post-traumatic stress and major depression (Bonanno et al., 2007; Prigerson et al., 2009). There appear to be a few reasons why bereavement researchers feel it is essential to establish the validity of a bereavement-related disorder.

Many veterans today have served multiple deployments in horrific circumstances, including those involving the death of close friends and comrades. This puts them at vastly greater risk for PTSD and traumatic grief. *Terrance Emerson/Fotolia*

When mental-health professionals assess people for suspected mental-health problems, they often use the current edition of the *Diagnostic and Statistical Manual*, usually just called the *DSM* (and the suffix for whatever edition is current, e.g., *DSM-IV-TR*) (American Psychiatric Association, 2000). First, there was no diagnostic category in *DSM-IV-TR* (the previous edition of the manual used by the American Psychiatric Association to classify mental disorders) specifically for complicated grief, yet the emerging research seemed clear in suggesting that a small but significant minority of bereaved people are plagued by intensely experienced and prolonged grief reactions. Second, there is also extremely strong evidence concerning the potential adverse health consequences of bereavement-related disturbance (Jacobs & Prigerson, 2000). Finally, interpersonal psychotherapy, which has been shown to be generally effective in treating a range of other mental-health concerns, does not seem to be very effective in treating bereavement-related issues (Shear, Frank, Houck, & Reynolds, 2005). Holly Prigerson, for one, expresses the hope that a recognized diagnosis might lead to the development of more effective therapies (Prigerson et al., 2009), similar to what happened after **post-traumatic stress disorder (PTSD)**, was recognized in the early 1980s.

The dust is just now starting to settle when it comes to the question of how to conceptualize bereavement-related disturbance. Prigerson has been a key figure in the fight for recognition. She and her team initially proposed the term *traumatic grief (TG)* for inclusion in *DSM-V* because they thought it captured the essence of the phenomenon. Other investigators have grouped experiences of distressing separation and traumatic symptoms into a single syndrome they refer to as *traumatic grief syndrome (TGS)* (Neria & Litz, 2004; Meagher, 2007). Prigerson and colleagues changed their proposed term from *traumatic grief* to *complicated grief (CG)* after the attacks on September 11th in order to avoid any possible confusion with post-traumatic stress disorder (Zhang, El-Jawahri, & Prigerson, 2006). Later, they changed it again to *prolonged grief disorder (PGD)* (Prigerson et al., 2009).

The American Psychiatric Association was considering a new category called something like **bereavement-related disorder** for inclusion in the fifth edition of the *Diagnostic and Statistical Manual (DSM-V)* (American Psychiatric Association, 2011). Although a new adjustment disorder related to bereavement and an *exploratory* bereavement related disorder have been included in an appendix to *DSM-V,* no broad diagnostic category for complicated grief has been included in the newly released *DSM-V* (Kaplow et al., 2012).

Bereavement Related Disorder

A. The person experienced the death of a close relative or friend at least 12 months earlier.
B. Since the death at least 1 of the following symptoms is experienced on more days than not and to a clinically significant degree:
1. Persistent yearning/longing for the deceased
2. Intense sorrow and emotional pain because of the death
3. Preoccupation with the deceased person
4. Preoccupation with the circumstances of the death
C. Since the death at least 6 of the following symptoms are experienced on more days than not and to a clinically significant degree:

Reactive Distress to the Death
1. Marked difficulty accepting the death
2. Feeling shocked, stunned or emotionally numb over the loss
3. Difficulty in positive reminiscing about the deceased
4. Bitterness or anger related to the loss
5. Maladaptive appraisals about oneself in relation to the deceased or the death (e.g., self-blame)
6. Excessive avoidance of reminders of the loss (e.g., avoiding places or people associated with the deceased)

Social/Identity Disruption
7. A desire not to live in order to be with the deceased
8. Difficulty trusting other people since the death
9. Feeling alone or detached from other people since the death
10. Feeling that life is meaningless or empty without the deceased, or the belief that one cannot function without the deceased
11. Confusion about one's role in life or a diminished sense of one's identity (e.g., feeling that a part of oneself died with the deceased)
12. Difficulty or reluctance to pursue interests since the loss or to plan for the future (e.g., friendships, activities)
D. The disturbance causes clinically significant distress or impairment in social, occupational, or other important areas of functioning
E. Mourning shows substantial cultural variation; the bereavement reaction must be out of proportion or inconsistent with cultural or religious norms

Specify if

With Traumatic Bereavement: Following a death that occurred under traumatic circumstances (e.g., homicide, suicide, disaster or accident), there are persistent, frequent distressing thoughts, images or feelings related to traumatic features of the death (e.g., the deceased's degree of suffering, gruesome injury, blame of self or others for the death), including in response to reminders of the loss.

FIGURE 11.1 Criteria for Proposed Bereavement Related Disorder in the DSM-V *Source:* This figure is based on APA, 2011.

If bereavement-related disorder (BRD) is adopted as a recognized disorder in some future edition of the *DSM,* we can probably expect whatever term is adopted to emerge as the generally accepted one. See Figure 11.1 for an outline of the specific criteria that were considered for the proposed new disorder.

As you can see from Figure 11.1, the criteria for BRD that was being considered by the American Psychiatric Association (2011) is consistent with many of the early observations of Collin Murray Parkes (1998a, 1998b) as well as conclusions of the emerging bereavement research about complicated grief (Bonanno et al., 2007; Prigerson et al., 2009). The specific features of the proposed bereavement-related disorder included loss at least one year earlier; severe separation distress; intense longing and searching for the deceased; preoccupation with thoughts of the deceased; symptoms of traumatic distress, such as feelings of disbelief, anger, and shock; avoiding people or places associated with the deceased; disruption in social relations or personal identity; impairment in social or occupational functioning; and the bereavement reaction is inconsistent with the person's cultural or religious norms (American Psychiatric Association, 2011).

The picture of the bereavement-related disorder that is coming into clearer focus for bereavement experts combines elements of profound sadness, denial, trauma, emotional reactivity, and impaired functioning that do not resolve quickly. As you might recall from the chapter introduction and discussion in Chapter 10, Parkes proposed that there are *traumatic*, *conflicted*, and *chronic* forms of complicated grief. There is a well-established body of evidence relating to traumatic loss and post-traumatic stress. There is *no* clear evidence supporting the contention that having a conflicted relationship with a deceased loved one causes complicated grief. But there is a growing body of evidence relating to the chronic or prolonged aspects of complicated grief. So, in the next two sections, we will look at the current state of the art in relation to traumatic loss and prolonged grief.

TRAUMATIC LOSS

Pebbles in the Pond

In Chapter 7, we looked at the experience of traumatic death. This exploration included several types of traumatic death: terrorism, murder, suicide, natural disasters, and large-scale health pandemics, such as AIDS. In this light, we briefly discussed the case of Tariq Khamisa, a 20-year-old San Diego State University art student who was murdered when delivering pizza (Dibsie, 1995; Hasemyer & Cantlupe, 1995). As you may recall, Tariq's father later teamed-up with the killer's grandfather in an effort to do something about the problem of youth violence. So, in this sense, something good came of the murder. But, some bad things also came of it. Let's call these "pebbles in the pond" to signify the little ripples, or aftershocks, of the initial tragedy.

Tariq, called TK, was not an isolated individual. He had a family, friends, dreams, and no doubt problems, too. He met Jennifer at San Diego State and the two of them fell in love. They were engaged to be married. They decided to move out of the dorm and into their own apartment, but in order to do so they had to have money. So, they formed a pact. They would take turns working while the other went to school. Jennifer had just finished a stint working and TK had just started a job at DeMille's Italian Restaurant, delivering pizzas. Jennifer, who was also a gifted artist and photographer, signed up for classes. Then tragedy struck. TK was murdered when delivering two large pizzas.

Jennifer wasn't present when the shot was fired. The case got a lot of local media attention, including clips of the murder scene and TK's lifeless body, lying bloody on the front seat of his "cool" tan-colored VW station wagon. And the case didn't go away quickly. For months in San Diego, the media covered the hearings, trials, and finally the sentencing in adult court of a boy who was 14 years old when he pulled the trigger.

Jennifer came from a good family. Her father was a respected army dentist. She had two brothers. Her mother was a stay-at-home mom. We can't know for sure exactly what she experienced after TK's murder. What we do know is that her life unraveled. For a time, she was living on the streets of San Francisco, working at a club. She developed a heroin addiction. Her mother tracked her down through contacts at a church shelter and then helped her get into treatment. After she left treatment she moved to be with her family. She kicked the heroin habit and things improved a little, but she was still deeply troubled.

Jennifer went from therapist to therapist after she came home. One of these mental-health professionals diagnosed her with schizo-affective disorder, a combination of mood disorder with psychotic symptoms. She was on and off her meds. She had sporadic conflicts at home, until her family moved her into her own little apartment. A girl with a history of eating disorders, she became isolated and reclusive after she lost her job at a local newspaper. Then, in late 2001, almost six years after TK was killed, she put a gun to her own head and pulled the trigger. When the body was found, her parents were called. More crime-scene yellow tape. More trauma. Ripples. After Jennifer's death, her mother wrote a poem. It is shared here, with permission.

Surviving...

In my Rude Awakening
I lost my compass,
the earth turned to sand
and the sky became hollow,
colorless & non-existent.

A shade was pulled down upon
the Window of my Life.
I was as one in, "The
Night of the Living Dead."
I slept the sleep of a drugged
victim.

All nerve-endings pulled
away from the wound.
I sought solace in solitude—
or mindless activity.
I stared a lot—I slept a lot.
I prayed.

My prayers were like one—
scratching...
on the interior surface of
a blackboard coffin.

Pleas—scribbled in the scrawl,
of a mad-woman
mad with grief—insane with pain.

There is no Common Prayer
for the newly bereft.
There are no words of comfort
no pill, no treatment—to ease the troubling pain.
Only time & space & Sonshine
can begin to soothe the cavity—we call
sudden tragic loss.

—C. Patchen

Early Research on Traumatic Grief

Among the first modern attempts to systematically study traumatic loss was the work done by Erich Lindemann (1944), who was then Chief of Psychiatry at Massachusetts General Hospital. Lindemann and other members of the staff at the hospital were called in to work with bereft families after a particularly tragic accident.

In the fall of 1942, there were two colleges in Boston that were renown for the spirited nature of their football rivalry: Holy Cross and Boston College (Lindemann, 1944, cited in Worden, 2002). At the end of the game, many of the attendees went to a local nightclub, the Coconut Grove, to celebrate. A busboy accidentally set a decorative palm tree on fire. The fire spread rapidly, killing 492 revelers at the club, which was filled beyond its stated 460 person capacity with nearly 1,000 people. In working with over 100 bereaved family members, Lindemann and his colleagues were able to identify a pattern of six key traumatic grief reactions:

1. Somatic, or bodily distress
2. Preoccupation with the image of the deceased
3. Guilt about the circumstances of what happened
4. Hostility
5. Difficulty functioning as before
6. Taking on characteristics of the deceased

In addition to Lindemann's early work with families and survivors, Alexandra Adler, the daughter of renowned psychoanalyst Alfred Adler, worked with more than 500 survivors of the Cocoanut Grove fire. Her work is now considered some of the earliest research on post-traumatic stress (Adler, 1943).

Assessing Reactions to Traumatic Loss

As discussed in Chapter 7, the experience of *trauma* conveys the idea of a shocking injury or to events outside the ordinary—for example, terrorism, murder, suicide, pandemic illness, or natural disaster. *Traumatic death* can contribute to problematic reactions among bereaved loved ones. Indeed, the proposed criteria for bereavement-related disorder (BRD) specify that evaluators should designate the loss as traumatic when this is the case (American Psychiatric Association, 2011). Although traumatic and prolonged forms of the proposed bereavement-related disorder have similarities and differences, there also seem to be similarities between a traumatically induced bereavement-related disorder and an anxiety-based disorder such as post-traumatic stress disorder, acute stress disorder, and various dissociative disorders. Indeed, the *DSM-IV-TR* criteria for post-traumatic stress disorder include exposure to situations involving threatened or actual death (American Psychiatric Association, 2000).

Currently, among the most commonly diagnosed anxiety-based reactions to psychological trauma is post-traumatic stress disorder. Post-traumatic stress disorder, or PTSD, is a disorder that itself didn't make it into the *Diagnostic and Statistical Manual* until the third edition, published in 1980. The designation PTSD was first officially used to describe a cluster of disturbing signs and symptoms experienced by a large number of Vietnam veterans suffering from the effects of their war-related experiences (Kemp, 1998).

Since then, it has been applied to people who develop similar symptoms in response to other traumatic experiences, such as auto accidents, witnessing violence, being threatened, the aftermath of suicide or murder, or severe abuse (Kemp, 1998). In addition to exposure to a traumatic event sufficiently severe to produce such a reaction, the diagnosis of the disorder requires that several other criteria be met. In addition to a **traumagenic event**, symptoms include **intrusive reexperiencing** (through such things as flashbacks and nightmares); **avoidance** of people, events, or situations that "trigger" the reexperiencing; and **hyperarousal** (vigilant scanning the environment, sleep disturbance, jumpiness, etc.). The symptoms must last more than a month, and may be of short duration (fewer than three months), chronic (more than three months), or have a delayed onset.

According to *DSM-IV-TR* (American Psychiatric Association, 2000) acute stress disorder is a disorder in which the person develops anxiety, dissociative, or other symptoms that occurs within a month of exposure to one of the stressors associated with post-traumatic stress disorder (American Psychiatric Association, 2000). The factor that distinguishes it from PTSD is that it surfaces within four weeks of the event and persists for no longer than four weeks. One other feature of this diagnosis that differs from PTSD is the presence of **dissociative symptoms**.

Dissociative symptoms refer to the process whereby a person separates, or splits away, the experience from conscious awareness. It can be expressed as numbing, feeling personally detached, absence of emotional responsiveness, reduction of awareness, a feeling that the experience isn't real, and amnesia to important aspects of the trauma. It should be noted that just because dissociative symptoms are not included within the criteria for PTSD does not mean that persons with PTSD don't also have dissociative symptoms.

In addition, there is a class of disorder linked to dissociation, called **dissociative disorders**. Rather than catalog each of them separately, we survey them here as a group. According to the *DSM-IV-TR* (American Psychiatric Association, 2000), "The essential feature of the dissociative disorders is a disruption in the usually integrated functions of consciousness, memory, identity, or perception of the environment."

Perhaps the most extreme, and famous, form of dissociative disorder is now called **dissociative identity disorder (DID)**, a relatively rare condition caused by extreme psychic trauma that usually first occurs in very young children, before their personalities are fully established. The disorder was formerly called *multiple personality disorder*, and involves the development of a number of distinct, autonomous, or semiautonomous personalities. As with other forms of dissociation, it develops as an attempt to cope with overpowering stress, and can be seen as a way to psychologically manage extreme levels of anxiety.

Other dissociative disorders include **dissociative amnesia** (loss of memory, usually about traumatic events, too extensive to be normal forgetfulness), **depersonalization disorder** (chronic feeling of being separated from one's mind or body, but having normal awareness of reality), and **dissociative fugue** (sudden travel away from home, confusion about identity, and loss of memory about one's past).

Dealing with Traumatic Reactions

As previously discussed, the new science of bereavement research has begun to establish bereavement-related grief as a distinct disorder (Bonanno et al., 2008; Prigerson et al., 2009; American Psychiatric Association, 2011). The current proposed criteria for BRD have both differences and similarities to such other disorders as post-traumatic stress disorder (PTSD) and major depressive disorder (MDD). Indeed, traumatic death is sometimes a factor in both bereavement-related disorder (BRD) and post-traumatic stress disorder (PTSD), just as profound sadness occur in both grief and major depressive disorder (MDD).

Treating trauma is a specialized field in itself. Attempting to address it thoroughly is beyond the scope of this chapter. Instead, we will briefly discuss some of the most important points. By way of introduction, we can say that any effort to treat trauma attempts to accomplish some basic goals: normalize the situation, shorten recovery time, reduce distress, restore functioning, and mobilize whatever resources may be available (Dyregrov, 2004; Marotta, 2000, cited in Meagher, 2007).

POSTTRAUMATIC STRESS The Veterans Administration is a major provider of care for patients with post-traumatic stress disorder (Rosen et al., 2004). It operates an extensive network of regional medical centers as well as a large number of community-based outreach clinics, called Vet Centers. In an effort to improve the quality of care for its patients, the VA system has begun to emphasize the use of evidence-based therapies and to disseminate knowledge about "best practices" in the treatment of post-traumatic stress disorder. It uses guidelines adopted by the International Society for Traumatic Stress Studies (ISTSS) (Foa, Keane, Friedman, & Cohen, 2009; Foa, Keane, & Friedman, 2000).

Solid research points to the effectiveness of a range of **cognitive-behavioral therapies (CBT)**, particularly **exposure therapy (ET)**. Exposure therapy refers to a series of procedures that progressively help the person confront distressing thoughts and memories (Foa et al., 2009). This usually involves asking the individual to imagine as realistically as possible the distressing thought or memory along with real-life exposure to reminders. The military has been using virtual reality technology to enhance the process (McLay, McBrien, Wiederhold, & Wiederhold, 2010; Freedman et al., 2010).

Other effective cognitive-behavioral therapies include systematic desensitization and stress inoculation training (SIT). *Systematic desensitization* involves pairing trauma-related memories and reminders with muscle relaxation (Foa et al., 2009). *Stress inoculation training* is an anxiety management program that includes education, muscle relaxation training, breathing, role playing, covert modeling, guided self-dialog, and thought stopping (Foa et al., 2009). There are also non-CBT therapies that have been shown to be effective in treating PTSD, including **eye movement desensitization and reprocessing (EMDR)**, group therapy, and psychopharmacotherapy, or the use of medications to address distressing symptoms (Foa et al., 2009). First developed by Francine Shapiro to help trauma victims, EMDR is an eight-phase psychotherapeutic process (Shapiro, 2001). It targets specific issues, events, feelings, and memories. Part of this process involves asking the patient to focus simultaneously on an image, negative thought, or disturbing feeling or body sensation, after which the patient is asked to follow a moving object. Group therapy provides a venue for efficiently delivering efficacious forms of treatment that also builds in social contact, social support, and modeling. The International Society for Traumatic Stress Studies believes that medications may play a role in targeting specific distressing symptoms of PTSD (Foa et al., 2009). There is good evidence that selective serotonin reuptake inhibitors (SSRI) can be used to target anxiety, mood, and reexperiencing symptoms. And some evidence suggests that adrenergic agents, such as clonidine, may help with hyperarousal, impulsivity, nightmares, and sleep problems.

DISSOCIATIVE PROCESSES The whole topic of dissociation and trauma is somewhat controversial in the mental-health field. This having been said, we should acknowledge that the International Society for the Study of Dissociation has adopted a set of evidence-based criteria to guide treatment of dissociative disorders. These are intended to supplement generally accepted principles of psychotherapy and psychopharmacology (International Society for the Study of Dissociation, 2005).

Dissociation is defined by the *DSM-IV-TR* as the "disruption in the usually integrated functions of consciousness, memory, identity, or perception" (American Psychiatric Association, 2000). In essence, it is a splitting or disintegration of consciousness, memory, identity, or perception in response to overwhelming trauma. It is the consensus of the ISSD community that the goal of treatment is to move the patient toward more integrated functioning.

Over the past two decades, a consensus has emerged in the ISSD that complex trauma-related disorders are most appropriately treated with a phase- or stage-oriented approach, as shown here (International Society for the Study of Dissociation, 2005):

1. Safety, stabilization, and symptom reduction
2. Working directly and in-depth with traumatic memories, and
3. Integration and rehabilitation

The ISSD suggests that the concept of **complex PTSD** may be an appropriate way to think of dissociative conditions, particularly dissociative identity disorder, since its victims have usually had repeated traumas starting in childhood (International Society for the Study of Dissociation, 2005). Dissociation, or "splitting," becomes a learned way of coping with trauma, so mental-health professionals who treat patients with dissociative disorders must help them confront their traumas but must also be somewhat tolerant of their use of dissociation until the person is able to manage without it.

During the initial stage of treatment, the focus is on managing the risk of suicide and a myriad of other safety concerns. During this phase, the ISSD recommends patient education on safety, identifying parts of the self that engage in unsafe behavior, entering into agreements about alternative strategies for managing problems, and developing strategies to deal with other symptoms (International Society for the Study of Dissociation, 2005). Efforts to help stabilize the individual may include use of skill building, soothing images, reaffirming statements, and calming imagery. The ISSD recommends that work with patients who have dissociative identity disorders requires interaction and communication with the "alters," learning about their roles in dealing with life events, and outlining a map of the dissociative "system."

During the second phase of work with dissociative patients, the International Society for the Study of Dissociation (2005) recommends communicating directly with the patients' about their traumatic memories and experiences. For patients with dissociative identity disorders, this involves interaction with alters that experience "themselves" as "holding" the traumatic memories. During this phase, efforts can be made to "detoxify" their experiences, framing them in a more understandable context, and looking for alternative meanings. The ISSD guidelines suggest that work during this phase may help the patient gain a sense of control.

In the third phase of treating dissociative patients, the goal is to help patients solidify the internal coordination and integration of the dissociative system (International Society for the Study of Dissociation, 2005). Patients are expected to function in a more integrated way. There is generally less discussion about past traumas and more attention on learning how to live better in the present. According to the ISSD, the experience of multiple losses, grief, and mourning is often experienced more profoundly during this stage. Finally, patients may need coaching about how to deal with the normal tribulations of life in a nondissociative manner.

The most common approach to treating dissociative disorders is individual psychodynamically oriented psychotherapy, sometimes supplemented with other therapies (International Society for the Study of Dissociation, 2005). These include behavior modification, cognitive behavior therapy, systematic desensitization, stress inoculation training, **dialectical behavioral therapy (DBT)** (e.g., Dimeff & Linehan, 2001), and the appropriate use of hypnosis in cases where the therapist is qualified to use it. In addition, the ISSD suggests consulting the distinct body of literature that has been developed on treating *complex PTSD*.

PROLONGED GRIEF

As discussed earlier in this chapter, the proposed diagnostic category of bereavement-related disorder (BRD) focuses on what used to be called *chronic* or *prolonged grief,* although it does admit traumatically induced cases. Recent research suggests that the difference between the experience of separation distress (e.g., yearning and longing) and traumatic distress (e.g., numbness, anger, and bitterness) appears to lie in the cause of death (Holland & Neimeyer, 2011). Generally, this research confirms that traumatic distress is influenced by the traumatic nature of the death, whereas separation distress is influenced by having had a close relationship with the deceased. In the preceding section we focused on the traumatic loss. In this section we focus on prolonged grief. Individuals with chronic, or prolonged, grief are sometimes described as being stuck in their mourning (Bonanno et al., 2004; Zhang et al., 2006). As discussed in Chapter 10, Collin Murray Parkes believed that the chronic form of complicated grief is largely caused by excessive dependency on the deceased (Parkes, 1998a, 1998b).

Indeed, George Bonanno, a leading contemporary bereavement researcher, whose work we discussed at length in Chapter 10, believes that dependency is the glue that holds the yearning, isolation, and emptiness of chronic grief together (Bonanno, 2009). By dependency Bonanno generally means emotional dependency—the exaggerated need to be cared for, nurtured, and protected, even when capable of doing so for oneself. Sometimes excessively dependent individuals are described as clingy, submissive, and fearful of separation.

Collin Murray Parkes was among the first in the West to observe that people in very long, dependent, relationships are at greater risk for the chronic form of complicated grief. *fotosergio/Fotolia*

The yearning of chronic grief tends to be focused on one thing: finding the lost beloved, but the pining fails to bring the loved one back (Bonanno et al., 2007; Bonanno, 2009; Prigerson et al., 2009). Instead, it only brings deeper pain, cycling again and again in the futile quest for the deceased. For most bereaved people, the memories of their deceased loved one brings a sense of comfort. We can sometimes call on our memories of lost loved ones to bring us temporary relief at times of stress and turmoil. According to Bonanno, the bonds we form with our caregivers give us internal representations of them we can call on in times of trouble (Bonanno, 2009). For those unfortunate bereaved individuals who lack secure bonds, memories of their deceased loved ones don't bring comfort. Instead, their lost loved ones haunt them in dreams, in faces in the crowd, or in the gait of a stranger who walks away. These experiences and the memories of their beloved remind them of their loss, not their connection, and tend to be experienced as disturbing.

RISKS AND RISK FACTORS

One of Collin Murray Parkes's greatest contributions to the field was calling attention to the mental and physical health of people with complicated grief. The specific factors that seem to put people at somewhat increased risk for chronic grief include death of a parent during childhood, having been abused or neglected as a child; childhood separation anxiety; insecure attachment style (see discussion of Bowlby in Chapter 10); having had a very close kinship relationship with the deceased; marital closeness and support; and inadequate preparation for death (Zhang et al., 2006; Prigerson et al., 2009).

In a study of long-term adjustment, the authors laud the general resilience and adaptability of most people who grieve, but warn of the potential adverse effects of bereavement (Arbuckle & de Vries, 1995). Comparing 184 bereaved persons (41 parents and 143 spouses) to nonbereaved adults, they found significantly reduced life satisfaction as well as increased feelings of depression and the sense of hopelessness. However, survivors emerged with a heightened awareness of their own ability to cope, especially so for women. They found that the type of loss the person experiences, gender, and social context all influence the outcome.

Wolfgang Stroebe and Henk Schut (2001), two leading researchers, conducted a review of the literature on the effects of bereavement on the health of survivors. They focus on three primary categories:

1. The bereavement situation (how the person died)
2. The person (personality, religiosity, gender, age)
3. The interpersonal context (social support and kinship)

Stroebe and Schut qualify the findings of their review by noting its three key limitations: (1) It encompasses only one type of grief experience—partner loss; (2) it looks primarily at health outcomes (and does not address personal growth or relationship issues); and (3) it covers only the most common factors that have been studied.

The bereavement situation refers to the mode of death, or how the person died. Stroebe and Schut (2001) observe it is generally thought that sudden, traumatic loss creates more difficulty for the bereaved than slow, expected loss (although the experience of expected loss might also bring with it anticipatory grief). Using the concept of attachment, sudden loss would seem to have the potential to impair the survivor's sense of safety and security. Stroebe and Schut report that the results of empirical studies are inconclusive on this point, even when the loss involves suicide. Some studies seem to indicate sudden loss leads to poor health outcomes, whereas other studies do not. Stroebe and Schut observe there may be other variables at play, such as the self-esteem of the survivor or the sense of personal control she or he has.

Personal Risk Factors

Personal risk factors include personality traits, religiosity, gender, and age. Stroebe and Schut (2001) count the survivor's pre-bereavement adjustment and sense of personal control as being among the important personality elements. Indeed, Stroebe and Schut (2001) concluded from their review that prior adjustment did seem to play an important role in bereavement outcomes—those with poor adjustment before their loss seem to have much more difficulty after. This conclusion gets support from a longitudinal study that was done with a sample of 125 bereaved spouses (Henderson, Hayslip, & King, 2004).

Religiosity

Religiosity can be understood as the degree to which a person has a commitment to a religious faith tradition. Stroebe and Schut (2001) suggest two possible mechanisms to explain any beneficial effects that might be found: (1) the belief system is an internal source of support and (2) social support networks are inherent in faith communities.

The findings, however, were mixed. Some studies found a positive influence, others found none, and still others even found an unhealthy influence. More recent studies conclude there appear to be beneficial effects (Holen-Hoeksema & Larson, 1999; Levy et al., 1994; McIntosh et al., 1993, cited in Stroebe & Schut, 2001). Much of the effect seems to relate to the role of social support. Some evidence, however, supports the notion that religion itself may help people find meaning even in difficult experiences and achieve a better long-term adjustment. In a study of 135 people close to a patient with end-stage cancer, the investigators found that people with spiritual beliefs seem to resolve their grief more rapidly and completely after a death (Walsh, King, Jones, Tookman, & Blizard, 2002).

Gender

In their review of the literature, Stroebe and Schut (2001) note that the evidence has been fairly clear for some time that grief affects spouses significantly and differently. After the loss of a spouse, both men and women have more health problems than people who still have their spouses. The evidence seems fairly clear in suggesting that men tend to have more physical health problems and die more quickly than women. Women, in contrast, seem to have more difficulty with depression. This outcome is often attributed to differing amounts of social support men and women are able to accept in response the loss of a spouse (Stroebe & Stroebe, 1983). Margaret and Wolfang Stroebe and their colleague, Henk Schut, use stress theory to develop an alternative explanation. Women seem better able to deal with the emotional, loss-oriented aspects of the loss, wherease men may be better at handling the more practical, restoration-oriented dimensions (Stroebe, Stroebe, & Schut, 2001). This may make it easier for men get back to a normal routine more quickly but without the emotional aspects of their loss having been resolved. This presumably results in the emotional aspects of their loss being "internalized" in the body.

Age

It is paradoxical that while age and health are normally inversely related (i.e., the older one gets the less healthy), it seems that when it comes to the impact of bereavement, the reverse is true. Older people seem to have an easier time adjusting to loss than younger people (Stroebe & Schut, 2001). There may be any number of variables that could contribute to this result, but it could result from older people having more experience with loss, better understanding the sudden nature of loss among those who are younger, or having more access to sources of help. In addition to the influence of age itself, it might be important to consider the generation the bereaved belongs to, since people experience different stressors depending on the era in which they live, as is especially seen during times when especially catastrophic events unfold, such as economic depression, natural disaster, war, or disease (e.g., polio and AIDS) (Folkman, 1997).

Interpersonal Factors

Identified by Stroebe and Schut (2001) as being major factors bearing on the experience of bereavement are *social support* and *kinship*. In a very simple but elegant model, John Briere, a trauma psychologist of some notoriety, suggests that crisis can ensue in the face of severe stress when either the person's internal strengths or external supports are not sufficient to face the situation at hand (Briere, 1992). In this model, either taking steps to support the individual's own coping abilities or providing extra support are appropriate.

Attachment Theory

Stroebe and Schut (2001) argue, however, that attachment theory may do a better job than stress theory in explaining grief associated with significant loss—a spouse, parent, child, or sibling. They observe that the literature is fairly clear. The loss of one's child, especially an adult child, seems to have the most severe impact on bereavement. They puzzle at these results, which seems to show that despite what they might expect on the basis of attachment theory, social support seems to benefit bereaved people. From their perspective, social support should not ameliorate a specific loss to a key attachment figure, yet it appears to do precisely this.

DISENFRANCHISED GRIEF

Grief is a normal response to loss. According to Kenneth Doka, who coined the term *disenfranchised grief,* this malady is grief is that is "not openly acknowledged, socially accepted, or publicly mourned" (Doka, 1989, p. 4). Examples of people who might be subject to disenfranchised grief include the illicit lover of a person who was married to someone else, the unmarried partners of gay men or lesbian women, women who have had a stillbirth or an abortion, mothers who have given up their babies for adoption, those who have lost a pet, or even the fan who had an idealized relationship with a celebrity who died.

Social acknowledgment, acceptance, recognition, or support for bereft individuals is withheld. Doka (1989, 2002) suggests there are five basic types of disenfranchised grief:

1. The relationship is not recognized (e.g., illicit lover, foster parent, or ex-spouse)
2. The significance of the loss is not acknowledged (e.g., the fan of the celebrity who has died)
3. The griever is excluded from public mourning (e.g., the very young, the very old, demented, mentally ill)
4. The circumstances of the death are stigmatized (e.g., death due to suicide, murder, AIDS, or the death penalty)
5. The way the individual grieves does not conform to social expectations (e.g., the person might appear "too cool" or, on the other hand, "too hysterical")

According to Doka (1989, 2002), disenfranchised grief interferes with the process of achieving a resolution to loss. Bronna Romanoff and Marion Terenzio (1998) suggest that the reasons for this are that getting through bereavement is a process that involves an intrapsychic transformation of one's sense of self, transition from pre-death to post-death social status, and continuation of one's sense of connection to the deceased.

The lack of recognition makes it more difficult for bereft individuals to internalize the significance of their loss (Romanoff & Terenzio, 1998). They might wonder, "If my relationship is not recognized, could it really have been that important?" Funerals are public rituals that mediate the transition from one status to the next—for example, from alive to dead or from spouse to widow. If one is not allowed to attend the funeral or one's status is not accepted, then negotiating the change can only be made without benefit of this activity. Bereavement experts now believe that maintaining a sense of connection to the deceased is important (Klass, 1993, 1997; Klass, Silverman, & Nickman, 1996; Klass & Walter, 2001). Being able to share helps keep a sense of relationship. Not being able to do so means that one cannot share one's loss with others.

COPING

Coping with loss, or adaptation, is considered a multidimensional process whereby one restructures one's self, one's relationships, and one's world to the reality of loss (Corr & Doka, 2001). It can be thought of as an ever-changing approach to trying to manage specific external and/or internal demands that are experienced as stressful or that exceed the resources of the individual (Lazarus & Folkman, 1984). The person's various efforts to cope or adapt can be directed to the problem itself or to the distressing feelings the person might be experiencing. While having to contend with the stresses that often surround the death of a beloved person is a clearly unpleasant prospect, it seems that human beings are far more resilient and adaptive than we may have realized.

Susan Folkman led a fascinating research effort that might go a long way in helping explain the rich possibilities in how people cope and adapt to extraordinarily stressful experiences (Folkman, 2001). Between 1990 and 1997, she and several of her colleagues conducted a longitudinal study of terminally ill gay men and their partners. In each case, death was expected. Anticipatory grief, coping, and adapting unfolded during a hugely challenging and poignant time in the lives of the affected individuals. It was not surprising that there were high levels of psychological stress.

One of the fascinating features of Folkman's study of gay men dying of AIDS is that she and her colleagues were able to study how the men and their partners coped with the disease and how the bereft partners coped with loss over a five-year period of time (Folkman, 1997, 2001; Folkman, Moskowitz, Ozer, & Park, 1997). The research unearthed a paradoxical mix of both depressive symptoms and positive emotions, both when dealing with the disease process and after bereavement. Using both classical quantitative methods (to test for the effects of the stress) and qualitative methods (to explore the experiential dimensions), Folkman and colleagues found surprisingly positive psychological states throughout caregiving and the bereavement period. Folkman identifies three key elements that seemed to contribute to the positive states these men experienced:

1. Problem-focused coping with the practical tasks associated with managing the disease
2. Positive reappraisal—redefining the situation in a more positive way
3. Using religious and spiritual beliefs

Despite the hardships, accomplishing such problem-focused tasks as changing bed linens, getting one's partner to the clinic, or hammering out an issue with an insurance company, was associated with improvement in negative mood, which Folkman (1997, 2001) believes was connected to gaining a sense of control over an uncontrollable disease process. When successful with a task it seems to have led to at least a temporary feeling of mastery. The ability to positively reappraise the situation, to "reframe" it, seems to have literally made it possible to see their life in a new light. Five years after the death of their partners, these men said they had achieved enhanced feelings of self-worth, strength, and wisdom, which they credit to their bereavement experience. Nearly one in five said they no longer feared death. In Folkman's study, the men claimed their religious and spiritual beliefs helped them find a sense of meaning and purpose in life that has stuck with them.

The work that Folkman and colleagues have done has led to some rethinking when it comes to our understanding of loss (Folkman, 1997, 2001; Folkman et al., 1997; Lazarus & Folkman, 1984). This and other recent work on bereavement has gone a long way to rouse the professionals, waking them, and stirring them to question and reevaluate conventional ways of approaching bereavement, grief, and mourning (Stroebe & Stroebe, 1987; Wortman & Silver, 1987, 1989; Bonanno & Kaltman, 1999, 2001). In the next section, we consider other emerging models and directions.

EMERGING MODELS

As discussed earlier, traditional approaches to psychotherapy and the use of medication haven't been very effective in treating people with chronic, or prolonged, grief. Indeed, one of the reasons why bereavement experts have been fighting so hard to gain recognition is in the hope that with it might come more effective approaches to treating it.

Complicated Grief Treatment

One such approach to treatment has already been developed. Katherine Shear and colleagues at the Columbia University School of Social Work have developed an approach called *complicated grief treatment (CGT)* (Shear et al., 2005). It uses an approach to cognitive behavior therapy (CBT) that targets specific symptoms of complicated grief. Much like the dual-process model discussed in Chapter 10, the CGT model simultaneously guides patients in dealing with their loss and helps them take steps to rebuild their lives. Consistent with treatment shown effective in treating post-traumatic stress disorder, clients are increasingly exposed to imagery related to their loss from within the safety of a clinical environment. See Box 11.1.

BOX 11.1

Treating Complicated Grief

As part of their research on complicated grief, Katherine Shear and colleagues (2005) developed a protocol for treating *complicated grief treatment (CGT)*. They have been able to empirically show that CGT is effective in treating complicated grief. It is a two-pronged approach in which the therapist simultaneously guides the patient to focus on the loss while at the same time helps the client take steps to rebuild his or her life.

- *Introductory phase:* The client is educated about normal and complicated grief and the dual-process model of adaptive coping that focuses on restoring a satisfying life and adjusting to the loss. Attention to personal life goals is included in this phase.
- *Middle phase*

   Revisiting: The patient is asked to close her or his eyes and tell the story of her or his loss. This is tape recorded and the patient is asked to listen to the recording at home.

   The patient is also asked to imagine situations related to the death he or she has been avoiding and gradually increase the exposure.

   A sense of ongoing connection with the deceased is also promoted by asking the patient to engage in a series of imagined conversations with the departed. The patient is also asked to complete a memories questionnaire, which primarily focuses on positive memories.

   Restoration focus: The patient is asked to articulate his or her personal life goals. The patient is also asked to consider what he or she would like for himself or herself if the grief was not so intense. The therapist assists the individual in working toward the identified goals.

- *Termination phase:* Review progress, discuss plans for the future, and talk about feelings regarding ending treatment.

Source: Shear, K. et al. (2005). Treatment of complicated grief: A randomized controlled trial. *Journal of the American Medical Association, 293*(21), 2601–2608. A copy of the protocol manual may be obtained from Katherine Shear, M.D., Department of Psychiatry, University of Pittsburgh, School of Medicine, 3811 O'Hara St., Room E-1116, Pittsburgh, PA 15213 (shearmk@upmc.edu).

Meaning and Story

Robert Neimeyer and his colleagues have been working for some time to develop an approach based on the idea that grief and complicated grief is mediated by how we find meaning in our experiences (Neimeyer, 2000, 2001, 2006; Neimeyer, Fontana, & Gold, 1984). In an edited volume, Neimeyer and colleagues address such issues as how we can reestablish a relationship after a loss, transcend trauma, make use of story, and achieve a new sense of meaning (Neimeyer, 2001).

Long before the new breed of thanatologist began to challenge the grief-work hypothesis, ordinary people had already begun their own grass-roots rebellion, clinging to the memories of their loved ones and refusing to establish "new" identities. What grief researchers really did was start asking the questions. In the renown Tübingen Longitudinal Study (Stroebe & Stroebe, 1989, 1991, 1993; Stroebe, Stroebe, & Domittner, 1988; Stroebe, Gergen, Gergen, & Stroebe, 1992; Stroebe, Stroebe, & Hanson, 1993), we learn that over two-thirds of widows and widowers said they planned to continue their previous life-styles as much as possible, a small number hoped for change, and a mere 17 percent reported seeking a new partner. Most said they planned to integrate their loss into their lives—not attempt to build a new identity. Nearly one-third claimed they could still sense the presence of their loved one over two years later, and over one-half said they "consulted" their deceased loved one when making important decisions. In a similar vein, Dennis Klass and colleagues have found in their work with bereft parents who have lost their children that these parents find it important to maintain a bond with their deceased children (see Chapter 3; Klass, 1993, 1997; Klass et al., 1996).

Margaret Stroebe and associates suggest that three basic principles can be derived from the emerging consciousness (Stroebe et al., 1992). The following brief summary attempts to capture the essence of these principles.

1. *Conceptual integration:* Rather than choosing from among apparently competing models of grief, it is beneficial to integrate or combine the best of each.
2. *Invitation to culturally embedded practices:* Instead of developing universal principles that attempt to apply in all situations, honoring the influence and rich textural variability of diverse cultures is advantageous in bereavement work. Intervention should be tailor-made for each situation.
3. *Expansion of responsibility:* Bereavement work should not be wedded to any particular theoretical "school," but should strive to honor and address the unique needs of each bereaved person.

As discussed in Chapter 10, Stroebe and Schut (1999) proposed what they call a *dual-process model of grief.* In this model, healthy coping is seen as a process in which people deal with their grief by using a strategy in which they alternate between using avoiding and confronting strategies to deal with both their current pain and future-oriented issues, depending on individual needs and the current issues at hand.

Torill Christine Lindstrom (2002) comments that excessive rumination, frequent crying and talking about it, and intrusive thoughts of the painful events does not help, but that the bereaved person must still come to terms with the "incomprehensible, unbelievable, and unacceptable fact that a loss has happened" (Lindstrom, 2002, p. 15). She observes that we probably should not recommend traditional grief-work approaches that coerce the bereaved to endlessly ruminate on their loss. We should also not encourage them to forget their grief at all costs, advocate they sedate or divert themselves, nor warn them about the possible adverse consequences of their loss-related thoughts or feelings. Rather, we should recommend that the bereaved recognize their emotional reactions as normal, accept their grief-related thoughts and feelings, encourage them to allow their feelings to heal naturally with time, unless there are clear reasons to do otherwise.

In Chapter 10, we discussed the insights of Tony Walter about the importance of being able to "tell the tale," or the story, about the deceased (Walter, 1996). As you may recall, he shared about the loss of his father and best friend. His point was, having the opportunity to tell the story with each other can help bereaved people heal from their loss. Walter observes that there are two *second-best* alternatives: professional counseling and self-help groups.

When Walter (1996) discussed the use of personal counseling as a second-best way to share one's stories of a deceased love one, he was specifically referring to the client-centered therapy of Carl Rogers (Rogers, 1965). This approach focuses on creating an atmosphere of trust, which allows the client to share and be listed to empathically. It is a cornerstone of most present-day approaches to psychotherapy. Self-help groups provide the opportunity to share with and be supported by other people who have similar experiences. What therapists and groups lack is firsthand experience with the deceased himself or herself. Therefore, the sharing that does occur is less likely to be as personal or meaningful and thus less healing.

"Storying"

The simultaneous existence of many apparently conflicting "truths" has led to an uneasiness about the prospects for discovering some universal truth that could someday explain human behavior (Corey, 2005, 2008). As a consequence, some argue that we have taken a postmodern turn (Best & Kellner, 1991, 1997, 2001; Corey, 2005, 2008; Kellner, 1999). Corey (2005, 2008) suggests that the postmodern turn in therapy involves a shift in which "truth" and "reality" have come to be understood as socially conditioned perspectives, shaped by history and social context.

In contrast to those who believe that there is an objective reality that can be systematically observed and measured, this new breed of theorists put more emphasis on subjective realities, which are not thought to be wholly independent of human observation (Corey, 2005, 2008; also see Chapter 2). From this frame of reference, a key to understanding experience comes from the meaning that emerges out of the use of language and by the sharing of stories. Although there is no single postmodern approach developed to address grief, several general ones have emerged from this perspective (Corey, 2005, 2008). Two seem particularly well suited for clients coping with the loss of a loved one. These are narrative therapy and collaborative therapy (Corey, 2005).

Gerald Monk uses the metaphor of "archaeologist" as a way to think about **narrative therapy** (Monk, 1997; Monk, Winslade, Crocket, & Eston, 1997). As the archaeologist goes about the business of exploring a site, he or she carefully brushes way the accumulated debris of untold ages with a small brush, gradually exposing various shards, fragments, and artifacts. With an eye for what is exposed and the imagination to sense what might yet lie beneath the surface, the archaeologist gradually pieces the story of a people together. The therapeutic archaeologist, however, is working with a living, breathing person. As Monk explains, "Narrative approaches to counseling invite clients to begin a journey of coexploration in search of talents and abilities that are hidden or veiled by a life problem" (Monk, 1997, p. 3). Therapists strive to build a collaborative relationship with an emphasis on listening to the clients' stories; searching for those times when they were skillful or successful; and using questions to engage with the client and facilitate the process (Corey, 2005, 2008). The approach assumes the stories we live by are socially created as a result of our interactions with others. A purpose of therapy is to uncover these stories, and transform their power in the lives of clients through a process of uncovering new meaning.

Corey (2005) describes the **collaborative therapy** approach (Anderson, 1993; Anderson & Goolishian, 1992; Carr, 1998) as a fairly unstructured style of counseling that emphasizes *caring for* and *being with* the client. Like the Rogerian person-centered approach, the collaborative language system approach asks the counselor to actively listen. Like narrative therapy, its parent, it starts with the premise that meaning is socially constructed. The client's story has emerged from the interaction between the person and the significant people in their lives. The purpose of counseling is to help the client tell or retell her or his story—not confront or challenge it. As the story unfolds, the intent is that the dialog will turn into a therapeutic conversation and new meaning will emerge. With this new meaning, problems are dissolved rather than solved. But, in order for this to happen, the counselor must take the stance of being a listener, eager to hear and operate from a position of "not knowing."

Chapter Summary

We began this chapter by noting that profound grief is a normal reaction to loss, but that the new science of bereavement research seems clear that a significant minority of grievers suffer from a more serious form of complicated grief that probably requires professional attention. They suffer from intense yearning and longing; symptoms of traumatic distress; avoiding people or place associated with the deceased; disruption in social relations or personal identity; and significant impairment for an extended period of time (American Psychiatric Association, 2011).

Several terms have been applied to this phenomenon. The American Psychiatric Association considered a new category of mental disorder, that was tentatively called

bereavement-related disorder (BRD), but ultimately declined to include it. We noted that Collin Murray Parkes had originally described three forms of complicated grief— traumatic, conflicted, and chronic—that he believed were caused by severe trauma, having had a conflicted relationship with the deceased, and dependency. The evidence suggests there is good evidence about the potential effects of trauma and dependency, but little about the impact of having had a conflicted relationship. So, we explored in some depth traumatic loss and prolonged grief.

We opened the discussion of traumatic loss by rerevisiting the murder of TK Khamisa, a 20-year-old San Diego State University student who was killed when trying to deliver two large pizzas, but we focused on the reactions of his fiancée, Jennifer, who had a great deal of difficulty coping after his death. Although TK's death got a great deal of attention in San Diego, Jennifer's difficulties got little attention, except from her friends and family, until she herself ended her own life.

Next we reviewed some of the earliest modern research on traumatic grief, done by Erich Lindemann and Alexandra Adler in response to the 1942 fire at the Coconut Grove nightclub, which ended in the death of 492 people. As a result of his work, Lindemann describes six traumatic grief reactions, which are quite consistent with the criteria being considered by the American Psychiatric Association for the new category of *bereavement-related disorder* (American Psychiatric Association, 2011).

According to Prigerson and colleagues, a key reason for considering a special category of bereavement-related disorder is in the hopes that doing so might result in more effective treatments, such as what happened when *post-traumatic stress disorder (PTSD)* was recognized in the early 1980s (Prigerson et al., 2009). Then we turned to a discussion of how we assess and treat traumatic stress and post-traumatic stress disorder. We paid particular attention to the "best practices" that have evolved, especially several cognitive behavior therapies (CBT) (Foa et al., 2009).

We also looked at another trauma-related reaction, the development of dissociative disorders, including *dissociative identity disorder (DID)*, which experts believe is often caused by the very severe abuse of young children. We reviewed the stage-oriented approach to treatment advocated by the International Society for the Study of Dissociation (ISSD).

We shifted our attention to a discussion of prolonged grief, which seems to be at the heart of much of the recent research on complicated grief. This new body of research appears to confirm Parkes's early observations about a form of grief that seems to develop in people who were very dependent on the deceased prior to their deaths. Described as clingy, submissive, and fearful of separation, these individuals have a very hard time returning to normal life after their losses.

Briefly we explored disenfranchised grief—that is, grief that is not openly acknowledged, socially accepted, or publicly mourned (Doka, 1989, 2002). According to Doka, disenfranchised grief can interfere with a bereaved person's ability to adjust to her or his loss. Doka (1989, 2002) discusses five types of disenfranchised grief, all of which relate to the refusal of society to acknowledge, recognize, and sanction certain types of loss.

We explored risks and risk factors associated with prolonged grief, including the influence of the bereavement situation, personal factors, and the interpersonal context: the role of how death occurred, personality characteristics, age, gender, religiosity, social support, and kinship. Then, we explored how people cope with, or adapt to, bereavement, drawing on the work of Susan Folkman, especially her study of gay men who cared for their terminally ill partners before they died. Despite the hardships, we learned how these men achieved an enhanced sense of life-mastery by successfully using problem-focused coping strategies, "reframing" techniques, and their own religious or spiritual beliefs.

In the final section, we took a postmodern turn, considering a couple recent challenges to traditional approaches. These insights now seem to be influencing the direction of bereavement studies. These included *narrative therapy* and the *collaborative therapy* approach, which draw on what some people like to think of as the postmodern imagination.

Key Terms

avoidance *245*

bereavement-related disorder (BRD) *240*

cognitive behavioral therapies (CBT) *246*

collaborative therapy *258*

complex PTSD *247*

depersonalization disorder *246*

dialectical behavioral therapy (DBT) *248*

dissociation *247*

dissociative amnesia *246*

dissociative disorders *245*

dissociative fugue *246*

dissociative identity disorder (DID) *246*

dissociative symptoms *245*

exposure therapy (ET) *246*

eye movement desensitization and reprocessing (EMDR) *247*

hyperarousal *245*

intrusive reexperiencing *245*

narrative therapy *257*

post-traumatic stress disorder (PTSD) *240*

religiosity *251*

traumagenic event *245*

Suggested Activities

1. Conduct an Internet search on the key words *complicated grief*. How many different terms were you able to find? What kind of materials did the links take you to? Did you notice any differences between materials put together by laypersons and those developed by professionals?

2. Consider some of the recent natural disasters you have become aware of because of media attention. Based on your understanding of trauma and traumatic reactions, what sorts of things do you think we ought to be aware of when considering how we should respond?

3. Consider any recent media account of traumatic death in your community. Who do these accounts focus on? Are there others that get little or no attention? What kind of issues do you think they are facing?

4. Keep a media file on traumatic death in your community. After you have gathered a body of clippings, what patterns do you see?

5. Explore the topic of prolonged grief in the literature. Which authors have devoted their creative talents to addressing personal loss? What can we learn from it? What do you think happens as a result of telling their story?

Suggested Reading

- Didion, J. (2007). *The year of magical thinking*. New York: Vintage.

  A memoir by one of America's premiere authors, this book tells the story of her husband's sudden death from a heart attack and her difficult adjustment during the year afterward. Described by one hospital worker as "a pretty cool customer," the dark side of cool is that she had an unnerving awareness of how things seemed to go badly.

- Kosminsky, P. (2007). *Getting back to life when grief won't heal*. New York: McGraw-Hill.

  This powerful book gives the reader a well-written description of complicated mourning. For those trying to deal with their own losses, this book takes you into the stories of others who have gone down this difficult path and ultimately helps you make some sense out of loss.

- Kroll, C. (2008). *Healing complicated grief: Reflections and exercises to mourn the loss of those who loved and hurt us*. Frederick, MD: PublishAmerica.

  This concise book for the bereft helps guide them through their grief with a series of reflections. The exercises help these individuals get in touch with memories of their loved ones, both glad and sad, venture through the mourning process, and embrace the future once again.

Links and Internet Resources

- **Complicated Grief Program at Columbia University**
  www.complicatedgrief.org/
  The Complicated Grief Treatment Program at Columbia University, School of Social Work and Department of Psychiatry, focuses on finding treatments that can help people with complicated grief. It also teaches professionals how to recognize and treat it. The program operates under the direction of Katherine Shear, MD.

- **Systematic Review of Literature on Complicated Grief**
  www.health.gov.au/internet/main/publishing.nsf/ Content/palliativecare-pubs-rsch-grief
  This site provides PDF downloadable documents published by the government of Australia, synthesizing the results of a systematic review of 88 peer-reviewed studies published between 1990 and 2005.

- **International Society for Traumatic Stress Studies**
  www.istss.org/Home.htm
  The society was created for professionals to share information about the effects of trauma. It is dedicated to the discovery and dissemination of knowledge about policy, program, and service initiatives to reduce traumatic stressors and their consequences.

- **National Child Traumatic Stress Network**
  www.nctsn.org/
  The National Child Traumatic Stress Network was established to improve access to care, treatment, and services for traumatized children and adolescents exposed to traumatic events.

- **Gift from Within**
  www.giftfromwithin.org/ http://www.istss.org/Home.htm
  This international nonprofit organization is dedicated to those who suffer post-traumatic stress disorder (PTSD), those at risk for PTSD, and those who care for traumatized individuals. Educational materials include videotapes, books, and articles for clinicians and those experiencing PTSD.

- **Bereaved by Suicide**
  www.bereavedbysuicide.com/
  Bereaved by Suicide is a global Internet resource devoted to connecting bereaved people and those who want to help them. Their goal is to help people bereaved by suicide find help—whether it is the personal story of a fellow survivor, information about programs around the world, or current research.

- **Sibling Survivors of Suicide**
  http://siblingsurvivors.com/
  Sibling survivors are often called the forgotten mourners. When a sibling dies, other siblings who are left behind, no matter their ages, are considered secondary mourners. This site, hosted by a sibling survivor and now clinical psychologist, attempts to provide a supportive venue for sibling survivors.

- **Open to Hope**
  www.opentohope.com/
  The *OpenToHope.com* website is an online community where people can find and share inspirational stories of life, loss, and love. It encourages its visitors to read, listen, share, and contribute with honesty and compassion.

Review Guide

1. Be fully familiar with all the major terms and concepts in **bold** print in this chapter.
2. What three forms of complicated grief were described by Collin Murray Parkes?
3. What is complicated grief? How many people do the experts think are affected by it?
4. What is bereavement-related disorder? What are the signs and symptoms? What are the implications if this new mental-health disorder is recognized by the *DSM?*
5. What kind of reactions did Lindemann find among the survivors of the Coconut Grove tragedy? How do the descriptions of these reactions fit with traditional approaches to understanding the experience of bereavement? How do they fit with your own understanding?
6. What is trauma? Posttraumatic stress? Posttraumatic stress disorder?
7. What are the signs and symptoms of posttraumatic stress disorder?
8. What do experts mean by "best practices" when it comes to the treatment of PTSD? What methods appear most reliable and effective? How is it done?
9. What are dissociative symptoms?

10. What are dissociative disorders?
11. What are "best practices" when it comes to the treatment of dissociative problems? Describe the phase- or stage-oriented approach to treating dissociative disorders.
12. Why do some experts think the concept of complex PTSD is important?
13. What are the characteristics of prolonged grief? How are those affected by it described by the experts? What happens to them as their grief unfolds?
14. What are the risks and risk factors for prolonged grief?
15. Based on research done by Stroebe and Schut (2001), what three factors seem to "mediate" prolonged grief?
16. What can attachment theory tell us about prolonged grief?
17. What is disenfranchised grief? What are the different types? Why is the concept of disenfranchised grief important?
18. What can we learn about coping, based on the work of Susan Folkman and her colleagues?
19. What is complicated grief treatment? Why was it developed? How effective is it?
20. What are some bereavement experts saying about "meaning" and "story"?
21. What are narrative therapy and collaborative therapy?

Legal and Ethical Borderlands

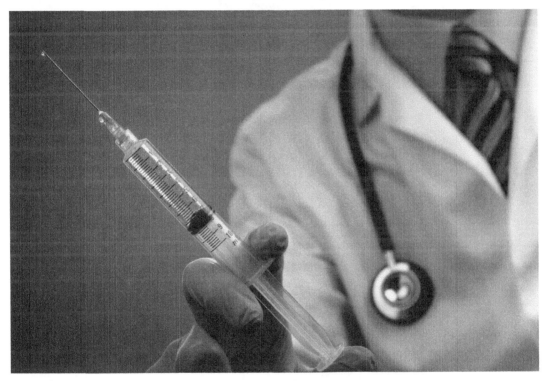

Brian Jackson/Fotolia

Part V contains two chapters that explore legal and ethical "borderlands" in death and dying. At one time, standards about life and death, good and bad, right and wrong, may have seemed fairly certain, but advances in technology and changing times have created fuzzier boundaries and difficult choices.

Chapter 12 explores the issues of physician-assisted suicide and euthanasia. Physician-assisted suicide, now legal in Oregon and Washington, and tolerated in Montana, is about using one's medical expertise to help terminally ill people end their own lives. The physician typically provides the drug, the patient must provide the will. Some patients—for instance, those suffering from ALS, or Lou Gehrig's Disease, may not be able to act on their wishes and may want more (i.e., voluntary euthanasia), or want someone else to take action that will end their lives. Tolerated in the Netherlands, Belgium, and Luxembourg, it is a much more difficult topic for health-care professional in North America.

Chapter 13 takes on the issues of withdrawing life supports and organ transplantation. It includes discussion of "brain death," harvesting human organs, and what to do when an individual falls into a persistent vegetative state, coma, or has "locked-in syndrome." Because technology makes it possible for us to artificially keep a body "alive" almost indefinitely doesn't necessarily mean we know when we ought or ought not do this.

12

Physician-Assisted Suicide and Euthanasia

- Core Concepts
- The Kevorkian Debate
- The Law and Hastened Death
- Unintentional Overdose

- Illicit Hastened Death
- Voluntary Euthanasia
- Moral and Ethical Concerns

In Chapter 8, we learned about Morrie Schwartz, a kindly retired sociology professor, who made it a point to learn as much as he could about dying and to share what he had learned about living. As you may recall, Morrie had ALS, or Lou Gehrig's disease. The course of illness with ALS varies from person to person. However, muscle degeneration usually leads to paralysis, often resulting in death from choking (PubMed, 2011). Morrie faced his death courageously at home, surrounded by his many friends and family. The kind of death Morrie achieved, however, is not always possible nor is it alwayss desirable. Many other patients with ALS report that they want the option of physician-assisted suicide. In one study of ALS patients in the Pacific Northwest, a majority of ALS patients said they would seriously consider physician-assisted suicide before their disease progressed to its final stages (Ganzini, Johnston, McFarland, Tolle, & Lee, 1998).

In Chapter 9, we discussed hospice and palliative care as considered by many to be the "gold standard" for end-of-life care. But what about those who prefer to end their suffering without going through the rigors of a long drawn-out process, such as what so often happens with life-threatening illnesses, such as cancer and ALS?

Only three states in the United States have laws that allow physician-assisted suicide, but several European countries are more permissive. In March 2010, the Public Broadcasting Service aired a *Frontline* episode highlighting the story of Craig Ewert. Craig and his wife,

As Long as One Person Remembers

Craig Ewert was 59 years old when he and his wife, Mary, came to Zurich, Switzerland. They were college sweethearts in Chicago, but would say their last good-byes in Zurich (Independent, 2008; Zaritsky, 2010). Since being diagnosed with ALS five months previously, Craig's condition deteriorated rapidly. By the time they arrived in Zurich, he had lost the use of his arms, was losing the use of his legs, and was dependent on a portable ventilator to breath. According to Mary, ALS was his worst nightmare, since for a long time he had had a fear of paralysis and suffocation (Independent, 2008).

Craig contacted Dignitas, a Swiss-based right-to-die organization. Physician-assisted suicide is legal in Switzerland and Swiss law did not require patients to be Swiss residents. John Zaritsky, a documentary film director, had also been in touch with Dignitas because he was interested in the topic. Dignitas put Craig in touch with Zaritsky and they agreed to film his ending (Independent, 2008). According to Mary, Craig agreed to film it because he felt it was important for all of us to learn how to face death honestly. After Craig and his medical records were examined by a doctor, Craig and Mary were taken to an apartment that had been rented by Dignitas. Everything was explained and Craig, still able to swallow, drank the deadly drugs through a straw. Before he died, Craig commented that a person "is not completely gone as long as one person remembers his name."

Mary, had been college sweethearts in Chicago—she a Catholic, he an agnostic. When their story was filmed, he was 59 years old and the couple were preparing to say their last good-byes. The disease had progressed quite rapidly. Rather than face the possibility of suffocating to death, he opted to go to Switzerland, where physician-assisted suicide is legal (Zaritsky, 2010).

In this chapter, we consider the issues involved with two highly controversial end-of-life topics: physician-assisted suicide and euthanasia. We look at definitions that are critical to understanding key issues linked to hastened death before exploring the topic itself, beginning with the one-man right-to-die crusade of Dr. Jack Kevorkian, a former pathologist turned "death counselor." He challenged the legal system and lost, but also managed to make the issue part of everyday conversation. We also review a few key U.S. legal cases that paved the way to the legalization of physician-assisted suicide in three states. We discuss the relaxation of voluntary euthanasia and physician-assisted suicide laws in several European countries. Finally, we explore a few of the moral and ethical concerns.

CORE CONCEPTS

It is a very fine line between using terminal sedation (medically induced coma) or using a potentially lethal dose of narcotics to control pain, and euthanasia or physician-assisted suicide. In Chapter 9, we briefly touched on the former. In this section of the present chapter we focus on the latter.

Hastened death is any act that speeds the dying process. **Euthanasia** is the act of deliberately causing the death of another for reasons that are believed to be beneficial. There are two basic types, active and passive euthanasia. **Active euthanasia** involves actively taking steps with the *intent* of ending another's life. **Passive euthanasia**, on the other hand, involves withholding necessary life-sustaining measures for the same purpose. **Physician-assisted suicide** refers to physicians using their medical expertise with the aim of helping another end their life.

Physician-assisted suicide can be accomplished in many ways, but it is perhaps most often done by prescribing a lethal drug or a fatal dose of an otherwise nonlethal medication. In the preceding paragraph, the word *intent* was emphasized because it is a key to distinguishing euthanasia and physician-assisted suicide from other acts that can result in death, but that are not explicitly intended to end life. When such an act is intended to relieve suffering and only incidentally causes death, it is consistent with the *principle of double effect* (which will be discussed in more detail later in the chapter). Thus, it does not constitute euthanasia or physician-assisted suicide (EPEC Project, 1999).

Euthanasia involves taking steps to hasten the death of another for reasons that are believed to be ultimately good or beneficial. *Web Buttons Inc/Fotolia*

There are two other categories of euthanasia:_nonvoluntary euthanasia and involuntary euthanasia. **Nonvoluntary euthanasia** is defined as deliberate administration of life-shortening substances with the *intent* of ending the life of a person who is not capable of making this choice for herself or himself (Giesen, 1997, cited in Amarasekara & Bagaric, 2004). **Involuntary euthanasia** was used by the Nazi regime to eliminate individuals it regarded as undesirable—the physically deformed, mentally incapacitated, and others it did not consider to be contributing members of the society. It is the act of ending another's life against their will and without their consent.

In recent days, voluntary euthanasia and physician-assisted suicide have become the focus of public debate about end-of-life choices. They achieved notoriety because of the controversy surrounding the activities of Dr. Jack Kevorkian, the debates about the legalization of physician-assisted suicide in three U.S. states, and because of decriminalization of voluntary euthanasia in three European countries, the focus of discussion in this chapter.

THE KEVORKIAN DEBATE

One-Man Campaign of "Dr. Death"

The public debate about physician-assisted suicide and euthanasia in the United States became noteworthy largely as the result of the ballyhoo surrounding the activities of the late Dr. Jack Kevorkian. When Kevorkian began his activities, he was a retired pathologist who had begun to advertise his services as a physician and "death counselor" in the local paper.

Kevorkian, dubbed "Dr. Death" early in his medical career by his colleagues because of his fascination with death, was sentenced to prison on April 13, 1999, for second-degree murder in the death of Thomas Youk (CNN, 1999). Youk, age 52, was suffering from ALS, or amyotrophic lateral sclerosis. He wanted physician-assisted suicide, and sought out Dr. Kevorkian, who by then had become quite well known. Youk wanted help in ending his life before ALS rendered him completely unable to do so.

Kevorkian assisted Youk and videotaped his death in Michigan, which he later gave to the CBS-TV show, *60 Minutes*. This time, Kevorkian actually injected Youk with the lethal drug. This turned out to be a final act of defiance. His one-man campaign to help people die humanely was both an affront to the legal system and the stuff

Dr. Jack Kevorkian may have done more than anyone in recent times to publicize the plight of people suffering from terminal illnesses. He is pictured here after his release from prison for assisting in the death of Thomas Youk, who was suffering from ALS, a degenerative nerve disease that often ends in death by suffocation and infection. *Jim West/AGE Fotostock*

of folk legend. With the *60 Minutes* footage there for all to see, Kevorkian was convicted. Melody and Terry Youk, Thomas's widow and brother, were prohibited from testifying during the trial but went to Kevorkian's defense during the sentencing phase. Mrs. Youk testified that by the time of his death, her husband had lost all but the use of a thumb and two fingers and was by then losing the ability to speak.

Although Kevorkian had previously been acquitted in three other cases and had one mistrial, this time, faced with the evidence from the *60 Minutes* tape and questions about whether or not Mr. Youk may have changed his mind at the last minute, the jury convicted Kevorkian of second-degree murder and violation of controlled substance laws. The murder conviction resulted from the act of administering the lethal drug. The controlled substance conviction is linked to his use of a controlled substance to kill Mr. Youk, since Kevorkian had been stripped of his license to practice medicine years before. As a result of these convictions, he was given a sentence of 10 to 25 years in prison.

In 1997, two years before his conviction, the Detroit Free Press, which had closely followed Dr. Kevorkian's duel with the legal system, ran a series of stories that chronicled 47 cases in which Kevorkian had a hand in someone's death (the links have since been removed from the paper's website). Sadly, a common feature in a great many of these cases was that the health-care system had failed to provide adequate symptom relief to patients who then turned to Dr. Kevorkian for help. By his own admission, Kevorkian was present at 130 suicides during his career (CNN, 1999). After his conviction in 1999, he became prisoner number 284797 at Thumb Correctional Facility in Lepeer, Michigan.

In December 2006, Michigan's parole board granted Kevorkian's request to leave prison on the basis of good behavior and his pledge to not assist in any further assisted suicides (Religion News Service, 2007). On June 1, 2007, he was released on parole. After his release, Kevorkian made an unsuccessful run for a seat in Congress. He continued to make public appearances advocating reforming laws on hastened death until 2011, when he died in the hospial at age 83 (McClellen, 2011).

The Law and Hastened Death

Although it seems that many seriously ill people want to have assisted suicide open to them as an option, in the vast majority of U.S. states it is not permitted. In 1997, two cases (*Washington* v. *Glucksberg* and *Vacco* v. *Quill*) came before the U.S. Supreme Court challenging the laws of Washington state and New York (Snyder & Sulmasy, 2001). Two separate federal appeals courts had previously invalidated state laws banning physician-assisted suicide. The Supreme Court was asked to revisit the rulings.

It did so, and in a 9-0 vote reversed the appeals court decision, ruling that the states had a legitimate stake in protecting human life. Therefore, it was lawful for states to use this authority to permit or prohibit physician-assisted suicide.

California, Michigan, Oregon, Maine, and Washington have all had initiatives on the ballot to legalize physician-assisted suicide, but so far only Oregon, Washington, and Montana now permit it (Lee et al., 1996; Steinbrook, 2002). In 1994, Oregon narrowly passed a measure permitting physician-assisted suicide for certain terminally ill patients (Steinbrook, 2002). After its passage, several legal challenges were launched in an attempt to reverse this decision. Despite these efforts, the voters took to the ballot boxes once again in 1997, resoundingly reaffirming their earlier decision. The new law known as the **Death with Dignity Act**—went into effect on October 27, 1997.

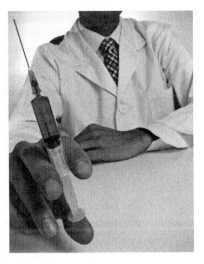

While many people believe it important to have access to professional help to achieve a good death, physician assisted suicide remains hotly controversial. *iStock © nito l 00*

Despite early attempts by former U.S. Attorney General John Aschroft to take punitive action against physicians who prescribed controlled substances under Oregon's new law, it remains in force today (Ashcroft, 2001, cited in Lowenstein & Wanzer, 2002). The case went all the way to the U.S. Supreme Court, which was unanimous in its 2005 ruling, saying Oregon had the authority to enact the law. It allows terminally ill Oregon residents (persons diagnosed as having six or fewer months to live) to get a prescription for a lethal dose of a controlled substance. It does not permit physicians to actually administer the drugs (which would constitute euthanasia). Refer to Figure 12.1 for a summary of the key provisions of Oregon's act.

During the first five years the law was in effect, 129 people died from a lethal prescription they received under the act (Sullivan, Hedberg, & Hopkins, 2001; Hedberg & Southwick, 2002; Hedberg, Hopkins, & Kohn, 2003). The vast majority of the deaths took place in the patient's own home (94 percent). The drugs most often prescribed were barbiturates: secobarbital and pentobarbital (98 percent). Death took place in 1 to 38 minutes, but most often in 5 or fewer minutes. The most common diagnoses among those who chose physician-assisted suicide were cancer and ALS. Through 2010, a total of 525 Oregonians have ended their lives using medications prescribed under the act (Oregon Public Health Division, 2011).

In neighboring Washington state, the campaign to legalize physician-assisted suicide picked up steam when Booth Gardner, a popular former governor, got involved. Then age 71, Gardner became sympathetic to the cause after being stricken with debilitating Parkinson's disease. He chose to make legalization of physician-assisted suicide in Washington his last campaign (Bergner, 2007). In November 2009, 58 percent of voters in Washington state passed a referendum based on Oregon's Death with Dignity Act. In 2010, its first full year in effect, 87 prescriptions were written under Washington's new law. Medication was used by 51 Washingtonians to end their lives that year. Nearly 80 percent of those who took the lethal medication had cancer and 10 percent had ALS or another similarly acting neurodegenerative disease (Washington State Department of Health, 2011).

1. *Oregon residency.* Oregon adult residents, who are capable, may initiate a written request under the act.
2. *Witnesses.* The request must be signed and dated by the patient and witnessed by at least two witnesses, who must attest that to the best of their knowledge the person is capable, acting voluntarily, and is not being coerced to sign the request. Witnesses may not be beneficiaries of the patient's estate, nor may the physician receiving the request serve as one of the witnesses.
3. *Responsibilities of the attending physician.* The attending physician must be attest to the person's capacity; ensure the patient is making an informed decision; state the medical diagnosis and probable prognosis; describe the potential risks of taking the medication; describe the feasible alternatives, including comfort care and hospice; refer the patient to another physician to confirm the diagnosis and the capacity of the patient; refer the person to counseling if appropriate; recommend the patient notify next of kin; and inform the patient that he or she may rescind the request at any time.
4. *Consultation.* A consulting physician must confirm the diagnosis, prognosis, and capacity of the patient.
5. *Oral and written requests.* The patient must make a written and oral request followed up by another oral request at least fifteen days after having made the first oral request.
6. *Waiting period.* The prescription may not be signed for at least fifteen days after the first oral request.

FIGURE 12.1 Summary of the Oregon Death with Dignity Act   *Source*: Oregon Revised Statute 127. 800-860.

On December 31, 2009, the Montana Supreme Court ruled by a vote of 5 to 2 that doctors in Montana are protected from prosecution if they help a terminally ill patient die. However, the court was not explicit in saying that physician-assisted suicide is a constitutionally protected right. The ruling was made in response to a case filed by Robert Baxter, a 76-year-old retired truck driver who was suffering from lymphocytic leukemia (Johnson, 2009a, 2009b; James, 2010). The following vignette tells his story.

By All Accounts He Was a Tough Man

By all accounts, Robert Baxter was a tough man. But the 76-year-old retired truck driver wasn't fighting traffic when he died. He was battling for the right to die with the help of his physician. He claimed that because his doctor was prevented by state law from helping him die, his rights under Montana's constitution were violated (Johnson, 2009a).

Once a robust man and avid outdoorsman, Baxter's body had been so ravaged by his 12-year fight with lymphocytic leukemia and the effects of chemotherapy that he could no longer enjoy the busy, active life he once had. He was miserable, his daughter told *ABC News*. He didn't have any fight left in him, and barely any meat on his bones (James, 2010). After stopping chemo in November 2008, he lost weight rapidly, shriveling into a mere shadow of what he had once been.

Baxter died on 31, 2009, the very day the lower court handed down its decision in his favor (Johnson, 2009a). The ruling affirmed that doctors are protected from prosecution when they help a terminally ill patient die. The state appealed that decision to the Montana Supreme Court. Exactly four months later, on December 31, 2009, the seven-member Supreme Court upheld the lower court decision by a vote of 5 to 2, making Montana the third state in the country to permit physician-assisted suicide (James, 2010).

UNINTENTIONAL OVERDOSE

When attempting to alleviate severe pain, powerful anelgesics, such as morphine, are often used. The appropriate amount and type of medication depend on the severity of symptoms and the tolerance to the effects of the drug. Too little medication and the person suffers; too much, and heart beat and respiration can become depressed enough to result in death. Sometimes health-care professionals admit there is a very fine line between the two. When strong medication is used to control pain and the person dies, it is generally presumed that the person has died because of the illness. In this situation, even if death actually results from the use of medication, it can be justified by the principle of double effect, a long established doctrine, discussed next.

The Principle of Double Effect

The **principle of double effect** is an ancient doctrine with application to today's tough medical dilemmas. With deep roots in Christian theology, it's a centuries-old precept of the Roman Catholic Church, used to help guide decisions on how to proceed when there are both desirable and undesirable outcomes (Krakauer et al., 2000). It's relevant today because the principle has been widely accepted by medical decision makers and church leaders alike. Bioethicists and those theologians who specialize in grappling with end-of-life moral questions have found the principle helpful in understanding those situations where individuals want to act in good faith yet are faced with the possibility of a bad outcome (Barry & Maher, 1990; Derse, 2000; Keenan, 1993; Krakauer et al., 2000; O'Rourke, 1989; Rousseau, 2001).

Without delving too deeply into the philosophical or theological issues, the principle asserts that an action with one good and one bad possible effect is morally defensible if four conditions are met:

1. Whatever action is taken cannot in itself be immoral.
2. The action must be undertaken with the intent of chieving the good effect, not the bad, even if it's possible to foresee the potential bad effect. The action cannot be intended to cause the bad effect.
3. The action must not achieve the good effect by means of the bad effect.
4. The action must be proportional (it accomplishes more good than bad).

To apply the principle to a case where an individual is being treated for severe pain, for example, one would need to consider the proposed course of action (administration of anagesic medication); the intent (good rather than bad, e.g., the action might be intended to normalize the dying process and ease the emotional strain on the family, not cause death, per se); that you do not accomplish the good (relief from suffering) through the bad (death); and that the course of action accomplishes more good than bad.

ILLICIT HASTENED DEATH

Unlike unintentional overdose, discussed earlier, illicit hastened death goes further. When it involves administering medication or engaging in acts to a critically ill person with the intent of causing a person's death, it is active euthanasia. When a health-care practitioner withholds something necessary for life with the intent of hastening the person's death, it is passive euthanasia. Active or passive, euthanasia, even voluntary euthanasia, is illegal in all 50 states in the United States and in all but three European countries. In health-care circles, however, there has been speculation for some time that euthanasia may be happening more often than we think.

Dr. David Asch, a Veterans Administration physician, conducted a study in an effort to find out about the attitudes and actions of critical care nurses about euthanasia (Asch, 1996). He found that of the critical care nurses who responded to his survey, about 17 percent said they had received requests from patients or family members for assistance; 16 percent of the nurses reported actually providing it. In addition, 4 percent said they had deliberately hastened a patient's death by only pretending to provide life-sustaining treatment.

In another study, this one involving physicians, Diane Meier and colleagues from the Mt. Sinai School of Medicine found that about 18 percent of physicians in specialties likely to face this issue had received a request for suicide assistance. According the study results, 11 percent of the physicians were asked to administer a lethal injection (Meier et al., 1998); 16 percent of those who had been asked provided some kind of assistance with suicide. About 5 percent followed through on a request for a lethal injection.

VOLUNTARY EUTHANASIA

The Netherlands became the first country in the world to formally decriminalize **voluntary euthanasia** when the country's senate passed legislation on April 10, 2001 (Netherlands Ministry of Foreign Affairs, 2001; Sheldon, 2001). In 2002, Belgium passed a similar law, based on the Dutch law. In 2008, Luxembourg, followed suit, making it the third member of the Benelux economic union to permit persons experiencing "unbearable suffering" to get assistance from a physician to end their lives.

The Dutch law, which went into effect on April 1, 2002 (Netherlands Ministry of Foreign Affairs, 2004), exempts doctors from the penalties of existing law so long as they act with "due care," follow strict guidelines, and report it. The law removed jurisdiction on physician-assisted suicide and voluntary euthanasia from the Public Prosecution Service and put the authority for oversight into the hands of newly created Regional Review Committees. See Figure 12.2 for an overview of the provisions of the Dutch law.

Although the law was new, the practice of physician-assisted suicide and voluntary euthanasia in the Netherlands was not. Tolerant attitudes toward many social issues—such as prostitution, homosexuality, recreational drug use—seems to be well-integrated in the national character. The acceptance of voluntary euthanasia and physician-assisted suicide seems entirely consistent with these attitudes. According to Gerrit Van der Wal, Medical Inspector for the Royal Dutch Medical Association, physician-assisted suicide and voluntary euthanasia have been practiced with ever greater openness in the Netherlands since the 1970s (Van der Wal et al., 1996; also see Emanuel, 1997). Although the issues are still hotly debated, acceptance of physician-assisted suicide and voluntary euthanasia probably reflects a high degree of acceptance of individual choice by the Dutch public and professional community. It is also etched in Dutch case law (Van der Maas, Van

- Establishes "Due Care" criteria that must be followed by the physician:
  a. Must be satisfied the patient made a voluntary and carefully considered request
  b. Must be satisfied the patient's suffering was unbearable with no prospect for improvement
  c. Informed the patient about his/her situation and the prospects
  d. Came to the conclusion with the patient that there was no reasonable alternative in light of the situation
  e. Consulted with one other independent physician who has seen the patientand who provided a written opinion on the "Due Care" criteria having beenfollowed
  f. Terminated patient's life or provided suicide assistance in accordance with due medical care and attention
- Provides for the possibility that minors over the age of 12 may receive assistance with suicide or the termination of life if they satisfy other provisions of the law
- Establishes Regional Review Committees, which consist of at least one legal expert (chair), one physician, and one expert on ethical or moral issues
- Exempts physicians from prosecution for helping another commit suicide or providing euthanasia if they fulfilled the "due care" criteria and notified the municipal pathologist of their actions

FIGURE 12.2 Summary of the Dutch Termination of Life on Request and Assisted Suicide (Review Procedures) Act   *Source*: Netherlands Ministry of Foreign Affairs (2001; 2004).

Delden, Pijnenborg, & Looman, 1991; Van der Maas, Van Delden, & Pijnenborg, 1992; Van der Maas, Pijnenborg, & Van Delden, 1995, cited in Van der Wal et al., 1996).

When doing field research for this text, I was briefly in the Netherlands. While there, I was privileged to meet with three individuals, each of whom had very different perspectives on euthanasia: Dr. Rob Jonquiere, who was then the chief executive officer of NVVE, the Dutch Voluntary Euthanasia Society; Dr. Theo Boer, a professor of systematic theology at Utrecht University; and Herman H. Van der Kloot Meijburg, a bioethicist, health-care educator, and pastoral counselor. Their reflections may help put a human face on the oftentimes emotional and contentious issues. Each of these are remarkable people with interesting things to say (Jonquiere, 2001; Boer, 2001; Van der Kloot Meijburg, 2001).

Dr. Rob Jonquiere: An Intensely Personal Experience

Dr. Rob Jonquiere is a physician who first became interested in the dilemmas surrounding death and dying when he was a young man in medical school. He came across the book, *Medical Power and Medical Ethics,* by Jan Hendrik Van den Berg, a famous Dutch psychiatrist (1969; English translation, 1978), which helped crystalize the issues for him. During his clinical training, like all doctors. he explained, he was confronted for the first time with dying people. He became a family physician, which put him in contact with all kinds of events in people's lives, most poignantly birth and death. He related that the aspects of being a doctor he liked most were linked to those circumstances when he could spend time with his patients discussing their life situations. It was during this period, Van den Berg claimed, that patients

(Continued)

naturally began to seek him out, asking for help with dying. The era was that of the late 70s and the beginning of the 80s, when the public debate on euthanasia in Holland was still new.

By the mid-80s, Dr. Jonquiere had helped two patients end their lives. When he described these experiences, I became very aware that for him the process leading to an agreement to end his patients' lives was a deeply personal one, in which he and his patients grew together in their relationship. To provide some context, Dr. Jonquiere related that in the Netherlands everyone is covered by health insurance and that people have a real relationship with their family doctor. Long before health declines, he explained, there's been plenty of opportunity to build a relationship. By the time death draws near, a lot has already been said. This is the kind of relationship where two people who respect and care about each other may speak freely about how to handle the end of life.

Dr. Jonquiere took his commitment to patient care into higher education, where he taught family practitioners at the university and nursing home physicians in the field. Eventually he was asked to lead the Dutch Voluntary Euthanasia Association, a step he describes as a natural one—the culmination of his experience and life career (Jonquiere, 2001).

Although the more tolerant policies on voluntary euthanasia and physician-assisted suicide enjoys the support of the vast majority of the Dutch people, perhaps as many as 80 percent, it is not unanimous. There are well-organized, vocal opponents, many of whom are strongly religious. Dr. Theo Boer's name was provided by contacts within the Dutch Reformed Church because he was regarded as a theologian who has been a valued consultant on issues associated with euthanasia.

Dr. Theo A. Boer: Maybe How We Die Indicates How We Live

Dr. Theo Boer is a theologian with considerable interest in the Calvinist heritage of the Netherlands. In explaining why the Dutch have been so willing to adopt liberal reforms, he suggests that because of the strong scriptural basis of this heritage that when the Dutch people began to question their religiously based beliefs, they were more willing to toss out the whole system and start from scratch.

Boer agrees with advocates of euthanasia that sometimes there are situations where circumstances are so bad—a *force majeure*—that one must depart from the rules. He believes that human life is sacred, but says he is not opposed to euthanasia when a person is experiencing severe physical suffering. He believes, however, that the new law goes too far. It allows suffering to be subjectively defined by the individual. Boer points out that it doesn't even require that the person be terminally ill. He cites two Dutch legal cases—*Shabot* and *Brongersmaa*—that establish psychological suffering as being sufficient to meet the requirements of the law.

I asked Dr. Boer about a concern that had been expressed to me about religiously oriented people imposing their values on others. He replied that the argument goes both ways. "When you're a society either way will influence the other," he said. "When you try to forbid euthanasia you impose your values on somebody else, but when you allow it…that will influence the society as a whole. I'm absolutely convinced about that." The crux of Boer's concern was that by making euthanasia normative, it has become more difficult for members of the society to refuse it when their health fails. This puts them in a position where they may think they must go along with it, he said, even if they might prefer to stay alive a while longer. There is a danger that issues of the expense of care and stress on the health-care system could come into play, he cautioned.

"In Holland people are very hard working. I think we may be one of the most productive countries in the world, with an unemployment rate of only 1.5 percent. Women are very much in the labor process…. This means people don't have very much time to be concerned about caring for their parents. When it takes longer…and it threatens to last for two or three years, people cannot take holidays any more…then, I think it could be a pressure." He observed. Boer's parting words were, "Maybe how we die indicates how we live" (Boer, 2001).

The Netherlands is a country with a population of approximately 16.7 million people. About 140,000 people die there each year. This figure includes the 3,600 actual cases of euthanasia and physician-assisted suicide that occur each year (Dutch Voluntary Euthanasia Society, 2001). Based on the anonymous reports of physicians, doctors comply with the law slightly more than 40 percent of the time by reporting it (Van der Maas et al., 1995). The country integrates palliative care into primary care, hospital care, nursing care, and seven integrated cancer centers. The hospice movement in the Netherlands is relatively small, mostly affiliated with various religious groups (Dutch Voluntary Euthanasia Society, 2001). Herman H. Van der Kloot Meijburg, an ethicist, educator, and pastoral counselor, was once a strong supporter liberalizing physician-assisted suicide and euthanasia in the Netherlands. In more recent days, however, this support for voluntary has waned as his conviction that there is a need for more hospice and palliative care in the Netherlands has increased. Read his following comments and reflections on the death of his own father through voluntary euthanasia.

Herman H. Van der Kloot Meijburg: Not Only Is It *You* Who's Dying, But *We* Will Have to Take Leave of You

Herman H. Van der Kloot Meijburg is an ethicist with a broad background in nursing education, workshop training, and pastoral care. For many years he had supported the efforts to liberalize policies on euthanasia. His father, who was nearly 90 years old, developed ALS in his old age. The senior Mr. Meijburg was married to Herman's mother for nearly 60 years. Unfortunately, she was afflicted with Alzheimer's disease and finally had to be placed in a nursing home. Herman's father visited his wife regularly until he himself moved into the same nursing home. His father's condition eventually deteriorated. His appetite waned. Finally, even the daily beer he had enjoyed didn't taste so good any more. The thickener they put in it because of his ALS ruined the flavor. He weakened. Finally, he lost interest in living.

(Continued)

> It seemed to Herman that something had changed—his father seemed to have one foot on the other side. One day the nursing home physician told Herman that his father had asked for help in ending his life. Herman recalls earlier conversations with his father about euthanasia. He remembers having said to him, "Not only is it you who's dying (in this situation), but we who will have to take leave of you." The message was that he shouldn't make a decision about euthanasia without talking with the rest of the family.
>
> Always before, Herman's father agreed to go on living. This time he and his doctor seemed to be in agreement. ALS had taken its toll. He was dependent on others for everything. The kind of death he would have with ALS wouldn't be pleasant. He would suffocate. Mr. Meijburg senior didn't want to continue. Herman recalls that he, his sister, and his father had said their last good-byes before the doctor administered the medication. Herman's father went to sleep and never woke up. It wasn't even recorded as a case euthanasia, Herman remembers. The municipal authorities wouldn't classify it this way. They said it was really just terminal sedation.
>
> One of the great moral issues in health care and one of the biggest differences between hospice and the Dutch euthanasia movements has to do with how we define euthanasia, Herman explained. With hospice, you allow the person to die, and with euthanasia, a medical person administers a drug. Who's really making the decision helps define it. It's vital that the moral issues be reckoned with, he said. I really support the idea of care, whatever the decision (Van der Kloot Meijburg, 2001).

MORAL AND ETHICAL CONCERNS

In the previous section, we concluded with a few reflections of Herman H. Van der Kloot Meijburg, whose father, suffering from ALS at age 90, died at his own request from a lethal injection. By Herman telling his father that not only would his father being taking leave of his family but that they would have to take leave of him, he was also pointing out that the consequences of even seemingly individual decisions, like choosing a death of one's own, also have an impact on others. While Meijburg had been at the forefront of the movement to decriminalize voluntary euthanasia in the Netherlands, in more recent years he became active in the development of hospice and palliative care programs in the Netherlands (see Van der Kloot Meijburg, 2003).

A concern about relaxing laws on physician-assisted suicide and euthanasia is that emphasizing the use of hastened death can detract from awareness about the need for and availability of hospice and palliative care. Dr. Ezekiel Emanuel is a leading opponent of physician-assisted suicide and voluntary euthanasia. As early as 1997, long before the Netherlands and other European countries enacted their permissive laws on hastened death, Emanuel wrote extensively about what he saw as potential pitfalls (Emanuel, 1997).

Professional Profile: Ezekiel J. Emanuel, M.D., Ph.D.

Ezekiel J. Emanuel is the Director of Clinical Bioethics at the National Institutes of Health; a fellow of the Hastings Center, a nonprofit bioethics think tank; and a Special Advisor on Health Policy in the Obama administration. He earned his medical degree and a doctorate in political philosophy from Harvard University. He is a medical oncologist, specializing in the treatment of breast cancer. Prior to his tenure at the National Institutes of Health, he was Associate Professor at the Harvard Medical School and a fellow at the Dana-Farber Cancer Institute.

His father was born Benjamin M. Auerbach, and his father's brother, Emanuel Auerbach, was killed during the 1936 Arab Riots in the former British Mandate of Palestine (present-day Israel, Jordan, the Palestinian territories, and parts of Saudia Arabia and Iraq). After Emanuel Auerbach's death, the family changed its name to Emanuel to honor his memory.

Ezekiel Emanuel is a leading opponent of physician-assisted suicide and euthanasia. He points to the Hippocratic Oath as evidence that medical technology in itself is not the cause of today's ethical dilemmas. He believes that legalizing physician-assisted suicide and decriminalizing euthanasia is harmful because it acts to decrease public support for pain management and mental-health care for individuals suffering from life-threatening illnesses. His brother, Rahm, is the present mayor of Chicago, and was President Obama's chief of staff.

In an article written for a general audience, Emanuel observed that in ancient Greece, at a time when physicians commonly provided euthanasia and assisted suicide for ailments ranging from foot infections to senility, the Hippocratic Oath actually represented a minority view (Emanuel, 1997). The oath enjoins physicians to "neither give a deadly drug if asked…nor make a suggestion to that effect" (Tyler, 2001).

Emanuel acknowledges that the majority of Americans support physician-assisted suicide and euthanasia on a conceptual level, but that this support is not resounding or universal (Emanuel, 1997). He observes that about one-third are strongly in favor, about one-third are opposed, and another one-third support it in some cases but not others, usually when patients are terminally ill *and* experiencing relentless pain. Emanuel points out that about two-thirds of Americans oppose state-sanctioned physician-assisted suicide and voluntary euthanasia when terminally ill patients are not in severe pain but want to ease the burden on their families or avoid a long drawn-out dying process.

A concern of opponents to voluntary hastened death centers on the so-called slippery slope hypothesis. It suggests that if society relaxes its laws on hastened death, it can result in a shift from permitting willing, competent, consenting adults to end their lives to imposing hastened death on those who cannot make this decision for themselves: the unconscious, demented, mentally ill, and children (Emanuel, 1997). As discussed earlier, it is the difference between *voluntary* and *nonvoluntary* euthanasia. Indeed, there is debate in the literature about the spread of nonvoluntary euthanasia in jurisdictions where laws on voluntary euthanasia have been relaxed (Amarasekara & Bagaric, 2004; Jotkowitz, Glick, & Gesundheit, 2008; Sayers, 2007).

Before the Dutch law was enacted in 2001, permissive attitudes toward hastened death had already become well rooted in the Netherlands. In 1981, the prosecution service and the nation's medical society came to an agreement about a set of guidelines. If physicians followed these guidelines, the government agreed not to prosecute (Emanuel, 1997). Based on information submitted in compliance with the new reporting rules, the Dutch government conducted a systematic review of hastened death, which became known as the Remmelink Report, named after Jan Remmelink, the head of the commission who conducted the review. The commission submitted its final report in 1990. A follow-up was completed five years later (Canady, 1998; Fenigson, 1997).

In 1990, there were 9,000 requests for hastened deaths (Fenigson, 1997). Some 2,300 people were given active voluntary euthanasia and 400 received medication from their physician with which to commit suicide. There were also 1,000 cases in which patients were given euthanasia without their explicit request. In addition, there were 4,941 cases in which patients were given lethal doses of morphine-like sedatives that resulted in death. In 1995, the number in each of these categories was slightly higher (Fenigson, 1997). For a visual display of results, refer to Table 12.1.

Although there were a significant number of nonvoluntary euthanizations, overall the Dutch authorities were generally pleased with improvements from 1990 to 1995. They seemed to feel that the agreement between the prosecution service and the country's physicians was a workable solution. As a result, the nation's controversial euthanasia and assisted suicide law was formally enacted in 2001. You might want to revisit Figure 12.2 for a summary of its requirements (Netherlands Ministry of Foreign Affairs, 2001, 2004).

Opponents of voluntary euthanasia and physician-assisted suicide, like Emanuel, observe that the people most concerned about these choices seem to be the people most likely to be abused and coerced: the old, the poor, and minorities (Emanuel, 1997). In addition, there is the question about what to do about the suffering of people with mental illness.

TABLE 12.1 Euthanasia and Physician-Assisted Suicide in the Netherlands, 1990–1995		
	1990	**1995**
Total Number of Deaths	128,786	135,675
Requests for Euthanasiaor Physician-Assisted Suicide	9,000	9,700
Active Euthanasia with Patient's Request	2,300	3,200
Assisted Suicides	400	400
Active Euthanasia without Explicit Patient Request	1,000	900
Intentional Lethal Overdose of a Morphine-Like Drug with Patient's Consent	3,159	2,046
without Patient's Knowledge	4,941	1,889

Source: Fenigsen, 1997. Dutch euthanasia revisited. Issues in Law & Medicine, 13, 301–311

In Oregon and Washington, physicians are required to refer anyone to counseling whose mental condition, such as depression, might have influenced their request (Oregon Public Health Division, 2011). In the Netherlands, this is not so. For example, Dr. Boudewijn Chabot, a psychiatrist, helped a 50-year-old depressed woman, who was otherwise in good health, to commit suicide because she wanted to die instead of treating her depression. Dr. Chabot was prosecuted for his actions. The Dutch Supreme Court ultimately heard the case. It ruled that mental suffering can be as intolerable as physical suffering. Therefore, the high court decided that the actions of Dr. Chabot could be legally justified (Canady, 1998).

In addition to the potential misuses of assisted death with people whose judgment is impaired by their mental condition, there is also concern about the abuse and coercion of other vulnerable populations. Advocates of the right to die suggest that many people are reassured when they know physician-assisted suicide and voluntary euthanasia are an option, but opponents argue that vulnerable populations may feel equally fearful, suspicious, and worried about having their lives ended prematurely without their consent.

Critics of legally sanctioned hastened death contend that once the relaxed standards become the new norm, it is all too easy for the general population to feel so complacent with hastened death that they also become less vigilant in protecting the vulnerable against its abuses. Emanuel (1997) advances the argument that once hastened death is legal, health-care providers are able to defend questionable behavior by asserting that it is legally protected. If true, we all become vulnerable.

Chapter Summary

The chapter began with a general discussion of some of the tough issues faced when dealing with life-threatening illness. Although many people are well served by hospice and palliative care, some do not want to endure the rigors of a long, painful death. For this reason, some seek out ways to alleviate their suffering by hastening their death. We briefly reviewed some of the particulars surrounding the ballyhoo of Dr. Kevorkian's one-man campaign to provide and publicize physician-assisted suicide.

Although the U.S. Supreme Court ruled in two precedent-setting cases (*Washington* v. *Glucksberg* and *Vacco* v. *Quill*) that states have the right to prohibit or permit physician-assisted suicide, it is lawful in only three U.S. states. Orgeon was the first to authorize physician-assisted suicide for terminally ill people. Even so, Oregon encountered stiff opposition

from then U.S. Attorney General John Aschcroft. Oregon appealed to the U.S. Supreme Court, which upheld Oregon's right to enact assisted-suicide legislation. Washington based their law on Oregon's. In Montana, the matter was settled by a State Supreme Court decision.

We discussed unintentional overdose and the principle of double effect as a way to distinguish between efforts to alleviate suffering and illicit hastened death. We noted that illicit hastened death is the deliberate ending of life, which research suggests might happen more often than we think.

Then we explored voluntary euthanasia, which was first decriminalized in the Netherlands, then Belgium, followed by Luxembourg. You heard from three Dutch professionals about their experience: the former head of the Dutch Voluntary Euthanasia

Society, a theologian, and a pastoral counselor. Each expressed quite different views.

The chapter concluded with a brief review of concerns raised by critics of relaxed standards with respect to physician-assisted suicide and voluntary euthanasis. We profiled Ezekiel Emanuel, one such critic, and examined some of the arguments he and others advance in support of erring on the side of caution.

Key Terms

active euthanasia *266*
Death with Dignity Act *269*
euthanasia *266*
hastened death *266*

involuntary euthanasia *267*
nonvoluntary euthanasia *267*
passive euthanasia *266*
physician-assisted suicide *267*

principle of double
   effect *271*
voluntary euthanasia *272*

Suggested Activities

1. Make a list of diseases that friends or family members have had. Consider what kinds of life-threatening illnesses you yourself might develop. Write a one-page description on how you would want to handle the situation.
2. Do some Internet research on the use of analgesic medication to control pain. What do the experts say about the effectiveness of these medications on life-threatening illnesses such as cancer. What would you do if the medications used to treat you or a loved one were not effective? What resources are available in your community?
3. Carefully review the interview summaries of Dr. Rob Jonquiere, Dr. Theo Boer, and Herman Van der Kloot Meijburg. Compare their positions and consider areas of agreement and disagreement. What issues or problems with physician-assisted suicide and euthanasia seem to surface when you reflect on what they had to say?

Suggested Reading and Viewing

- Zaritsky, J. (2010). *The suicide tourist.* Boston: WGBH/ Frontline, with Point Gray Pictures, Inc.
  This very moving *Frontline* documentary profiles the story of Craig Ewert, a 59-year-old man dying slowly of ALS who goes to Switzerland, where voluntary euthanasia is legal.
- Kuhse, H., & Singer, P. (Eds). (2006). *Bioethics: An anthology. (Blackwell Philosophy Anthologies).* Hoboken, NJ: Wiley-Blackwell.

This expanded and revised edition of the original is a definitive one-volume collection of key primary texts on the study of bioethics.
- Smith, W. J. (2006). *Forced exit: Euthanasia, assisted suicide and the new duty to die.* Jackson, TN: Encounter Books (Perseus Group).
  This text makes a case against legalized euthanasia and takes a closer look at other humane and compassionate alternatives.

Links and Internet Resources

- **The Hastings Center**
  www.thehastingscenter.org/
  This nonprofit research organization is dedicated to the study of fundamental ethical issues in the areas of health, medicine, and the environment. Especially interested in the interaction between these issues and the well-being of the society, its people, and institutions.
- **The Kevorkian File–PBS Frontline**
  www.pbs.org/wgbh/pages/frontline/programs/ info/1214.html

Aired on April 5, 1994, this *PBS Frontline* site highlights the exploits of Dr. Jack Kavorkian and the people he "helped" end their lives. Available for free viewing online.

- **The Kevorkian Verdict–PBS Frontline**
  www.pbs.org/wgbh/pages/frontline/kevorkian/
  This *PBS Frontline* profiles Dr. Jack Kavorkian after the 1999 verdict, in which he was convicted of second-degree murder of Thomas Youk. It includes interviews with four of Kevorkian's patients and their families; information on the legal rulings; views and practices of doctors; and a chronology in his life and cause. May be streamed online at no cost to the viewer.

- **Detroit Free News (Archives Search)**
  pqasb.pqarchiver.com/freep/advancedsearch.html
  The Detroit Free News began publishing articles about Dr. Jack Kevorkian and his suicide machine and his numerous trials in Oakland County, Michigan, beginning in the early 1990s.

- **Death with Dignity National Center**
  www.deathwithdignity.org/
  Death with Dignity National Center is an organization that led the legal defense of and education about Oregon's Death with Dignity Law.

- **Compassion and Choices**
  www.compassionandchoices.org/hemlock
  This site is hosted by the Hemlock Society, a right-to-die organization that advocates for alternative death choices.

- **Department of Bioethics and Interdisciplinary Studies: The Brody School of Medicine at East Carolina University**
  www.ecu.edu/medhum/
  This impressive website has some first-rate resources. These include a scholarly online newsletter (with archives of old editions); ethics codes and guidelines; directory of bioethics centers; legal resources; and more.

- **World Federation of Right to Die Societies**
  www.worldrtd.net/
  The World Federation of Right to Die Societies, founded in 1980, consists of 45 organizations from 26 countries around the world.

Review Guide

1. Be fully familiar with all the concepts **bolded** in the chapter.
2. Be able to discuss key "pro" and "con" arguments on each side of the physician-assisted suicide and euthanasia debate.
3. What lessons might society take from its experience in dealing with Dr. Jack Kevorkian's one-man campaign to help terminally ill people end their lives?
4. How can the *principle of double effect* be used to distinguish between withholding/withdrawing life support from physician-assisted suicide or euthanasia?
5. What legal and ethical issues surface as a result of the debate over physician-assisted suicide and voluntary euthanasia? What are the differences between these and nonvoluntary, or even involuntary, euthanasia?
6. What are the requirements of Oregon's Death with Dignity Act? What's the difference between physician-assisted suicide and euthanasia?
7. What is the difference between unintentional overdose and illicit hastened death?
8. What legal and ethical issues arise by the adoption of legislation about voluntary euthanasia, such as laws passed in the Netherlands, Belgium, and Luxembourg? What sorts of things can we learn from their experience?
9. What arguments are advanced in support of relaxed laws on physician-assisted suicide and voluntary euthanasia? What are the merits and weaknesses of these arguments?
10. What arguments are advanced by critics of relaxed laws on physician-assisted suicide and voluntary euthanasia? What are the merits and weaknesses of these arguments?

13

Withdrawing Life Support and Organ Transplantation

- **Defining Death**
- **Transplantation and Ethics**
- **Transhumanist Revolution?**
- **Withdrawing Life Support**

Today it is quite possible to keep people breathing and their hearts beating even when they have permanently lost all the normal attributes of their "personhood": the awareness of what is happening around them, thinking, and the ability to make decisions. When considering end-of-life issues, it is also common to hear people say things like, "I don't want to be kept alive with a bunch of machines" or "I don't want to be a vegetable."

However, on the practical level, what do statements like those really mean? The availability of sophisticated life-support technology coupled with uncertainty about the status of an individual when his or her brain has no activity make statements like the ones above hard to address. In this chapter, we will discuss our changing definitions of death: "clinical death" versus "brain death." We will also explore the issues at play when deciding to provide or withdraw mechanical **ventilation** (breathing), high-powered medications, artificial hydration (fluids), and **nutrition** (food). We will address questions like, When does an individual stop being a living person? When is it appropriate to withdraw life supports? When should we, or shouldn't we, "harvest" healthy organs from such individuals and transplant them in others who need them?

DEFINING DEATH

The technological advances of the last quarter century have challenged modern medicine, and indeed society, to rethink how it defines death. In the past, it was fairly easy to know when death occurred. It happened when such vital signs as heartbeat and breathing stopped. Although mistakes in determining death were sometimes made, signs such as the cessation of breathing and heartbeat, nonreactivity to light and pain, cool body temperature, stiffness followed by bloating, and the eventual signs of decomposition made the reality of death clear. With the arrival of mechanical ventilators, first developed in the 1950s to deal with the polio outbreaks of that era, it became much harder to define death (Waisel & Truog, 1997). Ventilators can artificially maintain patients who are unable to breathe on their own almost indefinitely. What's more, the patients are warm and alive-looking, even when there is little or no brain activity.

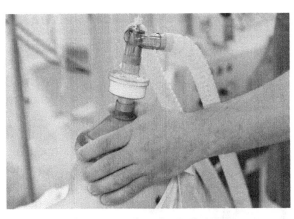

Intubation is the process of mechanically keeping a person breathing even when they can not do so on their own. With modern technology it is often possible to keep the body alive almost indefinitely. The question is, Should we do so? *beerkoff / Fotolia*

The old method of determining death— observing the cessation of heartbeat and breathing—no longer worked. Although the traditional methods could still define clinical death, defining this new phenomenon called **brain death** was far trickier. The term *brain death* is now used to denote the irreversible cessation of the activity of the whole brain (brain stem and neocortex), the brain stem, or the higher brain (neocortex) only, depending on the expert doing the defining and the criteria used. James Hughes refers to the two main camps as the "whole-brainers" and "neo-corticalists" (Hughes, 1995). This may sound flippant or even disrespectful, but the consequences are actually very serious. The cost of care and availability of organs for transplantation are hot issues.

Miracle in South Africa: The First Heart Transplant

On Saturday afternoon, December 2, 1967, Ann Washkansky saw a crowd gathered at the scene of an automobile accident in Cape Town, South Africa. Little did she know then that her fate would become linked with the victims of that accident. Nearby was Groote Schuur Hospital, which was nestled in the hills above the accident scene. Ann was in the neighborhood in order to be near her husband, Louis Washkansky, who was a cardiac patient at the hospital. Louis was in bad shape. He had a grossly enlarged heart, congestive heart failure, diabetes, and coronary artery disease. His skin blackened from lack of circulation, he was dying and he knew it. His cardiologist, Dr. Christian Barnard, who had put together a heart transplant team, approached Mr. Washkansky about his willingness to consider a transplant. Washkansky, who knew he was out of options, agreed (Ankney, 1998; Gustaitis, 2002).

The victims of the accident were Denise Ann Darvall and her mother. Denise had come to this part of Cape Town with her mother and father for a shopping trip. Coming out of a bakery, they were struck by a speeding car. Her mother died instantly. When Denise reached Groote Schuur Hospital, her heart was still beating but she was brain dead. Dr. Barnard approached her father, Edward Darvall, who gave his permission to use his daughter's heart in what would become the first successful human heart transplant. Louis would live for 18 days before succumbing to pneumonia (Ankney, 1998; Gustaitis, 2002).

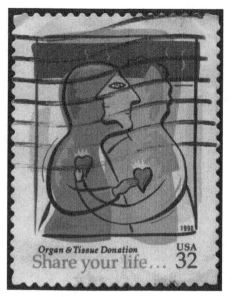

Since the early days of organ transplantation the practice has become vitally important to countless people with life-threatening illnesses. This U.S. postage stamp attempts to spread awareness about the widespread need for organ donors. *AlexanderZam/Fotolia*

TRANSPLANTATION AND ETHICS

Despite Mr. Washkansky's death, heart transplantation now seemed a plausible medical procedure. In addition to Dr. Barnard's team in South Africa, heart transplant teams from around the world were poised to do precisely what Barnard did (Ankney, 1998). With the "miracle in South Africa," a threshold had been crossed. The door was open for heart transplantation on a big scale. Indeed, it's estimated that between 3,000 and 4,000 heart transplants are now performed worldwide each year (Hetzer, 1994). It became a proven scientific fact that a human heart could be stopped, transplanted, and started up again in a different body. With the possibilities unfolding, it also seemed clear that healthy hearts would be needed. Would taking the beating heart from a comatose patient constitute homicide? This was a question that also concerned Dr. Barnard before doing that first transplant. Barnard was careful to wait until Denise's heart actually stopped and he had declared death before proceeding. He feared that if he didn't, he could be accused of homicide. He had good reason to be concerned.

The Dead Donor Rule

Within a few months after Dr. Barnard was hailed a hero for performing the world's first heart transplant, Dr. Juro Wada performed the first heart transplant in Japan (Masahiro, 2001). Instead of acclaim for the achievement, however, he was accused of unlawfully causing the death of both the donor and the recipient (Kerridge, Saul, Lowe, McPhee, & Williams, 2002; Masahiro, 2001). According to Japanese bioethicist Morioka Masahiro, Dr. Juro's actions were officially regarded as an act of illegal human experimentation and an example of poor judgment in declaring death (Masahiro, 2001).

Since then, policy makers and medical professionals alike have insisted that donors be declared dead according to recognized criteria before attempting to perform a transplant (Kerridge et al., 2002). This would become known as the **dead donor rule** (Kerridge et al., 2002). This rule establishes the legal and ethical principle that says organ retrieval in itself may not be the cause of death (Robertson, 1999). Redefining death in terms of brain functioning, then, is the only possible way to increase the pool of transplantable organs (Arnold & Youngner, 1993; Truog, 2003; Youngner & Arnold, 1993).

The Harvard Criteria

Almost immediately after Barnard's success in South Africa, the medical community in the United States seems to have anticipated the need for a consensus on a definition for brain death. Dr. Henry Beecher, who was an anesthesiologist at Harvard Medical

1. The patient is unreceptive and unresponsive—total unawareness of external stimuli; unresponsiveness even to pain
2. Complete absence of spontaneous breathing and muscular movement
3. There are no reflexes—i.e., eye pupils are fixed, dilated, and don't respond to light; lack of eye movement; no response to noxious stimuli; no tendon reflexes
4. There is a flat EEG (electroencephalogram)—i.e., there is no electrical activity in the brain

FIGURE 13.1   The Harvard Ad Hoc Committee Criteria for Determining Brain Death   *Source*: This figure is based on Beecher, H. K. (1968). A definition of irreversible coma. Report of the ad hoc committee of the Harvard Medical School to examine the definition of brain death. Journal of the American Medical Association, 205, 337–340.

School, approached the dean of the medical school and asked him to convene a panel of experts to discuss the situation of "hopelessly unconscious" patients. This panel, which included 10 physicians, an attorney, a theologian, and a historian, was called the Ad Hoc Committee of Harvard Medical School to Examine the Definition of Brain Death, or the Harvard Committee for short (Beecher, 1968; Beecher & Dorr, 1971).

The Harvard committee established four criteria, now called the **Harvard criteria**, for determining when someone was brain dead (Beecher, 1968). See Figure 13.1. The first three of the Harvard criteria are similar to the traditional indicators for clinical death: unreceptiveness and unresponsiveness; lack of spontaneous respiration and muscle movement; and absence of reflexes (e.g., to light and pain) (Beecher, 1968). The last criteria specifically relates to activity within the brain itself—the lack of electrical impulses in the brain. You may have noticed that the Harvard ad hoc committee adopted a "whole brain" definition of brain death, which includes the functioning of the brain stem (responsible for regulating involuntary life-sustaining activities) as well as the neocortex (associated with higher mental functions) (Beecher, 1968).

Uniform Death Determination Act

After the initial flurry of interest in heart transplantation in the late 1960s, professional interest in doing heart transplants waned, largely owing to problems of tissue rejection (Badone, 2004). The recipient body would recognize donor tissue as foreign. In 1981, when the immune suppressant cyclosporine came on the market, the rejection of donor tissue could be effectively managed. Interest in performing heart transplants resumed. Although the "Harvard criteria" were regarded as reliable, concern about a definition for brain death persisted. It soon became clear that a better consensus definition was needed.

In 1981, the medical consultants to a presidential commission issued a report recommending the use of criteria that would equate brain death with the integration of the organism as a whole (Kerridge et al, 2002; President's Commission for the Study of Ethical Problems in Medicine and Biomedical and Behavioral Research, 1981). The Commission arrived at a definition of brain death that emphasized the role of the brain as the organizer and regulator of integrated bodily functions. At the end of the day, the President's Commission, like the Harvard Committee before it, had adopted a whole brain definition of brain death. It recommended death be declared when all brain functions ceased "irreversibly." The recommendations of the Commission, along with the reasoning of recent court decisions and input from the American Medical Association, the American Bar Association, and the National Conference of Commissioners on Uniform State Laws, were grafted into a proposal for the **Uniform Determination of Death Act (UDDA)**. The act was intended to serve as a model in the United States. It contains two alternative criteria for declaring death when the determination is made in accord with "accepted medical standards" (Center for Bioethics, 1997a):

1. Irreversible cessation of spontaneous circulation and respiration
2. Irreversible cessation of all functions of the entire brain

Although the UDDA became a model, jurisdictions in the United States were never formally required to adopt it. In practice, however, it was enacted by over half the states. The remaining jurisdictions enacted legislation or relied on court decisions that used similar criteria (Center for Bioethics, 1997a). Like the Harvard criteria, the UDDA recognizes the cardiopulmonary standard for defining death, but it also provides an alternative to use in those cases where traditional criteria don't seem to apply—that is, when vital functions are artificially maintained.

Brain Stem Criteria

The brain stem is a small structure, about two and a half inches in length, that extends from the spinal cord to the base of the brain. Small in physical size, it nevertheless performs vital functions. Among them are breathing, heartbeat, alertness, and arousal. While the United States and other parts of the English-speaking world use "whole brain" definitions of brain death as described previously, the United Kingdom and many other parts of the English-speaking world define brain death as having occurred when competent medical authority determines that brain stem functioning is irreversibly gone (Conference of the Medical Royal Colleges, 1979; Kerridge et al., 2002; Machado, 2003; Youngner, 1992). The criteria, first proposed by Mohandas and Chou in Minnesota (1971), emphasizes the role of the brain stem as critical to the integration of all body functions. Proponents of the criteria (e.g., Pallis, 1983, 1985) argue that since the brain stem is essential to body integration, death should be equated with the irreversible loss of its functioning (Kerridge et al., 2002).

Neocortical Criteria

The cortex, usually referred to as the neocortex, is the large, outer portion of the brain. It is responsible for higher-thinking functions. Neocortical brain death occurs when the neocortex no longer functions. Often, the brain stem remains intact, leaving the person in a **persistent vegetative state (PVS)**. In contrast to whole brain and brain stem definitions, advocates of neocortical definitions are less interested with whether or not the brain is able to regulate or integrate bodily functions, and are more concerned with those mental activities most essential to being human. Robert Veatch, a bioethics pioneer and advocate for a neocortical definition, credits Henry Beecher, of Harvard Committee fame, with identifying the following qualities as essential characteristics of personhood: personality, conscious life, judging, reasoning, acting, enjoying, and worrying (Veatch, 1976, 1993a).

Neocortical death can occur in an otherwise healthy person when there is a lack of blood supply (called **ischemia**) and oxygen (called **hypoxia**) to the brain (Cranford, 1988). The most common causes of this, in order of frequency, are drug overdose, head trauma, and cardiac arrest (DeGeorgio & Lew, 1991). The loss of blood flow to the brain for 4 to 6 minutes is generally sufficient to cause extensive damage to the brain (Cranford, 1988). After experiencing loss of blood flow and oxygen, the person will frequently be in a coma, which by definition is caused by damage to the brain stem (Cranford, 1988). Because the brain stem controls choking and swallowing reflexes, long-term brain stem damage commonly results in death due to respiratory infection (Cranford, 1988). When a heart attack causes loss of blood flow and oxygen to the brain, 90 percent of those people die, even when CPR is attempted (DeGeorgio & Lew, 1991). Death is less likely when the origin of the brain trauma is head injury (50 percent) or drug overdose (1 to 5 percent) (DeGeorgio & Lew, 1991).

Because the brain stem is more resilient to ischemia and hypoxia than the cortex, the resulting loss of vital functions may be temporary. When the cortex is permanently damaged but the brain stem functions, it's possible for the individual to remain in a persistent vegetative state, often for years, so long as she or he is given nutrition and fluids. Adopting a neocortical definition of brain death would mean these individuals could be considered brain dead, and therefore possible organ donors. Indeed, one source points out that using the "higher-brain" criteria creates two new potential categories of "heart-beating" donors: those who exist in a persistent vegetative state and anencephalic infants—newborns who have intact brain stems but lack healthy neocortexes (Moskop, 2000).

This seems an appropriate place to reflect on the meaning of the terms *brain death, whole brain death, brain stem death, neocortical brain death, persistent vegetative state, coma, locked-in syndrome,* and *dementia.* Ronald Cranford (1988), a neurologist and a leading contributor to the discussion of these topics (e.g., Cranford, 1978, 1984, 1990), comments that even members of the medical community are prone to misuse them. He suggests, doing so leads to confusion and uncertainty among laypeople and professionals alike. See the terms in Table 13.1, which are based on his work (Cranford, 1988).

As you can see from reviewing Table 13.1, each of the terms used to describe brain death and unconscious states relates to distinct conditions and the functioning (or lack thereof) of the brain stem and neocortex. The terms *coma* and *persistent vegetative state* seem to relate to the same thing, but

Human organs from "deceased" or living donors are "harvested" and transported as quickly as possible to the medical facility where the transplantation will occur. *Dan Race/Fotolia*

TABLE 13.1	Terms Related to Brain Death, Coma, and the Persistent Vegetative State

Term	Description of the Condition to Which It Applies
Brain death	The irreversible cessation of the activity of the whole brain (brain stem and neocortex), the brain stem, or the neocortex (higher brain) only.
Whole brain death	Both neocortical and brain stem functioning stops although breathing is supported artificially.
Brain stem death	Brain stem ceases to maintain vital functions although activity in the neocortex may persist. The patient is unreceptive and unresponsive—total unawareness and unresponsiveness to external stimuli, even to pain.
Neocortical death	See *persistent vegetative state*, below.
Persistent vegetative state	The brain stem functions but the neocortex is no longer active. This is also known as neocortical death or eyesopen unconsciousness. It can persist for many years.
Coma	A sleep-like, eyes-closed, state of unconsciousness caused by brain stem damage. It is a temporary state that will result in death within months if brain stem functioning doesn't return.
Locked-in syndrome	The patient has cognitive (neocortical) functioning but does not appear conscious because the person is unable to move or communicate.
Dementia	Occurs when the neocortex loses its functioning over time. The process will result in death but the process tends to be very long and protracted. One of the best known types of dementia is Alzheimer's disease.

Source: This table is based on Cranford, R. E. (1988). The persistent vegetative state: The medical reality (getting the facts straight). *The Hastings Center Report*, 18(1), 27–32.

Cranford (1988) wants us to understand they are different. Comatose people will die relatively soon because of brain stem damage. Patients in a persistent vegetative state may survive almost indefinitely because their brain stems are relatively intact, yet they will have lost all those brain functions we previously said are hallmarks of being human.

A question that emerges from the preceding discussion is, Does the loss of consciousness mean the loss of personhood, with all this implies? Is the *person* truly dead? If so, can the person's vital organs be "harvested"? For Cranford (1988), the answer is *yes*. For the rest of society, it's not so clear. Indeed, the debate on the proper definition of death and brain death is ongoing.

Although Table 13.1 might help clarify the meaning of terms that are often misused or misunderstand, it can be all too easy to lose sight of the human condition when engaged in academic dialog. If you were someone who had a loved one in this condition, the subject would be far from academic. In doing the research for this book I interviewed the mother and grandmother of a young man who had been declared brain dead after a tragic accident (Kemp, 2001). At this juncture, I'd like to share a summary of that interview. Perhaps in doing so their story might help give the experience a human face.

For James's mother and grandmother, the idea that their son and grandson was really dead was hard to accept. The issues of the proper definition of death and brain death remain unresolved for bioethicists. Indeed, close study reveals that there is nearly always at least some residual activity even when brain death seems clear. Because of

---

He Was the Center of Everything

When I arrived at Philomena and her mother's home, a neighbor was in the dining room area conversing in Spanish with her mother. "I'm of mixed Spanish–Native American heritage," Philomena explained. The neighbor didn't speak much English, and they were about the only other Spanish speakers in the area. During the first part of the interview, her mother spoke with the neighbor while Philomena began telling their story. Philomena explained that this was hard for her. She'd thought about it all the previous night, she said, wondering how to explain it. "It was stupid circumstances," she said.

James was 20 years old. A graduate of an area high school with a reputation for excellence, he was a handsome young man who everyone in his large extended family liked to be with. "They come over now," Philomena commented with a smile, "and they tell me how boring it is over here compared to the way it used to be. 'He's gone.' I tell them, He was the center of everything." James had a good job, a car, and lots of friends. He lived at home and enjoyed the companionship of his mother and grandmother, she explained. He loved mama's cooking and talking with grandma. Philomena and her mother told me they both raised James. "I was only 15 when I had James, so she (pointing to her mother) had to teach me how to be a mother," Philomena told me, "She really raised both of us."

James was interested in the military and guns, perhaps because of a favorite uncle who was in the army. He also seemed to have a preoccupation with the grim reaper. "He wanted to get a tattoo of the grim reaper, and he'd draw him all the time. He had these grim reapers all over his room," Philomena said, "Like maybe he knew he was going to die." They went on to tell me that there were some other unexplained forebodings of James's death. They recalled how once they had all decided to play with a Ouija board. Everyone asked the Ouija board when they were going to die. "He asked the Ouija board when he was going to die. It said 19, from a gunshot." He turned 20 in June and died in October.

James was at a friend's home with four other young people. They were drinking and he had a gun. He removed the bullets and was showing the other kids the gun, passing it around and "dry shooting" the gun. The gun came back around and he put the bullets back in just before a girl wanted a closer look. He took the bullets out again. One of the girls swore to Philomena at the hospital that they saw six bullets in James's hand when he showed them the gun. They must have been talking about how to end your own life. Philomena related, "He said, 'This is how you do it' (she demonstrated by putting her index finger into the soft skin under the jaw). He pulled the trigger, the gun fired, and bullet went into his brain." James was kept functioning for a time using mechanical ventilation, but Philomena related that she was told, "He's brain dead." Someone asked her to consider donating selected tissue and organs. She agreed, but commented that even now it's hard to believe he is really dead. "He looked alive," she said.

this evidence, bioethicists such as Robert Veatch (1993a) and Robert Truog (1997) argue that the concept of whole brain death is no longer useful. Truog suggests abandoning it, returning to the old cardiopulmonary definition, and letting go of the dead donor rule. He would like to see physicians make full disclosure about the nature of the vegetative condition and ask families for permission to harvest the organs of their loved ones and allow them to die. Robert Veatch, on the other hand, prefers adopting a neocortical definition of brain death. Indeed, rapid technological advances continue to nudge the dialog into uncharted territory, which is addressed next.

TRANSHUMANIST REVOLUTION?

Considering the questions that have been raised as a result of the various definitions of brain death, you may have an appreciation of what a leap it would be to adopt a neocortical definition of brain death. Skeptics warn that adopting it could put us on the "slippery slope" of taking life from those most in need of protection. They warn that by deliberating on withholding and withdrawing life support, the idea of pulling the plug on severely demented or retarded individuals starts to sound rational, putting society close to, if not actually at the point of, accepting euthanasia, thereby devaluing the sanctity of human life.

Considering the life-and-death stakes, critics also express concern that commercial interests could come into play, making the sale of vital organs a lucrative business by providing financial incentives to organ "harvesters" (potentially at the expense of "donors"). On a practical level, the question arises about how to dispose of breathing "cadavers" with beating hearts, if, that is, they are to be considered truly dead (Angell, 1994).

Not balking at the criticisms of neocortical definitions, James Hughes (1995), a sociologist I introduced you to earlier, comments that the current whole brain definition of death is an unwieldy, historical compromise. Reviewing how the Harvard criteria and UDDA came into being, he suggests that the whole brain definition was, in the final analysis, a purely pragmatic one. It was easier to operationalize (determine when brain death occurred). It erred on the side of preserving life. Perhaps most important of all, it was the most radical definition the public would accept.

According to Hughes (1995), the whole brain definition may have been a necessary step in human progress. He predicts, however, that this definition will ultimately unravel as technological developments create unprecedented opportunities to repair, replace, and manipulate body and brain tissue. Hughes clearly wants society first to move toward adopting a neocortical definition of death and then to go beyond it (1995). He is one of a group of people allied with a movement called **transhumanism**, which sees technology as our chief hope to transcend our bodily limitations. (For a discussion, see, for example, Dvorsky, 2004; Elliott, 2003; Flynn, 1994; More, 1994.)

Far from endorsing euthanasia—the deliberate act of ending life—*transhumanists* want to find ways to enhance and extend it. They see the human body as a vital but fallible organism, which is nevertheless necessary as a host for human personality and consciousness. They are not interested in advancing neocortical definitions in the hopes of harvesting transplantable organs from "heart-beating cadavers." Rather, transhumanists are interested in human consciousness and using technology to enhance human intelligence, repair bodies, and extend human life. Reminiscent of TV's *Bionic Man*, they see a day when science will be able to create super intelligent human beings, with bodies capable of enormous feats, who will be able to live many times the span of those living today.

Hughes (1995, 2004) and other transhumanists see some of these technologies as existing now, at least in crude form—for example, using stem cells in neurogenesis, nanotechnology, neural-computer prostheses, and cryonic suspension. In one essay, Hughes (2004) reviews a number of developments. Among these is research that demonstrates infusions of stem cells (primitive brain cells that form in the brain stem) can be used to repair damaged brains (Kozorovitsky & Gould, 2003). With respect to neural-computer prostheses, he notes that scientists have designed chips that can be implanted in brain-damaged patients so that they can communicate through an external computer, by-passing damaged neural pathways. He and other transhumanists point to the possibility of cryonic suspension—freezing human heads or whole bodies—so they can be "reanimated" later, when technology is capable of repairing whatever problems may have caused their demise.

Most relevant to the discussion of defining death, transhumanists speak of taking human personalities and memories from the minds of living persons and "uploading" them, to use computer lingo, onto new "platforms," perhaps something like specialized hard disks (Dvorsky, 2004; Elliott, 2003; Flynn, 1994; Hughes, 1995, 2004; More, 1994). Residing on these new platforms, the consciousness of persons could continue to exist almost indefinitely—conceivably able to reflect, interact, and grow. In this kind of "postbiological" model, they might "live" and eventually "die" elsewhere than in a human body, giving a new twist to terms like "residing on a hard drive," "sparked up," and "pulling the plug."

WITHDRAWING LIFE SUPPORT

With the advent of life-supporting technology, new ethical issues surfaced, and with them, a relatively new field called bioethics evolved. It concerns itself with issues of withholding or withdrawing life supports, especially ventilation, nutrition, and fluids. The first time the issue was brought to light with the general public was with the publicity surrounding the case of Karen Ann Quinlan, which is briefly summarized here.

The Case of Karen Ann Quinlan

On the night of April 15, 1975, for reasons that are not clear, Karen Ann Quinlan stopped breathing for at least two 15-minute periods. Reports say she ingested alcohol and had taken tranquilizers. Friends tried to give her mouth-to-mouth resuscitation but their efforts failed. She was taken by ambulance to nearby Newton Memorial Hospital. When examined, she had a temperature of 100 degrees, her pupils would not respond to light, and she didn't react to even deep pain. While her doctors saved her life, Karen would exist in a "chronic persistent

(Continued)

vegetative state." She would eventually regain minimal brain activity, but it wasn't enough to regulate her breathing. She couldn't breathe without the help of a ventilator. There was no known treatment that could cure or improve her condition. Experts said she would never regain the ability to think or interact in a meaningful way. Her parents asked the doctors to remove the ventilator so she could die naturally. When they refused, her parents filed suit. The New Jersey Supreme Court would ultimately hear the case, and in 1976, they decided in favor of the parents (70 NJ 10 [1976] Supreme Court of New Jersey).

This case was the first to establish the rights of patients, or their proxies, to make end-of-life health-care decisions. In a twist of fate, she began to breathe on her own when the respirator was removed. She would live in a persistent vegetative state at a nursing home until she died about 10 years later, in 1985.

Robert Veatch was the first research associate for the Hastings Center, a think-tank devoted to issues in bioethics. He recalls the day when they got a call at the Hastings Center from a young lawyer from a legal aid office, Paul Armstrong (Veatch, 1993b). Armstrong had himself been approached by the parents of a young woman who had been rendered permanently unconscious and who was on a mechanical ventilator. The parents asked for the ventilator to be turned off, but the physician, Dr. Robert Morris, insisted he had the right and duty to continue life support indefinitely. The parents were Joseph and Julia Quinlan. Karen Ann was their daughter. As Veatch recalls, the case became a symbol of the ethics debates on withholding and withdrawing life support.

Since then, other cases have made their way through various U.S. courts. The decisions of these courts have given direction to the standards for withholding and withdrawing life support in the United States. For a summary of these key decisions and the precedents they established, refer to Figure 13.2.

As reflected in key court decisions, the most difficult ethical cases often involve withholding or withdrawing life support from patients who have been rendered permanently unconscious but who are capable of prolonged survival (in a persistent vegetative state [PVS]) (Center for Bioethics, 1997b). As we discussed in the previous section, cases of PVS involve severe neocortical damage with much less damage to the brain stem. The individual is thereby unconscious and incapable of higher cortical functions, but the brain stem keeps the heart beating and the lungs breathing. The question then becomes what should be done with the individual and who should decide.

In North America, societal values, considerable experience gained with cases involving persons in a persistent vegetative state, and key court decisions have each helped foster an emerging consensus about how to handle cases such as this. To summarize, it's been affirmed that individuals have the right to make choices about their own care, to refuse life support, including nutrition and fluids; for surrogates to make decisions for them when they are not able to do so for themselves; and for physicians to use **terminal sedation** to relieve any discomfort there might be during the dying process, even if it might hasten the process.

Case	Brief Description of the Case and the Court Decision
Quinlan (1976)	The New Jersey Supreme Court ruled that "substituted judgment" could be used to remove a permanently unconscious patient from advanced life support.
Saikewicz (1976)	The Massachusetts Supreme Court affirmed the decision of a Probate Court that ruled that a guardian ad litem appointed for a mentally incompetent patient could request that the patient not be subjected to chemotherapy because it was not believed to be in the patient's best interests.
Barber (1983)	A California Court of Appeals confirmed the principle of substituted judgment for legally incompetent patients. It also ruled that physicians could not be held liable for discontinuing life support when the situation is medically futile. Did not distinguish between nutrition/hydration and advanced life support.
Brophy (1983)	The Supreme Judicial Court of Massachusetts held that the wife of Paul Brophy, a fire fighter who was in a persistent vegetative state, could authorize the withdrawal of life support, including a gastrosomy tube (Gtube) that had been inserted in the wall of his abdomen so he could be fed artificially. Prior to being incapacitated, Brophy had made clear statements about not wanting life support were he to be in a persistent vegetative state. The U.S. Supreme Court declined to hear the case.
Cruzan (1990)	The U.S. Supreme Court ruled that states can constitutionally require "clear and convincing" evidence of a patient's wishes before allowing surrogates to discontinue life support. No distinction was made between advanced life support and hydration/nutrition. The decision also recognized the right of competent patient's to refuse treatment.
Glucksberg (1997) Vacco (1997)	The U.S. Supreme Court affirmed state laws prohibiting Vacco (1997) physician-assisted suicide. Distinguished between intended and unforeseen consequences of removing life supports, the so-called principal of double-effect. The decision included tacit approval of the practice of "terminal sedation," i.e. using sedation to ease the pain of terminal patients even when it may inadvertently hasten death.
Wendland (2001)	The California Supreme Court ruled that the feeding tube of a partially conscious person could not be removed without clear and convincing evidence that the patient would have wanted this done.

FIGURE 13.2   Key Court Decisions on Withholding and Withdrawing Life Support   *Source*: This table compiled from: Lo, Dorbbrand, Wolf, & Groman, 2002; Luce & Alpers, 2000; McCormick & Veatch, 1980; Raffin, 1991; Sharma, 2004.

The principles that have been used to answer questions about how to deal with cases in which a person resides in a persistent vegetative state reflect the cultural and professional values that have been adopted by the society. Among them are the principles of autonomy, nonmaleficence, beneficence, and justice (Gillon, 1994, 2003; Gillon & Lloyd, 1994; Rousseau, 2001). In addition to these, the competing value of respect for the **professional integrity** of the field of medicine is sometimes cited as a factor that must also be considered (Center for Bioethics, 1997b). Whereas medicine has an interest in fighting disease and prolonging life, using life support technology to do so may be at odds with the rights of patients and can create emotional and financial hardships for families.

The principle of **autonomy** relates to the prerogative of competent adults to make informed choices about their own care; it is well established by various court decisions. **Nonmaleficence** refers to the avoidance of doing harm, as reflected in the often quoted Latin expression, *primum non nocer,* "first do no harm." Nonmaleficence is rooted in the Hippocratic oath of the medical profession. Its companion principle, **beneficence**, calls on human beings to take the next step, to actively endeavor to do that which is good. **Justice**, a concept often equated with fairness, can be described as the obligation to distribute scarce resources equitably, respect human rights, and honor laws that contribute to the social good (Gillon, 1994; Gillon & Lloyd, 1994).

Although the state may have interests that conflict with the value of *autonomy* (especially the preservation of life and the protection of the integrity of the health-care professions), U.S. courts have been generally consistent in ruling that the individual's right to autonomy should prevail. This includes the right to be free from unwanted medical intrusions—such as ventilation, fluids, and nutrition—that are consistent with the person's values, desires, and goals. The preeminent place autonomy now holds in U.S. jurisprudence is grounded in common law and the right to privacy guaranteed by the U.S. Constitution.

In Canada, brain death is often defined as "according to accepted medical practice" (Shemie, Doig, & Belitsky, 2003). While the standards vary across provinces and territories in Canada, the whole brain definition is widely used (Lazar, Shemie, Greiner, Robertson, & Singer, 1996). The procedures for defining brain death may differ for each hospital, but the guidelines published by the Canadian Congress Committee on Brain Death and the Canadian Neocortical Care Group serve to provide a professional measuring stick for making them (Shemie et al., 2003). As in the United States, the Canadian courts often get involved when there's a dispute about the appropriateness of withdrawing life support.

In the United States, there are now three commonly agreed-on standards for making decisions about terminating life support (Center for Bioethics, 1997b). In the order of priority, they are:

1. *Subjective standard:* Oral or written instructions given by the patient before losing decision-making capacity. If the person has designated a proxy decision maker, the proxy is regarded as making decisions on behalf of the afflicted person.
2. *Substituted judgment standard:* A determination of what the patient would have wanted in the present circumstances, based on an understanding of the patient's prior preferences and value system.
3. *Best interests standard:* A determination of what is in the patient's best interests when the patient's preferences are unknown.

Although the *subjective standard* confers considerable autonomy to the individual, it isn't without its limits, especially when the individual hasn't made her or his wishes clearly known. A landmark case illustrating this is that of Nancy Cruzan, who suffered severe brain injury in an auto accident in 1983 (Villaire, 1992). By 1986, her family realized that she would remain in a persistent vegetative state so long as artificial feeding was continued. They asked that the feeding be stopped. As a result, the case found its way into the legal system. The case was filed in Missouri. Initially, Nancy's family received authorization to end the feeding but the state appealed. (As an interesting aside, the controversial former United States Attorney General John Ashcroft was the governor of the state during this era.) The matter was then heard by the Missouri Supreme Court, which overturned the lower court's ruling. The issue became a landmark case when it found its way to the U.S. Supreme Court, which refused to overturn the Missouri high court's decision. The U.S. Supreme Court did reaffirm, however, the right of patients to make decisions about life support, but ruled that the state also had the authority to require "clear and convincing" evidence about these wishes. This became known as the **Missouri Rule** (other states have the option of establishing their own rules). The case ultimately went back to the Missouri trial court. The Cruzans presented additional evidence and testimony. This time, the state didn't contest and the family won their motion. The feeding tube was removed. Twelve days later, on December 26, 1990, Nancy died. Her grave marker is inscribed as follows:

Born: July 20, 1957
Departed: January 11, 1983
At Peace: December 26, 1990

The "clear and convincing" standard established by the Missouri Rule essentially requires an advance directive, often called a living will, or the testimony of witnesses able to attest that before the person became incapacitated he or she had made explicit statements about not desiring specific forms of life support in particular circumstances. In this society, which some argue is still a death-denying one, it might be a stretch to think the citizenry will sign living wills or make the kind of declaration to friends and family required by the standard. Indeed, it's now estimated there are between 10,000 to 20,000 individuals who exist in a persistent vegetative state in various long-term care facilities throughout the United States. Nancy Cruzan's father, Joe Cruzan, and her sister, Chris Cruzan White, promote public awareness. White pursues this work through the Cruzan Foundation, which she founded.

As with the Karen Ann Quinlan story, the Cruzan case attracted considerable publicity. Indeed, the heart-wrenching ethical issues got the attention of an influential person—Nancy's own Missouri Senator, John C. Danforth, who was also an ordained Episcopal priest. In late 1989, Danforth, a conservative Republican, and New York's Daniel Patrick Moynahan, a liberal Democrat, teamed up to introduce a bill that would become the **Patient Self-Determination Act (PSDA)** (McCloskey, 1991; Milakovich, 1994). This bill, which was signed into law on November 5, 1990, requires hospitals, skilled nursing facilities, home health agencies, hospices, and health maintenance organizations (HMOs) that receive Medicare or Medicaid dollars to notify patients they have the right to give advance directives and to make decisions about their future care. For a summary, see Figure 13.3.

- Defines an advance directive as a written instruction, such as a living will or durable power of attorney for health care decisions, recognized by state law for the provision of health care when the individual is incapacitated.
- Requires that hospitals, skilled nursing facilities, home health agencies, hospice programs, and HMOs that participate in Medicare or Medicaid must maintain written policies and procedures guaranteeing that every adult receiving care is given written information and is made aware of their right to be involved in treatment decisions.
- Mandates that the patient's record must document whether or not he or she has executed an advance directive.
- Compels health care agencies to educate the staff and the community about advance directives.
- Charges agencies to develop written descriptions of their states' laws about advance directions, to be distributed to patients.
- Orders the responsible federal cabinet-department to develop and implement a national campaign to educate the public.

FIGURE 13.3 Summary of Provisions of the Patient Self-Determination Act *Source:* This figure is based on 101st Omnibus Reconciliation Act of 1990, *Public Law 101-508* [section] 4751 (1990).

Medical Futility

The Karen Quinlan and Nancy Cruzan cases highlight situations where families deemed medical intervention futile but were rebuffed by the medical experts. Today, the term **medical futility** has taken on quite a different meaning. Janet Cogliano, a nurse educator, comments, "Instead of physicians demanding that certain procedures be implemented.... we now find that patients and/or families are now demanding that 'everything be done'" (1999, p. 82). Used by the health-care professionals themselves, the term now refers to treatment medical experts don't believe will benefit the patient. Although there's no consensus on its precise meaning, health-care experts suggest it exists when one of the following conditions exists (Rousseau, 2001):

- The treatment does not serve a useful purpose
- The treatment causes needless pain and suffering
- The treatment does not restore the patient to an acceptable quality of life

There is continuing debate in the health-care community itself (Moskop, 1999). Much of it seems to hinge on a single question, should health care professionals be required to continue providing treatment even when they no longer believe it's beneficial to do so. There seems to be no easy answer and the discussion is ongoing (e.g., Cogliano, 1999; Reitman, 1996; Rousseau, 2001).

You might recall from the earlier discussions in this chapter that there are several key principles that come into play when discussing ethical decision making. Sometimes they conflict. In the debate on medical futility, the principles that seem most clearly at loggerheads are those of patient *autonomy* and *professional integrity* (Pellegrino, 1993). Although not necessarily wishing to return to the heyday of medical paternalism, many doctors nevertheless feel that as professionals they should be able to exercise their judgment even when at odds with the wishes of the patient or family. You probably won't be surprised to learn, however, that when the opinions of medical experts conflict with the wishes of families, the disagreements have found their way into the legal system. To the dismay of the health-care experts, the courts have almost always sided with patients and their families.

A case in point is the story of Helga Wanglie. She was an active, well-educated woman of 85 years when she tripped over a rug and broke her hip (Capron, 1991; Cranford, 1991). This began a saga that included series of admissions to the hospital, rehab centers, and nursing homes. After being successfully treated for her broken hip, Helga was discharged to a nursing home, where she developed respiratory problems serious enough to require mechanical ventilation. Over a span of months, her physicians tried several times to wean her from the respirator without success. It was during this period that she suffered a series of heart attacks. One of these deprived her brain of oxygen long enough to leave her in a persistent vegetative state. Her physicians recommended stopping life support. Her husband and children refused to go along with it. The medical facility attempted to negotiate with the family, but Helga's husband of 53 years wouldn't budge. The Fourth Judicial District Court, Hennipin County, Minnesota, ultimately ruled that Helga's husband was the best person to act on her behalf. It agreed with his request, refusing to grant the facility permission to discontinue life support. Three days after the judge handed down her decision, and after Helga had existed in a persistent vegetative state for over a year, she died.

A second landmark case centered on the opposite end of the life-course (Capron, 1994). It involved a newborn who became known as Baby K, a pseudonym she was given to protect her identity. Born in a Fairfax, Virginia, hospital on October 13, 1992, she was born without major portions of the skull and brain—a condition that affects about 1,000 infants each year. Generally, these infants—called **anencephalic infants**—receive comfort care without the benefit of life support. Because of the severe nature of the disability, it is uncommon for them to live longer than a few days.

Baby K was having difficulty breathing. Despite being told that the baby's condition was futile, her mother insisted that she be given artificial ventilation. After approximately two months, Baby K was stable enough to be discharged to a nursing home. She needed to return, however, to the hospital as a result of continuing respiratory problems. Upon the second admission, the hospital sought a judicial decision relieving it of the responsibility to provide what its health-care professionals regarded as futile treatment. The federal judge ruled against the hospital. It, in turn, appealed the decision. On appeal, the majority of the federal appeals court justices supported the decision of the federal District Court. Treatment was required. Two years later, a reporter from *USA Today* did a follow-up on the case (Castaneda, 1994). Contrenia Harrel, Baby K's mother, was having a birthday party for her. Stephanie, the name her mother gave her, was still alive and in a Virginia nursing home. Medical experts have suggested she was little more than a brain stem functioning to support her in a vegetative state, yet for Stephanie's mother, her daughter was alive and beautiful.

Withdrawing Life Support from the Actively Dying

The principle of double effect essentially states that an act is not unethical if a person inadvertently dies when attempting to alleviate suffering (see Chapter 12). This, as well as the other ethical precepts discussed so far in this chapter—autonomy, beneficence, nonmaleficence, and professional integrity—are all conceptual tools that can help frame the discussion about ethical decision making in end-of-life situations.

The discussion so far has focused on conditions where there is a lack of higher functioning but intact vital functions. Here, I want to shift the focus to the decision making that happens when a person is actively dying (when the vital functions are shutting down yet the person might still have the ability to use higher mental functions). In such situations, when is ventilation an intrusion? At what point does resuscitation cause harm? When is it best to let an infection take its natural course? When do providing food and fluids prolong dying instead of sustain functioning?

There are no easy answers to questions like these—no rote formulas, no clear-cut directions. Knowing what to do when someone is dying is uncertain business. Normal dying—the active dying process—often includes being bed bound; feeling weak and drowsy; having a hard time breathing; experiencing pain, restlessness, and agitation; having a short attention span; feeling disoriented; not being interested in food or fluids; and having difficulty swallowing (EPEC Project, 1999; Twycross & Lichter, 1998).

For family and friends, seeing a loved one in this situation is unsettling, to say the least. Feelings of fear, confusion, and helplessness are understandable. It's natural at such times to want to express one's love, ease discomfort, and do something that feels like helping. In our society, one way to try to do this is by giving food and drink. Loved ones may also mistakenly hope that by providing food and fluids they can help the person regain enough strength to overcome their current medical crisis. At an intuitive level, it may seem compassionate to continue providing such basics as air, fluids, and nutrition to a dying person. Recent studies, however, suggest that rather than providing comfort such acts can at times actually prolong the dying process and increase suffering.

The purpose of providing nutritional support, for example, will change as the disease progresses (Eberhardie, 2002). Early on, it might make a great deal of sense to provide nutrition in order to cope with the metabolic demands of the illness and treatment, to repair tissue and prevent infection, and to promote a sense of well-being. In the latter stages of the disease this may no longer make sense. Indeed, it's common for the appetite to naturally drop off when actively dying—perhaps the body's way of saying it no longer needs food the way it once did. What the body might need at this stage is the freedom to shut down and stop feeling discomfort.

It has been reported that at the end of life many terminally ill people paradoxically experience an *increase* in comfort that corresponds with a *decrease* in their nutritional intake. Shirley Smith and Maria Andrews (2000) work extensively with the terminally ill. They cite two theories that are used to explain why feelings of relative well-being might occur when eating stops. One suggests that the reduction in nutritional intake naturally stimulates the production of endorphins, an analgesic, or pain reliever, that's produced naturally in the body. The other submits that by cutting back on nutritional intake, the process of ketoacidosis (a condition that occurs in diabetes) is stimulated. The production of ketones that occurs in this process is thought to reduce feelings of pain and hunger (Printz, 1988, 1992). Regardless, based on recent research it seems that a sizable number of terminally ill people voluntarily forego taking in food and fluids when they are ready to die (Ganzini et al., 2003). Furthermore, the results of this research are fairly clear in suggesting that the quality of such deaths can be quite high, as rated by the hospice nurses who care for them.

Terminal dehydration is the loss of salt and water that occurs during the last days of life. Similar to what happens when a dying person loses interest in food, the dehydration may be adaptive—the body's way of adjusting to multisystem failure and the approach of death (Jackonen, 1997). It was once thought that terminal dehydration was accompanied by a marked reduction in fluid volume and the depletion of important electrolytes, substances necessary for the regulation of various bodily functions (Jackonen, 1997; Musgrave, 1990; Zerwekh, 1983). More recent evidence, however, hasn't shown electrolyte levels in the terminally ill to be especially problematic (Burge, 1993; Meares, 1994; Smith & Andrews, 2000; Vullo-Navich et al., 1998; Zerwekh, 1997).

Among actively dying persons, terminal dehydration seems to unfold naturally as a result of the gradual reduction in the amount of fluids the person takes in as well the normal secretion of urine, intestinal fluids, and perspiration (Jackonen, 1997). Similar to what happens when eating slows down, the evidence suggests that terminally ill dehydrated people may experience less discomfort and pain than those who are hydrated (Billings, 1985; Jackonen, 1997; Oliver, 1984; Printz, 1988, 1992; Smith & Andrews, 2000; Zerwekh, 1983). In addition, there's evidence to suggest that terminal dehydration may help reduce urinary output and incontinence, nausea and vomiting, and cardiopulmonary congestion, breathlessness, and cough (attributed to reduced fluids around the heart and in the lungs) (Jackonen, 1997; Musgrave, 1990; Rousseau, 1991; Zerwekh, 1983).

Although there are some surprising naturally occurring benefits associated with terminal dehydration, there is also clearly a down side. About 10 percent of terminally ill dehydrated patients may experience severe delirium—a state characterized by an increase in unpleasant symptoms such as agitation, restlessness, and hallucinations (Smith & Andrews, 2000). Research suggests that in these cases administering fluids, switching opioids (because of suspected opioid toxicity), and using less sedating types of medication can be successful in reducing the experience of terminal delirium to about 3 percent (Smith & Andrews, 2000).

As you may have already sensed from the discussion, there's no single kind of death. Indeed, we can say each death tells a different story. There do, however, seem to be some patterns that can distinguish "easy" and "difficult" deaths. Some have called these "two roads to death" (see Figure 13.4) (EPEC Project, 1999; Ferris et al., 1995). The first, referred to as the "usual road," is relatively peaceful. It is characterized by a gradually increasing sleepiness coupled with a decrease in consciousness, which ultimately leads to coma and death. The second, called the "difficult road," is trod by a relatively smaller percentage of the dying, perhaps 10 percent. It's marked by an agitated delirium. It can include any or all of the following: restlessness, fear, hallucinations, confusion, muscle spasms, and seizures.

The kinds of experiences of patients on the two roads to death are contrasted in Figure 13.4. The two columns merge into a single one at the bottom of the figure. This represents the point at which the two roads merge into a single path. In the end, those on both roads go through being semicomatose and then comatose before finally succumbing to death.

Some terminally ill patients are maintained on ventilators prior to death. If they are unable to continue living without the ventilator, these patients are called **ventilator dependent**. Because ventilators can artificially maintain the vital functions of even a terminally ill person for a very long time, at some point the patient (if conscious), family,

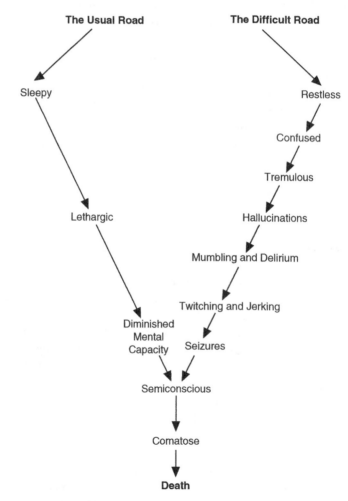

FIGURE 13.4 Two Roads to Death *Source:* Based on Ferris et al., 1995.

and the health-care team may feel compelled to discuss the appropriateness of discontinuing the use of artificial ventilation. This is always an extremely momentous event. The literature suggests that withdrawing ventilator support from a ventilator-dependent patient invariably spells death, sometimes within minutes, but almost certainly within hours (Ankrom et al., 2001; Campbell, Bizek, & Thill, 1999; EPEC Project, 1999; Gianakos, 1995; Gilligan & Raffin, 1995; Henig, Faul, & Raffin, 2001; Krieger, 2000; O'Mahony, McHugh, Zallman, & Selwyn, 2003; Tasota & Hoffman, 1996; Way, Black, & Curtis, 2002).

Once the health-care team and the family (or person able to make health-care decisions for the patient) and the patient (whenever possible) have discussed the current medical situation and the options, it may be desirable to make a decision about discontinuing ventilation. Health-care professionals suggest, and the principle of autonomy demands, that the decision be made with the full awareness of all parties that the likely result of taking this step would be death. The methods of carrying it out should also be discussed, with a full disclosure of the undesirable effects as well as the measures that would be used to address patient comfort needs (EPEC Project, 1999).

When the decision is made to withdraw mechanical ventilation, there are two general methods for doing so (EPEC Project, 1999; Henig et al., 2001; Gianakos, 1995; Gilligan & Raffin, 1995; Krieger, 2000). The first is called terminal weaning; the second is immediate extubation. Mechanical ventilation is a process whereby oxygen is artificially pumped to the lungs. The ventilator machine delivers pressurized artificial breaths infused with oxygen. In **terminal weaning**, the amount of oxygen and the breathing action of the ventilator are reduced while the tube, called an *endotracheal tube*, remains in place (EPEC Project, 1999). The goal is for the patient to resume spontaneous breathing until death occurs naturally. Some patients are incapable of spontaneous breathing, however. They will die immediately when artificial breathing stops. **Intubation** occurs when a patient is hooked up to mechanical ventilation. **Immediate extubation**, the opposite of *in*tubation, involves releasing the mechanism that holds the endotracheal tube in place and removing it from the airway. Secretions that might obstruct the airway are suctioned in an effort to clear the airway. An alternative to extubation is to put a T (valve) on the end of the endotracheal tube but leave it in place. In this case, medications and moisturized air may be infused by way of the T in an effort to provide additional comfort.

As you can imagine, foregoing oxygen and pressurized breath is understandably traumatic for a person who is ventilator dependent, if conscious. It can also be disturbing for members of the family and health-care team (Gilligan & Raffin, 1995). When weaning or extubation is done, minimizing the adverse effects and enhancing patient comfort becomes a medical priority. Opioids are used to control the uncomfortable sense of breathlessness, called **dyspnea**. Benzodiazapenes, or other anxiolytics (anti-anxiety medications), are used to control the anxiety. The doses are adjusted until the person is comfortable. If severe symptoms persist in a conscious patient, medically inducing a coma is sometimes the only effective way to ease the patient's suffering.

Chapter Summary

The world in which we live has changed. Technology has made it possible to artificially sustain life beyond when it would have been possible in the past. As a result, we've had to reexamine what we mean by death. This chapter began with an exploration of how to define death, beginning with the dichotomy of clinical death (heart beat and respiration) and so-called brain death (whole brain death, brain stem death, and neocortical brain death). As this examination progressed, the chapter explored some of the cultural context, particularly the need to find new ways to define death because of the ability to transplant vital organs. The chapter looked at the *dead donor rule*, the *Harvard criteria*, and the *Uniform Death Determination Act*.

Next, the issue of withdrawing life support was reviewed, starting with an examination of doing so when a person is existing is a *persistent vegetative state*, including a look at the case that seems to have begun the debate in North America—Karen Ann Quinlan. Since court cases have become important in dealing with questions about withholding and withdrawing life supports, I summarized some of the key legal decisions in Figure 13.2.

In addition, the chapter explored several key ethical concepts that often come into play when grappling with legal, moral, and ethical issues: *autonomy, nonmaleficence, beneficence, justice,* and *professional integrity*. The chapter also looked at the three key standards used when trying to decide about the appropriateness of withholding or withdrawing life support: the *subjective standard*, the *substituted judgment standard*, and the *best interest standard.*

In connection with the Nancy Cruzan case, the chapter also touched on the significance of the Missouri Rule as well as a new federal statute that established the rights of people to make decisions about health care in advance of experiencing a medical catastrophe: the Patient Self-determination Act. The chapter also looked at the application of this law and the principle of autonomy to cases of medical futility, defined by the physicians providing care, noting the supremacy of the principle of *autonomy* when there is a conflict with the medical profession's principle *professional integrity*.

Key Terms

anencephalic infants *297*
autonomy *294*
beneficence *294*
best interest standard *294*
brain death *283*
dead donor rule *284*
dyspnea *301*
Harvard criteria *285*
hypoxia *287*
immediate extubation *301*
intubation *301*

ischemia *287*
justice *294*
medical futility *296*
Missouri Rule *295*
nonmaleficence *294*
nutrition *282*
Patient Self-Determination
   Act (PSDA) *295*
persistent vegetative state *286*
professional integrity *293*
subjective standard *294*

substituted judgment
   standard *294*
terminal
   dehydration *299*
terminal sedation *292*
terminal weaning *301*
transhumanism *290*
Uniform Determination of
   Death Act (UDDA) *286*
ventilation *282*
ventilator dependent *300*

Suggested Activities

1. Consider those times when you've heard or read about a case of brain death, perhaps on TV or in a newspaper. Reflect on what you know about the different definitions of brain death. How does the way that brain death is defined change how people deal with such situation?

2. Using your favorite search engine, surf the Internet for sites having to do with organ donation and organ transplantation. See if you can get a sense of any differences that might exist between the need for organs and their availability.

3. Reflect on your own experiences with death. Consider how many instances in your own family or among your own friends involve persons who have spent long periods in a hospital or nursing home before dying. Briefly journal about your experience in light of the ability of modern technology to artificially sustain life. What are the pros and cons of using high-tech methods of sustaining life?

4. Develop a table that compares the different definitions of death and brain death. Which definition do you think works best? Are some definitions better in certain circumstances than others? Why?

5. List the advantages and disadvantages of using the dead donor rule.

6. If you know anyone who has been declared brain dead, journal about your recollections of the thoughts and feelings you had when you learned they had been given this diagnosis.

7. Seriously consider the claims of the transhumanists. If you had the option of living two or three times what is currently possible, would you choose it? What would the impact on life in the world be if everyone chose this option? Would you want to live an extended period of time if it meant you could only do so by "residing" on a hard drive?

8. Develop a set "advance directives" for yourself. Under what circumstances would you choose or not choose to have CPR and artificial ventilation? Under what conditions would you or wouldn't you want to be given fluids and nutrition artificially? Share with at least two other individuals your preferences about life-support therapies. What did you learn about the other person as a result of doing so? What did you learn about yourself?

9. After reviewing the ethical principles and decision-making priorities, develop a set of ethical principles that could be used to help guide your ethical decision making. How would you choose to use these principles in deciding about your own care? About the care of someone close to you? About any other person?

Suggested Reading

- Bauby, J-D. (1997). *The diving bell and the butterfly.* New York: Knopf.
  This is the profoundly moving memoir of Jean-Dominique Bauby, the former editor in chief of the French magazine *Elle.* At the age of 43, he experienced a rare stroke to the brain stem, which left him in a "locked-in" state. Fully conscious and aware, he was nevertheless left unable to move or communicate except to blink one eye. Developing a system of blinking to selected letters of the alphabet, he was ultimately able to tell his story in this amazing book.

- Colby, W. H. (2002). *Long goodbye: The deaths of Nancy Cruzan.* Carlsbad, CA: Hay House.
  This "spellbinding" book was written by William H. Colby, the attorney who represented the Cruzan family before the U.S. Supreme Court. In it, Colby recounts the poignant struggle of the family to secure Nancy Cruzan's right to die. The book personalizes the ethical issues and raises important questions about the meaning of life in the wake of the technological advances in medicine.

Links and Internet Resources

- **Aging with Dignity**
  www.agingwithdignity.org/
  This is home to an organization founded by Jim Towey in 1996 after his experiences at Mother Teresa's homes

  for the dying. It promotes and sells a document called *The Five Wishes*, which is intended to help people to express their wishes should they become seriously ill and unable to speak for themselves. It is an advanced directive designed to let family and physicians know (1) who should be empowered to make health-care decisions, (2) the kind of medical treatment wanted, (3) the comfort measures desired, (4) how the person wants to be treated, and (5) what the person would want his or her loved ones to know.

- **Center for Bioethics–University of Minnesota**
  www.bioethics.umn.edu/
  The Center for Bioethics strives to advance and disseminate knowledge concerning ethical issues in health care and the life sciences. It conducts original interdisciplinary research, offers educational programs and courses to foster public discussion and debate, and assists in formulating public policy. The website includes a variety of high-quality resources of interest to learners and teachers, especially their "reading packets."

- **Department of Medical Humanities, The Brody School of Medicine at East Carolina University**
  www.ecu.edu/medhum/
  This impressive website has some first-rate resources. These include a scholarly online newsletter (with archives of old editions), a resource page, and a link to the school's own bioethics center.

- **World Transhumanist Association**
  www.transhumanism.org/index.php/WTA/index/
  The World Transhumanist Association is an international nonprofit organization devoted to promoting the ethical use of technology to expand human capacities. Founded in 1998 by the philosophers Nick Bostrom and David Pearce, it supports the development of new technologies to enhance human intelligence, repair bodies, and extend life.

Review Guide

1. Compare definitions of death, clinical death, brain death (and various categories of brain death). Apply one or more of these definitions as you do one of the suggested activities.
2. Describe why definitions of death have become important.
3. What is the *dead donor rule*? In what ways does it or doesn't it make sense to use it when using a person's vital organs is considered.
4. Be familiar with the definitions of each of the terms printed in **bold** in this chapter.
5. What are the implications of adopting a transhumanist perspective when it comes to field of death and dying?
6. What are the kinds of life support discussed in this chapter? What considerations are important when considering providing, withholding, or withdrawing them?
7. Identify each of the major ethical principles that come into play in the field of bioethics. Describe the kinds of conflicts that can exist between them. What must be done to resolve conflicts between them?

8. Be familiar with the significant legal rulings relevant to withholding or withdrawing life support and with physician-assisted suicide. What ethical principles, if any, seem to hold sway in these decisions?
9. Be familiar with the standards that are used when consideration is given to withholding or withdrawing life support.
10. What are some of the possible effects of dehydration and lack of nutrition at the end of life? What might the impacts have on decision making about providing artificial hydration/nutrition when a person is nearing death?
11. What must be considered when deciding to remove artificial ventilation from a person who is ventilator dependent and in the final phase of life?

P A R T

VI

Into the Future

Part VI contains two chapters that relate to the future. Chapter 14 explores what happens after we die? Is there nothing? Do we simply cease to exist? Do we go to heaven? Do we go to the "other" place? Chapter 15 looks at the current trends.

According to *terror management theory*, which we discussed in some depth in Chapter 1, human beings are different from other animals in that we have the ability to think abstractly and even anticipate our own demise. Also according to this theory, we have come up with two strategies to help us deal with the reality of our own deaths: culture and self-efficacy. Culture includes religion, and one of the key functions of religion is to provide us with a sense of meaning, even it is about our deaths. Most religious systems suggest that some part of us survives our physical death, a "soul" of "continuity." So, in Chapter 14 we explore what several religious systems have to say about what happens when we die: the ancient Egyptian, Greek, Judaic, Christian, and Islamic traditions. Not only this, but we also look at something that in our culture became a topic of popular interest after we developed the ability to artificially resuscitate people when they ceased breathing or their hearts stopped breathing: the near-death experience. In an effort to try to understand the phenomenon, we investigate several theories and the evidence, such as it is.

In Chapter 15 we revisit some of the material presented the previous chapters. We ask the question, "Based on the way things are moving, what appears to lie ahead?" We explore modern trends, including the topics of "sequestration," "secularization," and "desecularization" in the context of death, dying, and bereavement. Also we look at how the currently living generations deal with death, the "Greatest Generation" and baby boomers, in addition to the Generation X-ers, Millennials, and Generation Z—the X-ers, Nexters, and Texters. We also explore the implications for health care. Next, we review end-of-life caring with an eye to some of the practical issues, such as funding. We then briefly look at how to live until we die, taking heed of the wisdom of those who have gone before us. Finally, we explore the "long good-bye," what we've learned about dealing with bereavement, grief, and mourning.

14

Life after Life

- Ancient Egyptian Beliefs
- Tibetan Buddhist Teachings
- Abrahamic Tradition
- The Near-Death Experience

There are certain questions that people throughout the ages have asked in relation to life and death. Does human experience end with death? Is there life after life? If so, what happens when we die? It is precisely this kind of question that has inspired so many people in various parts of the world and throughout history to wonder—and yet, there are no definitive answers. This chapter explores a few attempts to address the question of life after life.

ANCIENT EGYPTIAN BELIEFS

The beliefs of the ancient Egyptians regarding the afterlife are perhaps the most widely recorded. In ancient Egypt, when the body and organs were fully prepared, they were placed in a coffin inscribed with magical charms. The purpose of embalming was to preserve the body (Mackenzie, 1907), for the ancient Egyptians thought it necessary to preserve the body in order that the soul might survive. A papyrus roll was placed in the sarcophagus with the body, which provided the dead with a full set of instructions on traversing the treacherous territory on the way to the Egyptian heaven. These instructions, eventually to be known as the *Egyptian Book of the Dead,* served as a kind of road map, complete with detailed formulas thought necessary when encountering the gods and demons on the other side (Faulkner & Andrews, 1990; Faulkner, Goelet, & Andrews, 2000; Ashby, 2000).

As briefly discussed in Chapter 4, the ancient Egyptians believed that the body, soul (and personality) (**ba**), and spirit (**ka**) of the person were mystically interconnected. They believed that when the *ba* and *ka* come together in the afterlife it would reanimate the **akh**, a sort of living consciousness, causing the dead person to become a living *akh*.

In the Old Kingdom it was believed that only the Pharaoh, who was thought to be the earthly embodiment of the god Horus, could achieve reanimation. In the New Kingdom it was open to all. Heaven was a kind of spiritual counterpart to the Nile River Delta (Mackenzie, 1907; Schumann-Antelme & Rossini, 1998). Before reaching this heaven, called the **Paradise of Aalu**, the ancient Egyptians apparently believed they had to first undertake a long and arduous journey, for which the soul needed weapons, a staff, food, and water. Crossing barren deserts, it was thought that the soul would encounter beasts of all kinds, and climb the western mountains, before reaching the boundary of the kingdom of the dead. Upon arriving, the soul was said to come upon a colossal sycamore tree, which was full with clusters of fruit amidst luxuriant foliage. As the soul approached, it was believed that a goddess leaned out from an opening in the trunk of the tree and held a tray heaped with cakes, fruit, and a pot of clear, fresh, water. In order to proceed, it was thought the soul would need to nourish itself and drink of the pure water, and in the process become indebted to and a servant of the gods.

As the soul continued on its way, it was believed that it would encounter great dangers and endure arduous trials, including terrifying clashes with evil spirits and fierce demons, who would try to impede its passage, thereby causing the soul to experience a second and final death (Mackenzie, 1907). The ancient Egyptians thought that if the soul survived, it might contend with the most formidable enemy yet, **Seth**, an evil god who was said to take the form of a huge monster, with the head of a camel and the body of a hound. The murderer of the Osiris, Seth was feared as a threat to gods and humans alike. The ancient Egyptians thought that if the soul was able to drive back the evil god, it could proceed to the bank of a wide river, where a boat would await. This boat was believed to be crewed by silent divinities who awaited as the soul answered a series of questions put to it by the boat itself about its construction. The papyrus roll entombed with the body of the deceased contained the necessary secrets. When the soul answered the boat's questions and invoked the sacred formulas, the boat, guided by **Turnface**, a ferryman who always looked away from the soul of the deceased, would take the soul to the other side.

According to ancient traditions, on the other side lay the kingdom of the god **Osiris**—god of the dead and judge of all (Mackenzie, 1907). As the soul proceeded from the bank of the river, it was believed to come upon the great Hall of Justice, a fearsome place the soul needed to pass through before it could approach the Paradise of Aalu. No one was allowed to enter the hall without permission. To gain entrance, it was believed that the soul needed to pay homage to the god and recite a ritual confession in which it proclaimed its innocence from a litany of possible offenses (see Figure 14.1). The massive gates would swing open. The jackal-headed god Anubis then escorted the soul into the great hall and before the throne of Osiris, who sat with arms crossed, a crook in one hand and a flail in the other.

Before Osiris stood the **scales of justice**, where the person's heart would be weighed as the gods **Thoth**, **Horus**, and **Maat**, a recording god and the goddesses of truth and justice, waited nearby (Mackenzie, 1907). Again, the pilgrim would have to proclaim its innocence, with 42 animal gods watching, and ready to pounce on the deceased in the event of an unfavorable judgment. The heart of the deceased was placed on one side of the scales. On the other was an ostrich feather, symbol of the goddess Maat. According to tradition, the soul would cry out to its own heart, begging that the heart not to condemn the soul. If it was neither too heavy nor too light, the soul was acquitted. Thoth recorded the verdict on a papyrus, passing it on to Osiris, who would order the heart restored. The soul was then thought to be free to pass through the great hall and on to the Paradise of Aalu on the other side.

Pictured here is the heart of an individual placed on the scales of justice.   *rysp/Fotolia*

I have done no evil against another

I have not caused my kinsfolk to be put to death

I have not caused witnesses to speak falsely in the Hall of Justice

I have not done that which is hated by the gods

I am not a worker of wickedness

I have never oppressed a servant with too much work

I have not caused others to hunger or weep

I have not been without good works, nor have I acted weakly or with meanness

I am not a murderer

I have not conspired to have another put to death

I have not plotted to make another grieve

I have not stolen temple offering

I have not stinted the food offered to the gods

I have not despoiled the dead

I have not committed adultery

I have not failed to keep myself pure as a priest

I have not lessened the corn measure

I have not shortened the hand measure

I have not tampered with the balance

I have not deprived children of milk

I have not stolen cattle from the meadows

I have not snared the birds consecrated to the gods

I have not taken fish from holy lakes

I have not prevented Nile water from running in channels

I have turned aside the water

I have not stolen water from a channel

I have not put out the fire when it should burn

I have never kept from the nine gods what was their due

I have not prevented the temple cattle from grazing on my land

I have not obstructed a god's image when it came forth in a procession

FIGURE 14.1 Ancient Egyptian Ritual Confession *Source:* This figure is based on Mackenzie, 1907.

TIBETAN BUDDHIST TEACHINGS

The *Bardo Thodol Chenmo*, misnamed the *Tibetan Book of the Dead* by W. Y. Evans-Wentz, an American scholar, is perhaps the best known book on what happens after death, written from a Tibetan Buddhist perspective (Goss & Klass, 1997). As Goss and Klass suggest, the term **bardo** literally means "in between." In the context of the experience of death, it refers to the transitional condition that exists between this life and the one to come. The 49-day period after death is thought crucial to Tibetan Buddhists, for it is during this time that they believe the subtle mind, or consciousness, of the dead experiences a series of events in the bardo, before achieving its new birth, or reincarnation (Evans-Wentz, 1974; Fermantle & Trungpa, 1992).

The *Bardo Thodol Chenmo* is a manual for the dying and the dead. It has three major parts: one relating to the moment of death; another that describes experiences in the intermediate state between death and a new birth; and a third part, which addresses circumstances surrounding the mind undergoing new birth (Evans-Wentz, 1974; Fermantle & Trungpa, 1992). Containing a description of appearances the person can expect in the bardo, the book contains instructions that are to be read to the dying. The goal is to help the person make the transition from this life to the next.

In a recent book on death and dying, His Holiness the Dalai Lama, the spiritual of Tibetan Buddhists, suggests that the dying process has eight phases. The first four relate to the dissolution of **four basic elements**: earth (body), water (its fluids), fire (heat), and wind (energy or movement) (Gyatso, 2002). As the process unfolds, the body is no longer able to function as the foundation for consciousness. Normal feelings of pleasure and pain subside as fluids no longer course through the body. As the warmth of the body diminishes, attention to family and friends also diminishes. The breathing may become labored, and what in the West we call the "death rattle" may be heard. In the Tibetan tradition, the cessation of breathing also marks the start of the next four phases of the dying process.

These next four phases are all concerned with the **dissolution of consciousness** (Gyatso, 2002). Tibetan tradition holds that, similar to how the basic elements break down, consciousness dissolves from the grosser to more subtle—from sense awareness, emotion, to the conceptual. With this dissolution emerges the appearance of vivid white light, then orange-red, followed by that of a vivid black light, which recedes into the **clear light state**—the subtle consciousness of reality. This clear light is manifest because the ordinary states of mind, emotion, and ignorance that have obscured it up until then have dissolved (Sogyal, 1992). The clear light is said to carry with it the very substance of liberation, if only the mind can recognize it and act in a way to remain within that state. The Dalai Lama suggests that the clear light condition will usually last for about three days, although some very advanced practitioners may abide in it much longer (Gyatso, 2002). In the Tibetan tradition, it is important not to disturb the body during this period. Tibetans believe reading to the dead from the *Bardo Thodol Chenmo* is helpful at this time. Tibetan tradition suggests that although the body is no longer functioning, the subtle mind remains acutely aware.

Remarkable features are attributed to the clear light condition. For one, Tibetan tradition holds that the body does not decay when the mind is in clear light, even in warm climates (Gyatso, 2001, 2002; Thrangu, 1999). Anecdotally, His Holiness the Dalai Lama relates that his own senior tutor, Ling Rinpoche, existed in a state of clear light for 13 days—no heart beat or circulation but remarkably no decomposition of the body (Gyatso, 2001, 2002). Tibetan tradition holds that when the mind is in the clear light state, it is unimpeded by the body and is therefore able to travel anywhere in the world by merely conceiving it. If the mind does not find liberation during this phase, it is said to descend. Tibetan teachings contend that it is when the clear light state passes that the mind enters the intermediate state (when physical death actually occurs).

The mind will initially encounter 42 peaceful deities, who may remain for a seemingly long time (Thrangu, 1999). Then, 50 wrathful and 8 semiwrathful deities are believed to manifest. Tibetan tradition suggests that during the first six days in the bardo, a succession of individual deities and their attendant lights and retinue appear. On the first two days, the deities representing the creator god and the second most powerful deity appear. With the first comes the frightening bright blue light of heaven; with the other comes the dim, smokey, light reflecting the realm of hell (it's not good to be drawn to this one). On the seventh day, waves of wrathful and semiwrathful deities begin to appear. Although the mind can be easily drawn to the peaceful deities and frightened by the wrathful ones, Tibetan sages advise that these are all actually appearances of the mind that pervade the awareness (Evans-Wentz, 1974; Fremantle & Trungpa, 1992; Sogyal, 1992). If the mind is able to recognize them for what they really are, they dissolve, perhaps leading to liberation or enlightenment. Tibetans generally believe that the mind is able to achieve liberation anywhere in the bardo, but they think individual **karma**—good and bad merit earned in life—will usually lead to another cycle of *samsara*—birth, suffering, and death, until the individual achieves enlightenment.

ABRAHAMIC TRADITION

With their origins in the Middle East, the three monotheistic faiths of Judaism, Christianity, and Islam comprise what scholars often call the *Abrahamic tradition* (e.g., Ali, 2002; Islam Online, 2003; Institute for Advanced Study of Religion, 2003; Khan, 2000; Smith, 2004; Weizfeld, 1998). The name gets its meaning from the biblical figure Abraham, who is the acknowledged patriarch of Muslims, Jews, and Christians. According to Judaic and Muslim tradition, Abraham was the father of Isma'il, through Hagar, and of Isaac, through his wife Sarah—Ishma'il's descendants becoming the Arabs; Isaac's progeny the Jews (Metzger & Murphy, 1994, Gen 16:15, 21:3).

Semitic Traditions

In the eighteenth century of the current era, scholars coined the term *Semitic* to refer to peoples in the Middle East with certain similarities in language and culture (McDannell & Lang, 2001). This grouping includes Hebrews as well as Assyrians, Babylonians, Caananites, and Phoenicians. In pre-Judaic times, Semitic people pictured the world as something like a big house with an upper level for the gods (heaven), a middle level given to human beings by the gods (the earth), and an underworld called **Sheol**, with a great cave, where the gods of the netherworld and the dead were thought to reside—a very different concept from that of hell, which was conceived by Zoroastrians as a place of punishment, a concept that did not gain currency with the Jews until later in history.

The ancient Semites, living as they did between heaven and Sheol, saw their lives as precarious enterprises, influenced by forces from above and below (McDannell & Lang, 2001). To deal with these forces, they built temples, retained priests, sponsored choirs, offered sacrifices, chanted and prayed, listened to prophets, and consulted with wizards. Two forms of worship were practiced: private and public. Private worship involved the practice of venerating dead ancestors who had essentially achieved the status of underworld deities. The living made offerings and sought the help of ancestors to achieve personal or family benefits. When the whole community needed help, everyone prayed communally, appealing to the gods of heaven, usually led by priests with special training and knowledge.

Evolution of Jewish Beliefs about the Afterlife

The Jewish kingdoms of northern Israel and southern Judah were vassal states to various world powers at different points in history. After the destruction of the northern Israeli kingdom by the Assyrians in 722 B.C.E., a pious faction in Judah, which scholars now call "Yahweh-alonists," succeeded in prohibiting the practice of ancestor worship (McDannell & Lang, 2001). King Hezekiah (728–699 B.C.E.), of the southern kingdom of Judah, decreed that all first-born sons be consecrated to Yahweh, which would significantly change Jewish custom.

Traditionally, first-born sons had been obligated to care for, bury, and venerate their parents. By mandating first-born sons be consecrated to Yahweh, they were cleverly barred from venerating ancestors, thereby eroding this ancient practice. Although Jewish people were still allowed to put food and other offerings at the tombs of their ancestors, in 623 B.C.E. King Josiah banned all worship but to Yahweh alone. Further religious taboos were put on contact with dead bodies, creating a widening gap between the living and dead.

From the time of King Josiaha's decree to the fall of Jerusalem to the Babylonians in 586 B.C.E., veneration of ancestors and the gods of the underworld ended in Judah (McDannell & Lang, 2001; Ontario Consultants on Religious Tolerance, 2004). During their captivity in Babylon, members of the Jewish ruling and priestly classes were exposed to the teachings of Zoroaster, a Persian prophet and religious reformer. These teachings included the belief that individuals are judged after death; heaven exists as a reward for the righteous; hell is a place of punishment for the wicked; and body and soul would be reunited—resurrected when God came to vanquish evil on earth, once and for all.

The Jews in exile returned to Jerusalem 538 B.C.E. to reestablish the Jewish state (Bowker, 1997). Autonomy would be short-lived, however. Alexander, called "the great," would conquer it again in 332 B.C.E. With occupation came the beginnings of a Hellenization process. The Greeks brought their language and culture. Among their religious concepts were the ideas of an eternal soul and a "place" called **Hades**—where the Greeks claimed evil deeds were punished and virtuous ones rewarded. The term **Gehenna** refers to a valley outside Jerusalem where pagan sacrifices had once been performed and where the city's garbage was later burned. In the Christian New Testament, the name was used as a synonym for *Hades*. In addition, Greek tradition held there was a place called the **Elysian Fields**, a paradise that existed for the virtuous dead (McDannell & Lang, 2001).

On the death of Alexander, his empire was partitioned into three regions, one bequeathed to each of three long time friends and officers. Seleucus, founder of the Seleucid Empire, gained control of Alexander's Middle East territories, including the areas previously held by Israel and Judah. Eventually, not only did the Seleucid rulers oppress the Jews with heavy taxes but they also began to require submission to Seleucid religious customs, including the worship of Zeus and the emperor. The Jews revolted against Antiochus IV Epiphanes when the Seleucids defiled the Temple. This led to an intensification of the persecutions of 167–164 B.C.E. (McDannell & Lang, 2001). With the martyrdom of many righteous Jews, various factions came to believe God would resurrect the martyrs (Metzger & Murphy, 1994, Dan 12:2 , 2 Macc 6:1-7:42). With the added expectation that a promised messiah would soon rise to lead the people into freedom, there was also the anticipation of a general resurrection of righteous Jews sleeping in Sheol.

By the time the Romans occupied the Jewish territories in 63 B.C.E., there were three major sects within Judaism: the Sadducee, Pharisee, and Essene. As is well documented in Josephus's history (Whiston, 1987) and the Christian New Testament (Metzger & Murphy, 1994), the Saducess are said to have denied the immortality of the soul, the existence of an afterlife, and a resurrection of the dead. Scholars suggest they may have come from an affluent priestly class affiliated with the leadership of the Temple in Jerusalem. The Pharisees, a group that had been adamant in rejecting the secularization of the society, believed in the immortality of the soul, rewards and punishment in Sheol, and a bodily resurrection of the dead with the coming of the messiah. The Essenes were a politically neutral but pious group. Most Essenes were celibate, lived communally, shared their goods in common, and remained separate from what they viewed as a corrupt society. They believed human bodies to be corrupt. They also believed the soul is immortal, and that the souls of the righteous would ascend to a heavenly realm on death, and those of the wicked would descend to a dark and contemptuous place where punishment never ceases.

Christian Beliefs about the Afterlife

It was in this highly charged social milieu in which Christianity would emerge, first as a sect of Judaism and then as a distinct religious tradition. For Christians, Jesus was the messiah the Jews had been awaiting. His followers believe he died, was buried, and was resurrected. The Christian synoptic Gospels suggest that he preached the resurrection of a spiritual body, not just a physical one (Metzger & Murphy, 1994, Lk 20: 27-40; Mk 12: 18-27; Mt 22: 23-33).

Paul was a Pharisee who converted to the new religion soon after Jesus' crucifixion. He became a key evangelist to the non-Jewish gentiles, spreading the Christian message throughout much of the Roman world. Paul accepted the Pharisaic notion that the dead slept, but in keeping with Jesus' teachings he conceived of this resurrection not only as a profound physical-historical event but also as a present reality (McDannel & Lang, 2001). John of Patmos, author of the book of *Revelation*, had a slightly different vision. Like the author of Daniel in the Hebrew scriptures, he and his community had experienced persecution firsthand. For him, Rome was the incarnation of evil itself. Based on his mystical vision, John painted heaven as a post-apocalyptical spiritual experience—a divine liturgy, wholly focused on God, that would occur with the second coming of Christ and that would be a reward for persisting in the faith. Melding these visions, Christians of various orientations have argued for both an individual and general resurrection—the individual one is to take place in this life and at the time of death; the general one is to coincide with the Second Coming.

We should probably understand that Christianity is not a unified religion but one with many traditions, encompassing a diversity of denominations, jurisdictions, and sects that share but a few core beliefs, values, and practices. Some 2,000 years after Jesus' crucifixion, there is but one common Christian intuition about life after life: There is a continuation of life after this one. In Chapter 2, we briefly discussed the work of historian, Phillipe Aries, who suggested that in the medieval European Church, from the 6th through the 11st centuries, death was associated with the Gospel according to Matthew, in which the faithful were believed to sleep until the Second Coming (Aries, 1981). Aries also notes that by the late medieval period, from the 12th century to the Renaissance, there was a shift. This shift can be seen in the emphasis on the apocalypse of John, more commonly known as the book of *Revelation*, with its imagery about a judgment day, heaven, and hell.

What happened? New Testament references to the afterlife are brief and vague (see, for example, Mt. 13: 42; 23: 15; 25: 30, 41; Rev. 2: 11; 20: 14, discussed in Reicke, 1993; Cross & Livingstone, 1997). Some believe that the medieval imagination may have been influenced by the secular literature, especially Dante's *Divine Comedy* (Dante & Singleton, 1990). Dante Alighieri (1265–1321) wrote the *Divine Comedy*, which draws on fleeting New Testament references of the afterlife. On the surface, one can think of it as a description of Dante's mystical journey through purgatory, hell, and heaven (Bondanella, 2003). At a deeper level one can see it as a poem that attempts to explore the soul's journey to God (Dinsmore, 2010).

Christian conceptions of the afterlife have evolved, but there is little doubt that they are well rooted in the accepted creeds of the various Christian traditions. Although the particulars about the nature of heaven, hell, and purgatory are subject to interpretation by Christian leaders, belief in the resurrection of the dead and life in the world to come are

Images of heaven and hell in the late medieval period were heavily influenced by the imagination of authors, such as that of John's book of *Revelation* and Dante Alighieri's *Divine Comedy*.   *wjarek/Fotolia*

enshrined within the established creeds (Orr, 2012; Ayers, 2006). Clergy are generally expected to teach these received truths, and when they do not, they often run afoul of their denominations. Bishop James Pike, the fifth Episcopal bishop of California, was one such clergy member. He resigned from his post shortly after he was censured by his fellow bishops for his unorthodox beliefs, including the rejection of the notion of a literal hell (Pike, 1967).

Another example is that of Bishop Carlton Pearson who was an influential preacher in the African American Pentecostal movement (Pearson, 2007). An early protégé of evangelist Oral Roberts, he came to reject the existence of hell as a place of torment for nonbelievers; instead he adopted a "gospel of inclusion" and acceptance of a "universal reconciliation." As a result, Pearson, who had been the leader of a congregation in Tulsa, Oklahoma, that had had average Sunday attendance of 6,000, saw this drop to just a few hundred after his new beliefs became public. The Joint College of African American Pentecostal Bishops declared his views heretical, costing him his influence within the movement. No longer able to pay the mortgage, the bank foreclosed on the building the congregation had worshipped in. Today, Bishop Carlson is building a new ministry called "New Dimensions" in Chicago, Illinois, that emphasizes personal growth and redemption (New Dimensions Chicago, 2012).

Islamic Beliefs

The understanding of the afterlife in the Judeo-Christian heritage may be subject to interpretation. Such is not the case in Islam, however, in which the holy book, the *Qu'ran,* is explicit on the subject.

As discussed earlier, Arabs claim many of the same historical roots as other Semitic peoples. Islam, the religion established by Muhammad (c. 570–632 C.E.), is the dominant religious tradition among the Arab peoples. It continues to grow rapidly throughout the world (Bowker, 1997). The origins of Islam are attributed to the quest of Muhammad to find the absolute truth of God, after encountering the conflicting claims of the Jews, Christians, and Arab idol worshippers he met. He often went off to pray by himself, struggling to find **al-Haqq,** or the "true one." Islamic tradition holds that when he was praying in a cave on Mount Hira, he had a powerful mystical experience—an overwhelming sense of ultimate reality. The first words spoken from God, through the angel Gabriel, to Muhammad, would be the first words of the *Qur'an,* the holy book he compiled. Essential themes of this vision are that there is no god but Allah, Muhammad is his messenger, and all people should come together as one **'umma,** or community.

Death in Islam is sometimes regarded as the Return, for it is believed that before a breath was taken on earth, the soul existed with God (Murata & Chittick, 1994). There is a strong theme within Islam that it is God's wish that human beings return to Him, although they have some choice. In Islam, there are two possible types of Return: compulsory and voluntary. Human beings are thought to be compelled to submit to God with respect to expressing their created nature, but they have a choice with respect to accepting prophetic messages. That everyone dies and meets God is beyond the scope of individual choice.

In contrast to the other Abrahamic traditions, Islam is quite explicit in describing what happens to the person after death (Murata & Chittick, 1994). In Islam, it is taught that the dead have a life in the grave. Islam teaches that two angels, **Munkar** and **Nakir**, come to question the deceased in their graves. The questions are believed to be religious in nature, concerning belief in God, who they accept as prophet, and the holy scripture to which they subscribe. Based on the results, Islam teaches that the grave is either made very expansive and comfortable, or very constricted, dank, and miserable. In either case, death is not complete and the dead have a mixture of experiences, some of which have a dreamlike quality.

In Islam, the grave is only the first step on the path to the next world (Murata & Chittick, 1994). As in Christianity, there is the belief in resurrection. Also in Islam, there is the individual, or small resurrection, and a more general resurrection, called *qiyama*, that is thought to occur when the angel Seraphiel blows his trumpet in the last days. When the dead meet their Lord, it is thought their deeds are weighed and they're questioned about the reasons for their behavior. At this point, some may ascend to paradise; others are consigned to hell. Unlike other Abrahamic conceptions of hell, in the Islamic vision it is not necessarily an eternal one. The pain of hell can be conceived as a loving gesture on the part of God, influencing the soul to grasp the Real, which is God, and in so doing start the Return to His bosom, where Paradise is eternal.

THE NEAR-DEATH EXPERIENCE

In 1975, Dr. Raymond Moody, an Atlanta physician, wrote a best-selling book, *Life after Life*, that would rivet public attention on a phenomenon called the **near-death experience (NDE)** (Moody, 1975). In this book, Moody reported on the experiences of 150 persons who had died, or almost died, and then recovered. He summarized nine elements as being common to the NDE, including having an out-of-body experience, going through a tunnel toward a white light, meeting dead relatives on the other side, encountering a being of light, and having a highly vivid, "panoramic," review of one's life.

Moody's work was widely understood as providing a foundation for believing some essential part of the person survives death. His book stirred up considerable controversy, especially within the medical community. In 1980, psychologist Kenneth Ring published *Life at Death*, the first scientific attempt to describe the near-death experience itself (Ring, 1980). In this book, Ring, who has since become a principal investigator of NDEs, interviewed 102 people about their experiences. His landmark research was able to show that experiencing an NDE was not related to religious belief, race, or age. His research largely confirmed Moody's description, and is credited with legitimating Moody's original work.

Michael Sabom was an Atlanta cardiologist when he first learned of Moody's work in 1977. Initially skeptical, he began to speak informally with patients who had undergone life-saving procedures. To his surprise, many said they had had a near-death experience. As a result, he began a more formal study—one that would become a benchmark for later NDE research (Sabom & Kreutiziger 1977a, 1977b; Sabom, 1980, 1982). In this research, Sabom examined the experiences of 116 patients who said they had a near-death experience. He identified three types of experiences: **autoscopic** (out-of-body), **transcendental** (having a spiritual experience), and **mixed**. One of the interesting features of Sabom's classic research is that he interviewed 32 patients who said they had observed—floating above their bodies—as the medical team worked to resuscitate them. He compared the details of their reports with the educated guesses of patients who were resuscitated but did not claim to have had an NDE. Twenty-three of 25 of those who had not had a NDE made major errors in describing the procedure, whereas none of the patients who had reported a near-death experience made similar errors.

As a result of a developing body of research on the phenomenon, NDE researchers now generally agree on the core elements of the near-death experience, most of which are consistent with the original factors identified by Raymond Moody in 1975. Many of these classic elements have been reported by children (Morse, 1983, 1994a, 1994b; Morse, Connor, & Tyler, 1985; Morse, Castillo, Venecia, & Tyler, 1986; Serdahely, 1989–90) and those without sight (Ring & Cooper, 1999). See Figure 14.2 for a summary of these "core" elements.

A sense of being dead	Sudden awareness that one has had a fatal accident or has not survived an operation.
Feeling of peace	The experience of being completely at peace and feeling that ties to the world have been cut.
Out-of-body experience	Having the sensation of rising or floating above one's own body, and watching as the medical team attempts to intervene.
The tunnel experience	The sense of being drawn through a dark tunnel at high speed toward a golden, white, light.
People of light	Upon reaching the other side of the tunnel, or rising into the heavens, some people say they have met people who glow with an inner light. Sometimes the person has the experience of being greeted by dead friends or relatives.
Being of light	After being greeted, meeting a powerful spiritual being who may be identified as a religious figure.
Panoramic life review	A being of light shows the person an extremely vivid review of everything they have done in life. The person has the sense of actually reliving the experiences with an understanding of the impact on others. Sometimes described as causing the person to become really awares that love is the only important thing in life.
Reluctance to return	When told they must return, or given the choice to stay or return, feeling reluctant to return.
Personality transformation	A dramatic, and profound, personality change involving loss of the fear of death, increased spirituality, stronger feeling of connection with others and the environment, and a greater zest for life.

FIGURE 14.2   Elements of the Core Near-Death Experience   *Source:* This figure is based on Ring, K. (1980). *Life at death.* New York: Coward, McCann, & Geoghegan.

Although specific out-of-body experiences reported by those who have experienced near death have at times been independently verified, other aspects of the core *NDE* are hard to confirm. Rather than attempting to prove the veracity of the *NDE* itself, some researchers have turned their attention to what they regard as the clearest marker of authentic NDEs—the changed lives of the people who claim to have had them. P. M. H. Atwater (2001) and Kenneth Ring (1984) identify personal transformation as the *sine non qua* of a true near-death experience. Among the positive features of this transformation, they cite more appreciation for life, higher self-esteem, increased compassion for others, heightened self-understanding, increased drive to learn new things, enhanced spirituality, more attention to ecological issues, and an increased sensitivity to intuitive and psychic matters. Richard Kinnier and his colleagues similarly found that those who experienced near death were less materialistic, more spiritual, more caring, less worried about mundane issues, and more optimistic after their NDEs (Kinnier, Tribbensee, Rose, & Vaughn, 2001).

Dr. Bruce Greyson, a psychiatrist, now Director of the Institute for Personality Studies at the University of Virginia, has looked into how the lessons of the near-death experience might be applied to individuals with suicidal thoughts and impulses (Greyson, 1981, 1983, 1986, 2000). He says that suicide is generally unthinkable among individuals who have had an NDE, suggesting that the near-death experience somehow imparts a new sense of purpose and renewed hope about life.

How many people have NDEs? It was previously thought that between 30 and 40 percent of people who were close to death had near-death experiences, but recent studies suggest that 10 percent may be more accurate (Greyson, 2003; Parnia & Fenwick, 2002; Parnia, Waller, Yeates, & Fenwick, 2001). A team of researchers in the Netherlands conducted a prospective study, following 344 consecutive cardiac patients who were resuscitated after a cardiac arrest in 10 Dutch hospitals (Van Lommel, Van Wees, Meyers, & Elfferich, 2001). Eighteen percent reported having had a NDE, 12 percent said they had a "core" experience. Greyson (2003) similarly found that 10 percent of patients having had a cardiac arrest said they had a NDE. Parnia and Fenwick (2002) said 10 percent of their cardiac arrest patients had NDE memories.

Distressing Near-Death Experiences

Although the NDE literature paints a fairly positive picture, there are also reports of distressing NDEs, which suggest there may be a dark side to the near-death experience (Bush, 2002; Ellwood, 2001; Greyson & Bush, 1992, 1996; Rawlings, 1978; Rommer, 2000; Storm, 2000). Those who have had these negative brushes, describe **distressing near-death experiences**, or **DNDEs**, as being dominated by such tormenting feelings as horror, terror, anger, extreme loneliness, a sense of isolation, and overpowering guilt (International Association for Near-Death Studies, 2004).

Dr. Maurice Rawlings, a cardiologist who had resuscitated patients who were clinically dead (for a discussion of *clinical death* refer to Chapter 9), wrote an early book on distressing near-death experiences (Rawlings, 1978). Describing himself as having bet his life that there is no afterlife, he says his conversion to evangelical

Fearful	Individuals report some of the same things as those with pleasurable *NDEs* (e.g. going through the tunnel), except they experience them as frightening.
Voided	Sense of nonexistence or being completely cut off and alone in an absolute void.
Hellish	Includes hellish imagery, demonic beings, frightening animals, and loud noises.
Sobering	Instead of experiencing the life review as a supportive, learning, experience the person is made acutely aware of the wrongs committed in life and feels judged for these.

FIGURE 14.3 Distressing Near-Death Experiences This figure is based on: Greyson, B. & Bush, N. E. (1996). Distressing near-death experiences. In L. W. Bailey & J. Yates (Eds.), *The near-death experience: A reader*. New York: Routledge. Rommer, B. 2000. *Blessing in disguise: Another side of the near-death experience*. St. Paul, MN: Llewellyn.

Having the sense of journeying down a long tunnel with a bright light at the end is among the "core" near-death experiences. *Odina/Fotolia*

Christianity resulted from frightening accounts of hell his patients reported.

Based on research done with 50 patients reporting having had a distressing near-death experience, Greyson and Bush (1992, 1996) identify three major categories of distressing near-death experience. Barbara Rommer (2000) added a fourth. For the sake of simplicity, I've labeled these four as **fearful**, **voided**, **hellish**, and **sobering** in Figure 14.3. The *hellish* type comes closest to the category described by Dr. Rawlings. Greyson and Bush found this to be the rarest category of distressing NDE.

Kübler-Ross's Thinking about Life After Death

Dr. Elisabeth Kübler-Ross was profoundly affected by the dying people she worked with. Although hailed as a pioneer who got the modern world to take a second look at death and dying, in later years she became a controversial figure in the professional community simply because of her very unscientific views about what happens after we die. She suggests that as a result of her work with terminally ill patients, including children, and the research she and colleagues did with over 20,000 people who claim to have had near-death experiences, she came to know, not just believe, that life after death is a reality (Kübler-Ross, 2001).

First of all, based on Kübler-Ross's experience with the dying, she observes that those who are near death, especially children, often report the presence of deceased relatives or angels, who she says appear in order to help the dying transition into the next world (Kübler-Ross, 2001). In her view, children are closer to "reality" than adults, who have been taught not to believe in things that can't be proved. Because of the frequency of such reports, she suggests they are credible.

Based on her work with people who claim to have had a near-death experience, she suggests we can get something of a preview into what happens after we die. Her description is consistent, although not exactly like, the profoundly positive descriptions reported by Raymond Moody, Michael Sabom, and others.

Küubler-Ross uses the metaphor of the butterfly and cocoon to explain the three stages that unfold at the moment of death (Kübler-Ross, 2001). The cocoon is like the human body, she says. As soon as the cocoon is in irreparable condition it will release the butterfly, the soul. When the soul is released, it is supplied with psychic energy that makes it possible to "see" everything happening at the place of dying. Regardless of what has happened to the human body during life, at this stage of dying, according to Kübler-Ross, what the individual perceives to be her or her "soul" body becomes fully intact. There is no longer any pain. She says that this is also when you will meet up with those who will take you to the other side. During this stage, according to Kübler-Ross, space and distance have no meaning, and the individual is able to travel anywhere in the world simply by willing it.

Kübler-Ross suggests that after the person passes through a tunnel, crosses a bridge, or perhaps traverses across a mountain pass, the individual makes the transition from life to the afterlife. The person comes into the light of God, Christ, Truth, or whatever one cares to name this supreme higher power. In this light, she suggests, the person achieves full knowledge about himself or herself and are able to look back on the entirety of his or her life from the first day to the last, including every thought, word, and deed. With this knowledge, the individual also understands the impact of her or his life on others, and comes to understand that God, or whatever word one chooses for the supreme reality, is unconditional love.

Science and the Near-Death Experience

Although there are compelling accounts about life after life and the near-death experience, including those of Dr. Elisabeth Kübler-Ross, to the scientific community the jury is still out when it comes to the veracity of such experiences. There have been a number of criticisms leveled against NDE accounts, and skeptics have proposed a range of other explanations (Blackmore, 1991, 1993, 1998; Blackmore & Troscianko, 1988; Bonta, 2004; Britton & Bootzin, 2004; Carr, 1981, 1982; Gabbard & Twemlow, 1991; Gabbard, Tremlow, & Jones, 1981; Grosso, 1991; Holden & Joesten, 1990; Jansen, 1990, 1991, 1996a, 1996b, 1997; Kellehear, 1996; Martens, 1994; Noyes & Kletti, 1976a, 1976b, 1977; Parnia & Fenwick, 2002; Parnia et al., 2001; Persinger, 1983, 1984a, 1984b; Rodin, 1980, 1989; Siegel, 1992; Saavedra-Aguilar & Gomez-Jeria, 1989; Stevenson et al., 1989–90; Strassman, 2001; Vicchio, 1981, Woerlee, 2004). Figure 14.4 presents an overview of proposed alternative explanations.

Science likes hypotheses that are subject to direct observation and measurement. With the exception of out-of-body experiences, most of the phenomena associated with NDEs are subjective in nature and don't lend themselves easily to outside verification. Although many of the reports of near-death experiences seem credible—convincing accounts by reliable people—the idea of a reality that transcends the natural universe is hard to swallow, scientifically speaking.

Dying brain	*NDE* is the result of neurotransmitters in the brain shutting down, consistently creating the similar phenomena among many different individuals
Lack of oxygen	Cerebral anoxia, or lack of oxygen in the brain, produces a confusing dreamlike state in which delusions and hallucinations occur
Right temporal lobe	Activity in the brain's right temporal lobe is responsible for the sense of deep spiritual meaning and religious experience –*NDEs* result from instability and misfiring of neurons in that area
Cortical disinhibition	The tunnel and light experience are caused by the effects of oxygen deprivation and medication creating cortical disinhibition, creating light spots radiating from the center of a dark internal visual field
Hallucinations	*NDEs* and other highly imaginative experiences are hallucinations, similar to what is caused by hallucinatory drugs or anesthesia
Depersonalization	The stress associated with the situation causes the nervous system to become altered in order to psychically cope
Memory of birth	The tunnel and light experience is a reliving of the person's descent down the birth canal
Endorphins	Endorphins, the body's natural analgesics or narcotics, are produced in response to the pain and terror of the situation, creating feelings of pleasure, calm, and peace
Denial of death	The *NDE* serves as the psyche's defense against the prospect of ego annihilation
Fear of death	The severe anxiety and stress associated with the situation creates a dissociative state, whereby the individual separates the psyche from the body
Evolution	The *NDE* is an adaptive mechanism that functions to help the human race by giving its members a way to cope with the end of their lives
There is life after life	Consciousness actually survives physical death

FIGURE 14.4 Explanations for Near-Death Experiences *Source:* This figure is adapted from Williams, K. (2004). The NDE and Science: Kevin Williams' research conclusions. [On-line]. Available: http://www.near-death.com/experiences/research08.html

With the exception of Dr. Michael Sabom's early work (Sabom & Kreutiziger, 1977a, 1977b; Sabom, 1980, 1982), much of the *NDE* research has focused on the subjective experience of individuals, including the ways in which their lives have changed as a result of their experiences. Skeptics argue that few of the studies done so far make use of a control group or attempt to objectively verify reports, for example by reviewing medical records. Until recently, most of the NDE research has been retrospective—that is, done after the fact and relying on memory.

Perhaps in response to the paucity of confirming evidence coupled with the perplexing believability of near-death experience reports, various investigators have attempted to explain them medically and scientifically (see Figure 14.4). These explanations can be classified into two basic types: Neuropsychological and psychosocial. **Neuropsychological** explanations attempt to account for NDEs by using neurologically based theory—for instance, NDEs are caused by the dying brain (Blackmore, 1991, 1993, 1998); a lack of oxygen to the brain (Blackmore, 1991, 1993, 1998; Rodin, 1980, 1989); the brain is flooded with endorphins as a result of the stress associated with the dying process; that there is dysfunction in the right temporal lobe (Persinger, 1983, 1984a, 1984b). **Psychosocial** solutions explain near-death phenomena based on how we socially construct the meaning of the event (Kellehear, 1996) and how the psyche uses the NDE to defend itself from the awareness of its own impending annihilation.

Entire books are devoted to scientific approaches to explain near-death experiences. At the risk of oversimplifying, two of these seem appropriate to look at more closely here. The first is called the **cortical disinhibition theory**, which attempts to explain the tunnel phenomenon. The visual cortex part of the brain has many more cells devoted to seeing in the middle of the visual field than the periphery. In sum, the theory suggests that when the brain is deprived of oxygen, the cells begin firing randomly, producing the effect of a bright light in the center fading out toward darkness—in other words, the tunnel effect (Blackmore, 2002; Blackmore & Troscianko, 1988).

A second explanation for NDEs hinges on the properties of a drug called **ketamine**. Karl Jansen, a psychiatrist now practicing in London, has been a leading researcher into the relationship between the effects of this substance and the near-death experience (Jansen, 1990, 1991, 1996a, 1996b, 1997). Jansen's research suggests that *ketamine*, a drug used as an anesthetic for children and domesticated animals, when used at 10 to 25 percent of the anesthetic level, will fairly consistently produce an altered state of consciousness that reproduces all the classic features of the near-death experience: belief one is dead, the experience of going down a dark tunnel toward a bright light, telepathic communion with God, out-of-body experiences, and being in a mystical state.

Jansen (1996a, 1996b, 1997) explains that when events such as a cardiac arrest occur, blood flow in the brain stops, oxygen deprivation (anoxia) begins, and the brain produces in large quantities a substance called *glutamate*, a neurotransmitter used by the large neurons in the cerebral cortex. The large quantity of *glutamate* overstimulates the neurons, causing them to die through a process called *excitotoxicity*. Blocking the PCP receptor sites prevents cell death. Ketamine is one agent shown to effectively block the sites. Jansen hypothesizes that it is likely that the brain protects itself from the glutamate flooding by producing a ketamine-like substance. Glutamate is the key neurotransmitter in the temporal lobe, an area of the brain long shown to be associated with mystical experiences. Blocking receptor sites in this part of the brain by ketamine-like substances slows cell death, and has been shown to be linked to the kind of mystical experiences reported by those who have near-death experiences.

Corticol disinhibition and ketamine action, which both result from oxygen deprivation, are interesting alternative explanations for the near-death experience. However, they don't seal the verdict, especially since the recent prospective study done in the Netherlands shows that some near-death experiences occur even when the brain has not been deprived of oxygen (Van Lommel et al., 2001). The same study reports the story of a patient whose dentures were misplaced when the hospital team intubated him. Complaining that he wanted his missing dentures, he reported that during a near-death experience he saw a nurse put his dentures in the drawer of the "crash cart." Sure enough, when the staff went looking, they found them exactly where the man said they were.

So real are near-death experiences to those who have had them that these individuals often claim their lives were changed for the better. Skeptics reject the assertions of these people, claiming the evidence is far too inconclusive. One critic, Susan Blackmore, says that after more than 25 years since those first reports and after amassing an impressive body of research on the topic, the question of whether or not the near-death experience is real remains unresolved (Blackmore, 2002). Investigators of various types note that even credible accounts of near-death experiences do not prove the existence of an afterlife. On the other hand, proposed alternative explanations do not prove there isn't (e.g., Blackmore, 2002; Moody, 1975; Jansen, 1990, 1991, 1996a, 1996b, 1997). One can look at the evidence and reasonably argue both sides.

Chapter Summary

This chapter opened with the question of whether there is life after death. It began with a survey of ancient Egyptian beliefs, before turning to an exploration of Tibetan Buddhist teachings about the journey through the *bardo*—or intermediate state—believed to exist between this life and the one to come. Next, the chapter took an in-depth look at beliefs about the afterlife from the Abrahamic tradition—Judaism, Christianity, and Islam—tracing the history of Western views from Semitic times to the present.

The chapter concluded with a discussion of the near-death experience, looking at Dr. Raymond Moody's pioneering work, the classic studies by a cadre of early NDE researchers, the reflections of Dr. Elisabeth Kübler-Ross, and so-called distressing near-death experiences. Noting that debate on the near-death phenomenon is far from settled, the chapter also surveyed key research efforts to explain near-death phenomena scientifically.

Key Terms

akh *308*
al-Haqq *316*
autoscopic *318*
ba *308*
bardo *310*

clear light state *311*
cortical disinhibition
   theory *323*
dissolution of
   consciousness *311*

distressing near-death
   experience (DNDE) *319*
Elysian Fields *314*
fearful *320*
four basic elements *311*

Suggested Activities

1. Take about 15 minutes to write about what you think will happen to you after you die. Write a half page to a page. What do you think will happen at the moment of death? Will life fade to dark? Will you go on a journey? What do you think you will experience? If this is done in a class environment, you may wish to share your vision of "life" after life and compare it with others in the class.

2. Perhaps starting with the website of the International Association for Near-Death Studies, peruse the archived titles of articles in the *Journal for Near-Death Studies*. Identify both titles that seem to be open to near-death experiences as proof of an afterlife and those that are more skeptical. Consider getting copies of these articles and using them in a short library research paper.

Suggested Reading

- McDannell, C., & Lang, B. (2001). *Heaven: A history* (2nd ed.). New Haven, CT: Yale University Press.
  This is a well-researched, easy-to-read account of the Judeo-Christian imagination about heaven. It begins with an overview of Semitic beliefs, looks at developments in the Holy Land, and traces the evolution of Western concepts about heaven to the present day.
- Gyatso, T., 14th Dalai Lama. (2002). *Advice on dying: And living a better life*. New York & Toronto: Atria Books. In this remarkable book, His Holiness the Dalai Lama, offers an insightful overview of Tibetan Buddhist traditions in relation to what happens after death, as well as practical advice on how to prepare for and deal with the end of life, including discussion on how to achieve the best possible rebirth.
- Kübler-Ross, E. (2001). *On life after death*. Berkeley, CA: Celestial Arts.
  This is a very interesting compilation of four essays by the late Dr. Elisabeth Kübler-Ross that illumines her sensitive, original, and even controversial findings on death, dying, and the afterlife.

Links and Internet Resources

- **The International Association for Near-Death Studies, Inc.**
  www.iands.org/
  This association describes its mission as one that is dedicated to responding to the need for information and support in relation to near-death and similar experiences. The IANDS publishes two quarterly periodicals: the scholarly *Journal of Near-Death Studies* and a small newsletter called *Vital Signs*.

Review Guide

1. Consider ancient Egyptian beliefs about life after death. To what degree do you see similarities and differences with modern beliefs? What do you think these beliefs say about the culture?

2. Review Tibetan Buddhist teachings about "life" in the bardo. As you reflect, to what degree do you think such practices are helpful to the dead? To families of the dead? To the community? What kind of questions do they raise about the nature of death and the meaning of life?

3. Trace the development of belief in an afterlife from Semitic times to the present. Compare Abrahamic beliefs about the afterlife with your understanding of what people today believe. Did you notice any differences between historic beliefs and the beliefs that have become common? To what degree are religious beliefs about an afterlife influenced by other people and other cultures?

4. Review the research presented on the near-death experience. To what degree are you satisfied that this evidence supports belief in life after death? What problems, if any, do you see in this research? In what ways do you think this research is helpful to people? In what ways is it lacking?

5. Consider the research that strives to find alternative explanations for the near-death experience. To what degree does this evidence support the skeptics who regard belief in an afterlife based on the near-death experience to be misplaced?

6. What is your own position on the question of life after life and the near-death experience? On what basis do you hold these beliefs? What do you believe to be the most satisfactory evidence?

15

The Road Ahead

- **Modern Trends**
- **X-ers, Nexters, and Texters**
- **How We Are Dying**
- **End-of-Life Caring**
- **Learning to Live until We Die**
- **The Long Good-Bye**

We can predict with certainty that each of us is going to die. We can't predict with certainty the future of the field of thanatology or how we will deal with death, dying, and bereavement in the future. Too much remains unknown. However, we can look at trends that may help clarify how we got to where we are and that just might give us some clues about the road ahead. That is what we will explore in this chapter.

In Chapter 1, we discussed the concept of "the pall," a cloth covering placed over a casket during a funeral, the emotionally clammy reaction most of us have when we encounter the reality of death, and a metaphor for the "denial of death," to recycle the term first coined by Ernest Becker (1973) shortly before he himself died. Becker had probably put his finger on "what was happening" then. So focused were we in the West on modern science, technology, and a fascination with the idea of progress that we almost succeeded in convincing ourselves we could defeat death, one disease at a time (Callahan, 2000).

In Chapter 1, we also discussed the Hindu parable, in which four blind men were faced with the task of describing an elephant. Perhaps we can liken the early thanatology pioneers to the blind men in the parable. Each walked into the field blind and tried to describe what they encountered: Herman Feifel (1959), death anxiety; Elisabeth Kübler-Ross (1969), dealing with dying; Robert Fulton (1977), the social dimensions and the need for death education; and George Fitchett (1993), the nature of spirituality and its diverse dimensions.

MODERN TRENDS

Today, although the issues are complex, we do have more to draw on. Anthropologist Jenny Hockey (2007) suggests there are wider social trends reshaping our encounters with death. In Chapter 2, we already discussed the shift from industrial to postindustrial living, and between the modern and postmodern eras. The trends identified as being particularly important in the field include: **sequestration** of death (which relates to the process by which we isolate the experience of death from everyday life so that people don't directly experience it anymore); **secularization** (which refers to the abandonment of traditional religious belief systems, including about what, if anything, happens after we die); and **desecularization** (the process of strengthening faith in traditional religious systems, reclaiming spirituality, or imbuing things done by secular social institutions with meaning and purpose).

Sequestration

Sequestration is a term sometimes used to connote the idea that those touched by death are somehow isolated, or sequestered, from the rest of society, and as a result, even from the awareness of death itself (Hockey, 2007). The term is associated with the general idea of the *denial of death* and how we insulate ourselves—for example, through the *professionalization* of our death system: end-of-life professionals who care for the dying, "death care" workers who prepare the body and make the final arrangements, as well as the grief counselors who work with those left behind.

DENIAL OF DEATH   As you may recall, psychologists Tom Pyszczynski, Sheldon Solomon, and Jeff Greenberg built on Ernest Becker's pioneering work, developing *terror management theory (TMT)* (e.g., Greenberg et al., 1986; Greenberg et al., 1993; Greenberg et al., 2000; Pyszczynski et al., 1990; Pyszczynski et al., 1999a; Pyszczenski et al., 2003; Pyszczynski et al., 2006; Solomon et al., 1991; Solomon et al., 1996; Solomon et al., 2003). Terror management theory suggests that human beings are like all other animals in their desire to survive, but we are different in that we have the ability to imagine our own future demise. According to the theory, the awareness of one's mortality causes fear and the need to find means with which to protect the psyche. Also, TMT suggests we use culture (including religion) and self-efficacy, or the sense that one has the ability to control circumstances, to help us deal with this fear.

To understand how we arrived at the so-called denial of death, we can look to the early eighteenth century for part of the answer. The **Enlightenment**, or **Age of Reason**, began to emerge in Europe (Reill & Wilson, 2004). It gave birth to a worldview that challenged traditional religious belief. Indeed, August Comte, considered by many to be the father of modern sociology, went out there "in left field," so to speak, to characterize this new field of knowledge as the world's new great religion (Comte &

Congreve, 2009). With an emphasis on empiricism and the use of scientific method, the Enlightenment ushered into existence a new cosmology, or vision of the universe, and with it came the sense that we could somehow master it. So, in this way we can see the Enlightenment as both supplanting traditional culture (including religion) and giving Western civilization a sense of self-efficacy, or sense of control, through science and modern medicine.

In Chapter 2, we touched on the work of Phillipe Aries (1974, 1981), who as you may recall, pointed to two eras that stood in stark contrast to each other. In the early medieval period, the *tame death* was experienced intimately. It usually occurred at home, surrounded by family, friends, and neighbors. Death was real because people experienced it in their daily lives—it was a reality that was regularly "in their face," so to speak. This stands in contrast to the modern era when Aries was writing (1974, 1981), which he characterized as a time of the *invisible death,* or death denied. And, it is at this point in history when Becker (1973) published his Pulitzer Prize–winning treatise on the same theme.

PROFESSIONALIZATION   The healing arts evolved into scientific medicine and the healthcare system we have today (Kendall, 1980, 2010). Science and modern medicine made inroads in a variety of areas: increased life expectancy, reduced infant mortality, pasteurization of certain foods, the effective treatment of infectious diseases, the discovery of antibiotics, vaccination for life-threatening illnesses such as polio, and a host of others (Goldberg, 1998).

These advances also meant that people with life-threatening illnesses would be treated at major medical centers. This development moved the place of death from home to hospital, and with this move it put the care of seriously ill people into the hands of a new class of health-care professionals whose relationship with them was qualitatively more detached and dispassionate. When death occurred, the remains of the deceased were generally commended into the hands of another new class of professional—the funeral director (see Chapter 5). Because grief, the emotional response to the experience of bereavement, was seen as a threat to the mental health of the bereft, they were often thought to be in need of the services of yet another new class of professional—grief counselors and mental-health professionals (see Chapter 10). While one can make the case that these professionals were better equipped to deal with the specialized problems associated with death, one can also argue that the professionalization of death resulted in a loss of **agency**, or sense of personal control, over what was experienced in relation to death, dying, and bereavement (Hockey, 2007).

Secularization

Secularization is a big topic that is worthy of more discussion than we have space for here. Indeed, there is a lively debate going on about whether, how, and how much it is influencing Western culture (see, for example, Berger, 1999; Goldstein, 2009; Karpov, 2012; D. Lyon, 2010; Meisenberg, 2011; Paas, 2011; Taylor, 2004). For our purposes, we will limit discussion to the issues that seem most relevant to thanatology (Bregman, 2006).

Secularization is a term that was originally used in relation to the seizure monastic lands and property by the state (Paas, 2011). About a hundred years ago, Émile Durkheim (1912/1995) and Max Weber (1905/1976, 1922/1991) were among the first modern sociologists to suggest that the shifts they were observing in the West seemed to be influenced by secularization—a process by which society is transformed from a traditional way of life, grounded in religion (Bregman, 2006; Casanova, 1994; Lechner, 1997). Today, the term generally suggests the idea that society no longer falls under the "sacred canopy" of religion, and certainly not the hegemony of a single religion (Berger, 1967). Sometimes the term **disenchantment** is used in this regard. It is a term coined by sociologist Max Weber (1922/1991) to describe the process of displacing the mystique of religious belief with the certainty of science and reason.

When historian Phillipe Aries (1974, 1981) conducted his analysis on the evolution of attitudes toward death in Europe, he suggested that the shifting cultural beliefs toward death were largely influenced by various theological themes that were dominant in different historical eras. For example, he suggested that the *tame death* was influenced by the benign descriptions in the Gospel according to Matthew, with its emphasis on peace and sleep until the second coming. Similarly, he felt the era of *death of self* was influenced by the apocalyptic images of hell described in John's book of *Revelation* and Dante's *Divine Comedy*. Aries suggests that the later eras of *remote and immanent death* (alluring yet fearful) and *death of the other* (romantic loss of another) emerged with the same waves that brought in the *Renaissance* and *Enlightenment* (Aries, 1981).

Today, most sociologists of religion agree that secularization is an important concept although they may disagree about the particulars (Goldstein, 2009). Stefan Paas, a theologian who specializes in church missions, surveyed the literature. He identifies five basic themes in this discussion (Paas, 2011): differentiation, rationalization, privatization, pluralism, and individual loss of faith. **Differentiation** refers to the separation of church and state, the establishment of public institutions apart from religion, and the ability of people to have influence without being religious. **Rationalization** refers to an emphasis on the use of reason and scientific method and a reduced reliance on religious ideology. **Privatization** refers to a shift in the place of religion from the public sphere to the private. Religion becomes a matter of personal faith, not social obligation. **Pluralism** refers to an ideology that suggests society should accept diverse religious traditions. It begins to occur when the state stops favoring any specific religious tradition. Finally, the theme of individual **loss of faith** refers to what happens when people stop believing or quit attending religious services.

Let's consider how this relates to contemporary experience. Applying the five elements of secularization, we may well imagine the implications. Clergy administer the "last rites" less often at home. Instead, hospital or hospice chaplains, who are trained to keep their own personal religious convictions at bay, work at simply being "present" as "silent witnesses" for the dying. Dying people are more likely to experience death surrounded by professionals and are less likely to do so within a religious context. Funeral homes generally serve all-comers (for a fee), often changing the religious symbols in their chapels according to the declared faith, or no faith, of the deceased. Rented funeral home chapels often replace the church sanctuary for funeral services that may or may not be explicitly religious. The bodies are often planted in expansive commercial cemeteries instead of the local church graveyard that in North America rarely exists any longer. And the bereaved are less likely to make use of the framework provided by the mourning rituals of a particular faith tradition. Instead, they are more often referred to professional grief counselors.

In the following vignette, I briefly share a little about the death of our dad, Jack. He was not an explicitly religious man, nor did any of his children get much in terms of spiritual formation. Nevertheless, each would become a sojourner, albeit on diverse spiritual paths.

Our Dad Jack

Our dad, Jack, was 84 years old when he died suddenly from a heart attack at my sister's home, where he was visiting. Growing up on his family's homestead in Ryder, North Dakota, he left school after the eighth grade to work on the farm. Dissatisfied, he "hit the road" when he was just 15 years old, working odd jobs and playing pool in local saloons, until he settled in Santa Monica, California.

He married our mother and became father to four children, one of whom died of cancer when only age 4. By many accounts, our dad was a self-made man, becoming a key executive at the Douglas Aircraft Company during the Second World War. After the war, he opened his own business, a Schwinn bicycle dealership—a vocation he worked at until he retired at age 70.

Although his father was a Nazarene preacher, our dad never connected with formal religion. He was tolerant of the beliefs of others, but never made religion part of his own life. When he died, his body was placed in a hearse and driven from San Jose to North Hollywood, where a corporately owned funeral home took charge of the arrangements. A beloved figure in the southern California "cycling scene," he got quite a send-off, but there was no preacher in sight. Instead, each of his surviving children shared stories of him at the funeral and then hosted a pot-luck dinner at my brother Bob's home. As for his cremated remains, the four of us—mom, Bob, Peggy, and myself—poured them into the ocean off the Santa Monica pier, where a few years later we reunited mom's cremains with his.

Desecularization

One might think the Baby Boom generation grew up in a secular world. Indeed, Peter Berger was among the majority of sociologists of religion who took it as a given that we were enveloped in a secularized culture. More recently, however, Berger has had a change of heart (Berger, 1999). Now, he goes so far as to say that the notion we live in a secularized world is false. Indeed, he coined the term *desecularization* to describe what he sees as a counterbalancing reaction to secularization. Berger's work can also be seen as somewhat prophetic. Even before the events of 9/11, he was calling attention to the rise of Islamic fundamentalism, Christian evangelism, religious orthodoxy, and the resiliency of traditional forms of religion generally. He concedes, "Religious institutions have lost power and influence in many societies." But he suggests, "Both old and new religious beliefs and practices have nevertheless continued in the lives of individuals, sometimes taking new institutional forms and sometimes leading to great explosions of religious fervor" (Berger, 1999, p. 3).

Berger (1999) also suggests that the search for certainty is at the heart of desecularization, which he submits was the allure of science in the first place. He makes the following points. Modernity undermined the old certainties. This ambiguity is hard to bear. And, he suggests, "Therefore, any movement (not only a religious one) that promises to provide or to renew certainty has a ready market" (p. 7). This might also help explain why some religious movements that reject secular modernity, such as Islamic fundamentalism, Christian evangelism, Mormonism, and religious orthodoxies of all kinds, have been on the rise while those religious systems that seek accommodation, like the so-called mainline Protestant denominations, have been in decline.

Pictured here is an aging "baby boomer" sporting a peace symbol. In the 1960s, when the baby boomers were coming of age, the Vietnam War was raging. Young men were subject to involuntary induction into the military, called "the draft." Many boomers took refuge in eastern religion or experimented with drugs, sex, and rock-and-roll. *mariesacha/Fotolia*

RE-ENCHANTMENT The relationship between modernity, secularization, and desecularization is a complex one. Although Berger (1999) focuses on an exploration of fundamentalism and the allure of orthodoxy, he also makes mention of "new religion." In "the sixties," the expression, "God is dead," was widely quoted. Attributed to philosopher Friedrich Nietzche (1882/2008), it became something of an icon of the era, suggesting that traditional beliefs and values were no longer tenable. In North America, a hippie counterculture spread like wildfire (Gitlin, 1993). It was an unstructured wave that caught the imagination of a generation. While admittedly reveling in "sex, drugs, and rock-and-roll," it was a movement that rejected traditional authority and embraced a philosophy of peace and love (Miller, 2011). With it came an interest in alternatives, including a fascination with non-western spiritualities (e.g., Transcendental Meditation, Hare Krishna, Yoga, Nichiren Shoshu, Zen, Tibetan Buddhism, and Native American spirituality).

Such happenings as the "Summer of Love" and "Woodstock" have long since faded into the memories of burned-out hippies and aging Baby Boomers. However, the legacy of the hippie ethos arguably continues to permeate Western culture, including its disdain of authority; embrace of alternative lifestyles; rejection of rampant materialism; openness about sexuality; acceptance of diversity; emphasis on community; interest in natural living; and concern about the environment. You can detect its influence in the writings of Elizabeth

Kübler-Ross (Chapter 8), the "wellness paradigm" of hospice (Chapter 9), and in the spread of the death counterculture: funeral consumers' societies, the home funeral movement, and "green burial" (see Chapter 6).

Between religious orthodoxies of all stripes and the freewheeling hippie counterculture there is everything in between. Thomas Moore (1997), a former Roman Catholic monk and now married father of two, has written a book, *Re-Enchantment of Everyday Life*, which suggests that even though people may have issues about the religious orthodoxies of their youth and second-thoughts about counterculture alternatives, they still aspire to find meaning and purpose in life—the allure of spirituality (Fitchett, 1993). Enrollment in schools of theology and ministry is booming, especially among those who have already raised families and had careers. And, with new awareness about the realities of aging and death, they are also exploring how they might find meaning in this as well. According to Berger (1999), "The critique of secularity common to all resurgent movements is that human existence bereft of transcendence is an impoverished and finally untenable condition" (p. 13).

X-ers, Nexters, and Texters

I don't wish to alarm my death-denying Baby Boomer comrades. However, they may wish to consider that this generation is not too awfully far from the end of the road. Following on their heels will be what I would like to call the X-ers, Nexters, and Texters—the so-called X, Y, and Z generations (McCrindle & Wolfinger, 2010a, 2010b). The question arises, "Will they experience death, dying, and bereavement in the same way as their forebears?"

We used to think of generations in terms of the interval of time between the birth of parents and the birth of their offspring, a span of about 20 to 25 years. However, today we tend to think of it more in terms of cohorts of people born within a similar span of time, and who are influenced by its significant events, trends, and developments (McCrindle & Wolfinger, 2010a, 2010b). These days, generations are usually thought to span no more than about 15 years. As social change accelerates, we might expect these generations to be shorter and shorter. Table 15.1 summarizes a few recent generations.

Most of us have heard a lot of "buzz" about this or that generation. However, it was historians William Strauss and Neil Howe who became the first modern academicians to suggest there are recurring cycles that can help explain the rhythm of human history (see Strauss & Howe, 1991, 1997). Known as the *Strauss-Howe generational theory*, it suggests there is a dynamic in which each generation essentially reacts to the one that precedes it.

For example, the hippie excesses of the Baby Boom generation can be viewed as a reaction to the conformity of their parents—the so-called Greatest

Pictured here are three generations of the same family, the interval of time between the birth of parents and the birth of their offspring. *bst2012/Fotolia*

TABLE 15.1	Selected Cultural Generations	
Generation	**Birth Years**	**Defining Moments**
The Greatest Generation	1925–1945	The Great Depression World War II Jewish Holocaust
Baby Boomers	1946–1964	JFK Assassination Civil Rights Movement Vietnam War
Generation X "X-ers"	1965–1981	Cambodian Killing Fields Divorce Rates Peak AIDS
Generation Y "Millenials" "Nexters"	1982–1994	Fall of the Soviet Union Rwandan Genocide Yugoslav wars
Generation Z "Texters"	1995–present	9/11-War on Terror Sub-Prime Meltdown iPods-iPads-iPhones

Note: The birth years are arbitrary, but are loosely based on those published by various writers (e.g. Strauss & Howe, 1991, 1997; McCrindle & Wolfinger, 2010a, 2020b; Levickaité, 2010).

Generation. For those who came of age during World War II, that war was a symbol of standing up against evil and doing one's duty. For many of their "flower power" children, however, war was itself evil. For them, the Vietnam War in particular was an ever-present reminder of the possibility of an early, traumatic death. Some resisted vehemently. Others went, volunteering willingly or simply succumbing to the requirements of the "draft."

On December 1, 1969, the Selective Service System even began to draw lottery numbers to decide the order in which young men would be drafted. By the end of the war, over 58,000 U.S. soldiers, sailors, marines, and airmen had come home in body bags. Those who didn't die returned to a deeply divided nation. Perhaps because of tragedies like the My Lai massacre, they were often scorned. A measure of national healing began to occur in 1982, when the Vietnam Memorial, sometimes called "The Wall," was dedicated in Washington, DC. The memorial is a simple marble wall on which is inscribed the names of each American who died in the war. Today, it is a place of pilgrimage, where people come to honor and sometimes make a rubbing of the name of a fallen comrade or family member with paper and pencil. To the surprise of the memorial creators, people also began to spontaneously leave personal items at the site, which are now stored in a new building that is dedicated solely to this purpose.

X-ERS The so-called generation X, a group I'm calling X-ers, follows in the wake of the Baby Boomers. If the Strauss-Howe generational theory holds, we might expect this generation to move away from the excesses of the Baby Boom generation (Strauss & Howe, 1991). Although the specific years are probably somewhat arbitrary, and vary from author to author, the period from 1965 to 1981 is a close approximation. Sometimes feeling like a neglected group (Gordinier, 2009), X-ers are "tweeners," nestled in between the Baby Boomers and their "smug" offspring, the "Millennials." The X-ers were born during a time of transition, but they lived out their young-adult years in a time of relative economic peace and prosperity— after the tumultuous sixties but before the events of 9/11 (McCrindle & Wolfinger, 2010b). They also grew up at a time when the divorce rate peaked, when many families were breaking up, and when many people thought the family as a social institution was breaking down. Often, both parents worked. As a result, X-ers were more likely to be left home alone.

Academicians like to be cautious about the kind of generalizations they make. Indeed, when talking about generations it's easy to do. This having been said, contemporary author Douglas Coupland (1991), whose book, *Generation X: Tales for an Accelerated Culture*, is lauded as the inspiration for the name Generation X, suggests that the X-ers are a group of people who wanted to "hop off the merry-go-round of status, money, and social climbing that so often frames modern existence" (Levickaité, 2010, pp. 172–173). Coupland's book was also the inspiration for a punk band that gave the world pop-star Billy Idol. Generation X-ers have the reputation of being a bit more laid-back, less focused on career, and more attentive to friends and their own families. And frankly, they're tired of hearing about the sixties (Stephey, 2008).

X-ers are having a coming-of-age in the world of death-and-dying. Now in their mid-thirties to late forties, many may now be experiencing their own versions of a midlife crisis (Scott, 2010). Instead of trying to reclaim the glory of their youth, however, X-ers may have to confront a youth that to them never seemed that glorious to begin with. Less revolutionary than their predecessors and more attuned to the practicalities of daily life, this cohort might be expected to pay more attention to keeping up their friendships, staying home with their families, making the payments on their life-insurance policies, and putting their wills together. We can speculate that they might also be more conventional with respect to their final arrangements. Therefore, we should not be surprised if they wanted their loved-ones to share stories, play Kurt Cobain music, and display collages of photographs at funeral home services rather than organize home funerals.

NEXTERS "Life is good," "LG." This is the tag line for both a South Korean maker of consumer electronics goods and a generation that is variously known as "Generation Y," "The Millennials," "Generation Next," or the "Echo Boomers" (because they are often the children of Baby Boomers). Here, I am referring to them simply as "Nexters." Although we always need to be careful about generalizing, we probably can say that this group tends to be optimistic and satisfied with life (Pew Research Center, 2007). The birth years we see in print varies, but by blending dates used by a variety of sources we can estimate that this generation was born between about 1982 and 1994 (Pew Research Center, 2007; McCrindle & Wolfinger, 2010a, 2010b; Strauss & Howe, 1991, 1997; Lloyd, 2011).

Many Baby Boomer parents have attempted to provide their Nexter offspring with a safe and enriched environment, even if they sometimes hovered nearby. Although Nexters may be more materialistic than their "flower power" parents (81 percent say getting rich is their generation's top goal), they tend to admire their Boomer parents, and generally feel very close to them (Pew Research Center, 2007). If they don't actually live with their parents, they often live nearby and like to stay in close touch (Pew Research Center, 2007).

Like the X-ers who came before them, the parents of many Nexters were divorced or separated. Indeed, 36 percent of Nexters come from such families (Pew Research Center, 2007). As a result, many of them have grown up in a blended or binuclear family. **Blended families** are those in which the children live with a parent, step-parent, siblings, and step-siblings and also have another family in which they do not live. **Binuclear families** are those in which the children alternate between living with their mothers and fathers. As a result, many say they have a living step-parent and/or step-siblings who are important to them.

Not only do Nexters often come from more nontraditional families, as a group they also tend to be very accepting of other differences as well. Overwhelmingly, they support the idea that women should be able to take on nontraditional roles and that people from different racial backgrounds should be free to form romantic relationships. Sixty percent of Nexters completely disagree with the idea that women should return to traditional roles; 72 percent of them support interracial dating (Pew Research Center, 2007). In addition, they are far more supportive of gay rights than any generation that has come before them. Nearly half are in favor of gay marriage; 60 percent say that a homosexual lifestyle should be accepted; and 71 percent reject the idea that a school board ought to be able to fire a gay teacher (Pew Research Center, 2007). As a result of these shifts, we can probably expect even greater diversity in the kinds of families Nexters themselves create.

Like their Boomer parents, Nexters are a bit nontraditional in other ways as well. A substantial number say they have gotten tattoos, died their hair a nontraditional color, or have had a body part pierced. They are more likely to use marijuana or engage in heavy drinking. Over 80 percent say their generation is more likely to engage in casual sex than previous generations. In a formal sense, they are also less religious than any previous generation. About 44 percent say they are Protestant and about one-quarter are Roman Catholic. Fewer than 10 percent are affiliated with some other religion. However, even those that describe themselves as having a religious affiliation say they are not very likely to attend church on a regular basis (Pew Research Center, 2007).

While the Nexters are not necessarily native to digital technology, they did grow up with it. It is probably safe to say they tend to go online, send text messages, and use instant messaging. What sets them apart, however, is their increasing use of social networking sites. Three-quarters of Nexters say that most people they know use such sites as Facebook, MySpace, and MyYearbook (Pew Research Center, 2007). Nexters seem to understand both the advantages and disadvantages of using such sites. Almost three-fourths say they post too much personal information on these websites, but they also say that these sites provide a way to strengthen ties with old friends and family.

Except for the relatively small cadre of volunteers who went to war in Iraq or Afghanistan, most Nexters are less likely to have personally confronted death or dying than previous generations. However, their parents are now of an age where they are beginning to die. Since their parents are more likely than previous generations to pursue alternatives, we can anticipate that this will impact their children as well. The deaths that do occur among Nexters are more likely happen because of accident, violence, or suicide. The news is likely to travel fast via text messages, Twitter, or through messages left on Facebook, or other similar sites. Facebook even has a policy in place about how to handle the pages of someone who has died (Facebook, 2012).

When Facebook is notified the account is "memorialized." This means that the "privacy" is set such that only confirmed friends can see the profile or leave posts in remembrance. Members of the immediate family can also make a special request to take control of a deceased user's account. The youngest Nexters are now graduating from high school, but they may have already experienced the death of a classmate. Nexters tell me that the schools are increasingly bringing in grief counselors and critical incident response teams to help when a student dies.

With respect to dealing with death, Nexters are not only more likely to use social networking media to communicate about what has happened but they are also more likely to use digital technology to memorialize their losses. Since many Nexters are quite fluent with digital technology, we can anticipate that more and more of them will make use of the slide show technology available to them through such applications as iPhoto. We should also note that the Social Security Administration now publishes death records online. In addition, newspapers are networking with online outlets. For example, Legacy.com is a large organization that works with more than 800 newspapers in North America, Europe, Australia, and New Zealand to provide ways for readers to express their condolences and share their memories, photos, and digital clips online (Legacy.com, 2012).

TEXTERS   Not only is Generation Z, the cohort I'm calling Texters, growing up in a digital world, they were born in it (Lyon, 2010). Although the birth years cited vary from source to source, I am using the years 1995 to the present to represent this cohort. That means the oldest of them are now stepping onto college campuses. Often the children of X-ers, they are native to such technology as digital games, iPods, iPads, iPhones, iTunes, Droids, Kindle, Facebook, Twitter, and YouTube.

Although their X-er parents may have watched nervously from the sidelines, Texters were relatively free to explore this digital world on their own. As a result, Texters may be a bit more independent than their more conforming Nexter predecessors, who were weaned on group projects and collaborative learning approaches at school (Trunk, 2009). Taught multiculturalism but given ample

Members of Generation Z, "texters," are native to the digital world. Indeed, they use technology fluently in their daily lives. *ndoeljindoel/Fotolia*

opportunity for self-discovery, many of them also have a strong sense not only of themselves but of their own culture, which they quite prefer. As a result, they may not be as fascinated with other cultures as the generations that came before them.

Being native to digital technology and the Internet, this is a generation that is facile with finding, gathering, and processing information (Trunk, 2009). While accuracy may at times be an issue, they accomplish all of this at lightning speed. Referred to in this section as "Texters," it should come as no surprise that they very likely stay in regular touch with their friends through texting (Lenhart, 2012). Although digital technology seems to be at the heart of this generation, we should not neglect the "defining moments" of this generation: the 9/11 attacks and the war on terror; the so-called "subprime" meltdown; the 2008 collapse of the financial markets; and massive government bailouts of the U.S. banking and auto industries.

Since they are so new on the scene, we probably know less about this generation than any of the previous ones. However, since they are growing up at a time when there is concern that Baby Boomers might "break" the Social Security "bank," so to speak, we should not be surprised to learn that many of them are skeptical about Social Security retirement benefits being there when it comes time for them to retire. The Social Security Administration seems fairly certain that the Social Security Trust Fund is fully financed through the year 2036 (Social Security Administration, 2011), at which time benefits will have to be reduced or funding increased. This will conceivably occur when the oldest members of the Texter generation are about 40 years old.

The Texter generation has also been described as a cohort of multitaskers who are able to text their friends, find a resource online, and attend a college lecture at the same time, much to the chagrin of their professors. Contemporary commentators, such as Marc Prensky, chalk it up to the Texter generation being digital natives and their professors being digital immigrants who can only speak to their Texter students with a more or less heavy foreign (or alien?) accent (Prensky, 2006, 2008). Since the digital age appears to be here to stay, he suggests it may be wise to adapt to the novel ways and quantum speeds at which Texters learn. This might be better accomplished by giving them access to the technology with which to do it and the freedom to do it their own way.

In some ways, the Texter generation may be more spontaneous and socially linked. For example, the term "going viral" is often used to denote what happens when an event, YouTube clip, or product quickly attracts the attention of large numbers of people. It is self-validating in that once something has gone viral, others know something important has happened. This in itself gives it even more credibility and social importance. The attention it gets then has the power to influence public opinion and policy makers alike.

With respect to the implications for what this means with regard to death, dying, and bereavement, we may have to accept a certain amount of ambiguity. It is hard to predict how they will handle these experiences, and how it will be different from previous generations. Perhaps Texters will start up blogs should they become terminally ill and share instant updates with their entire network of friends and family. At funerals you may be more likely to have a room full of people networked to a "cloud" than folks decked out in black praying to a deity, if there is to be a traditional service at all. However they end up handling death and dying, we should rest assured they will move well beyond their Nexter, X-er, and Boomer predecessors, do so fully networked, with the latest digital technology, with ease, and at quantum speeds.

HOW WE ARE DYING

In Chapters 2 and 3, we discussed how we die. In this final chapter, I would like to shift the focus just a bit to the implications of how we are dying. Although death today is more common among the old, it happens in every season of life. Science and modern medicine have radically changed how and at what stage of life we are dying. As discussed in Chapter 3, "back in the day" it was fairly common for parents to lose one or more children before they reached adulthood. Death struck often in the early morning of life, when its victims were generally healthy. Beginning in the twentieth century, the practice of scientific medicine changed all that. Vaccinations and the widespread use of antibiotic medications are just two examples of how modern medicine became effective at treating acute illnesses, leading to far fewer deaths among the young.

Of the nearly 2.5 million deaths that occur each year in the United States, almost three-fourths are among people over age 65 (Xu et al., 2010). When older people die, they are sicker than ever, often suffering from an array of chronic illnesses, some of which can be only marginally managed with legions of sophisticated medications and generally ineffective "efforts" at making lifestyle changes. The leading causes of death among the old are heart disease, cancers, and stroke.

This having been said, looking at the most common causes of death during different seasons of life can be revealing (see Chapter 3, Table 3.1). Among infants, the most common causes are congenital birth defects, sudden infant death syndrome, and respiratory distress syndrome (Xu et al., 2010). People are waiting longer to get married and are having children later in life, which increases the risk for each. Among toddlers, those aged 1 through 4, the leading causes of death are accidents, birth defects, and homicide, usually by a parent. Cancer appears as the second leading cause of death among children, aged 5 to 14, with accidents and birth defects in first and third place, respectively. Among young people, aged 15 to 24, the leading causes of death, in order of frequency, are accidents, homicide, and suicide. It is not until the productive adult years, ages 25 to 44, that biological processes, such as cancer and heart disease, take center stage as leading causes of death.

What does all this tell us about ourselves? First of all, in some ways we are really quite bright. We continue to develop a science and technology that advances our ability to prevent and treat "unnatural," or untimely, death. There are some other social challenges, however. Both teen pregnancy and women waiting too long to have children increases the incidence of birth defects. As a society, we are somewhat angry, violent, and troubled, as evidenced by high rates of child abuse deaths and youth violence. It also seems we are somewhat careless, as evidenced by the number of people in a variety of age ranges who die as a result of "accidents" (Xu et al., 2010). Many people, young and old alike, overeat and are generally too sedentary, as evidenced by increased obesity rates, which in turn contributes to heart disease, diabetes, cancers, and other illnesses (Guh et al., 2009). Perhaps the greatest challenge of all, however, is not in our *ability* to treat acute and chronic illnesses but in our *commitment* to make the health-care resources we have developed available to all.

END-OF-LIFE CARING

I believe that health-care professionals are getting the message about the concerns related to the depersonalization and dehumanization of death and dying. There has been an increasing emphasis on more personalized and specialized end-of-life care, as evidenced by new physician training programs (EPEC Project, 1999; Stanford Faculty Development Center, 2003). Although awareness about the need for high-quality end-of-life care seems to be on the rise, it is still only a budding minority movement. Few physicians get even a single course on pain management in medical school. And, while end-of-life care for the dying may seem like a "no brainer," physicians who actually specialize in *palliative medicine*, like Dr. Diane Myers of Mt. Sinai Medical Center in New York, tell us that doing it well requires a high level of specialized knowledge and skill that few physicians actually have.

The health-care professionals who have the training and experience that leads to this kind of understanding are those who work in hospice and palliative care. The rise of the hospice and palliative care movements in the West is probably a response to the growing awareness that when medicine is no longer able to restore seriously ill people to health, it is only human and humane to relieve their suffering and make them as comfortable as possible until the end comes (see Chapter 9).

Traditional health care is rooted in the so-called "medical model" and is based on modern science. It tends to see death and disease as enemies that should be attacked; health as the absence of disease; and their mission as being concerned with responding to acute episodes of illness (Metzger & Kaplan, 2001). In contrast, the hospice and palliative care movements are rooted in the "wellness paradigm," which accepts death as the normal conclusion of life; health as being about the whole person—physical, social, psychological, and spiritual—and values quality of life as much as quantity of life (Metzger & Kaplan, 2001).

Hospice and palliative care are almost universally accepted as the "gold standard" when it comes to end-of-life care, but we should probably not be deceived into thinking they are a cure for end-of-life decision making. These programs are labor intensive. Only a minority of medical centers have palliative care services. Although hospice programs are marginally less expensive than traditional medicine at the end of life, they are still costly and subject to funding availability and eligibility requirements. Not all insurance programs provide an adequate hospice benefit and federally funded programs have their limitations. At the end of the day, programs reach only a relatively small minority of terminally ill people. In the United States, hospice typically requires a terminal diagnosis, the "prognosis" of six or fewer months to live, and the presence of a full-time caregiver in the home. On a practical level, those who do get into hospice are usually middle-class cancer patients, most of whom survive far fewer than six months.

In the early days of hospice, programs in the United States were usually staffed by volunteers who provided high-quality and very personal care but didn't worry much about eligibility requirements. After hospice became a Medicare benefit in 1983, all this changed. Health-care organizations began getting into the hospice business, largely because of the federal dollars that became available. With federal funding, however, also came mandates about who could be served and how their care was to be provided. Applicants for hospice had to agree to forego any further efforts to cure their illnesses in order to become eligible. Patients with uncertain prognoses, or who did not have full-time care-givers, were ineligible.

Most families try to care for their own at home, but sometimes the demands of the illness, such as with Alzheimer's, go well beyond what they can handle. Their loved ones may require long-term care, such as what can be provided in a nursing home. However, nursing homes are expensive. *Medicare*, the program that serves most elderly people, does not have a long-term care benefit. It only covers nursing home care for a relatively short period of time after a hospitalization. *Medicaid*, a health-care program intended to serve the poor, does have a long-term care benefit.

Higher-income families can qualify for Medicaid, but it is often heart breaking to see what they must go through to do so. Initially, they have to pay for the care themselves, using up their own assets (retirement funds, bank accounts, home, automobiles) with the exception of a very modest amount—the "spend down"—before they can qualify (see Chapter 9). This essentially means families who need long-term care for their loved ones must be either independently wealthy or become destitute before they can qualify.

By the time families get to this point, it is usually too late. When death finally does come, they are often exhausted, broke, or both. Indeed, there is good evidence to suggest that serious medical problems are to blame for over half of all personal bankruptcy filings in the United States (Himmelstein, Warren, Thorne, & Woolhandler, 2005; Himmelstine, Thorne, Warren, & Woolhandler, 2007). Most filers had health insurance, were well educated, owned their own homes, and had middle-class occupations. While few are able to actually pull it off, it may only be by anticipating the future need for long-term care that families are able to prepare, perhaps purchasing long-term care insurance or working out other creative care arrangements.

LEARNING TO LIVE UNTIL WE DIE

When I was doing my early research for this book I had the marvelous opportunity of interviewing His Holiness, the Dalai Lama, the spiritual leader of the Tibetan people. I had never met a person of his stature before and I was very serious about my topic. I tried my best to prepare for the interview by reading as much as possible about religious perspectives on death. In the Western tradition, St. Benedict suggests, "Mortem quotidie ante oculos suspectam habere," or "Keep death daily before your eyes" (Delatte,

1950, pp. 72–74). In reading Sogyal Rinpoche's book on Tibetan religious perspectives, I came to think that learning about death was extremely important to the Tibetan understanding about life (Sogyal, 1992). Indeed, devout Tibetan monks, including the Dalai Lama, meditate on death as part of their daily practice (Gyatso, 2002). So I brought this topic up when I met with His Holiness. I recall having said something like, "I understand that the purpose of life is to prepare for death." His Holiness looked surprised. He said, "The purpose of life is to live" (Gyatso, 2001).

Psychologist Erik Erikson, who died in 1994, remains alive as an icon in the field of human development (Erikson, 1963). You might recall from Chapter 3 that he suggested that an important part of learning to live involves moving progressively through a series of stages in which we struggle with specific challenges; accomplish life tasks; confront existential questions (such as "Who am I?" and "Why am I here?"); and achieve new strengths (see Table 3.4 in Chapter 3). All in all, he identified eight of these stages from infancy to old age, and eight struggles, from basic trust versus mistrust at the beginning of life to integrity versus despair in old age.

Erikson (1963) suggested that for those who achieve integrity in old age the strength they find is "wisdom." Joan Erikson, his wife, collaborated with Erik Erikson on his final project, *The Life Cycle Completed* (1982). Both Erik and Joan lived into their nineties. Based on years of discussions with her husband and the notes he wrote in the margins of his personal copy, Joan Erikson expanded *The Life Cycle Completed* to include a proposed ninth stage of development (Erikson & Erikson, 1997). During this final stage, she writes, the various strengths a person achieves in life often disintegrate. However, if one can somehow manage to come to terms with the indignities of old age, he or she may achieve *gerotranscendence*—a state of equanimity in which there is cosmic communion with the universe, one lives in the moment, space matches one's abilities, death is accepted as a natural part of life, and one's sense of self embraces a wide range of interrelationships with others.

The idea of *transcendence* in the face of death surfaces again in Chapter 8, where we profile the story of Dr. William Bartholome, a physician and medical bioethicist who was diagnosed with a terminal cancer (Bartholome, 2000a). As you may recall, he lamented that it took a death sentence to get him to change his whole attitude and approach to life. No longer shackled to things-to-do lists and calendars, he could learn to focus, he said, on the only thing we truly have: the present. Indeed, he described his new awareness about the certitude of impending death as being like "sugar," sweetening his life. He declared that he would never want to go back to living the way he did before.

THE LONG GOOD-BYE

When death occurs, bereavement, grief, and mourning follow. *The Long Goodbye* is the title of a novel written by Raymond Chandler (1953) when his own wife was terminally ill. I am using the title here as a metaphor for the experience of bereavement. While we used to think of "grief work," emphasis on work, as something that everyone who suffers a major loss had to get through, a new generation of bereavement researchers now think that the sorrow we experience when a loved one dies as something that remains with us as long as we live (Carnelley, Wortman, Bolger, & Burke, 2006, cited in Wortman & Boerner, 2007; Bonanno, 2009). In the beginning, there may be feelings of shock, sadness, and pain; loneliness, emptiness, and crying; and such physical manifestations as weakness, shortness of breath, or even a lump in the throat, all of which may be at first experienced acutely and profoundly. They tend to occur in waves, lessening in intensity over time until they recede into the background, but never completely go away.

We also can think of the grief we experience as a "long good-bye" because we are now coming to understand that most such losses are never fully "resolved." They continue to be with us as part of our experience and our own story until we ourselves take our leave. We are also coming to appreciate that for most people it is a normal part of what it means to be human. When you love someone, the sadness that comes with the loss of that loved one does not go away and neither do the memories nor the desire to keep their memory alive. For them, counseling may not be helpful. Indeed, it has been shown to be harmful in some cases.

The implications of these new revelations is that in most cases instead of encouraging people to work through their loss and move on, we should support them in their efforts to find a new place in their lives for their deceased loved one. It could mean having an opportunity to share stories, maintain a special place in the home for photos and mementos, keeping a candle lit, holding an anniversary gathering, or even sharing a special meal.

In only about 10 to 15 percent of cases do people experience complicated grief— grief so severe or that lasts so long that it requires professional attention (Bonanno et al., 2002; Bonanno et al., 2004; Ginzburg et al., 2002; Mancini, Prati, & Bonanno, 2011). Those most at risk appear to be people whose loved ones have had a traumatic death and those who have had an especially dependent relationship on the deceased (see Bonanno, 2009; Holland & Neimeyer, 2011). The American Psychiatric Association (2011) was considering including a new category of mental illness, that was tentatively labeled "bereavement-related disorder," into the forthcoming edition of its *Diagnostic and Statistical Manual*, a highly influential publication, often considered something of a "bible" by mental-health professionals.

One of the other things we are learning from the "new science of bereavement," as psychologist George Bonanno puts it (2009), is that not being adequately prepared for death also increases one's risk of *complicated grief* (see Chapter 11; Bonanno, 2009; Zhang, El-Jawahri, & Prigerson, 2006; Prigerson et al., 2009). For those of you who would like to take some practical steps, I've included a brief checklist in Figure 15.1.

Although it may be true that no one is ever fully prepared for the realities of death, taking a course on death and dying or reading a book like this are positive steps one can take in preparing for the inevitable—all of us will experience loss and we too will one day have to take leave of those we love.

A Checklist of "Things to Do" Before You Die: Compile Everything from the
Checklist and Put It All Together

1. **Make a List of Assets.** Make a list of your assets: bank account numbers, amounts, retirement funds, safe deposit boxes, IRA's, deeds, trusts, etc., along with names of institutions, locations, phone numbers. Put this information together in a single document and clearly label it so others can identify what it is. From time to time update this list.

2. **Compile a Summary of Insurance Coverage.** Consult with the HR department of your place of employment to determine what life, accident, long term care disability, accidental death, and funeral insurance you have with your company, if any. Copy down contact information for the HR department, amount of coverage, type of policy, policy numbers, and any other information that may be helpful to your survivors in terms of contacting insurance carriers in the event of your death. Put all this information on plainly labeled piece of paper. Consider if the amount of coverage you have will be sufficient for your survivors. If it isn't explore other coverage. From time to time update this list.

3. **Make a List of Debts.** Make a list of the account numbers, customer service phone numbers, and addresses of all creditors (mortgage company, car payment, credit cards, etc.). From time to time update this list.

4. **Sign a Will or Put Together a Living Trust.** Decide who you want to get what. Then, decide if you want a will or a living trust to make sure they get it. Consult an attorney, if need be. Or, use one of the many online legal services, software, or even forms available from the local office supply company. Develop your will or living trust, sign it and have it witnessed by a notary public or two witnesses. From time to time review it.

5. **Sign Your Advance Directives.** Consider the various possible health risks you might face, as discussed in this and other chapters. Follow "links-chapter resources" at the end of this chapter to the "Free Advance Directive & Durable Power of Attorney for Health Care." Review the forms and decide what kind of care you would want if you are no longer able to make this decision and decide who you would want to make health care decisions for you were you to wind up in this situation. From time to time review it.

6. **DNR Order.** Again, consider the possible health risks and think about whether or not you would want to have CPR should your heart stop beating or you stopped breathing in various situations. If appropriate in your situation, consider discussing a request for a DNR order with your physician. From time to time review it.

7. **Say Goodbye & Tell Your Story.** Think about what you want to say to those you will leave behind. Reconcile with anyone you need reconciling with. Consider writing your loved ones a letter, taping a message, of putting together a DVD about your life with photos, music, and a message from you to them that they can watch after you die. From time to time review it.

8. **Veteran's Status.** If you served in the military, you may be eligible for certain benefits, including a casket and plot or niche at a veterans' cemetery. If so be sure to put a copy of your Form DD 214 in with your other documents.

9. **Social Security.** Nearly everyone eligible for Social Security is eligible for a $255 death benefit. It may be a small thing, but be sure your survivor's apply. Also ascertain if your dependents may be eligible for survivors' benefits.

10. **Funeral Arrangements.** Consider what you want in terms of a funeral or memorial service, if any. Funeral home? Funeral consumer organization (membership number)? Home funeral? Who is going to do what and how easy will it be to pull this off? Who do you want to serve as celebrant? Who will make the arrangements? Who will tell your story? Who do you want there? How can they be contacted? Where do you want your remains or cremains to be put? From time to time review it.

FIGURE 15.1   A Checklist of "Things to Do" Before You Die: Compile Everything from the Checklist and Put It All Together

Chapter Summary

The field of thanatology—the study of death, dying, and bereavement—is not only an academic area of study but a very personal subject that affects all of us. In this text, we have broken down the discussion into chapters that address one topic, or one dimension, at a time. In this final chapter, I have attempted to bring it all together, integrating key insights drawn from various parts of the book, with an eye to understanding the road ahead.

We looked at the "pall," which we discussed in Chapter 1 as a metaphor for the denial of death. To do this, we revisited Ernest Becker's (1973) concept of the "denial of death," which he believed was at the root of many of today's biggest social problems. His thinking points out that human beings, like all animals, are mortal. We are going to die. Unlike most other animals, we also have consciousness, or the ability to anticipate the future. As a result, we can anticipate our own death. According to *terror management theory*, which was inspired by Becker's work, we are especially vulnerable to death anxiety, which we attempt to keep at bay through the use of *culture*—values, beliefs, norms, and practices—and trying to maintain a sense of *self-efficacy* (Pyszczynski et al., 2003). Unfortunately, these are socially constructed and easily shaken, which forces us to engage in a process of constantly defending our worldviews and sense of self-worth.

We explored the modern trends of sequestration, secularization, and desecularization as a way to explore how we got to present-day attitudes about death as well as other social developments in the West, including the social and intellectual waves that unfolded during the Renaissance and Enlightenment, or Age of Reason. As a result of the development of technology and scientific medicine, we increased average life expectancy and reduced infant mortality, but we also isolated, or sequestered, ourselves from the reality of death. A more emotionally detached and professional approach to dealing with death resulted–the medicalization of dying, the secularization of attending to spiritual needs, and the professionalization of undertaking. As a result, many people came to feel that they had lost something of their sense of *self* in relation to the universe and *agency*, or sense of control, over what happens at the end of life.

Terror management theory suggests that the reason we human beings have such a hard time with death is because we are like all other animals in wanting to survive but are different in that we are able to imagine our own demise. Accordingly, we use self-efficacy, or a sense of agency, along with culture and religion in order to fend off this encroaching awareness of our eventual demise. In the context of our discussion of desecularization and re-enchantment we discussed our continued reliance on religion and spirituality. We noted that sociologist Peter Berger suggested well before the events of 9/11 a rise of Islamic fundamentalism and other religious orthodoxies as a possible consequence of secularization. In reaction, he suggests a desecularization and re-enchantment, such as that which was expressed as an interest in "new" religion, the rise of Western interest in nonwestern religion, and the hippie ethos of the sixties.

As Baby Boomers began to age, they took on more traditional roles in society. Now approaching elderhood, many have reclaimed an interest in spirituality, bringing this re-enchantment full cycle. The X, Y, and Z generations—the X-ers, Nexters, and Texters—have arrived on the scene, each with its distinct character. We briefly explored some of these differences in an effort to understand "what's happening now," and to anticipate how young people might approach death, dying, and bereavement in the future.

We then revisited the topic of how we die, with a twist. How *are* we dying? We reflected on the changes made possible in average life expectancy and infant mortality by advances in health care, but took note of other influences on how we are dying, depending on where we are in the life cycle. Some of these include carelessness, violence, and suicide. Since on whole we are living longer, we also took note that acute illness is on the decline but chronic illnesses, such as obesity, diabetes, heart disease, cancer, and stroke, are on the rise, presenting us with the challenge of how to accommodate our changing health-are challenges.

In the context of recent concerns about the depersonalization and dehumanization of death and dying, we discussed the increasing emphasis on more personalized and specialized end-of-life care, as evidenced by physician training programs and popularity of hospice and palliative care programs as well as the "wellness paradigm" that has surfaced in response to the dominance of the biomedical model. Although the "wellness model," so popular in hospice and palliative care, has come to be seen as the "gold standard" when it comes to how to provide care to the dying, we also noted "cracks" in the system. These cracks seem to have relatively little to do with the state of the art. Rather, they relate to our commitment to provide this level of care to everyone who needs it.

We also discussed what it means to live until we die. I shared with you an anecdote about a meeting I had with His Holiness the Dalai Lama in which he told me that the purpose of life is not to learn how to die, but how to live. We reviewed the developmental model developed by Erik Erikson and refined by his wife, Joan, after he died. In the refinement of the model, she introduced a ninth stage of development concerned with gerotranscendence—the state of equanimity in which an individual gains a sense of cosmic communion with the universe and one learns to live in the moment.

Finally, we discussed the *long good-bye,* a term I used in this chapter as a metaphor for bereavement, grief, and mourning. In this regard, I noted that as a result of what we've learned from the "new science of bereavement research," we now can better understand our experience with grief—as intense and poignant as it can sometimes be—as a normal part of what it means to be a human being.

Key Terms

Age of Reason *328*
agency *329*
binuclear family *336*
blended family *336*
desecularization *328*

differentiation *330*
disenchantment *330*
Enlightenment *328*
loss of faith *330*
pluralism *330*

privatization *330*
rationalization *330*
secularization *328*
sequestration *328*

Suggested Activities

1. Conduct a search of the literature and see if you can find examples of literature that reflect different themes about death that have been popular in the West.

2. Interview people you know about death and religious belief, or no belief. What influence, if any, do religious beliefs seem to have in the lives of the people you interviewed?

3. Interview Baby Boomers, Generation X-ers, Nexters, and Texters about their experiences with and attitudes about death, dying, and bereavement. Are you able to detect any important differences between them? What similarities, if any, do they share?

4. Consider your own generation. What do you see as its attitudes about death, dying, and bereavement. Are these similar to those discussed in this text or are they different? Write a one- or two-page paper about this.

5. Consider what you've learned about end-of-life care. In a short paper, discuss what you think might be done to improve the way we care for people who are near the end of their lives.

6. Hypothetical situation: You are diagnosed with a life-threatening illness and you are told you are probably going to die soon. In a short paper, discuss what changes, if any, in how you would live the rest of your life.

7. Continuing with the hypothetical situation above, in a short paper discuss how would you want your loved ones to memorialize your life if you were to die soon.

8. Using the checklist outlined in Figure 15.1, come up with a plan for how you might tie up all the loose ends before you die.

Suggested Reading

- Reill, P. H., & Wilson, E. J. (2004). *Encyclopedia of the Enlightenment (Facts on File Library of World History)*. New York: Facts on File.
  This concise encyclopedia was conceived and written as a point of departure for anyone who wishes to begin encountering this world in all its complexities. It discusses key people, topics, terms, styles, works, and European locations important in history of the *Enlightenment* from the late 1600s to 1800.

- Berger, P. L. (1967). *The sacred canopy: Elements of a sociological theory of religion*. New York: Doubleday.
  This classic introduction to the sociology of religion helps the reader construct a sacred reality. It examines religion as a social construction, which we then accept as real and then internalize. It also explores secularization. This is a beautifully written provocative work.

- Berger, P. L. (1999). *Desecularization of the world: Resurgent religion and world politics*. Grand Rapids, MI: W. B. Eerdmans.
  Challenging the belief that we have become increasingly secular, Berger identifies the significance of Islamic fundamentalism and Christian evangelism well before the tragic events of 9/11.

- Gitlin, T. (1993). *The sixties: Years of hope, days of rage*. New York: Bantam.
  This book about "the sixties" describes in broad strokes a time when millions of young Americans questioned authority and thought they could change the world—through their openness to sexuality, mind-altering drugs, rock-and-roll music, communal living, universal love, and opposing a war they thought was wrong.

- Moore, T. (1997). *The re-enchantment of everyday life*. New York: Harper Perennial.
  Written by a former Roman Catholic monk and present-day father of two, this very sensitive book discusses the idea that we can no longer afford to live in a disenchanted world. Moore argues that an enchanted engagement with life should not be considered childish, but rather embraced as necessary for the sake of our personal and collective survival.

- Coupland, D. (1991). *Generation X: Tales for an accelerated culture*. New York: St. Martin's Griffin (Macmillan).
  This book gave a generation its name. Told as a tale about three twenty-somethings who embark on a regime of storytelling, boozing, and working meaningless jobs. A homage to a generation that is searching for a home.

- Gordinier, J. (2009). *X saves the world: How Generation X got the shaft but can still keep everything from sucking*. New York: Penguin.

  Generation X is the cohort I'm calling "X-ers." This is a funny yet thoughtful book about a generation that feels it got ignored and left out. Gordinier suggests they got lost somewhere between the self-indulgent Baby Boomers and their smug offspring, the millennials.

- McQueen, M. (2010). *The new rules of engagement: A guide to understanding and connecting with Generation Y*. Columbus, OH: McGraw-Hill.

  Generation Y, the cohort I'm calling "Nexters," are the children of the Baby Boomers. This is an eye-opening look inside the mind of the so-called millenials, a group that has decided it wants to accomplish something.

- Tapscott, D. (2008). *Grown up digital: How the Net[LG1] Generation is changing your world*. New York: Morgan James.

  Generation Z, the "Texters," is the first generation to have fully grown up digital. You may have noticed them texting their friends, downloading music, uploading videos, watching a movie on a two-inch screen, and networking on Facebook. In this book, *New York Times* best-selling author Don Tapscott takes you into their uniquely digital world.

Links and Internet Resources

- **Thinking Beyond Secularization**
  http://are.as.wvu.edu/sochange.htm
  This site wasv established by two Creighton University professors, Charles L. Harper and Bryan LeBeau, to help explore the topic of secularization.

- **Peter L. Berger's Blog**
  http://blogs.the-american-interest.com/berger/
  Hosted on site of *The American Interest* online magazine, Peter Berger regularly offers his reflections on a variety of issues and major trends.

- **American Experience: My Lai (Vietnam War)**
  www.pbs.org/wgbh/americanexperience/films/mylai/
  This PBS documentary attempts to explain why a company of American soldiers in Vietnam was the "worst American atrocity" in history.

- **PBS Newshour: Generation Next**
  www.pbs.org/newshour/generation-next/documentary/
  This is a website documentary about Generation Next, which aired on PBS in 2009. It covers careers and cash flow; role models, sex, and diversity; being engaged and informed; and the search for identity.

- *Legacy.com*
  www.legacy.com
  This online resource partners with 85 of the 100 largest newspapers in the United States. It features obituaries and guest books for about 75 percent of people who die in the United States. It also provides access to more than 78 million records from the Social Security Death Index, going back as far as 1937. In addition, it provides special memorial sites dedicated to such groups as World War II veterans, those who have died in Iraq and Afghanistan, as well as the victims of the 9/11 attacks.

Review Guide

1. Review Ernest Becker's concept of "denial of death" and key points made by those who propose *terror management theory*. Be able to discuss the significance of these concepts.

2. Review the concepts of *sequestration, secularization, desecularization, disenchantment,* and *re-enchantment*. How can we use these concepts to explain how we approach the topic of death, dying, and bereavement?

3. What is *agency*, and what is the significance of this concept in relation to our experience with death, dying, and bereavement?

4. What do the terms *differentiation, rationalization, privatization, pluralism,* and *individual loss of faith* mean? How might they help us "flesh out" the discussion of secularization?

5. Review the material related to Peter Berger's ideas about desecularization and re-enchantment. What does he say about the role of religious belief in people's lives? How might his ideas help explain why the perpetrators of the 9/11 attack did what they did? What did he suggest about why people turn to science or religion?

6. Review the material on the generational relationship between members of the Greatest Generation and the Baby Boomers. Would you be surprised to learn that members of the Greatest Generation sometimes looked on hippie Baby Boomers with disdain? Why or why not?

7. Be able to discuss the basic premises of the Strauss-Howe generational theory.

8. Be able to describe key characteristics of X-ers, Nexters, and Texters. How are these generations different from each other? What is the same about them? What is the influence of these groups on how they relate to death, dying, and bereavement?

9. In reviewing the material on how we are dying, how might we use this understanding to address the needs of those who face death, dying, and bereavement?

10. What are health-care needs? Is the current system adequately addressing them? How might we better address them?

11. Review the material on end-of-life caring. What are the advantages of how we are currently providing care to people near death? What are the challenges? How might we address them?

12. What does it mean to say "The purpose of life is to live"? What did Erik and Joan Erikson propose as a way to understand the end of life as the "final stage"? What is gerotransecndence?

13. What did Dr. William Bartholome say about how a terminal diagnosis changed his life?

14. What do we mean by the "long good-bye"? How should we understand grief? Complicated grief? What steps can one take that reduces the likelihood of experiencing complicated grief?

GLOSSARY

Abrahamic tradition A term used to describe the Abrahamic religions of Judaism, Christianity, and Islam, all of which accept the patriarch Abraham as their (spiritual) ancestor.

active euthanasia Actively taking steps with the intent of ending another's life that is believed to be beneficial.

acute pain Sharp pain due to a clearly identifiable injury or illness, with a definite onset and predictable duration.

adolescent egocentrism A term that is sometimes used in developmental psychology to explain the sense of invulnerability that seems so characteristic of adolescence and adolescents.

advance directive A general term for two types of legal documents: the *living will* and *medical power of attorney* in which a person communicates her or his wishes in the event the person becomes unable to do so at a later time.

Age of Reason Also known as the Enlightenment, it was a period from about the middle seventeenth century to the beginning of the eighteenth century which promoted science and discouraged recourse to superstition.

agency In the field of thanatology research, it is a term used to denote one's sense of personal control over what happens in relation to death, dying, and bereavement.

AIDS pandemic The widespread occurrence of AIDS, or acquired immune deficiency syndrome.

akh Egyptian term for the reanimated mind or consciousness of an individual.

al-Haqq In Islamic tradition, the pursuit of the "true one," Allah.

alienation A term coined by sociologist Emile Durkheim to describe a sense of estrangement from other people. In the context of terrorism, it refers to being cut off from mainstream society.

amyotrophic lateral sclerosis (ALS) More commonly known as Lou Gehrig's disease, an illness of the nerve cells controlling voluntary muscle movement that leads to a predictable death.

alternative container Containers used for dead bodies, made of inexpensive materials such as cardboard, that are used in place of a more expensive casket.

altruistic suicide A term coined by sociologist Emile Durkheim that refers to suicide that is an expression of an idealistic, but perhaps excessive, sense of personal responsibility.

Amended Funeral Rule Amendments to the Funeral Rule adopted by the FTC in 1994, which soften the requirements of the Funeral Rule and allow funeral directors to charge a "nondeclinable" basic service fee to all customers.

anatman The Buddhist notion of "not self," in contrast to other teachings, which include the concept of "soul" or "self," which is believed to be at the core of an individual.

anencephalic infants Infants born without major portions of the skull and brain.

anger turned inward A hypothesis put forward by Freud that suggests that when aggressive impulses are thwarted, they can be turned inward, leading to feelings of depression.

anomic suicide A term coined by sociologist Emile Durkheim that refers to the motivation to commit suicide as a reaction to a sense of normlessness that is experienced in a world in which the traditional social structures, roles, or rules have broken down.

anomie A term coined by sociologist Emile Durkheim to describe the sense of anxiety, confusion, and "normlessness" emerging after the industrial revolution.

anonymity The practice whereby a funeral service corporation continues to use the old name of the funeral home after buying it, not publicizing the new affiliation of the funeral home to the parent corporation, or its connection with other funeral homes in the area.

anorexia Reduced desire to eat.

anticipatory grief The kind of grief that the loved ones of a serious ill person experience in advance of the person's actual death.

antyesti The practice of cremation in Hindu tradition.

apotheosis The achievement of godlike stature as a result of the achievement of merit, perhaps as the result of successfully returning from a dangerous pilgrimage.

ativahika In Hindu tradition, the vaguely formed subtle body of the deceased.

atman A Hindu term that is translated as "soul."

attachment A concept attributed to psychiatrist John Bowlby that refers to the natural capacity and inclination to form emotional bonds with others.

autonomy In the context of medical ethics, the prerogative of competent adults to make informed choices about their own care.

autoscopic In the context of near-death experience phenomena, having an out-of-body experience in which the person can view his or her own body from above.

avoidance In the context of diagnosing post-traumatic stress disorder, attempting to evade people, places, things, or situations that that might trigger traumatic experiences or remind the individual of a prior traumatic event.

ba An ancient Egyptian term for something that is like the combined soul and personality of an individual.

bardo In Tibetan Buddhism, the state believed to exist in between death and the next incarnation.

basic services fee A "nondeclinable" fee charged to all customers of a funeral home, which allows the funeral home to pass on the cost of doing business to customers, and which also ensures that the funeral home will make a profit.

beneficence In the context of medical ethics, to do that which is good.

bereavement What happens as a result of the experience of loss, usually, but not always, from death.

bereavement-related disorder (BRD) A cluster of signs and symptoms related to the experience of loss being considered for recognition in a forthcoming edition of the *Diagnostic and Statistical Manual (DSM)*.

best interest standard In the context of medical ethics, a determination of what is in the patient's best interests when her or his preferences are unknown.

binuclear family A family in which offspring alternate between living with their mothers and fathers.

biomedical model A scientifically based approach to health care that is now the accepted paradigm in Western medicine.

blended family A family that consists of a parent and stepparent, and possibly siblings and/or stepsiblings.

brain death The irreversible cessation of the activity of the whole.

bramacarya In the Hindu Vedic divisions of the human life cycle, it is the period of the "student," or religious study under the tutelage of a guru, usually during the first 25 years of life.

breakthrough pain Pain that only occasionally erupts, or "breaks through," the otherwise effective treatment of chronic pain, which requires temporary additional measures to control it.

broken bonds A concept attributed to psychiatrist John Bowlby that refers to the undesirable consequences that result when important attachments are severed, for example, as a result of a loss.

Buddhism A religion or philosophy that uses scriptures, teachings, and practices attributed to Siddhartha Gautama, who has been called "Buddha," or "enlightened one."

burial vault A concrete, plastic, or metal container that completely encloses the casket and the body and that keeps the ground above from sinking.

burning ghat In Hindu tradition, the cremation grounds that are ideally situated near the steps of the river banks in India and other parts of South Asia.

cachexia Uncontrollable wasting associated with cancer, characterized by abnormally low weight, weakness, and a general bodily decline that interferes with the quality of life.

calacas In Mexican "days of the dead" tradition, the representations of skeletons that are a pervasive part of annual celebrations honoring dead ancestors.

casket A term coined by the funeral service industry for the long rectangular coffin used to contain the body of a deceased person.

casketing Dressing and preparing the body for viewing or the funeral and then placing it in the casket.

causality A concept related to our understanding of death, referring to the causes of death.

Chautauqua A place in upper New York state that has become a synonym for adult education and lifelong learning.

chemotherapy A medical procedure that uses drugs to stop or slow the activity of fast-growing cells, such as cancer.

chevra kadisha Jewish burial society in which members of the same sex stand vigil over the body and prepare it for burial.

Christianity A religion whose inspiration was a Jew named Jesus, from Nazareth. He was and is believed by the faithful to be their savior. The Greek term *Christ* means anointed.

chronic grief A type of complicated grief proposed by psychiatrist Colin Murray Parkes that comes about after the death of a person on whom one was very dependent.

chronic pain Pain caused by the effects of a long-term illness, which often has a gradual or poorly identified onset, continues without relief, and that may become progressively more severe with time.

clear light state A condition described in the Tibetan Buddhist tradition in which a person exists in a state of remarkable clarity after death and that can lead to liberation and enlightenment.

clinical death The state in which the heart stops beating, breathing ceases, the body cools, tissues begin to decompose, and foul-smelling gasses build up in the body.

clustering The practice of buying up several funeral homes within the same area and then centralizing its key services, such as cremation, embalming, and restoration, at a single location.

cognitive-behavioral therapies (CBT) Psychological therapies based on cognitive-behavioral theory that usually emphasize relationships between affects (feelings), behavior, and cognitions (thinking), and that are usually very observable and measurable in terms of process and outcomes

cognitive development A term used to refer to the process by which one's thinking matures.

collaborative therapy A fairly unstructured approach to psychotherapy that begins with the premise that meaning is socially constructed and that emphasizes caring for and being with the client.

collective trauma A term used by psychoanalyst to describe what happens when large numbers of people experience trauma, feelings of fear, and a sense of which leads to collapse of central functions of the self and a fundamental shock to the entire personality.

columbarium A special building at a cemetery with niches for the cremains of deceased persons.

committal The final service, held at the cemetery or crematorium before the body is sent off.

Compassionate Friends A support group of parents who have had a child die.

complex PTSD A term used by dissociation theorists as a way to think of "splitting" as a learned way of coping with extreme trauma.

complicated grief Sometimes called "pathological grief," a term coined by psychiatrist Colin Murray Parkes to describe grief that is experienced more profoundly or that lasts longer than ordinary grief.

concrete operations The stage of cognitive development from around age 7 to 11.

conflict theory A theoretical perspective which postulates that people from different strata in a society are in a state of natural conflict with one another over control of scarce resources (e.g., Marxist theory).

conflicted grief A type of complicated grief proposed by psychiatrist Colin Murray Parkes as resulting from the death of a person with whom one had a conflict-ridden relationship.

congenital malformations Structural deformities in the developing fetus.

continuity In the Buddhist tradition, the noncorporeal portion of a human being that continues after death.

coroner A government official who investigates human deaths, determines its causes, and issues the death certificate.

cortical disinhibition theory In the context of the near death experience, a neurologically based attempt to explain the "tunnel" phenomenon as resulting from oxygen deprivation that is believed to cause cells to fire randomly in the visual cortex.

cosmology A theory about the nature of the cosmos, or universe.

cremains The cremated and pulverized remains of a human body, usually a white, yellow, or gray colored mixture with a texture ranging from that of sand to powder.

crematoria Facilities in which bodies of deceased persons are cremated.

cryosurgery A medical procedure that uses extreme cold produced by liquid nitrogen to kill abnormal tissue.

cultural diffusion The exchange of cultural elements between cultures that occurs when cultures come in contact with one.

cultural universal A cultural element that occurs in all, or nearly all, cultures.

culture Everything that is part of the social environment—the language, beliefs, values, norms, behaviors, and material objects that are passed on from generation to generation.

culture contact What occurs when the people from one culture come in contact with those of another.

dead donor rule A rule that establishes the legal and ethical principle that says organ retrieval in itself may not be the cause of death.

death The cessation of life.

death anxiety A term coined by Herman Fiefel for fear of death.

death denied A term used by Philippe Aries to indicate a period in which death is not openly acknowledged and dealt with.

death of other One of five types of death discussed by Philippe Aries in which attitudes about death were highly sentimental, emphasizing the emotional experience of bereavement.

death of self One of five types of death discussed by Philippe Aries characteristic of a highly individualistic age in which people paid a great deal of attention to how they lived their lives.

death system A term coined by Robert Kastenbaum to signify the ideals, values, and practices that shape how people deal with death—including health-care system, laws, and the funeral service industry.

Death with Dignity Act A measure passed by Oregon voters in 1994 that permits physicians to prescribe lethal medications to certain terminally ill patients who want to end their lives.

deductive approach An approach to research that begins with a general idea, or theory; this starting point attempts to deduce a conclusion.

defense mechanisms A term used in Freudian theory to denote the psychological means by which an individual deals with threats to the psyche.

denial of death A term that became the title of a book by Ernest Becker for our modern reluctance to openly acknowledge and deal with the realities of death.

depersonalization disorder A dissociative mental disorder in which the sufferer is afflicted with persistent or recurrent feelings of depersonalization and/or derealization.

desecularization A term coined by sociologist Peter Berger to denote the worldwide renewal, resurgence, or persistence of religious belief and/or spirituality.

dharma A term used in Hinduism, Buddhism, Jainism, and Sikhism that denotes the idea of one's path, or obligations in life. In traditional Hinduism, one's dharma is associated with what is required of one in life and that is dependent on the state, or caste, in which one is born.

dialectical behavioral therapy (DBT) An approach to psychotherapy, especially for people with borderline personality disorders, that uses standard cognitive-behavioral therapy techniques to help people regulate their feelings and test what is really happening in their experience.

didactic An approach to teaching in which the instructor imparts knowledge, values, and skills believed to be beneficial to student learning through direct teaching.

differentiation One of five approaches to understanding *secularization* in the sociology of religion. Roughly, it is the separation of church and state, such that religion functions as a distinct social institution but loses its explicit authority to legitimate the society or its government.

direct cremation The practice of cremating the body after death without prior benefit of traditional mortuary services (embalming, viewing, and conducting a funeral).

disenchantment A way to describe the process of what happens in society when we replace personal spiritual experience with reason as the source of knowledge about ultimate truth.

disenfranchised grief A term coined by Kenneth Doka that refers to grief that is socially disallowed, hidden, and unaffirmed.

disequilibrium The destabilization of the family system that occurs after a significant loss, especially of a child.

dissociation Disruption in mental functioning that is usually well-integrated (i.e., consciousness, memory, identity, and perception).

dissociative amnesia A dissociative disorder, recognized in the *Diagnostic and Statistical Manual (DSM)*, characterized by the loss of memory, usually about traumatic events too extensive to be normal forgetfulness.

dissociative disorders A class of mental disorders recognized in the *Diagnostic and Statistical Manual (DSM)*, characterized by dissociative symptoms.

dissociative fugue A dissociative disorder, recognized in the *Diagnostic and Statistical Manual (DSM)*, characterized by sudden travel away from home, confusion about identity, and loss of memory about one's past.

dissociative identity disorder (DID) A relatively rare dissociative disorder, recognized in the *Diagnostic and Statistical Manual (DSM)*, in which a person forms more than one distinct personality, believed to be caused by extreme trauma, usually first occurring when very young, before one's personality forms.

dissociative symptoms Symptoms associated with splitting away, or separating, disturbing material from conscious awareness.

dissolution of consciousness In Tibetan Buddhism, the belief that during the last four phases of the dying process, consciousness or awareness dissolves from gross to subtle: sense awareness, emotions, and thinking.

distal reactions In terror management theory, longer-term reactions to terror that emerge over time.

distressing near-death experiences (DNDES) Reported by people who have been resuscitated after their hearts stopped beating.

do not resuscitate order (DNR) It is a document initiated by a person and signed by a physician that directs health-care providers not to attempt cardiopulmonary resuscitation (CPR) if their heart or breathing stops.

du'a In Islamic tradition, special supplications that are made on behalf of the deceased.

dual-defense model Two general modes of reacting to terror in terror management theory (see **distal reactions** and **proximal reactions**).

dual-process model (DPM) A model of coping with loss developed by Dutch researchers that suggests that bereaved people benefit from addressing both their loss experiences and working on restoring themselves to normal functioning.

dying The process of getting dead.

dying trajectory A term coined by sociologists Anselm Strauss and Barney Glasser that refers to four patterns by which death occurs, that depend on how certain death is and whether or not it is known when death will occur.

dyspnoea The uncomfortable sense of breathlessness.

dystonic In Erikson's model of social development, it denotes the challenges each person must face as he or she moves through successive developmental stages.

egoistic suicide A term coined by sociologist Emile Durkheim that refers to suicide that is a consequence of isolation or a lack of close ties with others.

Elysian Fields In ancient Greek mythology, a paradise that existed for the souls of the virtuous dead.

embalming Replacing the blood and other fluids with fluids that preserve the body and slow the process of decay.

emic An approach to documenting living cultures in which the observer uses concepts and categories that come from the culture one is studying.

Enlightenment Also known as the Age of Reason, the Enlightenment era spanned from about the middle seventeenth century to the beginning of the eighteenth century, which promoted science and the free exchange of ideas and discouraged recourse to superstition.

eros One of two primary drives proposed by Freud to explain human behavior, it relates to the desire for pleasure and sex.

ethnocentrism Group attitudes when people in one culture fail to appreciate the contributions or worth of people from a different culture.

etic An approach to documenting living cultures in which the observer uses concepts and categories from one's own culture to evaluate the observed culture.

expected loss The kind of loss people expect before the fact, usually experienced after a long illness.

eulogy A talk about the life of a deceased person delivered at his or her funeral.

euthanasia The act of deliberately causing the death of another for reasons that are believed to be beneficial.

experiential An approach to teaching in which the instructor engages the student in real-life activities designed to evoke one's feelings and perhaps even change attitudes.

exposure therapy (ET) A form of psychotherapy that uses a series of procedures to progressively confront distressing thoughts and memories.

extended family The family system, common in agricultural societies, in which more than two generations live together in the same home.

eye movement desensitization and reprocessing (EMDR) An eight-phase psychotherapeutic process that involves asking patients to focus simultaneously on an image, negative thought, and disturbing feeling or body sensation, after which the person is asked to follow a moving object.

fatalistic suicide A term coined by sociologist Emile Durkheim that refers to suicidal impulses as a way to escape excessive social regulation.

fearful In the context of *distressing near death experiences*, experiences that are frightening.

fifth vital sign A way of referring to pain as something that requires close monitoring, like the other recognized vital signs of temperature, heart rate, blood pressure, and respiration.

Five Wishes A specialized living will (available for a fee) that addresses the individual's personal, emotional, and spiritual needs as well as her or his medical wishes.

Flexner Report A report drafted in 1910 by Abraham Flexner that is credited with transforming medical education in the United States into a scientific enterprise.

floral tribute A euphemism used by the funeral service industry referring to a display of flowers.

formal operations stage The stage of cognitive development that begins at about age 11 and continues to be a critical part of thinking for the rest of one's life.

four basic elements In Tibetan Buddhist thanatology, earth (body), water (its fluids), fire (heat), and wind (energy of movement), which dissolve in the first four stages of the dying process.

four-facet model A multidimensional approach to thanatology used in this text that emphasizes the need to address the physical, social, cultural, and spiritual dimensions.

functionalism A theoretical perspective used in the fields of anthropology and sociology in which a variety of social institutions and practices are believed to contribute to the functioning of the society as a whole.

funeral Commemorative services for the dead in which the body is present.

funeral director Professionals who take care of picking up the body, preparing the body, and coordinating the funeral and burial or cremation.

funeral mass In Roman Catholic tradition, solemn mass, or Eucharistic liturgy, in which communion is received and the life of the deceased is celebrated.

Funeral Rule FTC regulations, which require funeral directors to disclose their price lists to consumers before any services are provided and which safeguards consumers from abusive funeral practices.

future shock A term coined by futurist Alvin Toffler to refer to human reactions to the breakneck changes characteristic of life after the mid-twentieth century.

Gehenna A valley outside Jerusalem, where pagan sacrifices were once performed and where the city's garbage was later burned; in the New Testament used as a synonym for *Hades.*

gemeinschaft A term coined by sociologist Ferdinand Tonnies to refer to the kind of relationships and sense of intimacy that comes from belonging and a sense of community.

gerotranscendence A state of equanimity that a minority of people experience before they die.

gesellschaft A term coined by sociologist Ferdinand Tonnies to describe a way of relating to others that is distant, formal, and impersonal.

globalization The increasing unification in the world's economies.

good death Idealized concepts about the preferred manner of dying.

grave liner Concrete liners that enclose the body in the grave completely or on three sides and that prevent the earth from sagging.

graveside service A simple service held at the cemetery, usually when there is no other service.

green burial An approach to disposing of human remains that causes the least amount of harm possible to the environment.

greenwashing The practice of misrepresenting a practice as environmental friendly.

grhasta In the Hindu Vedic divisions of the human life cycle, it is the second 25-year period of life, in which (in some cases) the person is a house holder, or married person, with adult responsibilities.

grief The emotional experience associated with a cluster of distressing symptoms that often occur in waves and that follow in the wake of a significant loss.

grief trajectories A term coined by psychologist George Bonanno to describe five distinct patterns that people exhibit after suffering a significant loss.

grief work A concept attributed to Freud that describes the psychological process by which an individual learns to uncover, confront, and work through emotionally threatening material related to significant loss.

Hades In ancient Greek mythology, a place where the soul was believed to go after death and where evil deeds were punished and virtuous ones rewarded.

Harvard criteria Criteria for determining when someone is brain dead; developed by an ad hoc committee of Harvard Medical School.

hastened death Any act that speeds the dying process.

hospital-based palliative care programs (HBPCP) Inpatient units or specialized consultation services concerned with providing high-quality palliative care for patients with life-threatening illness.

hellish In the context of *distressing near death experiences*, experiences in which the person feels he or she was in a place like hell.

Hinduism An ancient religion native to India.

HIV-positive Showing up positive for antibodies associated with the human immune deficiency virus that causes AIDS.

home funeral A practice in which family members and friends care for the remains of a deceased loved one instead of consigning this responsibility to a professional funeral director.

hope Visualizing positive outcomes.

Horus In ancient Egyptian mythology, the god of truth.

hospice A multidimensional, compassion-driven model for caring for people who are dying.

hospice palliative care A term used by the Canadian Hospice and Palliative Care Organization that refers to efforts designed to ease the suffering of people with life-threatening illness, regardless of where such services are offered.

hostess gown A euphemism used by the funeral service industry referring to a special dress that covers only the front of a deceased woman.

humiliation The experience of being publicly devalued or dishonored. In the context of terrorism, humiliation is considered a key motivation for international terrorism.

hydration Providing an individual with fluids.

hyperarousal In the context of diagnosing post-traumatic stress disorder, a predisposition to respond to threats from the environment, and that may include such things as jumpiness, sleep disturbance, and vigilant scanning of the environment.

hypoxia In the context of health care, the lack of oxygen.

ideal culture The values, beliefs, and behavior to which the culture aspires.

imaginary audience In developmental psychology, a term used to describe the experience, especially by adolescents, when they imagine that others are as preoccupied with them as they are themselves.

immediate extubation The immediate removal of the tube used to provide a person with air from a mechanical ventilator.

incident pain Pain that occurs only under certain circumstances, such as when a body part is in a particular position.

inductive approach An approach to research that begins with observations in the environment that generalize into a theory.

inevitability A concept developed by Maria Nagy that refers to the understanding of death as being the natural result of the breakdown of the body.

infant respiratory distress syndrome (IRDS) A syndrome that begins to unfold shortly after birth, characterized by irregular breathing and heart beat.

intrusive reexperiencing In the context of diagnosing post-traumatic stress disorder, distressing symptoms related to a past traumatic event, which may include flashbacks and nightmares.

intubation What occurs when a patient is hooked up to mechanical ventilation.

invisible death One of five types of death discussed by Philippe Aries, in which death is denied and in which it is considered ignominious and taboo.

involuntary euthanasia The act of ending another's life against his or her will and without his or her consent.

irreversibility A concept developed by Maria Nagy that refers to the understanding of death as permanent.

ischemia In the context of health care, lack of blood supply.

Islam A monotheistic religion in the Abrahamic tradition, founded by the Prophet Muhammad, and articulated in its holy book, the Qur'an, which is believed to be the direct message of God, called Allah.

Judaism A monotheistic religion in the Abrahamic tradition, considered to be an expression of the covenantal relationship established between God and the Jewish people, as told in Hebrew Bible.

justice In the context of medical ethics, the obligation to distribute scarce resources equitably, respect human rights, and honor laws that contribute to the social good.

ka In the ancient Egyptian tradition, the spirit of a person that continues to exist after death and that could combine with the Ba, or soul, to reanimate the Akh, or living mind or consciousness of the individual.

kaddish A special Jewish prayer recited in Aramaic that proclaims the goodness of God.

kafan In Islamic tradition, the shroud that is used to wrap the body.

Kaposi's Sarcoma A relatively rare cancer that is often associated with AIDS; until the advent of AIDS it was associated with elderly Jewish men, living near the shores of the Mediterranean.

karma A concept in Hinduism, Buddhism, and some other South Asian religions in which good or bad merit earned in this life is believed to result in good or bad conditions in one's next incarnation.

ketamine An anesthetic previously used with children and domesticated animals that, when diluted, will reliably produce symptoms similar to those associated with the near death experience.

lawn crypt A pre-dug chamber in the earth intended to contain the remains of more than one person, designed to keep the earth above in tact even after the casket and body begin to decompose in the earth.

liberation The release from the suffering of life.

libido A term coined by Freud to refer to sexual energy that is also used by psychiatrist John Bowlby to refer to emotional energy associated with relationships.

life insurance A contract between a policy holder and insurance company, in which the insurance company agrees to pay a designated beneficiary a sum of money in the event of the death of the insured.

life review The process of reflecting on one's life when approaching its end.

living trust A written document created when one is living that designates someone to manage one's property, which is often used in place of a will.

living will A document in which the individual provides specific information about the course of treatment to be followed by health-care providers if he or she is at the end of life or is unable to communicate.

loss of faith One of five approaches to understanding *secularization* in the sociology of religion; it refers to the experience of people turning away from their religious faith or practice.

Maat In ancient Egyptian mythology, the god of justice.

malignant neoplasm Cancers, a class of disease in which cells experience uncontrolled growth, destroying adjacent tissues, and sometimes spreading, or "metastasizing."

material culture The concrete, or material, part of culture that can be passed on from one generation to the next.

mausoleum A free-standing building or structure used as a burial space in which to intern the remains of the deceased.

mediators of mourning Things that William Worden believed influence the course of mourning.

Medicaid A medical insurance program, funded jointly by federal and state governments that covers low-income people with few assets.

medical examiner A medically qualified official whose duty it is to investigate deaths and determine its causes.

medical futility In the context of medical ethics, treatment medical experts don't believe will benefit the patient.

medical power of attorney Sometimes called a *health-care power of attorney, health-care proxy,* or *durable power of attorney for health care,* it is a document in which a person appoints someone to make health-care decisions in the event the individual becomes unable to do so.

Medicare A federally funded medical insurance program that covers most Americans over age 65.

memorial Commemorative services for the dead in which the body is not present.

Missouri Rule A rule based on a U.S. Supreme Court decision that establishes the right of patients to make decisions about life support, but also affirms the authority of a state to require "clear and convincing" evidence about those wishes.

mit A Hebrew term that refers to the body of a deceased person.

mixed In the context of the near death experience phenomenon, experience that has both *autoscopic* and *transcendental* features.

modernism A perspective, or worldview, associated with the scientific model and the European Enlightenment-era emphasis on reason.

modernity The epoch of time in history after the industrial revolution when modern empiricism as a philosophical paradigm reigned in the West.

moksha In Hinduism, and other Eastern religions, it refers to the "liberation," "release," "salvation," or "emancipation" of the soul.

morbidity Relating to illness, in demographics the occurrence of chronic illness or disability.

mortality Relating to death, in demographics the rate at which people die.

mortality salience Anything that increase one's awareness of death.

mourning The often culturally patterned process that people go through as they attempt to cope with loss.

multidimensional Refers to the many different aspects, or facets, of human experience, such as the physical, social, psychological, and spiritual.

multidisciplinary Knowledge associated with more than one existing academic discipline or profession.

Munkar In Islamic tradition, one of two angels who question the deceased in their graves.

Nakir In Islamic tradition, one of two angels who question the deceased in their graves.

narrative therapy An approach to psychotherapy that uses the metaphor of "archaeologist" to think about the process in which the therapist gradually helps people brush away the accumulated debris of experience and reveal significant shards, fragments, and artifacts to help them piece together their story.

Neanderthal A distinct species of people, *Homo sapiens neanderthalensis,* who were similar to our own species and who appeared in Europe as early as 250,000 years ago.

near-death experience (NDE) A phenomenon in which people who have been resuscitated after their hearts stop beating report having had an out-of-body experience, going through a tunnel toward a white light, meeting deceased relatives on the other side, encountering a being of light, and reliving significant life events.

neuropsychological explanations In the context of trying to understand the near death experience, explanations that attempt to use knowledge of neurology (e.g., lack of oxygen to the brain, the presence of chemicals in the brain, or the breakdown of brain tissue).

nirvana The merging with the universe, which can only take place when one's (selfish) desires completely dissolve.

noncorporeal continuity A concept related to one's understanding of death, referring to the more abstract idea that some form of personal existence—a self, soul, or psyche—will continue to exist after the demise of the body.

nonfunctionality A concept related to one's understanding of death, referring to death as something that makes it so that one's body cannot function.

nonmaleficence The avoidance of doing harm, as reflected in the often quoted Latin expression, *primum non nocere* ("first do no harm").

nonmaterial culture The nonmaterial aspects of culture—for instance, practices, behavior, beliefs, values, and norms.

nonvoluntary euthanasia The deliberate administration of life-shortening substances with the *intent* of ending the life of a person who is not capable of making this choice for herself or himself.

normative Relating to social norms, or standards of behavior, which in the death and dying field suggests that certain patterns of behavior are "normal," or preferred.

nuclear family A family pattern in which only parents and their children live together.

nutrition In health care, having the nutrients needed to sustain life.

opportunistic infections Infections that adversely affect health because the body's immune system has been compromised, as in the case of AIDS.

oscillation As suggested by Dutch researchers, the idea that bereft people should go back and forth between processing emotionally painful aspects of loss and distancing themselves from such pain.

Osiris In ancient Egyptian mythology, the god of the dead and the judge of all.

pall A cloth covering placed over the casket during a funeral service; a somber mood or tone that pervades a place; a metaphor for how people try to hide from the awareness of death.

palliative care Care intended to alleviate suffering but not necessarily cure disease.

palliative medicine An emerging subspecialization in medicine concerned with alleviating suffering.

Paradise of Aalu In ancient Egyptian belief, an idyllic place resembling the Nile River Delta, where the souls of people found worthy lived eternally after death.

passive euthanasia Withholding necessary life-sustaining measures with the intent of ending another's life that is believe to be beneficial.

Patient Self-Determination Act (PSDA) A federal law in the United States that requires hospitals, skilled nursing facilities, home health agencies, hospices, and HMOs that receive Medicare or Medicaid dollars to notify patients they have the right to give advance directives and to make decisions about their future care.

persistent vegetative state A state in which an individual has a beating heart and the ability to breathe but who lacks consciousness, or higher mental functions, and who must be given nutrients and fluid artificially to survive.

personal fable Associated with an adolescent's exaggerated feelings of invulnerability, perception of themselves as unique, and believing others to be incapable of relating to their experiences.

personal mortality A concept related to one's understanding of death, referring to the idea that not only does death end the lives of people but that it will happen to "me" personally.

physical facet Those aspects of material existence that people experience directly through the senses.

physician-assisted suicide What occurs when physicians use their medical expertise with the aim of helping another end her or his life.

pitr In Hindu tradition, the world of the ancestors.

pluralism One of five approaches to understanding *secularization* in the sociology of religion. As a result of *differentiation*, or the separation of church and state in a society, space is opened for "new" religious expressions, such as aboriginal religion, New Age spirituality, secular humanism, and non-Western religion.

pneumocystic carinni pneumonia (PCP) A relatively rare pneumonia that is also symptomatic of AIDS.

postmodern theory Theoretical speculation, originating in the work of several French philosophers, that suggests society is entering a postmodern era and that the older "grand narratives," or explanations, are no longer sufficient in explaining experiences.

postmodernism A perspective, or worldview, associated with a rejection of the unquestioned reliance on scientific method, deductive reasoning, and technology.

postmodernity The epoch of time in history, beginning in the mid-twentieth century that followed in the wake of discoveries in quantum science.

post-traumatic stress disorder (PTSD) A cluster of signs and symptoms related to the experience of a traumatic event that is recognized in the current edition of the *DSM* as a mental disorder.

postvention A term coined by Edwin S. Shneidman to denote what people do after a suicide to help the survivors; in contrast to prevention (what people do before) and intervention (what people do during a suicide or suicide attempt).

preoperational stage The stage of cognitive development from about age 1½ to about age 7.

prescriptive Relating to the idea that some process should unfold in a prescribed, or specific, way.

principle of double effect A centuries-old precept of the Roman Catholic Church, used to help guide decisions on how to proceed when there are both desirable and undesirable outcomes (e.g., taking steps to ease pain that inadvertently hasten death).

privatization One of five approaches to understanding *secularization* in the sociology of religion. As a result of religion's loss of authority to influence all of society, religion's primary focus shifts from the public sphere to the private, and concerns itself more with personal faith and family life.

professional integrity In the context of medical ethics, the obligation to fight disease and prolong life.

prognosis The expected outcome of a person's illness.

proximal reaction In terror management theory, reactions to terror that are likely to occur right away in response to an explicit threat.

psychological facet The facet of human experience that includes that most intangible of human phenomena, human consciousness, as well as the thoughts, feelings, and behaviors that are integral to human experience.

psychosocial explanations In the context of trying to understand the near death experience, explanations that are based on how people socially construct the meaning of the event.

psychosocial transition A term used by psychiatrist Colin Murray Parkes to refer to what happens when one must relearn how to function when someone becomes disabled or loses a body part.

purge Fluids that may seep from the lungs, stomach, or intestines after death.

qualitative approach An approach to research that emphasizes description of the natural environment, which is often inductive in nature.

quantitative approach An approach to research that emphasizes use of measurement and the scientific method.

radiation therapy The use of high-energy radiation to shrink tumors and kill cancerous cells.

Ramadan The month in the Islamic calendar when Muslims are expected to focus on their spiritual development by fasting during the daylight hours and observing other religious practices.

rationalization One of five approaches to understanding *secularization* in the sociology of religion. As a result of differentiation of religion as distinct social institutions with less authority, the society comes to rely on other sources of knowledge, such as science and reason.

real culture The beliefs, norms, and values that are actually played out in a culture.

religion A set of organized beliefs and practices about the supernatural, embracing the spiritual dimension of life.

religiosity As a risk factor for prolonged grief, it can be understood as the degree to which a person has a commitment to a religious faith tradition.

remote and imminent death One of five types of death discussed by Phillippe Aries, in which people attempted to push death out of consciousness yet were also strangely fascinated by it.

research The systematic process used by human beings to increase knowledge. It may be quantitative or qualitative in nature and include specific research methods, such as the experiment, field research, survey research, historical analysis, secondary analysis of existing data, and case study.

resilience The ability of a person to bounce back after experiencing adversity.

retort The cremation chamber, where gas or electric heaters raise temperatures to extreme levels that are sufficient to consume a human body, with only small fragments remaining.

rigor mortis The stiffening of the muscles that occurs after death.

salatul janazah In Islamic tradition, special prayers that are said on behalf of the deceased.

samnyasa In the Hindu Vedic divisions of the human life cycle, in some castes it is the final 25-year period of life, when the person withdraws from the affairs of this world and becomes an ascetic, or renunciate sheloshim.

samsara The cycle of birth, life, death, and rebirth, or reincarnation, which is a feature of Hinduism, Buddhism, and several other South Asian religions.

sati Sometimes called *sutee,* a traditional practice in some Hindu castes in which widows are expected to die on the funeral pyres of their deceased husbands.

scales of justice In ancient Egyptian mythology, the scales on which a person's heart is weighed before a final judgment is pronounced.

secularization A term used to denote the process by which things which were originally religious in nature are transformed for nonreligious use.

self-esteem One of two ways terror management theorists believe human beings psychologically protect themselves from the awareness of death.

sensorimotor stage The stage of cognitive development, beginning at birth and continuing until about 1½ years of age.

seppuku A form of ritualistic suicide carried out by members of Japan's feudal Sammurai, or warrior, caste.

sequestration A term used in thanatology research to connote the idea that those touched from death, and death itself, is sequestered, or isolated, from the rest of society.

Seth In Egyptian mythology, an evil God, the murderer of the God Osiris, who was said to have taken the form of a monster with the head of a camel and body of a hound.

sheloshim A 30-day period of mourning after shiva has concluded, when the restrictions on activities are relaxed and the bereaved begin to resume their usual activities.

Sheol In ancient Semitic cosmologies, an underworld, where the souls of the dead were thought to reside.

shiva In Judaism, the strict practice of mourning that lasts for one week during which loved ones remain home to receive condolences of well-wishers.

shradda In Hinduism, special rituals that are performed each of six times when the funeral procession stops on the way to the cremation site.

slumber room A euphemism used by the funeral service industry referring to the sales room where caskets are displayed.

sobering In the context of *distressing near-death experiences*, experiences that shakes a person up and causes the person to reconsider how she or he should live her or his life.

social facet The dimension of human experience concerned with social relations—family, groups, communities, social institutions, and the society itself.

social integration A term coined by sociologist Emile Durkheim in his exploration of suicide that refers to the degree to which individuals are included, or integrated, into the fabric of the society of which they are a part.

social regulation A term coined by sociologist Emile Durkheim in his exploration of suicide that refers to the process by which a society is able to manage, or regulate, the behavior of its members and their relationships with each other.

soul A religious or spiritual term that refers to the noncorporeal essence of a person, living thing, or object.

spend down The process of using up one's own assets until becoming eligible for Medicaid funding.

spirituality The sense about that which is beyond the ordinary, often linked to thanatology, perhaps because of widespread speculation about what, if anything, happens to us after death.

spirituality facet The dimensions of human living concerned with trying to understand death within the context of intuition about reality that transcends ordinary experience.

standard developmental account Our generally accepted understanding of how children conceive of death.

subjective standard In the context of medical ethics, oral or written instructions given by a patient before losing decision-making capacity.

substituted judgment standard In the context of medical ethics, a determination of what a patient would have wanted in the present circumstances, based on an understanding of the patient's prior preferences and value system.

sudden infant death syndrome (SIDS) Sometimes called "crib death," is an umbrella label used to describe the death of an infant that is not expected based on medical history, and that often remains uncertain, even after a thorough postmortem examination.

suffering Discomfort in any dimension of living: physical, social, psychological, or spiritual.

symbolic interaction A theoretical perspective in the field of sociology that suggests that people engage in a process of interaction in which they negotiate what experience means and that is believed to create their collective social reality.

syndrome of fanaticism In the context of terrorism, it refers to a phenomenon in which individuals have a firm belief in absolute truth, great zeal, utter faith in their view of good and evil, a standardized way of thinking, an aversion to anything contrary to their vision of truth, and such a complete commitment to an ideology that they are willing to end their own lives and partake in acts they might otherwise regard as criminal.

syntonic In Erikson's model of social development, it denotes the life tasks each individual strives to achieve.

tallit In Judaism, a shawl worn during prayer.

tame death One of five types of death discussed by Philippe Aries in which the people died at home, surrounded by family, friends, and neighbors.

tasks of mourning Tasks that grief expert William Worden believed everyone should accomplish as a result of going through the experience of loss.

teachable moment A real-life experience related to death that opens one to learn about it in a personal and meaningful way.

term insurance A form of *life insurance* that covers an individual for a specific period of time or term.

terminal dehydration The loss of salt and water that occurs during the last days of life.

terminal delirium An atypical state in which dying persons are agitated and restless despite efforts to comfort them.

terminal respiratory congestion Often called the "death rattle," it is the noisy, gurgling respiration heard in some people when they are dying.

terminal sedation Also called palliative sedation, it is the attempt relieve distress during the last hours or days of a dying person's life by administering a drug that causes her or him to sleep.

terminal weaning In the context of artificial ventilation, when the amount of oxygen and the breathing action of the ventilator with the hope that the individual will resume breathing on her or his own.

terror management theory (TMT) A theoretical model based on the original insights of Ernest Becker that posits that human beings, because of their consciousness about death, use culture and self-esteem to manage feelings of terror.

terrorism According to the FBI, it is the unlawful use of violence or threat of violence against a government, people, or any portion thereof, in pursuit of a social or political cause.

thanatology The study of death, dying, and bereavement.

thanatos One of two primary drives proposed by Freud to explain human behavior, it relates to death and destructive impulses.

theory A set of logically interrelated ideas generally used to describe, explain, and sometimes predict phenomenon.

theory-research cycle A graphic way of conceptualizing the relationship between theory and research developed in 1971 by Walter Wallace.

Thoth In ancient Egyptian mythology, the god who records the proceedings before a final judgment is rendered.

total pain A term coined by hospice pioneer, Dame Cicely Saunders that embodies not only physical discomfort but also psychological, social, and spiritual aspects as well.

Totten Trust A trust fund established between an individual and a bank that pays off only in the event of death and that is protected from forfeiture under Medicaid rules.

transcendental In the context of the near death experience phenomenon, a feature of the experience that transcends the ordinary.

transhumanism A movement to fundamentally transform the human condition by developing and making widely available technologies to vastly enhance human intellectual, physical, and psychological capacities.

trauma An experience that is sudden, violent, or shocking.

traumagenic event In the context of diagnosing post-raumatic stress disorder, an event powerful enough to trigger an adverse psychological adjustment.

traumatic death Death that is sudden, violent, inflicted, and/or intentional, and encounters with death that are shocking.

traumatic grief A type of complicated grief proposed by psychiatrist Colin Murray Parkes as being characterized by grief caused by death that is sudden, unexpected, or causes mutilation of the body.

trocar A pointed, hollow, surgical instrument approximately two feet long and three quarters of an inch in diameter used to pierce and then suction any gas or fluids from it organs in order to slow the process of decay.

Turnface In Egyptian mythology, a supernatural ferryman, who always looked away from the soul of the deceased, but who was responsible for taking the soul across a rive to the other side.

'umma In Islamic tradition, the community of believers.

Uniform Death Determination Act (UDDA) A consensus definition for brain death adopted based on the recommendations of a special presidential commission in the United States.

universality A concept developed by Maria Nagy, referring to the understanding of death as something that happens to everyone.

vanaprastha In the Hindu Vedic divisions of the human life cycle, it is the third 25-year period of life, when in some castes is a time of retirement, when the person begins to disengage from worldly affairs.

Vedas In Hindu tradition, the Vedas, which are hymns, are the most ancient and sacred scriptures.

ventilation In the context of health care, helping a person get air or oxygen.

ventilator dependent In the context of health care, patients who are unable to continue living without a ventilator.

viewing A time and place set aside for family and friends to see the body on display at the funeral home before the funeral.

voided In the context of *distressing near-death experiences*, experiences in which the person experiences utter emptiness.

wake A vigil held before the funeral, often held in the home of the deceased person.

whole life A form of *life insurance* in which there is a fixed annual premium, guaranteed death benefits, and guaranteed cash values, depending on when the policy is cashed out.

will A legal document in which you declare what will happen with your assets and who will manage your estate after you die.

wound filler A putty-like substance used by the funeral director to cover over wounds or injuries so the body will look more appealing to those who view it.

REFERENCES

Adamolekun, K. (1999). Bereavement salutations among the Yorubas of Western Nigeria. *Omega, 39*(4), 277–285.

Adler, A. (1943). Neuropsychiatric complications in victims of Boston's Coconut Grove disaster. *Journal of the American Medical Association, 123,* 1098–1101.

Adler, S. R. (1995). Refugee stress and folk belief: Hmong sudden deaths. *Social Science and Medicine, 40*(12), 1623–1629.

Agence. (2005, February 16). Gay concern over hyping AIDS "superbug." *Agence France Presse English.* Available: *www.highbeam.com.*

Aging with Dignity. (2011). Retrieved September 25, 2011, from *www.agingwithdignity.org/five-wishes.php.*

AIDS Treatment News. (2003a). Information fact sheets: What is AIDS? Available: *www.aids.org/factSheets/101-what-is-aids.html.*

AIDS Treatment News. (2003b). Drug names and manufactures charts. Available: *www.aids.org/factSheets/401-drug-names.html.*

Albom, M. (1991). *Tuesdays with Morrie: An old man, a young man, and life's greatest lesson.* New York: Doubleday.

Alderwoods Group. (2003). About Alderwoods. Available: *www.alderwoods.com/abAbout.cfm?Action=About.*

Ali, M. M. (2002). The Ka'abah and the Abrahamic tradition. Available: *www.bismikaallahuma.org/History/Makkah/kaabah-history.htm.*

Allan, G. (1994). Traditions and transitions. *Psychoanalytic Review, 81*(1).

Ahmedzai, S. (1998). Palliation of respiratory symptoms. In D. Doyle, G. W. C. Hanks, & N. MacDonald (Eds.), *Oxford textbook of palliative medicine* (2nd ed., pp. 583–616). New York: Oxford University Press.

Ainsworth, M. D. S. (1992). John Bowlby (1907–1990). *American Psychologist, 47*(5), 668.

Alighieri, D., Moser, B. (illus.), and Mandelbaum, A. (trans.). (1982). *The divine comedy of Dante Alighieri: Inferno.* New York: Bantam.

Amarasekara, K., & Bagaric, M. (2004). Moving from voluntary euthanasia to non-voluntary euthanasia: Equality and compassion. *Ratio Juris, 17,* 398–423.

American Academy of Hospice and Palliative Medicine (AAHPM). (2011). History growing stronger (1998–2008). Retrieved on May 23, 2011, from *www.aahpm.org/about/default/history.html.*

American Association of Retired Persons (AARP). (2011). Retrieved on September 27, 2011, from *www.aarp.org/money/estate-planning/.*

American Association of Suicidology (AAS). (2009). Survivors of suicide fact sheet. Available as a free download from *www.suicidology.org/.*

American Association of Suicidology (AAS). (2013). Facts, statistics, and current research. Available: *www.suicidology.org/stats-and-tools/suicide-fact-sheets.*

American Geriatrics Society (AGS). (2000). American Geriatrics Society (AGS) position statement: the care of dying patients. Available: *www.americangeriatrics.org/.*

American Medical Association (AMA). (1986). Current opinions of the Council on Ethical and Judicial Affairs, 12–13. Chicago: American Medical Association. Available: *www.ama-assn.org/resources/doc/code-medical-ethics/1005a.pdf.*

American Psychiatric Association (APA). (2000). *Diagnostic and statistical manual of mental disorders, 4th ed., text revised.* Washington, DC: Author.

American Psychiatric Association (APA). (2011). DSM-5 development. Proposed draft revisions to DSM disorders and criteria, trauma- and stressor-related disorders, G06 adjustment disorders, be reavement-related disorder. Retrieved July 3, 2011, from *www.dsm5.org/Proposed/Revision/Pages/proposedrevision.aspx?rid=367.*

Anderson, G. R. (1995). Walking through the valley of the shadow of death: Grief and fundamentalism. In J. K. Parry & Ryan, A. S. (Eds.), *A cross-cultural look at death, dying, and religion* (pp. 32-46). Chicago: Nelson Hall.

Anderson, H. (1993). On a roller-coaster: A collaborative language system approach to therapy. In S. Friedman (Ed.),

The new language of change (pp. 324–344). New York: Guilford.

Anderson, H., & Goolishian, H. (1992). The client is the expert: A not-knowing approach to therapy. In S. McNamee & K. J. Gergen (Eds.), *Therapy as social construction* (pp. 25–39). Newbury Park, CA: Sage.

Anderson, R. N., & DeTurk, P. B. (2002). United States life tables, 1999. *National Vital Statistics Reports, 50*(6). Hyattesville, MD: National Center for Health Statistics.

Andrade, M. J. (1996). *Through the eyes of the soul: Day of the dead in Mexico.* San Jose, CA: La Oferta Review.

Angell, M. (1994). After Quinlan: The dilemma of the persistent vegetative state. *New England Journal of Medicine, 330,* 1524–1525.

Ankney, R. N. (1998). Miracle in South Africa: A historical review of U.S. magazines' coverage of first heart transplant. Paper presented at the 1998 conference of the Association for Education in Journalism and the Mass Media. Available: list.msu.edu/cgi-bin/wa?A2=ind9811e&L=aejmc&F=&S=&P=55.

Ankrom, M., Zelesnick, L., Barofsky, I., Georas, S., Finucane, T. E., & Greenough, W. B. (2001). Elective discontinuation of life-sustaining mechanical ventilation on a chronic ventilator unit. *Journal of the American Geriatric Society, 49*(11), 1549–1554.

Aquinas, T., & McDermott, T. (Eds.). (1989). *Summa theologiae: A concise translation.* Allen, TX: Christian Classics.

Arbuckle, N. W., & de Vries, B. (1995). The long-term effects of later life spousal and parental bereavement on personal functioning. *The Gerontologist, 35*(5), 637.

Arias, E., Anderson, R. N., Hsiang-Ching, K, Murphy, S. L., & Kochanek, K. D. (2003). *National Vital Statistics Reports, 52*(3). Hyattesville, MD: National Center for Health Statistics.

Aries, P. (1974). *Western attitudes toward death: From the Middle Ages to the present.* Baltimore: Johns Hopkins University Press.

Aries, P. (1981). *The hour of our death.* New York: Knopf.

Arnold, R. M., & Youngner, S. J. (1993). The dead donor rule: Should we stretch it, bend it, or abandon it? *Kennedy Institute Ethics Journal, 3*(2), 263–278.

Arras, J. D. (1994). The technological teacher: An introduction to ethical and social issues in high-tech home care. *Hastings Center Report, 24*(5), S1–S2.

Arras, J. D., & Dubler, N. N. (1994). Bringing the hospital home: Ethical and social implications of high tech home care. *Hastings Center Report, 24*(5), S19–S28.

Asch, D. A. (1996). The role of critical care nurses in euthanasia and assisted suicide. *New England Journal of Medicine, 334*(21), 1374–1379.

Ashby, M. (2000). *The Egyptian book of the dead: The book of coming forth by day.* Miami, FL: Cruzian Mystic Books.

Ashcroft, J. (2001, September 6). Memorandum for Asa Hutchinson. Washington, DC: Office of the Attorney General.

Ashton, J., & Ashton, D. (2000). Dealing with the chronic/terminal illness or disability of a child: Anticipatory mourning. In T. A. Rando (Ed.), *Clinical dimensions of anticipatory mourning: Theory and practice in working with the dying, their loved ones, and their caregivers.* Champaign, IL: Research Press.

Associated Press (AP). (2002). Ted Williams signed frozen family pact. Available: *www.cbsnews.com/stories/2002/08/09/national/main518105.*

Association for Death Education and Counseling. (2009). *Handbook of thanatology.* New York: Routledge.

Atwater, P. M. H. (2001). *Coming back to life: The after-effects of the near-death experience* (rev. ed.). New York: Citadel Press.

Axline, V. M. *Play therapy.* New York: Ballantine.

Ayres, L. (2006). *Nicaea and its legacy.* Oxford, England: Oxford University Press.

Badone, E. (2004). Lecture notes for "Death & dying: The Western experience." Hamilton, ON: McMaster University, Department of Anthropology and Religious Studies. Available: *www.socsci.mcmaster.ca/relstud/undergraduate /summer_courses/cfm.*

Bailey, A. (2000). Pain as the fifth vital sign. On our own terms: Moyers on dying. Available: *www.pbs.org/wnet/onourownterms/articles/pain.html.*

Balk, D., Wogrin, C., Thornton, G., & Meagher, D. (Eds.). (2007). *Handbook of thanatology: The essential body of knowledge for the study of death, dying, and bereavement.* New York: Routledge/Taylor & Francis.

Barker, D. (2005). Dame Cicely Saunders: The founder of the modern hospice movement, she transformed the way we look at death and dying. *The Guardian,* July 16, 2005.

Retrieved May 22, 2011 from *www.guardian.co.uk/ news/2005/jul/16/guardianobituaries.health*.

Barnard, D. (1998). Palliative care: Whole-person care of the dying patient. *World Anasthesia, 2,* Article 16, 1. Available: *www.nda.ox.ac.uk/wfsa/html/wa02_01/ wa02_018.htm*.

Barry, R., & Maher, J. E. (1990). Indirectly intended life-shortening analgesia: Clarifying principles. *Issues in Law & Medicine, 6*(2), 117–152.

Barrett, T. W., & Scott, T. B. (1990). Suicide bereavement and recovery patterns compared with nonsuicide bereavement patterns. *Suicide and Life-Threatening Behavior, 29,* 1–5.

Bartholome, W. (1999). Address to the Midwest Bioethics Center on receiving the Founders' Award. Consult with Center for Practical Bioethics, Kansas City, MO.

Bartholome, W. (2000a). Lessons from the angel of death. *Bioethics Forum, 16*(1), 29–36.

Bartholome, W. (2000b). Living in the light of death. *Bioethics Forum, 16*(1), 17–18.

Bartholome, W. (2000c). A world unraveling. *Bioethics Forum, 16*(1), 13–16.

Bartholome, W. (2000d). STILL/HERE above ground. *Bioethics Forum, 16*(1), 19–22.

Bartholome, W. (2000e). May I be a cancerous survivor. *Bioethics Forum, 16*(1), 25–26.

Bartholome, W. (2000f). Meditations by William G. Bartholome. *Bioethics Forum, 16*(1), 13–36.

Bartholome, W. G. (1995). Care of the dying child: The demands of ethics. In L. E. DeSpelder and A. L. Strickland (Eds.), *The path ahead: Readings in death and dying*. Mountain View, CA: Mayfield.

Baudrillard, J. (1983). *Simulations*. New York: Semiotext.

Bayer, R., Callahan, D., Fletcher, J., Hodgson, T., Jennings, B., Monsees, D., Sieverts, S., & Veatch, R. (1983). The care of the terminally ill: Mortality and economics. *New England Journal of Medicine, 309*(24), 1490–1494.

Beck, A. T., Steer, R. A., Kovacs, M., & Garrison, B. (1985). Hopelessness and eventual suicide: A 10-year study of patients hospitalized with suicidal ideation. *American Journal of Psychiatry, 142,* 559–563.

Beck, A. T., & Weishaar, M. E. (1989). Cognitive therapy. In R. J. Corsini & D. Wedding (Eds.), *Current psychotherapies* (4th ed.). Itasca, IL: Peacock.

Becker, E. (1971). *The birth and death of meaning* (2nd ed.). New York: Free Press.

Becker, E. (1973). *The denial of death*. New York: Free Press.

Becker, E. (1975). *Escape from evil*. New York: Free Press.

Beecher, H. K. (1968). A definition of irreversible coma. Report of the ad hoc committee of the Harvard Medical School to examine the definition of brain death. *Journal of the American Medical Association, 205,* 337–340.

Beecher, H. K., & Dorr, H. I. (1971). The new definition of death: Some opposing views. *International Journal of Clinical Pharmacology, 5*(2), 120–124.

Bell, L. V. (1970). Death in the technocracy. *Journal of Human Relations, 18*(2), 833–839.

Bergner, D. (2007, December 2). Death in the family. *The New York Times*. Retrieved May 28, 2011, from *www. nytimes.com/2007/12/02/magazine/02suicide-t.html*.

Berman, A. L., Jobes, D. A., & Silverman, M. M. (2006). *Adolescent suicide: Assessment and intervention*. Washington, DC: American Psychological Association.

Benoliel, J. Q. (1987–1988). Health care providers and dying patients: Critical issues in terminal care. *Omega, 18,* 341–369.

Benoliel, J. Q. (1997). Death, technology, and gender in postmodern American society. In S. Strack (Ed.), *Death and the quest for meaning: Essays in honor of Herman Feifel*. Northvale, NJ: Jason Aronson.

Benoliel, J. Q., & Degner, L. F. (1995). Institutional dying: A convergence of cultural values, technology, and social organization. In H. Wass & R. A. Neimeyer (Eds.), *Dying: Facing the facts*. Washington, DC: Taylor and Francis.

Beresford, L. (1993). *The hospice handbook: A complete guide*. New York: Little, Brown.

Berger, P. L. (1967). *The sacred canopy: Elements of a sociological theory of religion*. New York: Doubleday.

Berger, P. L. (1970). *A rumor of angels: Modern society and the rediscovery of the supernatural*. Garden City, NY: Anchor.

Berger, P. L. (1977). *Facing up to modernity: Excursions in society, politics, and religion*. New York: Basic Books.

Berger, P. L. (1999). *The desecularization of the world: Resurgent religion and world politics*. Grand Rapids, MI: W. B. Eerdmans.

Berman, A. (2006, July/August). Risk assessment, treatment planning, and management of the at-risk-for suicide client: The "how to" aspects of assessing suicide risk and formulating treatment plans. *Family Therapy Magazine, 5*(4), 7–10.

Best, S., & Kellner, D. (1991). *Postmodern theory.* New York: Guilford.

Best, S., & Kellner, D. (1997). *The postmodern turn.* New York: Guilford.

Best, S., & Kellner, D. (2001). The *postmodern adventure.* New York: Guilford.

Beversluis, J. (Ed.). (1995). *Sourcebook for earth's community of religions.* Grand Rapids, MI: CoNexus Press and Global Education Associates.

Billings, J. A. (1985). Comfort measures for the terminally ill: Is dehydration painful? *Journal of the American Geriatrics Society, 33*(11), 808–810.

Billings, J. A., & Pantilat, S. (2001). Survey of palliative care programs in United States teaching hospitals. *Journal of Palliatve Medicine, 4*(3), 309–314.

Black, C. (1981). *It will never happen to me.* Denver: M. A. C., Printing and Publication Division.

Blackmore, S. J. (1991). Near-death experiences: In or out of the body? *Skeptical Inquirer, 16,* 34–35.

Blackmore, S. J. (1993). *Dying to live: Science and the near-death experience.* London: Grafton.

Blackmore, S. J. (1998). Experiences of anoxia: Do reflex anoxic seizures resemble NDEs? *Journal of Near-Death Studies, 17,* 111–120.

Blackmore, S. J. (2002). Near-death experiences. In M. Shermer (Ed.). (2002). *The skeptic encyclopedia of pseudoscience* (pp. 152–157). Santa Barbara, CA: ABC-Clio.

Blackmore, S. J., & Troscianko, T. (1988). The physiology of the tunnel. *Journal of Near-Death Studies, 8,* 15–28.

Blauner, R. (1966). Death and the social structure. *Psychiatry, 29,* 378–394.

Bluebond-Langner, M. (1978). *The private worlds of dying children.* Princeton, NJ: Princeton University Press.

Bluebond-Langner, M. (1989). Worlds of dying children and their well siblings. *Death Studies, 13*(1), 1–16.

Blumer, H. (1969). *Symbolic interaction.* Englewood Cliffs, NJ: Prentice-Hall.

Boelen, P. A. & Prigerson, H. G. (2007). The influence of symptoms of prolonged grief disorder, depression and anxiety on quality of life among bereaved adults: A prospective study. *European Archives of Clinical Neuroscience, 257,* 444–452.

Boer, T. A. (2001). Personal interview, December 3.

Boerner, K., Wortman, C. B., & Bonanno, G. A. (2005). Resilient or at risk? A 4-year study of older adults who initially showed high or low distress following conjugal loss. *Journal of Gerontology, 60B*(2), P67–P73.

Bolling, J. L. (1995). Guinea across the water: The African-American approach to death and dying. In J. K. Parry & A. S. Ryan (Eds.), *A cross-cultural look at death, dying, and religion* (pp. 145–159). Chicago: Nelson-Hall.

Bolton, I. (1986). Death of a child by suicide. In Therese Rando (Ed.), *Parental loss of a child.* Champaign, IL: Research Press.

Bonanno, G. A. (2004). Loss, trauma, and human resilience. *American Psychologist, 59*(1), 20–28.

Bonanno, G. A. (2009). *The other side of sadness: What the new science of bereavement tells us about life after loss.* New York: Basic Books.

Bonanno, G. A., & Kaltman, S. (1999). Toward an integrative perspective on bereavement. *Psychological Bulletin, 125,* 760–776.

Bonanno, G. A., & Kaltman, S. (2001). The varieties of grief experience. *Clinical Psychology Review, 20,* 1–30.

Bonanno, G. A., Neria, Y., Mancini, A., Coifman, K. G., Litz, B., & Insel, B. (2007). Is there more complicated grief than depression and post-traumatic stress disorder? A test of incremental validity. *Journal of Abnormal Psychology, 116*(2), 342–351.

Bonanno, G. A., Wortman, C. B., Lehmann, D. R., Tweed, R. G., Haring, M., et al. (2002). Resilience to loss and chronic grief: A prospective study from pre-loss to 18 months post-loss. *Journal of Personality and Social Psychology, 83,* 1150–1164.

Bonanno, G. A., Wortman, C. B., & Nesse, R. M. (2004). Prospective patterns of resilience and maladjustment during widowhood. *Psychology and aging, 19,* 260–271.

Bondanella, P. E. (2003). Introduction in Dante Alighieri & H. W. Longfellow (Trans.), *Inferno.* Lyndhurst, NJ: Barnes & Noble Classics.

Bonta, I. L. (2004). Schizophrenia, dissociative anesthesia and near-death experience: Three events meeting at the NMDA receptor. *Medical Hypotheses, 62*(1), 23–28.

Bower, B. (1994). Neanderthal tot enters human-origins debate. *Science News, 145*(1), 5.

Bower, B. (1995). Child's bones found in Neanderthal burial. *Science News, 148*(17), 261.

Bowker, J. (1993). *The meanings of death.* Cambridge: Cambridge University Press.

Bowker, J. (Ed.). (1997). *The Oxford dictionary of world religions.* New York: Oxford University Press.

Bowlby, J. (1969). *Attachment.* New York: Basic Books.

Bowlby, J. (1973). *Separation.* New York: Basic Books.

Bowlby, J. (1980). *Loss.* New York: Basic Books.

Bradnock, R., & Bradnock, R. (2000). *India handbook* (10th ed.) Chicago: NTC/Contemporary Publishing Group.

Bregman, L. (2006). Spirituality: A glowing and useful term in search of a meaning. *Omega, 53*(1–2), 5–26.

Brehony, K. A. (1996). *Awakening at midlife: A guide to reviving your spirit, crecreating your life, and returning to your true self.* New York: Riverhead Books.

Breitbart, W., Chochinov, H. M., & Passick, S. (1998). Psychiatric aspects of palliative care. In D. Doyle, G. W. C. Hanks, & N. MacDonald (Eds.), *Oxford textbook of palliative medicine* (2nd ed., 933–954). New York: Oxford University Press.

Briere, J. (1992). *Child abuse trauma.* Newbury Park, CA: Sage.

Brison, K. J. (1995). You will never forget: Narrative, bereavement, and worldview among Kwanga women. *Ethos, 23*(4), 474–488.

British Broadcasting Corporation (BBC). (2003). On this day, 18 November. *BBCNews. www.bbc.co.uk/onthisday/hi/date/stories/november/18/newsid2540000/254020t.stm.*

British Broadcasting Corporation News. (2005, July 14). Obituary: Dame Cicely Saunders. Available: *http://news.bbc.co.uk/2/hi/uk_news/4254255.stm.*

Britton, W. B., & Bootzin, R. R. (2004). Near-death experiences and the temporal lobe. *Psychological Science, 15*(4), 254–258.

Brosius, J. P. (1995). Signifying bereavement: Form and context in the analysis of Penan death names. *Oceana, 66*(2), 103–119.

Bruera, E. (2001). ABC of palliative care. Anorexia, cachexia, and nutrition. *British Medical Journal, 315,* 1219—1222.

Bruera, E., & Fainsinger, R. L. (1998). Clinical management of cachexia and anorexia. In D. Doyle, G. W. C. Hanks, & N. MacDonald, (Eds.), *Oxford textbook of palliative medicine* (2nd ed., pp. 534–548). New York: Oxford University Press.

Bryer, K. B. (1979). The Amish way of death: A study of family support systems. *American Psychologist, 34*(3), 255–261.

Brymer, M., Jacobs, A., Pynoos, R., Ruzek, J., Steinberg, A., Vernberg, E., & Watson, P. (2006). *Psychological first aid: Field operations guide* (2nd ed.). National Child Traumatic Stress Network & National Center for PTSD. Retrieved June 4, 2011, from *www.ptsd.va.gov/professional/manuals/psych-first-aid.asp.*

Burden, L. M. (2009, October). Teenage wasteland: A Chicago funeral home's business is growing, for all the wrong reasons. *The Atlantic Monthly,* 26–28.

Burge, F. I. (1993). Dehydration symptoms of palliative care cancer patients. *Journal of Pain and Symptom Management, 8*(7), 454–464.

Burgess, M. M. (1993). The medicalization of dying. *Journal of Medicine and Philosophy, 18,* 269–279.

Bush, N. E. (2002). Afterward: Making meaning after a frightening near-death experience. *Journal of Near-Death Studies, 21*(2), 99—133.

Butler, R. N. (1963). The life review: An interpretation of reminiscence in the aged. *Psychiatry, 26,* 65–76.

Butler, R. N. (1980–81). The life review: An unrecognized bonanza. *International Journal of Aging and Human Development, 12,* 35–38.

Byrne, G. J., & Raphael, B. (1994). A longitudinal study of bereavement phenomena in recently widowed elderly men. *Psychological Medicine, 24* (2), 411–421.

Byrne, P. A. & Nilges, R. G. (1993). The brain stem in brain death. *Issues in Law and Medicine, 9*(1), 3–21.

Cain, A. (Ed.). (1972). *Survivors of suicide.* Springfield, IL: Bannerstone House.

Callahan, D. (1990). *What kind of life: The limits of medical progress.* New York: Simon and Schuster.

Callahan, D. (2000). Death and the research imperative. *The New England Journal of Medicine, 342*(9), 654–656.

Campbell, J. (1949). *The hero with a thousand faces.* Princeton, NJ: Princeton University Press.

Campbell, J. (1988). *The power of myth.* New York: Anchor.

Campbell, M. L., Bizek, K. S., & Thill, M. (1999). Patient responses during rapid terminal weaning from mechanical ventilation: A prospective study. *Critical Care Medicine, 27*(1), 73–77.

Canadian Hospice Palliative Care Association (CHPCA). (2004). Available: *www.chpca.net.home.htm*.

Canady, C. T. (1998). Physician-assisted suicide and euthanasia in the Netherlands: A report to the House Judiciary Subcommittee on the Constitution–Executive Summary. *Issues in Law & Medicine, 14,* 301–324.

Candy-Gibbs, S. E., Sharp, K. C., & Petrun, C. J. (1985). The effect of age, object, and cultural/religious background on children's concepts of death. *Omega, 15*(4), 329–346.

Capron, A. M. (1991). In re Helga Wanglie (a long term patient in vegetative state whose husband chose not to terminate care. *The Hastings Center Report, 21*(5), 26–28.

Capron, A. M. (1994). Medical futility: Strike two. *The Hastings Center Report, 24*(5), 42–43.

Carnelley K. B., Wortman C. B., Bolger N., Burke C. T. (2006). The time course of grief reactions to spousal loss: Evidence from a national probability sample. *Journal of Personality and Social Psychology, 91*(3), 476–492.

Carlson, L. (1987). *Caring for your own dead.* Hinesburg, VT: Upper Access Publishers.

Carlson, L. (1998). *Caring for the dead: Your final act of love.* Hinesburg, VT: Upper Access Publishers.

Carr, A. (1998). Michael White's narrative therapy. *Contemporary Family Therapy, 20*(4), 485–501.

Carr, D. (1981). Endorphins at the approach of death. *Lancet, 826,* 390–398.

Carr, D. (1982). Pathophysiology of stress-induced limbic lobe dysfunction: A hypothesis relevant to near-death experiences. *Anabiosis: The Journal of Near-Death Studies, 2,* 75–89.

Casanova, J. (1994). *Public religions in the modern world.* Chicago: University of Chicago Press.

Cassel, C. K., & Foley, K. M. (1999). Principles for care of patients at the end of life: An emerging consensus among the specialties of medicine. New York: Milbank Memorial Fund. Available: *www.milbank.org/end-oflife/index.html*.

Cassell, J. J. (1993). The sorcerer's broom: Medicine's rampant technology. *Hastings Center Report,* November–December.

Cassidy, J., & Shaver, P. (Eds.). (2002). *Handbook of attachment: Theory, research, and clinical applications.* New York: Guilford.

Castaneda, C. J. (1994, October 13). Baby K—Now Stephanie—Turns 2. *USA Today,* p. A-3.

Castro, K. G, Ward, J. W., Slutsker, L., Buehler, J. W., Jaffew, H. W., & Berkelman, R. L. (1993). *1993 revised classification system for HIV infection and expanded surveillance case definition for AIDS among adolescents and adults.* Washington, DC: Centers for Disease Control, National Center for Infectious Diseases Division of HIV/AIDS.

CBS News. (2013). In depth: Boston Marathon bombings. Accessed May 24, 2013, from *www.cbsnews.com/2718-201_162-2153/boston-bombings/*.

Center for the Advancement of Palliative Care (CAPC). (2003). Palliative care programs rapidly growing in nation: AHA study highlights new trend in health care. Available: *www.capc.org/site_root/News/news_087160440.htm*.

Center for Bioethics, University of Minnesota. (1997a). *The determination of death.* Minneapolis, MN: Author. Available: *www.bioethics.umn.edu/publications/bov.shtml*.

Center for Bioethics, University of Minnesota. (1997b). *Termination of treatment of adults.* Minneapolis, MN: Author. Available: *www.bioethics.umn.edu/publications/bov.shtml*.

Center for Health Workforce Studies (CHWS). (2002). *The supply, demand and use of palliative care physicians in the United States.* Rensselaer, NY: Author. Available: *http://chws.albany.edu*.

Centers for Disease Control (CDC). (1981a). Pneumocystis pneumonia—Los Angeles. *Morbidity and Mortality Weekly Report, 30,* 250–252.

Centers for Disease Control (CDC). (1981b). Karposi's sarcoma and pneumocystic pneumonia. *Morbidity and Mortality Weekly Report, 30,* 305–308.

Centers for Disease Control (CDC). (1981c). Follow-up on Karposi's sarcoma and pneumocystic pneumonia among homosexual men—New York City and California. *Morbidity and Mortality Weekly Report, 30,* 409–410.

Centers for Disease Control (CDC), Divisions of HIV/AIDS Prevention. (2003a). *Basic statistics.* Available: ***www.cdc.gov/hiv/stats.htm#cumaids***.

Centers for Disease Control/National Center for Health Statistics. (1985). *Vital statistics of the United States, II, Mortality, part A, 1980.* Washington, DC: Public Health Service, National Vital Statistics System.

Centers for Disease Control and Prevention. (2003b). AIDS cases in adolescents and adults, by age—United States, 1994–2000. *HIV/AIDS Surveillance Supplemental Report, 9*(1), 1–25.

Centers for Disease Control and Prevention. (2003c). Characteristics of people living with AIDS and HIV, 2001. *HIV/AIDS Surveillance Supplemental Report, 9*(2), 1–27.

Centers for Disease Control and Prevention. (2011a). *Fact sheets: HIV in the United States.* Retrieved May 11, 2011, from ***www.cdc.gov/hiv/resources/factsheets/us.htm***.

Centers for Disease Control and Prevention. (2011b). *Diagnoses of HIV Infection and AIDS in the United States and Dependent Areas, 2009, 21.* Available: ***www.cdc.gov/hiv/pdf/statistics_2009_HIV_Surveillance_Report_vol_21.pdf***.

Centers for Disease Control and Prevention, National Center for Injury Prevention and Control. (2010, Summer). *Suicide, facts at a glance.* Retrieved May 24, 2013, from ***www.cdc.gov/violenceprevention***.

Chandler, R. (1953) *The long goodbye.* London: Hamish Hamilton.

Chin, A. E., Hedberg, K., Higginson, G. K., & Fleming, D. W. (1999). Legalized physician-assisted suicide in Oregon—The first year's experience. *New England Journal of Medicine, 340*(7), 577–583.

Chua, J. (2004/2005). Meth, men and myths: Substance use and the gay club scene. *CrossCurrents: Journal of Addiction and Mental Health.* Available: ***www.camh.net/***.

Clark, D. (1999). "Total pain," disciplinary power and the body of work of Cicely Saunders, 1958–1967. *Social Science and Medicine, 49,* 727–736.

Clark, M. (2000). *Interdisciplinary ministry collaboration.* Unpublished doctoral dissertation, St. Stephen's College, Edmonton.

Clark, M., & Olson, J. (2000). *Nursing within a faith community.* Thousand Oaks, CA: Sage.

CNN. (1999). Kevorkian gets 10 to 25 years in prison. Available: ***www.cnn.com/US/9904/13/kevorkian.03/***.

Cogliano, J. F. (1999). The medical futility controversy: Bioethical implications for the critical care nurse. *Critical Care Nursing Quarterly, 22*(3), 81–88.

Cohen-Almagor, R. Non-voluntary and involuntary euthanasia in the Netherlands: Dutch perspectives. *Issues in Law & Medicine, 18,* 239–257.

Comte, A., & Congreve, R. (trans.). (2009). *The catechism of positive religion: Or summary exposition of the universal religion in thirteen systematic conversations between a woman and a priest.* London: Cambridge University Press.

Conference of the Medical Royal Colleges. (1979). Diagnosis of death. *British Medical Journal, 1,* 332.

Connelly, R. J. (1997–1998). The medicalization of dying: A positive turn on a new path. *Omega, 36*(4), 331–341.

Connors, Jr., A. F., Dawson, N. V., Desbiens, N. A., Fulkerson, W. J., Goldman, L., Knaus, W. A., Lynn, J., & Oye, R. K., & the SUPPORT principal investigators (1995). A controlled trial to improve care for seriously ill hospitalized patients: The study to understand prognoses and preferences for outcomes and risks of treatments (SUPPORT). *Journal of the American Medical Association, 274,* 1591–1598.

Conrad, P. (1992). Medicalization and social control. *Annual Review of Sociology, 18,* 209–232.

Conrad, P, Nowacek, G., Adams, T., & Smith, L. (1996). Medical students' attitudes toward the autopsy. *Academic Medicine, 71*(6), 681–683.

Cooper, D. A. (1997). *God is a verb: Kabbalah and the practice of mystical Judaism.* New York: Riverhead Books (Penguin).

Coppleston, F. (1962). *A history of philosophy, 2 (II): Mediaeval philosophy, Albert the Great to Duns Scotus.* Garden City, NY: Image Books.

Coppleston, F. (1963). *A history of philosophy, 4: Modern philosophy, Descartes to Leibniz.* Garden City, NY: Image Books.

Coppleston, F. (1964). *A history of philosophy, 5 (I): Modern philosophy, the British philosophers, Hobbes to Paley.* Garden City, NY: Image Books.

Coppleston, F. (1967). *A history of philosophy, 8 (I): British empiricism and the idealist movement in Great Britain.* Garden City, NY: Image Books.

Coppleston, F. (1977). *A history of philosophy, 9 (I): Maine de Biran to Sartre, the revolution to Henri Bergson.* Garden City, NY: Image Books.

Corey, J. (2005). *Theory and practice of counseling & psychotherapy* (7th ed.). Belmont, CA: Brooks/Cole.

Corey, J. (2008). *Theory and practice of counseling & psychotherapy* (8th ed.). Belmont, CA: Brooks/Cole.

Corr, C. A. (1992). A task-based approach to coping with dying. *Omega, 24*(2), 81–94.

Corr, C. A. (1993). Coping with dying: Lessons that we should and should not learn from the work of Elisabeth Kübler-Ross. *Death Studies, 17,* 69–83.

Corr, C. A., & Doka, K. J. (2001). Master concepts in the field of death, dying, and bereavement: Coping versus adaptive strategies. *Omega, 43*(3), 183–189.

Corr, C. A., Nabe, C. M., & Corr, D. M. (2003). *Death and dying, life and living* (3rd ed.). Pacific Grove, CA: Wadsworth.

Corr, C. A., Nabe, C. M., & Corr, D. M. (2005). *Death and dying, life and living,* (5th ed.). Belmont, CA: Wadsworth.

Corr, C. A., Nabe, C. M., & Corr, D. M. (2008). *Death and dying, life and living,* (6th ed.). Belmont, CA: Wadsworth.

Corsini, R. J. & Wedding, D. (Eds.). (1989). *Current psychotherapies* (4th ed.). Itasca, IL: Peacock.

Cox, G. (2010). *Death and the Native American.* Omaha, NE: Grief Illustrated Press.

Coupland, D. 1991. *Generation X: Tales for an accelerated culture.* New York: St. Martin's.

Craig, G., & Baucum, D. (2002). *Human development* (9th ed.). Upper Saddle River, NJ: Prentice-Hall.

Cranford, R. E. (1978). Brain death. Concept and criteria. *Minnesota Medicine, 61*(10), 600–603.

Cranford, R. E. (1984). Termination of treatment in the persistent vegetative state. *Seminars in Neurology, 4*(1), 36–44.

Cranford, R. E. (1988). The persistent vegetative state: The medical reality (getting the facts straight). *The Hastings Center Report, 18*(1), 27–32.

Cranford, R. E. (1990). Cruzon: Hostage to technology. *The Hastings Center Report, 20*(5), 9–10.

Cranford, R. E. (1991). Helga Wanglie's ventilator. *The Hastings Center Report, 21*(4), 23–24.

Craven, M. (1973). *I heard the owl call my name.* New York: Laurel, a division of Doubleday.

Cremation Association of North America (CANA). (1997). Special report: 1996/97 cremation container, disposition and service survey. Available: ***www.cremationassociation.org/html/publications/html.***

Cremation Association of North America (CANA). (2004a). The cremation process: Step by step. Available: ***www.cremationassociation.org/html/publications/html.***

Cremation Association of North America (CANA). (2004b). Historical data: United States vs. Canada. Available: ***www.cremationassociation.org/html/publications/html.***

Cremation Association of North America (CANA). (2004c). Table of international statistics. Available: ***www.cremationassociation.org.html/publications/html.***

Crosby, A. E., Ortega, L., & Stevens, M. R. (2011). Suicides—United States, 1999–2007. *Morbidity and Mortality Weekly Report, Supplements, 60*(01), 56–59. Available: ***www.cdc.gov/mmwr/pdf/other/su6001.pdf.***

Cross, F. L., & Livingstone, E. A. (Eds.). (1997). *The Oxford dictionary of the Christian church.* New York: Oxford University Press.

Cummings, I. (1998). The interdisciplinary team. In D. Doyle, G. W. C. Hanks, & N. MacDonald (Eds.), *Oxford textbook of palliative medicine* (2nd ed., pp. v–ix). New York: Oxford University Press.

Daaleman, T. P. & VandeCreek, L. (2000). Placing religion and spirituality in end-of-life care, *Journal of the American Medical Association, 284 ,* 2514-2517.

Dante, A., & Singleton, C. S. (1990). *The divine comedy, I. Inferno. Part 2.* Princeton, NJ: Princeton University Press.

Dean, L. (1995). The epidemiology and impact of AIDS-related death and dying in New Yorks' gay community. In L. Sherr (Ed.), *Grief and AIDS.* New York: Wiley & Sons.

DeGeorgio, C., & Lew, M. F. (1991). Consciousness, coma, and the vegetative state: Physical basis and definitional character. *Issues in Law & Medicine, 6*(4), 361–371.

Delatte, P. (1950). *The rule of Saint Benedict: A commentary by the Right Reverend Dom Paul Delatte, Abbot of Solesmes and Superior-General of the Congregation of Benedictines of France* (J. McCann, Trans.). Eugene, OR: Wipf and Stock Publishers.

Dimeff, L., & Linehan, M. M. (2001). Dialectical behavior therapy in a nutshell. *The California Psychologist, 34,* 10–13.

Derse, A. R. (2000). Is there a lingua franca for bioethics at the end of life? *Journal of Law, Medicine, & Ethics, 28*(3), 279–285.

DeSpelder, L. A., & Strickland, A. L. (1995). *Readings in death and dying: The path ahead.* Mountain View, CA: Mayfield.

DeSpelder, L. A., & Strickland, A. L. (1999). *The last dance: Encountering death and dying.* Mountain View, CA: Mayfield.

DeSpelder, L. A., & Strickland, A. L. (2004). *The last dance: Encountering death and dying* (7th ed.). New York: McGraw-Hill.

DeSpelder, L. A., & Strickland, A. L. (2008). *The last dance: Encountering death and dying* (8th ed.). New York: McGraw-Hill.

DeWalden-Galuszko, K., Majkowicz, M., Trzebiatowska, I. A., & Kapala, P. (1998). Medical staff's attitude towards death and psychological distress of care for cancer patients. *New Trends in Experimental and Clinical Psychiatry, 14*(2), 71–74.

Dibsie, P. (1995, January 25). Slaying victim adapted his life to "follow his passion" for art. *San Diego Union-Tribune.* Retrieved from ***http://nl.newsbank. com/nl-search/we/Archives***.

Dickinson, G. E., & Field, D. (2002). Teaching end-of-life issues: Current status in United Kingdom and United States medical schools. *American Journal of Hospice & Palliative Care, 19*(3), 181–186.

Dills, C. R., & Romiszowski, A. J. (Eds.). (1997). *Instructional development paradigms.* Englewood Cliffs, NJ: Educational Technology Publications, p. 299.

Dimeff, L., & Linehan, M. (2001). Dialectical behavior therapy in a nutshell. *The California Psychologist, 34,* 10–13.

Dinsmore, C. A. (2010). *The teachings of Dante.* Charleston, SC: Nabu Press.

Doka, K. J. (Ed.). (1989). *Disenfranchised grief: Recognizing hidden sorrow.* Lexington, MA: Lexington Books.

Doka, K. J. (1995–1996). Coping with life-threatening illness: A task model. *Journal of Death and Dying, 32*(2), 111–122.

Doka, K. J. (Ed.). (2002). *Disenfranchised grief: New directions, strategies, and challenges for practice.* Champaign, IL: Research Press.

Dolan, M. B. (1983). Another hospice nurse says. *Nursing, 33*(1), 51.

Donnelly, S. (1999). Folklore associated with dying in the West of Ireland. *Palliative Medicine, 13*(1), 57–62.

Doyle, D., Hanks, G., & Macdonald, N. (Eds.). (1998a). *The Oxford textbook of palliative medicine* (2nd ed.). New York: Oxford University Press.

Doyle, D., Hanks, G., & Macdonald, N. (1998b). Introduction. In D. Doyle, G. W. C. Hanks, & N. MacDonald, (Eds.), *The Oxford textbook of palliative medicine* (2nd ed., pp. 3–8). New York: Oxford University Press.

Dossey, L. (1982). *Space, time, and medicine.* Boulder, CO: Shambala.

DuBois, P. M. (1980). *The hospice way of death.* New York: Human Sciences Press.

Dufault, K., & Martocchio, B. C. (1985). Hope: Its spheres and dimensions. *Nursing Clinics of North America, 20*(2), 379–391.

Dunn, R. G., & Morrish-Vidners, D. (1988). They psychological and social experience of suicide survivors. *Omega, 18,* 175–215.

Dunne, E. J., McIntosh, J. L., & Dunne-Maxim, K. (Eds.). (1987). *Suicide and its aftermath.* New York: Norton.

Durkheim, E. (1893/1964). *The division of labor in society.* Ann Arbor: University of Michigan Press.

Durkheim, E. (1897/1951). *Suicide.* New York: Free Press.

Durkheim, E. (1912/1995). *The elementary forms of religious life.* Trans. Karen E. Fields. New York: Free Press.

Durkheim, E. (1915). *The elementary forms of religious life.* Trans. Karen E. Fields. New York: Free Press.

Dutch Voluntary Euthanasia Society (NVVE). (2001). *Facts about the Netherlands.* Amsterdam: Author.

Dvorsky, G. (2004, May–June). Better living through transhumanism: More than just a philosophy and social movement, transhumanism is for many a way of life. *The Humanist, 64*(3), 7–10.

Dyregrov, A., & Dyregrov, K. (1999). Kupst long-term impact of sudden infant death: A 12- to 15-year follow-up. *Death Studies, 23*(7), 635–661.

Dyregrov, K. (2004). Strategies of professional assistance after traumatic deaths: Empowerment or disempowerment? *Scandinavian Journal of Psychology, 45,* 181–189.

Eberhardie, C. (2002). Nutrition support in palliative care. *Nursing Standard, 17*(2), 47–52.

Eberhardt, M. S., Ingram, D. D., & Makuc, D. M. (2001). *Health, United States, 2001.* Hyattsville, MD: National Center for Health Statistics.

Ebert, R. H. (1986). Medical education at the peak of the era of experimental medicine. *Daedalus, 115,* 55–81.

Edwards, B. K., Ward, B., Kohler, B. A., Eheman, C., Zauber, A. G., Anderson, R. N., Jemal, A., Schymura, M. J., Lansdorp-Vogelaar, I., Seeff, L. C., van Ballegooijen, M., Goede, S. L., & Ries, L. A. G. (2010). *Annual report to the nation on the status of cancer, 1975–2006, featuring colorectal cancer trends and impact of interventions (risk factors, screening, and treatment) to reduce future rates.* Bethesda, MD: Nation Cancer Institute.

Eitzen, D. (Director). (1998). The Amish and us. [Film]. (Available from Direct Cinema, Ltd. P. O. Box 10003, Santa Monica, CA 90410.)

Elkind, D. (1976). *Child development and education: A Piagetian perspective.* New York: Oxford University Press.

Elkind, D., & Bowen, R. (1979). Imaginary audience behavior in children and adolescents. *Developmental Psychology, 15,* 38–44.

Elliott, C. (2003). Humanity 2.0: Transhumanists believe that human nature's a phase we'll outgrow, like adolescence. Someday we'll be full-fledged adult posthumans, with physical and intellectual powers of which we can now only dream. But will progress really make perfect? *The Wilson Quarterly.*

Ellwood, G. F. (2001). *The uttermost deep: The challenge of near-death experiences.* New York: Lantern.

Ely, M., Anzul, M., Friedman, T., Garner, D., & Steinmets, A. M. (1991). Doing qualitative research: Circles within circles. New York: Falmer.

Emanuel, E. J. (1997, March). Whose right to die? *The Atlantic.* Retrieved May 28, 2011, from theatlantic.com/magazine/archive/1997/03/whose-right-to-die/4641.

Encyclopedia of Death and Dying. (2009). Available: **www.deathreference.com/.**

End-of-Life Nursing Education Consortium (ELNEC). 2005. *End-of-life care.* Available: **www.aacn.nche.edu/elnec.**

Engel, G. L. (1977). The need for a new medical model: A challenge for biomedicine. *Science, 196,* 129–136.

EPEC Project. (1999 and 2003). *EPEC (education for physicians on the end-of-life care): Participant handbook.* Available: **www.epec.net/.**

Erikson, E. H. (1963). *Childhood and society* (2nd ed.). New York: Norton.

Erikson, E. H. (1982). *The life cycle completed.* New York: Norton.

Erikson, E. H. & Erikson, J. M. (1997). *The life cycle completed: Extended version with new chapters on the ninth stage of development.* New York: Norton.

Estes, C. L., & Binney, E. A. (1989). The biomedicalization of aging: Dangers and dilemmas. *The Gerontologist, 29*(5), 587–596.

Evans, W. E. D. (1963). *The chemistry of death.* Springfield, IL: Charles C. Thomas.

Evans-Wentz, W. Y. (1974). *Tibetan book of the dead* (3rd ed.). New York: Oxford University Press.

Facebook. (2012). What does memorializing an account mean? Retrieved on March 30, 2012, from *www.facebook.com/help*.

Fainsinger, R. L., Bruera, E., Miller, M. J., Hanson, J., & MacEachern, T. (1991). Nutrition and hydration for the terminally ill. *Journal of the American Medical Association, 273,* 1736.

Faiver, C., Ingersoll, R. E., O'Brien, E., & McNally, C. (2001). *Explorations in counseling and spirituality: Philosophical, practical, and personal reflections.* Pacific Grove, CA: Brooks/Cole.

Farran, C. J., Herth, K. A., & Popovich, J. M. (1995). *Hope and hopelessness: Critical clinical constructs.* Thousand Oaks, CA: Sage.

Farrell, J. J. (1980). *Inventing the American way of death.* Philadelpha: Temple University Press.

Farrugia, D. The experience of the family when a child dies. *Family Journal, 4*(1), 30–36.

Faulkner, K. W. (2001). Children's understanding of death. In A. Armstrong-Dailey & S. Zarbock (Eds.), *Hospice care for children* (2nd ed.). New York: Oxford University Press.

Faulkner, R. O., & Andrews, C. (1990). *The ancient book of the dead.* Austin, TX: University of Texas Press.

Faulkner, R. O., Goelet, O., & Andrews, C. (2000). *The Egyptian book of the dead: The book of going forth by day.* San Francisco: Chronicle Books.

Federal Bureau of Investigation (FBI). (2000). *Terrorism in the United States 1999, Counterterrorism, threat assessment and warning unit.* Available: *www.fbi.gov/publications/terror/terroris.htm*.

Federal Trade Commission (FTC). (2003). Complying with the Funeral Rule. Available: *http://ftc.gov/bcp/conline/pubs/buspubs/funeral.htm*.

Feifel, H. (Ed.). (1959). *The meaning of death.* New York: McGraw-Hill.

Feifel, H. (Ed.). (1977a). *New meanings of death.* New York: McGraw-Hill.

Feifel, H. (Ed.). (1977b). Death in contemporary America. In H. Feifel (Ed.), *New meanings of death.* New York: McGraw-Hill.

Fenigsen, R. (1997). Dutch euthanasia revisited. *Issues in Law & Medicine, 13,* 301–311.

Ferris, F. D., Balfour, H. M., Bowen, K, Farley, J., Hardwick, M., Lamontagne, C., Lundy, M., Syme, A., & West, P. (2002). *A model to guide hospice palliative care: Based on national principles and norms of practice.* Ottawa: Canadian Hospice Palliative Care Association. Available: *www.chpca.net*.

Ferris, F. D., Flannery, J. S., McNeal, H. B., Morissette, M. R., Cameron, R., & Bally, G. A. (Eds.). (1995). Module 4: Palliative care. *A comprehensive guide for the care of persons with HIV disease.* Toronto: Mt. Sinai Hospital and Casey House Hospice.

Ferruolo, S. (1998). *The origins of the university: The schools of Paris and their critics, 1100–1215.* Stanford, CA: Stanford University Press.

Field, M. J., & Cassel, C. K. (Eds.). (1997). *Approaching death: Improving care at the end of life.* Washington, DC: National Academy Press.

Fields, D. M. (1995). Postmodernism. *Premise* (2), 8.

Final Passages. (2003). Available: *www.finalpassages.org*.

Fingerthut, L. A., Hoyert, D. L., & Pickett, D. (2003). Classification of deaths resulting from terrorism. *Homicide Studies, 7*(1), 85–91.

Fisher, D. (2006). Helping teenagers get through suicide. *Phi Delta Kappan, 87,* 9–13.

Fitchett, G. (1993). *Assessing spiritual needs: A guide for caregivers.* Minneapolis: Augsburg Fortress.

Flynn, T. W. (1994, Fall). Defending Prometheus: Rekindling humanity's love affair with science and technology. *Free Inquiry.* Available: *www.questia.com/library/1G1-16378912/defending-prometheus-rekindling-humanity-s-love-affair*.

Foa, E. B., Davidson, J. R. T., & Frances, A. (1999). The expert consensus guideline series: Treatment of posttraumatic stress disorder. *Journal of Clinical Psychiatry, 61* (Suppl. 5).

Foa, E. B., Keane, T. M., & Friedman, M. J. (2000). *Effective treatments for PTSD: Practice guidelines from the International Society for Traumatic Stress Studies.* New York: Guilford.

Foa, E. B., Keane, T. M., Friedman, M. J., & Cohen, J. A. (Eds.). (2009). *Effective treatment for PTSD: Practice guidelines from the International Society for Traumatic Stress Studies* (2nd ed.). New York: Guilford.

Folkman, S. (1997). Positive psychological states and coping with severe stress. *Social Science and Medicine, 45,* 1207–1221.

Folkman, S. (2001). Revised coping theory and the process of bereavement. In M. S. Stroebe, R. D. Hanson, W. Stroebe, & H Schut (Eds.), *Handbook of bereavement research: consequences, coping, and care* (pp. 563–584). Washington, DC: American Psychological Association.

Folkman, S., Lazarus, R. S., Pimley, S., & Novacek, J. (1987). Age difference in stress and coping processes. *Psychology and Aging, 2,* 171–184.

Folkman, S., Moskowitz, J. T., Ozer, E. M., & Park, C. L. (1997). Positive meaningful events and coping in the context of HIV/AIDS. In B. H. Gottlieb (Ed.), *Coping with chronic stress* (pp. 293–314). New York: Plenum.

Foucault, M. (1980). *Power/knowledge.* New York: Pantheon.

Frame, M. W. (2003). *Integrating religion and spirituality into counseling.* Pacific Grove, CA: Brooks/Cole.

Frankl, V. E. (1984). *Man's search for meaning: An introduction to logotherapy.* New York: Simon and Schuster.

Frazer, J. G. (1909). *Psyche's task: A discourse concerning the influence of superstition on the growth of institutions.* London: Macmillan.

Frazer, J. G. (1911–1915). *The golden bough: A study in magic and religion, 12 vols.* (3rd ed.). London: Macmillan.

Freedman, S. A., Hoffman, H. G., Garcia-Palacios, A., Weiss, P. L., Avitzour, S., & Josman, N. (2010). Prolonged exposure and virtual reality–enhanced imaginal exposure for PTSD following a terrorist bulldozer attack: A case study. *Cyberpsychology, Behavior, and Social Networking, 13*(1), 95–101.

Fremantle, F., & Trungpa, C. (Trans.). (1992). *The Tibetan book of the dead: The great liberation through hearing in the bardo by Guru Rinpoche according to Karma-Lingpa.* Boston: Shambhala.

Freud, S. (1913/1959). Thoughts for the times on war and death. In *Collected works, 4,* 288–317. London: Hogarth.

Freud, S. (1917/1959a). *Collected papers.* London: Hogarth.

Freud, S. (1917/1959b). Mourning and melancholia. In *Collected papers, 4,* 152–172. London: Hogarth.

Freud, S. (1918/1952). Totem and taboo: Resemblances between the psychic life of savages and neurotics. A. A. Brill (trans.). New York: Moffat Yard & Co. Paperback edition. New York: Vintage Books.

Fulton, R. (1997). Death, society, and the quest for immortality. In S. Strack (Ed.), *Death and the quest for meaning: Essays in honor of Herman Feifel.* Northvale, NJ: Jason Aronson.

Fulton, R., & Owen, G. (1988). Death and society in the twentieth century. *Omega, 18*(4): 379–394.

Funeral Consumer's Alliance (FCA). (2009). Testimony on behalf of Funeral Consumer's Alliance, Inc. before the House Committee on Energy and Commerce, Subcommittee on Consumer Protection. July 27, 2009. Available: *www.funerals.org/newsandalerts/consumer-alerts/1099-hr900bereavedconsumersact.*

Funeral Consumer's Alliance (FCA). (2010). Testimony on behalf of Funeral Consumer's Alliance, Inc. before the House Committee on Energy and Commerce, Subcommittee on Consumer Protection, re: HR 3655. January 27, 2010. Available: *www.funerals.org/newsandalerts/consumer-alerts/1099-hr900bereavedconsumersact.*

Funeral Consumer's Alliance (FCA). (2011a). Available: *www.funerals.org.*

Funeral Consumer's Alliance (FCA). (2011b). Retrieved September 6, 2011, from *www.funerals.org/faq/198-preneedpitfalls.*

Funeral Consumer's Alliance of Connecticut (FCA-CT). (2004). Simple and cheap my father said. Available: *www.funerals.org/faq/judge.htm.*

Gabbard, G. O., & Twemlow, S. W. (1991). Do "near-death experiences" occur only near-death?—Revisited. *Journal of Near-Death Studies, 10*(1), 41–48.

Gabbard, G. O., & Twemlow, S. W., & Jones, F. C. (1981). Do "near-death experiences" occur only near-death? *Journal of Nervous and Mental Disorders, 169*(6), 374–377.

Ganzini, L., Goy, E. R., Miller, L. L., Harvath, T., Jackson, A., & Delorit, M. A. (2003). Nurses' experiences with hospice patients who refuse food and fluids to hasten death. *New England Journal of Medicine, 349*(4), 359–365.

Ganzini, L., Johnston, W. S., McFarland, B. H., Tolle, S. W., & Lee, M. A. (1998). Attitudes of patients with amyotrophic lateral sclerosis and their care givers toward assisted suicide. *New England Journal of Medicine, 333*(14), 967–973.

Geertz, C. (1973). *The interpretation of cultures.* New York: Basic Books.

Getzel, G. S. (1995). Judaism and death: Practice Implications. In J. K. Parry & Ryan, A. S. (Eds.), *A cross-cultural look at death, dying, and religion* (pp. 18–31). Chicago: Nelson-Hall.

Gianakos, D. (1995). Terminal weaning. *Chest, 108*(5), 1405–1406.

Gilligan, T., & Raffin, T. A. (1995). Rapid withdrawal of support. *Chest, 108*(5), 1407–1408.

Gillis, C. L., Moore, I. M., & Martinson, I. M. (1997). Measuring parental grief after childhood cancer. Potential use of the scl-90r. *Death Studies, 21,* 277–287.

Gillman, N. (2000). *The death of death: Resurrection and immortality in Jewish thought.* Woodstock, VT: Jewish Lights Publishing.

Gillon, R. (1994). Medical ethics: Four principles plus attention to scope. *British Medical Journal, 309,* 184–188.

Gillon, R. (2003). Four scenarios. *Journal of Medical Ethics, 29,* 267–268.

Gillon, R., & Lloyd, A. (Eds.). (1994). *Principles of health care ethics.* Chicester: Wiley.

Ginzburg, K., Geron, Y., & Solomon, Z. (2002). Patterns of complicated grief among bereaved parents. *Omega, 45,* 119–132.

Gitlin, T. (1993). *The sixties: Years of hope, days of rage.* New York: Bantam.

Glaser, B. G., & Strauss, A. L. (1965). *Awareness of dying.* Chicago: Aldine.

Glaser B. G., & Strauss A. L. (1967). *Discovery of grounded theory: Strategies for qualitative research.* Mill Valley, CA: Sociology Press.

Glaser, B. G., & Strauss, A. L. (1968). *Time for dying.* Chicago: Aldine.

Glesne, C. (1999). *Becoming qualitative researchers: An introduction* (2nd ed.). New York: Longman.

Goffman, I. (1959). *Presentation of self in everyday life.* Garden City, NY: Anchor.

Goldberg, V. (1998). Death takes a holiday, sort of. In J. Goldstein (Ed.), *Why we watch: The attractions of violent entertainment.* New York: Oxford University Press.

Goldstein, W. S. (2009). Secularization patterns in the old paradigm. *Sociology of Religion, 70*(2), 157–178.

Goodman, A. M. (2003). *A plain pine box: A return to simple Jewish funerals and eternal traditions.* Jersey City, NJ: KTAV Publishing.

Gordinier, J. (2009). *X saves the world: How Generation X got the shaft but can still keep everything from sucking.* New York: Penguin.

Gorman, E. M., Nelson, K. R., & Applegate, T. (2003). Club drug and poly-substance abuse and HIV among gay/bisexual men: Lessons gleaned from a community study. *Journal of Gay & Lesbian Social Services, 17,* 1–17.

Goss, R. E., & Klass, D. (1997). Tibetan Buddhism and the resolution of grief: The Bardo-Thodol for the dying and the grieving. *Death Studies, 21,* 277–395.

Grassie, W. (1997, March). Postmodernism: What one needs to know. *Zygon: Journal of Religion and Science.*

Gray, M., Prigersson, H., & Litz, B. (2004). Conceptual and definitional issues in complicated grief. In B. Litz (Ed.), *Early intervention for trauma and traumatic loss* (pp. 65–84). New York: Guilford.

Green, B., Krupnick, J., Stockton, P., Goodman, L., Corcoran, C., & Petty, R. (2001). Psychological outcomes associated with traumatic loss in a sample of young women. *American Behavioral Scientist, 44,* 817–837.

Greenberg, J., Arndt, J., Simon, L., Pyszczynski, T., & Solomon, S. (2000). Proximal and distal defenses in response to reminders of one's mortality: Evidence of a temporal sequence. *Personality and Social Psychology Bulletin, 26,* 91–99.

Greenberg, J., Pyszczynski, T., & Solomon, S. (1986). The causes and consequences of a need for self-esteem: A terror management theory. In R. F. Baumeister (Ed.), *Public self and private self* (pp. 189–212). New York: Springer-Verlag.

Greenberg, J., Pyszczynski, T., Solomon, S., Pinel, E., Simon, L., & Jordan, K. (1993). Effect of self-esteem on vulnerability-denying defensive distortions: Further evidence of an anxiety-buffering function of self-esteem. *Journal of Experimental Social Psychology, 29,* 229–251.

Greenberg, J., Simon, L., Pyszczynski, T., Solomon, S., Rosenblat, A., Burling, J., Lyon, D., et al. (1992). Assessing the terror management analysis of self-esteem: Converging evidence of an anxiety-buffering function. *Journal of Personality and Social Psychology, 63,* 913–922.

Greenleigh, J., & Beimler, R. R. (1998). *The days of the dead: Mexico's festival of communion with the departed.* San Francisco: Pomegranate.

Griffiths, B., & Edwards, F. (Eds.). (1989). *A new vision of reality: Western science, Eastern mysticism, and Christian faith.* Springfield, IL: Templegate Publishers.

Greyson, B. (1981). Near-death experiences and attempted suicide. *Suicide and Life Threatening Behavior, 11*(1), 10–16.

Greyson, B. (1983). Near-death experiences and personal values. *American Journal of Psychiatry, 140*(5), 618–620.

Greyson, B. (1986). Incidence of near-death experiences allowing attempted suicide. *Suicide and Life Threatening Behavior, 16*(1), 40–45.

Greyson, B. (2000). Resasons for living versus reasons for dying. *Suicide and Life Threatening Behavior, 30*(2), 179–180.

Greyson, B. (2003). Incidence and correlates of near-death experiences in a cardiac care unit. *General Hospital Psychiatry, 25*(4), 269–276.

Greyson, B., & Bush, N. E. (1992). Distressing near-death experiences. *Psychiatry, 55*(1), 95–110.

Greyson, B., & Bush, N. E. (1996). Distressing near-death experiences. In L. W. Bailey & J. Yates (Eds.), *The near-death experience: A reader.* New York: Routledge.

Grosso, M. (1991). The myth of the near-death journey. *Journal of Near-Death Studies, 10*(1), 49–60.

Groves, R., & Klauser, H. A. (2005). *The American book of dying: Lessons of healing spiritual pain.* Berkeley, CA: Celestial Arts.

Guh, D. P., Wei, Z., Bansback, N., Amarsi, Z., Birmingham, C. L., & Anis, A. H. (2009). The incidence of co-morbidities related to obesity and overweight: A systematic review and meta-analysis. *BMC Public Health, 9,* 1–20.

Gustaitis, J. (2002, December). *Special feature: Frontiers of heart medicine. The World Almanac E-Newsletter.* Available: *www.worldalmanac.com/200212WAE-Newsletter.html.*

Gyatso, T., 14th Dalai Lama. (1996). *The good heart: A Buddhist perspective on the teachings of Jesus.* Boston: Wisdom Publications.

Gyatso, T., 14th Dalai Lama. (1999). *Ethics for the new millennium.* New York: Riverhead Books.

Gyatso, T., 14th Dalai Lama. (2001). Personal interview, December 12, 2001.

Gyatso, T., 14th Dalai Lama. (2002). *Advice on dying: And living a better life.* New York: Atria Books.

Hall, H. I., Hughes, D., Dean, H. D., Mermin, J. H., & Fenton, K. A. (2011, January 14). HIV infection—United States, 2005 and 2009. *Morbidity and Mortality Weekly Report,* Supplement 60, 87–89. Washington, DC: Centers for Disease Control and Prevention.

Hamama-Raz, Y., Solomon, Z., & Ohry, A. (2000). Fear of personal death among physicians. *Omega, 41*(2), 139–149.

Harmer, R. M. (1963). *The high cost of dying.* New York: Collier.

Hasemyer, D., & Cantlupe, J. (1995, March 10). Three boys barely old enough to shave are accused of killing a man over two large pizzas, exemplifying the source of juvenile violence. *San Diego Union-Tribune News.* Retrieved from *http://nl.newsbank.com/nl-search/we/Archives.*

Haskins, C. H. (1972). *The rise of universities.* Ithaca, NY: Cornell University Press.

Hayek, C. (2003). Personal interview, August 27, 2003.

Hayes, R. P., Stoudemire, A. S., Kinlaw, K., Dell, M. L., & Loomis, A. (1999). Changing attitudes about end-of-life decision making of medical students during third-year clinical clerkships. *Psychosomatics, 40*(3), 205–211.

Hedberg, K., & Southwick, K. (2002). Legalized physician-assisted suicide in Oregon, 2001. *New England Journal of Medicine, 346*(6), 450–452.

Hedberg, K., Hopkins, D., & Kohn, M. (2003). Five years of legal physician-assisted suicide in Oregon. *New England Journal of Medicine, 348*(10), 961–964.

Hellerstein, D. (1983, August/September). Overdosing on medical technology. *Technology Review,* 13–17.

Henderson, J. M., Hayslip, B., & King, J. K. (2004). The relationship between adjustment and bereavement-related distress: A longitudinal study (research). *Journal of Mental Health Counseling, 26*(2), 98–124.

Henig, N. R., Faul, J. L., & Raffin, T. A. (2001). Biomedical ethics and the withdrawal of advanced life support. *Annual Review of Medicine, 52,* 79–92.

Henslin, J. M. (2001). *Sociology: A down-to-earth approach* (5th ed.). Boston: Allyn & Bacon.

Henslin, J. M. (2005). *Sociology: A down-to-earth approach* (8th ed.). Boston: Allyn & Bacon.

Hetzer, R. (1994). The present state of heart transplantation. *Forensic Science International, 69*(3), 251–257.

Hewa, S. (1994). Medical technology: A Pandora's Box? *Journal of Medical Humanities, 15*(3), 171–181.

Himmelstein, D. U., Thorne, D., Warren, E., & Woolhandler, S. (2007). Medical bankruptcy in the United States, 2007: Results of a national study. *American Journal of Medicine, 122*(8), 741–746.

Himmelstein, D. U., Warren, E., Thorne, D., & Woolhandler, S. (2005, January–June). Illness and injury as contributors to bankruptcy. *Health Affairs, Web Exclusives,* W5-63–W5-73.

Hockey, J. (2007). Closing in on death? Reflections of research and researchers in the field of death and dying. *Health Sociology Review, 16*(5), 436–446.

Holden, J. M. & Joesten, L. (1990). Near-death veridicality research in the hospital setting: Problems and promise. *Journal of Near-Death Studies, 9*(1), 45–54.

Holen-Hoeksema, S., & Larson, J. (1999). *Coping with loss.* Mahwah, NJ: Erlbaum.

Holland, J. M., & Neimeyer, R. A. (2011). Separation and traumatic distress in prolonged grief: The role of cause of death and relationship to the deceased. *Journal of Psychopathology & Behavioral Assessment, 33*(2), 254–263.

Home Box Office (HBO). (2013). About the show. Six feet under, HBO website. Available: ***www.hbo.com/ sixfeetunder***.

Horrowitz, M. J., Siegel, B., Holen, A., Bonanno, G. A., Milbrath, C., & Stinson, C. H. (1997). Diagnostic criteria for complicated grief disorder. *American Journal of Psychiatry, 154,* 904–910.

Hoyert, D. L., Arias, E., Smith, B. L., Murphy, S. L., & Kochanek, K. D. (2001). Deaths: Final data for 1999. *National Vital Statistics Reports, 49*(8). Hyattesville, MD: National Center for Health Statistics.

Hughes, J. J. (1995). *Brain death and technological change: Personal identity, neural prostheses and uploading.* Paper presented at the Second International Symposium on Brain Death. Available: ***www.change-surfer.com/Hlth/BD/Brain.html***.

Hughes, J. J. (2004). The death of death. *Advances in Experimental Medical Biology, 550,* 79–87.

Hummel, K. (2013, May 2). Staying safe after Boston bombings. *The Pioneer, 46*(12), 1. Published by Pierce College, Lakewood, WA.

Illich, I. (1975). *Medical nemesis.* New York: Pantheon Books.

Illich, I. (2002). *Limits to medicine: Medical nemesis.* New York: Marion Boyars.

Independent. (2008, December 10). *Mary Ewert: 'Why I want the world to see my husband die': As the final moments of a terminally ill man who committed suicide in a Zurich clinic are shown on television, his widow explains why.* Retrieved May 27, 2011, from ***www. independent.co.uk/life-style/health-and-families/ health-news/mary-ewert-why-i-want-the-world-to-see-my-husband-die-1059442.html***.

Ingles, T. (1980). St. Christopher's Hospice. In M. P. Hamilton and H. F. Reid (Eds.), *A hospice handbook.* Grand Rapids, MI: William B. Eerdmans Publishing.

Institute for the Advanced Study of Religion, University of Chicago. (2003). D. R. Sharpe Lectures, October 21–23, 2003: *Humanity before God—Contemporary faces of Jewish, Christian, and Islamic ethics.* Conference description. Available: ***http://sharpelectures.uchicago. edu/description.htm***.

Insurance Information Institute. (2011). Retrieved September 25, 2011, from ***www.iii.org/***.

International Association for Hospice and Palliative Care (IAHPC). (2004). Manual of palliative care. Available: ***www.hospicecare.com/manual/IAHPCmanual.htm***.

International Association for Near-Death Studies (IANDS). (2004). Available: *www.iands.org/distressing.html*.

International Commission on English in the Liturgy. (1990). *Order of Christian funerals: Complete text of the order approved for use in the United States of America.* Chicago: Liturgy Training Publications.

International Society for the Study of Dissociation (ISSD). [Chu, J. A., Loewenstein, R., Dell, P. F., Barach, P. M., Somer, E., Kluft, R. P., Gelinas, D. J., Van der Hart, O., Dalenberg, C. J., Nijenhuis, E. R. S., Bowman, E. S., Boon, S., Goodwin, J., Jacobson, M., Ross, C. A., Sar, V., Rine, C. G., Frankel, A. S., Coons, P. M., Courtois, C. A., Gold, S. N., & Howell, E. J.] (2005). Guidelines for treating dissociative identity disorder in adults. *Journal of Trauma & Dissociation, 6*(4), 69–149.

Iserson, K. (2001). *Death to dust: What happens to dead bodies.* Tucson, AZ: Galen Press.

Islam Online. (2003). The symbolism and related rites of the Ka'bah. Available: *www.islamonline.net/English/Introducingislam/Worship/Pilgrimage/article 02.shtml*.

Jackonen, S. (1997). Dehydration and hydration in the terminally ill: Care considerations. *Nursing Forum, 32*(3), 5–13.

Jackson, J. (2003). *SOS: A handbook for survivors of suicide.* Washington, DC: American Association of Suicidology.

Jacobs, S. C. (1993). Pathological grief: Maladaptation to loss. Washington, DC: American Psychiatric Press.

Jacobs, S., & Prigerson, H. (2000). Psychotherapy of traumatic grief: A review of evidence for psychotherapeutic treatments. *Death Studies, 24,* 479–495.

James, S. D. (2010). *Daughter hails Montana's right-to-die ruling.* ABC News/Health. Retrieved on May 28, 2011, from *http://abcnews.go.com/Health/doctor-assisted-suicide-approved-montana/story? id=9492923*.

Jamison, K. R. (2000). *Night falls fast: Understanding suicide.* New York: Vintage.

Jansen, K. L. (1990). Neuroscience and the near-death experience: Roles for the NMSA-PCP receptor, the sigma receptor and endopsychosins. *Medical Hypotheses, 31*(1), 25–29.

Jansen, K. L. (1991). Transcendental explanations and the near-death experience. *Lancet, 337,* 244.

Jansen, K. L. (1996a). Neuroscience, ketamine and the near-death experience: The role of glutamate and the NMDA receptor. In L. J. Bailey & J. Yates (Eds.), *The near-death experience: A reader* (pp. 265–282). New York: Routledge.

Jansen, K. L. (1996b). Using ketamine to induce the near-death experience: Mechanism of action and therapeutic potential. In C. Ratch & J. R. Baker (Eds.), *Yearbook for ethnomedicine and the study of consciousness* (pp. 55–81). Berlin: VWB.

Jansen, K. L. (1997). The ketamine model of the near-death experience: A central role for the N-methyl-D-aspartate receptor. *Journal of Near-Death Studies, 16,* 5–26.

Jarret, B. (1999). Pilgrimages. In K. Knight (Ed.), *The Catholic Encyclopedia,* v. 12 (online edition). Available: *www.newadvent.org/cathen/12085a.htm*.

Jennings, B., Ryndes, T., D'Onofrio, C., & Baily, M. A. (2003). Access to hospice care: Expanding boundaries, overcoming barriers. *Hastings Center Report Special Supplement, 33*(2), S3–S59.

Jevne, R. F., & Nekolaichuk, C. L. (2003). Threat and hope in coping with cancer for health care professionals. In R. Jacoby & G. Gleinan (Eds.), *Between stress and hope: From disease-centered to a health-centered perspective.* Santa Barbara, CA: Praeger (ABC-CLIO).

Jitatmananda, S. (2002). Personal interview, January 1, 2002.

Johnson, C. J., & McGee, M. G. (Eds.). (1998). *How different religions view death and afterlife* (2nd ed.). Philadelphia: Charles Press.

Johnson, K. (2009a, August 31). Montana court to rule on assisted suicide case. *The New York Times.* Retrieved on May 28, 2011, from *www.nytimes.com/2009/09/01/us/01montana.html*.

Johnson, K. (2009b, December 31). Montana ruling bolsters doctor-assisted suicide. *The New York Times.* Retrieved on May 28, 2011, from *www.nytimes.com/2010/01/01/us/01suicide.html*.

Johnson, T. F. (1995). Aging well in contemporary society: Introduction. *American Behavioral Scientist, 39*(2), 120–130.

Joint Commission on the Accreditation of Healthcare Organization (JCAHO). (2004). *Pain monograph.* Available: *www. jcaho.org/standard/pm*.

Jonquiere, J. (2001). Personal interview, December 3, 2001.

Jordan, J. R., & Neimeyer, R. A. (2003). Does grief counseling work? *Death Studies, 27,* 765–786.

Jotkowitz, A., Glick, S., & Gesundheit, B. (2008) A case against justified non-voluntary active euthanasia (the Groningen Protocol). *The American Journal of Bioethics, 8*(11), 23–26.

Joyce, J. (1939). *Finnegan's wake.* New York: Viking.

Jung, C., & Reed, H. (Ed.). (1981). Archetypes of the collective unconscious. In C. Jung (Ed.), *Collected works of C. G. Jung,* Vol. 9, Part 1. Princeton, NJ: Princeton University Press.

Kalat, J. W. (2002). *Introduction to psychology* (6th ed.). Belmont, CA: Wadsworth.

Kalff, D. M. (1980). *Sandplay.* Boston: Sigo Press.

Kaplan, H. I., Sadock, B. J., & Grebb, J. A. (1994). *Synopsis of psychiatry* (6th ed.). Baltimore: Williams & Wilkins.

Kareem, A. (2001). Personal interviews, December 15–16, 2001.

Kariyawasam, A. G. S. (1995). *Buddhist ceremonies and rituals of Sri Lanka.* Kandy, Sri Lanka: Buddhist Publication Society.

Kaplow, J. B., Layne, C. M., Pynoos, R. S., Cohen, J. A., & Lieberman, A. (2012). *DSM-V* diagnostic criteria for bereavement in children and adolescents: Developmental considerations. *Psychiatry: Interpersonal I Biological Processes, 75*(3), 243–266.

Karpov, V. (2012). Descularization: A conceptual framework. *Journal of Church and State, 52*(2), 232–270.

Kastenbaum R. (1972). On the future of death: Some images and options. *Omega, 3,* 306–318.

Kastenbaum, R. (1982). New fantasies in the American death system. *Death Education, 6*(2), 155–166.

Kastenbaum R. (1986). *Death, society, and human experience* (3rd ed.). Boston: Longman.

Kastenbaum, R. (1987–1988). Theory, research, and application: Some critical issues for thanatology. *Omega, 18*(4), 397–410.

Kastenbaum, R. (1993). Reconstructing death in postmodern society. *Omega, 27*(1), 75–89.

Kastenbaum, R. (1995). Reconstructing death in a postmodern society. In L. E. DeSpelder & A. L. Strickland (Eds.), *Readings in death and dying: The path ahead.* Mountain View, CA: Mayfield.

Kastenbaum, R. (1997). What is the future of death? In S. Strack (Ed.), *Death and the quest for meaning: Essays in honor of Herman Feifel.* Northvale, NJ: Jason Aronson.

Kastenbaum, R. (1998). *Death, society, and human experience* (6th ed.). Boston: Allyn & Bacon.

Kastenbaum, R. (2001). *Death, society, and human experience* (7th ed.). Boston: Allyn & Bacon.

Kastenbaum, R. (2003). *Death, society, and human experience* (8th ed.). Boston: Allyn & Bacon.

Kastenbaum, R. (2006). *Death, society, and human experience* (9th ed.). Boston: Allyn & Bacon.

Kastenbaum, R. (2008). *Death, society, and human experience* (10th ed.). Boston: Allyn & Bacon.

Kato, P. M., & Mann, T. (1999). A synthesis of psychological interventions for the bereaved. *Clinical Psychology Review, 19,* 275–296.

Kearl, M. (1989). *Endings: A sociology of death and dying.* New York: Oxford University Press.

Kearl, M. (1996). Dying well: The unspoken dimension of aging well. *American Behavioral Scientist, 39*(3), 336–360.

Kearl, M. (2002). *Death and medicine. Kearl's guide to the sociology of death.* Available: ***www.trinity.edu/mkearl/deathmed.html***.

Keenan, J. F. (1993). The function of the principle of double effect. *Theological Studies, 54*(2), 294–316.

Kellehear, A. (1996). *Experiences near death: Beyond medicine and religion.* New York: Oxford University Press.

Kellner, D. (1990). Postmodern turn: Positions, problems, and prospects. In G. Ritzer (Ed.), *Frontiers of social theory: The new syntheses* (pp. 255–286). New York: Columbia University Press.

Kellner, D. (1999). Postmodern turn: Positions, problems, and prospects. In G. Ritzer (Ed.), *Frontiers of social theory: The new syntheses* (pp. 255–286). New York: Columbia University Press.

Kelly, E. W. (2001). Near-death experiences with reports of meeting deceased people. *Death Studies, 25,* 229–249.

Kelly, E. W., Greyson, B., & Stephenson, I. (2000). Can experiences near death furnish evidence of life after death? *Omega, 40,* 513–519.

Kemp, A. R. (1998). Abuse in the family: An introduction. Florence, KY: Brooks/Cole (Cengage Learning, Inc.).

Kemp, A. R. (2001). A time to mourn: *Qualitative research on the experience of parents who have had a child die.* Unpublished research report, St. Stephen's College, Edmonton.

Kendall, D. (1980). *Square pegs in round holes: Non-traditional students in medical schools.* Unpublished doctoral dissertation, Department of Sociology, The University of Texas at Austin.

Kendall, D. (2005). *Sociology in our times.* Belmont, CA: Wadsworth.

Kendall, D. (2009). *Sociology in our times: The essentials* (7th ed.). Belmont, CA: Wadsworth.

Kendall, D. (2010). *Sociology in our times* (8th ed.). Belmont, CA: Wadsworth.

Kenyon, B. L. (2001). Current research in children's conceptions of death: A critical review. *Omega, 43*(1), 63–91.

Kerridge, I. H., Saul, P., Lowe, M,, McPhee, J., & Williams, D. (2002). Death, dying and donation: Organ transplantation and the diagnosis of death. *Journal of Medical Ethics, 28,* 89–94.

Khan, M. (2000). Re-imagining Jerusalem: One faith, one city. Available: ***www.themodernreligion.com/jihad/jeru-onecity.html.***

Killen, P. O., & De Beer, J. (1999). *The art of theological reflection.* New York: Crossroad.

Kingsbury, A. (2010, July 16). Gangs in the U.S. *CQ Researcher, 20*(25), 581–604. Retrieved from ***http://library.cqpress.com/cqresearcher/.***

Kinnier, R. T., Tribbensee, N. E., Rose, C. A., & Vaughan, S. M. (2001). In the final analysis: More wisdom from people who have faced death. *Journal of Counseling & Development, 79,* 171–177.

Klass, D. (1988). *Parental grief: Resolution and solace.* New York: Springer.

Klass, D. (1993). Solace and immortality: Bereaved parents' continuing bonds with their children. *Death Studies, 17,* 343–368.

Klass, D. (1996). Ancestor worship in Japan: Dependence and the resolution of grief. *Omega, Journal of Death and Dying, 34*(1), 1–14.

Klass, D. (1997). The deceased child in the psychic and social worlds of bereaved parents during the resolution of grief. *Death Studies, 21*(2), 147–175.

Klass, D., & Goss, R. (1999). Spiritual bonds to the dead in cross-cultural and historical perspective: Comparative religion and modern grief. *Death Studies, 23*(6), 547–567.

Klass, D., & Goss, R. (2002a). Politics, religions, and grief: The cases of American spiritualism and the Deuteronomic reform in Israel. *Death Studies, 26*(9), 709–729.

Klass, D., & Goss, R. (2002b). The politics of grief and continuing bonds with the dead: The cases of Maoist China and Wahhabi Islam. *Death Studies, 27*(9), 787–811.

Klass, D., & Goss, R. (2003). Politics, religions, and grief: The cases of American spiritualism and the Deuteronomic reform in Israel. *Death Studies, 26*(9), 709–729.

Klass, D., Silverman, P. R., & Nickman, S. L. (1996). *Continuing bonds: New understandings of grief.* Philadelphia: Taylor and Francis.

Klass, D., & Walter, T. (2001). *Processes of grieving: How bonds are continued.* In M. S. Stroebe, R. D. Hanson, W. Stroebe, & H. Schut (Eds.), *Handbook of bereavement research: consequences, coping, and care* (pp. 431–448). Washington, DC: American Psychological Association.

Kobak, R. (2002). The emotional dynamics of disruptions in attachment relationships: Implications for theory, research, and clinical intervention. In J. Cassidy & P. Shaver (Eds.), *Handbook of attachment: Theory, research, and clinical applications* (pp. 21–43). New York: Guilford.

Koehler, K. (2010). Helping families help bereaved children. In C. A. Corr & D. E. Balk (Eds.), *Children's encounters with death, bereavement, and coping.* New York: Springer.

Konefes, J. L., & McGee, P. K. (1996). Old cemeteries, arsenic, and health safety. *Cultural Resource Management (National Park Service), 19*(10), 15–18.

Kotler, D. P. (2000). Cachexia. *Annals of Internal Medicine, 133,* 622–634.

Kozorovitskiy, Y., & Gould, E. (2003). Adult neurogenesis: A mechanism for brain repair? *Journal of Clinical Experimental Neuropsy, 25*(5), 721–732.

Krakauer, E. L., Penson, R. T., Truog, R. D., King, L. A., Chabner, B. A., & Lynch, T. J. (2000). Sedation for intractable distress of a dying patient: Acute palliative care and the principle of double effect. *The Oncologist, 5,* 53–62.

Krieger, B. P. (2000). Futile ventilator support: Clinical and ethical aspects of withdrawal. *Journal of Critical Care Medicine, 161*(5): 1450–1458.

Krous, H. F. (2010). Sudden unexpected death in infancy and the dilemma of defining the sudden infant death syndrome. *Current Pediatric Reviews, 6,* 5–12.

Kübler-Ross, E. (1969). On death and dying: *What the dying have to teach doctors, nurses, clergy and their own families.* New York: Collier.

Kübler-Ross, E. (2001). *On life after death.* Berkeley, CA: Celestial Arts.

Kuhn, T. (1962). *The structure of scientific revolution.* Chicago: University of Chicago Press.

Kupst, M. J. (1986). Death of a child from a serious illness. In T. Rando (Ed.), *Parental loss of a child.* Champaign, IL: Research Press.

Kurlick, T., Holiday, B. & Martinson, I. M. (Eds.). (1987). *The child and the family facing life-threatening illness* (pp. 120–125). Philadelphia: Lippincott.

Kurtz, E., & Ketcham, K. (1992). *The spirituality of imperfection.* New York: Bantam.

Kutner, L. (1969). The living will: A proposal. *Indiana Law Journal, 44*(1), 539–554.

Lamb, S. (1997, September). The making and unmaking of persons: Notes on aging and gender in North India. *Ethos, 25*(3), 279–302.

Lanser, P., & Gessell, S. (2001). Pain management: The fifth vital sign. *Healthcare Benchmarks, 8*(6), 68–70.

Last Acts. (1997). *Precepts of palliative care.* Washington, DC: Last Acts National Program Office.

Last Acts. (2003a). *On the road from theory to practice: Progressing toward seamless palliative care.* Washington, DC: Last Acts National Program Office.

Last Acts. (2003b). On the road from theory to practice: A resource guide to promising practices in palliative care near the end of life. Washington, DC: Last Acts National Program Office.

Lazar, N. M., Sheimie, S., Greiner, G. G., Robertson, G., & Singer, P. A. (1996). Bioethics for clinicians: Substitute decision-making. *Canadian Medical Association Journal, 155*(10), 1435–1437.

Lazar, N. M., Sheimie, S, Webster, G. C., & Dickens, B. M. (2001). Bioethics for clinicians: Brain death. *Canadian Medical Association Journal, 164*(6), 833–836.

Lazarus, R. S., & Folkman, S. (1984). *Stress, appraisal, and coping.* New York: Springer.

Lechner, F. J. (1997). The "New Paradigm" in the sociology of religion: Comment on Warner. *American Journal of Sociology, 103,* 182–192.

Lee, M. A., Nelson, H. D., Tilden, V. P., Ganzini, L., Schmidt, T. A., & Tolle, S. W. (1996). Legalizing assisted suicide—Views of physicians in Oregon. *New England Journal of Medicine, 334*(5), 310–315.

Lee, R. L. M. (2002). Modernity, death, and the self: Disenchantment of death and symbols of bereavement. *Illness, Crisis, & Loss, 10*(2), 91–107.

Leenaars, A. A. (1995). Suicide. In H. Wass & R. A. Neimeyer (Eds.), *Dying: facing the facts.* Washington, DC: Taylor and Francis.

Leenaars, A. A. (2010). Edwin S. Shneidman on suicide. *Suicidology Online, 1,* 5–18. Available: ***www.suicidology-online.com.***

Legacy.com. (2012). About Legacy.com. Retrieved on March 30, 2012, at ***www.legacy.com/NS/about/.***

Lenhart, A. (2012). *Teens, smartphones, and texting.* Pew Internet & American Life Project. Washington, DC: Pew Research Center. Retrieved on March 31, 2012, from ***www.pewinternet.org/~/media//Files/Reports/2012/PIP_Teens_Smartphones_and_Texting.pdf.***

Leppaniemi, A. K. (2004). Global trends in trauma. *Trauma, 6,* 193–203.

Lessa, W. A., & Vogt, E. Z. (1979). *Reader in comparative religion: An anthropological approach* (4th ed.). New York: Harper & Row.

Levickaité, R. (2010). Generations X, Y, Z: How social networks form the concept of the World Without Borders (The Case of Lithuania). *LIMES, 3*(2), 170–183.

Levy, J. A., & Gordon, A. (1987). Stress and burnout in the social world of hospice. *Hospice Journal, 3*(2/3), 29–51.

Levy, L. H., Martinkowski, K. S., & Derby, J. F. (1994). Differences in patterns of adaptation in conjugal bereavement: Their sources and potential significance. *Omega, 29*(1): 71–87.

Ley, D. C. H., & Corless, I. B. (1988). Spirituality and hospice care. *Death Studies, 12,* 101–110.

Leyn, R. (1976). Terminally ill children and their families. *Maternal Child-Rearing Journal, 5*(3), 179–188.

Lindemann, E. (1944). The symptomology and management of acute grief. *American Journal of Psychiatry, 101,* 141–148.

Lindemann, E., & Greer, I. M. (1972). A study of grief: Emotional responses to suicide. In A. C. Cain (Ed.), *Survivors of suicide* (pp. 63–69). Springfield, IL: Bannerstone House.

Lindsey, L. L., & Beach, S. (2002). *Sociology* (2nd ed.). Upper Saddle River, NJ: Prentice-Hall.

Lindstrom, T. C. (2002). It ain't necessarily so… Challenging mainstream thinking about bereavement. *Family Community Health, 25*(1), 11–21.

Lloyd, D. (2011, March 23). Five new facts about Generation Y. *Huffington Post.* Retrieved March 17, 2012, from *www.huffingtonpost.com/delia-lloyd/millennial-generation_b_836931.html*.

Lo, B., Dornbrand, L., Wolf, L. E., & Groman, M. (2002). The Wendland case—Withdrawing life support from incompetent patients who are not terminally ill. *New England Journal of Medicine, 346*(19), 1489–1493.

Lofland, L. H. (1978). *The craft of dying: The modern face of death.* Beverly Hills: Sage.

Logan, J. E., Smith, S. G., & Stevens, R. R. (2011, January 14). Homicides—United States, 1999–2007. *Morbidity and Mortality Weekly Report,* Supplement, 60, 67–70. Washington, DC: Centers for Disease Control and Prevention.

Lowenstein, E., & Wanzedr, S. H. (2002). The U.S. Attorney General's intrusion into medical practice. *New England Journal of Medicine, 346*(6), 447–448.

Luce, J. M., & Alpers, A. (2000). Legal aspects of withholding and withdrawing life support from critically ill patients in the United States and providing palliative care to them. *American Journal of Respiratory Critical Care Medicine, 162,* 2929–2032.

Ludden, J. (Interviewer). (2005, February 12). Interview: Dr. Thomas Frieden talks about a rare and drug-resistant strain of the AIDS virus detected in a New York patient. *Weekend Edition (NPR).*

Lynch, M. (2001a). Pain as the fifth vital sign. *Journal of Intravenous Nursing, 24*(2), 85–94.

Lynch, M. (2001b). Pain: The fifth vital sign: Comprehensive assessment leads to proper treatment. *Advanced Nurse Practitioner, 9*(11), 28–36.

Lynn, J., Harrell, Jr., F. E., Cohn, F., Hamel, M. B., Dawson, N., & Wu, A. (1996). Defining the "terminally ill": Insights from SUPPORT. *Duquesne Law Review, 35,* 311–336.

Lynn, J., Harrell, Jr., F. E., Cohn, F., Wagner, D., & Connors, Jr., A. F. (1997). Prognoses of seriously ill hospitalized patients on the days before death: Implications for patient care and public policy. *New Horizons, 5*(1), 56–61.

Lynn, J., Schuster, J. L., & Kabcenell, A. (2000). *Improving care for the end of life: A sourcebook for health care managers and clinicians.* New York: Oxford University Press.

Lyon, D. (2010). Being post-secular in the social sciences: Taylor's social imaginaries. *New Blackfriars, 91*(1036), 648–664.

Lyon, E. (2010). Examining Generation Z: Stats, demographics, segments, predictions. Retrieved on March 31, 2012, from *http://sparxoo.com/2010/02/23/examining-generation-z-stats-demographics-segments-predictions/*.

Lyotard, J. F. (1984). *The postmodern condition.* Minneapolis: University of Minnesota Press.

Machado, C. (2003). A definition of human death should not be related to organ transplants. *Journal of Medical Ethics, 29,* 201–202.

Macionis, J. J. (1999). *Sociology* (7th ed.). Upper Saddle River, NJ: Prentice-Hall.

Macionis, J. J. (2005). *Sociology* (11th ed.). Upper Saddle River, NJ: Prentice-Hall.

Maciejewski, P. K., Zhang, B., Block, S. D., & Prigerson, H. G. (2007). An empirical examination of the stage theory of grief. *JAMA, Journal of the American Medical Association, 297*(7), 716–723.

Mackenzie, D. A. (1907). *Egyptian myth and legend with historical narrative, notes on race problems, comparative beliefs, etc.* London: Gresham Publishing.

Malinowski, B. (1931). Culture. In E. R. A. Seligman & A. S. Johnson (Eds.), *Encyclopedia of the social sciences,* vol. IV, pp. 634–642.

Malone, M. M. (1982). Consciousness of dying and projective fantasy of young children with malignant disease. *Journal of Developmental and Behavioral Pediatrics, 3,* 55–60.

Malone, M. M. (1987). Consciousness of dying and projective fantasy of young children with malignant disease. In T. Kurlick, B. Holiday, & I. M. Martinson (Eds.), *The child and the family facing life-threatening illness* (pp. 165–174). Philadelphia: Lippincott.

Mancini, A. D., Prati, G., & Bonanno, G. A. (2011). Do shattered worldviews lead to complicated grief? Prospective and longitudinal analyses. *Journal of Social and Clinical Psychology, 30*(2), 184–215.

Mannix, K. A. (1999). Palliation of nausea and vomiting. In H. Feifel (Ed.), *New meanings of death* (pp. 489–499). New York: McGraw-Hill.

Martignoni, M. E., Kunze, P., & Friess, H. (2003). Cancer cachexia. *Molecular Cancer, 2*(1), 36–38.

Marone, R. (1997). *Death, mourning, and caring.* Pacific Grove, CA: Brooks/Cole.

Marotta, S. A. (2000). Best practices for counselors who treat posttraumatic stress disorder. *Journal of Counseling and Development, 78,* 492–495.

Marshall, V. W., & Levy, J. A. (1990). Aging and dying. In R. H. Binstock & L. K. George (Eds.), *Handbook of aging and the social sciences* (3rd ed., pp. 245–260). New York: Academic Press.

Martens, P. R. (1994). Near-death experiences in out-of-hospital cardiac arrest survivors: Meaningful phenomena or just fantasy of death. *Resuscitation, 27*(2), 171–175.

Marwit, S. J., & Klass, D. (1995). Grief and the role of the inner representation of the deceased. *Omega, 30,* 283–298.

Marx, K. (1843/1970). *Marx's critique of Hegel's philosophy of right.* A. Jolin & J. O'Malley (Eds.). Cambridge: Cambridge University Press.

Marx, K. (1867). *Capital: Critique of political economy.* Berlin: Verlag von Otto Meisner.

Masahiro, M. (2001). Reconsidering brain death: A lesson from Japan's fifteen years of experience. *The Hastings Center Report, 31*(4), 41–46.

Matthews, G. B. (1989). Children's conceptions of illness and death. In L. M. Kopelman & J. C. Moskop (Eds.), *Children and health care: Moral and social issues.* Boston: Kluwer.

Maxwell, J. S. (2002). *What is Chautauqua? The complete Chautauqua: A guide to what "Chautauqua" means in America.* Available: ***www.members.aol.com/ AlphaChautauquan/what.html***.

McClellen, D. (2011, June 4). Dr. Jack Kevorkian dies at 83; "Dr. Death" was advocate, practitioner of physician-assisted suicide. *Los Angeles Times.* Retrieved on June 3, 2011, from ***www.latimes.com/news/obituaries/la-me-jack-kevorkian-20110604,0,4504790.story***.

McCloskey, E. L. (1991). The spirit of the PSDA (Patient Self-Determination Act) (Practicing the PSDA). *The Hastings Center Report, 21*(5), S1–S16.

McCormick, R. A., & Veatch, R. (1980). The preservation of life and self-determination. *Theological Studies, 41*(2), 390–396.

McCourt, F. (1996). *Angela's ashes: A memoir.* New York: Touchstone, published by Simon & Schuster.

McCrindle, M., & Wolfinger, E. (2010a). Generations defined. *Ethos, 18*(1), 2–13.

McCrindle, M., & Wolfinger, E. (2010b). *The ABC of XYZ: Understanding the global generations.* Sydney, Australia: University of New South Wales Press.

McDannell, C., & Lang, B. (2001. *Heaven: A history* (2nd ed.). New Haven, CT: Yale University Press.

McIntosh, D. N., Silver, R. C., & Wortman, C. B. (1993). Religion's role in adjustment to a negative life event: Coping with the loss of a child. *Journal of Personality and Social Psychology, 65,* 812–821.

McIntosh, J. L. (2002). *U.S.A. Suicide: 2000 official final data.* Available: ***www.suicidology.org***.

McLay, R. N., McBrien, C., Wiederhold, M. D., & Wiederhold, B. K. (2010). Exposure therapy with and without virtual reality to treat PTSD while in the combat theater: A parallel case series. *Cyberpsychology, Behavior, and Social Networking, 13*(1), 37–42.

McManners, J. (Ed.). (1990). The Oxford history of Christianity. New York: Oxford University Press.

McMillan, A., Mentnech, R. M., Lubitz, J., McBean, A. M., & Russell, D. (1990). Trends and patterns in place of death for Medicare enrollees. *Health Care Financing Review, 12*(1), 1–7.

McQueen, M. (2010). *The new rules of engagement: A guide to understanding and connecting with Generation Y.* Columbus, OH: McGraw-Hill.

Mead, G. H. (1934/1962). *Mind, self, and society: From the standpoint of a social behaviorist.* Chicago: University of Chicago Press.

Meagher, D. K. (2007). Ethical and legal issues in traumatic death. In D. Balk, C. Wogrin, G. Thornton, & D. Meagher (Eds.), *Handbook of thanatology: The essential body of knowledge for the study of death, dying, and bereavement.* New York: Routledge/Taylor & Francis.

Meares, C. J. (1994). Terminal dehydration: A review. *American Journal of Hospice & Palliative Care, 11*(3), 10–14.

Med Health. (2011). *Amyotrophic lateral sclerosis: Lou Gehrig's disease, or ALS; Upper and lower motor neuron disease; Motor neuron disease.* Retrieved May 27, 2011. from *www.ncbi.nlm.nih.gov/pubmedhealth/PMH0001708/.*

Meier, D. E., Emmons, C., Wallenstein, S., Quill, T., Morrison, R. S., & Cassell, C. K. (1998). A national survey of physician-assisted suicide and euthanasia in the United States. *New England Journal of Medicine, 338*(17), 1193–1201.

Meisenberg, G. (2011). Secularization and desecularization in our time. *The Journal of Social, Political and Economic Studies, 36*(3), 318–359.

Memorial Ecosystems. (2011). Available: *www.memorialecosystems.com/.*

Mendoza, M. J. G. (2001). *Dia de muertos: The dead come to life in Mexican folk art.* Locally published paper. Oaxaca, Mexico: La Mano Magica, M. Alcala 203. Centro.

Metzger, B. M., & Coogan, M. D. (1993). The Oxford companion to the Bible. Oxford, England: Oxford University Press.

Metzger, B. M., & Murphy, R. E. (Eds.). (1994). *The Oxford annotated Bible with the Apocryphal/Deuterocanonical books.* New York: Oxford University Press.

Metzger, M., & Kaplan, K. O. (2001). *Transforming death in America: A state of the nation report.* Washington, DC: Partnership for Caring.

Middleton, W., Burnett, P., Raphael, B., & Martinek, N. (1996). The bereavement response: A cluster analysis. *British Journal of Psychiatry, 169,* 167–171.

Middleton, W., Moylan, A., Raphael, B., Burnett, P., & Martinek, N. (1993). An international perspective on bereavement related concepts. *Australian and New Zealand Journal of Psychiatry, 27,* 457–463.

Milakovich, M. (1994). *Rationing and ethical considerations (Medical resource allocation, part 2). Physician Executive.* Available: *www.highbeam.com.*

Miller, D. N., & Eckert, T. L. (2009). Youth suicide behavior: An introduction and overview. *School Psychology Review, 38*(2), 153–167.

Miller, J. P. (2000). *Education and the soul: Toward a spiritual curriculum.* Albany: State University of New York Press.

Miller, P. J., & Mike, P. B. (1995). The Medicare hospice benefit: Ten years of federal policy for the terminally ill. *Death Studies, 19,* 531–542.

Miller, T. S. (2011). *The Hippies and American values.* Knoxville: University of Tennessee Press.

Milo, E. M. (1997). Maternal responses to the life and death of a child with a developmental disability. *Death Studies, 21*(5), 443–476.

Minino, R. M., & Smith, B. L. (2001, October 9). Deaths: Preliminary data for 2000. *National Vital Statistics Reports, 49*(12). Hyattesville, MD: National Center for Health Statistics.

Mitford, J. (1963). *The American way of death.* New York: Simon & Schuster.

Mitford, J. (1998). *The American way of death—Revisited.* New York: Vintage.

Mohandas, A., & Chou, S. N. (1971). Brain death. A clinical and pathological study. *Journal of Neurosurgery, 35,* 211–218.

Monat, A., & Lazarus, R. S. (Eds.). (1991). Stress and coping: An anthology (3rd ed.). New York: Columbia University Press.

Monk, G. (1997a). How narrative therapy works. In G. Monk, J. Winslade, K. Crocket, & D. Eston (Eds.), *Narrative therapy in practice: The archaeology of hope.* San Francisco: Jossey-Bass.

Monk, G., Winslade, J., Crocket, K., & Eston, D. (Eds.). (1997). *Narrative therapy in practice: The archaeology of hope.* San Francisco: Jossey-Bass.

Moody, H. R. (1997). *The five stages of the soul: Charting the spiritual passages that shape our lives.* New York: Anchor.

Moody, R. (1975). *Life after life.* New York: Bantam.

Moon, M., & Boccuti, C. (2002). *Medicare and end-of-life care.* Washington, DC: Last Acts.

Moore, J., & Moore, C. (2010). Talking to children about death-related issues. In C. A. Corr & D. E. Balk (Eds.), *Children's encounters with death, bereavement, and coping.* New York: Springer.

Moore, T. (1997). *Re-enchantment of everyday life.* New York: Harper Perennial.

Moos, N. (1995). An integrative model of grief. *Death Studies, 19,* 337–364.

More, M. (1994, Fall). On becoming posthuman. *Free Inquiry.* Available: ***http://www.maxmore.com/becoming.htm***.

Morse, M. (1983). A near-death experience in a 7-year old child. *American Journal of Diseases of Children, 137*(10), 959–961.

Morse, M. (1994a). A near-death experience and death-related visions in children: Implications for the clinician. *Current Problems in Pediatrics, 24*(2), 55–83.

Morse, M. (1994b). Near-death experiences of children. *Journal of Pediatric Oncology Nursing, 11*(4), 136–144.

Morse, M. (1995). *Transformed by the light.* New York: Random House.

Morse, M., Castillo, P., Venecia, D., & Tyler, D. C. (1986). Childhood near-death experiences. *American Journal of Diseases of Children, 140*(11), 1110–1114.

Morse, M., Conner, D., & Tyler, D. (1985). Near-death experiences in a pediatric population: A preliminary report. *American Journal of Diseases of Children, 139*(6), 595–600.

Moskop, J. C. (1999). The great futility debate of the 1990's: A brief review. *Ethics and Health Care, 2*(1), 1–3. Available:*www.ecu.edu/medhum/newsletter/spring1999_p2.htm*.

Moskop, J. C. (2000). Increasing the supply of transplant organs: Prospects and problems. *Ethics & Health Care, 3*(1), 1–3. Available: ***www.ecu.edu/medhum/newsletter/spring2000_p2.htm***.

Mount, B. M. (1976). The problem of caring for the dying in a general hospital: The palliative care unit as a possible solution. *Canadian Medical Association Journal, 115*(2), 119–121.

Moyers, J. D., & Moyers, B. (Exec. Eds.) (2000). *On our own terms: Moyers on Dying.* (Video). Educational Broadcasting Corporation/Public Affairs Television, Inc.

Murata, S., & Chittick, W. C. (1994). *The vision of Islam.* St. Paul, MN: Paragon.

Murdock, G. P. (1945). The common denominator of culture. In R. Linton (Ed.), *The science of man in the world crisis.* New York: Columbia University Press.

Museum of Funeral Customs. (2006). *Formaldehyde: Its development and history since 1906.* Available: ***www.greatriverroad.com/quincy/kibbemuseum.htm***.

Musgrave, C. F. (1990). Terminal dehydration: To give or not to give intravenous fluids? *Cancer Nursing, 13*(1), 62–66.

Nagy, M. A. (1948/1959). The child's theories concerning death. *Journal of Genetic Psychology, 73,* 3–27.

Names Project Foundation (NPF). (2005). *The AIDS memorial quilt: About the quilt.* Available: ***www.aidsquilt.org/about/htm***.

National Association for Home Care and Hospice (NAHC). (2002). *Hospice facts and statistics.* Updated November 2002. Available: ***www.nahc.org/consumer/hpcstats.html***.

National Cancer Institute (NCI). (2011). Cancer treatment. Retrieved May 21, 2011, from ***http://www.cancer.gov/cancertopics/treatment***.

National Center for Health Statistics. (2011). *Health, United States, 2010. With special feature on death and dying.* Hyattsville, MD: Author.

National Funeral Directors Association (NFDA). (2001). *General Price List Survey.* Complete GPL Report available from NFDA InfoCentral: ***http://www.nfda.org***.

National Funeral Directors Association (NFDA). (2003). *Federal Trade Commission (FTC) Funeral Rule compliance summary.* Available: ***www.nfda.org/page.php?plD=121***.

National Funeral Directors Association (NFDA). (2004). What happens dujring the cremation process. Available: ***www.nfda.org/page.php?plD=160#what***.

National Funeral Directors Association (NFDA). (2006a). *About NFDA.* Available: *www.nfda.org/missionhistorystructure.php.*

National Funeral Directors Association (NFDA). (2006b). *Code of professional conduct: Approved October 19, 2002.* Available: *www.nfda.org/missionhistorystructure.php.*

National Funeral Directors Association (NFDA). (2006c). *Code of professional conduct enforcement procedures.* Available: *www.nfda.org/missionhistorystructure.php.*

National Hospice and Palliative Care Organization (NHPCO). (2004a). History of hospice care. Available: *www.nhpco.org/i4a/pages/index.cfm?pageid=3285.*

National Hospice and Palliative Care Organization (NHPCO). (2004b). *What is hospice and palliative care?* Available: *www.nhpco.org/i4a/pages/index.cfm?pageid=3281.*

National Hospice and Palliative Care Organization (NHPCO). (2004c). *HHPCO facts and figures.* Alexandria, VA: Author.

National Hospice and Palliative Care Organization (NHPCO). (2010, September). *NHPCO Facts and Figures: Hospice Care in America.* Alexandria, VA: Author.

National Hospice and Palliative Care Organization (NHPCO). (2011). *Glossary of end of life terms.* Accessed September 23, 2011, from *www.caringinfo.org/files/public/ad/Appendix_A_Glossary.pdf.*

National Institute of Mental Health. (2010). *Suicide in the U.S.: Statistics and prevention.* Retrieved May 24, 2013 at *www.nimh.nih.gov/health/publications/suicide-in-the-us-statistics-and-prevention/index.shtml.*

National Pharmaceutical Council (NPC) and Joint Commission on the Accreditation of Healthcare Organizations (JCAHO). (2001). *Pain: Current understanding of assessment, management, and treatment.* Reston, VA: National Pharmaceutical Council.

Naumes, M. (2002). Personal conversation, October 1, 2002.

Neimeyer, R. A. (2000). Searching for the meaning of meaning: Grief therapy and the process of reconstruction. *Death Studies, 24,* 541–558.

Neimeyer, R. A. (Ed.) (2001). *Meaning reconstruction and the experience of loss.* Washington, DC: American Psychological Association.

Neimeyer, R. A. (2006). Complicated grief and the quest for meaning: A constructivist contribution. *Omega—Journal of Death and Dying, 52*(1), 37–52.

Neimeyer, R. A., Fontana, D. J., & Gold, K. (1984). A manual for content analysis of death constructs. In F. R. Epting & R. A. Neimeyer (Eds.), *Personal meanings of death.* Washington, DC: Hemisphere.

Neimeyer, R. A. & Fortner, B. (1997). Death attitudes in contemporary perspective. In S. Strack (Ed.), *Death and the quest for meaning: Essays in honor of Herman Feifel.* Northvale, NJ: Jason Aronson.

Neria, Y., & Litz, B. T. (2004). Bereavement by traumatic means: The complex synergy of trauma and grief. *Journal of Loss and Trauma, 9,* 73–87.

Netherlands Ministry of Foreign Affairs. (2001). *Q & A euthanasia: A guide to the Dutch Termination of Life on Request and Assisted Suicide (Review Procedures) Act.* The Haag, Netherlands: Author. Available: *www.minbuza.nl.*

Netherlands Ministry of Foreign Affairs. (2004). *Termination of Life on Request and Assisted Suicide (Review Procedures) Act.* Available: *http://www.minbuza.nl.*

New Dimensions Chicago. (2012). Retrieved January 28, 2012, from *http://bishoppearson.com/.*

New York Voice. (2004, April 28). Health commissioner warns NY's about crystal methamphetamine use, the increased risk it poses for new HIV/AIDS infections. Available: *www.highbeam.com.*

Nichols, J. A. (1986). Newborn death. In T. A. Rando (Ed.), *Parental loss of a child.* Champaign, IL: Research Press.

Nietzche, F. (1882/2008). *The gay science.* New York: Barnes and Noble Library of Essential Reading.

Nightmare, M. (1997). *Pagan book of living and dying.* San Francisco: Harper Collins.

Nordquist, G. (1999, Spring/Summer). American health care and the medicalization of dying. *Journal of Applied Social Sciences, 23*(2), 31–42.

Noyes, R., & Kletti, R. (1976a). Depersonalization in the face of life-threatening danger: A description. *Psychiatry, 39,* 19–27.

Noyes, R., & Kletti, R. (1976b). Depersonalization in the face of life-threatening danger: An interpretation. *Omega, 7*(2), 103–114.

Noyes, R., & Kletti, R. (1977). Panoramic memory: A response to the threat of death. *Omega, 8*(3), 181–194.

Nuland, S. (1994). *How we die.* New York: Knopf.

Nuland, S. (1997). Heroes of medicine. *Time.* (Fall special edition): 6–10.

Nuland, S. (2000). *The way we die.* New York: Random House.

Oaklander, V. (1988). Windows to our children. Gouldsboro, ME: The Gestalt Journal Press.

Oden, T. C. (1992). *Two worlds: Notes on the death of modernity in America and Russia.* Downers Grove, IL: InterVarsity Press.

O'Donnel, M. (1996). *HIV/AIDS: Loss, grief, challenge, and hope.* Washington, DC: Taylor & Francis.

O'Halloran, C. M., & Altmaier, E. M. (1996). Awareness of death among children: Does a life-threatening illness alter the process of discovery? *Journal of Counseling & Development, 74,* 259–262.

Okholm, D. L. (1999, July/August). I don't think we're in Kansas anymore, Toto! Postmodernism in our everyday lives. *Theology Matters 5*(4).

Olbricht, T. H. (1998). The Churches of Christ. In C. J. Johnson & M. G. McGee (Eds.), *How different religions view death and afterlife* (2nd ed., pp. 76–89). Philadelphia: Charles Press.

Oliver, D. (1984). Terminal dehydration. *Lancet, 2*(8403), 631.

Oliver, L. (1999). Effects of a child's death on the marital relationship: A review. *Omega, 39*(3), 197–227.

O'Mahony, S., McHugh, M., Zallman, L., & Selwyn, P. (2003). Ventilator withdrawal: Procedures and outcomes. Report of a collaboration between a critical care division and a palliative care service. *Journal of Pain Symptom Management, 26*(4), 954–961.

Onions, C. T., Friedrichsen, C. W. S., & Burchfield, R. W. (Eds.). (1966). *The Oxford Dictionary of English Etymology.* New York: Oxford University Press.

Ontario Consultants on Religious Tolerance (OCRT). (2004). *Teachings in the Hebrew scriptures about the afterlife.* Available: *www.religioustolerance.org/aft_bibll.htm*.

Open Society Institute (OSI). (2004). *Transforming the culture of dying: The project on death in America, October 1994 to December 2003.* New York: Open Society Institute. Available: *www.soros.org/initiatives/pdia*.

Oregon Public Health Division. (2011). Oregon's Death with Dignity Act—2010. Retrieved on May 28, 2011, from Oregon Health Authority website *http://public.health.oregon.gov/Pages/Home.aspx*.

Orr, J. (2012). The Apostles' Creed, in *International Standard Bible Encyclopedia.* Retrieved January 28, 2012, from *www.reformed.org/documents/index.html?mainframe=http://www.reformed.org/documents/apostles_creed_orr.html*.

O'Rourke, K. (1989). Should nutrition and hydration be provided to permanently unconscious and other mentally disabled persons? *Issues in Law & Medicine, 5*(2), 181–196.

Paas, S. (2011). Post-Christian, post-Christendom, and post-modern Europe: Towards the interaction of missiology and the social sciences. *Mission Studies, 28,* 3–25.

Page, T. (1999). The attachment partnership as conceptual base for exploring the impact of child maltreatment. *Child & Adolescent Social Work Journal, 16*(6), 419–437.

Pallis, C. (1983). ABC of brain stem death. The arguments about the EEG. *British Medical Journal, 286,* 123–124.

Pallis, C. (1985). Diabetes insipidus with brain death. *Neurology, 35,* 1086–1087.

Palmer, G. (1993). *Death: The trip of a lifetime.* New York: HarperCollins.

Palmer, P. J. (1993). *To know as we are known: Education as a spiritual journey.* New York: Harper.

Palmer, P. J. (1998). *The courage to teach: Exploring the inner landscape of a teacher's life.* San Francisco: Jossey-Bass.

Pan, C. X., Morrison, R. S., Meier, D. E., Natale, D. K., Goldirsch, S. L., Kralovec, P., & Cassel, C. K. (2001). How prevalent are hospital-based palliative care programs? Status report and future directions. *Journal of Palliative Medicine, 4*(3), 315–324.

Papadatou, D. (1988). Adolescents dying from cancer. *Acta Oncologica, 27,* 937–839.

Papadatou, D. (1997). Training healthcare professionals in caring for dying children and grieving families. *Death Studies, 21,* 575–592.

Parkes, C. M. (1998a). Bereavement. In D. Doyle, G. W. C. Hanks, & N. MacDonald (Eds.), *Oxford textbook of palliative medicine* (2nd ed., pp. 995–1010). New York: Oxford University Press.

Parkes, C. M. (1998b). Coping with loss: Bereavement in adult life. *British Medical Journal, 316*, 856–859.

Parkes, C. M. (2001). *Bereavement: Studies of grief in adult life* (3rd ed.). New York: Routledge.

Parnia, S., & Fenwick, P. (2002). Near death experiences in cardiac arrest: Visions of a dying brain or visions of a new science of consciousness. *Resuscitation, 52*(1), 5–11.

Parnia, S., Waller, D. G., Yeates, R., & Fenwick, P. (2001). A qualitative and quantitative study of the incidence, features and aetiology of near death experiences in cardiac arrest survivors. *Resuscitation, 48*(2), 149–156.

Parry, J. K., & Ryan A. S. (1995). *A cross-cultural look at death, dying, and religion.* Chicago: Nelson-Hall.

Parsons, T. (1952). Sociology and social psychology. In H. N. Fairchild (Ed.), *Religious perspectives in college teaching* (pp. 286–305). New York: Ronald Press.

Parsons, T. (1963). Death in American society: A brief working paper. *American Behavioral Scientist, 6*, 61–65.

Patten, S. B., Gatz, Y. K., Jones, B., & Thomas, D. L. (1989). Posttraumatic stress disorder and the treatment of sexual abuse. *Social Work, 34*(3), 197–203.

Pattison, E. M. (1977). *The experience of dying.* Englewood Cliffs, NJ: Prentice-Hall.

Pattison, E. M. (1978). The living-dying process. In C. A. Garfield (Ed.), *Psychosocial care of the dying patient* (pp. 133–168). New York: McGraw-Hill.

Pearson, A. M. (1998). Hinduism. In C. J. Johnson & M. G. McGee (Eds.), *How different religions view death and afterlife* (2nd ed., pp. 109–131). Philadelphia: Charles Press.

Pearson, C. (2007). *The gospel of inclusion.* Tulsa, OK: Council Oak Books.

Pellegrino, E. D. (1993). Ethics. *Journal of the American Medical Association, 270*, 202–203.

People's Memorial Society (PMS). (2011). Sample cemetery cost calculation. Available: *www.peoplesmemorial.org*.

Persig, R. (1974). *Zen and the art of motorcycle maintenance: An inquiry into values.* New York: Bantam.

Persinger, M. A. (1983). Religious and mystical experiences as artifacts of temporal lobe function: A general hypothesis. *Perceptual and Motor Skills, 57*(3 pt 2), 1255–1262.

Persinger, M. A. (1984a). People who report religious experiences may also display enhanced temporal lobe signs. *Perceptual and Motor Skills, 58*(3), 963–975.

Persinger, M. A. (1984b). Propensity to report paranormal experiences is correlated with temporal lobe signs. *Perceptual and Motor Skills, 59*(2), 583–586.

Pew Research Center. (2007). *How young people view their lives, futures, and politics: A portrait of "Generaton Next."* Washington, DC: Author.

Pfefferbaum, B., Call, J., Lensgraf, S., Miller, P., Flynn, B., Doughty, D., et al. (2001). Traumatic grief in a convenience sample of victims seeking support services after a terrorist incident. *Annals of Clinical Psychiatry, 13*, 19–24.

Phipps, W. E. (1988). The origin of hospices/hospitals. *Death Studies, 12*(2), 91–99.

Piaget, J. (1937/1954). *The construction of reality in the child* (M. Cook, Trans.). New York: Basic Books.

Pickrell, J. (1989). "Tell me a story": Using life review in counseling the terminally ill. *Death Studies, 13*, 127–135.

Pike, J. (1967). *If this be heresy.* New York: Harper & Row.

Ponn, A. L. (1998). Judaism. In C. J. Johnson & M. G. McGee (Eds.), *How different religions view death and afterlife* (2nd ed., pp. 145–159). Philadelphia: Charles Press.

Prensky, M. (2006). Listen to the natives. *Educational Leadership, 63*(4), 8–13.

Prensky, M. (2008). Turning on the lights. *Educational Leadership, 65*(6), 40–45.

President's Commission for the Study of Ethical Problems in Medicine and Biomedical and Behavioral Research. (1981). Guidelines for the determination of death: Report of the medical consultants on the diagnosis of death. *Journal of the American Medical Association, 246*, 2184–2186.

Prigerson, H. G., Horowitz, M. J., Jacobs, S. C., Parkes C. M., Aslan, M., et al. (2009) Prolonged Grief Disorder:

Psychometric validation of criteria proposed for *DSM-V* and *ICD-11*. *PLOS Medicine 6*(8): e1000121. doi:10.1371/journal.pmed.1000121.

Prigerson, H. G., & Jacobs, S. C. (2001). Caring for bereaved patients: All the doctors just suddenly go. *Journal of the American Medical Association, 286*(11), 1369–1376.

Prigerson, H. G., & Maciejewski, P. K. (2006). A call for sound empirical testing and evaluation of criteria for complicated grief proposed for *DSM-V*. *Omega–Journal of Death and Dying, 52*(1), 9–19.

Prigerson, H. G., Shear, M. K., Jacobs, S. C., et al. (1999). Consensus criteria for traumatic grief: A rationale and preliminary empirical test. *British Journal of Psychiatry, 174,* 67–73.

Printz, L. A. (1988). Is withholding hydration a valid comfort measure in the terminally ill? *Geriatrics, 43*(11), 84–88.

Printz, L. A. (1992). Terminal dehydration: A compassionate treatment. *Archives of Internal Medicine, 152,* 697–700.

Public Broadcasting System (PBS). (2001). *Terrorist attacks on Americans, 1979–1988.* Available: *www.pbs.org/wgbh/pages/frontline/shows/target/etc/cron.html*.

Pyszczynski, T., Abdollahi, A., Solomon, S., Greenberg, J., Cohen, F., & Weise, D. (2006). Mortality salience, martyrdom, and military might: The great Satan versus the axis of evil. *Personality & Social Psychology Bulletin, 32*(4): 525–537.

Pyszczynski, T., Greenberg, J., & Solomon, S. (1999a). A terror management analysis of self-awareness and anxiety: The hierarchy of terror. *Anxiety Research, 2,* 177–195.

Pyszczynski, T., Greenberg, J., Solomon, S., & Hamilton, J. (1990). A terror management analysis of self-awareness and anxiety: The hierarchy of terror. *Anxiety Research, 2,* 177–195.

Pyszczynski, T., Solomon, S., & Greenberg, J., (1999b). A dual-process model of defense against conscious and unconscious death-related thoughts: An extension of terror management theory. *Psychological Review, 106,* 835–845.

Pyszczynski, T., Solomon, S., & Greenberg, J. (2003). *In the wake of 9/11: The psychology of terror.* Washington, DC: American Psychological Association.

Quittner, J. (2004, March 16). Crystal's destructive path: Gay men continue to be systematically ravaged by the deadly drug as officials try to stop an epidemic. (Health). *The Advocate* (The national gay and lesbian newsmagazine).

Radcliffe-Brown, A. R. (1939). *Taboo.* Cambridge: Cambridge University Press.

Raffin, T. A. (1991). Withholding and withdrawing life support. *Hospital Practice, 26*(3), 133–136, 140–141, 145.

Rando, T. A. (1986). *Parental loss of a child.* Champaign, IL: Research Press.

Rando, T. A. (Ed.). (2000). *Clinical dimensions of xanticipatory mourning: Theory and practice in working with the dying, their loved ones, and their caregivers.* Champaign, IL: Research Press.

Rawlings, 1978. *Beyond death's door.* New York: Bantam.

Reed, P. G. (1986). Religiousness among terminally ill and healthy adults. *Research in Nursing and Health, 9,* 35–41.

Reed, P. G. (1987). Spirituality and well-being in terminally ill hospitalized adults. *Research in Nursing and Health, 10,* 335–344.

Reicke, B. (1993). Hell. In B. M. Metzger & M. D. Coogan (Eds.), *The Oxford companion to the Bible.* Oxford, England: Oxford University Press.

Reill, P. H., & Wilson, E. J. (2004). *Encyclopedia of the Enlightenment* (Facts on File Library of World History. New York: Facts on File.

Reinhold, N. (1993). Gastrointestinal intubation. In D. Drossman (Ed.), *Manual of gastroenterologic procedure* (pp. 10–21). New York: Raven Press.

Reitman, J. S. (1996). The dilemma of "medical futility"—A "wisdom model" for decision making. *Issues in Law & Medicine, 12*(3), 231–264.

Religion News Service. (2007, June, 26). Assisted suicide has national support as Kevorkian leaves jail. *Christian Century, 124,* 16.

Reynolds, R. M., & Cimbolic, P. (1988–1989). Attitudes toward suicide survivors as a function of survivors' relationship to the victim. *Omega: Journal of Death and Dying, 19*(2), 125–133.

Richmond, C. (2005, July 16). Dame Cicely Saunders: Founder of the modern hospice movement.

British Medical Journal, 331(7509). Retrieved May 22, 2011, from *www.bmj.com/content/331/7509/suppl/DC1*.

Ring, K. (1980). Life at death: A scientific investigation of the near-death experience. New York: Coward, McCann, & Geoghegan.

Ring, K. (1984). *Heading toward omega: In search of the meaning of the near-death experience.* New York: Quill-William Morrow.

Ring, K., & Cooper, S. (1999). *Mindsight.* Palo Alto, CA: Institute of Transpersonal Psychology.

Ritzer, G. (Ed.). (1990). *Frontiers of social theory: The new syntheses.* New York: Columbia University Press.

Ritzer, G. (1997). *Postmodern social theory.* New York: McGraw-Hill.

Ritzer, G. (1998). *The McDonaldization thesis.* London: Sage.

Ritzer, G. (2000). *Sociological theory.* New York: McGraw-Hill.

Robertson, J. A. (1999). The dead donor rule. *The Hastings Center Report, 29*(6), 6–14.

Robinson, P. J., & Fleming, S. (1989). Differentiating grief and depression. *Hospice Journal, 5*(1), 77–88.

Robinson, P. J., & Fleming, S. (1992). Depressotypic cognitive patterns in major depression and conjugal bereavement. *Omega, 25*(4), 291–305.

Robinson, W. G. (1997). Heaven's Gate: The end? *Journal of Computer-Mediated Communication, 3*(3). Available: *www.ascusc.org/jcmc/vol3/issue3/robinson.html.*

Rodin, E. (1980). The reality of death experiences: A personal perspective. *Journal of Nervous and Mental Disorders, 168*(5), 259–263.

Rodin, E. (1989). Comments on "A neurobiological model for near-death experiences." *Journal of Near-Death Studies, 7,* 255–259.

Rodriguez, R. J., Martin, R. J., & Fanaroff, A. A. (2002). Respiratory distress syndrome and its management. In A. A. Fanaroff & R. J. Martin (Eds.), *Neonatal-perinatal medicine: Diseases of the fetus and infant* (7th ed., pp. 1001–1011). St. Louis: Mosby.

Rogers, C. (1965). *Client-centered therapy.* Boston: Houghton Mifflin.

Romanoff, B. D., & Terenzio, M. (1988). Rituals and the grieving process. *Death Studies, 22*(8), 697–711.

Rommer, B. (2000). Blessing in disguise: Another side of the near-death experience. St. Paul, MN: Llewellyn.

Rosen, C. S., Chow, H. C., Finney, J. F., Greenbaum, M. A., Moos, R. H., Sheikh, J. I., & Yesaavage, J. A. (2004). VA practice patterns and practice guidelines for treating posttraumatic stress disorder. *Journal of Traumatic Stress, 17*(3), 213–222.

Rosenblatt, A., Greenberg, J., Solomon, S., Pyszczynski, T., & Lyon, D. (1989). Evidence for terror management theory I: The effects of mortality salience on reactions to those who violate or uphold cultural values. *Journal of Personality and Social Psychology, 57,* 681–690.

Rosenblatt, P. (2001). Social constructionist perspective on cultural differences in grief. In M. S. Stroebe, R. D. Hanson, W. Stroebe, & H Schut (Eds.), *Handbook of bereavement research: Consequences, coping, and care* (pp. 285–327). Washington, DC: American Psychological Association.

Rousseau, P. (2001). Ethical and legal issues in palliative care. *Palliative Care, 28*(2), 391–400.

Rousseau, P. C. (1991). How fluid deprivation affects the terminally ill. *RN, 51*(1), 73–74, 76.

Rupp, J. (1996). *Dear heart, come home: The path to midlife spirituality.* New York: Crossroad.

Saavedra-Aguilar, J. C., & Gomez-Jeria, J. S. (1989). A neurobiological model of near-death experiences. *Journal of Near-Death Studies, 7*(4), 205–222.

Sabom, M. B. (1980). The near-death experience. *Journal of the American Medical Association, 244*(1), 29–30.

Sabom, M. B. (1982). *Recollections of death: A medical investigation.* New York: Simon and Schuster.

Sabom, M. B., & Kreutiziger, S. (1977a). Near-death experiences. *Journal of the Florida Medical Association, 64*(9), 648–650.

Sabom, M. B., & Kreutiziger, S. (1977b). Near-death experiences, *New England Journal of Medicine, 297*(19), 1071.

Sakr, A. H. (1995). Death and dying: An Islamic perspective. In J. K. Parry & A. S. Ryan (Eds.), *A cross-cultural look at death, dying, and religion* (pp. 47–73). Chicago: Nelson-Hall.

Sanders, C. (1986). Accidental death of a child. In T. Rando (Ed.), *Parental loss of a child.* Champaign, IL: Research Press.

Sanders, C. (1989). *Grief: The mourning after.* New York: Wiley & Sons.

Sankar, A. (1993). Images of home death and the elderly patient: Romantic versus real. *Generations 17*(2): 59–63.

Sanskrit Religions Institute (SRI). (2003). Hindu funeral rites and ancestor worship: Antyesti, sradda and tarpana. Available: *www.sanskrit.org/Rites%20of%20 Passage/ancestors1.html.*

Santaniello, C. (2003). Personal interview, September 5, 2003.

Santrock, J. W. (2002). *Life-span development* (8th ed.). Boston: McGraw-Hill.

Saunders, C. (1977). Dying they live: St. Christopher's Hospice. In H. Feifel (Ed.), *New meanings of death* (pp. 154–179). New York: McGraw-Hill.

Saunders, C. (1998). Foreword. In D. Doyle, G. W. C. Hanks, & N. MacDonald (Eds.), *Oxford textbook of palliative medicine* (2nd ed., pp. v–ix). New York: Oxford University Press.

Sayers, G. M. (2007). Restraint in order to feed: Justifying a lawful policy for the UK. *European Journal of Health Law, 14,* 221–240.

Schmidt, J. D. (1986). Murder of a child. In T. Rando (Ed.), *Parental loss of a child.* Champaign, IL: Research Press.

Schneidman, E. S. (1977). Aspects of the dying process. *Psychiatric Annals, 8,* 25–40.

Schowalter, J. E., Buschman, P., et al. (Eds.). (1987). *Children and death: Perspectives from birth through adolescence.* New York: Praeger.

Schulz, R., & Schlarb, J. (1991). Two decades of research on dying: What do we know about the patient? In A. Monat & R. S. Lazarus (Eds.), *Stress and coping: An anthology* (3rd ed.). New York: Columbia University Press.

Schumann-Antelme, R., & Rossini, S. (1998). *Becoming Osiris: The ancient Egyptian death experience.* Rochester, VT: Inner Traditions International.

Schuurman, D. L. (2002). The club no one wants to join: A dozen lessons I've learned from grieving children and adolescents. *Grief Matters, 5*(2). Melbourne, Victoria, Australia: The Centre for Grief Education. Available: *www.dougy.org/default.asp?pid=4985010.*

Schwab, R. (1996). Gender differences in parental grief. *Death Studies, 20*(2), 103–113.

Schwartz, M. (1996). *Morrie: In his own words.* New York: Delta Trade Paperbacks.

Scott, A. O. (2010, May 7). Gen X has a midlife crisis. *The New York Times.* Retrieved March 18, 2012, from *www. nytimes.com/2010/05/09/weekinreview/09aoscott.html.*

Searl, E. (2000). *In memoriam: A guide to modern funeral and memorial services* (2nd ed.). Boston: Skinner House.

Seidman, S. (1994). *Contested knowledge: Social theory in the postmodern age.* Oxford: Blackwell.

Senate of Canada, Standing Committee on Social Affairs, Science & Technology. (2002). *The Health of Canadians—The Federal Role Final Report.* Volume 6, Recommendations for reform. Available: *www.parl. gc.ca/37/2/parlbus/senate/com-e/soci-e/rep-e/repoct 02vol6-e/htm.*

September11News.com. (2003). *News images and photos of the September 11, 2001 attack on the World Trade Center.* Available: *www.september11news.com/ AttackImages.htm.*

Serdahely, W. J. (1989–1990). A pediatric near-death experience: Tunnel variants. *Omega, 20*(1), 55–62.

Service Corporation International. (2003). Service Corporation International. Available: *www.sci-corp.com.*

Shapiro, E. R. (1996). Family bereavement and cultural diversity: A social developmental perspective. *Family Process, 35,* 313–332.

Shapiro, F. (2001). *EMDR: Eye movement desensitization of reprocessing: Basic principles, protocols, and procedures* (2nd ed.). New York: Guilford.

Sharma, B. R. (2004). Withholding and withdrawing of life support: A medicolegal dilemma. *American Journal of Forensic Medicine and Pathology, 25*(2), 150–155.

Shear, K., Frank, E., Houck, P. R., & Reynolds, C. F. (2005). Treatment of complicated grief: A randomized controlled trial. *Journal of the American Medical Association, 293*(21), 2601–2607.

Shear, K., & Shair, H. (2005). Attachment, loss, and complicated grief. *Developmental Psychobiology, 47*(3), 253–267.

Sheehan, D., & Forman, W. B. (1996). *Hospice and palliative care: Concepts and practice.* Boston: Jones and Bartlett.

Sheldon, T. (2001). Holland decriminalizes voluntary euthanasia. *British Journal of Medicine, 322,* 947.

Shemie, S. D., Doig, C., & Belitsky, P. (2003). Advancing toward a modern death: The path from severe brain injury to neurological determination of death. *Canadian Medical Association Journal, 168*(8), 993–995.

Sherr, L. (Ed.). (1995). *Grief and AIDS.* New York: Wiley & Sons.

Shneidman, E. (1975). Postvention: The care of the bereaved. In R. Pasnau (Ed.), *Consultation in liaison psychiatry* (pp. 245–256). New York: Grune and Stratton.

Shneidman, E. (1998). "Suicide" in the Encyclopedia, 1777–1997 Britannica. *Archives of Suicide Research, 4,* 189–199.

Siegel, R. K. (1992). *Fire in the brain.* New York: Dutton.

Silverman, E., Range, L, & Overholser, J. (1994). Bereavement from suicide as compared to other forms of bereavement. *Omega, 30,* 41–51.

Singer, P. A., & Bowman, K. W. (2002). Quality care at the end of life. *British Medical Journal, 324,* 1291–1292.

Sloan, S. L. (1992). The hospice movement: A study in the diffusion of innovative palliative care. *The American Journal of Hospice & Palliative Care, 8*(2), 24–32.

Slocum, J., & Carlson, L. (2011). *Final rights: Reclaiming the American way of death.* Hinesburg, VT: Upper Access.

Smith, H. (1982). *Beyond the post-modern mind.* New York: Crossroad.

Smith, J. I. (1998). Islam. In C. J. Johnson & M. G. McGee (Eds.), *How different religions view death and afterlife* (2nd ed., pp. 132–144). Philadelphia: Charles Press.

Smith, L. (2004). *Once and future Islam: A Sufi imam challenges moderate Muslims to fashion a new American faith.* Available: *http://slate.msn.com/id/210698/.*

Smith, S. A., & Andrews, M. (2000). Artificial nutrition and hydration at the end of life. *Medical Surgical Nursing, 9*(5), 233–244.

Snyder, L., & Sulmasy, D. P. (2001). Physician-assisted suicide. *Annals of Internal Medicine, 135*(3), 209–216.

Social Security Administration. (2011). *2011 OASDI Trustees Report.* Retrieved April 1, 2012, from *www.ssa.gov/oact/tr/2011/II_D_project.html.*

Society for the Promotion of Buddhism (SPB). (1966). *The teaching of Buddha.* Tokyo: Kosaido Printing.

Sogyal, R. (1992). The Tibetan book of living and dying. New York: Harper Collins.

Solecki, R. (1975). Implications of the Shanidar Cave Neanderthal flower burial. *Annals of the New York Academy, 293*(1), 114–125.

Solomon, C. (2003). *How to plan an $800 funeral.* MSN-CNBC. Available: moneycentral.msn.com/content/Retirementandwills/Planyourestate/P57926.asp.

Solomon, S., Greenberg, J., & Pyszczynski, T. (1991). A terror management theory of social behavior: The psychological functions of self-esteem and cultural worldviews. In M. Zanna (Ed.), *Advances in experimental social psychology* (Vol. 22, pp. 91–159). Orlando, FL: Academic Press.

Solomon, S., Greenberg, J., & Pyszczynski, T. (2003). Fear of death and human destructiveness. *Psychoanalytic Review, 90*(4), 457–474.

Solomon, S., Laor, N., & McFarlane, A. C. (1996). Acute posttraumatic reactions in soldiers and civilians. In B. A. van der Kolk, A. C. McFarlane, & A. C. L. Weisaeth (Eds.), *Traumatic stress: The effects of overwhelming experience on mind, body, and society* (pp. 102–114). New York: Guilford.

Sommer, J. D. (1999). The Shanidar IV "flower burtial": A re-evaluation of Neanderthal burial ritual. *Cambridge Archaeological Journal, 9*(1), 127–129.

Sormanti, M., & August, J. (1997). Parental bereavement: Spiritual connections with deceased children. *American Journal of Orthopsychiatry, 67*(3), 460–469.

Soubbotina, T. P., & Sheram, K. (2000). *Beyond economic growth: Meeting the challenges of global development.* Washington, DC: The World Bank (The International Bank for Reconstruction and Development).

Sourkes, B. M. (1995). *Armfuls of time: The psychological experiences of the child with a life-threatening illness.* Pittsburgh: University of Pittsburgh Press.

Speck, P. (1998). Spiritual issues in palliative care. In D. Doyle, G. W. C. Hanks, & N. MacDonald, (Eds.),

Oxford textbook of palliative medicine (2nd ed., pp. 805–814). New York: Oxford University Press.

Speece, M. W., & Brent, S. B. (1984). Children's understanding of death: A review of three components of a death concept. *Child Development, 55*(5), 1671–1686.

Speece, M. W., & Brent, S. B. (1992). The aquisition of a mature understanding of three components of the concept of death. *Death Studies, 16*(3), 211–229.

Speece, M. W., & Brent, S. B. (1996). The development of children's understanding of death. In C. A. Corr & D. M. Corr (Eds.), *Handbook of childhood death and bereavement* (pp. 29–50). New York: Springer.

Spinetta, J. J. (1974). The dying child's awareness of death: A review. *Psychological Bulletin, 81*(4), 256–260.

Spinetta, J. J., & Maloney, L. J. (1975). Death anxiety in the outpatient leukemic child. *Pediatrics, 56*, 1034–1037.

Spinetta, J. J., Rigler, D., & Karon, M. (1973). Anxiety in the dying child. *Pediatrics, 52*, 127–131.

Spinetta, J. J., Rigler, D., & Karon, M. (1987). Anxiety in the dying child. In T. Kurlick, B. Holiday, & I. M. Martinson (Eds.), *The child and the family facing life-threatening illness* (pp. 120–125). Philadelphia: Lippincott.

Stanford Faculty Development Center. (2003). End-of-Life Care Curriculum for Medical Teachers. Palo Alto, CA: Stanford University School of Medicine.

Stanley, J. M. (2003). What people would want if they knew more about it: A case for the social marketing of hospice care. *Hastings Center Report Special Supplement, 33*(2), S22–S23.

Starhawk. (1997). *The Pagan book of living and dying: Practical rituals, prayers, blessings, and meditations on crossing over.* New York: HarperCollins.

Statistics Canada. (2002). *Selected leading causes of death by sex.* Available: *www.statcan.ca/english/Pgdb/People/Health/health36.htm*.

Steinbrook, R. (2002). Physician-assisted suicide in Oregon—An uncertain future. *New England Journal of Medicine, 346*(6), 460-464.

Steele, H. (2002). State of the art: Attachment theory. *Psychologist, Special Issue: The changing family, 15*(10), 518–522.

Stephey, M. J. (2008, April 16). Gen-X: The ignored generation. *Time.* Retrieved March 18, 2012, from *www.time.com/time/printout/0,8816,1731528,00.html*.

Stern, J. (2003). *Terror in the name of God: Why religious militants kill.* New York: HarperCollins.

Stevens, M. M., Rytmeister, R. J., Proctor, M-T., & Bolster, P. (2010). Children living with life-threatening or life-limiting illnesses: A dispatch from the front lines. In C. A. Corr & D. E. Balk (Eds.), *Children's encounters with death, bereavement, and coping.* New York: Springer.

Stevenson, I., Cook, E. W., & McClean-Rice, N. (1989–1990). Are persons reporting "near-death experiences" really near death? A study of medical records. *Omega, 20*(1), 45–54.

Stewart Enterprises. (2003). *Profile.* Available: *www.stewartenterprises.com/profile/profile.cfm*.

Stillion, J. M., & Papadatou, D. (2002). Suffer the children: An examination of psychosocial issues in children and adolescents with terminal illness. *American Behavioral Scientist, 46*(2), 299–315.

Storm, H. 2000. *My descent into death, and the message of love which brought me back.* Edinburgh, Scottland: Clairview.

Strack, S. (1997). *Death and quest for meaning: Essays in honor of Herman Feifel.* Lanham, MD: Jason Aronson.

Strassman, R. (2001). *The spirit molecule.* Rochester, VT: Park Street Press.

Strauss, A. L. (1985, June 7). *Research on chronic illness and its management.* Fifth Helen Nahm Research Lecture. San Francisco: University of California, San Francisco. Available: *http://sbs.ucsf.edu/medsoc/anselmstrauss/chronic.html*.

Strauss, W., & Howe, N. (1991). *Generations: The history of America's future, 1584–2069.* New York: Harper Perennial.

Strauss, W., & Howe, N. (1997). *The fourth turning: What the cycles of history tell us about America's next rendezvous with destiny.* New York: Broadway.

Stroebe, M. (1992–1993). Coping with bereavement: A review of the grief work hypothesis. *Omega, 26*(1), 19–42.

Stroebe, M., Abakoumkin, G., & Stroebe, M. (2010). Beyond depression: Yearning for the loss of a loved one. *Omega, 61*(2), 85–101.

Stroebe, M., Gergen, M. M., Gergen, K. J., & Stroebe, W. (1992). Broken hearts or broken bonds: Love and death in historical perspective. *American Psychologist, 47*(10), 1205–1212.

Stroebe, M. S., Hansson, R. O., Stroebe, W., & Schut, H. (2001). Introduction: Concepts and issues in contemporary research on bereavement. In M. S. Stroebe, R. O. Hansson, W. Stroebe, & H. Schut (Eds.), *Handbook of bereavement research: Consequences, coping, and care.* Washington, DC: American Psychological Association.

Stroebe, M. S., Hansson, R. O., Stroebe, W., & Schut, H. (Eds.). (2001). *Handbook of bereavement research: Consequences, coping, and care.* Washington, DC: American Psychological Association.

Stroebe, M. S., & Schut, H. (1999). The dual process model of coping with bereavement: Rationale and description. *Death Studies, 23*(3), 197–224.

Stroebe, M. S., & Schut, H. (2001). Meaning making in the dual process model. In R. Neimeyer (Ed.), *Meaning reconstruction and the experience of loss* (pp. 55–73). Washington, DC: American Psychological Association.

Stroebe, M. S., Schut, H., & Stroebe, W. (2005). Attachment in coping with bereavement: A theoretical integration. *Review of General Psychology, 9*(1), 48–66.

Stroebe, M. S., & Stroebe, W. (1983). Who suffers more? Sex differences in health risks of the widowed. *Psychological Bulletin, 93,* 297–301.

Stroebe, M. S., & Stroebe, W. (1991). Does "grief work" work? *Journal of Consulting and Clinical Psychology, 59,* 57–65.

Stroebe, W., & Stroebe, M. S. (1987). *Bereavement and health.* Cambridge: Cambridge University Press.

Stroebe, W., & Stroebe, M. S. (1989). Who participates in bereavement research? A review and empirical study. *Omega, 20*(1), 1–29.

Stroebe, W., & Stroebe, M. S. (1993). Determinants of adjustment to bereavement in young widows and widowers. In W. Stroebe, M. S. Stroebe, & R. D. Hanson, (Eds.), *Handbook of bereavement.* New York: Cambridge University Press.

Stroebe, W., Stroebe, M. S., & Domittner, G. (1988). Individual and situational differences in recovery from bereavement: A risk-group identified. *Journal of Social Issues, 44,* 143–158.

Stroebe, W., Stroebe, M. S., & Hanson, R. D. (Eds.). (1993). *Handbook of bereavement.* New York: Cambridge University Press.

Sullivan, A. D., Hedberg, K., & Hopkins, D. (2001). Legalized physician-assisted suicide in Oregon, 1998–2000. *New England Journal of Medicine, 344*(8), 605–607.

Sullivan, M. A. (1995). May the circle be unbroken: The African-American experience of death, dying, and spirituality. In J. K. Parry & A. S. Ryan (Eds.), *A cross-cultural look at death, dying, and religion* (pp. 160–171). Chicago: Nelson-Hall.

Sykes, N. P. (1998). Constipation and diarrhea. In D. Doyle, G. W. C. Hanks, & N. MacDonald (Eds.), *Oxford textbook of palliative medicine* (2nd ed., pp. 513–526). New York: Oxford University Press.

Tamm, M. E., & Granqvist, A. (1995). The meaning of death for children and adolescents: A phenomenographic study of drawings. *Death Studies 19,* 203–222.

Tapscott, D. (2008). *Grown up digital: How the Net Generation is changing your world.* New York: Morgan James.

Tasota, F. J., & Hoffman, L. A. (1996). Terminal weaning from mechanical ventilation: Planning and process. *Critical Care Nursing Quarterly, 19*(3), 36–51.

Taylor, C. (2004). *Modern social imaginaries.* Durham, NC: Duke University Press.

Teasdale, W. (1999). *The mystic heart: Discovering a universal spirituality in the world's religions.* Novato, CA: New World Library.

Teno, J. J., Clarridge, B. R., Casey, V., & Welch, L. C. (2004). Family perspectives on end-of-life care at the last place of care. *Journal of the American Medical Association, 291*(1), 88–93.

Thrangu, K. (1999). A brief overview of the bardo. Boulder, CO: Namo Buddha Publications. Available: ***www.dharma-media.org/media/kagyu/thrangurinpoche/Bardo_nbp.pdf.***

Tilly, J., & Wiener, J. (2001). *Medicaid and end-of-life care.* Washington, DC: Last Acts.

Tisdale, M. J. (2001). Cancer anorexia and cachexia. *Nutrition, 17,* 438–442.

Toffler, A. (1970). *Future shock.* New York: Random House.

Tolstoy, L., & Edmonds, R. (Trans.). (1960). *The death of Ivan Ilyich and other stories.* New York: Penguin.

Tonnies, F. (1887/1963). *Community and society (Gemeinschaft und gesellschaft).* New York: Harper & Row.

Torma, L. (1999). Pain—The fifth vital sign. *Pulse, 36*(2), 16.

Tornstam, L. (1993). Gerotranscendence: A theoretical and empirical exploration. In L. E. Thomas & S. A. Eisenhandler (Eds.), *Aging and the religious dimension.* Westport, CN: Greenwood.

Toynbee, A. (1968). Traditional attitudes towards death. In A. Toynbee, A. K. Mant, N. Smart, J. Hinton, S. Yudkin, E. Rhode, R. Heywood, & H. H. Price (Eds.), *Man's concern with death.* London: Hodder and Stroughton.

Toynbee, A., Mant, A. K., Smart, N., Hinton, J., Yudkin, S., Rhode, E., Heywood, R., & Price, H. H. (Eds.). (1968). *Man's concern with death.* London: Hodder and Stroughton.

Trinkaus, E., & Shipman, P. (1993). *The Neanderthals—Changing the image of mankind.* New York: Knopf.

Trunk, P. (2009). What Generation Z will be like at work. Retrieved on March 23, 2012, from *http://blog.penelopetrunk.com/2009/07/27/what-work-will-be-like-for-generation-z/.*

Truog, R. D. (1997). Is it time to abandon brain death? *Hastings Center Report, 27*(1), 29–37.

Truog, R. D. (2003). Role of brain death and the dead-donor rule in the ethics of transplantation. *Critical Care Medicine, 31*(9), 2391–2396.

Turner, J. H. (1991). *The structure of sociological theory* (5th ed.). Belmont, CA: Wadsworth.

Tweit, S. (2010). *Dying to be green.* Available: *www.audubonmagazine.org/audubonliving/audubonliving1009.html.*

Twycross, R., & Lichter, I. (1998). The terminal phase. In D. Doyle, G. W. C. Hanks, & N. MacDonald (Eds.), *The Oxford textbook of palliative medicine* (2nd ed., pp. 977–992). New York: Oxford University Press.

Tyler, E. B. (1873). *Primitive culture: Research into the development of mythology, philosophy, religion, language, art, and custom* (2nd ed., 2 volumes). London: John Murray.

Tyler, P. (2001). *The Hippocratic Oath: Modern version.* Nova. WGBH Educational Foundation. Retrieved May 29, 2011, from *www.pbs.org/wgbh/nova/body/hippocratic-oath-today.html.*

United Nations Aids/World Health Organization (UNAIDS/WHO). (2003). *Epidemiological fact sheets on HIV/AIDS and sexually transmitted infections.* Geneva, Switzerland: UNAIDS/World Health Organization Working Group on Global HIV/AIDS.

United States Government Accounting Office (GAO). (2000). *Medicare: More beneficiaries use hospice but for fewer days of care.* GAO/HEHS-00-182. Washington, DC: Author.

USA Today. (April 25, 2011). Japan's tsunami waves exceed historic heights, p. 5.

Vacco v. Quill, 117 S. Ct. 2293 (1997).

Van den Berg, J. H. (1978). *Medical power and medical ethics.* (English translation). New York: Norton.

Van der Kloot Meijburg, H. H. (2001). Personal interview, December 3, 2001.

Van der Kloot Meijburg, H. H. (2003). From the Netherlands. *Palliative Medicine, 17,* 176–177.

Van der Maas, P. J., Pijnenborg, L., & Van Delden, J. J. M. (1995). Changes in Dutch opinion on active euthanasia, 1966 through 1991. *Journal of the American Medical Association, 273*(18), 1411–1414.

Van der Maas, P. J., Van Delden, J. J. M., & Pijnenborg, L. (1992). Euthanasia and other medical decisions concerning the end of life. *Health Policy, 22*(1–2), vi–x, 1–262.

Van der Maas, P. J., Van Delden, J. J. M., Pijnenborg, L., & Looman, W. W. N. (1991). Euthanasia and other medical decisions concerning the end of life. *Lancet, 338*(8768), 669–674.

Van der Wal, G., Van der Maas, P. J., Bosma, J. M., Onwuteaka-Philipsen, B. D., Willems, D. L., Haverkate, I., & Kostense, P. J. (1996). Evaluation of the notification procedure for physician-assisted death in the Netherlands. *New England Journal of Medicine, 335*(22), 1706–1711.

Van Dongen, C. J. (1990). Agonizing questioning: Experiences of survivors of suicide victims. *Nursing Research, 39,* 224–229.

Van Dongen, C. J. (1991). Experiences of family members after a suicide. *Journal of Family Practice, 33,* 375–380.

Van Dongen, C. J. (1993). Social context of postsuicide bereavement. *Death Studies, 17*(2), 125–141.

Van Dongen-Melman, J. E. W. M., Van Zuuren, J. J., & Verhulst, F. C. (1998). Experiences of parents of childhood cancer survivors: A qualitative analysis. *Parent Education and Counseling, 34,* 185–200.

Van Eys, J. (1987). The definition of dying and the personhood of the child. In J. E. Schowalter, P. Buschman, et al. (Eds.), *Children and death: Perspectives from birth through adolescence* (pp. 113–122). New York: Praeger.

Van Lommel, P., Van Wees, R., Meyers, V., & Elfferich, I. (2001). Near-death experience in survivors of cardiac arrest: A prospective study in the Netherlands. *Lancet, 358,* 2039–2045.

Van Setten, H. (1999). Album angels: Parent-child relations as reflected in 19th century photos, made after the death of a child. *Journal of Psychohistory, 26,* 819–834.

Veatch, R. M. (1976). *Death, dying, and the biological revolution.* New Haven, CT: Yale University Press.

Veatch, R. M. (1993a). The impending collapse of the whole-brain definition of death. *The Hastings Center Report, 23*(4), 18–24.

Veatch, R. M. (1993b). From forgoing life support to aid-in-dying. *The Hastings Center Report, 23*(6 Suppl), S7–S8.

Verbrugge, L. M. (1984). Longer life but worsening health? Trends in health and mortality of middle-aged and older persons. *Health and Society (Milbank Memorial Fund Quarterly), 62*(3): 475–519.

Vicchio, S. J. (1981). Near-death experiences: A critical review of the literature and some questions for further study. *Essence: Issues in the Study of Ageing, Dying and Death, 5*(1), 77–89.

Villaire, M. (1992). The Cruzans talk about Nancy, the critical care experience and their new mission. Interview with Michael Villaire. *Critical Care Nurse, 12*(8), 80–87.

Von Bertalanffy, L. (1968). *General systems theory.* New York: George Braziller.

Von Gunten, C. F., Ferris, F. D., Portenoy, R. K., & Glajchen, M. (Eds.). (2001). *CAPC manual: How to establish a palliative care program.* New York: Center to Advance Palliative Care. Available: *http://64.85.16.230/educate/content.html.*

Vullo-Navich, K., Smith, S. A., Andrews, M., Levine, A. M., Tischler, J. F., & Veglia, J. M. (1998). Comfort and incidence of abnormal serum sodium, BUN, creatinine, and osmolality in dehydration of terminal illness. *American Journal of Hospice and Palliative Care, 15*(2), 77–84.

Waechter, E. H. (1971). Children's reactions to fatal illness. *American Journal of Nursing, 71,* 1168–1172.

Waechter, E. H. (1984). Dying children: Patterns of coping. In H. Wass & C. A. Corr (Eds.), *Childhood and death* (pp. 1–68). Washington, DC: Hemisphere.

Waechter, E. H. (1987). Children's reactions to fatal illness. In T. Kurlick, B. Holiday, & I. M. Martinson (Eds.), *The child and the family facing life-threatening illness* (pp. 108–119). Philadelphia: Lippincott.

Waisel, D. B., & Truog, R. D. (1997). The end-of-life sequence. *Anesthsiology, 87*(3), 676–686.

Walker, R. J., & Pomeroy, E. C. (1996) Anticipatory grief and AIDS: Strategies for intervening with caregivers. *Health and Social Work, 21*(1), 49–58.

Wallace, S. E. (1973). *After suicide.* New York: Wiley-Interscience.

Wallace, W. (1971). *The logic of science in sociology.* New York: Aldine de Gruyer.

Walsh, K., King, M., Jones, L., Tookman, A., & Blizard, R. (2002). Spiritual beliefs may affect outcome of bereavement: Prospective study. *British Medical Journal, 324,* 1551–1556.

Walter, T. (1994). *The revival of death.* London: Routledge.

Walter, T. (1996). A new model of grief: Bereavement and biography. *Mortality, 1*(1), 7–25.

Walter, T. (2006). What is complicated grief? A social constructionist perspective. *Omega—Journal of Death and Dying, 52*(1), 71–79.

Washingtgon v. Glucksberg, 117 S. Ct. 2258 (1997).

Washington State Department of Health. (2011). *Washington State Department of Health 2010 Death with Dignity Act Report.* Retrieved May 28, 2011, from *www.doh.wa.gov/dwda/.*

Wass, H. (1997). Children, adolescents and death. In S. Strack (Ed.), *Death and the quest for meaning: Essays in honor of Herman Feifel*. Northvale, NJ: Jason Aronson.

Wass, H., & Neimeyer, R. A. (Eds.). (1995). *Dying: Facing the facts*. Washington, DC: Taylor & Francis.

Watson, P. J., Morris, R. J., & Hood, R. W. (1988). Sin and self-functioning part 2: Grace, guilt and psychological adjustment. *Journal of Psychology and Theology, 16,* 270–281.

Way, J., Black, A. L., & Curtis, J. R. (2002). Withdrawing life support and resolution of conflict with families. *British Medical Journal, 325,* 1342–1345.

Weber, M. (1905/1976). *The Protestant work ethic and the spirit of capitalism*. Talcot Parson (Trans.). New York: Scribner.

Weber, M. (1922/1991). *The sociology of religion*. Boston: Beacon.

Weber, M. (1947). *The theory of social and economic organization*. New York: Free Press.

Wedemeyer, N. (1986). Transformation of family images related to death. *Journal of Family Issues, 7,* 337–351.

Wegscheider, S. (1981). *Another chance*. Palo Alto, CA: Science and Behavior Books.

Weijer C. (2005). A death in the family: Reflections on the Terri Schiavo case. *Canadian Medical Association Journal, 172*(9), 1197–1198.

Weinrib, E. L. (2004). *Images of the self: The sandplay therapy process*. Cloverdale, CA: Temenos Press.

Weizfeld, A. (1998). *The Abrahamic tradition*. Available: ***www.eccmei.net/E/E018.html***.

Westrate, E. (Producer & Director). (2003). *A family undertaking*. [Film]. (Available from Fanlight Productions, P.O. Box 1084, Harriman, NY 10926.)

Whiston, W. (1987). *The works of Josephus: Complete and unabridged*. Peabody, MA: Henrickson Publishers.

Whyte, William F. (1955). *Street corner society* (2nd ed.). Chicago: University of Chicago Press.

Wikipedia. (2004). Thomas Samuel Kuhn. Available: ***http://en.wikipedia.org/wiki/Thomas_Kuhn***.

Wilkinson, A. M., & Lynn, J. (2001). The end of life. In R. H. Binstock & L. K. George (Eds.), *Handbook of aging and the social sciences* (5th ed., pp. 444–461). New York: Academic Press.

Williams, B. K., Sawyer, S. C., & Wahlstrom, C. M. (2009). *Marriages, families, and intimate relationships: A practical introduction*. Boston: Pearson.

Williams, K. (2004). *The NDE and Science: Kevin Williams' research conclusions*. Available: ***www.near*** death.com/experiences/research08.html.

Wilson, B. G. (1997). The postmodern paradigm. In A. A. Romiszowski & C. R. Dills (Eds.), *Instructional development paradigms*. Englewood Cliffs, NJ: Educational Technology Publications.

Wirth, J-H. (2003). 9/11 as a collective trauma. *Journal of Psychohistory, 30*(4), 363–388.

Woerlee, G. M. (2004). Darkness, tunnels, and light (near-death experiences). *Skepitcal Inquirer, 28*(3). Available: ***www.csicop.org/si/2004-05/near-death-experience.htm***.

Wogrin, C. (2007). Professional issues and thanatology. In D. Balk, C. Wogrin, G. Thornton, & D. Meagher (Eds.), *Handbook of thanatology: The essential body of knowledge for the study of death, dying, and bereavement*. New York: Routledge.

Worden, J. W. (1991). *Grief counseling and grief therapy: A handbook for the mental health practitioner* (2nd ed.). New York: Springer.

Worden, J. W. (2002). *Grief counseling and grief therapy: A handbook for the mental health practitioner* (3rd ed.). New York: Springer.

Worden, J. W. (2008). *Grief counseling and grief therapy: A handbook for the mental health practitioner* (4th ed.). New York: Springer.

World Health Organization (WHO). (1990). *Cancer pain relief and palliative care: Report of a WHO expert committee*. Geneva, Switzerland: Author.

World Health Organization (WHO). (1996). *Cancer pain relief and palliative care: Report of a WHO expert committee* (3rd ed.). Geneva, Switzerland: Author.

World Health Organization (WHO). (2004). *WHO definition of palliative care*. Available: ***www.who.int/cancer/palliative/definition/en/***.

Wortman, C. B., & Boerner, K. (2007). Beyond the myths of coping with loss: Prevailing assumptions versus scientific evidence. In H. S. Friedman & R. C. Silver

(Eds.), *Foundations of health psychology* (pp. 285–324). New York: Oxford University Press.

Wortman, C. B., & Silver, R. C. (1987). Coping with irrevocable loss. In G. R. VandenBos & B. K. Bryant (Eds.), *Cataclisms, crises, and catastrophes: Psychology in action* (pp. 189–235). Washington, DC: American Psychological Association.

Wortman, C. B., & Silver, R. C. (1989). The myths of coping with loss. *Journal of Consulting & Clinical Psychology, 57,* 320–333.

Xu, J. Q., Kochanek, K. D., Murphy, S. L., & Tajada-Vera, B. (2010). *2007 Annual Mortality File. National Vital Statistics Reports, 58*(19). Hyattsville, MD: National Center for Health Statistics.

Yalom, I. (1980). *Existential psychotherapy.* New York: Basic Books.

Yamamoto, J., Okonogi, K., Iwasaki, T., & Yoshimura, S. (1969). Mourning in Japan. *American Journal of Psychiatry, 125*(12), 1660–1665.

Youngner, S. J., & Arnold, R. M. (1993). Ethical, psychological, and public policy implications of procuring organs from non-heart-beating cadaver donors. *Journal of the American Medical Association,* 269, 2769–2774.

Yum, Y. O., & Schenck-Hamlin W. (2005). Reactions to 9/11 as a function of terror management and perspective taking. *Journal of Social Psychology, 145,* 265–286.

Zaritsky, J. (Ed.). (2010). *The suicide tourist.* PBS Frontline episode, aired March 2, 2010. Available from ***www.pbs.org/wgbh/pages/frontline/suicidetourist/***.

Zerwekh, J. V. (1983). The dehydration question. *Nursing, 13*(1), 47–51.

Zerwekh, J. V. (1997). Do dying patients really need IV fluids. *American Journal of Nursing, 97*(3), 26–30.

Zhang, B., El-Jawahri, A., & Prigerson, H. G. (2006). Update on bereavement research: Evidence-based guidelines for the diagnosis and treatment of complicated bereavement. *Journal of Palliative Medicine, 9*(5), 1188–1203.

Zohar, D. (1990). *Quantum self: Human nature and consciousness defined by the new physics.* New York: Quill-William Morrow.

INDEX